The Talking Cures

The Talking Cures

The Psychoanalyses and the Psychotherapies

Robert S. Wallerstein, M.D.

Yale University Press   *New Haven and London*

Published with assistance from the foundation established in memory of Philip Hamilton McMillan of the Class of 1894, Yale College.

Designed by Sonia L. Scanlon.

Set in Bembo type by Rainsford Type, Danbury, Connecticut.

Printed in the United States of America by Vail-Ballou Press, Binghamton, New York.

Library of Congress Cataloging-in-Publication Data
Wallerstein, Robert S.
The talking cures : the psychoanalyses and the psychotherapies / Robert S. Wallerstein.
p.   cm.
Includes bibliographical references and index.
ISBN 0-300-06107-2
1. Psychodynamic psychotherapy.   2. Psychoanalysis.
I. Title.
RC489.P72W35 1995
616.89'17—dc20   95-1548
                                                  CIP

A catalogue record for this book is available from the British Library.

The paper in this book meets the guidelines for permanence and durability of the Committee on Production Guidelines for Book Longevity of the Council on Library Resources.

10   9   8   7   6   5   4   3   2   1

With love and gratitude to
Judy, our three children and their spouses, and our five grandchildren,
who have together made everything possible

The most unfortunate invalids on earth came in search of health: a poor woman who since childhood had been counting her heartbeats and had run out of numbers; a Portuguese man who couldn't sleep because the noise of the stars disturbed him; a sleepwalker who got up at night to undo the things he had done while awake; and many others with less serious ailments.

Gabriel García Márquez
"A Very Old Man with Enormous Wings:
A Tale for Children" (short story)

Contents

Acknowledgments

There is a particularly heavy indebtedness of intellectual acknowledgments when a book represents, as this one does, forty-five years of involvement in psychotherapy and psychoanalysis as a student, teacher, clinician, supervisor, theorist, and researcher. Many, indeed, have helped along the way in the development, critique, and refinement of my perspectives on the issues of this volume, actually a never-ending process.

They include, of course, my own patients over all those years and the special forty-two patients who were the subjects of the Psychotherapy Research Project of The Menninger Foundation; my students in each of my professional homes, the Menninger School of Psychiatry in Topeka, Kansas, and the Mount Zion Hospital and then the Langley Porter Institute of the University of California, both in San Francisco; the participants in supervision seminars at the Winter VA Hospital (which I co-led with Rudolf Ekstein) and the Topeka State Hospital, both in Topeka, and at the Langley Porter Institute in San Francisco; the candidates of the San Francisco Psychoanalytic Institute, including especially all the participants in my course "Psychoanalysis and Psychoanalytic Psychotherapy"; my teachers and mentors in Topeka, especially Rudolf Ekstein and Lewis Robbins, with a particular debt of gratitude to Gardner Murphy, who from the start placed such high confidence in my untested potential as a psychotherapy researcher; my comrades, too numerous to mention, in the organizational life of the American Psychoanalytic Association and the International Psychoanalytical Association over now three and one-half decades, of whom I single out only four, each for special reasons: Serge Lebovici, Joseph Sandler, Jock Sutherland, and Edward Weinshel; my colleagues on the Education Committee of the San Francisco Psychoanalytic Institute, with whom I have discussed these issues over many years, especially Stanley Goodman and Edward Weinshel; and my colleagues around the country with whom I have many times discussed and debated the issues of this book, especially Merton Gill, Otto Kernberg, and Leo Rangell; and last, the participants in an informal psychoanalytic seminar of good friends and colleagues for the discussion of "semibaked ideas," which has been meeting monthly for three years now and where the final two chapters of this book were specifically discussed and shaped.

I also have particular indebtedness to a group of British colleagues who have guided my study of the special British contributions to the themes of the book (detailed in chapter 19), foremost among them Jane Pettit, for overall guidance and on the special role of the Tavistock Clinic, and also Mervin Glasser on the

Portman Clinic, Jennifer Johns on the Cassel Hospital, Moses Laufer on the Brent Consultation Centre (now renamed Johnston House), Jonathan Pedder on the Maudsley Institute of Psychiatry, and Malcolm Pines for his several articles of overview of the development of psychoanalytic psychotherapy in Britain. I also owe thanks to the *Journal of the American Psychoanalytic Association* for permission to reprint sections from my 1966 book essay, "The Current State of Psychotherapy: Theory, Practice, Research," from my 1986 book review of *Severe Personality Disorders: Psychotherapeutic Strategies* by Otto Kernberg, and from my 1989 article "Follow-Up in Psychoanalysis: Clinical and Research Values"; to the *International Journal of Psychoanalysis* for permission to reprint sections from my 1989 article "One Psychoanalysis or Many?" and from my 1989 article, "Psychoanalysis and Psychotherapy: A Historical Perspective"; and to *Psycho-analytic Inquiry* for permission to reprint sections from my 1990 paper "The Corrective Emotional Experience: Is Reconsideration Due?"

The title of this book I owe to the reflective comments of Allen Wheelis. The manuscript was entered into the word processor by Barbara Lehman with great diligence, accuracy, and expeditiousness. All correspondence relating to it has been handled by Ali Anderson. Special thanks are due to Gladys Topkis, Senior Editor at Yale University Press, who was interested in the book from its inception and with whom I established a most felicitous editing relationship. The improvements she wrought are clear to me throughout the text. I also appreciate very much the diligent and painstaking editorial clarifications of Lawrence Kenney at Yale University Press. And finally in this array of credits, my very great gratitude goes to the Rockefeller Foundation and its Study Center at Bellagio on Lake Como, Italy, for providing me with a five-week Fellowship in May and June 1992, where this book was organized and the first seven chapters drafted under idyllic circumstances. These thanks go particularly to Susan Garfield in the New York office and to Pasquale Pesce and Gianna Celli, the managers in Bellagio.

All that remains to be stated is my deep gratitude for a lifetime marital and intellectual partnership with my wife, Judy. No brief words can express her influence upon my entire career, including in every way the thinking that has gone into this book. And, of course, no such impressive array of credits and thanks can absolve me of my own full responsibility for its contents.

Preface

The intertwined relationship between psychoanalysis as a therapy and the range of psychoanalytically informed psychotherapies, as they have evolved over half a century, has represented the promise of the productive application of a scientific psychology and a scientific psychotherapy to as broad a segment as possible of the mental and emotional ills of society. It has also stood at the intersect of my own ongoing clinical, theoretical, and research interests since I started my training in psychiatry in 1949 and in psychoanalysis in 1951.

As has always been customary among psychiatrists coming to psychoanalytic training, my first clinical experiences were in psychotherapy, the tenets of which I had been taught in one of the psychoanalytically oriented psychiatric residency training programs established in the immediate wake of World War II. The central psychology taught was psychoanalysis, and the central therapeutic was psychoanalytically oriented, or, as it was also called, psychodynamic psychotherapy. The prevailing American metapsychology paradigm, as architected principally by Heinz Hartmann and his many colleagues and systematized by David Rapaport, was ego psychology. My professional reading was built around the clinical and theoretical psychoanalytic literature but included the beginning literature on psychoanalytic psychotherapy, the dynamic application of psychoanalytic understanding to a wider array of patients than those designated as classically amenable to the standard psychoanalytic procedure. Toward the beginning of my psychoanalytic training several panel discussions—actually debates—took place on what constituted proper psychoanalysis and how it resembled and differed from the psychoanalytic psychotherapies in their then crystallizing variants. These panels, brought together as a sequence of twelve papers in a single issue of the *Journal of the American Psychoanalytic Association* in 1954, sought to define the emerging consensus (as well as a distinctive minority dissent) within American psychoanalysis on these issues. For reasons developed in this book, the year 1954 marked a watershed in the history of psychoanalytic psychotherapy vis-à-vis psychoanalysis, and I was among those who responded readily to its conceptual as well as its practical intellectual challenge.

Another major determinant of my professional interests occurred during that same time period. After completion of my psychiatric residency at the Menninger School of Psychiatry in 1951 and coincident with the start of my candidacy at the Topeka Institute for Psychoanalysis, I took a job at the affiliated Winter Veterans Administration (VA) Hospital in Topeka, where, together with a group of collaborators, I undertook a comparative research study of four treatment approaches to a chronic alcoholic patient population on an inpatient unit at the hospital (Wallerstein et al. 1957). This study came to the attention of Gardner Murphy, the recently arrived Director of Research at the Menninger Foundation, who thereupon offered me a position in his department as Assistant Director with the charge of developing a *clinical* research program that would better link the research department—then peopled exclusively by psychologists and focused on various experimental and developmental researches—to the main clinical enterprise of the Menninger Foundation, the long-term psychoanalytic and psychoanalytically based therapy, inpatient and outpatient, of individuals who came or were brought to this protected sanatorium setting and who presumably were unable, because of the nature of their character or illness, to tolerate treatment in the usual outpatient consulting-room practice.

Out of that offer evolved a position (starting in January 1954), half-time in the Department of Research and half-time doing outpatient psychotherapy and psychoanalysis in the Department of Adult Psychiatry (DAP). First with Lewis L. Robbins, then Director of DAP, and then also principally with Helen D. Sargent and Lester Luborsky, I fashioned what came to be known as the Psychotherapy Research Project (PRP) of the Menninger Foundation, a comprehensive and successful effort to involve both the clinical and the research community at the Foundation in a prolonged research quest to learn more about the nature of the enterprise to which we were devoting our professional lives. The two seemingly simple (though not at all simpleminded) questions to which we addressed ourselves were (1) *what* changes actually take place in psychoanalysis and in psychoanalytic psychotherapies (the outcome question)? and (2) *how* do those changes come about or how are they brought about, through the interaction of what factors or variables (the process question)? The history of that research program has been written up by some fifteen to twenty research and clinical collaborators in some seventy articles and half a dozen books, including my own final clinical accounting of the treatment-careers and subsequent life-careers of the entire research cohort over a thirty-year span, *Forty-two Lives in Treatment: A Study of Psychoanalysis and Psychotherapy* (Wallerstein 1986a).

Material from the PRP, both its original conceptualization in the 1950s within the framework of the emerging consensus about the distinctions and relationships between psychoanalysis and the psychoanalytic psychotherapies and the final assessment of its findings and conclusions in the much altered psychoanalytic climate of the 1980s around these issues, will be presented at appropriate places in this book. This should serve to demonstrate the ongoing close articulation between the empirical research activity and the evolving clinical and theoretical perspectives on psychoanalysis and psychoanalytic psychotherapy over that time span, consequent to both shifts in the nature of the patient population and new developments in theory.

Lastly, much of my professional lifetime of teaching, both psychiatric residents and trainees in the other mental health disciplines, in departments of psychiatry, in psychoanalytic institutes, in supervision seminars, and in psychotherapy and psychoanalytic supervisions has been built around the problems and issues of psychoanalytic psychotherapy vis-à-vis psychoanalysis. This has kept me constantly renewing and critically reevaluating my thinking as shaped in the interactions with often critical and challenging students as well as constantly rereading many of the most significant books and articles in the field. The new perspectives I thus acquired were, of course, always being refracted through the constantly ongoing evolution of therapeutic and analytic theory and practice. In recent years I have been teaching a new course at the San Francisco Psychoanalytic Institute specifically focused on the topic of this book: the relationship of psychoanalytic psychotherapy to psychoanalysis.

So much for my background and motivation to write this book. I undertook the task with one somewhat limiting problem in mind, and others emerged as I reread my sources. The problem clearly in mind at the start was that mine is an essentially parochial—American—perspective and experience in relation to these topics. In one sense that is appropriate and not just a reflection of the happenstance of my own educational and experiential provenance: for reasons developed *in extenso* in chapter 3, there were special circumstances that made America both the logical and the necessary locus for the development of psychotherapies based on the psychoanalytic understanding of the mind but adapted to the needs of patient populations with deeper and wider disorders than those for whom Freud initially developed psychoanalysis as a therapy.

It is clear, however, that by now psychoanalytic psychotherapy has become a worldwide enterprise carried out in all the centers of psychoanalytic activity (with varying degrees of clarity in regard to its distinctness from and relationship with psychoanalysis proper), and in both its conceptual development and its practice it is no longer uniquely or even predominantly American. I try in part to correct this bias by devoting a chapter (19) to the distinctive institutional history of psychotherapy in Britain. I simply have had less access to the specifically psychoanalytic psychotherapy literature in other countries (and language areas). Recently, articles have appeared in the major English-language psychoanalytic journals, especially the *International Journal* and also the *International Review of Psychoanalysis,* from psychoanalytic centers around the world (but mostly from various European countries) mostly as part of a current common worldwide dialogue, not as simply distinctive national voices. Nonetheless, there are still limitations posed by language, perhaps especially as regards the French-language literature concerned with the impact of the Lacanian perspective on the theory and practice of psychotherapy as well as the literature produced by French psychoanalysts strongly opposed to Lacanian theory and practice. On the other hand, my active involvement, both scientifically and organizationally, in the affairs of the International Psychoanalytical Association, including all its biannual Congresses over the past two and a half decades, and my growing acquaintance with the various regional and national streams of the psychoanalytic (if not always the psychotherapeutic) enterprise have at least partially mitigated whatever distorted (American) emphases may have colored this account.

Two other, not quite anticipated, problems arose as I undertook to organize this book conceptually. The first is that the book necessarily grew broader and correspondingly less precisely focused than I originally envisaged. Certainly in what I have called the "era of the converging consensus" that emerged with the 1954 publication of the panel discussions held in the early 1950s, the parameters of a book on this topic were then much clearer. Over the intervening years, not only has the psychoanalytic psychotherapy enterprise expectedly evolved and changed with cumulating clinical practice and theoretical developments, but the anchoring reference point—the specific psychoanalytic enterprise—has itself increasingly diversified. The now fully accepted pluralism of theoretical perspectives or metapsychologies (see Wallerstein 1988a), basically both destabilizes the psychoanalytic psychotherapies and psychoanalysis and makes their similarities and differences less clear. For when their conceptual distinctness was established, in the 1940s and 1950s, it was within the context of the unified American psychoanalytic mainstream, the ego psychology paradigm called classical or traditional psychoanalysis, putatively derived in an unbroken lineage from Sigmund Freud's *The Ego and the Id* (1923) and *Inhibitions, Symptoms and Anxiety* (1926), elaborated by Anna Freud in *The Ego and the Mechanisms of Defence* (1936) in relation to the defensive functions of the ego and by Heinz Hartmann in *Ego Psychology and the Problem of Adaptation* (1939) in relation to the adaptive functions of the ego and subsequently further developed and extended by a host of colleagues and coworkers, Ernst Kris, Rudolph Loewenstein, Edith Jacobson, Margaret Mahler, and David Rapaport among the most significant.

The unquestioned hegemony of so-called classical ego psychology in America has long since splintered (see Wallerstein 1988a), and with the increasing acceptance of the clinical and theoretical contributions of the Kleinian and, even more, the various object-relational perspectives arising within the British Independent Group, as well as the growth in America of Kohut's self psychology and the rising awareness of contributions from the contemporary exponents of the Sullivanian interpersonal school (cf., for example, Levenson 1972, 1983,

1991), it has become much more difficult to compare the dimensions and the technical practices of the psychoanalytic psychotherapies and psychoanalysis proper. It has in effect become a question of *which* psychoanalysis: is one person's proper psychoanalysis someone else's "mere" psychotherapy? This set of considerations has necessarily enlarged the scope of the literature and the clinical practice encompassed in this book and led me to pluralize the word "Psychoanalyses" in its title. At the same time, it has opened the door to justifying the inclusion of almost the totality of the psychoanalytic literature within this book's purview. I will simply indicate in the concluding section of this introduction some of the major areas of psychoanalytic inquiry and scholarship, both clinical and theoretical, that I have (somewhat arbitrarily) elected to exclude from specific attention except as aspects of them become momentarily germane to the main thread of my argument.

The other unanticipated problem I have encountered exists in regard to the presentation of historical development in any scholarly discipline: a historical effort is presumably clearest and most logical when it can be presented in a reasonably chronological unfolding. However, it became evident as I tried to outline the book in my mind that to keep the main themes as orderly and as comprehensible as possible, I would have to depart from a strictly temporal sequence in the very first chapter, describing Freud's beginning creation of psychoanalysis as a therapy out of its forebears and origins in hypnosis and suggestion, along with his tenacious efforts thenceforward to purge psychoanalysis of any hint of continuing suggestive influence, while simultaneously often acknowledging its concomitant smuggling back in as a component of the interpretive process and its postulated therapeutic action. This dialectical interplay between stern efforts to expunge or deny suggestion as an influence within psychoanalysis and, on the other hand, the willingness to acknowledge its ready presence within the work of interpretation is then traced in that first chapter through the early contributions of Ferenczi, Jones, and Glover (all supportive of Freud's basic position) to the later commentaries of Waelder and Gitelson in much the same vein and finally to a contemporary (1990) assessment by Hayley laying out the much more complexly nuanced current majority view configuring the inherent (and helpful) place of suggestion within the interpretive process.

The organizational schema for this first chapter proved to be a felicitous template, and from that beginning I have chosen to follow discrete topical areas longitudinally, knowing that this could mean that specific issues or considerations did not fall properly into place in relation to concurrent developments until all of the interrelated areas were in turn presented. I have made the best compromises and accommodations in these regards that I could within the overarching schema I have conceived for the book as a whole. And it should of course be understood in this connection that the sequencing of chapters and topics does follow in some rough way the temporal origin and rise of those topical areas as major concerns within the unfolding evolution of the psychoanalytic psychotherapies. In this sense, the plan of the book is still intrinsically chronological.

It should be clear from the foregoing why this has become a larger and more comprehensive book than I had originally planned. However, it is not an effort at a full historical presentation of all the significant contributions to the issues dealt with and to the *Zeitgeist* in which I have appreciatively participated. The relevant psychoanalytic literature is simply too vast for that. I hope only that I have given due credit to those whose thinking has most selfconsciously helped shape and guide mine. Nor have I tried to be exhaustive in presenting Freud's initiating and almost always seminal contributions to each area I cover, and it is well known of course that salient forerunners can be found in Freud for just about every subsequently developed line of psychoanalytic inquiry and scholarship, even of course for developments that are antithetic and seemingly incompatible. I have only tried to supply illustrative specimens of his originating statements in each relevant area; the existence of the Freud Concordance (Guttman, Jones, and Parrish 1980) makes it possible to readily trace out the full panoply of Freud's evolving views in regard to any topic his writings have touched on. Actually, even with the topics selected for particular attention within this book, I do not claim exhaustive coverage, only what I feel is most relevant to my central focus in the English-language literature available to me.

I turn now to indicate the areas excluded from specific consideration, except where germane to the main thread of my argument. In no particular logical order, these areas are:

1. The very important and currently rapidly growing literature on the countertransference. The interested reader is referred to the landmark article by Paula Heimann (1950), the excellent review article by Douglass Orr (1954), the presentation of the concept of the countertransference neurosis by Heinrich Racker (1968), the comprehensive overview of the current literature on this topic in the four main psychoanalytic language areas in Horacio Etchegoyen's encyclopedic *Fundamentals of Psychoanalytic Technique* (1991), and Theodore Jacobs's (1991) recent courageous explorations of the pervasiveness and range of countertransference pressures even in everyday psychoanalytic work.
2. The whole corpus of the literature on child (and adolescent) analysis and psychotherapy. This could well be the focus of a very comparable

book. I have learned from my years of participation in the annual scientific Colloquia at the Anna Freud Centre in London that whatever our problems in conceptualizing the similarities and differences in psychoanalysis and psychotherapy with adults, the problems are compounded in work with children, where the usual distinguishing accoutrements of adult psychoanalytic work are absent and the central distinguishing operative approach of adult analysis, the method of free association, is either absent or severely modified. Reference of course can be made to the whole oeuvre of Anna Freud, Melanie Klein, Donald Winnicott, and all those who have come after. A particular locus of Anglo-American contributions is the annual series *The Psychoanalytic Study of the Child,* started in 1945.

3. With a small exception, the whole body of literature beginning with Paul Federn (1952) on the psychoanalytic therapy of the overtly, and usually institutionalized, psychotic (cf. Gertrud Schwing [1954], Marguerite Sechehaye [1951], and John Rosen [1953] as well as, more recently, Harold Searles [1965, 1986] in the United States, Herbert Rosenfeld [1965] in England, and David Rosenfeld [1992] in Argentina). Though now diminished in urgency because of the widespread deployment of the neuroleptic drugs among such patients, this was once a major arena of efforts to extend (very modified) psychoanalytic techniques—on the basis of a very diverse array of psychoanalytic rationales as represented by the just mentioned authors—to this population, much sicker than the usual psychoanalytic patients. The small exception referred to has to do with some aspects of the work of Frieda Fromm-Reichmann (1950, and Dexter Bullard 1959), whose theoretical and clinical endeavors with the institutionalized overtly and flagrantly psychotic related to the important debates in the early 1950s over the issue of 'blurring' or 'sharpening' the conceptual boundaries between psychoanalysis and the psychoanalytic psychotherapies.

4. Specific patient categories treated by varieties of psychoanalytical techniques, from the essentially unmodified to the most sharply transformed: the so-called psychosomatic, or the impulse-disordered like the addictions and the perversions, or the delinquent and criminal; also, patients in specific age groups representing such phases in the life cycle as adolescence or old age. For pioneering and representative—and quite diverse—attention to these groups, one can turn to Franz Alexander (1950a, with Thomas French, 1948), Felix Deutsch (1953, 1959), Pierre Marty and Michel de M'Uzan (1963), Joyce

McDougall (1989) (psychosomatic); Charles Socarides (1968, 1975, 1978, 1988), Janine Chasseguet-Smirgel (1984), Adam Limentani (1989) (perverse); Robert Knight (Stuart Miller, 1972) (alcoholic); August Aichhorn (1935, Otto Fleischmann et al., 1964), Kurt Eissler (1949), Fritz Redl and David Wineman (1951, 1952), Edward Glover (1960a) (delinquent and criminal); Peter Blos (1962, 1979) (adolescent); and Martin Berezin and Stanley Cath (1965) (the elderly).

5. Specialized applications of psychotherapeutic work, such as brief, time-limited therapy, family therapy, or group therapy. Some of these endeavors are designedly psychoanalytic in conceptualization and application; most are within other-than-psychoanalytic psychological explanatory frameworks, like the Rogerian client-centered, the phenomenological-existential, family or systems theory, behavior modification, or simply the avowedly 'eclectic.' Of the purportedly more specifically psychoanalytic, reference is made to the pioneering contributions of David Malan (1963), Peter Sifneos (1972), James Mann (1973), Mardi Horowitz (1976), Habib Davanloo (1978), and Paul Crits-Christoph and Jacques Barber (1991) for the brief therapies, and to Samuel Slavson (1943, 1947, 1950), S. H. Foulkes (1948), Henry Ezriel (1950, 1952), Saul Scheidlinger (1952, 1982), and Murray Bowen (1978) for group and family therapies.

6. This leads of course to the vast realm, by now probably larger than the psychoanalytic, of psychotherapy literature conceived within nonpsychoanalytic psychological paradigms. No reference to that body of literature will be made here; however, I do want to draw attention to a distinction made by John Benjamin during a consultation visit to the Psychotherapy Research Project in the late 1950s, between the effort to help forge a theory of psychoanalytic therapy (to which the PRP was directed) as against the much more ambitious and currently far less attainable goal of forging a psychoanalytic theory of all therapy, whether conceived within the framework of psychoanalytic theoretical understanding or not. Ultimately, of course, if we assume that psychoanalytic theory provides a more comprehensive understanding of human mental functioning than any of the rival theories of mind, we should be in a position to provide a psychoanalytic understanding of the results achieved and *how* they are achieved within other, even radically different, purported understandings, such as the results achieved with phobic illnesses or sexual dysfunctions by behavior-modification methods.

7. Quite apart from the nonpsychoanalytic therapies are the various

streams of psychoanalytic theoretical development other than the (American) ego psychological, which has provided the main conceptual framework for this book: The Kleinian, the Bionian, the British object-relational (Suttie, Fairbairn, Guntrip, Winnicott, Balint, Bowlby, and their successors), the Lacanian, Kohut's self psychology, and even Sullivan's interpersonal analysis and Horney's cultural psychoanalysis—each of these has a major body of literature readily accessible to every psychoanalytic reader, albeit with language barriers in some instances. A very small segment of the literature in these areas will be referred to as it bears on the central themes of this book. Reference is made here to three recent books which attempt to compare some of these theoretical perspectives: Jay Greenberg and Stephen Mitchell (1983), Judith Hughes (1989), and Howard Bacal and Kenneth Newman (1990).

8. Another large, somewhat related realm is that of the literature on the nature of psychoanalysis as science—whether psychoanalysis is akin to natural science, or all science, is a different kind of science, a social or behavioral science with presumably different canons of evidence and validation, or a special and unique science ("our science," Saul Harrison 1970), or a "hermeneutic science," if there is such a thing (Merton Gill 1983a)—or no science at all but an avowedly hermeneutic endeavor like literary criticism or the exegetical Biblical criticism from which the term *hermeneutics* derived in the first place. My own position on what I have termed "the great metapsychology debate" is elaborated elsewhere (Wallerstein 1976, 1986b); this body of inquiry is only tangentially related to the concerns of this book and will not be directly addressed. For a contemporary overview of both the philosophical-psychological debates around these issues as well as full consideration of the implications for the therapeutic enterprise (whether proper psychoanalysis or psychoanalytic psychotherapy), reference is made to the counterposed books by Adolf Grunbaum (1984) and Marshall Edelson (1984).

9. Still another excluded area is the currently burgeoning literature on psychoanalytic therapy *research* directed toward the fuller understanding of the processes and outcomes of psychoanalytic therapies, whether in psychoanalysis proper or in the varieties of psychoanalytic psychotherapies. Some of this research will be covered in this book where it bears centrally on the book's main concerns; this includes the Psychotherapy Research Project of the Menninger Foundation, treated in various places throughout this book, and also a chapter

devoted to the assessment of results achieved, judged at treatment termination and in some instances also at follow-up. For comprehensive statements of the cutting edge of contemporary psychoanalytic *process* research, reference is made to the books of Hartwig Dahl et al. (1988), Lester Luborsky et al. (1984, 1988, 1990), and Mardi Horowitz et al. (1979, 1984, 1991).

10. Last in this listing of topics wholly or mostly excluded from consideration in this book is the whole arena of the sociopolitical and economic problems in the professional practice of psychoanalysis and psychotherapy—the seemingly universally shrinking patient base, the increasing numbers of nonpsychoanalytically based alternative therapies (some verging on the cultist) and of self-help groups, the growing preoccupation everywhere with cost effectiveness and cost containment within both private and national health insurance systems, the growing requirements for peer review and utilization review, with their inevitable impingements on the privacy and confidentiality of the two-party therapeutic transaction, etc. I have dealt with these issues, so vital to our future as a professional activity, in my article entitled "The Future of Psychotherapy" (1991) and as a significant part of another article, "The Future of Psychoanalysis" (Wallerstein and Edward Weinshel 1989).

Given all these major arenas of exclusion from central consideration, I trust that I have brought this book's dimensions, large as they are, within manageable compass and that I have managed a reasonable and reasonably comprehensive rendering of the many issues and problems, both for theory and for clinical practice, in the ever-changing relationship between psychoanalysis (or the psychoanalyses) as therapy and all the derived and related psychoanalytic psychotherapies.

I. The Emergence of Psychoanalysis and of Psychoanalytic Psychotherapy

1 Sigmund Freud: The Origins of Psychoanalysis from Hypnosis and Suggestion

The story of psychoanalysis as a theory and as a therapy starts, of course, with Sigmund Freud. The first article I wrote on the subject of this book (Wallerstein 1966) began as follows: "Though their roots can be traced far back into history, to soothsayers and ancient prophets, and to priests and primitive medicine men, modern dynamic psychology and psychotherapy derive firmly from the scientific psychology innovated by Freud. The psychoanalysis developed by Freud as a purified product out of the congeries of therapeutic approaches in vogue in his time or experimentally introduced by him and his first co-worker, Breuer—electrical stimulations, rest cures, hypnotic suggestion, forced associations on command, etc.—soon became *the* scientific psychology and *the* scientific therapy" (183–84).

Actually, Freud laid down the fundaments of this scientific therapy as early as 1905, in his lecture "On Psychotherapy" (1905b).[1] There he made his famous distinction between the "cathartic or analytic method of psychotherapy" and hypnotic/suggestive techniques: "There is, actually, the greatest possible antithesis between suggestive and analytic technique—the same antithesis which, in regard to the fine arts, Leonardo da Vinci summed up in the formulas: *per via di porre* and *per via di levare*" (260). This was the analogy between painting, *per via di porre*, applying pigment to cover the canvas, and the hypnotic covering up of psychic distress by either positive or negative suggestions (to behave, think, or feel in particular ways counter to the neurotic symptoms or inhibitions or to give up particular symptoms or dysfunctional behaviors). On the other hand,

1. It is a semantic issue of this book that throughout it the word "psychotherapy" is used in two senses. In the broad usage, the word is used to encompass the whole range of psychotherapies as psychological or "talking" therapies, though in almost all instances this will mean only those based on psychoanalysis as the underlying theory of mental functioning, excluding the nonpsychoanalytically based psychotherapies. This usage does, however, include psychoanalysis proper among these psychoanalytic psychotherapies. In the narrow usage, the word "psychotherapy" is meant to be distinguished from psychoanalysis proper as therapy, in the sense of being counterposed to it, but again as *psychoanalytic* psychotherapy. Which usage is meant, the broad or the narrow, should be clear from the context. In this particular instance, Freud's usage is neither one of these because he means here psychotherapy as *equated* with psychoanalysis as therapy. As I develop in this chapter, Freud never distinguished any psychoanalytically derived psychotherapies; he knew only psychoanalysis as a specific therapy—other than the various forms of suggestion and/or hypnosis, that is, nonpsychoanalytically based therapies.

sculpture, *per via di levare,* is removing marble to uncover and reveal the statue hidden within it, analogous to the psychoanalytic uncovering and revealing of repressed and disavowed traumatic memory, strangled affect, or unconscious inner conflict.

Freud then set down the criteria of analyzability. Those amenable to this rationally understood and powerful new psychotherapeutic tool must suffer from a chronic neurotic syndrome (of the kind that later came to be called transference neuroses), be past adolescence but still in the prime of adulthood, of good intelligence, with "a reasonable degree of education . . . a fairly reliable character . . . [and] driven to seek treatment by their own sufferings"; all in all, they must "possess a normal mental condition" 263–64).[2] On the other hand, "neuropathic degeneracy, . . . psychoses, states of confusion and deeply-rooted (I might say toxic) depression are . . . not suitable for psycho-analysis; at least not for the method as it has been practiced up to the present. I do not regard it as by any means impossible that by suitable changes in the method we may succeed in overcoming this contraindication—and so be able to initiate a psychotherapy of the psychoses."[3] He also ruled out as prospective analysands those near or over the age of fifty, who, he believed, lacked sufficient "elasticity" to be "educable."

Freud then addressed the common conception that psychoanalysis was only the application of a commonsense psychology and required no special training or skill: "It seems to me that there is a widespread and erroneous impression among my colleagues that this technique of searching for the origins of an illness and removing its manifestations by that means is an easy one which can be practiced off-hand, as it were . . . They think that there is nothing to enquire about, that the thing is perfectly self-evident. . . . Reports reach my ears that this or that colleague has arranged appointments with a patient in order to undertake a mental treatment of the case, though I am certain he knows nothing of the technique of any such therapy" (261). Clearly, Freud heartily disapproved of such presumptuous practices.

But psychoanalysis is neither an ideal nor a speedy treatment and, no doubt

2. This conception of a "normal mental condition," meant to exclude the psychotic and the organically mentally ill, was later picked up by Eissler (1953) in his elaboration of Freud's conception of "the hypothetically normal ego" (125), the vital criterion of amenability to the "classical" psychoanalytic technique.

3. Here is a very early reference to Freud's hope that someday ("by suitable changes in the method") even the overtly psychotic could be drawn within the orbit of the psychoanalytically treatable. This later developed into a very specific literature that, as has been indicated, will be touched on only tangentially here, and that in reference to Frieda Fromm-Reichmann's contribution (1954) to the landmark debates of the early fifties.

with suggestive and hypnotic techniques in mind, Freud went on to say, "I consider it quite justifiable to resort to more convenient methods of treatment as long as there is any prospect of achieving anything by their means. That, after all, is the only point at issue. If the more difficult and lengthy method accomplishes considerably more than the short and easy one, then, in spite of everything, the use of the former is justified" (262). And finally, where it *is* appropriately used, by a proper practitioner, psychoanalysis will not cause harm: "You will no doubt wish to enquire about the possibility of doing harm by undertaking a psycho-analysis. In reply to this I may say that if you are willing to judge impartially, if you will consider this procedure in the same spirit of critical fairness that you show to our other therapeutic methods, you will have to agree with me that no injury to the patient is to be feared when the treatment is conducted with comprehension. Anyone who is accustomed, like the lay public, to blame the treatment for whatever happens during an illness will doubtless judge differently" (265).

In another paper of the same year (1905c), Freud reviewed the psychotherapeutic uses of hypnosis and suggestion, spoke to the severe limitations of these modalities as psychic treatments, and described the evolution of his own more scientific (i.e., etiologically causal) efforts to manage dysphoric affects, thoughts, and behaviors. Though there is no specific mention of psychoanalysis at all in this paper, at the end he stated, "It is not surprising that physicians, to whom hypnotic mental treatment promised so much more than it could give, are indefatigable in their search for other procedures, which would make possible a deeper, or at least a less unpredictable, influence on a patient's mind" (302).

With these very early articles, Freud established his central conception of psychoanalysis as a mental therapy, originally built out of, but to be sharply distinguished from, suggestion and hypnosis.[4] Freud's concern here was to keep the conceptual distinctions between psychoanalysis and suggestive/hypnotic techniques clear, though he also (e.g., in his *Autobiographical Study*, 1925b) acknowledged the persistence of elements of suggestion in the handling of the transference: "It is perfectly true that psycho-analysis, like other psychotherapeutic methods, employs the instrument of suggestion (or transference). But the difference is this, that in analysis it is not allowed to play the decisive part in determining the therapeutic results. It is used instead to induce the patient

4 His later sequence of six papers on technique (1911 to 1915, *S.E.* 12:83–173) elaborated his technical prescriptions for carrying out this psychoanalytic treatment. These will be discussed in chapter 7 in connection with the controversy that arose many years later concerning what constituted Freud's "actual technique" and its relation to what came to be described as the "classical technique" (Eissler 1953; Lipton 1977).

to perform a piece of psychical work—the overcoming of his transference-resistances—which involves a permanent alteration in his mental economy" (42–43). (Note how, in this passage, Freud even conflated transference and suggestion, something he generally did not do.)

Even earlier, in his technical paper "On Beginning the Treatment" (1913), Freud had remarked on the positive role of suggestion in psychoanalytic technique. In response to a question as to when to offer interpretations ("the moment for disclosing to him [the patient] the hidden meaning of the ideas that occur to him," 139), Freud stated, "The answer to this can only be: Not until an effective transference has been established in the patient, a proper *rapport* with him. It remains the first aim of the treatment to attach him to it and to the person of the doctor. To ensure this, nothing need be done but to give him time. If one exhibits a serious interest in him, carefully clears away the resistances that crop up at the beginning, and avoids making certain mistakes, he will of himself form such an attachment and link the doctor up with one of the imagos of the people by whom he was accustomed to be treated with affection" (139–40). (Again, note the conflation of transference and rapport/suggestion.) And in the very next of the series of technical papers, "Remembering, Repeating, and Working-Through" (1914a), Freud went on to say, "If the patient starts his treatment under the auspices of a mild and unpronounced positive transference, it *makes it possible* at first for him to unearth his memories just as he would under hypnosis" (151, italics added)—that is, the suggestive influence of the transference enables the analyst to overcome the patient's resistances.[5]

In another famous passage, from his 1918 Budapest address, Freud (1919) spoke of an admixture of analytic and suggestive techniques. He began, "Our therapeutic activities are not very far-reaching. There are only a handful of us, and even by working very hard each one can devote himself in a year to only a small number of patients. Compared to the vast amount of neurotic misery which there is in the world, and perhaps need not be, the quantity we can do away with is almost negligible. Besides this, the necessities of our existence limit our work to the well-to-do classes" (166). "On the other hand," he added, "it is possible to foresee that at some time or other the conscience of society will awake and remind it that the poor man should have as much right to assistance for his mind as he now has for the life-saving help offered by surgery; and that

---

5. This aspect of Freud's view of the transference was picked up much later by Macalpine (1950) and made the fulcrum of her reconceptualization of the unfolding of the transference in psychoanalysis as being profoundly suggestively induced, as against the till then conventional wisdom that it was a spontaneous evolution, with the analyst's central role being the avoidance of interference with this evolution—the view espoused in many passages by Freud and followed by almost all who came after. This is discussed *in extenso* in chapter 12.

the neuroses threaten public health no less than tuberculosis, and can be left as little as the latter to the impotent care of individual members of the community. . . . We shall then be faced by the task of adapting our technique to the new conditions" (167).

These remarks led to the famous statement, "It is very probable, too, that the large-scale application of our therapy will compel us to alloy the pure gold of analysis freely with the copper of direct suggestion; and hypnotic influence, too, might find a place in it again, as it has in the treatment of the war neuroses. But, whatever form this psychotherapy for the people may take, whatever the elements out of which it is compounded, its most effective and most important ingredients will assuredly remain those borrowed from strict and untendentious psycho-analysis" (167–68).

Yet, despite these well-known statements, in many places in his voluminous writings Freud made clear his intention to sharply differentiate psychoanalysis from the hypnosis and suggestion out of which it was born, insisting on the need to remove as far as possible—by thorough analysis—any vestige of suggestive impact upon the process of change and cure. Sandor Ferenczi, whose technical innovations and seeming deviations, under the rubric of "active therapy," led ultimately to a severe strain in his relationship with Freud, nonetheless was very much at one with Freud in regard to this goal. In his most explicit statement, in "Suggestion and Psycho-Analysis" (1912), Ferenczi began by outlining the drawbacks of suggestive/hypnotic therapies: not everyone can be influenced by these means, their good effects may be only temporary, and, above all, they are an education in blindness, in the narrowing of consciousness, and therefore are at best only palliative, whereas "analysis desires to be called a 'causal process of healing' " (61). Though "there have been people who declared that analysis itself is nothing else than a form of suggestion" (62), Ferenczi outlined the differences: the suggester fosters belief, whereas the psychoanalyst fosters skepticism by exposing the resistances; the suggester wishes to impress his patient favorably, whereas the psychoanalyst interprets the negative transferences; the suggester wants only to convey pleasant things, whereas the psychoanalyst unflinchingly faces unpleasant truths.

Yet, like Freud, Ferenczi was aware of the suggestive influence that could lurk within the transference: "A similar inclination to unquestioning submission on the part of the patient certainly manifests itself also in analysis, and in so far the presence of suggestive factors in analysis also must be acknowledged; but this 'suggestion' in analysis is only a transitional stage, and no patient can analytically be held to be cured who has not sobered down out of this condition" (64–65). And, like Freud, Ferenczi called for constant vigilance concerning this risk to the possibility of proper psychoanalytic cure: "The analysing doctor must keep strict watch that he is not content with a success due to suggestion" (65). But the analyst is also specifically armed against this possibility: "Not only is analysis not any kind of suggestion but [it is] a constant battle against suggestive influences, and . . . the technique of analysis uses more protective measures against blind belief and unquestioning submission than any methods of teaching and enlightenment that have ever been used in the nursery, the university, or the consulting room" (66).

Twelve years later, Ferenczi and Otto Rank (1924) indicated their awareness that the active therapy methods they were advocating could be experienced as a Trojan horse, readmitting the specter of suggestion into psychoanalytic work. Concerning the search for a shorter, more effective analytic treatment process, they said, for example, "This possibility of readmitting hypnosis, or other suggestive methods, into our analytic therapy would perhaps be the culmination of the simplification of the analytic technique, towards which, according to our interpretation, we should be and are actually tending. The final goal of psychoanalysis is to substitute, by means of the technique, affective factors of experience for intellectual processes. It is well known that this is just what is achieved in an extreme way in hypnosis, in which conscious material is called forth or eliminated according to need" (62). Lest they be thought heretical for drawing analytic and suggestive techniques conceptually closer, the authors by implication called on Freud's pure gold of analysis and copper of suggestion metaphor: "We should not wonder if the point were finally reached when other psycho-therapeutic methods which had proven themselves useful according to analytic understanding (as we tried to show, for example, in hypnosis) were legitimately combined with psycho-analysis" (64).

It was, however, Ernest Jones, followed closely by Edward Glover, who was most uncompromising in insisting that the therapy world was totally dichotomous, divided into psychoanalysis on the one side and all the varieties of suggestion on the other. In a long paper on suggestion in psychotherapy, Jones (1910) argued,

> Suggestion plays the chief part in all methods of treatment of the psychoneuroses except the psycho-analytic one. It acts by releasing the regressed desires that are finding expression in the form of symptoms, and allowing them to become attached to the idea of the physician; psychologically this means the replacement of one symptom by another—namely, psychosexual dependence on the physician. This is often of temporary, and sometimes of permanent benefit, but in severe cases the replacement is inconvenient and detrimental. In psycho-analysis, on the contrary, the repressed tendencies are permanently released by being made conscious,

and hence can be directed, by sublimation, to more useful, non-sexual, social aims. (359)

This view, that proper psychoanalysis, purged of any suggestive components, was the only truly curative and scientific psychotherapy and that psychoanalysts had little or nothing to offer patients who lacked the characteristics that would make them suited to the classical method (as spelled out by Freud 1905b), pervaded almost all of Freud's lifetime. It marked the period that I have called the prehistory of psychotherapy (Wallerstein 1989a)—now more narrowly considered as psychotherapy other than psychoanalysis proper—within psychoanalysis.

The position that all psychotherapy other than psychoanalysis was merely suggestion was carried to its extreme by Glover. In his powerfully influential paper "The Therapeutic Effect of Inexact Interpretation" (1931), he began, "We are periodically stimulated to reconsider the relation between different forms of psychotherapy, more particularly when any advance is made in analytic knowledge" (397). He went on to develop the view that all psychotherapy other than psychoanalysis, correctly and exactly applied, was indeed *nothing but* suggestion. I have described Glover's view as follows:

> His thesis was that all therapies other than thorough psychoanalysis are merely varieties of suggestion since they rest on elements (which can even include interpretations of unconscious conflicts) that are not fully analyzed back to their genetic-dynamic roots and hence must ultimately be based on the strong transference authority of the therapist. Even inexact interpretations conveyed in the course of an effort at analysis become, in this view, only displacement substitutes, not so inappropriate as the neurotic symptoms and yet sufficiently remote from the real sources of anxiety so that the patient is all too willing, unconsciously, to live up to them. (Wallerstein 1966, 184)

Glover (1931) posed the specific underlying problem created here: "What is the effect of inexact as compared with apparently exact interpretation? If we agree that accuracy of interpretation amongst other factors contributes towards a cure, and if we agree that fresh phantasy systems are discovered from time to time, what are we to make of the cures that were effected before these systems were discovered?" (398). His not surprising response was, "If in former times analysts did not completely uncover unconscious content, then surely the analytic successes of earlier days must have been due in part to an element of suggestion" (406) because whatever is not fully analyzed rests ultimately on the "strong transference authority" of the analyst. This applies even, and perhaps especially, to (hidden) suggestions "of the pseudo-analytical type—that is, suggestions based on some degree of interpretative appreciation" (403).

Almost a quarter of a century later, during which time psychoanalytic psychotherapy had developed as a complex, multifaceted therapeutic enterprise, Glover still held this view: "A further case exists: should the analyst's interpretations be consistently inaccurate, then quite clearly he is practising a form of suggestion, whatever else he himself may call it. It follows then that when analysts differ radically as to the aetiology or structure of a case—as they nowadays do with increasing frequency—one side or the other must be practising suggestion" (1955, 394).[6] Five years later, Glover (1960b) added words of alarm on this subject. He talked of the "hotch-potch" (74) of psychotherapeutic activities that had burgeoned in England and then opined sadly, "There seems no reason to suppose that in course of time, the sharp distinction between psychoanalysis and rapport therapies [the varieties of suggestion] will not become blurred in this country," as he felt had already happened in the United States (81–82).

We can see readily enough the kind of narrowed reasoning—that there must be only a single "correct" interpretive line in every analytic situation and that any deviation from it, willing or not, based on inexactness, ignorance, countertransference, or whatever—must therefore be only suggestion (in a pejorative sense)—that led Glover, building on Freud and Jones, to this sharp dichotomization of all psychotherapy into either "pure" psychoanalysis or simply a variation of suggestion. In this way, he, along with Jones and Freud, did an unwitting disservice to the future development of psychoanalytically informed and guided psychotherapy with a sound theoretical base in psychoanalytic psychology by obscuring the theoretical and technical complexities it involved. The encompassing rubric of suggestion was used to cover (and thereby blur) a diversity of distinct principles and practices.

Thus, the prehistory of psychoanalytic psychotherapy was marked by the delineation of psychoanalysis as a clearly articulated therapy with consensually agreed-upon principles and practices and specific indications and contraindications; all else—for all categories of patients deemed not amenable to psychoanalysis—was swept into the ill-defined, encompassing category of suggestion. Since at least the early 1940s a now-dominant counterstream has existed that views psychotherapy as distinct from both psychoanalysis *and* suggestion, yet the position of Freud and Ferenczi and Jones and Glover on this

6. But Glover had earlier softened the blow: "bad analysis may conceivably be good suggestion" (1931, 407).

issue has nonetheless persisted, continuingly skeptical and critical of psycho-*therapeutic* efforts that are not "strict and untendentious psycho*analysis*."

For example, Robert Waelder (1960), in his otherwise valuable book on the basic theory and practice of psychoanalysis, held to this same simplified view of psychotherapy. He distinguished between psychoanalysis, an *exploratory* psycho-therapy that investigates the unconscious and renders it conscious to the patient, and *educational* (his word for suggestive) psychotherapy, the generic term for all forms of influence that try to bring about better adjustment of an individual to the outside world through advice, suggestion, guidance, retraining, occupational therapy, community living, or other means. Like Freud (and Ferenczi), Waelder talked of mixing the two in an effort to effect a mass application of psychoan-alytic therapy. But he said that such a mixture, usually called "psychoanalytically oriented psychotherapy," was bound to meet with difficulties because analysis requires an attitude of neutrality and education an attitude of guidance. Taking educational measures necessarily interferes with the possibility of doing analysis. Waelder summed up pessimistically: "The partnership between psychoanalysis and educational psychotherapy may therefore well end up somewhat like the coalitions between democratic and totalitarian parties in which the former are likely to be swallowed up by the latter; in the end, only education remains" (216).

Another voice along these lines was that of Maxwell Gitelson, who helped shape the development of psychodynamic psychotherapy in America but none-theless straddled this issue of the possibility of an analytic psycho*therapy* that is more than suggestion. On the one hand, he could say,

> Psychotherapy today is rational because it is based on what we know about psychopathology and psychodynamics as psychoanalysis has elu-cidated them. From this standpoint, good psychotherapy looks so much like psychoanalysis that on paper we almost cannot tell the dif-ference! And yet, I believe there are very important differences. Mod-ern psychotherapy deserves its position in psychiatry because it is in a real sense the psychiatrist's reason for being.[7] Moreover, it has become

7. This could hardly be said today. Psychiatry has become much more diversified in structure and scope, especially with the recent explosive growth of neurobiology (and molecular biology and molecular genetics) as basic sciences, and the derived psychopharmacology as their clinical therapeutic expression. Today, there are many intellectually gratifying career paths in psychi-atry, a far cry from the psychoanalytically congenial days of the 1950s, when psychoanalytic theory and psychodynamic psychotherapy were practically the whole of psychiatry and when most young physicians who entered psychiatric residency training did so with the explicit intent of seeking psychoanalytic training and becoming psychoanalysts.

a truly effective instrument. Nothing I have to say about it is intended to give the impression that I depreciate its validity and its usefulness. Nevertheless it is not psychoanalysis even when it is psychoanalytic. (1956, 247)

And yet, within a page he could collapse the total theoretic understanding of this developing psychotherapy onto the familiar base of suggestion. He stated then that in skilled psychotherapy, the results ultimately "depend for their effectiveness on what is dynamically a repression of a basic conflict, following on some partial solution of derivative conflicts, and finally accepted on the *fundamentally suggestive* basis of an unresolved transference" (248). The italics here are Gitelson's and the date (1956) is *after* the fullest flowering, in 1954, of what I have called the second era, the era of converging consensus, in the historical development of our conceptions of a psychotherapy grounded in psychoanalysis as theory, yet clearly distinct from it in goals, technical implementation, and range of application (Wallerstein 1989a).[8]

But these efforts by Freud and others to expunge all vestiges of suggestive influences from psychoanalysis and concomitantly to consign all psychotherapy other than psychoanalysis to the realm of *nothing but* suggestion have never been—nor could they be—fully successful. The place of suggestion as an inseparable element within the operative mechanism of the transference has been acknowledged by many outstanding psychoanalysts from Freud's time to the present. For example, James Strachey (1934) spoke of the transference as abetted by the familiar powers of suggestion, albeit not in the service of repression but rather of overcoming it. Almost a half-century later, Leo Stone (1982) stated, "When Freud speaks of the 'gold' of analysis (in contrast with the 'copper' of suggestion), he means that this *element of suggestion* is no longer the authoritarian curative element in itself. But it continues to function as a component of a facilitating interpersonal vehicle, the transference, to launch the new adventure of insight, self-understanding, and confrontation with conflict, ultimately itself to be subject to the analytic scrutiny intended to dissolve it" (82). And, as already indicated, Ida Macalpine (1950) made the powerful role of suggestion in the unfolding of the regressive transference

8. Gitelson (1951) had come to this same conclusion five years earlier, although he expressed it in somewhat different language (more akin to Glover's 1931 concept of "inexact interpretation" and in that sense again ultimately reducible to suggestion). There he said, "Yet psychoanalytic scrutiny will disclose such a [psychotherapeutic] 'cure' to have been based on elaborate rationalization, which depends for its effectiveness on what is dynamically a repression of the basic conflict after some partial solution of derivative conflicts has been attained and accepted as a compromise" (286).

neurosis the centerpiece of her understanding of the evolution of the transference (see chapter 12).[9]

A final illustration of the persistent vitality of concern with the role of suggestion in the psychoanalytic treatment process is Tom Hayley's "Charisma, Suggestion, Psychoanalysts, Medicine-Men, and Metaphor" (1990), a paper whose observational bases are the twin pillars of anthropological fieldwork (in Uganda and India) and clinical psychoanalysis. Hayley began with the statement, "We know how psychoanalysis has been denigrated as being *merely* an organized way in which to impart suggestions to patients and that, partly as a result, this is something psychoanalysts have usually denied" (2). He went on to frame his own inquiry: "The issues really narrow themselves down to how much is suggestion at work in our psychoanalytical psychotherapy and what is this 'decisive factor' postulated by Freud [1925b, 43], which is the really effective part of an interpretation?" (2). His response was, "We think we know what the decisive factor is. We think it is the nearness we can reach to psychic truth—how accurately we manage to hit the nail on the head—which we try to effect by our metaphorical interpretations. Since our interpretations are metaphorical, it is very difficult to know whether the effect they may have is due to the psychic truth they reveal or the suggestion conveyed by charismatic authority" (6).

Hayley then amplified what he meant by suggestion in this context:

> I wish to make it quite clear that when I talk about "suggestion" involved in charismatic influence, I do not mean any form of overt suggestion, such as reassurance, or the blatant suggestion advocated by Coue or contained in hypnotism. In fact psychoanalytical method rightly avoids all overt forms of reassurance or suggestion. I am referring in this paper to the hidden forms of suggestion latent in charismatic influences and the phenomenon of positive transference, and the hidden forms of reassurances involved in the clinical setting, the psychoanalyst's couch, the reliability of his time-keeping, etc. Psychoanalysts appear to turn a blind eye to all this covert suggestive influence in their need to demonstrate their studious avoidance of suggestive practices. (6)

And in further amplification, "The effect of five sessions a week, or rather a greater daily continuity of treatment, is to strengthen the transference feelings.

9. Other echoes of the acknowledgment of suggestive influence in the ongoing work of psychoanalysis as well as in psychoanalytic psychotherapy will be discussed under such headings as parameters (chapter 7), the psychoanalytic relationship and the role of new experience (chapters 16 and 17), and most directly Bibring's (1954) delineation of the basic therapeutic principles of all psychodynamic psychotherapies, including psychoanalysis (chapter 5).

This means, if my thesis is correct, that it strengthens the suggestive quality of the charismatic authority of the psychoanalyst at the same time as it gives more time for the mutative process to work" (8).

Hayley concluded,

> This paper shows how anthropological observations may throw light on psychoanalytical theory and practice. The suggestive power of role and personal charisma in medicine-men and psychoanalysts works in aid of the decisive factor of revealing psychic truth in psychic change. This is conveyed through the metaphor of interpretations (in the case of psycho-analysts) and/or enacted metaphors (the ceremonies, in the case of med-icine-men). The psychoanalyst is exhorted to preserve anonymity, confine his interventions to interpretation, maintain the daily continuity of treat-ment, etc. This has the effect of enhancing the positive transference and with it the charismatic suggestive influence of the psychoanalyst, stem-ming from the earliest charisma of parents which lies behind early learning processes and the building up of the inner world of psychic truth or unconscious phantasy. (9)

I would guess that these views (contra Freud and the efforts to deny sugges-tion in psychoanalysis) represent a majority opinion in contemporary psychoa-nalysis, though there have been strong efforts to maintain and extend Freud's thinking in this area—notably by Kurt Eissler (1953, 1958), Charles Brenner (1979, 1982), and Paul Gray (1973, 1982, 1986, 1987, 1988, 1990, 1991), whose contributions are elaborated in chapters 7, 11, 13, and 21.

2 Sandor Ferenczi: The Psychoanalytic Relationship and the Active Technique

Though Sandor Ferenczi, Freud's closest psychoanalytic collaborator and intellectual companion, played no direct role in the development of psychoanalytic psychotherapy out of psychoanalysis, his lifelong efforts to enhance the effectiveness of psychoanalysis as therapy, through the development of the techniques of active therapy and an intensifying focus on the affective therapeutic relationship as a central vehicle of the curative process, became the acknowledged forerunners of several of the most significant trends that later became linked to the developing psychoanalytic psychotherapy enterprise.

Ferenczi began his experimentation in an effort to deal with regularly recurring resistances in the analytic situation. For example, he undertook to force obsessionally indecisive patients to make necessary life decisions: "The analyst can, and must from time to time, practice 'active therapy' in so far as he forces the patient to overcome the phobia-like incapability of coming to a decision. By the change in the affective excitations that this overcoming will occasion he hopes to obtain access to as yet inaccessible unconscious material" (1919a, 184). He analogized this kind of activity to Freud's "parameter" of requiring the phobic patient, after sufficient interpretive analytic work, to finally enter the phobically avoided situation in order to unearth the still-hidden phobic anxieties for psychoanalytic scrutiny.

Ferenczi developed this line of thinking more fully in a companion paper of the same year (1919b). He first described a hysterical patient who was caught up in an erotic transference and who kept her legs crossed during an entire hour in what Ferenczi considered to be a larval form of masturbation. After a while, he hit upon the idea of forbidding the patient to adopt this position. The result was "staggering": a major affective mobilization and recovery of forgotten memories. When the stagnation recurred, Ferenczi extended the interdiction to the patient's whole day and to further masturbatory equivalents as he unearthed them, including sudden urgent needs to urinate. He called this "a new rule in analysis . . . as follows: during treatment one must also think of the possibility of larval onanism and onanistic equivalents, and where indications of these are observed, abolish them" (193). Whether the analyst *commanded* the patient to perform an action or *forbade* one, the intent of Ferenczi's "active technique" was therapeutic: to mobilize otherwise warded-off anxiety for analytic scrutiny.

Of the case described in the second paper, Ferenczi said, "I was compelled . . . to give up the passive part that the psycho-analyst is accustomed to play in the treatment, which is confined to the hearing and interpretation of the patient's ideas, and had by active interference in the patient's psychic activities to help her over dead points in the work of the analysis." He claimed in support that Freud himself had directed patients to just such critical situations that elicited attacks of anxiety. Ferenczi called this the "method of experiment": "Since our knowledge of transference and of 'active technique' we are able to say that besides observation and logical deduction (interpretation) psychoanalysis has also at command the method of experiment . . . in suitable cases we can and must shut off psychic excitement from unconscious paths of discharge, in order by this 'rise of pressure' of energy to overcome the resistance of the censorship and of the 'resting excitation' by higher psychic systems" (196–97).

Ferenczi developed these "experiments" even more systematically in a 1920 paper on the array of interdictions and commands that could be deployed in active therapy: "In requiring what is inhibited, and inhibiting what is uninhibited, we hope for a fresh distribution of the patient's psychic, primarily of his libidinal, energy that will further the laying bare of repressed material. . . . Active technique desires nothing more and nothing less than to lay bare latent tendencies to repetition and by this means to assist the therapy to these triumphs a little oftener than hitherto" (212, 217). Ferenczi again stressed that such activity was not new in analysis. The original Breuer-Freud cathartic procedure was indeed very active, and an active "education of the ego" was always part of the work of analysis.

In another example, Ferenczi wrote about a musician suffering from performance fright. He first commanded this patient to sing and play the piano in the analytic hour in order to uncover the hidden (and avoided) masturbatory pleasures. He then forbade these very activities so that the now-frustrated hidden pleasures could be forced further into psychic consciousness. In all, active therapy became a series of alternating or simultaneous commands and prohibitions. In this connection, Ferenczi mentioned urinary urgency, bodily movements, and playfulness in the analytic hours [205–06].

At the same time, Ferenczi raised a series of cautions about these techniques. First of all, they should be used only "in certain exceptional cases" and only to the extent necessary: "As soon as the stagnation of the analysis, the only justification for and the only motive of the modification, is overcome, the expert will immediately resume the passively receptive attitude most favourable for the efficient co-operation of the doctor's unconscious" (198). Active techniques should also be avoided at the beginning of analysis, when they could be a "wild" analytic activity and frighten the patient away; however, " 'the end-game' of the analysis is seldom successful without active interference or tasks respectively that the patient must perform beyond the exact adherence to the fundamental rule" (209). Here Ferenczi mentioned a range of interventions: forcing necessary decisions, setting the termination date, even temporarily forbidding sexual intercourse.

All this, of course, relates to the way in which the analyst can further the treatment by deliberately and planfully manipulating his own behavior in relation to the patient: "One has in fact sometimes to cool down a too impetuous transference by something of reserve, or to make some advances to the shy and by these means to establish the 'optimum temperature' of the relations between doctor and patient. Within the limits of complete sincerity there is room for tactical measures as regards the patient" (216). Once this "optimum temperature" is reached, the analyst is enjoined to return to the main (interpretive) tasks of the analysis. Statements like these have been regarded, properly, as precursors of the concept of the "corrective emotional experience" (see chapter 4) later developed by Franz Alexander and his co-workers (1946, 1954a, 1954b, 1956).

In *The Development of Psycho-Analysis* (1924), Ferenczi and Rank elaborated the theoretical bases for the interventions that characterized active therapy; these centered on the task of transforming repetition into memory:

> The first practical necessity . . . is not only not to suppress the tendency to repetition in the analysis, but even to require it, provided, of course, that one knows how to master it, for otherwise the most important material cannot be expressed and dealt with. . . . Thus we finally come to the point of attributing *the chief role in analytic technique to repetition instead of to remembering*. This, however . . . consists . . . in a gradual *transformation of the reproduced material into actual remembering*. . . . We undoubtedly emphasize greater "activity" by which we mean absolutely requiring the tendency to reproduce. . . .
>
> It is really the insight gained from understanding the repetition compulsion which just makes the results of "active therapy" comprehensible and gives the theoretic reason for its necessity. (4–5)

Toward the end of the book, the same conception is stated even more clearly—and with a caution: "The moderate, but, when necessary, energetic activity in the analysis consists in the analyst taking on, and, to a certain extent, really carrying out those roles which the unconscious of the patient and his tendency to flight prescribe. By doing this the tendency to the repetition of earlier traumatic experiences is given an impetus, naturally with the goal of finally overcoming this tendency by revealing its content. When this repetition takes place spontaneously, it is superfluous to provoke it and the analyst can simply call forth the transformation of the resistance into remembering (or plausible reconstruction)" (43–44). But they conceded that the technique of active therapy can be overused: "The newness of a technical point of view introduced by Ferenczi under the name of 'activity' resulted in some analysts, in order to avoid technical difficulties, overwhelming the patient with commands and prohibitions, which one might characterize as a kind of 'wild activity.' This, however, must be looked upon as a reaction to the other extreme, to holding too fast to an over-rigid 'passivity' in the matter of technique" (43).

"The extravagant praise of a few young persons . . . [who] were ready to see in this 'activity' the dawn of a new kind of psycho-analytical freedom" (1925, 218) impelled Ferenczi to call attention to the weaknesses of the technique. The first was theoretical: " 'Activity' unquestionably stimulates the resistance of the patient in so far as it seeks to increase the psychological tension by painful frustrations, injunctions, and prohibitions, and so gain new material. . . . I have the impression that the analyst who is sure in his *knowledge* and is ready to take a chance on this method may make a part of the 'future prospects of psycho-analytic therapy' which Freud hopes to see realized. In the hands of those who know less of the subject a reversion to the pre-analytic suggestive and enforcing method may very easily result from active technique" (218–19).

The second weakness was countertransferential: forcible injunctions and prohibitions can be a sadistic acting out by the analyst. The third was the risk of excess, acknowledged in Ferenczi's feeling that he had gone too far in his book with Rank in calling for the accelerated ending of analysis, based on the technical application of Rank's birth trauma theory. Ferenczi now stated that this "far exceeds what I wish to comprehend under the term 'activity' " (223). He added, "The wish of the patient to receive signs of positive counter-transference must remain unfulfilled; it is not the task of the analysis to bring happiness to the patient by tender and friendly treatment (he must be referred to the real world after the analysis to get these claims satisfied)" (225).

In a later paper (1928), Ferenczi expressed his concern about the potential for misuse of his innovation even more strongly: "I entirely share my critics' views that these technical precepts of mine, like all previous ones, will inevitably be misused and misunderstood, in spite of the most extreme care taken in drafting them. There is no doubt that many—and not only beginners, but all who have a tendency to exaggeration—will seize on what I have said about the importance of empathy to lay the chief emphasis in their handling of patients on the subjective factor, i.e., on intuition, and will disregard what I stated to be the all-important factor, the *conscious* assessment of the dynamic situation" (99–100). In this paper Ferenczi again stated his caution, this time with a specific technical retrenchment, in effect rendering it much less coercive and more tentative: "Experience . . . taught me that one should never order or forbid any changes of behaviour, but at most advise them, and that one should always be ready to withdraw one's advice if it turned out to be obstructive to the analysis or provocative of resistance. . . . In other words, it is the patient himself who must decide the timing of activity, or at any rate give unmistakable indications that the time is ripe for it" (96–97).

But in Ferenczi's last writing on this subject, the important "Confusion of Tongues" paper (1933) given shortly before his death, he reverted to even more extreme claims. A major obstacle to realization of the full benefits of active therapy, he said, was "professional hypocrisy" (159), by which he meant the analyst's reluctance to forthrightly acknowledge technical errors and counter-transference deformations to patients. He said of one patient, "Something had been left unsaid in the relation between physician and patient, something insin-cere, and its frank discussion freed, so to speak, the tongue-tied patient; the admission of the analyst's error produced confidence in his patient. . . . It is this confidence that establishes the contrast between the present and the unbearable traumatogenic past, the contrast which is absolutely necessary for the patient in order to enable him to re-experience the past no longer as hallucinatory repro-duction but as an objective memory" (159–60). Along this line and, one would hope, tongue in cheek, Ferenczi even advised the analyst to deliberately make mistakes so as to give the patient the therapeutic experience of the analyst's confessions. But he added that there really was no need for such a recommen-dation; we all make mistakes enough as it is, without trying.[1]

In other papers, however, Ferenczi talked of the technique of "mutual" or "reciprocal" analysis, the analyst alternating with the patient on the couch in transferential confession—though he did point out a major technical obstacle to the implementation of this extreme therapeutic mode: the analyst's obligation to the confidentiality of his other patients would preclude full free association confessionals to any one patient.

What I trust has emerged in this brief description of Ferenczi's technical innovations and experiments is his organizing therapeutic premise, his overrid-ing emphasis on an affective heightening of the transference experience as the necessary precondition for effective interpretive work and a successful analytic outcome. This elevation of the (transferential) analytic relationship as a central vehicle of therapeutic change within analysis, alongside Freud's focus on inter-

---

1. This was stated as follows: "It would almost seem to be of advantage occasionally to commit blunders in order to admit afterwards the fault to the patient. This advice is, however, quite superfluous; we commit blunders often enough, and one highly intelligent patient became justifiably indignant, saying: 'It would have been much better if you could have avoided blunders altogether. Your vanity, doctor, would like to make profit even out of your er-rors' " (159).

pretation leading to insight, is the hallmark of Ferenczi's contribution to our conceptions of the therapeutic action of psychoanalysis and the source of his continuing influence within psychoanalysis.

Ferenczi's technical recommendations and innovations have always been a passionately controversial matter. Michael Balint undertook the role of carrier and interpreter of the Ferenczi legacy to the psychoanalytic world, both amplifying and clarifying the theoretical basis of Ferenczi's technique. In a 1967 paper, he insisted that Ferenczi was often "misunderstood, misquoted, and misrepresented. . . . The usual misunderstanding [of active technique] is that, in contrast to the classical analytical passivity, the analyst should be more active. However, it is not the analyst but the patient who is induced to be more active, that is, to do something or to avoid doing something" (154); he adds, "The analyst's activity should be restricted to suggesting to the patient what he should do and then encouraging him to do it" (157).

Whether the analyst's intervention took the form of proposing that the patient cease to indulge in a particular habit—that is, give up the concealed satisfaction of his repressed wishes—or of encouraging the patient to enjoy it openly and freely, "it was hoped that a successful intervention by the analyst would cause a considerable increase of tension [i.e., heightened affectivity] in the patient and that this, in turn, would produce . . . a breakthrough into consciousness of a hitherto repressed instinctual urge or drive, changing an unpleasurable symptom into a pleasurable satisfaction, thereby strengthening and extending the rule of the patient's ego; and further, by removing resistances, it would start the patient's dried-up or stagnant associations flowing again" (156).

It was such considerations that led to Ferenczi's conviction, as paraphrased and summarized by Balint, that "any event in this [analytic] situation must be understood as an interplay between the patient's transference, that is, his compulsion to repeat, and the analyst's countertransference, that is, his technique. As the former had to be accepted as a constant, almost unalterable, factor (at any rate for the time being), if he [the analyst] wanted to get out of the impasse, he had to accept the task of changing the other factor, his technique" (160). Hence, the panoply of commands and prohibitions, advice and suggestions, flexibility and forbearance, and even ultimately severe indulgence that marked the technical experiments of active therapy. And since it would only repeat the original childhood traumata for the analyst to be uninvolved in the repetitions of the originating traumatic events in the transference (as the patient's parents had been uninvolved and detached at the time), principled departures from Freud's call for analytic abstinence also became necessary.

Andre Haynal (1988) has updated our understanding of Ferenczi's psychoanalysis vis-à-vis Freud's and of Balint's role as mediator between Ferenczi and the modern developments in psychoanalysis to which he gave impetus. Haynal first outlined some of Ferenczi's major technical and conceptual contributions: his willingness to experiment with technique; his declared incorporation of subjectivity into analytic thinking; his exposition of the analyst's contributions to the creation of an adequate analytic atmosphere; his delineation of the range of possible analytic postures, from that of "stern father" in the imposed frustrations of active technique to that of "indulgent mother" in the gratifications, such as his well-known tolerance of Clara Thompson's kisses; his highlighting of the real traumata of the "unbearable traumatogenic past," which had to be unearthed and rendered fully conscious; his correction of the overestimation of instinctual vicissitudes and unconscious fantasy and the consequent underestimation of the traumatic past reality in pathogenesis; and his emphasis on the need for the fullest therapeutic regression in analysis with, then, the possibility for a healthier "new beginning."

Haynal then indicated Balint's extensions of the Ferenczi heritage. Balint's central thrust was the shift of analytic investigative focus onto the personality of the analyst. For Balint, psychoanalysis was not only a technique but, much more, a relation between two people, and the analyst played the central role in the creation and maintenance of the psychoanalytic situation. Haynal quotes Balint as stating that "it is as true for the patient as for his analyst that no human being can in the long run tolerate any relationship which brings only frustration." And Balint importantly espoused "the 'two-body' view, in which the analyst participates fully in the relation with his own economy and dynamics, with his own reactions and personality [which] seems to have been [now] recognized as a basic stance for dealing with analytic problems" (78). Balint's conceptions of "primary love" and "new beginning" he acknowledged as being rooted in Ferenczi's insistence that "the formal elements of the transference and the whole analytic situation derive from very early infant-parent relationships" (79) reactivated in the psychoanalytic transference neurosis. All in all, a variety of developmental lines in psychoanalysis take their inspiration from Ferenczi's original basic contributions.

Aaron Esman (1991), reviewing Haynal's book, further highlights some distinctions between the psychoanalyses of Ferenczi and of Freud:

> Haynal suggests that Freud favored the concept of *Einsicht*, the "insight" of the Age of Enlightenment, while Ferenczi opted for *Erlebnisse*, or genuine experiences. . . . Ferenczi "always considered that the analyst should be active." . . . At the same time, he emphasized the need for the analyst always to be aware of his own contribution to the analytic exchange; it

was he who first underscored the central role of empathy[2] in psychoanalytic technique, and with it the "incorporation of subjectivity into analytic thinking." . . . Unlike Freud, who was explicit about his distaste
for working with severely disturbed or regressed patients, Ferenczi ea-
gerly undertook to treat them and to follow them into their regressed
states. . . . By doing so he believed he was better able to uncover early
traumata—events of the preoedipal period whose importance, he felt, was
underestimated in the Freudian canon. (291)

On Ferenczi's enduring influence in psychoanalysis, Esman said, "This technical divergence between the neutral, nongratifying, purely interpretive stance
of the 'classical' analyst and the active participatory 'empathic' stance of the
Hungarian school and its followers persists today and cannot be easily dismissed.
Ferenczi's influence, mediated by Balint's concept of the 'new beginning,' can
be seen not only in the work of the English 'independents,' but also in that of
the self psychologists and . . . those mainstream American analysts who emphasize the primary role of the 'holding environment,' at least in the treatment of
borderline and narcissistic patients. It is true that . . . with the widening scope
of psychoanalysis outlined by Stone (1954), there is a tendency toward an assimilation of these approaches, a blending of technical measures, a less categorical
concern about 'parameters' than was the case a generation ago. But, at least in
principle, the difference remains and must be acknowledged—and with it, the
role played by Ferenczi and his followers in the shaping of modern psychoanalytic technique" (291–92).

These last considerations are reflected in what Lewis Aron and Therese Ragen (1990) have called "a remarkable resurgence of interest in the clinical and
theoretical contributions of the Hungarian psychoanalyst Sandor Ferenczi. . . .
Psychoanalysts from around the world and representing a wide variety of theoretical persuasions seem to have simultaneously rediscovered the significance
of his contributions. . . . It is clear that Ferenczi had a direct effect on the founders of . . . major schools of contemporary psychoanalysis including British object relations theory, the American interpersonal school, the French school of
Lacan, and American self psychology" (3–4).

2. In his 1928 paper "The Elasticity of Psycho-Analytic Technique," Ferenczi said, "I have come
to the conclusion that it is above all a question of psychological tact whether or when we
should tell the patient some particular thing. . . . But what is 'tact'? The answer is not very
difficult. It is the capacity for empathy" (89). Of the verbal work required of the analyst, he
said, "One might say that his mind swings continuously between empathy, self-observation,
and making judgments" (96). This is a clear forerunner of a central theme in Kohut's subsequent theory building (see chapter 20).

A mark of the current renaissance of interest in Ferenczi is the recent publication of the complete Freud-Ferenczi correspondence (1993) as well as of the
Clinical Diary of Sandor Ferenczi (Dupont 1988), intended, according to the fly-
leaf, as "Ferenczi's last filial appeal—albeit an unsuccessful one—to the father
of psychoanalysis to sanction his work." The editor's introduction to the diary
suggests that the motive for Ferenczi's restless therapeutic searching—which can
be considered to be either an ebullient, unquenchable optimism or, in Freud's
words, more pejoratively, a *furor sanandi*—can be understood as follows: "To
maintain that a patient who could not be cured with this theory or with this
technique was unanalyzable appeared to him unsatisfactory and, moreover, in
itself traumatizing. He believed that all patients who asked for help should receive it, and that it was up to the psychoanalyst to devise the most appropriate
response to the problems presented to him. Thus, Ferenczi became the last resort
for cases considered hopeless, cases that his colleagues referred to him from all
corners of the earth" (xix).

Dupont then has this to say on Ferenczi's reluctant retreat from his most
extreme technical experiment, "mutual analysis": "Gradually Ferenczi encountered a whole series of problems stemming from the techniques of mutual analysis . . . he lists some of these: the risk of seeing the patient 'deflect attention
from himself' and search for complexes in the analyst in a paranoid way; the
impossibility of letting oneself be analyzed by every patient; the imperative need
to respect the patient's sensibilities; the problem posed by the discretion owed
to other patients whose secrets the analyst would in principle be obliged to
reveal to the patient-analyst" (xxi–xxii).

Ferenczi's technical innovations had a very mixed and often quite critical
reception—beginning with Freud. In his "Lines of Advance" address in Budapest (1919), Freud stated as "a fundamental principle" that "analytic treatment
should be carried through, as far as is possible, under privation—in a state of
abstinence" (162). (This entire sentence was italicized by Freud when the speech
was published.) Freud then developed this thought:

> The patient looks for his substitutive satisfactions above all in the treatment
> itself, in his transference-relationship with the physician; and he may even
> strive to compensate himself by this means for all the other privations laid
> upon him. Some concessions must of course be made to him, greater or
> less, according to the nature of the case and the patient's individuality.
> But it is not good to let them become too great. Any analyst who out of
> the fullness of his heart, perhaps, and his readiness to help, extends to the
> patient all that one human being may hope to receive from another,
> commits the same economic error as that of which our non-analytic in-

stitutions for nervous patients are guilty. Their one aim is to make everything as pleasant as possible for the patient, so that he may feel well there
and be glad to take refuge there again from the trials of life. In so doing
they make no attempt to give him more strength for facing life and more
capacity for carrying out his actual tasks in it. In analytic treatment all
such spoiling must be avoided. As far as his relations with the physician
are concerned, the patient must be kept with unfulfilled wishes in abun-
dance. It is expedient to deny him precisely those satisfactions which he
desires most intensely and expresses most importunately. (164)

Ilse Grubrich-Simitis (1986), in her paper on six newly discovered letters
from the Freud-Ferenczi correspondence, quoted more of Freud's misgivings:
that Ferenczi's experiential emphasis on the management of the transference
repetitions came too close to the early, but now sharply diminished, emphasis
on the importance of cathartic discharge and abreaction; that his technique of
"mother-tenderness" could lead to the degeneration of psychoanalysis as an
etiologic uncovering therapy, and so forth. In one of the letters, dated February
24, 1924, Freud wrote to Ferenczi of "my impression that the path opened up
here could lead away from psychoanalysis, that it promises to become a path for
travelling salesmen. But, undoubtedly, this must not be the case. The warning
should suffice" (267). There are other such comments throughout the correspondence.

Characteristically, it was Glover (1924) who carried these cudgels on Freud's
behalf even further. In " 'Active Therapy' and Psychoanalysis: A Critical Review," after reviewing Ferenczi's efforts to devise special procedures to meet
especially difficult analytical situations and to render psychoanalysis in general
more effective and speedier, Glover posed a series of questions, some of them
in declarative form, to Ferenczi and the other advocates of active therapy:

1. Do not active interferences on the part of the analyst disturb the transference picture as a spontaneous repetition, since the recognition by
   the patient of transference materials *as such* is greatly facilitated by the
   passive role of the analyst and his impersonality? (281)
2. How far . . . [should] repetitions . . . be merely interpreted, or assuming that they may be actively interfered with, what interval should be
   allowed for working through? . . . The question of determining the
   optimum amount of repetition in analysis is obviously one requiring
   the nicest judgment. (285)
3. It was suggested that one of the dangers of applying active technique
   was the production of a "second fixation" in that the analyst's injunc-

tions would lend colour in reality to the unconscious identifications of the patient. (287)

4. The use of orders and prohibitions with their avowed intention of causing "pain" is surely calculated to play into the hands of the masochist. (288)

5. It is at any rate a legitimate suggestion that before applying the direct active technique of Ferenczi, a persistent analysis should be made. (296)

These considerations led Glover to ask, "How far has the case for universal application of 'active methods' been satisfactorily established?" (299). His answer, surprisingly moderate in view of his polemical character, was that it was still open for investigation and discussion: "The active therapist definitely shoulders the responsibility of actually playing to some extent the imago-role thrust upon him by the patient" (305). But has the active therapist "like the *hypnotiseur* gained immediate progress at an ultimate sacrifice?" (306). Glover then sounded his final warning: " 'Do this', 'Don't do that' . . . are, after all, the battle-cries of the nursery and, however laudable their intent, are calculated to reactivate, this time in reality, the associated ideas of parental tyranny and judgment. . . . Whoever says 'Don't' may also smack. . . . It may well be that in certain cases at certain times the empirical advantages may outweigh any drawbacks inherent in the application of active technique. On the other hand, we are entitled to enter a plea for more prolonged consideration of phenomena and against too rapid a crystallization of set principles" (307, 309).

These views of Freud and Glover prevailed for a very long period of time within the mainstream American ego psychological paradigm. However, it is clear that today, even in America, many of Ferenczi's viewpoints have been widely revived, albeit not in their original form. Indeed, as early as 1962, Arthur Valenstein, a steady representative of this American ego psychological mainstream position, said of the place of abreaction in the evocation of insight (with specific reference to Freud's original cathartic theory of analytic cure), "One aspect of tension management through abreaction remained, however, valid and pertinent to the goal of insight through psycho-analytic interpretations. . . . By providing an opportunity for emotional release through the verbalization of affect-charged impressions and ideas, the strongly disturbing ideas are at least temporarily weakened in their disturbing effect. At this moment they are more accessible to ego-corrective influence, including evaluation against reality, and the application of cognitive self-reflective intellectual considerations" (319–20). Further on, with specific reference to the 1924 book by Ferenczi and Rank, Valenstein added,

The emphasis was really upon *repeating* and *experiencing* rather than re-membering and understanding (insight-gaining) which was seen as dis-tinctly limited. . . . They implied the necessity of a form of acting out within the transference . . . as a means of helping the patient to reproduce repressed situations which he could not remember as such, because "they never had been conscious". By this formulation they gave the term "ex-periencing" a literal significance and technical connotation which amounted to a major revision of psychoanalytic technique. It led finally to a therapy based almost entirely on interpersonal considerations and experiential learning through the active manipulation of the transference. (320)

Obviously Valenstein did not agree with this last, extreme position—which was actually the impetus for Alexander's development of the concep-tion of the "corrective emotional experience," discussed in chapter 4—but Ferenczi's influence in shaping Valenstein's assessment was nonetheless un-mistakable, as witness these remarks by Valenstein: "Affects have a special place in the insight process, especially in the treatment of more extreme dis-turbances brought within the widening scope of psycho-analysis" (319); "Treatment of such disorders [these sicker patients] is necessarily much more a literal reliving, is predominantly interpersonal and reeducationally corrective in nature" (321); and finally (and more broadly applicable than just to the "sicker patients"), "In psycho-analysis the element of emotion, as it bears upon a proportionate and properly time-integrated degree of emotional reliv-ing, would seem to be of fundamental significance to the final development of insight" (322).

Just such considerations have led to increasing attention to the technical problems posed by the new paradigmatic patients of our time, those sicker pa-tients with wider and deeper ego disorders than patients classically amenable to an unmodified psychoanalytic technique. John Gedo (1986) has described Ferenczi's seminal role in this regard: "Was Ferenczi alone in the psychoan-alytic community in the 1920s to realize that adults whose ego development led to maladaptations require departures from the standard technique of con-temporary psychoanalysis if they are to profit from treatment? Clearly, we are in no position to answer this question. All that we can say about it is that other analysts who were dissatisfied with Freud's methods, such as Otto Rank and (somewhat later) Wilhelm Reich, left organized psychoanalysis, while Ferenczi persevered in trying to persuade his colleagues that technical modi-fications might enable them to broaden the therapeutic scope of their disci-pline" (50).

Anthony Bass (1992), in his review of Margaret Little's (1990) autobiographical book, stressed the importance of Ferenczi's early emphasis on the potential therapeutic values of deep regression with seriously disturbed patients—an emphasis that has provided the therapeutic rationale for much of the literature on the psychoanalytical treatment of the overtly and flagrantly psychotic.[3] And Axel Hoffer, in a review of the Ferenczi diary (1990), emphasized Ferenczi's brief period of experimentation with mutual analysis:

The *Clinical Diary* contains the only published description of "mutual analysis." In it we are told how and why Ferenczi—reluctantly and temporarily—takes his approach to its extreme yet "logical" conclusion in this radical technique of "mutual analysis." Pressed by a severely traumatized patient in a stalemated analysis openly to acknowledge with her his unresolved countertransference difficulties, Ferenczi consents out of desperation to reverse roles and position. He allows the analysand to be his analyst and to sit behind him. Ferenczi experiments for several months with the "mutual analysis" of two—and possibly three—such patients, carried out by alternating the role of analyst and analysand in daily or twice-daily sessions. Although he finds the approach therapeutically useful, he soon abandons and renounces that technique for practical reasons, citing in particular the threat to the confidentiality of his other patients in his freely associating—"like conducting analysis with the door open." His renunciation notwithstanding, the egalitarian, "anti-hypocritical" role-reversal clearly appeals to him. . . .

In my opinion, history will best remember Sandor Ferenczi for his interest in the analytic relationship and his passionate concern about the impact on the analysand of the analyst's contribution to what is repeated in the transference. . . . In the *Diary* Ferenczi highlights the opportunities and dangers of enactments and re-enactments which occur on the microscopic level in the analytic hour with neurotic analysands and in the macroscopic level in the acting out of patients belonging to the "widening scope of psychoanalysis." (725–27)

3. "The controversy began to take shape in the 1920s when Ferenczi began to explore, through his psychoanalytic experiments, the therapeutic value of regression. He found that the more deeply disturbed patients with whom he worked were unresponsive to the rather contained, mainly interpretive classical psychoanalytic regimen developed by his own analyst and mentor, Freud. 'Analysis must make possible for the patient, morally and physically, the utmost regression, without shame', wrote Ferenczi in his June 1932 entry in his clinical diary" (Bass 1992, 119–20).

But Hoffer also acknowledged the controversy still surrounding the work of Ferenczi: "Some see Ferenczi as the 'loose cannon' on the foredeck of psychoanalysis, a man whose daring, impulsive innovations are not undone by an outpouring of 'mea culpas'; others see him as the courageous pioneer who protects his patient rather than himself, unafraid to say the emperor has no clothes" (725).

In a subsequent article, Hoffer (1991) stressed Ferenczi's emphasis on reactivation of the early mother-child relationship in the therapeutic regression and also on the two-person interactional matrix: "His technique of 'relaxation' [meaning gratification and indulgence] contained an implicit reenactment of Ferenczi's conception of the idealized early mother-infant bond, characterized by an ambience of total acceptance and indulgence of the help-seeking, traumatized child-within-the-analysand" (467). Quoting Ferenczi on this point ("We see then that, while the similarity of the analytical to the infantile situation impels patients to repetition, the contrast between the two encourages recollection" [1930, 124]), Hoffer commented, "We can hear in this passage the beginning of the concept of 'corrective emotional experience' developed by Alexander and French." Similarly, of Ferenczi's emphasis on a "two-body" interactional psychology, Hoffer said, "Ferenczi simultaneously created an increasingly explicit two-person psychology with a new emphasis on the recreation of the mother-infant relationship in the analytic situation" (468). Hoffer then somewhat lyrically contrasted Freud's psychoanalytic stance and Ferenczi's: "The disagreements between Freud and Ferenczi are conflicts inherent not only in psychoanalysis but in human nature. These polarities include those between the heart and the mind, passion and reason, indulgence and frustration, mother and father, and, finally female and male" (469).

Grubrich-Simitis (1986) likewise focused on the meaning of Ferenczi's regression-inducing "maternal indulgences." She put it very graphically: "Ferenczi soon increased these liberties to indulgences and finally, to spoiling and the exchange of those physical expressions of tenderness between analyst and patient that characterize the mother-child relationship. The analyst's behaviour is thus rather like that of an affectionate mother, who will not go to bed at night until she has talked over with the child all his current troubles . . . and has set them at rest" (272-73). In this connection, she quoted from the same 1930 Ferenczi paper about patients with "unusually profound traumas in infancy": "For them the usual methods of analytical therapy are not enough. What such neurotics need is really to be adopted and to partake for the first time in their lives of the advantages of a normal nursery" (124). But Grubrich-Simitis concluded quite critically, "Ferenczi, swept away by his *furor sanandi*, finally manoeuvred himself and his patients into situations that could no longer be dealt with analytically, because aspects of the transference were indissolubly mingled with phenomena belonging to the real relationship" (273).

Jacob Jacobson (1994), in a very appreciative assessment of Ferenczi's enduring psychoanalytic contributions, focused on the early legitimation he gave, in the 1933 "Confusion of Tongues" paper, to the validation of the patient's real traumatic experiences:

> He describes the repetition of childhood traumatic states in the analysis; urges that we examine the plausibility of patients' rageful criticisms of us in the transference; raises the possibility that standard analytic technique may in certain cases not be experienced as neutral at all, but can unwittingly replicate early traumatic situations; describes vividly the traumatization which sexual assault visits upon a child, the splitting of consciousness which frequently attends it, the helpless submission and paradoxical clinging of the child to the abuser, the "terrorism of suffering" of the sexually abused child, the introjected guilt, precocious pseudo-maturity, and hypertrophied sense of responsibility with which children emerge from such experiences.[4] (27)

Though this paper was not well received when Ferenczi delivered it in 1932, at a time when he was engaged in a variety of extreme and questionable therapeutic behaviors and involved in an ambivalent conflict with Freud, "sixty years later, the paper, and the idea it presents of the analyst acknowledging and validating the reality to the patient in cases of actual sexual abuse, have been the subject of renewed interest, as issues of sexual abuse and the treatment of adults who suffered sexual abuse as children have become important areas of concern" (27).

Jacobson then added an explanatory codicil:

> The problem with Ferenczi's paper was not that he was re-introducing an unwelcome return of an abandoned [seduction theory] hypothesis [since Freud never said that seduction does not occur, only that it is not universal while drive-rooted fantasies *are* universal], but rather that he was emphasizing the importance of *acknowledging* to the patient the fact of

---

4. Hoffer (1990) also emphasized Ferenczi's central focus on the actual traumata in the life experience of the more disturbed patients: "In keeping with the consistent portrayal of the patient as childhood victim of the insensitive parent and analyst, overwhelming trauma to the ego serves as the paradigm for Ferenczi's understanding of his disturbed patients. . . . The analyst's task, repeatedly articulated by Ferenczi, is to provide a safe, accepting, loving, empathic, relaxed setting where the trauma necessitating these disruptive defences can be reexperienced, remembered and thereby ultimately resolved" (725).

seduction in appropriate cases, rather than maintaining a focus on the
fantasy components alone. I believe it was the fear of diluting the analysis
of the fantasy contributions, seen to be the lever of therapeutic change,
that created the adverse reactions to the paper. Over time, we have come
to see that validating for a patient the actuality of sexual abuse [or other
real trauma] where it clearly has been present, has powerful therapeutic
value, and how *not* offering such validation may unwittingly repeat the
typical situation around the original trauma, where a conspiracy of silence
and ambiguous lack of validation within the family so often would have
prevailed. (28–29)

Juxtaposing Freud and Ferenczi, Carlo Strenger (1989) talks of "the tension
between the classic and the romantic vision of human reality" (593), with Freud
and those who have followed his emphasis representing the classic stance, and
Ferenczi, followed by Balint, Winnicott, Kohut, and others, the romantic. If
"psychoanalysis for Freud is the relentless pursuit of the truth about ourselves,
the penetration beyond appearances to reality which was once too threatening
to face" (598), then the antithesis is between "Freud's basic polarity [which] is
that between the pleasure principle and the reality principle, [and] Kohut's [an
ideological descendant of Ferenczi], . . . [which is] between joy and vitality on
the one hand and depletion and depression on the other hand" (599–600).

Because "the idea that the material of the patient lends itself to only one
interpretation, if we look at it in a sufficiently close manner, is illusory," it
follows that "we can look at every utterance, every action of the patient under
the perspective of how truthful he is. . . . It means that we must listen with a
certain amount of suspicion, must always question the face value of what we
hear. We can also listen from the romantic point of view. We will then listen
for the thwarted attempts to feel wholesome and alive, to feel enthusiasm and
love behind the self-destructive, perverse and unintelligible aspects of the patient's actions and words" (602). Depending on which orientation toward life
the analyst espouses and inevitably reflects in his/her interpretive strategy, the
therapeutic task posed to the patient can vary in emphasis: "The classic approach
tries to make the patient maximally conscious of his ways of acting in order to
allow him to take more responsibility for himself. The romantic approach focuses on factors in the patient's environment during his development which did
not allow him to flourish, thus trying to mobilize frozen intrapsychic constellations which developed as a result of these intrusions" (605). (And, of course,
"what the patient internalizes is not just a set of interpretations. It is no less an
attitude towards life and towards himself" [601]).

In the best of cases, good interpretations should somehow combine the two attitudes: "Ideally, interpretations both allow the patient to step back and understand his feelings and behaviour from a more objective point of view and allow him to come closer to aspects of himself which were experienced as intolerable before" (605). But the two visions still stand separately as philosophical choices: "I think that it is important to see that the tension between the classic and the romantic stance is *not* a purely technical problem. It cannot be resolved through amassing more knowledge about curative factors in psychotherapy" (606). With reference to this realm of life orientation choices, Valenstein (1989) remarked that the pendulum seems to be swinging from the Vienna thinkers to the Budapest feelers.

And in the most recent assessment, Gerald Fogel (1993) summarized the Freud-Ferenczi juxtaposition as follows: "These necessary dialectics [in the Freud-Ferenczi interplay] include the relative emphasis on remembering versus reliving in the here-and-now, reconstruction versus construction, observation versus experience, intellectual versus affective understanding, interpretive versus relational aspects of analytic work, conflictual versus developmental aspects, dyadic versus triadic, object-instinctual versus narcissistic, and old versus new experience. One side of this series of crucial polarities—roughly the relational and existential, and later the preoedipal and developmental—can be considered Ferenczi's theoretical discovery, his great contribution to psychoanalysis" (598). Fogel added, "Freud's 'objectivity' and intellectual detachment and Ferenczi's 'subjectivity' and emotional immersion—observation and experience—both will retain their importance. How to maintain appropriate involvement *and* perspective in a self-reflexive relational field, where empirical validation of important experiences and understandings is difficult or impossible, will preoccupy theorists into the present" (599).

Finally Fogel indicated that Freud and Ferenczi held opposed concerns about the risks to proper analysis: "Freud worried that an overemphasis on the factors of experience and the analyst's empathy would lead beginners and inferior analysts to justify the substitution of arbitrary subjective factors for correct impartiality and disciplined technique. Ferenczi worried that without experiential and relational factors made explicit, passivity and intellectualism could hide behind a banner of orthodox Freudianism and kill the life blood of psychoanalysis" (597).

3 The Development of the Psychoanalytic Psychotherapies out of Psychoanalysis

As I have stated, the emergence of specifically (and self-consciously) *psychoanalytic* psychotherapies out of the psychoanalysis created by Freud was a distinctively American phenomenon.[1] I have recounted some of this history elsewhere (Wallerstein 1974, 1980). Essentially, psychoanalysis was the single-minded creation of the genius of one man, working in what he called a "decade of splendid isolation" in fin de siècle Vienna. Starting around 1905, some students and colleagues began to adhere to him, but the enterprise was totally private, outside the established university, medical, and psychiatric world. This enforced isolation was caused partly by the reaction against the scandalous doctrines of infantile sexuality that Freud espoused and partly by the more or less official anti-Semitism of the Austro-Hungarian Empire, which denied Freud the academic recognition to which he aspired all his life. (Freud remained just a *Privat-Dozent* at the University of Vienna and only once—during the academic year 1916–17, in the midst of World War I—was he invited to give a year-long series of weekly lectures, subsequently published as the *Introductory Lectures* [1916–17].)

Psychoanalysis thus grew in Vienna—and in the other major cities of the central European heartland through which it first spread, Zurich, Budapest, and

---

1. Dynamic psychotherapy is indeed the one distinctively American contribution to modern-day clinical psychiatry and mental healing albeit a glorious one. Psychoanalysis was created by Freud in Austria; the descriptive nosology of the major mental disorders was the work of Kraepelin and his school in Germany; electro-convulsive therapy was inaugurated by Cerletti and Bini in Italy, insulin coma by Sakel in Hungary, and the ill-starred lobotomy operation by Egas Moniz in Portugal; the concept of the therapeutic community was developed by Maxwell Jones in England; the modern psychoactive drug era was inaugurated in Switzerland with Largactil, later brought to America by way, first, of Canada, as Thorazine; and lithium for manic-depressive disorders was first successfully employed by Cade in Australia.

However, it is certainly not true that dynamic psychotherapy had no roots or independent beginnings in other countries. Chapter 19 is devoted to the story of its development in Great Britain, from the founding of the Tavistock Clinic in 1920, situated ideologically between the antipsychoanalytic psychiatric establishment and the (comparably antipsychiatric) psychoanalytic establishment (the British Psycho-Analytical Society), essaying to provide a receptive meeting ground for both psychiatrists and psychoanalysts who were interested in the development of a British dynamic psychotherapy. Similar indigenous developments of a psychoanalytic psychotherapy, distinct from psychoanalysis but quite clearly derived from and related to it, no doubt also took place elsewhere, I would say especially in Holland, Germany, and Scandinavia.

Berlin—as a private enterprise, and its educational system as a private night school. Its first medical practitioners were predominantly clinical neurologists, like Freud. A major clinical issue in their practices was the differential diagnosis of multiple sclerosis (for which there was no specific therapy) from the various sensory and motor hysterical disorders that could be mistaken for it, and with whom and for whom Freud, after his initial experiments with hypnosis and other suggestive techniques, evolved first the in-between method of forced associations and then psychoanalysis, built on the method of free association. Psychiatric patients proper, those seen in psychiatric clinics in medical schools and psychiatric hospitals, were in the hands of the Kraepelinian nosologically oriented psychiatrists, and their treatment at best comprised humane care, rest cures, at times electrical stimulations, and so on.[2]

Despite its spread to Holland, England, and even America in the first decades of the century, psychoanalysis continued within this private-practice framework, divorced from the university world and the world of organized medicine and isolated therefore from psychiatry and the care of the severely mentally ill. Hitler's accession to power in Germany in 1933 and his subsequent march across Europe transformed this situation. The major psychoanalytic strongholds of Berlin, Vienna, and Budapest were one by one depopulated as the Jewish majority among the psychoanalysts (and some of their non-Jewish colleagues) fled into exile, the overwhelming majority to America, a very significant minority (including, of course, Freud and his family) to England, and a handful to Australia, Palestine, Asia, South America, and other places. The demography of psychoanalysis changed totally and seemingly overnight. Whereas the Americans in 1931 had numbered only 22 percent of the world cadre of recognized psychoanalysts, by 1952, their numbers swelled by the flood tide of Hitler refugees, that figure had risen to 64 percent (Knight 1953a, 209).

In contrast to the European growth and development of psychoanalysis outside of psychiatry, medicine, and academia, the American psychoanalysts em-

2. This situation was a major source of Freud's delight when Jung joined the beginning psychoanalytic circle toward the end of the first decade of the twentieth century. Jung was established at Bleuler's Burgholzli Sanatorium in Zurich and thus brought a very welcome access to psychiatry and to the potential psychoanalytic study of the psychotically ill. And Jung, descendent of a line of Swiss Protestant pastors, was the first non-Jew to espouse psychoanalysis and thus could rescue it from the fate Freud feared, that of being designated a Jewish science and therefore discounted in the wider world. On both accounts, Freud selected Jung as the first designated president of the International Psycho-Analytical Association (established at the first Congress in Salzburg in 1908). All of this weighed heavily in Freud's heartache when the collaboration ended with Jung's departure in 1913 to found his own school of "Analytical Psychology," which totally abjured Freud's sexual doctrines.

barked upon a self-conscious and largely successful effort to penetrate the peculiarly receptive soil of American psychiatry,[3] to capture academic psychiatry and its formal training centers and become its prevailing psychological theory and therapeutics, and thus to be firmly planted in medicine, the medical schools, and, at least via this route, the universities as well. This radical transformation of American psychiatry over a short span of years reached its high-water mark in the 1950s, when in one major department of psychiatry after another, the retiring chairman, characteristically an Adolf Meyer–trained psychobiological psychiatrist, was replaced by a psychoanalytically trained psychiatrist committed to making the department thoroughly psychoanalytic in its understandings and in its therapies.[4]

This systematic capture of American psychiatry by psychoanalysis brought both the opportunity and the obligation to develop technical applications of psychoanalytic theory to the amelioration of that wide spectrum of patients seen in psychiatric clinics and hospital psychiatric wards and not amenable to psychoanalysis proper. It was marked by the emergence of a distinctive literature on what came to be called psychoanalytic or psychoanalytically oriented psychotherapies.

Lawrence Kubie (1943) was one of the first psychoanalysts to describe this development as a—to him—confluence of commonsense psychology and, where that was insufficient, the uncommonsense psychology of psychoanalysis. He stated, "In this loose sense, psychotherapy embraces any effort to influence human thought or feeling or conduct, by precept or by example, by art or

3. This receptivity of American psychiatry to the psychoanalytic idea reflected a particular Zeitgeist that prevailed at the time within American intellectual and professional life: the wide acceptance within American psychiatry of the psychological doctrines of Adolf Meyer, with their emphasis on detailed case and life histories to indicate the causal relationships of experiential events; the growth of the "mental hygiene movement," with its melioristic call for professionally guided interventions via mental hygiene clinics and child guidance clinics; the impact of John Dewey's "progressive education" and other pragmatically optimistic ideas, etc. Psychoanalysis, with its promise of etiological understanding of human emotional distress and misery and of radical and definitive cure for these disorders, fitted well into this overall optimistic spirit of progressive betterment.

4. It would be a digression here to elaborate on the concomitants of that effort, the decision of the American Psychoanalytic Association, arrived at after bitter and divisive debate, to effect what was called the 1938 rule, barring thenceforward the training of nonmedical candidates under the auspices of the American and barring membership to nonmedical analysts unless trained before that date. As if to strengthen its claim to psychological hegemony within psychiatry, American psychoanalysis tried to divest itself of its nonmedical cohorts, no matter how illustrious their contributions had been. Whether this sacrifice was necessary it is hard to know in hindsight. But certainly it was a heavy sacrifice, and one that many felt was unwise; it was literally a half-century before this exclusionary policy was reversed.

humor, by exhortation or appeals to reason, by distraction or diversion, by rewards or punishments, by charity or social service, by education, or by the contagion of another's spirit. . . . As a *science* psychotherapy begins only where these leave off" (183, italics added). He described three main groupings of psychotherapeutic activity:

> (a) Practical support—consisting primarily of advice, guidance, and assistance in the management of life situations and environmental difficulties . . . (b) Emotional support—consisting essentially of sympathy, exhortation, admonition, encouragement, humor, art, recreation, companionship, etc., (c) Reorienting education—consisting primarily of efforts to alter the patient's habitual attitudes of guilt, fear, hate, and depression, by educating him to tolerate his own conscious and unconscious needs and cravings, his instinctual hungers, his familial jealousies and hates, etc. The third of these groups requires extensive knowledge of unconscious psychological forces, and hides many subtle dangers . . . the first two, however, can hardly be called a discovery of the psychiatrist. They are the homely, nonspecific, common-sense weapons of every wise parent and educator. They must always be tried first. (186)

Kubie defined "palliative psychotherapy" as consisting "primarily of an effort to teach patients how to live with some measure of comfort within the confines of their uncured neuroses" (187). This could often be accomplished by the environmental and emotional manipulations comprised in the first two groups, and much neurotic suffering could thereby be relieved. When this failed, Kubie would call on a "scientific psychotherapy," an exploration by the third group of methods of the sources of the patient's rigidly repetitive and compulsively driven behavior patterns that are refractory to the influence of experience and reality. "During recent years various methods have been developed by which this goal is pursued. The most important of these is psychoanalysis" (194). Kubie listed some of these other methods as hypnotherapy and narcotherapy but did not attempt to establish theoretically grounded conceptual linkages or distinctions other than by the tripartite grouping quoted above.

Bernhard Berliner, at about the same time (1941, 1945), tried to distinguish "short psychoanalytic psychotherapy" from psychoanalysis proper. Short therapy is more active, though always "analytically minded" (1941, 205). It offers advice, guidance, and educational influence, but mostly techniques of "ego-analysis" (1941, 210), by which Berliner meant consistent confrontations with reality. "The principle which I have in mind," he wrote, "is to understand within a short period of time the central problem of the patient from the point of view of his libido situation and to make it understandable to him in a way his ego is able to accept" (211–12). Berliner adduced several indications for this approach: that the ego resistances be at a minimum, that a good positive transference pertain during the whole period of the treatment ("so that no time will have to be spent on transference analysis" [1941, 210]), and that the patient derive significant narcissistic gratifications from the process of treatment itself. The presence of significant secondary gain from the illness was declared a contraindication. Berliner felt that the possibilities for a satisfying outcome of treatment in such cases did not correlate with either the acuteness or the duration of the illness.

In a later paper (1945), Berliner spelled out the distinctions between psychoanalysis and short psychoanalytic psychotherapy: "If much analysis of transference is necessary to work out resistance and to mobilize the neurotic conflicts, we are doing a full classical analysis. If the case is such that little or no analysis of transference is required on the way to the desired therapeutic result, we are doing a treatment which may deserve the name of short psychoanalytic psychotherapy. But if the therapist, in order to do a short treatment, neglects the analysis of a transference which produces resistances, he does no treatment at all." Berliner then summarized as follows: "Cases suitable for short psychoanalytic psychotherapy are those in which the patient can be helped to see and to discuss his central conflict in its own right and in terms of its realities without extensively reliving it or acting it out in relation to the therapist" (156).

These beginning efforts to delineate a scientific psychotherapy apart from but also derived from and related to psychoanalysis were already so numerous that Otto Fenichel, in his encyclopedic *Psychoanalytic Theory of Neurosis* (1945), made the statement (oft-quoted since), "*There are many ways to treat neuroses but there is only one way to understand them.* Many attacks against psychoanalysts have been based on the notion that they 'swear exclusively by their own method.' That is in no way true. There are many reasons why a nonanalytic treatment might be preferable to an analytic one. What is true, however, is that psychoanalysts are of the opinion that only psychoanalytic science understands what is going on in neurosis, and that there is but one theory to give a scientific explanation of the effectiveness of *all* psychotherapies" (554, italics added).

It was Robert Knight, a leader in American psychoanalysis *and* psychiatry at the time, who played the truly pioneering role in framing the fundamental conceptions that have marked psychoanalytic psychotherapy as *psychoanalytic* therapy that is, nonetheless, distinct from psychoanalysis proper and that remain at the very center of the still ongoing controversies around those distinctions. Knight's principal concern was the relationship of American psychoanalysis to psychiatry. He stated that until the advent of psychoanalysis, "psychiatry still lacked a psychology" (1945, 121), and he devoted himself to articulating what he called "a basic science of dynamic psychology . . . on which all competent psychotherapy must rest . . . [and] the chief contributions to which have been made by psychoanalysis" (1949, 101). In the 1945 paper, Knight had stated that the "most significant trend in psychoanalysis, as it relates to the broad field of psychiatry, is that toward modification of the so-called 'orthodox' technique, including the general application of psychoanalytic principles to other types of psychotherapy" (126).[5] What those modifications would be Knight undertook to formulate authoritatively in the 1949 paper: "Of the various possible ways of classifying psychotherapeutic attempts, most psychiatrists would agree that two large groups could be identified—those which aim at *support* of the patient, with suppression of his symptoms and his erupting psychological material, and those which aim primarily at *expression*" (107, italics added). The scope of supportive psychotherapy was defined as follows: "Suppressive or supportive psychotherapy, also called superficial psychotherapy, utilizes such devices as inspiration, reassurance, suggestion, persuasion, counseling, reeducation, and the like and avoids investigative and exploratory measures" (107).[6]

The bias in favor of the more expressive approach, as more definitive already implied in the designation "superficial" for the supportive approach, was then made more explicit: "Suppressive or supportive psychotherapy . . . may be indicated, even though the psychotherapist is well-trained and experienced in expressive techniques, where the clinical evaluation of the patient leads to the conclusion that he is too fragile psychologically to be tampered with, or too

5. Knight at this point joined the growing chorus of those who dissented from Freud's conviction about the inaccessibility of the grossly psychotic to psychotherapeutic influence. Knight wrote, "Intensive psychotherapy using psychoanalytic principles or 'modified psychoanalytic treatment' of the psychoses by many psychoanalysts has shown that psychotics are capable of an especially intrusive, unpredictable, and stormy kind of transference requiring far more skillful technique on the part of the therapist [and far more attention to scrutiny of the countertransference] than in the treatment of the neuroses" (1945, 127)—meaning that he felt such patients to be psychotherapeutically treatable. Here he was referring to his own experiences (1939, 1946) and those of colleagues at the Menninger Clinic as well as of such contemporaries as Harry Stack Sullivan, Frieda Fromm-Reichmann, and John Rosen.

6. Like so much else in psychoanalysis, the precursor of this conception of a supportive psychotherapeutic approach can be found in Freud—in this case in his earliest clinical writing, *Studies on Hysteria* (1893–95), coauthored with Breuer—albeit as an essential component of the evolving conceptions of psychoanalysis as a therapeutic modality. Freud put it thus: "One works to the best of one's power, as an elucidator (where ignorance has given rise to fear), as a teacher, as a representative of a freer or superior view of the world, as a father confessor who gives absolution, as it were, by a continuance of his sympathy and respect after the confession has been made. One tries to give the patient human assistance, so far as this is allowed by the capacity of one's own personality and by the amount of sympathy that one can feel for the particular case" (282–83).

inflexible to be capable of real personality alteration, or too defensive to be able to achieve insight. . . . The decision to use suppressive measures is made actually because of contraindications to using exploratory devices" (107–108). Knight added that, of course, transference (and countertransference) manifestations can and do arise in these supportive therapies and must, of course, be appropriately handled.

The scope of expressive therapies (called "major psychotherapy") was also defined: "Expressive psychotherapies utilize such devices as exploratory probing through questioning, free-association, abreaction, confession, relating of dreams, catharsis, interpretation, and the like, all with the purpose of uncovering and ventilating preconscious and unconscious pathogenic psychological material" (108). Here, Knight made another distinction (critical to all the future debates in the field): that expressive psychotherapy, though closely allied to psychoanalysis proper (psychoanalysis itself can be described as one variant of a reasonably "pure" *expressive* psychotherapy), is also distinct from psychoanalysis, in fact, unlike psychoanalysis:

> Competent expressive psychotherapy may have goals which vary considerably. In cases where there has been an acute onset of neurotic symptoms in reaction to a discoverable precipitating event and the patient's history shows a comparatively healthy course, the therapy may properly consist of thorough ventilation of the reaction to the upsetting event, with the therapist pointing out connections, relationships, and hidden motivations in the limited life area of the setting prior to the event, of the event itself, and of the patient's immediate and later reactions to the event. In skillful hands this is a most rewarding type of expressive psychotherapy. Recovery may be achieved in a very few interviews and the patient is restored to his previous good functioning with insights he would not otherwise have achieved. In such instances there is no therapeutic aim of exhaustive investigation, recovery of infantile memories, or altered ego structure. (109)

Such "major psychotherapy," Knight declared, should "not be undertaken without thorough grounding in dynamic psychology, adequate experience in clinical evaluation, practice under supervision, and personal suitability" (109)— again, tacitly downgrading supportive psychotherapy, as if it did not require the same thorough training and experience. Knight then placed psychoanalysis itself within this context: "In other cases which may at first seem similar, the early clinical evaluation uncovers more neurotic difficulties than were at first apparent, and it becomes clear that the patient's adjustment prior to the precipitating event was a precarious one at best. The therapeutic aim may now change to one of more thoroughgoing alteration of the neurotic personality structure, and the expressive techniques lead into psychoanalysis" (109).[7]

In a subsequent paper (1952), Knight pushed his dichotomization of the therapeutic arena further, and also distinguished more precisely the goals and intentions of supportive and exploratory (expressive) approaches. Within the latter, he further distinguished the goals and indications of psychoanalysis proper. He began with a statement of what should be obvious: "The therapy should fit the patient, being modified to continue to fit him as he improves or worsens; the patient should never be forced into the single therapeutic method a given therapist knows. . . . I would like, then, for purposes of discussion, to designate two fundamental kinds of psychotherapeutic measures or approaches—one which is primarily supportive and one which is primarily exploratory" (118).

Knight then clarified his usage of these key rubrics, though "all kinds of psychotherapy—in good hands at least—involve support of some kind, even if no word of encouragement or reassurance is voiced by the therapist. . . . By the term 'primarily supportive' I mean to imply the *intention* to support and reconstruct the defense mechanisms and adaptive methods customarily used by this patient before his decompensation, and the *implementation* of this intention by explicit supportive techniques." The techniques of external support, he wrote, include hospitalization where indicated, reduction of environmental demands upon the patient, counseling with key persons in the patient's life, and the like. As to the internal supports, "Reinstituting of defenses may also include the cultivation of related but new defense mechanisms, the encouragement to invest interest and effort in cultivating new sublimatory activities, and the instruction of the patient in areas of knowledge and social adaptation where he is deficient" (118). Finally, Knight attempted a somewhat systematic listing of the techniques of supportive psychotherapy: "encouragement, advice, active help in feasible management of the environment; appropriate coaxing, exhortation, kidding and praise; suggestion; prescription of daily activities, including mental hygiene read-

---

7. Somewhat further on, Knight again spoke to the treatment of the openly psychotic by "modifications of technique to meet the therapeutic problems in patients who are too ill to cooperate in the usual analytic procedure. These modifications . . . used chiefly with psychotics . . . involve approaches by the analyst which actively cultivate a treatment relationship, communication with the sick patient being established on whatever level is possible in the individual case. The success of such attempts depends on the resourcefulness of the analyst in coping with the patient's inaccessibility and his capacity for empathy and intuition in understanding what is communicated by the patient's verbalizations, behavior, and attitudes" (111–12). By way of example, Knight spoke particularly about John Rosen's (1953) "direct psychoanalysis" and his very idiosyncratic approach—throwing all usual cautions to the winds and fearlessly and relentlessly making early and regular deep interpretations of archaic impulses and fantasy systems.

ing; provision of temporary, recurrent, or permanent support through a nurse or companion; long range support through less frequent but continuing supportive interviews as the patient improves." And with all this, Knight conceptually upgraded the requirements of supportive psychotherapeutic work (as compared with his earlier article) to a more nearly equal status with the expressive approaches. He said, "This is a perfectly respectable, valuable, and effective psychotherapy which may require the utmost in skill and resourcefulness from the therapist" (119).

Among the expressive modes, psychoanalysis is clearly the most far-reaching, "the best method available to achieve the more ambitious goal of fundamental alteration of character structure, with eradication or reduction to a minimum of neurotic mechanisms. . . . Psychoanalysis attempts the ultimate in exploration, with a goal of the maximum in self-knowledge and structural alteration of the personality" (120). Other expressive psychotherapy is accorded a distinctively different place: "The greatest field, and often the most rewarding one for exploratory psychotherapy which does not involve the more ambitious goals of psychoanalysis, lies in those clinical conditions which are appraised as relatively recent decompensations arising out of upsetting life experiences. . . . The psychotherapist's capacity to detect the nature of the event and the reasons for the patient's excessive reaction to it . . . enables him to penetrate the neurotic conflict, actively conduct the exploration, and finally expose the whole sequence of predisposition, overtaxing event, and neurotic response" (120). Knight concluded with an epigrammatic statement of the common factors (albeit in different admixtures) in *all* effective psychotherapies—*support, rapport* (the therapeutic relationship), and *import* (the meanings expressed) (124).

Thus, the first clear declaration of the distinctions among psychoanalytic therapies, from the most supportive to the most expressive.[8] Knight was also the

8. These were the distinctions embodied in the psychoanalytic psychotherapies being taught at that time in the psychiatric training centers rapidly coming under psychoanalytic influence— departments of psychiatry in medical schools and general hospitals, the Veterans Administration hospitals charged with treating the continuing psychiatric casualties among those who had been in the military during World War II, mental hygiene clinics including special clinics for returning veterans, etc. The word "psychodynamics" was the euphemism under which the psychoanalytic thinking represented by Knight was so enthusiastically incorporated into American psychiatry in that immediate post–World War II decade. This was officially recognized in the very influential NIMH-supported American Psychiatric Association Conference on Psychiatric Education held at Cornell University in the summer of 1952. In the published proceedings of that conference, the chapter on "the role of psychoanalysis in residency training" stated, "It is now almost universally agreed that a necessary part of the preparation of a

first popularizer of the notion of the borderline state. In a 1953 article he wrote, "The term 'borderline state' has achieved almost no official status in psychiatric nomenclature, and conveys no diagnostic illumination of a case other than the implication that the patient is quite sick but not frankly psychotic. . . . Thus the label 'borderline state,' when used as a diagnosis, conveys more information about the uncertainty and indecision of the psychiatrist than it does about the condition of the patient" (1953b, 1).

But Knight *was* certain that psychoanalysis proper was contraindicated for the treatment of this borderline state:

> The ego of the borderline patient is a feeble and unreliable ally in ther-apy. . . . If [such a patient is] encouraged to free associate in the relative isolation of recumbency on the analytic couch, the autistic development is encouraged, and the necessary supportive factor of positive transference to an active, visible, responding therapist is unavailable. . . . Even though a trial analysis may bring forth misleading "rich" material, and the analyst can make correspondingly rich formulations and interpretations, the pa-tient's ego often cannot make use of them, and they may only serve the purpose of stimulating further autistic elaborations. Psychoanalysis is, thus, contraindicated for the great majority of borderline cases, at least until after some months of successful analytic psychotherapy. Psychotherapists can take their cue from the much better front these patients are able to present and maintain in face-to-face psychiatric interviews, where the structured situation and the visible, personal, active therapist per se pro-vides an integrating force to stimulate the patient's surviving adaptive, integrative, and reality-testing capacities. Our therapeutic objective, then, would be the strengthening of the patient's ego controls over instinctual impulses and educating him in the employment of new controls and new adaptive methods, through a kind of psychotherapeutic lend-lease.[9] With our analytic knowledge we can see how he defends himself, and what he defends himself against, but we do not attack those defenses except as we may modify them or educatively introduce better substitutes for them. Our formulations will be in terms of his ego operations rather than of his

---

competent psychiatrist is the development of and understanding of principles of psychody-namics," and "It seems obvious that an understanding of psychodynamics presupposes—in-deed necessitates— . . . knowledge of Freudian concepts and of psychoanalytic theory and practice" (Whitehorn et al. 1953, 91).

9. A phrase derived from the American shipment of military supplies to the Soviets for use against the Germans during World War II.

id content, and will be calculated to improve and strengthen the ego operations.[10] (10–11)

Leo Stone (who had earlier been with Knight at the Menninger Foundation) and Merton Gill (who remained at Menninger until 1947 and then left with Knight to go to the Austen Riggs Center in Stockbridge, Massachusetts) significantly extended and at the same time, in different ways, modified Knight's proposals concerning this emerging delineation of the range of psychoanalytic psychotherapies vis-à-vis psychoanalysis. Gill (1951) began with Freud's definition of psychoanalysis in his *History of the Psycho-Analytic Movement:*

> It may thus be said that the theory of psycho-analysis is an attempt to account for two striking and unexpected facts of observation which emerge whenever an attempt is made to trace the symptoms of a neurotic back to their source in his past life: the facts of transference and of resistance. Any line of investigation which recognizes these two facts and takes them as the starting-point of its work has a right to call itself psychoanalysis even though it arrives at results other than my own. But anyone who takes up other sides of the problem while avoiding these two hypotheses will hardly escape a charge of misappropriation of property by attempted impersonation, if he persists in calling himself a psycho-analyst. (1914b, 16)

Gill's modification, in the light of Knight's formulations, was as follows: "In point of fact the designation 'psychoanalysis' is reserved for the technique which *analyzes* transference and resistance. Psychoanalytic therapy is any procedure which *recognizes* transference and resistance and rationally utilizes this recognition in the therapy, though this may be done in many different ways, and part or all of the transference and resistance may not be analyzed" (1951, 62).

These "many *different* ways," of course, represent the various expressive and supportive modes of psychoanalytic therapy. Gill stated these differences in terms of goals and strategies:

> In psychoanalysis the goal is relatively clear: a progressive analysis from the surface to the depth; analysis of the defenses and the motives for defense; the development and analysis of the transference neurosis; a res-

10. These views were the starting point for Kernberg's enormously influential reformulations on the borderline state, although he departed sharply from Knight on the precise nature of the borderline pathology and its amenability to a (very expressive) "modified" psychoanalytic approach (see chapter 20). Kernberg began his career in America at the Menninger Foundation, as a participant in the Psychotherapy Research Project—a context very much influenced by the views of Knight and his colleagues and students.

olution of symptoms, and as complete a 'structural' alteration of the neurotic aspects of the personality as possible. In psychotherapy the goal may be anything from as quick relief of a symptom as possible, with the restoration of the previous integrative capacity of the ego, through a whole range of more ambitious goals *up to* analysis, the most ambitious of all. *The choice of therapy may be divided into that which determines the minimum necessary to restore the ego to functioning, and that which strives for the maximum change that is possible.* (63, italics added)

In terms of strategy, Gill said, "The gross major decision is whether the defenses of the ego are to be *strengthened* or *broken through* as a preliminary toward a reintegration of the ego. . . . The decision to strengthen the defenses is made in cases in which this is *all that is necessary*, or in those in which this is *all that is safely possible*." At the other end of the spectrum, "Analysis . . . is clearly the procedure for a *middle range* in which the ego is sufficiently damaged that extensive repair is necessary, but sufficiently strong to withstand pressure" (63–64, italics added).[11] And then determinedly at the end, in connection with the question of the therapeutic inevitability and necessity of the transference neurosis and Freud's famous statement that an enemy cannot be slain in effigy, Gill stated, "Psychotherapy must determine how thoroughgoing an alteration in personality can be achieved by only partial development of the transference neurosis" (70).

Of course, Gill allowed, "While the two poles of either strengthening the defenses, or of analyzing them as first steps toward reintegrating the damaged ego, stand as the gross opposites of two theoretical modes of approach, the psychotherapy of any specific case will show intricate admixtures of both" (65). Concerning the borderline, he pretty much went along with Knight, though in somewhat different words: "In borderline cases with marked regression one cannot strengthen the defenses of the ego with the aim of restoring a previous satisfactory adjustment because there was none. In such cases modified analysis is used: it analyzes the transferences and the resistances, but only with the assistance of strong supportive techniques to avert the danger of impairing whatever small degree of integration the ego has retained" (64).

Finally, Gill elaborated ways of "strengthening the defenses":

11. Erikson (1982) explicitly added a third defining characteristic of this so-called middle range of patients for whom psychoanalysis is the indicated therapy. He said, "This [psychoanalysis] has proven to be a meditative procedure which can yield unheard of healing insight for those individuals who feel disturbed enough to need it, *curious enough to want it,* and healthy enough to 'take' it—a selection that can make the psychoanalyzed in some communities feel, indeed, like a new kind of elite" (87, italics added).

A first principle, then, for techniques of strengthening defenses is to encourage, praise, or in general to give narcissistic support for those ego activities in which defense is combined with adaptive gratifications [for example, compulsive hard work], and to discourage by subtle or direct techniques those activities which are maladaptive gratifications, whether or not they are combined with defense. . . . A second principle . . . is that one must take great care not to unwittingly attack an important defense [like the denial of dependency longings]. . . . Another way in which the theory of strengthening of defense may be formulated is the one proposed by Glover. He suggests that artificial neuroses of various kinds may be set up which offer a partial discharge for derivatives of instinct. . . . For the theory of the results achieved by such a technique Fenichel suggests that "by this partial discharge the instinct becomes relatively weaker and the work of defense against the remainder becomes easier." The defense may then be said to have been relatively strengthened. (66–67)

This specification of the nature and modus operandi of supportive psychotherapeutic techniques was the first such (psychoanalytic) conceptualization. The simplistic assumption to that point had been that support meant no more than reassurance, encouragement, and so on—despite the clear knowledge that simple reassurance might not be at all reassuring.

Stone, who also published his first paper on this topic in 1951, covered much the same ground, but in a more complexly modulated and subtly nuanced way as compared with Gill's characteristic very precise language. Like Gill, Stone began with a definitional statement about psychoanalysis as a therapy, an "intricate and relatively constant configuration of techniques. . . . Regardless of one's objective judgment of their value, these precepts, interpreted with varying degrees of flexibility or rigidity, with occasional modifications or elaborations for special reasons, and the development of certain interpretative trends from ego and character analysis have continued to provide the broad outlines of technical procedures for most analysts" (216–17). He then listed eight such fundamental techniques of psychoanalysis: free association, frequency, regularity, recumbency, the analyst's general passivity, neutrality, abstinence, confinement to interpretation and declared that their overall coordinated deployment comprised the "fairly constant and unique ensemble" (218) that characterizes psychoanalysis.

By contrast, psychotherapy was much less clear: "Psychoanalysis, as is any science, is full of unsolved problems. However, it is a relatively well-defined and systematized procedure, compared to this large and chaotic field, ranging from simple suggestion to the procedure most usually referred to as 'psychotherapy' which bears a superficial resemblance to psychoanalysis but which, because of the inclusion of important variables, is very poorly defined, highly unpredictable, and exceedingly difficult to evaluate" (215). To make the distinction (or, rather, the boundaries) between psychoanalysis and psychotherapy conceptually even more problematic, Stone added, "The actual functional distinction between psychoanalysis and brief psychotherapy [Stone's phrase at the time for all psychoanalytic psychotherapy other than psychoanalysis] is, of course, really in doubt only in the area where there are certain resemblances; but it is precisely in this area that it is most important that the distinction be maintained" (216).

Not surprisingly, Stone saw the relationship among these various (psychoanalytic) therapies along a continuum, whereas Gill thought in terms of more distinctly modal crystallizations, albeit also arranged along a spectrum. In Stone's words, "One may think of a continuum from the free play of human relationships in which there is no conscious psychotherapeutic intention—but which obviously play an enormously important psychotherapeutic role in the lives of relatively normal people—to the objective and precise relation between the surgeon and his patient, which Freud idealized. The well-defined psychoanalytic technique and brief psychotherapy are both far from either pole, and yet definitely removed from one another in these opposite directions" (221–22).

In keeping with such fuzziness of conceptual borders, and his practice of lumping together all psychoanalytically based therapies under the ill-chosen rubric "brief psychotherapy," Stone, in his attempt to list the principles differentially operative in psychotherapy and psychoanalysis, conflated the supportive and expressive approaches. Similarly, in his listing (the most elaborated to that point) of the indications for psychotherapy over psychoanalysis (or of contraindications to psychoanalysis, if you will), Stone also conflated the supportive and the expressive psychoanalytic psychotherapies. Here he first mentioned the practical indication for psychotherapy: "the great numbers of patients who because of limitations of money or time cannot be analyzed" (224). He then proposed seven conceptual and technical indications:

(1) people who are so sick mentally, or whose situation in life is so unpropitious, that the effort toward extensive revision of the personality is not justified, or might even lead to greater difficulties; (2) those whose illness is so slight that radical and lengthy procedures are not justified; (3) acute reactive disorders in those who have given evidence of healthy adaptation under reasonable circumstances, exacerbations of mild disorders, fulminating conditions, incipient conditions in general; (4) transitional states as, for instance, the readaptation to civilian life of some

veterans, or certain problems of adolescence; (5) preparatory preanalytic therapy for borderline patients or psychotics, follow-up treatment for certain unresponsive patients who have had long or multiple analyses; (6) more specific indications, mentioned by individual writers, as certain masochistic marital problems, monosymptomatic impotence, "psychosomatic" illnesses, certain mild chronic neuroses, certain schizoid personalities; (7) a high degree of secondary gain is mentioned by a few writers as a contraindication whereas a slight degree is believed a conceivable avenue of approach to a patient. (225)

Although Stone did not try to separate those patients most appropriately treated by expressive approaches from those most appropriately treated by supportive methods, he did clarify the basis for Gill's (1951) statement that psychoanalysis is the treatment of choice for a "middle range" of patients and that there are both those too healthy for it (appropriate for expressive psychotherapies) and those too sick for it (requiring more supportive approaches).

Gitelson also published an article in this area in 1951. He was quoted in chapter 1 as somewhat ambivalently (in a 1956 article) seeming to support Freud's original notion that any psychotherapy other than proper psychoanalysis must be only a variant of suggestion. However, in his 1951 article, he, too, took cognizance of a psychoanalytic psychotherapy (or "dynamic psychiatry," as he called it) as a distinct offshoot of psychoanalysis, close to psychoanalysis in conception and distinct from, and far from, suggestion. He defined dynamic psychiatry as an "indigenous American expression . . . meaning treatment of the mind on the basis of the management of the forces of the mind" (283) and declared that the psychotherapy so conceived need no longer be qualified as psychoanalytically oriented any more than modern medical therapeutics need be qualified as pathophysiologically oriented. "*Rational psychotherapy* is based on everything we know today about psychopathology and psychodynamics . . . we can look upon psychoanalysis [as a theory] as the pathophysiology of the psyche" (284, italics added). And, "So complete is the rapprochement of psychiatry and psychoanalysis today (particularly as regards psychotherapy) that there has been increasing confusion, not only among lay people but also among psychiatrists and psychoanalysts, as to where the boundary between dynamic psychiatry and psychoanalysis proper is to be found. And yet there is a boundary, and it shall be my attempt now to establish it" (283). Here, Gitelson introduced the metaphor of the chemical reaction, quite in accord with the developing views of Knight, Gill, and Stone, to explain the relatedness of the psychotherapies (at least of the expressive psychotherapies) along a spectrum leading to psychoanalysis as one end point:

A metaphor may be helpful in this connection. Let us look upon a complex chemical reaction. Assuming that all things remain equal, once it is underway, it will continue until it has reached a final state of dynamic equilibrium. Transitional to this state, many intermediate reactions will have occurred, and many intermediate compounds will have been synthesized and broken down. . . . Psychotherapy is not oriented toward an end point in the interaction between therapist and patient which approaches a final dynamic equilibrium. Psychoanalysis is oriented toward such an end point and, in contrast to psychotherapy, is potentially capable of attaining it. . . .

The psychoanalytic reaction is the transference neurosis, the recapitulation of the pathogenic infantile past in the relationship to the analyst. The end point is the resolution of that neurosis. The technique is directed toward the establishment of the reaction and the maintenance of the optimum conditions . . . for its completion. In contrast, psychotherapy, whether from necessity or from choice, will bring the reaction to an end at any point of stability. Thus, psychotherapy must of necessity intervene, contribute, and manipulate. It must be more or less active. . . . In contrast, psychoanalysis . . . dealing interpretively with the resistances and the manifestations of the transference neurosis . . . must be more or less passive. (287)

This chemical metaphor, Gitelson felt, gave him warrant to state that modern psychotherapy "is not psychoanalysis even when it is psychoanalytic. . . . The differences between psychoanalysis and the most extensive psychotherapy are to be found in the difference in technique and in the goal which is striven for and attainable" (286).

Thus the beginning crystallization of views (in America) about a psychotherapy (or, rather, psychotherapies) derived from psychoanalysis, with modified techniques, but firmly grounded in the *theory* of psychoanalysis as the way to understand human mental functioning, to be applied to a far broader array of psychopathology than was amenable to psychoanalysis.

Before leaving this point, I note a more recent article by Robert Michels (1985) covering the same terrain from the opposite perspective, with a striking and provocative figure-ground reversal. His thesis begins familiarly enough: "The prototype . . . [is] psychoanalysis and the psychoanalytic or psychodynamic psychotherapies that are usually described as derived from it, but that, in fact [and here Michels begins to shift the usual conceptual ground] share a common origin with it" (7). He ventures further with "The common view of dynamic psychotherapy is that it was derived from psychoanalysis, influenced by external factors, the desire to make the treatment briefer, to broaden its applicability to patients who for one reason or another were not suitable for traditional psychoanalysis, and to diminish some of the undesirable side effects of psychoanalysis, particularly those associated with the regression and prolonged dependency believed to be less intense in psychotherapy. However, there are problems both with this rationale and with the historical assumptions underlying it" (8).

Michels then expounds his reverse thesis:

> His [Freud's] early patients suffered from neurotic symptoms, and were treated by relatively brief (less than 10 months) courses of talking therapy that focused on identifying the dynamics and genetics of their symptoms and then persuading the patient of the validity of the interpretations. Resistance, when recognized, was dealt with by direct persuasion. Transference was recognized only as a problem in the treatment. The relationship between symptom and character was not understood. By contemporary psychoanalytic standards, Freud's clinical work in those early decades of discovery was not only psychotherapy rather than psychoanalysis, it was quite a modified psychoanalytic psychotherapy, with little attention to the central dynamic themes of transference and resistance and heavy admixtures of suggestion and direction. Modern psychoanalysis and modern psychodynamic psychotherapy were both born out of this early process; but it is clear that psychoanalysis has been modified far more extensively than psychotherapy in the ensuing years. The later "discovery" of psychoanalytic psychotherapy was really a rediscovery, required in part by the growing "purity" of what had now come to be called psychoanalysis, with the consequent loss of some of its earlier flexibility as the theoretical advances of the earlier phase were translated into technical developments that made it more "analytic" but less "psychotherapeutic." (9)

Michels then modifies this austere judgment a little: "He [Freud] came to see the analysis of transference and resistance as the essence of psychoanalysis rather than a preliminary or prerequisite, as important sources of data to be studied carefully rather than merely obstacles or facilitators of the treatment proper" (9). In other words, Freud became more psychoanalytic (in the modern sense).

This perspective on the relationship between psychoanalysis and psychotherapy is, of course, a retrospective view, almost a half-century after the fact, and is made possible by Eissler's (1953) description of what he proclaimed to be "classical" psychoanalytic technique and Samuel Lipton's (1977) later challenge to Eissler's version as a major misreading of Freud's "actual technique," which Lipton declared (with supporting evidence) was much more "humane" and relaxed. In chapter 7, I develop this controversy in detail. It is still not a settled issue, as attested by George Allison's recent evenhanded appraisal (1994) of what he calls the current "homogenization" of psychoanalysis and psycho-analytic psychotherapy: "There is also agreement that historically *both modalities* derive from Freud's original version of psychoanalysis, which by today's stan-dards many consider instead to define psychoanalytic psychotherapy" (350).

4 Franz Alexander and the
Corrective Emotional Experience

The "corrective emotional experience" was one of the major innovative psychoanalytic concepts introduced in the 1940s and 1950s, a time when a distinctive array of psychoanalytic psychotherapies was emerging from their psychoanalytic matrix and the relationship between the two developments was itself the focus of much disputation. The concept and its technical precepts were first spelled out in *Psychoanalytic Therapy* (Alexander, French, et al. 1946) and achieved great popularity in the first post–World War II decade in America. Indeed, the ferment these new ideas aroused and the prospect that they might actually split the American psychoanalytic world into two rival camps were a major impetus for a series of panel discussions and conferences,[1] later published in a single issue of the *Journal of the American Psychoanalytic Association* (1954, 2: 4). Alexander spoke at both panels of the American, and his views were generally supported, albeit with their own nuances, by fellow panelists Frieda Fromm-Reichmann and Edith Weigert. Edward Bibring, Merton Gill, Leo Rangell, Leo Stone, and Anna Freud were the principal speakers for the opposition majority view (at the time called the classical or traditional position). From these discussions—which were, in their spirit, more like debates—came the crystallization of the consensus on what at that time constituted psychoanalysis, what constituted psychoanalytic psychotherapy, and what the relationship of the Alexander modifications was to each. This consensus on boundaries and definitions held sway within American psychoanalysis and the wider community of psychodynamic psychiatry for the next quarter century.

What was the nature of Alexander's concept, which played such a role in galvanizing the American psychoanalytic world into a more explicit articulation of the relationship between psychoanalysis and psychoanalytic psychotherapy in order to frame a proper response to the challenge that it posed?[2] Actually, the

---

1. A panel at the December 1952 meeting of the American Psychoanalytic Association entitled "The Traditional Psychoanalytic Technique and Its Variations" (Zetzel 1953); another at the May 1953 meeting of the American entitled "Psychoanalysis and Dynamic Psychotherapy: Similarities and Differences" (Rangell 1954a); and a conference (May 1954) sponsored by the New York Psychoanalytic Society entitled "The Widening Scope of Indications for Psychoanalysis" (Stone 1954; Anna Freud 1954).
2. This concept was not the only major innovation in the Alexander and French book. It also set forth a number of related (and equally controversial) concepts: the "principle of flexibility," which included alteration of (usually diminishing) the frequency of sessions, planned inter-

opening statement of the 1946 book did not develop the concept fully or un-
ambiguously. The five-page section (66–70) entitled "The Principle of Corrective Emotional Experience" described the example of Jean Valjean, the
convicted thief in Victor Hugo's *Les Misérables* (1862), who stole from the
bishop who had befriended him and, in response to being forgiven and then
protected by the bishop, had a conversion experience (an emotional metamor-
phosis) that fundamentally changed him from confirmed sinner to saint. Building
on this literary example, Alexander defined the corrective emotional experience
as follows:

> The analyst assumes an attitude different from that which the parent has
> assumed toward the child in the original conflict situation. . . . This makes
> the patient's transference behavior a one-sided shadow boxing, and thus
> the therapist has an opportunity to help the patient both to see intellec-
> tually and to *feel* the irrationality of his emotional reactions. . . . When
> one link (the parental response) in this interpersonal relationship is
> changed through the medium of the therapist, the patient's reaction be-
> comes pointless. . . . Because the therapist's attitude is different from that
> of the authoritative person of the past, he gives the patient an opportunity
> to face again and again, under more favorable circumstances, those emo-
> tional situations which were formerly unbearable and to deal with them
> in a manner different from the old. (Alexander and French 1946, 66–67)

Stated in these words, and seen from the perspective of its time, the corrective
emotional experience hardly seems to differ from the then prevailing under-

---

ruptions of the treatment, termination by "weaning," etc.; the consciously planned "manipulation of the transference," usually via the corrective emotional experience but also in other
ways; counteracting the propensity toward the development of an "insoluble transference
neurosis," especially in those with passive-dependent and masochistic character structures, by
curtailing the frequency of sessions and thus the intensity of the analytic process, thereby
inhibiting the development of the regressive transference neurosis; and presenting the case for
far-reaching personality changes consequent to "brief therapy," which they declared to range
from a single interview up to sixty-five sessions. All these proposals, singly or in combination,
were ostensibly designed to make the analytic method more flexibly adapted to the clinical
exigencies posed by patient pathologies, to fit the therapy to the patient, rather than (as the
authors claimed) the more traditional analytic stance of fitting the patient to the therapy. The
concept of the corrective emotional experience bore the brunt of the attacks on the Alexandrian positions, though it was in effect an umbrella covering most of these proposals. Taken
as a whole, the Alexander-French position was attacked as undermining the very structure of
psychoanalysis as a specific and unique therapy with its distinctive and constant "ensemble"
(Stone 1951, 218) of techniques.

standing of the transference. In 1950, Alexander ventured further in differentiating his position: "The crucial therapeutic factor," he wrote,

> is that the analyst's reactions are different from those of the parents. The simplest example is the repression of self-assertive and aggressive attitudes due to parental intimidation which encourages dependence and causes all kinds of inhibitions in human relations. In the transference the therapist's attitude must *reverse* that of the intimidating parent. The fact that the patient's aggressions are met objectively without emotional response or retaliation on the part of the analyst corrects the original intimidating influence of the parent. The parental intimidation is undone by the more tolerant and sympathetic attitude of the therapist who replaces the authoritarian parent in the patient's mind. (1950b, 486, italics added)

Even more specifically, in describing an outstanding therapeutic success (in twenty-six sessions over ten weeks), he wrote,

> My attitude was not simply objective and helpful; it was consistently tolerant and definitely encouraging, *exactly the opposite* of his father's attitude. While the father was overbearing and omniscient, the analyst emphasized repeatedly the limitations of psychiatry and of his own knowledge, encouraging the patient to express his disagreement with interpretations. The father had been extremely critical of the patient; the analyst openly displayed admiration for certain of the patient's qualities. This was of course all within the limits of the usual attitude of the analyst, but I gave a definite emotional coloring to the transference, which might be criticized as not psychoanalytic but psychotherapeutic because of its openly encouraging connotation. (488–89, italics added)

In these quotations, Alexander went further in asserting that the analyst should reverse the patient's transference expectation, but he did not quite separate this as distinct from (more than) the usual expectation of evenhanded analytic neutrality and objectivity in the transference relationship.

In 1953 Alexander felt called upon to defend his recommendations against the charge that they constituted a deliberate assumption of roles, or role-playing. He said, "Some analysts have contested these recommendations with the argument that if these assumed attitudes are artificial, they will fail to achieve their purpose; the patient will sense their insincerity." Alexander's answer was that "the detached objective attitude of the analyst required by classical theory is also highly studied. Certainly, it is not a spontaneous attitude in human intercourse. Moreover, since the therapist's whole orientation is to help a suffering human being, trying to act in a manner which is in the interest of his patient is by no means artificial. Every educator should do this; we as psychiatrists require such changes in attitude in a psychiatric nurse, for instance" (1953, 120–21).

Alexander further specified these "changes in attitude" in terms of the "principle of the contrast": "The analyst's basic attitude should remain always objective, non-evaluative, and helpful. In the framework of this basic attitude, however, the more subtle interpersonal climate should, in each phase of the treatment, be preferably the *opposite* to that which prevailed in the original situation being repeated in the transference at that particular time" (1954a, 692, italics added).

Finally, in another full-length book, Alexander (1956) carried his conceptual development to its logical extreme and offered a full-fledged rebuttal of his opponents' counterarguments. He began by insisting that "the corrective emotional experience is . . . the central therapeutic agent in the original and now standardized psychoanalytic procedure" (42). He went on to say, "The standard procedure can be *improved* by rendering the corrective influence of the transference situation more effective by giving increased attention to the interpersonal climate of the treatment situation" (76, italics added).[3] He explicated this further on:

> Knowledge of the early interpersonal attitudes which contributed to a patient's neurosis can help the analyst to assume *intentionally* a kind of attitude which is conducive to provoking the kind of emotional experience in the patient which is suited to undo the pathogenic effect of the original parental attitude. . . . The proposition made here is that the analyst should attempt to replace his spontaneous countertransference with attitudes which are *consciously planned* and adopted according to the dynamic exigencies of the therapeutic situation. This requires the analyst's awareness of his spontaneous countertransference reactions, his ability to control them and substitute for them responses which are conducive to correcting the pathogenic emotional influences in the patient's life. . . . In this connection it should be considered that the objective detachment of the psychoanalyst [in traditional analysis] is itself an adopted, studied attitude and not a spontaneous reaction to the patient. (92–94, italics added).[4]

3. In this phrase, "increased attention to the interpersonal climate of the treatment situation," we can discern Alexander's indebtedness to Ferenczi's emphasis on affectivity in the reexperiencing within the transference.
4. Many would assert here that everything we know about how the countertransference operates would argue against this recommendation as a simplistic misunderstanding of the complex

Finally, Alexander defended the corrective emotional experience as a vital and logical addition to and improvement upon the traditional psychoanalytic handling of the transference. First, "If we declare that [the deliberate and controlled substitution of attitudes] cannot be achieved, or that it is some kind of artificial manipulation of the therapeutic situation, it follows that the range of a psychoanalyst's effectiveness must be restricted to those patients whose problems fit his own personality and particularly his own residual neurosis."[5] And second, "It could be argued that the personality of the analyst is something given, it is perceived by the patient, and no 'play-acting' will cover it up convincingly. This is partially correct but it does not exclude the possibility of assuming attitudes prescribed by the nature of the patient's conflict situation. Conscious modification of the interpersonal climate is a much less radical proposition than any role playing" (101).

This in full development is the exposition of the corrective emotional experience, the hallmark of Alexander's various modifications of theretofore traditional psychoanalysis to meet the new clinical exigencies of his time and the need in all science for incremental growth, and in all disciplines for flexible renewal. Alexander's critics were not slow to remark that these conceptions were prefigured in Ferenczi's espousal of a more active therapy and greater emotional expressiveness on the part of the analyst in the transference-countertransference interplay, to make up for the emotional deprivations of the patient's past. In chapter 2, I indicated several passages in Ferenczi that could be seen as intellectual forerunners of the trends that Alexander later developed. Indeed, in several places Alexander (e.g., 1954a, 688) acknowledged his specific indebtednesses to Ferenczi, as well as expressing a more general feeling of gratitude for the "healthy experimental spirit" (689) he felt psychoanalysis owed to Ferenczi.[6]

---

nature of the countertransference and of our inevitable human limitations in the ability to fathom it, let alone deliberately titrate it so precisely.

5. Alexander himself thought of this as an (inevitable?) human limitation to the applicability of (good) analytic technique: "I fully recognize the fact that the analyst cannot change himself and not every analyst is a good enough actor to create, convincingly, an atmosphere he wants. Here seem to lie the limitations of our technique, and we may have to accept the fact that every therapist is better suited to one type of patient than to others" (Alexander 1961, 331).

6. Of all Alexander's severe critics, Gill alone took exception to this claim that Alexander's central theses derived from ideas originating in Ferenczi, with the implied psychoanalytic legitimation that Alexander could thus claim. Gill (1954) put it thus: "Ferenczi, whom Alexander declares to be the forerunner of his innovations, is really unjustly accused of such parenthood. It is true that Ferenczi felt that emotional factors were being neglected in favor of intellectual and that repetition in the transference was being neglected in favor of remembering, but in his joint book with Rank he stressed vigorously the need for the development of a full and regressive

The intensity of the debate stirred up by Alexander's concept of the corrective emotional experience and the related technical precepts he introduced attest to the widespread impact these ideas had on the American psychoanalytic world at the time and to the depth of the fear that they threatened the very heart of the psychoanalytic enterprise. The onslaught was initiated by Ernest Jones's (1946) review of the Alexander and French book. Jones said that the authors were "describing something other than the technique of psycho-analysis. Instead they describe various other useful methods of treatment, and their justification for the title of the book [*Psychoanalytic Therapy*] is that in their opinion any method of treatment informed by psycho-dynamic principles deserves to be called psychoanalytic" (163). Jones then listed some of the specific techniques the authors advocated and declared, to Jones's dismay, to be psychoanalytic. Jones concluded, "To practitioners having little or no knowledge of psychoanalysis, and perhaps holding a position at a clinic attended by a large variety of patients, it [the book] should prove not only valuable but illuminating. Such penetration, skill and tactfulness in the handling of patients as are here demonstrated will show other workers the advantages of an inspired and highly trained team. Our only criticism is that such a reader would be left in ignorance of the important fact that besides the various methods here described there is such a thing as real psycho-analysis" (163). In the light of the presentation in chapter 3 of the development of psychoanalytic psychotherapy vis-à-vis psychoanalysis, it can be inferred from this review that Jones might have been quite content if Alexander had only claimed that his modifications constituted a variant of psychoanalytic psychotherapy rather than psychoanalysis proper.

The attack was pursued with equal vigor on the American side of the Atlantic. Eissler (1950) devoted an entire fifty-five-page article to a review of the Alexander and French book. He charged that the approach advocated was behaviorist and therefore merely palliative rather than etiologically curative, that it constituted essentially a "magical" (suggestive?) rather than a rational therapy, and that it was not directed toward structural change based on insight. (For example, the authors "do not take the attitude that more knowledge is necessary for their patients, they do not request that better understanding of dependency reactions is required in order to combat them successfully, but they proclaim that here the analytic situation per se has found a limit, or causes, so to speak,

---

transference and just as vigorously the absolute necessity for the resolution of the transference by interpretation. Ferenczi anxiously asked himself whether his activity was introducing a suggestive factor into the treatment which could not subsequently be resolved, and he candidly admitted failures in which just this happened" (790–91). Footnote 2 in this chapter outlines Alexander's opposite position from that of Gill on this matter.

a sickness and has to be discarded" [128]). In overall judgment, Eissler stated, "Alexander and French's book will be a challenge to those who still believe that Freud in his theories of the human mind and his technique of investigation and therapy laid the foundation not only for a scientific psychology but also created an instrument with which to liberate the individual from the shackles of his ancestors and of his society" (104). Toward the end of the essay he stated, "Alexander reverts to magical treatment in psychoanalytic phraseology. It is exactly that which Freud had warned against and which he made a supreme effort to keep out of psychoanalysis. . . . This does not mean that magical therapy is ill-advised; it only means that a physician using magical therapy should know that he is outside the bounds of psychoanalysis" (150). It would seem that Eissler too would be agreeable if only Alexander and French had talked of psychoanalytic (or "magical" or suggestive) psychotherapy rather than of psychoanalysis itself.

Many other leading psychoanalysts soon joined the critics of the Alexandrian proposals. For example, Robert Knight (1949, 114) felt that the authors had abandoned fundamental analytic principles and had substituted mere symptom relief and conventional social adaptation for its goals and methods; Max Gitelson (1952, 9) felt that the assumption of roles and the choice of therapeutic attitudes (described as techniques) were far too close to rationalized expressions of countertransferential enactments; Heinz Hartmann (in Zetzel 1953) felt that these proposals would not work because "the patient could easily see through repeated changes of attitude on the part of the analyst" (534); Phyllis Greenacre (1954, 675–76) saw them as "little more than old-fashioned habit training with especially strong suggestive influencing"; and both Rudolph Loewenstein (1951, 3) and Elizabeth Zetzel (1956, 374) lamented that the Alexandrian techniques devalued the importance of dynamic changes produced by insights gained from interpretations and that they suggested instead that the corrective emotional experience alone could bring about qualitative dynamic alterations in mental structure leading to a satisfactory therapeutic goal.

The critiques offered by Gill, Rangell, and Stone were the most systematic, the least polemical, and the most definitive, and therefore warrant more extended consideration. Gill (1954) tackled the conceptual issues most comprehensively. First, he stated that Alexander's vaunted principle of flexibility confused

> what is transference and what is reaction to the therapist's behavior. Neutrality does not mean mechanical rigidity of behavior with the effort to suppress any spontaneous responses, as for example, to use an often-cited example of Alexander's, a spontaneous show of anger by the analyst. But

he seems to have overlooked that this kind of response from a therapist may have been occasioned by his failure to make appropriate interpretations early enough, that it is not justifiable to generalize and say that in all cases such techniques are best, that the possible good effect of such a spontaneous event does not absolve the analyst from looking into himself to observe how it was precipitated, that he is not justified in generalizing such an outburst into a consistent role, and that it may also be true that such techniques have disadvantages as great as their apparent advantages. (776)

Gill went on to challenge the corrective emotional experience as simply not psychoanalytic:

I think there is little doubt that Alexander is correct in stating that by overt behavior toward the patient one can more quickly get him to change some aspects of his behavior. But what is the meaning of such a change? It is an adaptation to this particular interpersonal relationship—as it exists between patient and analyst. But this is not the goal of analysis. The goal of analysis is an intrapsychic modification in the patient, so that for example his dependent behavior is given up not because he has learned that if he acts too dependent he will be punished by a loss of therapy hours, but because despite the invitation to regress and the maintenance of the frequency of his hours he has come to feel and understand his dependency in such a way that he no longer needs it or wants it—and that this is a conclusion valid not simply for this particular interpersonal relationship but has more general applicability, in short has the status of an intrapsychic change. (781)

Although Gill did not state it explicitly, his conclusion is clear: Alexander's innovations have taken his endeavors outside the realm of analysis proper. Despite Alexander's claim that they were merely more effective analysis better geared to the needs of his patients, to Gill they were a form of psychoanalytically oriented psychotherapy, which may or may not be appropriate depending on the particular clinical circumstance.

Rangell (1954b) considered the same example—Alexander's handling of his patient's unduly dependent behaviors—from a complementary perspective, reaching the same conclusion as Gill:

The various maneuvers engaged in by the therapist in Alexander's system, and in general with "the corrective emotional experience," are at times, to be sure, dynamically indicated, but when they are, they distinctly constitute dynamic psychotherapy in contrast to psychoanalysis. When they are indicated, the dynamic condition is such as to make necessary or desirable an intermediate point of stability rather than the psychoanalytic end point [Gitelson's chemical reaction analogy]. . . . As an example of the contrasting formulae in the two therapies, one can consider the patient who is "becoming too dependent" upon the therapist. Alexander "does something," e.g., cuts the frequency in order to show the patient that he is wrong, that he need not be dependent, in order to educate him to something different. To the analyst, on the other hand, the patient is right, he *is* too dependent, this being a facet of the transference neurosis which exists. The direction, however, now continues inward, toward the infantile neurosis, to answer the question, "Why this phenomenon?" The analyst continues inward toward the infantile hub, while the psychotherapist, for good or bad reasons, stops at an intermediate concentric layer or turns back toward the current periphery. (743–44)

Stone (1951), in his characteristically multifaceted and nuanced way, undertook to challenge even more comprehensively the whole interrelated fabric of underlying assumptions and technical modifications comprised in Alexander's system. He began with the statement that Alexander and French had conveyed the misleading impression that one can control powerful dynamic forces, "best exemplified in the impression given that the transference can not only be distributed almost at will, but can be controlled in intensity by the frequency of visits" (223). In a review (1957) of Alexander's definitive 1956 book, he first outlined Alexander's system:

Alexander's principal explicit technical recommendations in the text are: variations in frequency of hours, planned interruptions of treatment, and "control of the interpersonal climate of treatment." The latter . . . is not the "playing of a role." Nevertheless, it is rooted in the idea of being "different" in attitude from the decisive historical personage who dominates the transference, to the extent that the "corrective emotional experience" is sharpened. . . . Alexander, in a tour de force of logic, recommends that the variety of human attitudes present in analysts be bent to specific attitudes toward their patients, while at the same time believing that the classical analytic attitude is impossible of attainment. (400–01)

Here Stone explicitly registered his deep disagreement with the basic principles involved:

If Alexander does not believe that most individuals can successfully adopt the standard "analytic technique," toward which their entire training is rationally directed, how will they fare with personal attitudes specifically prescribed for specific individuals? How does the patient's reality sense deal with the change from the pretransference neurosis neutrality (which is admittedly necessary) to the tendentious attitude adopted after its establishment? In his combined "role" as analyst, as physician, as friendly human being, there is a considerable reservoir of attitudes with which the analyst may appropriately and unaffectedly respond, to the degree *proved necessary* by the diseased ego with which he deals, without illusory or artificial historically specified "oppositeness." Otherwise, and indeed in most instances, he does better to adhere, to the best of his ability, to that tested clinical attitude which alone permits a relatively uncontaminated transference neurosis to arise, and to be resolved. (402–03)

Stone pressed this argument even more incisively in his 1961 monograph, in which he differentiated between his own modifications of Eissler's austere image of "classical" psychoanalysis then being propagated (see chapter 7) and Alexander's proposals: "Ferenczi's principle that the analyst should, in effect, provide the love (tenderness) of which neurotic patients, in his view, had been deprived in their developmental years, and Alexander's proposal that the analyst facilitate a 'corrective emotional experience' by 'control of the interpersonal climate of treatment' (i.e., by being different from the parent whose attitudes are retrospectively judged as importantly pathogenic), are . . . relevant to this discussion. In both, there would be, in effect, the *neutralization* of a basic element in the transference neurosis, via an attitude which would presumably undo the effects of an injurious parental attitude in early years" (56–57). Stone then summed up his objections to this as a line of *psychoanalytic* thought:

(1) While either one *might,* in a given case, have a psychotherapeutic effect, both (if effective!) substitute direct interpersonal response for the analysis of emergent elements judged to be crucial in the transference neurosis. (2) Both call for a current attitude to undo the effect of a genetically earlier attitude as if they were interchangeable; whereas the situations of origin of the respective attitudes are, in fact, remote from one another in time, place, real functional significance, state of development of the patient, actual personal meaning of the object (i.e., the analyst), and in many other lesser details. (3) Both, to varying degrees . . . call on the analyst to "adopt" attitudes which are not necessarily immanent in the analyst's identity—i.e., in his specific (analytic) functions, in his role as physician, in his specifically personal reactions to the analysand. (57–58)

What Stone called for was a reaffirmation of the traditionally neutral (in the sense of being "objective" but still concerned, compassionate, and "physicianly")[7] posture of the analyst in the transference-countertransference interaction: "In following correct precepts, in doing what is technically appropriate at a given time, in assuming an attitude required by the particular medical specialty which he practices, the analyst does assume a role, in the realistic sense that all adults assume specific adult occupational responsibilities" (1957, 401–02). Seemingly paradoxically, Stone declared this adherence to traditionally correct precepts to be more in the service of a true corrective emotional experience than Alexander's advice that the analyst assume a role deliberately opposite to the dominant transference imagos from the past: "Any attitude not directly derived from or germane to the therapist's role is perforce 'less unlike' the patient's past experience than the classical analytic attitude, which, as Alexander explicitly recognizes, *is* different from all other human attitudes, past and present" (402).

That properly neutral (and ultimately properly "corrective") analytic stance, Stone avers, is properly *expectable:* "It is *not* an excessive expectation that an analyst, in his capacity as physician, feel a kindly and helpful, broadly tolerant and friendly interest in his patients, expressed largely in the channels provided by his special work. . . . This is, to be sure, a 'role,' in a sense; however, a role which represents a lifelong vocation, a profound sense of identity and commitment, and a real functional relationship to another individual, is easily distinguished from the others which we are considering" (1961, 59). (I would here interpolate an additional consideration. Suppose Alexander's way were the better way, in the sense of being analytically more efficacious. How sure could Alexander, or anyone else, always be that he or she had correctly judged the dominant or salient transference expectation from the past that required specific counteracting at each changing moment of the analytic progression?)

Gill (1954) used Stone's argument as his own summary statement in redefin-

---

7. This is, of course, specifically different from the conception of the proper stance in the transference field that Freud seemingly propounded with his famous surgical and mirror models. In his "Recommendations to Physicians" (1912b) Freud said, "I cannot advise my colleagues too urgently to model themselves during psycho-analytic treatment on the surgeon who puts aside all his feelings, even his human sympathy, and concentrates his mental forces on the single aim of performing the operation as skillfully as possible" (115); and further on, "The doctor should be opaque to his patients and, like a mirror, should show them nothing but what is shown to him" (118). Eissler's (1953) declaration of a very austere model as reflecting classical psychoanalysis (i.e., imputed to be based on Freud's technique) and Lipton's (1977) counterargument that this represented a misreading of Freud's actual technique are discussed at length in chapter 7.

ing a *true* corrective emotional experience: "Certainly to meet the patient's transference behavior with neutrality *is* to give him a corrective emotional experience without the risks attendant on taking a role opposite to that which he expects, as Alexander suggests" (782). Many years later (1982), Stone restated this point: "A physician can only give that form and degree of love which is integrated in and compatible with his enduring and dependable professional role, a measure of love which can always be available to the patient should he need it. . . . There is thus always a 'corrective emotional experience,' the correction of infantile distortions of the object by the increasingly correct perceptions of the present object, aided by interpretive work" (97). In these assertions, Gill and Stone reverse the entire argument by insisting that the proper corrective emotional experience, which every effective psychoanalysis (and every effective psychotherapy, as well) imparts, rests upon the properly neutral posture of the analyst (therapist) in the analytic (therapeutic) situation, and that contrived departures from this stance specifically intended to correct the inferred transference expectations of the patient are not appropriate, effective, or even very possible. Therefore, often these experiences are far less than the kind of corrective emotional experiences they are intended to be.

At the time of these debates, Alexander's following was impressively large, and the outcome in terms of widespread acceptance or rejection by the psychoanalytic community seemed uncertain. Over time, however, it became abundantly clear that the majority of psychoanalysts agreed essentially with the counterarguments of Jones, Eissler, Gill, Rangell, Stone, and the others quoted that the so-called corrective emotional experience rested on a dubious rationale; that even if indicated in specific clinical situations, it would require an accurate inferential knowledge of the most salient transference expectations of the patient, which would not necessarily be available even to the most insightful or intuitive analyst; that, further, even if successfully carried out in a specific instance, it would be, par excellence, a psychotherapeutic rather than a properly psychoanalytic maneuver in the sense indicated by Gill (1954, 781) and Rangell (1954b, 743–44); and that greater psychoanalytic rewards would be secured by adherence to time-tested precepts of technical neutrality in the frame of "physicianly concern"—and that this is a *true* corrective emotional experience (cf. Gill's redefinition, 1954, 782, and Stone's 1982, 97).

Gradually, preoccupation with this issue of the corrective emotional experience (and the related Alexandrian concepts) dwindled away. Edward Bibring's 1954 paper (discussed in chapter 5) came to be taken as the definitive delineation of the major technical principles that distinguished the psychoanalytic psychotherapies from proper psychoanalysis; and Eissler's famous 1953 paper on parameters (discussed in chapter 7) was widely taken to set the standard for proper psychoanalysis—i.e., a treatment resting solely on resolution of intrapsychic conflict through interpretation and working through, leading to insight and change. All deviations from this exclusively interpretive mode Eissler designated "parameters," perhaps temporarily necessary on occasion, but in any case to be fully analytically resolved, again by interpretation alone, before the appropriate termination of the analytic work.

In this context the Alexander concept of the corrective emotional experience could perhaps find a (circumscribed) place as but one of a variety of possible psycho*therapeutic* maneuvers, to be conceptualized in Bibring's terms as some combination of abreaction and manipulation (nonpejoratively intended), and invoked in a psychotherapeutic effort when a properly psychoanalytic intervention would be less useful to the overall treatment endeavor or even contraindicated. And just as the proposals of Alexander (and before him, Ferenczi) were a reaction to the sterile intellectualizing of the time, so the Eissler article was taken as the specific "establishment" response to the deviations from the traditional technique that Alexander proposed.

Over the years, however, the concerns Alexander raised about the need for proper attention to the affective and interpersonal climate of the psychoanalytic (and psychotherapeutic) interaction have far from disappeared. Stone acknowledged this in his 1961 monograph as an important broadening of the total psychoanalytic discourse that had been permanently implanted by Alexander, building on Ferenczi, whose work had, at the time, fallen into an era of relative neglect. Stone said, "To my knowledge . . . only Ferenczi and Alexander have tried to establish broad and systematic generalizations regarding the purposive utilization of the analyst's affective responses in the analysis of neurotic patients, within the original framework of psychoanalytic theory" (132). These concerns with the affective and relationship components of the psychoanalytic treatment process have continued ever since, but under a variety of rubrics and in ways that do not necessarily relate clearly to Alexander's original propositions.

To indicate just some of the lines of theoretical development that subsequently unfolded: In America, there was concern with the various proposed "alliances" (therapeutic, working) as equal partners in the analytic process, alongside the vicissitudes of the transference; or with disentangling the various transference elements and components ("primal" or "core" transferences and the diatrophic relationship within which they operate) from the maturationally unfolding object-related transferences; or, in other words, with the earliest mother-child matrix and its growth-facilitating interactions as the proper prototype for the renewed developmental processes that proper analysis tries to promote; or with the so-called interpersonal (Sullivanian) theory of psychoanalysis arising mostly outside the organizational frame of the American Psychoanalytic Association. In Britain, concern with the analytic relationship was a major component of the Kleinian development (albeit embodied in an instinct-based language that could obscure the essential relational nature of the theory—cf. Greenberg and Mitchell 1983) and also of the developing object relational perspective (Suttie, Fairbairn, Guntrip, Balint, Winnicott, Bowlby, and a host who came after). In both countries and elsewhere around the world (see Racker 1968 in Latin America) a growing interest in the (inevitable) countertransference coloring of the analytic work has contributed importantly to this focus on the affectively charged nature of the analytic relationship. Most recently, Gill and Irwin Hoffman, together and separately, have pushed furthest in this direction with their focus on the "patient's *experience* of the psychoanalytic relationship" embedded in an uncompromisingly "two-body" psychology, leading to what Hoffman has dubbed the "social-constructivist" paradigm of psychoanalysis. All these development are discussed in later chapters.

I do not imply identity or even much similarity among the various perspectives on the affective nature of the analytic relationship. The writings alluded to in the preceding paragraph simply share (with Ferenczi and Alexander) a focus on the affective patient-analyst relationship as a salient dynamic in the treatment process. None of them restates the particular Alexander concept of the corrective emotional experience, though some of these writers have felt it necessary to specifically distinguish their views from the Alexander position. And yet it is precisely these developments, maturing gradually over the past four decades, that have raised anew the question of whether the current widespread acceptance of the centrality of affective relationship factors in the psychoanalytic process represents, if not a return of the concept of the corrective emotional experience in a new guise, at least a warrant for its critical reconsideration.

Such considerations led the editors of *Psychoanalytic Inquiry* to devote an issue in 1990 to a reconsideration of Alexander's concept. The papers in that issue took a number of surprising turns, including both new critiques and new affirmations, with a plea to continue to find a place for the corrective emotional experience, in more modern garb perhaps, in psychoanalytic ranks. I will select comments from two of the most critical and two of the most positive papers.

First from the critical side: Hanna Segal (1990) gave a Kleinian critique (this, interestingly, from a camp that had at first almost completely ignored Alexander's work, presumably as irrelevant to proper psychoanalysis). Segal actually agreed with Alexander's intent: "Indeed it is a general psychoanalytical tenet, that psychoanalysis is a corrective emotional experience and that purely intellectual insight produces no changes. . . . I doubt if anyone today holds totally to the view criticized by Alexander" (409). But, from a Kleinian perspective, she found Alexander's approach highly flawed:

It seems to me that this approach completely ignores the existence of splitting. Where in the patient's internal world was the good aspect of father in the first case, or the bad aspect of father in the second and third cases? The analyst doing the opposite of the patient's expectations in these cases acted out the split-off other aspect of the original object, which I think is as damaging as acting out the expected role. In both situations splits are ignored and conflict avoided. It is my contention that, far from giving a corrective emotional experience, such acting out in fact shortcuts the experience. Presenting the patient with some firm demonstration— "I am a good object, not a bad one as you expected"—cuts short any exploration of the splitting process. . . . It also takes for granted that the fathers in these cases were in reality exactly as the patient conceived them. It ignores the fact that transference is not a linear repetition of the real past with the real external object, but is a projection onto the analyst of an internal figure which has a long history. (411)

This reasoning led Segal to charge, in fact, that acting oppositely to what the patient expects can mean that the analyst is being "unconsciously manipulated by the patient. Presenting oneself as a victim of the father's tyranny may be devised precisely to call forth a sympathetic response. It could, for example, be inviting the mother aspect of the analyst to collude against the father" (415).

Patrick Casement's critical remarks came from within the British Independent (object-relational) perspective and centered even more squarely on the object-tie or object-relationship between patient and analyst. He questioned sharply Alexander's "*deliberate* provocations—selected on the basis of a 'principle of contrast'—[with] the analyst consciously choosing to respond in ways that are opposite to the manner in which the parents had behaved" (1990b, 327, italics added). After presenting a case from his own therapeutic work, Casement developed his differing perspective: "I had not provided this patient with an experience that was designed to *contrast* with what she had experienced in her childhood. Instead, Mrs. K. had found her own way to use me as if I were the *same* as her mother. Only then could she find a therapeutic difference in her experience with me that could help to bring about real and lasting change. The difference was that I could tolerate being treated as if I were the rejecting mother of her early life, and I could survive being subjected to those feelings that had first been associated with that early experience of rejection" (342).

And it is this experience of living through sameness rather than repetition that Casement feels patients require: "Analysts often find in their clinical work that to attempt (actively) to provide good experience for a patient almost invariably deflects the analytic process because it interferes with the patient's use of the analyst in the transference. A prime reason for this is that patients often need to use the analyst in order to work through feelings about early experiences *as they had been:* it is not enough simply to have experience in the analytic relationship that might seem to be 'corrective' " (343). Casement put it thus: "How then does this fit in with the notion of 'corrective emotional experience'? The main difference, in my opinion, is that *therapeutic experience in analysis is found by the patient—it is not provided.* Earlier bad experience may be repeated in the search for understanding or for 'mastery' of the anxieties related to it. But when better experience is also found in an analysis it is always important that it should have arisen spontaneously. It cannot be a matter of deliberate technique, for if it is any way set up by the analyst, it will be artificial and will eventually be experienced as false" (343–44). In an earlier book, Casement had gone over much the same ground, emphasizing additionally the notion of the patient's autonomy. The deliberate adoption of a role in relation to a patient "becomes a way of influencing what he or she experiences in the analysis. In that sense it infringes on the patient's autonomy and is antithetic to the analytic process" (1985, 169) and thereby "fails to allow an analytic freedom to use the therapist in those ways that relate to the earlier experience and inner world of the patient" (172).

Two American analysts, as it happened, were arrayed on the other side of this renewed debate of 1990. Jule Miller's conclusion was that "Alexander's concept of the corrective emotional experience, and the term itself, are felicitous and should be retained. I believe the concept should be used in the core sense, without the addition of contrived attitudes" (1990, 386). Miller had earlier indicated what he meant by "core sense" and "contrived attitudes" when he talked about Alexander's "experiments" in deliberately choosing an emotional posture opposite to that of the major operative transference disposition: "While I believe it was a reasonable experimental suggestion, in retrospect I think it unfortunate that it was advanced, and an unnecessary addition. It afforded a vulnerable spot which facilitated the rejection of the entire concept. Throughout his writings, Alexander made it clear that the standard neutral analytic atmosphere itself would provide a corrective emotional experience in the substantial majority of clinical instances. It would have been better if he had left it there" (376).

Miller saw two advantages in retaining Alexander's concept. First, it complemented the therapeutic effects of insight gained through interpretation and working through and in that sense served as a conceptual underpinning for the more current analytic acceptance—as compared with Alexander's day—of the coequal status, if not the real primacy, of new experience alongside interpretation and insight as vehicles of analytic change. Second, the corrective emotional experience as an explanatory concept "allows us to understand how the use of very different analytic theories can produce lasting and far-reaching beneficial changes in patients" (385)—though, of course, other explanations of these same facts have been adduced without the need for Alexander's formulations (see Wallerstein 1988a). The problem with Miller's defense of Alexander's conceptions, of course, is that in dumping the excess (or misleading) baggage of role-playing (or providing the appropriate contrast in the transference-countertransference interplay), Miller may have come quite close to accepting the redefinitions of Gill and Stone of the *true* corrective emotional experience, thus preserving only the name rather than the substance of what made Alexander's views distinctive.

Theodore Jacobs, in contrast, made a more spirited and at the same time more persuasive defense of Alexander's conceptions in a way quite consonant with modern analytic sensibilities and stripped of what Lawrence Friedman (1988) called Alexander's "naivete."[8] Jacobs's reformulation, in the paraphrased words of one of his seminar leaders—back in *1963*—was, "Every good analysis contains elements of a corrective emotional experience. We do not always like to acknowledge that fact because it is not part of accepted theory and because that dimension of our work does not separate us sufficiently from therapists of other persuasions. But it is true nonetheless, and it is important that we recognize that fact and without apology accord to it its rightful place in our theory of cure" (438).

Such corrective action operates, Jacobs indicated, quite spontaneously, by using intuitive understanding to make "unconscious adjustments in . . . technique" (445). Therefore, "as he works, the analyst often finds himself intuitively responding to patients in ways that are clearly different from those of parents and other caretakers. . . . Inevitably we act in 'corrective' ways, and in my view every good analysis includes a measure of this ingredient in its therapeutic mix" (446). Jacobs then explained in greater detail:

> The corrective actions of the analyst . . . are an inevitable and necessary part of treatment. With most patients they are employed in minimal, quite subtle, and unobtrusive ways. With some individuals, however, it may be necessary to utilize them in a more planned and deliberate manner. Along with certain aspects of the analyst's behavior, including his attentive listening, his benevolent neutrality, his honesty, reliability, and analytic tact, the intuitive "corrective" moves that he makes as he attunes himself to

8. "He [Alexander] thought that a pathogenic issue might be simple enough and wrong enough to be symbolized by the analyst in a single contrary attitude"—and therefore, "If Alexander is a bad example of something, that something is not manipulativeness, but naivete" [p. 522]).

certain needs of the patient have the effect of offering the patient a unique object relationship, one that is different from others he has known. To the extent that the patient can experience the relationship as it is offered, internalization of "corrective" attitudes, values, behaviors, and self-representations take place. Over time these affect both ego and superego and play a not unimportant role in producing changes in these structures. (453)

Put this way, Jacobs's rendering of Alexander's ideas will resonate very acceptably with many present-day analysts and certainly comes close, if not to Gill's (1954) quite precise redefinition of the true corrective emotional experience, at least to Stone's (1961) overall perspectives on the nature of the psychoanalytic situation and of the psychoanalytic process that occurs within it. The question persists, however, whether this intervening history of consideration and reconsideration warrants a specific revival of Alexander's language, with all the meanings he gave to it. In my own historical overview, included in that same 1990 issue of *Psychoanalytic Inquiry,* my conclusion was in the negative. Despite the various expressions of concern with affective relationship factors as major components of analytic understanding in the almost fifty years since Alexander's first writings in this area, it would be neither necessary nor particularly useful to reconsider the corrective emotional experience in Alexander's language and with his meanings and restore it to the psychoanalytic scheme of things.

Arnold Modell (1988b) set his ideas about the therapeutic action of psychoanalysis squarely in relation to his reading of Alexander's conception of the corrective emotional experience: "The theory of therapeutic action of psychoanalysis that I am proposing can be placed under the heading of a 'corrective emotional experience.' There is hope that this much maligned term may be undergoing a rehabilitation, but it should be clear that this term does not mean that the analyst subverts the analytic process by assuming a role different from that of the patient's archaic objects. This emotional reliving is not to be taken as a naive correction that psychoanalysis works simply by providing a corrective gratification that repairs a developmental deficit" (237–38). Both implied and explicit in this article is a view of the refurbished conception of the corrective emotional experience quite clearly in line with the redefinitions of Stone and Gill. This redefinition, of course, again runs the risk that different meanings may adhere to the same phrase.

For my part, I still feel it best to accord the concept the meaning Alexander gave it and to see it in the same light that Gill (1954), Rangell (1954b), Stone (1961), and a host of others did: as a specifically psychotherapeutic rather than psychoanalytic concept, a technical maneuver possibly justifiable and even indicated in specific clinical circumstances, albeit always difficult to pinpoint and chancy in its effect. I would, however, add two caveats. The boundaries between what is psychoanalytic and what is psychotherapeutic are far from clear and fixed for all time; both enterprises have changed significantly over time as our understandings of both have grown. And, of course, psychoanalytic psychotherapy is neither more nor less honorable or effective than psychoanalysis proper. The basis for both these caveats has been developed elsewhere (Wallerstein 1986a, 1988b, 1989a) and will, of course, be in evidence throughout this book.

Clearly, however, Alexander and his co-workers had a major impact on the psychoanalytic world, and related ideas can be traced in many important developments since. To illustrate that one can hardly take a position on the theory of psychoanalytic technique now adays without some reference to Alexander, I will mention only Veikko Tahka's *Mind and Its Treatment: A Psychoanalytic Approach* (1993), essentially a developmental and hierarchical organization of the principles of therapeutic intervention in relation to the psychopathological spectrum of illness, somewhat related to the more familiar writings of John Gedo and of Hans Loewald.

Tahka's contribution to the issues of this book will be discussed in detail in chapter 18. Here I want to call attention to his perceived need to compare his ideas with Alexander's. Tahka put it this way:

> Provided that the analyst has received the position of a past parental object for the patient, an obvious requirement for his becoming a new developmental object is that he behaves in an *unexpected* way from the patient's point of view. Objects, behaving in an expected way are familiar objects, with whom the patients, without being aware of it, expect to repeat or continue relationships that are determined by their repressed or continually actualized past. The new and unexpected ways of the analyst to approach his patients in his role or function as a new developmental object, could be regarded as providing the patient with a corrective experience, although not in the original Alexandrian (Alexander and French, 1946) sense of the term. Unlike the latter, the analyst's becoming a new developmental object for the patient has nothing to do with purposeful role-playing, regarded as opposite to the patient's prevailing transference expectations. Instead, the analyst's approach as a new object is, or ought to be, based on his empathic and/or complementary recognition of the patient's frustrated and arrested developmental needs and potentials, that are present alongside of the repetition and continuation of his failed developmental interactions in the analytic relationship. (231)

II. *The Eras of Consensus and of Fragmentation*

5 The Crystallization of the Majority Consensus: 1954

The emerging consensus within the American psychoanalytic world on what constituted psychoanalysis proper, what constituted the array of varyingly supportive and varyingly expressive psychoanalytic psychotherapies, and how they were related was crystallized, as noted, in the publication in 1954 of an issue of the *Journal of the American Psychoanalytic Association*. The issue comprised a dozen papers from three major panels, two held at meetings of the American, *The Traditional Psychoanalytic Technique and Its Variations* (panel report, Zetzel 1953) and *Psychoanalysis and Dynamic Psychotherapy: Similarities and Differences* (panel report, Rangell 1954a), and one held by the New York Psychoanalytic Society, *The Widening Scope of Indications for Psychoanalysis.*[1] An important impetus for the outpouring of contributions on this theme was the intense ferment stirred up by the bold technical proposals of Alexander and his co-workers. These proposals were received with reactions ranging from great enthusiasm to dismay; some believed that they pointed the way to a more effective and also speedier psychoanalytic treatment, others that the feared dilution of proper psychoanalysis into an amorphous psychotherapy, all the more dangerous because it masqueraded as psychoanalysis and so could hoodwink the uninformed, was under way—a feared logical but extremely unhappy outcome of the growing closeness in America between psychoanalysis and psychiatry. An even stronger impetus to the publications of 1954 was the growing controversy over the similarities and differences between psychoanalysis and psychotherapy. Out of that controversy emerged what I have called the second era in the relationship of psychotherapy to psychoanalysis, that of established diversity of goals and techniques within a unity of theory, an era of converging consensus that lasted for approximately twenty years albeit with increasing strain after its full delineation in these manifestos of 1954.

The central controversy had to do with the most appropriate way to conceptualize the relationship between dynamic psychotherapy and psychoanalysis. Alexander (1956, Alexander and French 1946), Fromm-Reichmann (1950),

---

1. Other panels on aspects of this topic took place at other meetings of the American during this same period but were not separately published as a group: *The Essentials of Psychotherapy as Viewed by the Psychoanalyst* (panel report, English 1953), *Psychoanalysis and Psychotherapy: Dynamic Criteria for Treatment Choice* (panel report, Ludwig 1954), and *Psychoanalysis and Psychotherapy* (panel report, Chassell 1955).

Stanislaus Szurek (1958), Dexter Bullard (1959), and their adherents, but altogether a distinct minority, saw the historical trend as blurring, if not obliterating, the technical distinctions between dynamic psychotherapy and psychoanalysis. The majority of analysts, for whom Bibring (1954), Gill (1951, 1954), Rangell (1954b), and Stone (1951, 1954) served as major spokesmen, advocated the full preservation of the conceptual and operational distinctions between the two via a process of ever more adequate clarification. The former group took two somewhat discrepant positions. The more popular, and seen by its opponents as the more dangerous in its push toward the dissolution of the distinctness of psychoanalysis, was that associated with Alexander and his followers. One of Alexander's two contributions to the panels published in 1954 expressed the position well, calling for the total integration of psychoanalysis into academic psychiatry and medicine: "That psychoanalytic concepts, the theoretical knowledge of psychodynamics and neurosis formation, are necessary for every psychiatrist is by now rather generally accepted, both by analysts and nonanalytic psychiatrists . . . psychoanalytic theory [has become] the common property of whole psychiatry and through psychosomatic channels of the whole of medicine" (1954b, 724). With the "absorption" of psychoanalytic theory and practice into psychiatry, a "unification" would be accomplished, "dictated by the immanent logic of the field" (725).

Alexander declared that this was already happening and that what kept the situation from being more generally recognized was simply the guild interests of organized psychoanalysis. "A sharp distinction between psychoanalytic treatment and other methods of psychotherapy which are based on psychoanalytic observations and theory is becoming more and more difficult, . . ." he wrote. "In their actual practice . . . all psychiatrists become more and more similar, even though one may practice pure psychoanalysis and the other psychoanalytically oriented psychotherapy" (725). Indeed, any distinction between psychoanalysis proper and other uncovering or expressive procedures was, he declared, only "quantitative," and all distinctions based on the frequency of interviews, the duration of the treatment, or the use or not of the couch were nonvital and even "spurious" (729). For after all, "as long as the psychological processes in the patient are the same and the personality changes achieved by these processes are of similar nature, it is not possible to draw a sharp dividing line where psychoanalysis proper ends and psychoanalytically oriented psychotherapy begins." The only solution, therefore, "is to identify as 'psychoanalytic' *all* these related procedures which are essentially based on the same scientific concepts, observations and technical principles" (730–31, italics added).

In this connection Alexander added the battle cry of flexibility as opposed to the rigidity of his opponents: "It should be emphasized that to use psychoanalytic principles in a more flexible way does not require less but more knowledge" (731). Weigert (1954), in her contribution to these panels, made flexibility her central theme: "Any rigidity, any automatization of attitude or procedure can become a defense against intuitive insight and block the passage from the unconscious to the conscious processes of the analyst" (702–03). After quoting Fenichel that "everything is permissible, if only one knows why," she added, "Fixation of rules is a danger for a science that has set liberation from compulsion as an essential goal" (710).

"The *only* realistic distinction," Alexander insisted, "is . . . that between primarily supportive and primarily expressive methods" (730, italics added), thus collapsing all of expressive psychotherapy and psychoanalysis into a single category of psychoanalytic (i.e., expressive) therapy. Alexander then adumbrated the specifically supportive therapeutic techniques: gratification of dependent needs, abreaction with reduction of emotional stresses, intellectual guidance through objective review of stressful pressures, aiding of the ego's neurotic defenses when the patient is unable to deal with the unconscious material, and manipulating of the life situation when the patient is unable to cope with life circumstance (728). This list was actually quite similar to Knight's (1952) (presented in chapter 3), though it was conceptually more distinct. On the other side of the dichotomy Alexander placed all expressive approaches, psychoanalysis included, which he declared varied only in quantitative and not in critical parameters. In his definitive presentation of his views on all the issues of psychoanalysis and psychotherapy, Alexander (1956, 152–61) restated every one of the propositions from his panel presentation in practically the identical language.

Fromm-Reichmann (1950, 1954; Bullard 1959) on the other hand, took the somewhat different position that the psychoanalytic treatment of the borderline and even the blatantly psychotic required not just major modifications of technique (with which all would agree) but also systematic revision, or rather conversion, of the theory of classical psychoanalysis into the more modern "interpersonal theory," or "dynamically oriented psychiatric theory" (173) based on the interpersonal conceptions of Harry Stack Sullivan. Fromm-Reichmann's conceptual development was stepwise a seemingly logical one. She started with the patients she treated at the Chestnut Lodge Sanatorium, primarily the hospitalized overtly schizophrenic. She stoutly (and rightly) took issue with two major articles of faith that had stood in the way of a therapeutic approach to schizophrenics: the preanalytic notion that their mental manifestations were meaningless and could not be understood and the analytic notion, stemming from Freud's paper "On Narcissism" (1914c), with its statement of the narcissistic origin of the schizophrenic disorder, that a workable therapeutic relationship could not be effected with the schizophrenic.

In the most convincing—and inspiring—passages in her book, Fromm-Reichmann demonstrated both her understanding of her psychotic patients and her capacity to work effectively with them by means of a technique drastically modified from that which originated in a quiet Vienna consulting room with inhibited neurotic patients. Most of the external accoutrements of the analytic method, like the couch and the call for free associations, simply had to be dispensed with, and in this most of the psychoanalytic world would certainly concur. But here Fromm-Reichmann called on new theory, as if necessary to bolster new, or modified, technique. She first defended the thesis that even treatment so modified is still psychoanalysis, calling on Freud's well-known dictum that "every science and therapy that accepts his teachings about the unconscious, about transference and resistance, and about infantile sexuality may be called psychoanalysis. According to this definition, we believe that we are practicing psychoanalysis with our schizophrenic patients" (1959, 126). But then Fromm-Reichmann not only declared that traditional psychoanalysis and her brand of psychoanalytic psychotherapy were almost indistinguishable on a merely quantitative continuum but also undertook to systematically redefine psychoanalysis as theory, now in Sullivanian terms. Dynamic psychiatry, she claimed, is nothing but the art and science of interpersonal relationships. And within this framework, classical libido theory, anchored in the biological rooting of the drives, was replaced by interpersonal developmental theory; the concepts of the dynamic unconscious and the ego as the executor of compromise formations that mediated the conflicting pressures of id, superego, and outer reality were replaced by an ego concerned with security operations that warded off the anxieties consequent to threatening and dysphoric interpersonal relations.

In effect, Fromm-Reichmann had, in a sequence of steps, starkly modified standard psychoanalytic technique to make it applicable to the requirements of the most grossly disturbed patients, the flagrantly schizophrenic; called the new technical procedures (in which only the rationale of understanding was recognizably psychoanalytic in its original sense) still the same psychoanalysis; altered the theory from the classical (American) ego-psychological paradigm to the Sullivanian interpersonal system, which she believed was conceptually more directly congenial to the psychological phenomena encountered with her schizophrenic patients; and even declared this severely modified analytic therapy based now on Sullivanian principles the treatment of choice not only with hospitalized schizophrenics but also with neurotics in the outpatient, private practice consulting room. Like Alexander, she argued that psychoanalysis and psychoanalytically based psychotherapy had become indistinguishably close on a merely quantitative continuum, but in Fromm-Reichmann's case with a transformed theory, and with psychoanalysis assimilated to the new interpersonal theory of dynamic psychiatry rather than, as with Alexander, with psychoanalytic psychotherapy assimilated to psychoanalysis. For both of these contributors, coming from opposite directions, the distinctions between psychoanalysis and psychoanalytic psychotherapy had indeed been blurred, if not yet entirely obliterated.

Like Alexander's, Fromm-Reichmann's views were specifically countered in the 1954 panel debates. Gill, for example, in a critique directed primarily at the technical issues, called Fromm-Reichmann's movement a "regrettable development . . . from the direction of intensive psychotherapy with deformed ego structures, with the modifications in technique *necessary* in that field *unjustifiably generalized back* into the psychoanalytic treatment of the neurosis. . . . Reasoning correctly that regression should be avoided if possible in these severely distorted egos, she cautions against free association, recumbency, and similar measures. But then she proceeds to argue that such measures are likewise not necessary in psychoanalysis but only waste time. I think this can only mean that she does not see the need for regression in the analytic situation when dealing with the relatively strong ego" (1954, 794–95, italics added).

In a critique directed primarily at the theoretical issues, Rangell pointed to Fromm-Reichmann's shift to the interpersonal theory of dynamic psychiatry as a basically different conception of the genesis of mental illness. His own view, he said, "differs from this position, holding instead that both technical approaches [classical psychoanalysis and dynamic psychiatry] must rest on a single, we hope correct, estimation of psychodynamics and pathogenesis. A piece of hysteria does not have a different origin depending on which form of treatment is selected to combat it" (1954b, 738). This is in direct line, of course, with the earlier quotation from Fenichel, "There are many ways to treat neuroses but there is only one way to understand them" (1945, 554). Stone, in his impromptu comments on this same panel (Rangell 1954a), similarly said that Fromm-Reichmann "had applied the question of similarities and differences to a comparison between classical psychoanalysis and what is apparently regarded as an equivalent or alternative system of dynamic psychotherapy, rather than to the distinction between psychoanalysis proper and the methods based on it or derived from it" (155).

It is clear from these comments that both Rangell and Stone saw Fromm-Reichmann as operating with two theoretical systems, the interpersonal for the psychotic and the classically psychoanalytic for the neurotic. My reading of her work, however, is that she had shifted her entire understanding from the theoretical system of classical ego psychology to the interpersonal Sullivanian system. The confusion I think may stem from the fact that there are passages in Fromm-Reichmann's book (1950) and selected papers (Bullard 1959) that can be read in either way. All could readily agree, however, with Bernard Bandler's impromptu remarks at the same panel (Rangell 1954a) that Fromm-Reichmann "generalized her work with psychotics to extend it to the entire psychoanalytic framework" (159).

Both Alexander's and Fromm-Reichmann's views had considerable popular appeal at the time, though they were also the distinct minority and deviant perspectives within the dominant ego psychological paradigm. Since then, the Alexander conceptions have essentially dropped out of psychoanalytic discourse as such, though his focused attention on the affective factors in the psychoanalytic relationship has indeed influenced many subsequent developments. The notion itself is one that all subsequent contributors in this area have had to come to terms with, if only to deny or affirm similarities and/or differences. Fromm-Reichmann's views (rather, her *techniques*) have survived more directly but essentially within a group of colleagues and their students working in the arena in which these ideas originally grew, the (modified) psychoanalytic psychotherapy of the severely psychotic, usually in institutional settings. Because her major influence seemed confined to that special arena, it was perceived as a lesser threat to the overall structure of psychoanalysis and was less intensely attacked.

By contrast to Alexander and Fromm-Reichmann, those, actually the dominant psychoanalytic majority, who strove to maintain and sharpen the distinctions among the range of psychoanalytically based psychotherapies, including psychoanalysis, aimed in their differential treatment planning to select the therapeutic modality that best fit the psychological structure of the individual patient, in terms of the more or less "classical" or current indications, recognizing that even classical indications shift slowly with accumulating clinical experience and changing theory and technique. This, of course, was the opposite of the position taken by those who would blur these distinctions, in effect collapsing all psychoanalytic treatment modalities into the position that good psychotherapy is all analytic or is all analysis, and then pushing the logical limits of this "analysis" to its utmost extension—to cases of marginal or experimental indication. On one level, this can be conceptualized as a concern with the limits of applicability of a particular treatment method as against the choice of the most appropriate treatment method for each patient.

The initial problem for those who sought to sharpen the distinctions among the various psychoanalytically grounded therapies was, of course, definitional. Rangell (1954b) put this as follows: "That this investigation is not focusing on an already settled problem is attested to by the experiences of the Committee on Evaluation of Psychoanalytic Therapy, set up with the American Psychoanalytic Association in 1947. In the years of its work since then, this Committee was never able to pass the initial and vexatious point of trying to arrive at some modicum of agreement as to exactly what constitutes psychoanalysis, psychoanalytic psychotherapy, and possibly transitional forms" (734). Actually, Gill, Rangell, and Stone all sought to begin with a definitional statement for psychoanalysis, the parent therapy. Gill's statement was most succinct and came to enjoy the widest currency: "Psychoanalysis is that technique which, employed by a neutral analyst, results in the development of a regressive transference neurosis and the ultimate resolution of this neurosis by techniques of interpretation alone" (1954, 775).[2]

This definition (and the others cited from the same group of panels) circumscribes psychoanalysis far more precisely than Freud's (1914b) definition, which stated that *any* therapy that *recognizes* the two facts of transference and resistance and takes them as the *starting point* of its work can call itself psychoanalysis, and is totally consistent with Gill's earlier (1951) modification of Freud's 1914 definition, cited in chapter 3, which had distinguished between psychoanalysis which *analyzes* transference and resistance, and pyschoanalytic psychotherapy which *recognizes* transference and resistance and utilizes this recognition in the therapy. In that paper, Gill, following Knight, made the point that the "gross major decision is whether the defenses of the ego are to be strengthened or broken through as a preliminary toward a reintegration of the ego" (63). In 1954, he reiterated that "methods of psychotherapy . . . are primarily supportive or primarily exploratory, with all grades in between. . . . Exploratory psychotherapy may be brief or it may be long, even longer than the usual psychoanalysis" (772). Here Gill put aside Stone's (1951) misleading designation of all psychotherapy other than psychoanalysis as "brief therapy" and also indicated his interest in "grades in between," especially in exploratory (or expressive) psychotherapy as an entity "in between" supportive psychotherapy and psychoanalysis on the spectrum of therapies. A primarily supportive psychotherapy is the preferred mode for those patients too ill for analysis (or expressive therapies), patients whose egos are not sufficiently strong to withstand pressure—i.e., those whose failed psychic equilibrium is to be restored by "strengthening

---

2. Rangell's definition, though wordier, was in substance almost identical: "Psychoanalysis is a method of therapy *whereby* conditions are brought about favorable for the development of a transference neurosis, in which the past is restored in the present, *in order that,* through a systematic interpretative attack on the resistances which oppose it, there occurs a resolution of that neurosis (transference *and* infantile) *to the end of* bringing about structural changes in the mental apparatus of the patient to make the latter capable of optimum adaptation of life" (1954b, 739–40).

Stone's definitional statement was characteristically less formally precise than either Gill's or Rangell's but covered the same ground: "I would think that the mobilization of as full and undistorted a transference neurosis as may be possible, and its ultimate dissolution (or minimization) by interpretative means, would be regarded as essential to a genuinely analytic outcome" (1954, 574).

the defenses" through the variety of supportive techniques spelled out now by Knight, Gill, Alexander, even Stone. Gill discussed this category of patients this way: "A major contraindication [to psychoanalysis] is the presence of severe regressive factors or the dangers that such may develop. The instances of rather sudden onset of psychosis shortly after beginning psychoanalysis are to be attributed to the regressive pressure of the technique *per se* in a precariously balanced personality" (1954, 780).[3] These are the patients "too sick" to be amenable to psychoanalysis. (To go forward several decades for a moment, a major current controversy, initiated primarily by Kernberg (1975), is the degree to which borderline patients *can* be treated by a "modified psychoanalysis," a variant expressive psychotherapy or should rather continue to be treated by a more supportive therapy as explicitly recommended in this earlier era by Knight and Gill and others.)

A primarily expressive psychotherapy is the preferred mode for patients whose illnesses are slight, those with acute reactive disorders, or those in transitional states, whose egos are not so deformed (Gill) that they cannot tolerate the effort to analyze the defenses to the extent necessary via the established methods of interpretation and working through, leading to the requisite insights and resolutions. These patients can be considered "too well" for psychoanalysis in the sense that they do not require or warrant so ambitious and far-reaching, intensive and extensive, a treatment. This way of conceptualizing the different therapeutic modes and their differential indications puts expressive psychotherapy exactly into an intermediate position—certainly in techniques—between supportive therapy and psychoanalysis itself. Two quotations from Gill's 1954 paper indicate the delicate balancing he had in mind. First, "In contrast to our analyst . . . , the psychotherapist is willing to permit many transference manifestations to remain unresolved on the one hand and on the other to behave in ways which would make it more difficult to resolve [them] if he were to attempt it" (784). However, "I believe we have failed to carry over into our psychotherapy enough of the nondirective spirit of our analyses. . . . My stress on this point arises from my feeling that discussion of therapeutic results in psychoanalysis and psychotherapy too often views them as polar opposites, with psy-

3. With an eye probably to the work of Fromm-Reichmann, Gill said a little later of patients with such weakened egos: "Freud's early statement [on the inaccessibility of such patients] . . . has been revised. It is not that these patients do not develop a transference. Rather, that transference is florid, wild, and fluctuating. What they are able to develop only with great difficulty is a stable object relationship within which the transference can become a usable therapeutic instrument" (784). Here Gill balanced his severe criticism of Fromm-Reichmann's *theoretical* ventures with his acknowledgment of the high value (and difficulty) of the *clinical* venture in which she, and others like her, was engaged.

choanalysis regarded as producing structural changes, and psychotherapy as unable to produce any significant intrapsychic change, but only altering techniques of adjustment through transference effects and shifts in defensive techniques" (786–87). And further: "I would raise the question . . . as to whether there is not more to be said on results and mechanisms in prolonged psychotherapy with more ambitious goals by a relatively inactive therapist and in intensive [he means expressive] psychotherapy" (789).

In this connection, Gill made the statement, surprising for that time, that after all, psychoanalysis was not such a totally definitive therapeutic reconstruction as its theory perhaps promised: "It is generally the more experienced analysts who are not so optimistic about the sweeping character changes often hoped for from psychoanalysis. And there is no doubt that we can still recognize our friends and colleagues, even after they have been analyzed. In 'Analysis Terminable and Interminable' [1937a], Freud wryly observes, 'Every advance is only half as great as it looks at first' (786–87). Given this, Gill could more readily see the similarities in goals, methods, and results—albeit with real differences—between psychoanalysis and the expressive psychotherapies that he now called "intermediate types of psychotherapy": "This is the psychotherapy done by people analytically oriented or trained whose goals are intermediate between rapid symptom resolution [i.e., supportive psychotherapy] and character change [i.e., psychoanalysis], where techniques are in a sense intermediate—for example, relative neutrality and inactivity; transference dealt with, though not a full regressive transference neurosis; interpretation the principal vehicle of therapist behavior—and, I suggest, where results are likewise intermediate" (789) "I am not suggesting that psychotherapy can do what psychoanalysis can do; but I am suggesting that a description of the results of intensive [again, he means expressive] psychotherapy may be not merely in terms of shifts of defense but also in terms of other intra-ego alterations" (793). And in his final statement: "I have tried to say that techniques and results in psychoanalysis and intensive, relatively non-directive psychotherapy are not the polar opposites which they are often declared to be, and that a more positive and detailed description of changes both in psychoanalysis and in psychotherapy which will take account of our newer formulations in ego psychology and include descriptions in terms of intrapsychic alterations and techniques of adaptation, will help to make this clear" (795–96). But, of course, "the psychotherapist is willing to permit many transference manifestations to remain unresolved . . . and . . . to behave in ways which would make it more difficult to resolve if he were to attempt it" (784).

All this brings up the question of the degree of real conflict resolution that is possible outside of psychoanalysis proper, which at least aims at unravelling the genetic-dynamic roots of conflict to their infantile prototypes. On this issue,

Gill (1954) said, "I would still like to hold open the question that even though the basic [i.e., infantile] conflict is unsolved and under sufficient stress can once again reactivate the derivative conflicts, the derivative conflicts develop a relative degree of autonomy, and exist in a form which allows a relatively firm resolution even under psychotherapeutic techniques, of the more intensive and less directive form I have described" (793). In a related way, Stone (1954) said, "In certain well-managed psychotherapeutic situations, where many ordinary emotional needs of the patients are met, within the limits of the physician-patient relationship, significant *pathological fragments* of the transference relationship . . . may separate from integrated expression in this real professional situation, and be utilized to great and genuine interpretive advantage by a skillful therapist" (578). Of course, the whole possibility of a truly interpretive expressive psychotherapy that can resolve circumscribed neurotic conflicts in individuals who do not need full psychoanalysis—that is, a resolution of chronic and ingrained neurotic conflicts to their infantile genetic-dynamic origins—rests on this conception of derivative conflicts that have achieved at least a *relative* autonomy from their infantile sources. Needless to say, this has always been a central issue in the debate over the possibility of a truly *definitive* psychotherapy outside of psychoanalysis for any category of patient.

All this adds up to the statement that, in contrast to psychoanalysis, with its maximalist goals in terms of fundamental conflict resolution and character reorganization, all other psychotherapies range in goals from the most minimal to the increasingly more ambitious, with no agreement as to how asymptotically closely they can approach those of psychoanalysis with different kinds of patients. Gill put it similarly in 1954 as in 1951: "The goals of psychotherapy extend over a very wide range. To take first the goals in psychotherapy with a relatively strong ego. The goal may be the resolution of a crisis, assistance through a troubled period, or symptom amelioration. . . . But goals may range up to more ambitious aims in cases where there is no pressing problem, but where psychoanalysis is impossible or not used for external reasons . . . goals are much more ambitious than in palliative psychotherapy, and . . . more important results are achieved than I believe is often admitted" (785).

A related issue was also not resolved in these debates of the early 1950s except by argument and fiat: the degree of real distinctiveness among the various psychoanalytic therapeutic approaches. Are supportive psychotherapy, the "intermediate form," expressive psychotherapy, and psychoanalysis really qualitatively distinct, or are they crystallized nodal points along a continuum, or are they just a (quantitatively varying) continuum, as Alexander and Fromm-Reichmann contended?—another way of stating the blurring vs. sharpening argument at the heart of these debates.

Gill, as is clear, made the sharpest conceptual distinctions. Stone, characteristically, tempered his commitment to this distinction, already quoted, from the free play of human relationships to the precise professional relationship between the surgeon and his patient, with all the psychotherapies far from either pole but with supportive psychotherapy and psychoanalysis clearly remote from each other. Rangell (1954) perhaps best expressed the degree of consensus achieved within the group of those who sought to clarify and sharpen these distinctions: "The two disciplines [psychoanalysis proper and psychoanalytic psychotherapy], at far ends of a spectrum, are qualitatively different from each other, though there is a borderland of cases between them. An analogous comparison can be made to the fact that conscious is different from unconscious, even though there exists a preconscious and different degrees of consciousness. Day is different from night, though there is dusk; and black from white, though there is gray" (737).

Rangell's principal contribution to the debates published in 1954 was his effort to articulate the major similarities and differences between what he called psychoanalysis and dynamic psychotherapy. In regard to the similarities, he stated the obvious: both are psychological treatments influencing other human beings through verbal discourse, and both are rational therapies built on an "identical body of metapsychology" (737). Here he presented his sharp disagreement with Fromm-Reichmann, who he felt modified the metapsychology into something other than what he understood it to be. The differences, Rangell wrote, lay in technique and in goals. As regards technique, "The crucial differentiating point relates to the role and position of the therapist," or the centrality of what he called "the analytic attitude":

> Let us consider that the mental apparatus exerts around it a field of magnetic energy. In psychoanalysis, the therapist takes up his position at the periphery of this magnetic field of his patient, not too far away so that he is useless and might just as well not be there, nor too close, so that he is in the field interacting with it with his own magnetic field (he can err equally in both directions). Immune from repulsion or attraction (at least optimally, within the limits set by his own unconscious), he sits at the margin, like a referee in a tennis match so that he can say to the patient, "This is what you are doing." . . . In psychotherapy, in contrast, the therapist does not sit consistently in the seat, though he may sit there momentarily. He is, rather, generally on the court with his patient, interacting with him, the two magnetic fields interlocked, with the therapist's own values, opinions, desires, and needs more or less actively operative. Where is the line which distinguishes activity of one type from that of the other?" (741–42)

In regard to differences in goals, Rangell again used an analogy, this one Gitelson's (1951) description (quoted in chapter 3) of the complicated chemical reaction that once under way could continue to a state of final dynamic equilibrium, but that could also be altered or interrupted by external interfering agents that would halt the reaction at some intermediate point of relative stability: "The therapeutic process can be looked at from this same point of view. Psychoanalysis aims at the establishment of the reaction (transference neurosis) and the maintenance of optimum conditions for its final complete resolution. It is not only oriented toward such a final end point, but in contrast to psychotherapy, is potentially capable of attaining it. Psychotherapy, on the other hand, either from necessity or from choice, introduces the external agent and brings the reaction to an end at any intermediate point of stability" (743).

Lest value judgments be inadvertently introduced, Rangell continued, as between psychoanalysis and dynamic psychotherapy, "one method is neither better nor worse nor more or less praiseworthy than the other. There are indications and contraindications for each" (744). Joseph Chassell put this same thought even more strongly and in fact tipped it in the opposite-than-expected direction in another panel (English 1953): "We keep assuming that psychotherapy is a watered-down procedure or is bound to be pure psychoanalysis alloyed with the baser metals of suggestion, and so on. My present thesis is that really psychodynamic psychotherapy is an approach as strong or stronger than classical psychoanalysis, has increasingly greater range of applicability than classical psychoanalysis, is more inclusive theoretically, and that classical psychoanalysis may turn out to be a special procedure of limited but significant usefulness in certain cases" (550–51).

The debates published in 1954 also included Bibring's delineation of basic therapeutic principles, which are intended, through differential selection and combination, to be capable of explaining all psychoanalytic therapies, from psychoanalysis to supportive psychotherapy, and the Leo Stone–Anna Freud discussion of the problem of the "widening scope" of psychoanalysis. Bibring's (1954) widely influential article delineated and defined five distinct "basic therapeutic principles," each with a particular goal:

1. Suggestion, the induction of mental processes in the patient, independent (or to the exclusion) of the patient's rational or critical thinking
2. Abreaction, emotional discharge, which, with the abandonment of Freud's original traumatic theory of the neuroses, had become progressively less salient

3. Manipulation,[4] a mobilization (or neutralization or redirection) of emotional systems existing in the patient in the service of the therapy or the exposure of the patient to novel experiences, a form of "experiential manipulation" (close indeed to Alexander's corrective emotional experience)

4. Insight through clarification, i.e., enhanced self-awareness, clarity, and differentiation of self-observation in the absence of resistance (in the technical sense), but rather received with "surprise and intellectual satisfaction"—e.g., the presentation to the patient of mental processes which are not conscious, but which he/she readily recognizes when attention is called to them

5. Insight through interpretation, which is dynamically different—i.e., the processing of conflicted unconscious material with resistance, intense ego-involvement, and working through (747-59).

According to Bibring, all psychotherapies, even those conceptualized within other psychological reference frames (client-centered, existential, behavioral, etc.), could be classified by some combinations of these five central therapeutic principles, differing in their spread, frequency, and saliency. For example, "In psychoanalysis proper, all therapeutic principles are employed to a varying degree . . . but they form a hierarchical structure in that insight through interpretation is the principal agent and all others are—theoretically and practically—subordinate to it" (762). Therefore, "*interpretation* is the supreme agent in the hierarchy of therapeutic principles characteristic of analysis . . . all other principles . . . are employed with the constant aim of making interpretation possible and effective" (763).

By contrast, in psychotherapy, the therapist deploys "different selections and combinations . . . which imply a corresponding difference in goal . . . a general trend to shift the emphasis from insight through interpretation toward 'experiential' manipulation; that is, learning from experience seems to become the supreme agent rather than insight through interpretation" (765–66). Bibring even tried to assess the nature of Rogerian client-centered therapy in this (psychoanalytic) frame, declaring manipulation and clarification to be the most salient of the five therapeutic principles in that therapy, with the goal of establishing "a realistic, objective perspective to oneself and to the environment,

---

4. Bibring explicitly disavowed the pejorative connotation of the word "manipulation" as customarily used. He also did not include under manipulation such crude forms of intervention as advice, guidance, and similar ways of trying to run a patient's life.

in an ego which is at the same time strongly manipulated toward independence and self-reliance" (767). Bibring's classification continues in active use today.[5]

In his almost equally influential contribution on "the widening scope of indications for psychoanalysis," Stone (1954) wrote, "One might say that in the last decade or two, at least in the United States, any illness or problem which has a significant emotional component in its etiology has become at least a possible indication for psychoanalysis . . . scarcely any human problem admits of solution other than psychoanalysis. . . . Hopeless or grave reality situations, lack of talent or ability (usually regarded as 'inhibition'), lack of an adequate philosophy of life, or almost any chronic physical illness may be brought to psychoanalysis for cure" (568). So may the most trivial disorders: "If the personality illness were judged really slight . . . I would regard the indications for psychoanalysis as very seriously in doubt. For psychoanalysis represents a tremendous investment of many complicated elements by two people; it should not be invoked for trivial reasons" (570). Stone was thus warily skeptical of this widening trend, albeit also cautiously receptive. It is, again, the argument over extending the applicability of the true (or best) therapy to its possible limits against fitting differentiated treatment approaches to the nature and needs of the patient.

Stone's final assessment on this issue was as follows: "If one reads the indications [for psychoanalysis] as given by a reasonably conservative authority like Fenichel, it soon appears that practically every psychogenic nosological category can be treated psychoanalytically, under good conditions, although—obviously—they vary extremely in availability and prognosis" (591). And finally, "the scope of psychoanalytic therapy has widened from the transference psychoneurosis, to include practically all psychogenic nosologic categories. The transference neuroses and character disorders of equivalent degree of psychopathology remain the optimum general indications for the classical method. While the difficulties increase and the expectations of success diminish in a

5. Valenstein (1979) in an assessment of Bibring's contribution a quarter-century later stated that Bibring "was establishing that there might be a legitimate adaptation of psychoanalysis for the elaboration of a whole range of dynamic psychotherapies extending from those close to psychoanalysis, which aim at insight predominantly through interpretive methods, to those which perhaps necessarily depend upon interpersonal experiential methods for those conditions, including borderlines . . . for whom interpretation and insight is only limitedly effective" (118). On this point, Bibring (1954) had called attention to "the shift in emphasis from insight through interpretation to experiential manipulation. It seems to have become a common trend in various methods of dynamic psychotherapies. Alexander and French's statements may serve as illustrations of this shift. 'Insight is frequently the result of emotional adjustment and not the cause of it.' And, 'the role of insight is overrated' " (768).

general way as the nosological periphery is approached, there is no absolute barrier" (593).

Anna Freud (1954), in her discussion, though expressing herself as being in profound agreement with Stone's paper almost in its entirety, nonetheless singled out his guarded and even skeptical reception of the trend toward a widening scope, indicating that her own predilections ran counter to such receptive sentiments. She said,

> For years now, our most experienced and finest analysts have concentrated their efforts on opening up new fields for the application of analysis by making the psychotic disorders, the severe depressions, the borderline cases, addictions, perversions, delinquency, etc., amenable to treatment. I have no wish to underestimate the resulting benefits to patients, nor the resulting considerable gains to analysis as a therapy and science. But I regret sometimes that so much interest and effort has been withdrawn from the hysteric, phobic and compulsive disorders, leaving their treatment to the beginners or the less knowledgeable and adventurous analytic practitioners. If all the skill, knowledge and pioneering effort which was spent on widening the scope of application of psychoanalysis had been employed instead on intensifying and improving our technique in the original field, I cannot help but feel that, by now, we would find the treatment of the common neuroses child's play, instead of struggling with this technical problem as we have continued to do. (610)

This was truly a call for narrowing the scope of indications for psychoanalysis, a position to which Anna Freud steadfastly adhered all her life, against all the popular and current trends.

It is in the context of this debate in the early 1950s that a group at the Menninger Foundation undertook a major empirical study (the Psychotherapy Research Project [PRP]) of what changes occur with psychoanalytic and psychotherapeutic treatments (the outcome question) and *how* those changes come about or are brought about (the process question). The differential treatment indications for the range of psychoanalytic therapies being studied was originally set forth, in the context of the definitions and conceptualizations elaborated in the papers here reviewed, as follows:

1. Psychotherapeutic counseling [a treatment intervention that in fact was never recommended or implemented with any of the forty-two patients who took part in the research study] is indicated when an individual with a basically healthy personality reacts in an unhealthy way to a life problem largely because of not perceiving or knowing the facts

needed for the solution of a particular dilemma. . . . Counseling is appropriate in cases of situational maladjustments; occupational misplacement . . . some marital problems. It usually requires a shorter period of treatment. . . .

2. Supportive psychotherapy is indicated for: (a) Basically healthy individuals overwhelmed by a severe problem or anxiety so that their optimal effective functioning is temporarily paralyzed. . . . Acute combat fatigue. . . . Acute reactive states . . . states of object loss (some depressive reactions) . . . some traumatic neuroses, (panic states) . . . Like psychotherapeutic counseling, this form of supportive psychotherapy is brief. (b) Chronic, severe personality disorders with major ego-defects of several varieties . . . principally "character disorders" with disruptive, alloplastic symptoms. . . . Treatment is aimed to help them discharge their impulses in a more socially acceptable way which will reduce their overt symptoms and ameliorate the disruptive consequences of the symptoms. The borderline states—those with "fragile egos" (as against "ego strength") are another group in this category. . . . Treatment is often sought at a point of accelerating collapse and represents an effort to stop the regression and stabilize the individual on whatever possible level of functioning. . . . Appropriate to this treatment modality are the borderline psychotic, some overtly psychotic, plus a large group of patients who suffer from "impulse neuroses." Many cases of addiction and perversion likewise fall here. . . .

3. Expressive psychotherapy is the treatment of choice for persons with the requisite ego strength, intelligence, and tolerance for anxiety who have a serious, but *relatively circumscribed* neurotic conflict . . . significant help and change can be effected without having to uncover the infantile genetic roots. . . . Appropriate here . . . are patients who fall into the categories "symptom neuroses," and "character neuroses." . . .

4. Psychoanalysis is the therapy of choice where ego strength, anxiety tolerance, intelligence and capacity for developing insight are of requisite degree and where *the neurotic conflict is sufficiently intense and pervasive* that satisfactory resolution can only come, it is felt, through the development of the transference neurosis and the re-creating, in consciousness, of its prototype—the repressed infantile neurosis. As distinct from patients treated by expressive psychotherapy, the neurotic conflict is more pervasive and less circumscribed; and the psychotherapeutic effort, likewise, less specifically goal-directed. (Wallerstein et al. 1956, 252–56, italics added)

Here is the full application of the conception of dynamic psychotherapy and its relationship to psychoanalysis that came to dominate the American psychoanalytic scene from the 1940s into the 1960s, as elaborated in the design of a program of empirical research devised in the early 1950s. PRP followed the treatment careers and subsequent life careers of the forty two research patients over a thirty-year span (1952–82). Its final clinical accounting was written up in my book *Forty-Two Lives in Treatment: A Study of Psychoanalysis and Psychotherapy* (1986).

6 The Persisting Influence of the Formulations of 1954

Following the crystallizing consensus achieved in the publications of 1954, there was substantial agreement—at first very solidly but later on with increasing uncertainty and erosion—on the differential indications (and contraindications) for each of the therapeutic approaches, the goals to be striven for, the techniques most appropriate to the different nosologic categories of patient, and the expectable results in terms of the maximal reach of each of the differentiated therapeutic approaches. Despite the conception of the widening scope of psychoanalysis, the prevailing mood was that the treatment should be fitted to the clinical exigencies and needs of the patients, contrary to the stance in Freud's day, when proper psychoanalysis had been conceived as the only scientific and truly etiologic treatment approach, to which the patients should be fitted if at all possible. The focus on adapting the treatment to the patient brought with it an emphasis on careful clinical assessment and treatment planning, at least in some clinical centers (notably the Menninger Clinic and the Austen Riggs Center), and the development, by David Rapaport (1945, 1946) and others, of the psychological projective test battery as an aid to those tasks. This, again, was in contrast with practice in Freud's day, when characteristically there was a two- to three-week "trial analysis" to determine the patient's amenability to the only therapy the analyst at that time felt equipped to carry out.

The 1950s and 1960s also represented the high-water mark of enthusiasm for the far-reaching goals that all therapies, but centrally psychoanalysis, were confidently expected to reach.[1] Despite the relative neglect of Ferenczi's writings during this period and the quite overwhelming rejection of the technical innovations he had pioneered, the era was nonetheless caught up in his ebullient therapeutic optimism (as against Freud's more sober realism) and in his conviction that every patient was reachable and treatable if only one could devise the

1. I wrote two survey papers on this issue: "The Goals of Psychoanalysis: A Survey of Analytic Viewpoints" (1965), in the heyday of the hegemony in America of the ego-psychology metapsychological paradigm and, within that, of the 1954 consensus on the clearly differentiated nature of the psychoanalytic therapeutic approaches; and, a quarter-century later, an update and revision of these views, "The Goals of Psychoanalysis Reconsidered" (1992b), in light of the theoretical advances and clinical and empirical research experience during the intervening period and the vastly altered current climate on these issues. See also in this connection, Weinshel, "How Wide Is the Widening Scope of Psychoanalysis and How Solid Is Its Structural Model? Some Concerns and Observations" (1990a).

proper therapeutic approach. Freud, on the other hand, was from the start as mindful of the limitations of psychoanalysis as of its possibilities. This is usually thought of in connection with his last great clinical paper, "Analysis Terminable and Interminable" (1937a), in which he spelled out the three major factors that he felt importantly affected the outcomes potentially achievable in any analytic treatment: the severity of the traumata experienced by the patient, the constitutional strength of the instinctual pressures, and the enduring deformations of the ego resulting from the particular interactions of experiential and maturational vicissitudes. He then ended the paper with a consideration of what he felt to be the biological bedrock that ultimately limited the individual's ability to surmount the constraints our biology imposed on our psychology: penis-envy in the woman, the repudiation of femininity in the man. It is less often remarked that Freud had this same modest approach to the therapeutic possibilities of psychoanalysis at the very start of his therapeutic career, as expressed in *Studies on Hysteria* (Freud and Breuer 1893–95), in which he addressed the patient: "But you will be able to convince yourself that much will be gained if we succeed in transforming your hysterical misery into common unhappiness" (305). Actually, what was new in "Analysis Terminable and Interminable" was not the impression of realistic pessimism of Freud's final (1937a) assessment of the therapeutic potential of psychoanalysis or his emphasis on the difficulties of the procedure and the obstacles in its way but, rather, his new skepticism about the power of even the most successful of analytic outcomes to truly safeguard the individual, in the face of sufficiently adverse life circumstance, against a future outbreak of neurosis, either a differently constituted neurosis or the return of the old one.

It was Glover who most closely followed Freud, even during this optimistic era after World War II, in calling attention to the limitations of psychoanalytic cure. In "The Indications for Psycho-Analysis" (1954), he listed three main categories of patients with whom one could apply the analytic method: (1) those he declared flatly to be "accessible"—the anxiety hysterics (phobic illness), conversion hysterics, reactive depressions, and "equivalent" sexual disorders and character neuroses. With these, there was a "reasonable expectation of cure." (2) The "moderately accessible," including the obsessionals and some perversions, alcoholics, and drug-addicted. With these, one could look forward to "substantial improvement but with no certainty of cure." And (3) the "intractable or only slightly accessible," those with "wider or deeper ego disorders," such as the endogenous depressions, severe alcoholics, paranoids, hysterics with a psychotic substructure, psychotic characters, and psychopaths. With these the best prospects were for only "mild betterment." For Glover this outcome might be worthwhile since he was convinced (along with Freud and Jones) that psychoanalysis was the only properly scientific psychotherapy available and that it therefore should be tried even in such refractory instances; nothing else could offer even that much hope (399–400). Glover concluded about this, "Therapeutic failure is an honourable failure which may in course of time lead to an improvement of the therapeutic instrument" (401).[2]

But aside from such voices as Glover's, the prevailing mood in the psychoanalytic world was optimistic indeed, and the 1954 consensus was relatively unchallenged for about two decades, at least within America. Since then, with major efforts to extend the applicability of psychoanalysis to the narcissistic personality disorders (Kohut 1971, 1977, 1984) and of "modified" psychoanalysis to the borderline personality organizations (Kernberg 1975, 1976, 1980, 1984, 1992; Kernberg et al. 1989), the consensus on indications has fallen away (see chapter 20). Significant disagreements have emerged, depending upon the theoretical perspective within psychoanalysis to which one adheres and on one's conception of the nature of psychoanalytic psychotherapy and its relationship to psychoanalysis. All that will be the subject of later chapters. Here I want only to emphasize that there is still a very substantial body of psychoanalytic opinion that continues to support the formulations on indications and contraindications reached during the 1950s.

David Werman (1988), for example, staunchly adhered to the clear conceptual distinctions of psychoanalysis, expressive psychotherapy, and supportive psychotherapy worked out in the 1950s. Writing about the indications for supportive psychoanalytic psychotherapy in which he had a special interest, he said, "Although many patients in the borderline group are appropriate candidates for supportive treatment, such psychotherapy may properly be recommended for some patients in virtually every diagnostic category, whether it be psychoneurosis, psychosis, or organic brain syndrome. Thus, individuals who, for example, have little or no insight into their psychological disorder, who seem unable to identify their feelings, who are overwhelmingly dependent, who cannot regulate affect, whose motivation for change is minimal or nonexistent, or who routinely somaticize their conflicts may benefit from supportive psychotherapy" (159). In

2. It was, incidentally, this conception of "heroic indications" for psychoanalysis that led the clinical staff at the Menninger Foundation at that time, impressed with the theoretical possibilities for the intensive psychoanalytic treatment of such sicker patients within the protective context of the psychoanalytic sanatorium, to undertake prolonged efforts at psychoanalysis with such borderline, addicted, and paranoid patients who, in terms of the consensus of the 1954 publications, should more appropriately have been taken into varyingly supportive and/ or expressive face-to-face psychotherapies. (And, parenthetically, it was from this group of so-called "heroic" indications for psychoanalysis that most of the failed cases in that cohort of forty-two patients came.)

1984, even more tersely, Werman gave two opposite indications for supportive psychotherapy: for relatively healthy individuals overwhelmed by acute stress, and for the sicker ones who suffer chronic and profound deficits in psychic functioning. It is unlikely that such a statement would have met much dissension in 1954.

Jerome Oremland, with a special interest in the more expressive approaches, has recently (1991) proposed a new tripartite division into psychoanalysis, psychoanalytically oriented psychotherapy, and interactive psychotherapy (roughly approximating the traditional designations of psychoanalysis, expressive psychotherapy, and supportive psychotherapy, but differing in ways to be discussed in chapter 9). He sees psychoanalytically oriented psychotherapy as having a broader range of applicability than psychoanalysis—in fact, as applicable to all patients deemed suitable for psychoanalysis proper. He stated that he begins his therapeutic work with all patients "in ad hoc psychoanalytically oriented psychotherapy sessions" (125) and then decides: "For the patient who is equally suitable for either modality, I equally favor continuing the psychoanalytically oriented psychotherapy [usually twice weekly] or increasing frequency and beginning psychoanalysis" (127–28). Oremland elaborated: "When the psychotherapist proceeds incrementally, patients outside the mental health field tend to continue in psychoanalytically oriented psychotherapy, seeing it as the more conservative choice [more economical of time, energy, money]. Mental health professionals, on the other hand, tend to select psychoanalysis because of the greater prestige that psychoanalysis carries within the field itself. These tendencies, which largely are disguised transference-countertransference imperatives, transcend the thoroughness of the interpretive investigation of the various factors involved" (128–29). And all this is possible because of the perceived overlap between psychoanalysis and psychoanalytically oriented psychotherapy; the main difference is that the former puts greater emphasis on the historical aspects of life experience and the latter on the transferential actualities of the dynamic interaction in the present. Except for his declared equal willingness to employ either of these modalities with patients who are suitable (appropriate?) for psychoanalysis, Oremland's account is also fully in line with the distinctions arrived at in the 1950s.

And last, Edward Weinshel (1992), who, like many others today, is much less sure of where the dividing lines among these various therapeutic approaches should be placed, or whether they make the same kind of sense at all in today's psychoanalytic world, nonetheless also undertook to spell out indications for psychoanalytic psychotherapy vis-à-vis psychoanalysis, very much along the lines that Stone did in 1951, not distinguishing particularly between supportive and expressive psychotherapy. Weinshel's list of indications for psychotherapy comprises patients sicker than those amenable to analysis; healthier patients, including those returning for therapeutic work after a "reasonable analysis"; older patients (over sixty?); those precluded from analysis by reality considerations, such as money, geography, or physical health; those who are unmotivated or who resist analysis; and the psychosomatic (341)—a list practically indistinguishable from Stone's of 1951. This persistence of shared thinking about differential indications and contraindications for varied therapeutic approaches among individuals with otherwise differing views is but one manifestation of the impact on subsequent psychoanalytic development of the writings of the early 1950s and especially of the 1954 publication of the papers from the three major panels.

At this point, I want to move from the consideration of the issue of differential diagnosis and differential indications to a broader set of issues—via the discussion of a sequence of books dealing specifically with psychotherapy from a psychoanalytic viewpoint. These books clearly show how the thinking embodied in those panels and publications of the 1950s has continued to shape a major sector of psychoanalytic theory and practice—in the face of the conceptual and technical flux that has otherwise come to characterize present-day psychoanalysis in its relationship to what we understand by psychoanalytic psychotherapy.

The first in this group of books, a self-styled primer for neophyte psychotherapists by Kenneth Mark Colby (1951), actually preceded most of the panel debates and publications I have been discussing; it was simply a product of the same Zeitgeist. I mention it here because of its pride of place as the first book— and for some time the only book—from within the psychoanalytic tradition to address the issues and the specific techniques of general psychotherapy completely apart from psychoanalysis.[3] Colby distinguished psychoanalysis proper from a basically expressive psychoanalytic psychotherapy, resting on the interpretation of transference and resistance, and in a form to be learned by young therapists in training in psychiatric residency and clinical psychology training programs. He also discussed mechanisms of strengthening (as against analyzing) defenses by means of direct support, guidance, and reassurance, though he did not always make clear distinctions among what we would see as supportive and

---

3. Almost a decade earlier, Maurice Levine (1942), a psychoanalyst interested in the application of psychoanalytic understanding to the medically ill, had published *Psychotherapy in Medical Practice*. Although Levine declared that it was written for "general practitioners and medical specialists, and for medical students, . . . not . . . for psychiatrists or psychoanalysts, or for students of psychiatry" (vii), it is a book on psychotherapy (within the presumed scope of the interested medical practitioner) and not on psychiatry in general (e.g., the somatic treatment methods available at that time).

expressive therapeutic components. Colby's main reiterated distinction was between psychoanalysis and other psychotherapy: "Thus psychotherapy and psychoanalysis have a similar theory of neurosis and treatment, but they differ
quantitatively and to some extent qualitatively in their theory, and hence practice, of technique" (9).

The fact that Colby's book was for a number of years the only book on the
theory and practice of psychoanalytically oriented psychotherapy written specifically for psychotherapists in training seemed to reflect a mythos that experienced analysts know all about psychotherapy which was—for so many
analysts—after all, at best but a diluted application of analysis (echoing the
position of Freud, Jones and Glover); if it needed to be written about, it would
only be for the newcomer to the field of mental treatment. This situation was
substantially remedied by the publication of Paul Dewald's *Psychotherapy: A
Dynamic Approach* (1964), a book squarely about the theory and practice of
psychoanalytic psychotherapy, dichotomized into expressive and supportive approaches in terms of the consensus of 1954 and addressed to psychoanalysts and
(other) psychotherapists alike.[4] (Dewald throughout employs the term "insight-
directed" in preference to "expressive," a usage that indeed has some advantages, as indicated in chapters 10 and 11.)

The Dewald (1964) book was set explicitly within the mainstream of American ego psychology. The first two-thirds of the book consisted of an exposition
of psychoanalysis as a theory of mental functioning and, within that, a theory
of psychopathology. It spelled out the fullest implications of the distinctions
between the expressive and supportive approaches for every aspect of psychotherapeutic work. As Dewald put it, "the material is deliberately presented in
the form of a somewhat artificial dichotomy of supportive vs. insight-directed
psychotherapy. This is being done for pedagogic reasons, with full recognition
that in the usual clinical situation such sharp dichotomies do not always exist or
persist" (xvii).

The last section of the book, "Psychotherapy," opens with a chapter on
therapeutic strategy and goals. In relation to the now-familiar issue of strengthening versus interpretively undoing defenses, Dewald wrote, "One of the therapist's tasks in supportive treatment is to survey the various defenses available to

---

4. There had been an intervening book, *The Teaching and Learning of Psychotherapy* (Ekstein and
Wallerstein 1954), but that book was focused specifically on the supervision process and the
(psychoanalytically understood and conceptualized) skills and attitudes that characterize it and
that could be applied (generically) to the supervision of any interpersonal helping process—in
this instance, psychoanalytic psychotherapy as taught in a psychoanalytically oriented psychiatric hospital training program. An understanding of the nature of the psychoanalytically informed psychotherapy process was presupposed in the writing and reading of that book.

the patient and determine which of these can most effectively be introduced, strengthened, encouraged or reinforced" (101). By contrast, "in insight therapy, where the goal is to make unconscious and preconscious conflicts and mental processes conscious, the therapist gradually helps the patient reduce or give up his resistances and defenses in order that conflicts can emerge more clearly into consciousness. This means interpreting resistances and defenses at appropriate times." He then summarizes as follows: "Whereas in supportive therapy the attempt is to allay and reduce anxiety by strengthening defenses, in insight-directed therapy it is necessary, through lowering of defenses, temporarily to mobilize and increase anxiety in amounts that can be tolerated by the patient as part of the process of making unconscious material conscious" (102).

Similarly in regard to mechanisms of conflict reduction or resolution: In supportive therapy, "at times it may become necessary for the therapist actively to assume certain ego functions that ordinarily the patient would carry out himself. In this sense, the therapist temporarily takes over a surrogate-ego role, in that he may actively make decisions for the patient, intervene in the patient's life, arrange for various things to be done to and for the patient, etc."—and thereby dampen the behavioral expressions of inner conflict. By contrast, "in insight-directed therapy, the relationship and the therapeutic interventions are used to bring previously unconscious conflicts to the patient's conscious awareness in an emotionally meaningful way. In other words, the strategy is to re-establish and recreate the earlier conflicts which have resulted in the formation of neurotic symptoms or character traits" (103).

And again, with regard to the issue of identifications and their therapeutic role: "In supportive therapy, strategy involves encouraging and promoting identification with the therapist" (104), whereas "in insight therapy, the goal is the greatest possible degree of independent development and self-fulfillment." In other words, "the concept of 'reinforcement by rewards' involves reliance on an external authority for motivation, control, and judgment, and as such is opposed to one of the basic goals of insight-directed therapy, namely the development of independent judgment and motivation" (105). And still again, on the nature of therapeutic rapport in relation to the transference: "In supportive therapy, the strategy is to maintain a positive relationship based on conscious rapport, in which the conscious elements of the relationship are emphasized, and distortions are diminished. . . . Strategy in insight-directed therapy calls for relative frustration of drive-derivatives in the treatment situation. This will tend to enhance the development of a transference relationship in which the conflicts may become increasingly conscious as the first step towards definitive resolution" (106–07).

Dewald ended this chapter with a statement that encapsulates both the spirit and the style of the entire book:

> In summary, the strategy of supportive psychotherapy involves limited goals, and the direct relief of symptoms, by focusing chiefly on current conscious conflicts, and supporting and strengthening defensive and adaptive ego functions in an attempt to re-establish a dynamic steady state. Underlying unconscious conflicts and personality distortions are not significantly altered. Insight therapy involves the attempt, in whatever degree is possible, to resolve unconscious conflicts and to promote more effective personality organization and development towards maturity. Immediate symptom relief becomes secondary, in the sense that, after the resolution of underlying conflict, there will be a shift in intrapsychic forces which then makes the symptoms superfluous and permits the patient to give them up. (108)

The same kind of drawing of contrasts pervades the succeeding chapters: on differential treatment indications;[5] on the differing kinds of therapeutic contract; on the patient's role in the therapeutic process ("in supportive therapy, the therapist focuses the patient's attention primarily on *conscious* ego mechanisms and attitudes, and emphasizes the role that they play in the patient's overall adaptation. In insight-directed treatment, on the other hand, the therapist also emphasizes and helps the patient to become aware of the *unconscious* conflicts, mechanisms and methods of adaptation, and as the patient becomes increasingly aware of these unconscious forces, he must then attempt to put this *now conscious* awareness to active use" [171–72]); on the therapist's contrapuntal differential role and the techniques employed to implement it; on the handling of the transference ("In supportive treatment, strategy calls for the use of the transference as a tool for the immediate reduction of conflict and strengthening of defenses, thereby as quickly as possible re-establishing a stable dynamic equilibrium. In insight-directed treatment, strategy calls for the use of the transference as a tool for the mobilization of previously unconscious conflicts, and their ultimate conscious resolution to whatever degree possible" [219]); on the comparably different handling of resistance, regression, and conflict; on the place of insight and working through ("In the type of face-to-face psychotherapy discussed here, insight generally is not achieved [except for intellectual reconstructions] to ages more remote than the latency period" [242]—in contrast, of

5. And almost totally in accord with the conceptualizations of the Psychotherapy Research Project of the Menninger Foundation. See for comparison Dewald (1964, 109–36) and Wallerstein et al. (1956, 239–62).

course, to the major insights sought in *insight*-directed psychotherapy); and on the problems and manners of terminating (with the far-reaching and ambitious termination goals of insight-directed psychotherapy compared with the modest goals of supportive psychotherapy—the remission of symptoms and the reversal of decompensating or regressive processes to a preexisting stable dynamic state).

At each point in the book, the statement is in the familiar and usually (for heuristic purposes) overschematized form of specifying the distinct characteristics of the supportive versus insight-directed therapeutic modes. Often the simple format and the clear-cut distinctions seem to imply comparable clarity and separateness in the actual hurly-burly of psychotherapeutic interactions, which is, of course, *not* intended. And at times a difference in approach is categorically stated (in sharply distinct terms) without a concomitant statement about the difficulties of translating it into practice or, for that matter, about *how,* indeed, to translate it at all. But however much one agrees or disagrees with the particulars of the distinctions and the categorizations—and there is room for a wide range of individual opinions—it was clear when it was published that this book was a major step toward fulfilling the promise for the practice of the psychoanalytic psychotherapies created by the publications of 1954.

Dewald also offered the first systematic effort to improve on Bibring's (1954) outline of the various techniques that define the place of a therapy in the spectrum of psychoanalytically based psychotherapeutic modes. Dewald set forth a similar but larger grouping, arranged along a logical spectrum from those implying the least intrusive activity by the therapist to those calling for the most— recognizing, of course, that even the least active of the techniques listed, quiet listening, is an intensely active process. His ordering of therapeutic techniques along this activity spectrum was as follows: listening (including processes of empathy, transient identification, and regression in the service of the ego), clarification, confrontation, suggestion and/or prohibition, and active control (manipulation) (173–90).[6]

Toward the end of the book, there is a chapter on the conceptual relatedness of insight-directed therapy and psychoanalysis. Here, Dewald also took his stand with the consensus of 1954 that psychotherapy, even the most insight-directed, deals with derivative conflicts only, does not lift infantile amnesia (the recall of genetic conflictual material being chiefly from latency forward to adult life), does not involve a regressive transference neurosis (called not only unnecessary

6. It can, of course, be said that Bibring's list—suggestion, abreaction, manipulation, clarification, interpretation—is also a logical ordering, along the dimension from the most suppressive to the most uncovering of unconscious conflict. In any case, the dimensions laid out by the two authors seem orthogonal to each other and clearly have different usefulness.

but, in these circumstances, unwise and potentially disruptive), and does not rest on adherence to the basic rule and the free association method. At its most extensive and intensive, it is a "segmental" approach that "helps the patient to gain insight and understanding in the resolution of certain conflicts while leaving others deliberately untouched or unexplored" (293). For "the strategy of psychotherapy . . . involves the establishment of a transference relationship (as opposed to a regressive transference neurosis) in which there is an emotionally meaningful experience of the *derivatives* of the infantile and early childhood conflicts, with an attempt to resolve or modify patterns of integration, structural organization, and behavior at the level of these derivative conflicts. . . . The lifting of infantile amnesia is not a goal of insight-directed therapy, and the recall of genetic conflictual material is focused chiefly from latency and adolescence forward towards adult life" (289).

Set in this frame, insight-directed psychotherapy "stands roughly midway on a spectrum between supportive psychotherapy and psychoanalysis. And furthermore, the distinctions in the strategy and tactics of insight-directed therapy as compared with analysis are of a similar magnitude to those that distinguish insight-directed treatment from supportive psychotherapy" (293). This is a major message of Dewald's book and further embedded it in the mainstream of the 1954 consensus effort.[7]

A year before Dewald's book, Sidney Tarachow (1963) published a work that also sought to elucidate the nature of analytic psychotherapy by setting out its conceptual distinctions from psychoanalysis proper. *An Introduction to Psychotherapy* was aimed at psychiatric residents, therefore neophytes in psychotherapy, but it developed a theoretically highly sophisticated albeit idiosyncratic viewpoint toward both psychoanalysis and psychotherapy. Tarachow believed that there is "a clear theoretical and clinical difference between psychotherapy and psychoanalysis and that this difference can be conceptualized even for a beginner in psychotherapy" (6). Further, "the technique of psychotherapy is not the technique of psychoanalysis, but the theory of both involves an understand-

---

7. In a contemporaneous article, Louis Paul (1963) designated the major variants of psychoanalytic psychotherapy as "non uncovering psychotherapy" and "insight psychotherapy." His list of the mechanisms of non uncovering (supportive) psychotherapy is quite comparable to the earlier listings of Knight, Alexander, Gill, and Stone: strengthening repression (including via symptom-muting medications), manipulating the environment, supplying general information, supplying advice on the conduct of life, and ("hypnotic") suggestion (akin to Glover's [1931] "pseudo-analytic suggestions"). He described the mechanism of insight psychotherapy (also Dewald's phrase for expressive psychotherapy) as twofold, first instructing and educating the patient to look within, at his psychic interior, and then interpreting what comes into view— leading thus to insight.

ing of the same factors in therapists and patients, and in terms of the same concepts. . . . Classical psychoanalytical technique is a theoretical baseline of thinking and a springboard to the understanding of psychotherapy as a theory and technique" (4).

So far, this statement could have been made by Dewald or any of the other writers discussed in this chapter. But Tarachow's rendering of the conceptual and technical distinctness of psychoanalytic psychotherapy, while broadly compatible with Dewald's mainstream view, was nonetheless distinctively his own and provides a worthwhile vantage point on the conceptual struggles with these issues at the time. Tarachow outlined his conception of the therapeutic relationship and task in both his book (1963) and a preparatory article a year earlier (1962). In every therapy, of whatever kind, he averred, the therapist and patient face a common basic problem, that of object need. Each is tempted to regard and use the other as a real object, tempted thereby toward a mutual acting out.

How then is a therapeutic—a psychoanalytic—situation created out of this real relationship? By an act of the analyst, imposing a "therapeutic barrier" against reality. This barrier creates a "therapeutic task" for both analyst and patient: to transform a real situation into an "as if" situation demanding attention and comprehension. The act that brings about this transformation is interpretation, which treats the real event, not as reality, but as the expression of the patient's fantasies and as determined by his unconscious conflicts. At this point, the therapist has made the salient choice which (if consistently adhered to) distinguishes psychoanalysis from psychoanalytic psychotherapy. The therapist may either join the patient in a mutual acting out of the patient's unconscious fantasies or he may act in such a way as to create the therapeutic barrier by interpretation so that the patient develops (ultimately) a full-fledged transference neurosis. Interpretation creates the condition under which each party to the analytic situation must deprive himself of the other as a real object and must tolerate the ensuing deprivation and its awesome loneliness. For every interpretation of a transference wish is a deprivation (of a fantasy, a defense, a gratification). "The principal consequence [of an interpretation]," writes Tarachow, "is object loss. A correct interpretation is followed by a mild depression" (1962, 383).

Deprivation cannot be total, and the object hunger of the patient is satisfied (to some necessary minimal degree) in the therapeutic alliance: "It would probably be impossible to find any analyst who could rigorously maintain the detachment necessary not to use the patient as an object at all. . . . There is also the real relationship. . . . In fact, the reality of the analyst is a factor which keeps the treatment going. . . . The oscillation between the real and the 'as if' relationship can actually facilitate analyses . . . considered in terms of oscillation be-

tween gratification and deprivation. . . . The real relationship supplies the
motivation [aside from the stimulus of the patient's neurotic suffering] to face
the pain of the transference deprivations. In effect, there are two concurrent
relationships, the real and the 'as if' " (1962, 383). And, naturally, every analysis
oscillates between the amount of real and as if relationships it imposes, between
gratification (as little as possible) and deprivation (as much as possible).

To this model of the psychoanalytic situation Tarachow counterposed psychotherapy, which, in the logic of his scheme, is for those sicker patients who
cannot tolerate the task of setting the other aside as a real object to the maximal
interpretive extent, who need more of the real relationship than analysis allows.
Psychotherapy, in this conceptualization, consists technically of the variety of
ways (rationally understood and undertaken according to psychoanalytic understanding) in which the other, the therapist, can be allowed to be taken as a
real object: "If it [the relationship] is taken as real, then the symptoms and life
events are also taken as real, and both therapist and patient turn their backs on
the unconscious fantasies and anxieties." If, contrariwise, "the real relationship
is set aside, then both therapist and patient turn toward an understanding and
working through of the unconscious fantasies" (1962, 378).

Tarachow then enunciated the three major principles, each a way of taking
the relationship with the object as real, that together characterize all psychotherapies. The first consists of supplying the infantile object in reality, by way
of the uninterpreted, unanalyzed transference. In psychotherapy, "the patient is
permitted to act out his basic object needs as well as his infantile projections
with the collusion of the therapist, to whatever degree the latter deems necessary
for purposes of treatment" (1962, 380). The second principle is that of supplying
displacement—that is, new symptoms and/or resistances. As Gill (1951) had
done before in outlining the techniques of supportive psychotherapy, Tarachow
here built on Glover's (1931) paper on inexact interpretations, since he saw
displacement (like inexact interpretation) as offering a pseudoexplanation that
the patient would seize on in order to suppress the truth. Displacements could
be into the uninterpreted or incompletely interpreted transference, into new
symptoms in Glover's sense of a benign phobia, into projection or joining the
patient in a benign psychotherapeutic paranoia that ascribes the source of difficulty to the environment or to specific people in it, or by introjection, blaming
something in the body that can then be treated medically.

The third principle of psychotherapy is supplying stability—ego-support
through education and information, and superego-support by commands, prohibitions, and expressions of moral values. If all this is properly done, a psychotherapeutic result is achieved, "a rearrangement rather than a resolution of
elements. . . . The transference, repression, and resistances are dealt with in such

a way that their stability is preserved, while trying at the same time to effect whatever of the therapeutic goals are desirable or possible" (1963, 41). To do this well, Tarachow asserted, "requires even greater sensitivity and empathy than psychoanalysis does" (54).

Tarachow also pursued many related and subsidiary themes—for example: (1) the application of the same (supportive) basic model to still sicker patients, those who need to be hospitalized. Here, the whole hospitalization is conceived (in its therapeutic, not its protective function) as a means of offering the patient an opportunity to act out neurotic behavioral patterns under controlled and observed conditions that can then be used in a manner exactly analogous to the verbal exchange in individual psychotherapy; (2) the plea to make use of the flexibility allowed by psychotherapy in both goals and duration—from a few interviews to a lifetime of support; (3) the clarification of the concept of support as being not simply overt verbal reassurance, encouragement, etc., but rather the dynamically more significant acceptance of the role of a real object and interaction with the patient and his feelings as real; and (4) the point that in psychotherapy real and enduring change can come about without significant interpretation, working through, and insight.

On the other hand, Tarachow was clearly at odds with a major theme of the 1954 publications and with Dewald on the implementation of the conceptualizations of 1954. Tarachow clearly distinguished between psychoanalysis, as carried out through consistent interpretation (an austere view, moderated, however, by Tarachow's attention to the need for the oscillating gratification-deprivation aspects of the therapeutic relationship), and psychotherapy, viewed as an elaborate and sophisticated delineation of the premises and techniques of supportive (psychoanalytic) psychotherapy. What is missing is what Gill (1954) called the "intermediate type of psychotherapy" or what Dewald (1964) called "insight-directed psychotherapy," in which there is a consistent, albeit circumscribed and goal-directed, use of interpretation (i.e., setting the other aside as object), in addition to important components of unanalyzed transference (i.e., accepting the other as object). After all, this form of psychotherapy is what most analytically oriented psychotherapists practice as much of the time as they can with as many of their patients as they adjudge suitable, and what they feel most distinguishes them from their nonanalytically oriented confreres. Unless this modality is sharply distinguished as an in-between "third force," we are in danger of reverting to the oversimplified dichotomization of all therapies into psychoanalysis on the one hand and (nothing but) suggestion (Freud, Jones, Glover) or education (Waelder) on the other hand.

As a side-motif to these major developments in the psychoanalytic psychotherapy literature, I want to mention the contemporaneous efforts of Roy

Grinker, a somewhat maverick psychoanalyst, to create a variant that he called "transactional" psychotherapy, a general psychological theory that he claimed encompassed and transcended psychoanalysis as a theory of mental functioning. Actually, Grinker's approach deviated more in name than in substance from the established principles and methods of *expressive* psychoanalytic psychotherapy.[8]

Grinker's main theses about psychotherapy are expressed primarily in two articles (1959, 1961), both entitled "A Transactional Model for Psychotherapy." His is avowedly an operational approach to dynamic psychotherapy that makes the therapeutic activity appropriate to the structural requirements and possibilities within the clinical setting, the needs of the patients being served, and the realities of trainee and staff life within psychiatric hospitals and clinics, including factors of deployment, turnover, and the like. The major focus of the therapeutic endeavor (as distinct from that of psychoanalysis proper) is on current rather than remote (infantile) conflict, what Grinker (and others) came to call primary involvement with the "here and now." Describing transactional psychotherapy, Grinker said, "We do not emphasize the so-called genetic processes or the past experiences of childhood . . . past experiences of dissatisfaction. These form the neurotic core of the personality and will persist." Rather, "we are content to work with what the psychoanalysts call derivative conflicts and we are not especially interested in his uncovering the so-called primary conflicts" (1961, 207–08). This statement could be taken directly from Gill's 1954 paper or Dewald's 1964 book and the rationales stated there for the reasonable resolution of derivative conflicts, at least those that have achieved a reasonable autonomy from their instigating sources, in exploratory or expressive psychotherapies.

In his articles, Grinker implicitly employed the same psychoanalytic theory that he was ostensibly setting aside. Yet, he acknowledged that, "of all the theoretical systems in psychiatry, psychoanalytic psychodynamics yields most satisfaction because of its completeness, its sense of closure, and its analogical fit" (1961, 192) and that therefore "the basic core of our pedagogical processes in psychiatric training is the psychodynamics of Freudian psychoanalysis" (1959, 133). Grinker's apparent need to put explicit psychoanalytically based theorizing

8. I have elsewhere (Wallerstein 1972) described in detail my understanding of Grinker's theory of transactionalism and its derived therapeutic application. Another variant psychoanalytic formulation of that time, the "adaptational" perspective and technique, promulgated by Sandor Rado (1956) and his collaborators, divided psychoanalytically based therapeutic approaches into *reconstructive methods,* akin to psychoanalysis proper, except ostensibly more focused on realistic adaptation, on the here and now in the transference, and on future orientation, and *reparative methods,* akin to psychoanalytic psychotherapy, "less ambitious treatment methods that would attain limited goals in much shorter time" (92). As with transactional therapy, this is a dated nomenclature that has not survived into current use.

aside in describing his transactional psychotherapy stemmed from his conviction that psychoanalysis placed a "heavy load of interference" on the psychotherapist by requiring him or her to organize the data of observation into psychologically meaningful configurations. This constraining bias operates presumably because of the central significance of interpretation as a therapeutic change agent in psychoanalytically conceived psychotherapies (as if any ascription of meanings could ever be totally free of theory and a conceptual framework within which the meaning makes sense). Grinker's subsequent explanation in terms of the language of role theory, field theory, and communication theory (all intermingled in the language of the general theory of transactionalism) did not demonstrate that this was any less interfering or prejudicial. In fact, he went on to talk of the interpretation of repetitive behavior patterns in the here and now, of dealing with transference phenomena, the varying possible goals of the therapy, the activity of the therapist, and the use of dreams in psychotherapy (Wallerstein 1972, 128–30) in ways that can be read quite simply as good expressive (psychoanalytically based) psychotherapy resting on principles derived from thinly disguised psychoanalytic theory and appropriately extrapolating different kinds of technical interventions for differing kinds of patients not amenable to classical psychoanalysis. Grinker chose to call this the application of a commonsense psychology (transactionalism) instead of the uncommon sense that is psychoanalytic psychology, devoted to rationally comprehending the irrational.

All told, Grinker's work can be conceived as a major effort to put the main tenets of psychoanalytic thinking about the psychotherapeutic enterprise into a more palatable, seemingly commonsense language for (presumably resistant or skeptical) psychiatric circles. Certainly Grinker was in the vanguard of the successful effort in the 1950s and 1960s to capture the strongholds of American psychiatry for the psychoanalytic idea. He was for many years the editor of one of the two most influential and widely read general psychiatric journals, the *Archives of General Psychiatry,* and he brought many psychoanalysts to its editorial board and many psychoanalytically informed articles to its very large readership.

I turn now to two quite recent books specifically on psychoanalytically based supportive psychotherapy. Werman's *The Practice of Supportive Psychotherapy* (1984) is clinically focused, essentially a handbook on technique; Lawrence Rockland's *Supportive Therapy* (1989) is more theoretically focused. Both books are contemporary statements of the tripartite nature of the psychoanalytic psychotherapy enterprise arrived at in the publications of 1954.[9] Both seem to have

9. A paper by William Offenkrantz and Arnold Tobin (1974) entitled "Psychoanalytic Psychotherapy" was also written from this spirit of 1954 for the *American Handbook of Psychiatry*. It listed the techniques of psychoanalytic psychotherapy, drawing on George Goldman (1956):

been written to prevent the clear formulations of that era from being obscured by the evolving trends in psychoanalytic thinking about psychoanalysis and psychoanalytic psychotherapy over the intervening decades. Both books also accord major status and conceptual dignity to the work of supportive psychotherapy, which is always at risk of being denigrated as trivial or inconsequential by therapeutic tyro and seasoned expert alike, something that "does itself," without particular conceptualization or specification.

Werman, in the 1984 book and in papers of 1988 and 1990, first explicated the goals of supportive psychotherapy: to "provide patients with the psychological functions they lack" (1988, 158) by being a "benevolent, level-headed parent . . . lending ego" to the patient whose ego functions are inadequate to the situation. This was, then, a "substitutive form of treatment, one that supplies the patient with those psychological elements that he either lacks entirely or possesses insufficiently" (1984, 7–8). Supportive psychotherapy viewed in this way could fulfill three main functions for the patients: "[It] provides them with the opportunity to air their feelings; it may offer them a symbolic form of love through the contact with an empathic, helping therapist; and it can help soothe angry, frightened, guilty, despairing or humiliated feelings, when the patient is unable to do so himself" (9). This is accomplished in a variety of ways: "He [the therapist] will provide the opportunity for the patient to ventilate his problems and painful feelings; he may recommend changes in the patient's external life . . . ; he may assist the patient to clarify maladaptive patterns in his behavior; he may use suggestions, prescribe medications, and work with family members" (1984, 43).

The balance of the book is a rather unsystematic chronicling of various interventions designed to accomplish these ends, with clinical illustrations covering a wide range indeed: helping the patient limit destructive impulses, make life decisions, and find sublimatory channels; validating his perceptions when appropriate; making suggestions regarding the handling of difficult relationships, manipulating the outer reality, setting realistic limits (nonpunitively), tactfully and repeatedly confronting the patient with the consequences of untoward be-

---

"Management of dependency needs, evaluation of emotional reactions with positive focus, objective review of stress situations, emotional decompression [abreaction], reinforcement of ego defenses, educative guidance, effecting changes in the life situation, modification of patient's goals, use of magical omnipotence, and limited use of transference interpretation." All these worked, according to these authors, to facilitate "covert dependency gratification and the identification [with the therapist] that results from it" (596), leading to "symptom relief through identification" (598)—as against psychoanalysis, which operates through the evocation and interpretive resolution of the transference neurosis.

haviors, encouraging positive behaviors, maintaining positive rapport, bypassing significant resistances, providing plausible and reasonable explanations of behaviors, undermining grossly maladaptive defenses, mitigating the most blatant distortions of reality, fostering healthier identifications, including that with the therapist, softening a harsh and punitive conscience, helping the patient avoid anxiety-triggering situations, supporting the intellectualizing and rationalizing defenses—and many more. It is clear from this long list that a variety of mechanisms is permissible so long as they are in the service of rational goals, clearly (psychoanalytically) conceptualized. Further, the entire enterprise is accorded respectful attention as a serious and worthwhile therapeutic endeavor, requiring and warranting all our skill and experience.

Rockland (1989) conceives the goal of "psychodynamically oriented supportive therapy" (POST) to be "improving ego functions, either directly—for example, by strengthening reality testing or the ability to delay gratification— or indirectly, by decreasing the strain on the ego from the id, superego, and external reality. All this is in the service of promoting better adaptation to both inner and outer worlds" (6–7). POST is distinguished from the general support inherent in all effective psychotherapy by the specific formulation and then implementation through selected techniques of the *intent* to support, via the specific enhancement of ego functioning. This is accomplished by a variety of strategies: being a "real" figure, keeping the therapeutic focus on the conscious and preconscious productions of the patient, maintaining a benignly positive transference through interpretive undermining of negative or erotized transference elements, and encouraging adaptive defenses while counteracting maladaptive ones (81–83). These strategies are then said to be implemented by the same bewildering variety of interventions that Werman had catalogued (84–97).

The last part of Rockland's book is devoted to his conception of how supportive treatment works, discussing the nonspecific effects of all psychotherapies (with references to Jerome Frank's seminal book of 1961 on this subject):[10] dependence on unanalyzed positive transferences, selective reliance on unanalyzed negative transferences, the provision of "corrective emotional experiences" (more in Gill's 1954, sense), the fostering of identifications with the therapist, the establishment of positive feedback loops and the disruption of negative ones, and the consequent overall strengthening of ego functions. Neither of these books broke new conceptual ground but both represent important

10. For an extended review and critique of Frank's book—a major nonpsychoanalytic effort to explicate the common characteristics of all successful psychotherapies as well as their relationship to cognate efforts at interpersonal influence, from shamanistic rites to political brainwashing—see Wallerstein 1966.

reminders that the spirit of '54 is alive and well in American psychoanalysis today.[11]

I end this chapter with a tabular summary of the results of ongoing efforts by a San Francisco research group to formulate a logical and comprehensive ordering of supportive psychotherapeutic interventions, extending some aspects of the Psychotherapy Research Project of the Menninger Foundation (Wallerstein, unpubl. ms.d):

I. "Utilizing" rather than "analyzing" defenses
   A. Actions
      1. gratification of needs
      2. encouragement of adaptive defensive configurations (and discouragement of maladaptive ones) (Gill 1951)
      3. avoidance of undermining vital defenses (Gill 1951)
      4. incomplete interpretation in the service of more effective repression (Gill 1951)
   B. Mechanisms
      1. transference cure
      2. "anti-transference cure" (Wallerstein 1986a, 439–51)
      3. collusive bargain (Wallerstein 1986a, 476–89)
      4. displacement of neurosis into the treatment situation (Wallerstein 1986a, 432–39)
II. Manipulation of intratreatment situation with "learning from experience" (Bibring 1954) and bolstering self-esteem
   A. "Corrective emotional experience" (in Gill's, 1954, sense; also Wallerstein 1986a, 451–58)
   B. Use of indicated parameters (Eissler 1953)—but not necessarily to be eliminated
   C. Fostering identifications with the therapist
      1. advice and guidance
      2. educational measures (Wallerstein 1986a, 458–66)
      3. buttressing reality testing (Wallerstein 1986a, pp. 458–66)
      4. "corrective emotional experience" (in Alexander's sense)

11. This is not, of course, without controversy. Friedman (1988), in his vast and ambitious book *The Anatomy of Psychotherapy* seems to go out of his way to denigrate and trivialize supportive psychotherapy. He said, for example, "Anyone can just accept a fixed role. That is probably the best definition of 'supportive therapy.' At that point the therapist might more accurately consider himself a counselor, an advisor, or friend. He is no longer pursuing the goal of psychotherapy, although the patient may experience a therapy fortuitously related to the therapist's efforts" (534).

III. Manipulation of external life situation
   A. Provision of protected and nurturant life setting
   B. Planned and prescribed daily regimen
   C. Disengagement from noxious life situation (Wallerstein 1986a, 466–76)
   D. Maintaining engagement in needed life situation (Wallerstein 1986a, 466–76)
   E. Limit setting
   F. Altering interactions with, or attitudes of, significant others
IV. Concomitant prescription of psychoactive drugs

The administration of drugs always carries a variety of psychological meanings specific to the particular patients and their characteristic transference expectations, fears, and wishes. These various meanings—for example, gratification, avoidance, encouragement, a corrective emotional experience—can place drug administration under a variety of relevant headings in the above listing.

7 Kurt Eissler and Parameters: "Classical" Technique and Freud's Actual Technique

A year before the 1954 publications that sought to clarify the dimensions of psychoanalysis as therapy vis-à-vis the psychoanalytically based psychotherapies derived from it, Kurt Eissler published a paper attempting to define psychoanalysis as distinct from all its cousins and imitators. Eissler's paper could be, and was, widely read as the establishment response to the major deviations proposed by Alexander in understanding the nature of the psychoanalytic enterprise and how it brought about desired changes. Eissler had already (1950) published a detailed critique of the work of Alexander and his colleagues, which he dubbed a "magical therapy" in contrast to proper psychoanalysis, a "rational therapy."

In his 1953 article, Eissler focused explicitly on psychoanalysis as a therapy without direct reference to Alexander's work. His argument was straightforward. He began by restating the basic model of psychoanalysis as he felt it had originated with Freud: the central tool is interpretation and working through, and the central goal is insight and consequent change based on insight. "In the ideal case," he wrote, "the analyst's activity is limited to interpretation; no other tool becomes necessary" (108), though he did allow room for an ancillary tool, usually taken for granted: the judicious asking of appropriate questions to facilitate the flow of associations and thereby to help furnish the data for interpretations. Eissler felt that this basic model could be achieved with relative ease in classic cases of hysteria with Freud's "hypothetically normal ego."

However, in the treatment of the phobic, analytic progress would sometimes come to a halt. Then, "a new technical tool becomes necessary. As is well known, this new tool is advice or command" (110), and it is this deviation from the basic model technique that Eissler designated a "parameter."[1] Eissler's reference—"as is well known"—was to Freud, for it was he who had first identified and proposed such deviations. For example, in "Lines of Advance" (1919), Freud stated,

> Our technique grew up in the treatment of hysteria and is still directed
> principally to the cure of that affection. But the phobias have already made
> it necessary to go beyond our former limits. One can hardly master a

1. This is, of course, a misuse of the word "parameter," which means limits or dimensions, but so influential and persuasive was Eissler's article that this particular usage of the word has persisted unaltered in the psychoanalytic literature ever since.

phobia if one waits till the patient lets the analysis influence him to give it up. He will never in that case bring into the analysis the material indispensable for a convincing resolution of the phobia. One must proceed differently. Take the example of agoraphobia. . . . One succeeds only when one can induce them by the influence of the analysis . . . to go into the street and to struggle with their anxiety while they make the attempt. One starts, therefore, by moderating the phobia so far; and it is only when that has been achieved at the physician's demand that the associations and memories come into the patient's mind which enable the phobia to be resolved. (165–66).

In the same paper, Freud alluded to his other well-known parameter, often required, he felt, in dealing with obsessive-compulsives: "Their analysis is always in danger of bringing to light a great deal and changing nothing. I think there is little doubt that here the correct technique can only be to wait until the treatment itself has become a compulsion, and then with this counter-compulsion forcibly to suppress the compulsion of the disease" (166). The "counter-compulsion" Freud alluded to he made explicit in his report on the Wolf-Man case (1918). When the Wolf Man's analysis seemed to be bogged down, he finally set a fixed termination date. Freud felt that this forced the Wolf Man to bring up the relevant and necessary associations that, in turn, exposed the conflicted unconscious material and made it possible to resolve the neurotogenic intrapsychic conflicts.

In his preface to August Aichhorn's *Wayward Youth,* Freud (1925a) presented what could be construed as another, an educational, parameter, useful in the psychoanalytic therapy of the juvenile delinquents Aichhorn was reporting on. Freud said, "The possibility of analytic influence rests on quite definite preconditions which can be summed up under the term 'analytic situation'; it requires the development of certain psychical structures and a particular attitude to the analyst. Where these are lacking—as in the case of children, of juvenile delinquents, and as a rule, of impulsive criminals—something other than analysis must be employed, though something which will be at one with analysis in its *purpose*" (274). Freud did not specify further, and this passage has usually not been remarked when Freud's proposals about needed parameters have been discussed.

Ferenczi, whose technique seemed to deviate so much from Freud's, was nonetheless at one with Freud in the requirements for such parameters. For example, in their 1924 book, Ferenczi and Rank stated, "He [the analyst] sets a definite period of time for completing the last part of the treatment in which the libido of the patient, following an automatic course, now shows the tendency to fix itself in the analysis as a substitute for the neurosis" (13). This was even seen as *part* of the active therapy that Ferenczi always claimed was only the logical extension of Freud's psychoanalysis to the more difficult cases.[2]

Eissler, after defining what he meant by a parameter, laid down the three conditions a parameter had to meet to qualify as such: "(1) A parameter must be introduced only when it is proved that the basic model technique does not suffice; (2) the parameter must never transgress the unavoidable minimum; (3) a parameter is to be used only when it finally leads to its self-elimination, that is to say, the final phase of the treatment must always proceed with a parameter of zero" (111). These very rigorous conditions could presumably be met by directing the phobic patient to finally enter the phobic situation so as to unmask still-hidden intrapsychic conflict. In theory, one would have the opportunity after these events to analytically uncover and undo the meanings to the patient of having submitted to the analyst's coercive pressure. But with the obsessional patient, the third of Eissler's criteria could not be met even in theory, because once a termination date is set and adhered to there is no longer open time—as long as it takes—to analyze completely the meanings of this intervention. Speaking of Freud's Wolf-Man case, Eissler pointed to what he believed were two distinct parameters: the fixing of the termination date and the promise of complete recovery (the transference authority and the meaning of the unanalyzed fantasy of the analyst's omnipotence). Eissler asserted that both of these manifestly fulfilled the first criterion, questionably met the second criterion, but failed completely in regard to the third. Later Eissler commented, perhaps ruefully, with Freud in mind, that "the effect of the parameter on the transference relationship must never be such that it cannot be abolished by interpretation" (113).

In the more theoretical section of the article, Eissler developed the idea that the basic model technique can be applied only if the patient has "an ego not modified to any noteworthy degree" (116). This is Freud's "hypothetically normal ego" (121), which would guarantee unswerving loyalty to the analytic compact: "A normal ego is one which, notwithstanding its symptoms, reacts to rational therapy with a dissolution of its symptoms" (122). It may suffer disease, but with nonetheless unharmed possibilities and resources. Of course, only the classical instance of pure hysteria can even claim the possibility of such a hy-

---

2. Rank, when he later departed from psychoanalysis and developed his Will Therapy, took this concept of a predetermined termination date as almost the defining element of a process that in nine months should be able to bring about the proper psychological (re)birth of a now autonomously functioning individual, developed on the template of the biological gestational period of nine months to the time of physical birth.

pothetically normal ego. It follows that parameters are inevitably introduced in all other cases beyond that theoretic possibility.³ For the rest, the nature of the ego is progressively modified up to the psychotic end of the scale, where the analytic compact becomes completely impossible.⁴

When Eissler's strictures are scrupulously adhered to, proper psychoanalysis can be done, and required deviations from classical technique are justified in terms of the clinical needs of patients with less than perfectly suitable ("normal") egos. As Eissler put it, "Freud's concepts—(1) the hypothetically normal ego as defined by the response in the situation of the basic model technique; (2) a scale leading by degrees to a state of absolute unresponsiveness to the analytic concept; and (3) the intervening variety of ego modifications to which a variety of techniques must be correlated—provide, in my estimation, a system which is ideally flexible and superbly adaptable to actual clinical work" (125). And it has built-in safeguards: "I think that the concept of a parameter and adherence to the . . . rules I mentioned may prevent us from falling into wild analysis" (141).

In a follow-up article in 1958, Eissler reasserted his position of 1953: "The science of interpretation is the bulk and main chapter of the classical psycho-

3. Freud (1937a) had expressed himself very explicitly on the hypothetically normal ego in his last great clinical paper, "Analysis Terminable and Interminable" (1937): "But a normal ego of this sort is, like normality in general, an ideal fiction. The abnormal ego, which is unserviceable for our purposes, is unfortunately no fiction. Every normal person, in fact, is only normal on the average. His ego approximates to that of the psychotic in some part or other and to a greater or less extent; and the degree of its remoteness from one end of the series and its proximity to the other will furnish us with a provisional measure of what we have so indefinitely termed an 'alteration of the ego' " (235). A half-century later, Helmut Thoma and Horst Kachele (1987) spoke of this same stark ideal in much the same vein: "It has never been possible to treat patients with the basic model technique [which] is a fiction created for a patient who does not exist. The specific [technical] means, led by interpretation of transference and resistance [Eissler's declared technique], are embedded in a network of supportive and expressive (i.e., conflict-revealing) techniques, even though particular means are emphasized" (p. 41).

4. Like others in his day, Eissler was quite skeptical of the claims by Fromm-Reichmann and others who thought like her about the accessibility, however difficult, of the openly psychotic to (modified) psychoanalytic therapy. He said, "This incapacity to lift himself out of the context of phenomena at one point at least must make the technique of treating schizophrenics essentially different from that of neurotics if one extends the treatment to the treatment of the ego modification. It is strange to notice that this technical problem which is most typical of the treatment of schizophrenics is barely mentioned in the contemporary literature on the psychotherapy of schizophrenia" (135–36). What Eissler was of course referring to here was the focus in that literature on the analysis of the drives as expressed in the transference with a bypassing of the impaired capacities of the crippled ego of the psychotic to deal responsibly with those drive expressions.

analytic technique. Where we interpret from the surface down or in the opposite direction, it is either correct or incorrect classical technique but not a variation of that technique. That term [variation] should be reserved exclusively for the introduction of tools that lie outside interpretation. . . . Classical technique is . . . one in which interpretation remains the exclusive or leading or prevailing tool" (222–23).

But in this same paper, he allowed for the possibility that this dictum could not always be adhered to: "In the classical technique the analyst lends the patient at most one function, merely the ability to draw from scattered bits of evidence general and specific conclusions about the patient's unconscious" (227). He also acknowledged how difficult (if not impossible) this could be: "It may even be worthwhile to experiment and investigate, in properly selected instances, what the effect upon the patient is when strictly and consistently all other technical tools are excluded and only interpretations are given. No doubt this would put a strain on the patient as well as on the analyst." And then Eissler departed from his own strict tenets: "With the help of *pseudo-parameters* one may be able to smuggle interpretations into the pathognomonic area with a temporary circumvention of resistances. A frequent device of this kind is the right joke told at the right moment" (224, italics added); or "I presume every analyst has had the experience of a patient grasping the full meaning of a remark he has made casually, when the analyst [simply] repeats it" (225).

But these were minimal concessions in an otherwise uncompromising restatement of so-called classical psychoanalytic technique, widely accepted as both the full establishment response to the threatening Alexander heresy and, pari passu, the definitive version of the classical psychoanalytic technique inherited from Freud. However, Eissler did not long have this definitional field entirely to himself. Leo Stone's 1961 monograph *The Psychoanalytic Situation* was one of the most influential in mitigating Eissler's austere image of proper psychoanalysis. Actually, Stone's treatise was far more than a softening of Eissler's conceptions; it was an expression of a trend in psychoanalysis, initiated with Ferenczi, to focus on the multifaceted nature of the psychoanalytic situation and the psychoanalytic relationship as major determinants of therapeutic progress, and it was also an authoritative mark of the perceived legitimation of this countertrend within organized psychoanalysis. This will be discussed in detail in chapter 16; here I want only to draw upon some of Stone's earlier (1954) responses to Eissler's 1953 paper.

In his more immediate riposte, Stone said that though he agreed in general with the spirit and intent of Eissler's formulations, "this rule seems altogether too severe. There are very sick personalities who, to the very end of analytic experience, may require occasional and subtle or minimal emotional or technical concessions from the analyst, in the same sense that they will carry with them into their outside lives, vestiges of ego deficits or modifications, which, while not completely undone, are—let us say—vastly improved" (1954, 576). And further: "Probably all analyses include certain formal and subtle emotional deviations somewhere along the line, aside from the fact that no two analysts would ever give precisely the same interpretations throughout an analysis" (574). Stone then posed the critical question: "How far can the classical analytic method be modified, and still be regarded as psychoanalysis, 'modified psychoanalysis,' if you wish, rather than another form of interpretative psychotherapy?" (575).

An even more fundamental challenge to Eissler's articulation of classical technique was posed in a sequence of papers by Lipton (1967, 1977, 1979, 1988) challenging head-on Eissler's assumption that he was only conveying and clarifying the technique inherited from Freud. In the first of these, Lipton (1967) presented an exhaustive exegetical survey of all of Freud's later writings to glean whatever technical precepts and recommendations he could, especially any that would indicate modification of the precepts laid down in his six papers on technique (Freud [1911–15], SE 12:pp. 83–173). He conducted a comparable survey, with the same ends in view, of the practices revealed in the many accounts by Freud's analysands. Lipton concluded that Freud's fundamental technique seemed to have crystallized no later than 1920 and was not significantly altered thereafter.

In this paper, Lipton stated his understanding of Freud's work under two headings, technical and personal. Under the technical rubric, he listed Freud's principles of technique as follows: "the central importance of the psychoanalytic situation; the juxtaposition of free association by the patient and evenly hovering attention and interpretation and construction by the analyst; the interpretation of resistances; the development and resolution of the transference; the aim of genetic reconstruction of pathogenic experiences; the impossibility of directly attacking symptoms; the necessity of consistently starting from the current surface of the material; and the proper place of dream interpretation" (90). Lipton then listed Freud's personal qualities as expressed in the treatment situation: "The first is intellectual brilliance. . . . The second is the warmth, empathy, candor, and benign humor that shine through the clinical descriptions. The stubborn misunderstanding that in using the screen analogy Freud was recommending that the analyst actually be detached or impassive is regularly refuted in his case reports. In fact, he meant only that the analyst should confine his personal attributes to establishing and maintaining a working alliance, or positive transference in a realistic sense, and devote all his efforts to expanding the patient's understanding rather than attempting to influence him directly" (99–91).

In his next (1977) paper, Lipton undertook to compare what he called

Freud's actual technique with the version of standard or classical technique expressed and codified by Eissler. Lipton based this paper on a detailed study of Freud's Rat-Man[5] case (1909b) as well as on the subsequently published, much more detailed notes Freud kept on this patient. Lipton warned that even this detailed record is incomplete, which should make one cautious indeed in drawing conclusions about issues that Freud failed to write about.

Lipton set out to demonstrate that what is called modern technique is not a continuation of Freud's original technique but rather a gross redefinition that broadened the concept of technique far beyond what Freud intended or practiced. This redefinition began, he said, when several highly respected analytic authorities, some forty years after Freud's original statements about (his) technique, began to express criticisms of Freud's actual practices: that he talked too much and tended to indoctrinate his patients intellectually, that he paid inadequate attention to the analysis of the transference or of acting out, and so on.[6] In relation to one of these critics Lipton explained, "The problem which Zetzel found in these interchanges lies [to my mind] in the expansion of the concept of technique to incorporate matters which Freud did not consider technical but instead considered only as part of his own non-technical personal relationship with Lorenz. . . . Exigencies which impel the analyst to offer the patient some courtesy or some assistance on a personal basis occur occasionally, and every experienced analyst I have spoken to about this subject has had his own unique confirmatory experiences to report. In designating such interchanges as these as outside of technique I must emphasize that I *by no means imply that their repercussions are excluded from the analysis*" (259). This occasional "assistance on a personal basis" extended even to such extreme-sounding things (to our modern ears) as feeding Lorenz a meal when he arrived hungry one day or giving a gift of a book to Smiley Blanton. It was just these sorts of things, which Freud

5. Lipton referred to the patient by his pseudonym, Paul Lorenz, rather than by the unattractive, though commonly employed designation, Rat-Man, taken from the patient's frightening obsession with rats.

6. For example, Lipton quoted the following from an article by E. Kris (1951): "If we reread Freud's older case histories, we find . . . that the conspicuous intellectual indoctrination of the Rat Man was soon replaced by a greater emphasis on reliving in the transference, a shift which has no apparent direct relation to definite theoretical views" (17). Lipton (1977) commented, "This astonishing claim was not supported by specific citations but was advanced simply as if it were a known or easily recognizable fact, although, as far as I know, it had not been made before" (257). He similarly challenged other unfavorable comments on Freud's actual technique—made by Jones, Kanzer, Grunberger, Weiner, Zetzel, Morgenthaler, Beigler, Rangell, Gedo—with the assertion that in no case was adequate evidence adduced in support of the criticisms or, for that matter, in support of the view that Freud's technique subsequently changed in a more properly psychoanalytic direction.

considered not matters of technique at all but rather part of his nontechnical (personal) relationship with his analysands, that have now been redefined as technique and then widely labeled as bad technique.

Yet Lipton declared that despite the common exculpatory assumption that after the analysis of Lorenz Freud had changed his technique in a more rigorously classical direction, there is no evidence of this in Freud's writings or the writings of his analysands, and indeed, no one raised this issue for many years after Freud's death. Freud always established a cordial personal relationship with his patients (as attested to by many accounts) and felt that this was nontechnical. Overall, "the areas in which Freud is thought to have changed his technique, Freud did not think of as technical at all" (261).

However, by 1977, analysis had been stripped of these personal elements, and technique had been broadened to encompass what Freud put out of bounds. And this modern technique had been defined as classical and declared to be the direct heir to Freud's percepts and practices. As part of this movement, analytic silence has been elevated to correct technique, and the most trivial matters are given weighty significance (granted that a trivial matter may indeed be important in a patient's eyes). All this, of course, has simplified the everyday work of analysis because we could now be less alert to the *effect* of our responses, technical or nontechnical, on the patient; we could now feel that we are doing the right thing if we adhere to "correct" technique. Technique is now judged not by intent or outcome so much as by technical behavior.

Lipton saw this whole development as a redefinition of technique, beginning in the 1940s (after Freud's death), mainly as a reaction against the possibility that Alexander's concept of the corrective emotional experience would win popular acceptance. Alexander could be regarded as trying to systematize technically many of the things Freud did that Freud would say were natural and spontaneous, not part of technique at all. The answer of modern technique and its central exponent, Eissler (1950, 1953), was to avoid these issues altogether: "It was in the period after this paper [Eissler 1953] was published that the exclusion of the personality of the analyst and the expansion of technique to cover all utterances of the analyst gained acceptability. . . . It seems to be in accord with the view that every word which the analyst utters should be an interpretation, or more realistically, should be governed by technical rules, that silence itself has become idealized to some extent" (Lipton 1977, 265). Modern technique, according to Lipton, seems to have three simple rules: (1) say nothing but interpretations; (2) otherwise be silent; and (3) remember that every word is governed by technical rules.

Lipton felt that the concepts of the therapeutic and the working alliances (see chapter 15) were being proposed during this period to rescue the human being in the analyst from the dilemma created by Eissler's austere image of proper analysis. These concepts could provide the analyst with a new (technical) rationale for saying a good many things that should get said in any going analysis—and do get said. To Lipton, these concepts were no more than the personal relationship Freud established with his patients and simply excluded from considerations of technique: "Technique of analysis is best restricted to what might be called analysis proper, that is, the interpretation of the patient's associations, and the corollary view that the personal relationship between the analyst and patient be excluded from technique" (267). Lipton took pains to point out that excluding the personal relationship from consideration of technique did not mean anything goes. The analyst's conduct should at all times be civil, courteous, sensible, and ethical, and the analyst should at all times be alert to repercussions within the analysis of personal exchanges between analyst and patient.

Yet Lipton felt that the weight of opinion had swung behind Eissler's presentation. To Lipton, modern technique had dehumanized psychoanalysis; Freud's technique was simply better: "Without the actuality of the non-technical personal relationship, irrational elements of the transference remain imaginary or intellectual. With this actuality and its kernel of truth, the patient can gain conviction about the importance of his covert feelings, about their undue intensity and importance, about their timing and about the importance of tracing them to their historical roots" (271). Lipton granted that what is personal and what is technical cannot always be precisely demarcated, but nevertheless it was important to try to retain the distinction.

He ended the paper with a restatement of his purpose and his thesis: "to prove that the technique which Freud used with Lorenz was his definitive technique, fully developed before that analysis, never changed for the rest of Freud's life and accepted as classical analysis for some 40 years. Only after that time was Freud's technique in that case repudiated. Only after that time did the tenacious myth arise that [it] . . . was only a precursor of his imaginary later technique" (271). To Lipton, Freud's mirror and blank screen metaphors, used by Eissler as justification for equating Freud's technical stance with modern technique, were intended to apply only to matters of technique, never to the personal relationship.

Lipton wrote two more papers on this topic (1979, 1988). The first is a very short addendum to Freud's newly published notes on the first eight analytic sessions with Lorenz, which Lipton compared with the version of those sessions in the Standard Edition. Nothing in the new material caused him to want to alter a word of his earlier paper. His last paper (1988) related this issue to the larger consideration of what constitutes psychotherapy vis-à-vis psychoanalysis. For example: "Freud's technique incorporated various procedures which were

later excluded from psychoanalysis proper and relegated to psychotherapy."
And, discussing Freud's close co-worker Abraham: "He found that some of
these [older] patients found it difficult to begin an hour, and that therefore he
had to begin with 'a little stimulus,' perhaps an allusion to a previous session.
What is pertinent here is that he simply incorporates this measure into analysis
with, of course, no concern about what we might now think of as psychotherapy" (21). Most pointedly: modern technique "seems to overemphasize the
behavior of the analyst, instead of his purpose, and attempts to prescribe and
codify his conduct excessively. It seems to me that modern technique has the
purpose not only of conducting analysis but also guarding against its contamination by psychotherapy" (22). In this statement, Lipton seems to have caught
the main concern, to preserve psychoanalysis from any hint of dilution, whether
by suggestion and hypnosis (as was feared by Freud, Jones, and Glover), by the
corrective emotional experience, or by any variant of psychotherapy (as was
feared by Eissler and all the other proponents of modern/classical technique).

Lipton devoted the bulk of the paper to the potentially untoward effects of
the modern enshrinement of silence as a technique: the analyst's silence can lead
to an idealization of his presumed superior understanding; the patient is not
supposed to mention anything the analyst remains silent about, such as not
acknowledging his tardiness in starting a session; the patient will get unnecessarily discouraged and frustrated by the impassivity reflected in the silence; the
analyst might refrain from confronting the patient with a clear danger when
doing so might be a higher priority than the search for latent meanings. The
sanctification of silence, of course, is based on the concept of not interfering
with the patient's flow of associations. Of this Lipton said, "This principle . . .
is the most astonishing single element of modern technique. . . . One of the
most obvious indications of resistance is the patient's silence about something
which the analyst knows perfectly well that he is aware of. It seems to me that
the failure of the analyst to bring such an exclusion to the attention of the patient
will tend to slow down the analysis, and, if he never brings it up, lose material
altogether" (27).[7]

7. Substantial support for Lipton's concern about the proper place of silence, talk, and asking
questions in the analytic discourse was offered by Boesky's "The Questions and Curiosity of
the Psychoanalyst (1989). Boesky is usually seen, properly, as one of the present-day proponents of the so-called modern or classical position on matters of technique, albeit modified—
as with most present-day analysts—from the purified position exemplified by Eissler.

Boesky developed a multifaceted argument: "We do not ask questions merely to obtain
answers, but, more important, to evoke associations in the aftermath of a newly altered psychic
equilibrium which has been destabilized by the question of the analyst" (581). And further,
"It is precisely what the patient learns about what the analyst wants to know that constitutes

Lipton also commented on the imputed risks of "wild analysis": "Possibly the concern about formal correctness in analysis has kept alive the anachronistic concept of wild analysis. We might recall that even in 1910 Freud noted that wild analysts he cited did less harm than some respected authority could have done (Freud, 1910b, p. 227). If there is any danger now, I think that it is more from tame analysis than from wild analysis" (31).

Almost a quarter of a century had elapsed between Eissler's 1953 paper on parameters and Lipton's 1977 main paper on Freud's actual technique. By that time, the tone of American psychoanalysis established by Eissler and accepted almost unquestioningly by so many, had undergone a sea change, and Lipton's challenge to Eissler's version of psychoanalytic history found widespread acceptance. In an article entitled "Changes in Psychoanalytic Ideas" (focused on models of transference interpretation), Arnold Cooper (1987a) summarized the story of this chapter:

> Corresponding to the swings of analytic culture between classical and romantic, there were swings in analytic technique from Freud's actual technique, as reconstructed from his notes and the reports of his patients, to the so-called "classical" technique that held sway after Freud's death. . . . Lipton (1977) has insisted that in the 1940s and 1950s the so-called "classical" technique replaced Freud's own more personal and relaxed technique, probably in reaction to Alexander's suggestion of the corrective emotional experience. It was Lipton's view that the misnamed "classical" technique, in contrast to Freud's, emphasized rules for the analyst's behavior and sacrificed the purpose of the analysis. Eissler's 1953 description of analysis as an activity that ideally uses only interpretation became the paradigm for "classical" analysis. It was, Lipton says, a serious and severe distortion of the mature analytic technique developed by Freud. Freud regarded the analyst's personal behaviors, the personality of the analyst, and the living conditions of the patient as nontechnical parts of every analysis, as exemplified for Lipton in the case of the Rat Man. The so-called "classical" (and in his view non-Freudian) technique attempted to

---

one of the important antecedent events that paves the way to insight. It is what the analyst learns about what the patient does not want to know that paves the way toward interpretation" (581). And questions, as a form of discourse, carry the weight of being the most insistently forceful. The consequences can be various: "There can be no systematic classification of questions in the clinical psychoanalytic situation just as there can be no taxonomy of psychoanalytic discourse. A question like any other intervention of the analyst can *facilitate or hinder* the analytic process" (592, italics added). Surely a supportive warrant for Lipton's more relaxed stance on the place of questions as an acceptable aspect of analytic dialogue (contra Eissler).

include every aspect of the analytic situation as a part of technique, and led to the model of the silent, restrained psychoanalyst. (86–87)

Support for Lipton's perspective on Freud's technique as against Eissler's came from other influential quarters, notably Stone (1981a) and Haynal (1988). After a detailed recapitulation of Lipton's argument, Stone noted tartly, "If one had to choose, one would do better to choose Freud's early latitudes and naturalness over the robotlike 'anonymity' of our own neoclassical period, when it reached absurd heights" (106). And Haynal (1988), in his book on the relationships of Freud, Ferenczi, and Balint, listed an impressive array of Freud's analysands—Smiley Blanton, Medard Boss, Hilda Doolittle, Abram Kardiner, Jeanne Lampl-de Groot, Roger Money-Kyrle, and Alix Strachey—who attested to their generally positive reaction to Freud's actual technique.

Peter Buckley (1989), like Lipton, has related these concerns specifically to the issue of psychotherapy vis-à-vis psychoanalysis: "The impact of personal interactions between the therapist and the patient has been a neglected subject in the literature, perhaps because of the uneasy feelings that are stirred up in clinicians who fear that the 'purity' of the therapeutic field is compromised by such occurrences" (1402). But "Freud was not unaware of the therapeutic relationship as a mutative factor in treatment. In one of his last papers [he is referring to "Analysis Terminable and Interminable," 1937a] he stated that the positive transference 'is the strongest motive for the patient's taking a share in the joint work'; however, he does not develop the theoretical implications of the therapeutic relationship and, specifically, of *supportive measures* in therapy, although as is clear from the Rat-Man and the Wolf-Man cases, he empirically used them" (1401, italics added). Here Buckley is explicitly referring to such instances as Freud's feeding the Rat-Man, his giving the Wolf Man free treatment and even financial support when he was impoverished, his influencing Ruth Mack Brunswick to continue the Wolf-Man's treatment without charge, and so forth. These are exactly the kinds of events Lipton called personal interactions outside of technique rather than supportive therapeutic measures *within* technique.

Buckley went on to cite a paragraph from Anna Freud's widening scope discussion of 1954, in which she had expressed these same ideas but, writing at a time when Eissler's views held unquestioned sway, had expressed them very cautiously: "Concerning the 'real personal relationship' between analyst and patient versus the 'true transference reactions' " she had said:

> To make such a distinction coincides with ideas which I have always held on this subject. . . . So far as the patient has a healthy part of his personality, his real relationship to the analyst is never wholly submerged [by the

progressive evolution of the transference neurosis]. With due respect for the necessary strictest handling and interpretation of the transference, I feel still that we should leave room somewhere for the realization that analyst and patient are also two real people of equal adult status, in a real personal relationship to each other. I wonder whether our—at times complete—neglect of this side of the matter is not responsible for some of the hostile reactions which we get from our patients and which we are apt to ascribe to 'true transference' only. But these are technically subversive thoughts and ought to be 'handled with care.' " (618–19)

Another perspective on the analytic posture epitomized by Eissler has come from the current broad retreat from what Richard Simons (1990) called the idealizations of analysis—the perfectionistic implication that proper and correct technique would lead ineluctably to complete analysis and expectable cure. Simons wrote,

I believe that . . . during our so-called halcyon days . . . along with the idealization of the structural model came the emphasis on interpretation and insight as the exclusive hallmarks toward which all other techniques and processes of change were contributory but not central. In this value system all deviations from the "basic model technique" were to be viewed as "parameters" (Eissler, 1953). Such certainty offers a powerful security and therefore exerts a powerful appeal, and we saw emerge during this same period the grand illusion that there was a psychodynamic explanation or etiology for all mental disorders, and by implication a psychodynamic therapeutic approach or cure for all these disorders. The inevitable end result was the "myth of perfectibility" (Gaskill, 1980; Blum, 1989) of the fully terminated analysis, whose goal was the attainment of some idealized state of transference and conflict resolution, without a more balanced view of the relative immutability of both transference . . . and psychic conflict. (18)

This same perception of the current retreat from the counsels of complete conflict resolution and cure has been articulated by Weinshel (1990a), a prominent spokesman for the post-ego-psychological era in mainstream American psychoanalysis, which is nonetheless still identified with Freud's structural theory and its implications for technique. In "How Wide is the Widening Scope of Psychoanalysis, and How Solid is its Structural Model?" Weinshel drew inspiration from Gitelson's much earlier suggestion (1963) that "the time may be appropriate to propose a counsel of modesty for psycho-analysts" (522)—a remark directed in its day at all the talk of complete cures and an ever-widening scope. In this connection, Weinshel remarked, "I have always been grateful to Gill (1954) for his pithy, pungent reminder that 'there is no doubt that we can still recognize our friends and colleagues, even after they have been analyzed' " (278). Within this context, Weinshel set forth his own "central thesis . . . that in the past thirty-five years American psychoanalysis, at least that portion of it closely associated with the ego-psychological structural model, has been engaged in a relatively unobtrusive campaign to bring psychoanalysis within a more realistic—more modest—frame of reference" (277).

Weinshel outlined the evidence of this more modest posture:

1. We now speak of psychoanalytic changes, not cures
2. We no longer talk of eliminating conflict, just modifying it so that it is more manageable and less constraining
3. Analyses are not completed or finished, just brought to a reasonable state that allows stopping
4. Transferences are never completely resolved
5. We no longer "overcome" or "demolish" resistances, just analyze them
6. We no longer focus on evidence of parameters as deviations from "correct" technique
7. There is no longer a single-minded focus on the retrieval of buried memories and consequent great insights
8. Dream analysis is no longer *the* royal road to the unconscious
9. We no longer focus on the transformative effects of "good hours" (E. Kris 1956) but are content with plenty of "not-so-good hours"
10. We acknowledge the increased importance of the affective participation of the analyst in the effectiveness of the analytic work

All in all, an ensemble of interrelated perspectives reflecting the extent of the change in analytic thinking in America since the hegemony of Eissler's paradigm. Yet Weinshel has in no way defected from his staunch adherence to the theoretical and clinical usefulness of modern-day structural theory in its current more complex and sophisticated guise. He said, in fact, "The structural theory's stress on conflict and compromise formation *virtually* guarantees an emphasis on multidetermination and a premium on searching for the unexpected"—that is, it *supports* the new emphasis on a "counsel of modesty." Yet Weinshel also acknowledged that "one of the greatest pressures on the structural theory has been to provide more effective techniques in treating the sicker patients in our clientele, the so-called borderline and narcissistic personality disorders" (290–91).

Two other recent papers round out the contemporary assessment of Eissler's effort to define the classical technique of psychoanalysis and of Lipton's claim that it is a misreading of Freud and the Freudian legacy. Hoffman (1992a) undertook to clarify Lipton's position on Freud's technique in relation to both Eissler's *and* Alexander's views:

> Lipton (1977) argues that it is an error to subsume the personally expressive aspects of the analyst's behavior under the rubric of technique. Using the example of Freud's offering the Rat Man a meal, Lipton differs both with those who would object to such behavior on the grounds that it is technically incorrect (because it may have unanalyzable transference repercussions) [clearly Eissler's position] and with those like Alexander and, perhaps, certain deficit theorists [a reference to Kohut?] who, depending on the diagnosis of the patient, might regard it as technically correct, and who might even consider incorporating it into a systematic program to provide the patient with a corrective emotional experience. Instead, in keeping with an attitude he attributes to Freud, Lipton favors regarding such behavior as merely personal and spontaneous, with no major technical implications unless transference repercussions surface subsequently in the patient's associations (4).

Here Hoffman put Lipton squarely—and I think correctly—at odds with both Alexander's proposals and Eissler's response to them; both of them, in Lipton's view, missed the main point that this was not a matter of good or bad technique, but in fact didn't concern technique at all.

Statements made by Freud (to Ferenczi) about his own technique in practice and how it related to the technical precepts he had put into the literature were cited by Jacobson (1994) in relation to the correspondence between Freud and Ferenczi published in Grubrich-Simitis's paper (1986). Jacobson said,

> A letter from Freud to Ferenczi on the occasion of the latter's 1928 paper on "The Elasticity of Technique" bears on this point. Remarking on Ferenczi's introducing there the notion of tact in interpretation, Freud told him: "The title is excellent and would deserve to be made more of—as my recommendations on technique [of 1912–15] were essentially negative. I thought it most important to stress what one should not do, to point out the temptations that run counter to analysis. Almost everything one should do in a positive sense, I left to the "tact" that you have introduced. What I achieved thereby was that the Obedient submitted to these admonitions as if they were taboos and did not notice their elasticity. This would have had to be revised someday. . . ." Then, ever concerned with possible wild or self-indulgent misuse of the analytic situation, Freud's caution returns as he now worries about Ferenczi's use of the word "tact,"

stating: "All those without tact will see therein a justification . . . for the influence of personal complexes that have not been overcome" (Grubrich-Simitis, 1986, p. 271). The technical rules and admonitions, in other words, were intended to keep the inexperienced, the unruly, and the neurotically unresolved analyst in line, but intended to be used in a flexible manner by the reliable and "normal" analyst. Who gets to decide which analysts are normal, which unreliable, and which overly Obedient and rigid, and just how that determination is to be made, are rather touchy questions. (17–18)

We of course can see at once the very different ways in which Eissler and Lipton have dealt with these "rather touchy questions."

Ferenczi, from his side, spoke in an exactly counterpart manner in his interchanges with Freud over the proper understanding of Freud's technique and the ways in which it could be understood (or misunderstood) in the context of a literal reading of Freud's technical papers. Quoting an unnamed colleague's "criticism," but no doubt referring to that same letter from Freud unearthed and published by Grubrich-Simitis so many years later, he said, " 'The title ["Elasticity"] is excellent,' he replied, 'and should be applied more widely, for Freud's technical recommendations were essentially negative. He regarded it as his most important task to emphasize what one should not do, to draw attention to all the pitfalls that stand in the way of analysis, and he left all the positive things that one should do to what you called "tact." The result was that the excessively docile did not notice the elasticity that is required and subjected themselves to Freud's "don'ts" as if they were taboos. This is a situation that requires revision, without, of course, altering Freud's rules' " (1928, 99).

Two years later, in "Relaxation and Neocatharsis" (1930), Ferenczi spoke in his own voice, even more categorically. After describing his own technical innovations and experiments, Ferenczi commented, "I had the greatest conscientious scruples about all these infringements of a fundamental rule . . . until my mind was set at rest by the *authoritative information* [presumably from Freud] that Freud's 'Recommendations' were really intended only as warnings for beginners and were designed to protect them from the most glaring blunders and failures; his precepts contained, however, hardly any positive instructions, and considerable scope was left for the exercise of the analyst's own judgment, provided that he was clear about the metapsychological consequences of his procedure" (114–15, italics added). As between the interpretations of Eissler and of Lipton, Freud and Ferenczi would obviously have positioned themselves more with Lipton, albeit in Freud's case with more cautions.

A final note on what classical technique means, based on two papers by

Valenstein (1962, 1979), seventeen years apart. In the earlier paper, during the period when Eissler's views were so widely accepted, Valenstein offered a very positive appreciation of the connotation of "classical": "The effectiveness of the classical or standard psycho-analytic method, as it has developed and endured for sixty years, is due to its being in itself (to paraphrase Hartmann) much more preadapted to the average expectable clinical situation than may usually be realized. That is to say, it is applicable to a considerable range of clinical situations, unless it is prejudiced by irreversible or unanalyzable deviations in technique or innovations which make it no longer psycho-analytical in a classical sense" (319).

In his later paper (1979), written after Lipton had entered the fray and the concept of classical had lost some of its shine, Valenstein began with a set of questions: "Just what is meant by 'classical analysis?' Is it simply a euphemism to indicate a technical continuity with analysis as it was elaborated and practiced by Freud and his immediate followers—i.e., 'Freudian' psychoanalysis? Or does it imply more than historical kinship?" (114). He quoted three definitions of "classical" from Webster's Third New International Dictionary (1965). Two seem expected and standard: "regarded as of first historical significance" and "of any form or system felt to be the authentic, authoritative, or time-tested one." But the third meaning—"used of a coherent and authoritative theory, method, or body of ideas commonly after new developments or general change of view have made it generally less authoritative"—may convey Valenstein's implicit message. In his effort to take account of the changes in theory and practice since his earlier paper, Valenstein ruefully admitted that "commonly, classicism is understood to signify rigidity" (115), though he hastened to add that this need not necessarily be the case. The implicit plea might, however, be that perhaps the word had outlived some of its usefulness, that it had gotten caught in polemics and become too much either a beleaguered defensiveness or a pejorative dismissal, that perhaps it should even possibly be retired—though this is my reading, not Valenstein's explicit statement.

8 The Fragmenting of the Consensus: 1954–1979

As I have emphasized, for a significant period after the forging of the consensus in 1954 on what constituted psychoanalysis and what constituted the supportive and expressive psychoanalytic psychotherapies, the debates over these issues seem to have been stilled. The technical proposals of Alexander and his colleagues gradually receded in popularity; the techniques of Fromm-Reichmann and her like-minded confreres were pursued primarily within specialized psychoanalytic sanatoria; and to only a very limited degree with very sick individuals in outpatient settings. Grinker's propositions about "transactional psychotherapy" were hardly noticed by the psychoanalytic world; nor did Rado's altered nomenclature take root. Eissler's defining propositions about the nature of psychoanalysis as therapy were widely accepted almost as self-evident. And most of the psychoanalytically influenced psychiatric institutions and training centers were practicing and teaching psychoanalytically oriented psychotherapy in both the expressive and supportive variants. Many of the graduates of these programs naturally went on to seek full psychoanalytic training in the proliferating psychoanalytic institutes around the country to which the psychoanalyst faculty members in their psychiatric training programs belonged.

Few relevant papers appeared during that period, but one noteworthy exception was Herbert Schlesinger's (1969) attempt to clarify the semantics of the "expressive-supportive" issue. He pointed out that when we evaluate patients and prescribe a course of treatment, "we tend to resort to a nomenclature of treatment modalities that provide only a few widely spaced categories of psychological treatment"; the time-honored terms "expressive" and "supportive" "have come to be misapplied and, as used, no longer capture with any precision the distinctions they were coined to preserve" (270). Schlesinger's basic premise was that all therapies worthy of the name, including psychoanalysis, were always supportive and at the same time always expressive. For example, psychoanalysis, the quintessentially *expressive* approach, is, nonetheless, at the same time exquisitely *supportive*. (Where else does one have the opportunity—day after day, and for as many years as both parties deem it worthwhile—to unburden oneself fully to another human being devoted totally, during that time together, to listening, understanding, and conveying that understanding, without moral judgment, bias, or ulterior motive?) On the other hand, these are talking therapies, and, even in the most supportive mode, the patient is clearly *expressing* something of his concerns and anguishes. Schlesinger said, "By arrogating the name 'supportive' for a polar example of psychotherapy in which the purpose of supporting a patient is pursued in a particular way with particular techniques and with limited aspirations, we . . . tend to obscure the fact that support is one of the essential purposes of all psychotherapy, and we use it to imply a specific *kind* of psychotherapy—which it is not." He then offered a modifying suggestion: "It would not be amiss on logical grounds to term the treatment 'supportive' in which the psychotherapist must be ever mindful of the patient's need for support. But when used to denote a brand or type of psychotherapy this term has psychological pitfalls and may have unsought and even pernicious consequences. When 'supportive' is used as a type-modifier of psychotherapy, some therapists understand that the term requires the *exclusive* use of certain explicit supportive techniques and prohibits the use of certain other techniques (notably content and even defense interpretations)" (271). He recommended that the term be used to denote one of several interlocking purposes of *all* psychotherapy: "Thus, one must not only ask 'support what?' but also 'support *how?*'"—and then also "support when?" And, of course, "the therapist should also ask himself, when is support *un*necessary? After support, *then what?* . . . The fallacy which this question contains is the implication that the terms supportive and expressive as applied to psychotherapy are antithetical" (273). Reciprocally, every one of these considerations concerning the potential for mischief in using the term "supportive" to denote a distinct *kind* of therapy could be applied in reverse to the use of the term "expressive."

Schlesinger then described how these terms interlock in potentially confusing ways: "When we consider that a psychotherapist may help a patient *suppress* something by encouraging the *expression* of something else, the clarity of the logical distinction is lost. . . . Similarly 'expressive,' while not really of the same order, also characterizes all psychotherapy. A psychotherapy in which the patient is not helped to express something of the depth of himself would be quite unthinkable" (274). In a comparable paper written in the same year, Ira Miller (1969) proposed dealing with this dilemma by speaking of supportive and expressive measures, not therapies; he illustrated the interpenetration of these concepts by pointing to the potentially very supportive, anxiety-reducing aspects of an appropriate, well-timed interpretation.

This issue had, of course, not been unremarked before. Nearly all those involved in creating the distinctions articulated in the early 1950s pointed at one time or another to the difficulty of drawing clear-cut conceptual boundaries among the varying admixtures of intents and techniques that characterized actual therapies. Alexander (1954b), for example, noted that "supportive measures knowingly or inadvertently are used in all forms of psychotherapy, and conversely some degree of insight is rarely absent from any sound psychotherapeutic approach" (726). And the Menninger Psychotherapy Research Project had explicitly made room for "expressive-supportive psychotherapy as an admixture varyingly balanced, as one of the possible treatment recommendations, and as one of the possible judgments on the nature of a completed treatment" (Wallerstein et al. 1956)

Louis Paul (1963) had actually presaged much of Schlesinger's specific argument:

> One reason for distinguishing the two types of psychotherapy as uncovering and non-uncovering is that the customary term for the latter type, supportive psychotherapy, is inadequate because all psychotherapy is supportive in the sense that it augments temporarily reduced resources. To call one great class of psychotherapy supportive implies that the other is not, which is misleading. Predominantly uncovering psychotherapy has strong supportive elements; in fact without the supportive elements the patient would be unable and perhaps unwilling to undergo the discomfort of looking into himself. The distinguishing element between these two kinds of treatment is whether the *goal* is predominantly insight or uncovering, or whether it is a goal of not uncovering, or repressing or in some sense assisting the person without attempting to encourage him toward insight (287, italics added).

Of course, Schlesinger could argue that in an important sense Paul missed the point by maintaining a conceptual dichotomization under another rubric—non-uncovering instead of supportive—and with a different distinguishing criterion—goal instead of method. But whatever the arguments, as is so often the case, established semantic usage is difficult to alter and the terms "expressive" and "supportive" psychotherapy continued to be used as before, with, however, perhaps somewhat more explicit concern for the cautionary note sounded by Schlesinger.

The next significant marker in the psychoanalytic world's concern with the issues of psychoanalysis and psychotherapy was the decision by the Program Committee of the International Psychoanalytical Association to have a plenary session panel discussion entitled "The Relationship of Psychoanalysis to Psychotherapy—Current Issues" at the Rome Congress in 1969, the first such panel in its sixty-year history. I was invited to chair that panel and began my opening presentation (Wallerstein 1969) by noting, "This marks in effect the growing concern within the world-wide family of psychoanalytic endeavor with what has seemed for so long primarily a peculiarly American creation," (117) and, further, that the issues and controversies regarding the relationship between psychoanalysis and the dynamic psychotherapies that had been discussed so comprehensively in the United States fifteen years earlier still seemed very much with us, not appreciably altered, let alone resolved. This international congress would afford an opportunity to consider these issues from the wider vantage point of the experiences of psychoanalysts in diverse national and regional centers of psychoanalytic activity with differing historical developments and ecological settings.

I then reviewed and summarized the discussions of the early 1950s within the framework of a sequence of questions addressed to the international panel, each followed by a brief statement of the major positions expressed in the original panels. These questions were stated in summary as follows:

1. Is there a scientific psychotherapy apart from psychoanalysis?
2. What are the similarities and the differences between psychoanalysis and dynamic psychotherapy?
3. How important are the differences (or the similarities)? Should the differences be blurred or should they be sharpened?
4. What are the proper boundaries of each therapeutic modality? or When does "modified" psychoanalysis or psychoanalysis with parameters become psychotherapy?
5. How are differential treatment indications determined? Is the patient fitted to the treatment, or the treatment fitted to the patient?
6. What are the proper dividing lines across the range of psychotherapies conceptualized within the framework of psychoanalytic theory? Is the major dividing line between the expressive-uncovering therapeutic modalities (of which psychoanalysis is one) and the suppressive-supportive therapeutic modalities? Which divisions are meaningful, in theory and in practice?
7. What is the relation to non-psychoanalytic therapy? Can a theory of psychoanalytic therapy extend to a psychoanalytic theory of all therapy?
8. Can derivative conflicts, can any conflicts, be substantially resolved by means short of psychoanalysis?
9. What are our problems as psychoanalysts in doing psychotherapy? (125–26)

Although the issues that had concerned the panels a decade and a half earlier could be framed in 1969 in very much the same terms, despite whatever advances and changes had taken place in the meantime, both in widening clinical experience with extended categories of patients, and significant theoretical changes, it is nonetheless clear that much was happening in psychoanalysis that did bear clearly on the issue of psychotherapy vis-à-vis psychoanalysis—and that would need to find expression at some point in the modification of the dialogue around these specific issues. I am referring here to such trends as the delineation of the therapeutic alliance (or working alliance) as distinct from the transference evolution, with the postulated interactive relationship between the two; the growing focus on the affectively charged therapeutic relationship as a coequal determinant, with veridical interpretations leading to working through and mutative insights, in bringing about meaningful therapeutic change; the burgeoning of a dynamic psychotherapy derived from psychoanalysis in other centers around the world, most particularly Great Britain; the increasing acceptance of theoretical diversity within psychoanalysis around the world, with all the inevitable issues that that would inevitably raise of where then the boundaries between psychoanalysis and the derivative psychotherapies could be properly drawn and where one person's psychoanalysis would readily become another's psychotherapy; and, finally, the new diagnostic and therapeutic conceptualizations being advanced in regard to the widening arc of patients appearing in psychoanalytic consulting rooms, particularly the borderline personality organizations and the narcissistic personality disorders, and the extent to which these new conceptualizations should be marked as still psychoanalytic or as clearly psychotherapeutic. These trends will be considered in detail in parts IV and V. All together, they clearly added both urgency and cogency to efforts within psychoanalytic ranks to maintain the distinctiveness of psychoanalysis and of psychoanalytically based psychotherapy with their clearly (or not so clearly) differentiated spheres of application to the array of psychopathological formations subjected to psychotherapeutic intervention. This was all the more striking as the more classical symptom pictures, around which our theory and practice were originally conceptualized, were seeming to dwindle in our consulting rooms.

Clearly, the landscape of psychotherapies required reassessment in the light of these developments in theory and these shifts in patient population. Toward this end, the Southern Regional Psychoanalytic Societies (in the United States) sponsored a symposium in 1979 to which three of the central protagonists in the discussions published in 1954, Gill, Rangell, and Stone, were invited to present their updated views on the similarities and differences between psychoanalysis and psychotherapy, a 25-year perspective. Gill, Rangell, and Stone had been essentially in agreement during the debates of the early 1950s, representatives of the majority classical position that there was a spectrum of psychotherapies, with clearly differentiated modalities along that spectrum from psychoanalysis to expressive psychotherapy, the "intermediate therapy," to supportive psychotherapy—each with specific applicability to a particular nosologically reasonably coherent segment of patients.[1]

1. For an illustration of the firm concordance of their views during the discussions of the early

The forceful and united voice with which the three contributors to the Atlanta panel had spoken a quarter-century earlier made their divergence of views in 1979—on precisely the same questions and issues—all the more impressive—reflecting at that point substantial shifts in the climate of thinking about psychotherapy and psychoanalysis and their relationship that I had indicated seemed in 1969 (just a decade earlier) to have persisted essentially unchanged. It is this shift that I have called the era of fragmented consensus, the third era in the development of psychoanalytic psychotherapy (after the first era of the prehistory and the second era of the emerging consensus). This third era is one in which the broad consensus that had characterized mainstream psychoanalytic thinking in this area and that reflected the rise of psychodynamic psychotherapy as a distinctive, differentiated, and prized off-shoot of psychoanalysis had clearly given way by the end of the 1970s (Wallerstein 1989a). It is this 1979 panel that I now review.

It was Leo Stone's views that were the most subtly nuanced in 1954 and also survived most nearly intact in the 1979 retrospective. Basically, Stone (1982) adhered to his earlier distinctions between the psychoanalytic psychotherapist and the psychoanalyst practicing psychoanalysis in the (quantitatively) greater reality orientation and more manifest "physicianly attitudes" of the former. For example: "The therapist's activity, instead of taking a reductive direction slanted toward the genetic-infantile environment or its currently unconscious representations, tends to preserve the patient's cathexis of his real and immediate environment—his cathexis of persons, or problems as such, and conflicts as such—and (very importantly) his cathexis of the essential realities of the patient-doctor relationship" (86–87).[2] And again: "The psychotherapist remains avowedly a physician, employing a specialized psychological technique; whereas the analyst, in his technique, sets aside the manifest physicianly attitudes except as they remain implicit in the long-term goals and purposes of the treatment" (86).

Stone then added a characteristically subtle new distinction between the special character of the interpretation in psychotherapy as compared with psychoanalysis:

1950s, see their definitional subscriptions of psychoanalysis, pp. 76-77 and footnote 2, chapter 5).

2. Stone's presentation at the 1979 Atlanta Symposium was never published as such. The ideas in it were incorporated into a paper he was preparing at the same time for the Eighth Conference on Training held in July 1979 as part of the 31st Congress of the International Psycho-Analytical Association (personal communication). The topic of the IPA Conference on Training was "Psychotherapy: Impact on Psychoanalytic Training." Stone's address to that conference was entitled "The Influence of the Practice and Theory of Psychotherapy on Education in Psychoanalysis" (Stone 1982). My quotations are from that 1982 paper.

[Interpretation in psychotherapy,] instead of orienting itself to facilitating the spontaneously evolving transference neurosis of the basic psychoanalytic situation, . . . is usually based on the therapist's conception of what constitutes the major and currently active conflict or conflicts in the patient's presenting illness or disturbed adaptation, and the relationship of such conflict or conflicts to his actual objects. . . . Interpretations, moreover, tend to be holistic, integrative (Stone, 1951), minimizing the distinctions between defense and impulse, infantile and current, emphasizing large, accessible, and readily intelligible personality dynamisms, except as more detailed elements present themselves unequivocally for such understanding.

Now, what is the basic differentiating element that emerges from this non-authoritarian but firm maintenance of the central position of current reality in all references, and from the marked diminution of the specifically and uniquely analytic abstinences (e.g., from the maintenance of the critical sensory input of visualization of the doctor, the communicative give and take of discussion, and the evident physicianly role of the therapist)? The adult representations of the basic positive child-parent longings of early life . . . are gratified in integrated form; the tendency toward regression and manifest fantasy formation is diminished; and the ungratified transference assumes a less diffuse, more selective form. (87–88)

Summarizing his views, Stone wrote, "Interpretations remain largely 'in situ,' so to speak, in relation to individuals involved in the patient's actual daily life . . . because the principal libidinal and aggressive investments reside, in fact, in these relationships" (89). Neither in the 1950s nor in 1979 did Stone explicitly try, within the range of psychoanalytic psychotherapies, to demarcate the more interpretive (expressive) from the less interpretive or noninterpretive (supportive) modes—as Knight and Gill and the PRP had done. Stone's long-time consistency in this regard was expressed in a skeptical discussion in this 1979 presentation of Knight's original proposal of the expressive-supportive distinction:

The essential idea [of supportive psychotherapy] is that the therapist aligns himself with the patient's defenses, fostering them rather than seeking to weaken them. While this is conceptually and schematically reasonable, it does not lend itself readily to technical specification; and I would feel some doubt that it can often be achieved in a direct and purposive sense. That the negative side of the same coin—the avoidance of the literally analytic type of interpretation, especially defense interpretations—may be feasible and useful remains true, as it remains true that the therapist's informed interest in and support for the patient's current and potential adaptive struggle in his real environment may itself be beneficial. (1982, 92)

But Stone did allow for some crystallization of nodal points along the expressive-supportive psychotherapeutic continuum when he said of the more supportive approach, "The effort is to provide a sense of friendly and reliable alliance in the therapeutic situation, involving the ordinary modalities of sympathetic listening, rational encouragement, sometimes simple advice and guidance. To varying degree, there may be added whatever modicum of broad understanding of himself and his environment that may seem to contribute directly to the patient's greater comfort and effectiveness, or to be required by the emergence of confronting conflict. This type of supportive effort should be taken very seriously" (93). And this, in Stone's view, can be compatible with distinctive interpretive work: "Interpretation always remains distinctively and often critically useful even in essentially noninterpretive contexts. Thus the relationship between interpretation and other psychotherapeutic modes (even those apparently opposite) is often truly dialectical. . . . I do not believe that support and interpretation are intrinsically and inevitably opposed, except perhaps in the choice of intervention with respect to a given specific issue" (94–95).

Finally, Stone essentially restated the indications for psychotherapy versus psychoanalysis he had laid down in 1951 (224–25)—despite his articulation in his "widening scope" paper of 1954 of the multitudinous efforts to expand the scope of psychoanalysis to ever-widening circles of less specifically amenable patients. In 1979, he again identified the chronic transference neuroses (in Freud's original sense) and the reasonably severe character neuroses as the proper candidates for "strict and untendentious psychoanalysis": "Yet it is quite likely that many such cases, of milder grade, especially when incipient, would do well with a proximal form of interpretive psychotherapy" (100)—again in keeping with the conviction voiced in 1951 and 1954 that many typical neurotics, though clearly amenable to psychoanalysis, are not sufficiently ill or emotionally incapacitated to warrant such an effort at thoroughgoing character reorganization. And as for the indications for psychotherapy, "For acute fresh neurotic conditions, for panics of uncertain nature, for situational entanglements, problems of transition, and personal crises of varied nature, it seems to me that psychotherapy represents the treatment of choice, sometimes to be followed by analysis in the future" (102).

Stone's remarkable steadiness of perspective contrasts sharply with the significantly altered views of the other principal protagonists in the 1979 panel discussion. The individual whose views I think shifted most radically over the intervening years (though he would not necessarily agree) is Merton Gill. In the early 1950s, following upon Knight, Gill was clearest in his distinctions among psychoanalysis, expressive psychotherapy, and supportive psychotherapy. The very radical shift I see in his views is to me, a direct consequence of his evolving preoccupation over this period with the interpretation of the transference as *the* overriding criterion of psychoanalysis and what is psychoanalytic. His newer views on the nature and place of transference interpretation—the distinction between resistance to the awareness of transference and resistance to the resolution of transference; the emphasis on the earliest possible interpretation of the transference (including making the implicit transferences explicit from the very start of the treatment); the focus on the here and now as against the genetic thrust ("there and then") in the transference interpretation; and the elaboration of the implications of what Gill calls the two-person as against the one-person view of the two participants' contributions to the transference—are discussed in detail in chapters 12 and 21. Here I will pursue only their implications for Gill's (now very significantly altered) views on the nature of psychoanalysis and psychotherapy and their relationship as specified in his contribution to the 1979 Atlanta Symposium.

Gill developed these new views with his customary logical precision. "The thrust of my 1954 paper," he said, "was to *insist on the difference* [between psychoanalysis and psychotherapy] and at the same time to *recognize* that the two are on a *continuum*" (1984, 162, italics added). He then reviewed the "intrinsic criteria" by which analysis is usually defined ("the centrality of the analysis of transference, a neutral analyst, the induction of a regressive transference neurosis and the resolution of that neurosis by techniques of interpretation alone, or at least mainly by interpretation"—all strikingly the same as his 1954 definition) as well as the often commonly indicated "extrinsic criteria" or markers ("frequent sessions, the couch, a relatively well integrated patient, that is, one who is considered analysable, and a fully trained psychoanalyst" [161]). Then: "The question of the relationship between psychoanalysis and psychotherapy is even more important in practice today than it was in 1954 because of the practical difficulties in maintaining the ordinarily accepted extrinsic criteria of analysis. . . . The question becomes: How widely can the range of extrinsic criteria be expanded before the analyst must decide for psychotherapy rather than psychoanalysis?" (162).

After reviewing the sociocultural and economic difficulties analysts have today in maintaining the usual external criteria of psychoanalysis, Gill went on to say, "The changes I will propose are more radical than a simple extension of the recommendation I made in 1954 that we carry more of the non-directive spirit of psychoanalysis into our psychotherapies." Rather,

> I will argue that with the definition of analytic technique at which I will finally arrive, it should be taught to *all psychotherapists* and that how well it will be employed will depend on their training and natural talent for the work. . . . I mean that analytic technique as I will define it should be employed as much as possible even if the patient comes less frequently than is usual in psychoanalysis, uses the chair rather than the couch, is not necessarily committed to a treatment of relatively long duration, is sicker than the usually considered analyzable patient and even if the therapist is relatively inexperienced. In other words, I will recommend that we sharply *narrow* the indications for psychoanalytic *psychotherapy* and *primarily practice psychoanalysis as I shall define it* instead (163, italics added).

What we see here, of course, is a proposal to assimilate to psychoanalysis what Gill in 1954 had taken such pains to demarcate as expressive psychotherapy—in other words, to blur, perhaps to obliterate, the differences between psychoanalysis and this "intermediate" psychoanalytic psychotherapy that he once felt it so vital to maintain. In effect, this is a revival of the position of Alexander and his followers on this issue that Gill had once led the (largely successful) effort to reject.

Gill acknowledged the basis for these radically altered views: "The recommendation I am proposing is an outgrowth of my changed views on transference and its analysis" (164). And further: "My reconceptualization of these intrinsic criteria of analysis, namely transference and its analysis, the neutral analyst, the regressive transference neurosis, free association, and the role of experience in addition to interpretation, leads me to the conclusion that the centrality of the analysis of transference, as I have defined transference, . . . is alone the distinguishing characteristic of . . . psychoanalysis. It is what distinguishes it from psychotherapy. It remains for me to try to show that it can be maintained *even in an expanded range of external criteria*" (172, italics added).

Gill then developed his ideas that even a certain frequency and the use of the couch may be dispensable in proper psychoanalytic work—depending on the patient and, implicitly, on the patient-analyst duo:

> While the couch is ordinarily considered to be conducive to regression, it may enable an isolation from the relationship which has a contrary effect. No universal meaning of any aspect of the analytic setting may be taken for granted. It follows that no universal prescription can be given for this or that type of case. One may generalize that analytic work goes

better with healthier patients lying down and sicker patients sitting up and with frequent sessions for both kinds of patients, but a particular patient may not conform to the rule. The meaning of the setting must be analyzed in each instance. Nor is degree of pathology the only variable which determines a patient's response to the analysis of transference. Apart from pathology, some take to it like a duck to water and can work despite infrequent sessions, while others never seem to find it congenial. (174)

Gill then dealt once again with the impact of each of the usual external parameters of the psychoanalytic situation. On frequency: "It would seem obvious that one can accomplish more with greater frequency simply because there is more time to work. But if greater frequency is frightening to a particular patient, frequent sessions may impede the work despite interpretation. One cannot simply assume that more is better. The optimal frequency may differ from patient to patient. We must not confuse optimal frequency with obligatory ritualized frequency" (174). About the couch, similarly: "The argument that psychoanalytic technique cannot be used in the face-to-face position because of the reality cues afforded the patient is a variant of the mistaken idea that it is the external stimulus rather than the patient's interpretation of that stimulus that matters. Discussions of the issue seem to gravitate to quantitative terms as though there are fewer stimuli if the patient cannot see the analyst. It may be that the patient facing the analyst is exposed to a wider range of stimuli but the patient's response is to the quality, not the quantity, of stimuli." And about the experience of the therapist: "Therapists use the technique to whatever degree their skill and comfort in exposing the transferential experience of the relationship permits." Finally, on the relatively long duration and open-endedness of analytic work: "I do not know the lower limit in duration for the use of the technique I advocate, but I have used it successfully in once-a-week therapy preset to last no longer than nine months" (175). And so on.

Gill declared that central to all the aspects of the psychoanalytic situation he was challenging was the "implicit assumption" that "analysis is a kind of all-or-none proposition, yielding its positive results only if carried through to the end. It is this belief which may sustain patient and analyst through long periods of apparent stagnation and stalemate, but this belief is often a vain illusion. Freud compared interrupting an analysis to the interruption of a surgical operation. I suggest, on the contrary, that in the changed way of conducting it which I am proposing, analysis may be a process with progressively cumulative benefits, interruptible at various points without necessary loss of what has been gained" (176). Surely, thus defining the prevailing view of psychoanalysis is setting up something of a straw man since analysis can assuredly stop in all stages of incompleteness, quite aside from the understanding that in theory, analysis is *never* complete in any but an asymptotic sense. None of this, however, is the same as amalgamating every expressive-interpretive psychotherapy to psychoanalysis, as Gill wants to do, with the sole stipulation that the therapeutic thrust be unswervingly focused on interpretation of the (implicit as well as explicit) transferences in the here and now.

In this whole uncompromising statement of such a radically altered perspective Gill made only one small concession to the generally prevailing views he was challenging. At the beginning of his article he said, "Although I will propose that psychoanalysis . . . as I define it is applicable across the whole range of psychopathology, my convictions are the strongest for its application to patients ordinarily considered analysable for whom issues of time and money preclude the usual setting of an analysis" (161).

Where, then, would this leave the field of psychotherapy vis-à-vis psychoanalysis? Gill asked the question this way: "Should the use of the technique I describe in less than the optimal setting for an analysis still be called psychoanalysis?" Gill obviously felt that the answer was yes, though he did say that "other things being equal, obviously an analysis conducted at lesser frequency cannot accomplish what otherwise could be" and "There ought to be different names for an analysis carried through as fully as it could be and one which is partial and incomplete." The only variant name he proposed at this point was "psychoanalytic psychotherapy," which he now said "should be reserved for a technique which *does not* deal with the transference in the way I have suggested is the essential criterion of analytic technique" (176, italics added).[3] In other words, "psychoanalytic psychotherapy" should be the designation for that therapeutic approach which is *not* psychoanalysis (i.e., does not systematically interpret transference)—what Knight originally, and Gill after him, called in the 1940s and 1950s psychoanalytically oriented *supportive* psychotherapy. In a further retrograde perspective, there is even more than passing allusion to the feeling that this psychotherapy-which-is-not-psychoanalysis rests fundamentally on "witting and unwitting suggestion" (177)—a return to what I have called the first era in the developmental history of dynamic psychotherapy, the era of

---

3. At this point Gill both proposed and withdrew what would have been a truly confusing change of nomenclature: "If a therapy which uses analytic technique with less than optimal extrinsic criteria and without the intention of going as far as one could be called neither psychoanalysis nor psychoanalytic psychotherapy, what should it be called? Psychoanalytic therapy might be a solution though that name was used by Alexander for what I would call psychoanalytic psychotherapy" (176). Gill clearly decided to let the matter rest at calling it *all* psychoanalysis or psychoanalytic—except for what he was segregating off as psychoanalytic psycho*therapy*.

the views of Freud and Ferenczi and Jones and Glover on suggestion as the "all-else" in therapy other than "strict and untendentious psycho-analysis."

Gill's radically altered views on these issues stemmed, as he acknowledged, from the evolution of his own particular conceptions of the nature of the transference and the role of transference interpretation in the therapeutic process. There is yet a third position to be distilled out of the 1979 Symposium, one much more influenced by and in tune with the changing Zeitgeist in psychoanalysis between 1954 and 1979. That is the position enunciated by Leo Rangell (1981b) at the 1979 Symposium and one, incidentally, for which the data of the Menninger Psychotherapy Research Project provide compelling support. It can be situated between the relatively unchanged position propounded by Stone and Gill's radical return to the once-rejected views of Alexander and his co-workers, albeit far closer to Stone's position. Rangell stated that the views he was now expressing came from the experiential vantage point of forty years of clinical practice, and he invited his readers to compare them with their own cumulated clinical experience.

Since the Atlanta Symposium was set up in a debate format, it was perhaps inevitable that a significant segment of Rangell's presentation was devoted to a rebuttal of Gill's revisionist views. Rangell's repeated call for *balance* in perspective was clearly at variance with Gill's central thesis. The concept of balance was stated thus: "The analyst roams with free-floating attention over these *three* pillars of every analytic hour [present, past, and then transference], without allowing himself to become excessively attached to one. It is like a needle on an instrument panel designed to record a certain area. If the needle gets stuck, it may need a little tap to continue to survey the *entire* area" (1981b, 677, italics added). And "There is no analysis from dreams alone. The analyst hovers, equidistant not only from the three psychic structures but between intrapsychic and interpersonal, the internal and external world, past and present, transference and original objects. There is also no analysis from resistances alone, from defenses, without coming to what is defended against. If a patient relates only to the analyst, or to external objects and not the transference figure, or if he speaks of the past and not the present, or only about sex, or only the deep unconscious without the daily and trivial, the needle has become stuck and needs a tap" (678).[4]

But Rangell's main concern in the 1979 Symposium was to stake out his own (modified) position in regard to the relationship between psychotherapy and psychoanalysis, a position I have called (Wallerstein 1986a, 1988b) the "infiltration" of psychoanalysis by psycho*therapeutic* techniques, while nonetheless

4. The balance of Rangell's many-sided response to Gill's views will be presented in chapter 10.

maintaining conceptual clarity around their differences. Rangell stated this conception as follows:

> But just as analysts apply analytic principles freely and copiously to their practice of dynamic psychotherapy, reciprocally and empirically, with ever-increasing complexity and length of psychoanalysis, the opposite also holds. There is no analysis without its share of each of the technical maneuvers noted by Bibring (1954) [i.e., suggestion, abreaction, manipulation, and clarification, along with interpretation], which he also described as occurring in both techniques but which typically are considered to characterize mainly psychotherapy. . . . There is no analysis without some of these mechanisms, which are not inadvertent but built-in and by design. Nor are they of themselves necessarily parameters [a response also to Eissler] but accessory and preparatory modes *intrinsic* to the treatment. There is no analytic case treated by interpretation alone, in spite of Gill's definition of 1954. If this were a prerequisite, no treatment would qualify as analytic. This is an empirical conclusion based not on theoretical preconception but on my composite experience. (670–71).

This is the crux of Rangell's argument; the rest was amplification. For example, returning to the theme of the similarities and differences between psychoanalysis and dynamic psychotherapy, he stated, "Since the comparisons of 1954, increasing experience and precision of technique have led to a *lessening of the differences between the two.* Structural change of time-enduring quality, although thought previously to characterize mainly psychoanalysis, can be achieved in analytic therapy carefully chosen and performed. Leo Stone noted this in his 1954 paper and has since confirmed and strengthened this view. I have been able to reach convincing elements of patients' infantile neuroses in consistent analytic psychotherapy, with results comparable to what I have come to expect in psychoanalysis" (679–80, italics added). And "Empirically, it is not uncommon in practice for there to be a gap between the trains of free associations and the infantile experiences to which we believe they lead. While it might be assumed to be a distinguishing mark between psychotherapy and psychoanalysis that such a gap between data and interpretation exists only in psychotherapy, I would like to point out that this also occurs regularly in psychoanalysis and that this point is not sufficiently appreciated. . . . The link from current associations or behavior to castration anxiety is not typically made without what one of my patients described as 'the creative leap' which he felt was necessary from the analyst to him" (680).

The essence of this position, this intermingling of analytic and therapeutic techniques in all therapies, is nonetheless that psychoanalysis and psychotherapy are still distinct, with separately categorizable techniques. Rangell put this in relatively simple quantitative terms:

> While I have been largely discussing overlapping areas, there are also lines of demarcation between the two fields today as there were in 1954. I said then that there is day and night, although there is dusk (Rangell, 1954b). There are still differences in quality and quantity, in consistency and goals, in the uniformity and relentlessness of approach. The distances between the observational data and the genetic mysteries to which they open doors are generally less in psychoanalysis than in dynamic psychotherapy. Again a disclaimer: it is possible in an individual case to bridge this synapse effectively in psychotherapy while the distance may remain wide and the links over it sterile and theoretical even in a well-conducted analysis. (682)

And in conclusion, "As a long-range observation over the years, empirically there is . . . a large borderland in which therapeutic procedures are practiced in a gray area between 'psychoanalysis with parameters' and steady intensive psychotherapy which is not quite psychoanalysis. My belief today is that it is still possible to draw a line between the two, although it is also true that in many cases this line is difficult to define" (682–83). This, overall, was the panorama of the new third-era debate, with its crystallized and quite discrepant positions on the nature of the relationship between psychoanalysis and the derivative psychoanalytically based psychotherapies, as epitomized by the three protagonists in the 1979 Symposium, Gill, Rangell, and Stone, who were so together in their viewpoints during the critical panels of the early 1950s that had staked out the then-emergent second-era consensus on these issues. It is clear from these views that that consensus had fragmented by 1979.

In this context, it is worthwhile to consider the findings of the Psychotherapy Research Project (Wallerstein 1986a, 1988b), which resonate impressively with Rangell's position in the 1979 Atlanta debate. PRP had been conceived and designed in the early 1950s within the crucible of the crystallizing second-era consensus on the spectrum of psychoanalytic therapies.[5] The PRP results were written up shortly after the 1979 Atlanta Symposium and in the context of the

---

5. The definitions we used, the indications (and contraindications) we prescribed, and the procedures and techniques that we said differentially characterized the different therapeutic modes have already been at least partially stated in chapter 5. They are described at length in the initial publication from PRP (Wallerstein et al. 1956). The final clinical accounting of the treatment courses and outcomes of the forty-two patients and their subsequent life courses over a thirty-year time span has been published in book form (Wallerstein 1986a); a summary of the main conclusions from that work has been published in article form (Wallerstein 1988b).

new ferment that characterized what I have called the third era in the history of dynamic psychotherapy. Our systematic empirical findings bore directly on these very issues, and in a manner most congruent with the conclusions of Rangell, which were based, in his instance, on his clinical observations in a solo practice. To summarize drastically from the published article (Wallerstein 1988b), itself a summary of a very long book:

The project cohort consisted of forty-two patients, half in psychoanalysis and half in varying admixtures of expressive and supportive psychoanalytic psychotherapy. During the course of treatment some patients were deliberately and some were de facto shifted from psychoanalysis to psychotherapy; within the group in psychotherapy there were also some planned as well as some unplanned shifts along the expressive-supportive dimension, and these were uniformly in the supportive direction. In studying the individual case write-ups of these patients, from their pretreatment Initial Studies to their post-treatment Termination Studies and then the planned Follow-up Studies (with data on 100 percent of the cohort), I elaborated our data-based reorganization and amplification of the various supportive mechanisms and interventions (some twelve in all, see Wallerstein 1988b, 135–40), presented earlier by Knight, Alexander, Gill, Stone, and others. Using our project data as the base, I spelled out the operation of each of these twelve mechanisms in the patient case histories (and subsequent life histories) (Wallerstein 1988b, 135–40; 1986a, 373–510). In my paper (1988b), I brought our overall Project conclusions together as a series of sequential propositions regarding the appropriateness, efficacy, reach, and limitations of psychoanalysis (varyingly classical and modified) and of psychoanalytic psychotherapies (varyingly expressive and supportive) (see 1988b, 144–49):

1. In regard to the distinctions between so-called structural change, presumably based on the interpretive resolution of unconscious intrapsychic conflicts, and behavioral changes (or changes in "manifest behavior patterns"), which presumably are all that can come out of nonexpressive, noninterpretive, non-insight-aiming change mechanisms, I strongly question the continued usefulness of the effort to link the *kind* of change achieved so tightly to the intervention mode by which it is brought about. The changes reached in our more supportive therapies and via intrinsically supportive modes often seemed just as "structural" as the changes reached in our most expressive-analytic cases.

2. Therapeutically induced change will be at least proportional to the degree of achieved conflict resolution (the so-called proportionality argument)—though it is clear that significant change can additionally

be brought about on bases other than interpretation, working through, and achievement of insight.

3. Effective conflict resolution turned out *not* to be necessary to thera-peutic change (the so-called necessity argument). An almost overriding finding was that a substantial range of changes was brought about via the more supportive psychotherapeutic modes and techniques, cutting across the gamut of declared supportive *and* expressive (even analytic) therapies, and these changes were (in many instances) quite indistin-guishable from the changes brought about by typically expressive-analytic (interpretive, insight-producing) means.

4. Counterpart to the proposition based on the tendency to overestimate the necessity of the expressive (analytic) treatment mode to effect ther-apeutically desired change has been the happy finding that the sup-portive psychotherapeutic approaches and techniques often achieved far more than was initially expected of them and did so in ways that often represented indistinguishably structural changes in terms of the usual indicators of that state. Most of the treatments (psychotherapeutic and psychoanalytic alike) had been substantially altered during their course in varyingly supportive directions, and more of the patients had changed on the basis of designedly supportive interventions and mech-anisms than had been initially predicted.

5. Just as more was accomplished than expected with psychotherapy, es-pecially in its more supportive modes, so psychoanalysis, as the quin-tessentially expressive therapeutic mode, was more limited—at least with these patients—than had been anticipated. This, of course, sig-nificantly reflected the nature of the patient population at the Men-ninger Foundation, considerably "sicker" than those in the usual outpatient private practice setting. Certainly, these disappointing out-comes of analytic treatments with these sicker patients invite a reposi-tioning of the pendulum in the direction of narrowing the indications for (proper) psychoanalysis, along the lines marked out by Anna Freud (1954).

6. Taken together, the psychoanalyses as a whole, as well as the expressive psychotherapies as a whole, were systematically modified in the direc-tion of introducing more supportive components in widely varying ways, they had more limited outcomes than promised (hoped), and an often substantial amount of that was accomplished by noninterpre-tive—i.e., supportive—means. The psychotherapies, on the other hand, often accomplished a good deal more than was initially expected.

Given these observations and conclusions from the PRP, what can be said overall about the evolving relationship of psychoanalysis and its derivative dynamic psychotherapies? This is summarized in the final pages of my 1988 article:

1. The treatment results, with patients selected either as suitable for trials at psychoanalysis, or as appropriate for varying mixes of expressive-supportive psychotherapeutic approaches, tended—with this population sample—to converge, rather than diverge, in outcome.

2. Across the whole spectrum of treatment in the 42 patients, ranging from the most analytic-expressive, through the inextricably blended, on to the most single-mindedly supportive, in almost every instance—the psychoanalyses included—the treatment carried more supportive elements than originally intended, and these supportive elements accounted for substantially more of the changes achieved than had been originally anticipated.

3. The nature of supportive therapy, or better the supportive aspects of all psychotherapy as conceptualized within a psychoanalytic theoretical framework and as deployed by psychoanalytically knowledgeable therapists, bears far more respectful specification in all its form variants than has usually been accorded it in the psychodynamic literature.[6]

4. When studying the kinds of changes reached by this cohort of patients, partly on an uncovering, insight-aiming basis and partly on the basis of the opposed covering-up varieties of supportive techniques, the changes themselves—divorced from how they were brought about—often seemed quite indistinguishable from each other, in terms of being so-called real or structural changes in personality functioning.

In the light of the conceptual and predictive framework within which the Psychotherapy Research Project of the Menninger Foundation was planned and implemented three decades earlier, there is, of course, considerable real surprise to the overall project findings: that these distinctive therapeutic modalities of psychoanalysis, expressive psychotherapy, supportive psychotherapy, etc., hardly exist in anywhere near ideal or pure form in the real world of actual practice; that real treatments in actual practice are inextricably intermingled blends of more or less expressive-interpretive and more or less supportive-stabilizing elements; that almost all treatments (including even presum-

---

6. For a detailed exposition of the dozen differing supportive mechanisms and modes delineated by PRP, see Wallerstein 1986a, 373–510; for a summary of these, see Wallerstein 1988b, 135–40.

ably pure psychoanalyses) carry many more supportive components
than are usually credited to them; that the overall outcomes achieved
by those treatments that are more "analytic" as against those that are
more "supportive" are less apart than our usual expectations for those
differing modalities would portend; and that the kinds of changes
achieved in treatments from the two ends of this spectrum are less
different in nature and in permanence, than again is usually expected,
and indeed can often not be easily distinguished. (Wallerstein 1988b,
149–50)

Overall, these conclusions from an intensive empirical study of the processes
and outcomes of psychoanalysis and psychoanalytically based psychotherapies,
as conceptualized within the formulations of the mainstream consensus of the
early 1950s—conclusions that emerged in the midst of "the era of fragmented
consensus" among once like-minded colleagues—fell, like Rangell's between
the later views of Gill and Stone. They did not support Gill's effort in effect to
collapse all expressive and exploratory approaches into "more or less" psychoanalysis while pushing all supportive approaches back toward an undifferentiated
suggestion. The one part seems a revival in new form of the movement spark-
plugged by Alexander with its effort toward merger of dynamic psychiatry with
psychoanalysis; the other part seems a revival in new form of the original positions of Freud, Ferenczi, Jones, and Glover from the era that predated the
theoretical articulation of psychotherapies that were derived from psychoanalysis
but were distinct from it. Nor did the PRP findings support reiterations of the
1950s consensus on the clear-cut distinctions among psychotherapeutic modalities. Though the differences between psychoanalysis and expressive and supportive psychotherapy are real, the boundaries and the seemingly specific
deployments are also much less clear-cut, with—and this is the major understanding of the results of the Menninger Project—inevitable infiltrations, advertent or inadvertent, of more supportive techniques and modes into even the
purest of expressive-analytic approaches.

I will close this chapter with a few additional references that each bring a
special perspective to these issues. Otto Kernberg (1983) (who had been an
active member of PRP and took on the principal directing role when I left the
Menninger Foundation in 1966) laid out his way of demarcating expressive from
supportive psychotherapy within the constraints of PRP. Expressive psychotherapy, he stated, rested centrally on clarification, confrontation, and interpretation, and he emphasized the importance of the unremitting effort to do this
within the framework of precise "technical neutrality." Transference interpretations, the central technical tool, should also be codetermined by the patient's

predominant transference position, the immediate external reality, and the specific treatment goals. By contrast, supportive psychotherapy rested on clarification and confrontation, in order to highlight "inappropriate" or "unrealistic" aspects of the transference (but not interpretation in a technical sense) plus varieties of adjunct cognitive and emotional supports. Here "the use of suggestion, advice, and environmental intervention eliminates technical neutrality by design" (257). This specific emphasis on the maintenance or, oppositely, the abrogation of technical neutrality as the hallmark of expressive as against supportive psychotherapies seems implicit in all the other authors cited in this chapter.

Paul Myerson (1981) cautioned against the allure of ad hominem argumentation in the to-and-fro of debates (whether in 1954 or 1979) in this arena: "Where the analyst has decided not to use a classical approach and has decided to apply a more confronting, manipulative, or supportive technique, the critical observer can always suggest that the analyst's departure from the classical, more normative approach was unnecessary and was brought about by countertransference or by an idiosyncratic theoretical orientation. On the other hand, the analyst and his defenders can respond to his critics by claiming that the analysand's personality structure made it essential to modify the classical approach" (173). This is a caution to be borne in mind in all scientific discourse, especially, of course, in our field.

And finally Fred Pine (1984), in an article entitled "The Interpretive Moment," began with recommendations based on conceptions similar to those advanced by Schlesinger (1969) and discussed at the beginning of this chapter: that the distinction "expressive-supportive" is often specious or mischievous or both. He ended with his own effort to redefine this distinction. At the "interpretive moment" with the normal-neurotic (analyzable) patient, the therapist would bend his efforts to heighten the affective impact of interpretation; with the more "fragile" patients, who are most vulnerable when they are most influenceable, the therapist might choose to "strike [interpretively] while the iron is cold" (60)—that is, when the intensity of affective involvement has diminished. This is done via a variety of "supportive" maneuvers, for example, preparing the patient for the fact that the interpretation may not be pleasant to hear, rendering it tentatively, according the patient the explicit right to accept, modify, or reject it, and so on. These measures to facilitate interpretive work with sicker patients (described more explicitly in chapter 11) have necessary implications for the expressive-supportive dichotomy. Pine put it as follows: "The clinical procedures I have described blur the distinction between insight and supportive therapies in at least two ways. The first way is that *support* (a style of intervention that attempts to keep the patient's defenses functioning at their best and that provides a 'holding' object-related context in the patient-therapist relationship) helps to advance interpretations, i.e., to work toward *insight*. The second stems from the underlying belief that insight is one of the best forms of *support*" (66). This thinking led Pine quite logically to the statement that "too great a separation between insight and supportive therapies has been detrimental to theory-building regarding supportive work" (67)—and to his own efforts to conceptually integrate expressive and supportive approaches. In this sense, "this supportive approach in the here and now of the therapy relationship makes it possible to introduce interpretive work and its potential benefits into treatments that might otherwise not be amenable to interpretation" (69). Pine's proposed redefinition would be not between expressive and supportive approaches but between interpretations given in the context of abstinence (expressive approaches, including, of course, psychoanalysis proper) and interpretations given in the context of support (the work Pine described with the more fragile patients).

9 A World without Consensus: 1979–1994

The conceptual untidiness produced by the fragmenting of the 1954 consensus, which became so evident in the 1979 reconceptualizations of three of the major protagonists of this earlier theory building, Gill, Rangell, and Stone, who had been so together in 1954 and were so apart in 1979, has persisted ever since. We have essentially been living in a vastly enlarged psychoanalytic world, with many diverse lines of theoretical and clinical development (to be described in detail in later chapters); it is now a world without consensus.

In one sense, there have been no significant conceptual changes in this arena since the events detailed in the preceding chapter. At the December 1989 meeting of the American Psychoanalytic Association, three major panels were held on the overall theme "Psychoanalysis and Psychoanalytic Psychotherapy—Similarities and Differences." Separate panels focused on theory, on technique, and on indications and contraindications; they brought together most of the individuals who had made significant contributions to these issues over the years. To indicate the scope and range of present-day thinking on these issues, I will briefly survey the three panel reports (Hoch 1992; McNutt 1992; and Morris 1992), several of the individual papers on those panels, and a few related papers published or presented between 1989 and 1992. In addition, I will take up some incidental remarks in a book by Friedman (1988) concerning the relationship of psychotherapy to psychoanalysis, as set within his kaleidoscopic effort to elucidate the "anatomy" of the psychotherapy enterprise[1] by exploring the meanings and uses of theory in its forever dialectical interplay with the meanings and processes of therapy; chapters by Gray and Jacobs[2] from Arnold Rothstein's (1988) book, *How Does Treatment Help? On the Modes of Therapeutic Action of Psychoanalytic Therapy;* and, most specifically pertinent to the issues of this chapter, Oremland's (1991) ambitious reassessment of the terms of the debates of 1954 and 1979. These articles and books will be assessed in this chapter in order to bring up to date all the lines of thinking about the distinctions between psychoanalytically oriented and derived psychotherapies from psychoanalysis proper that were given their initial organization and thrust

1. Meaning any "talking therapy" grounded in a scientific (or, at least, a theoretical) psychology— i.e., psychoanalysis. His book is entitled *The Anatomy of Psychotherapy*.
2. These are the only chapters in that book that address the similarities and differences between psychoanalysis and psychoanalytic psychotherapy; the other chapters refer to their subject under the conflated rubric of "psychoanalytic therapy" as an overall umbrella term, or simply as analysis, in its widest possible scope and meaning.

in the seminal and enduring contributions of Knight and his colleagues a half-century ago (see chapter 3).

Most of the contributors to the December 1989 panels of the American Psychoanalytic Association reaffirmed their familiar positions as presented in earlier chapters. Dewald (unpubl. ms) restated his conception of the distinction between psychoanalysis and (expressive) psychoanalytic psychotherapy in terms of the therapeutic focus on "core" as against "derivative" conflicts, fantasies, elements of psychic structure and function, and so on. He then went systematically down the line again, noting such quantitative distinctions as the fact that in psychoanalysis the derivatives are traced to a deeper level, there is more intense regression, more primary process fantasies, and more primitive affects are reached—all in terms of the distinction between working at the "level" of derivative conflicts as opposed to trying to reach the core (meaning ultimately the infantile core) via the evolving regressive transference neurosis. The whole issue (and the whole distinction) he stated as "how far proximal or distal to the core of psychic function the process is focused" (13).

Rangell (unpubl. ms) also started with his familiar views on the increasing difficulty since 1954 of establishing the similarities and differences between psychoanalysis and the psychoanalytic psychotherapies, but this time he attributed it to the proliferation and increasing worldwide acceptance of a diversity of psychoanalytic theories and technical precepts—with the ensuing problem that what the adherents of one theoretical position call psychoanalysis, adherents of another would designate as "only" psychotherapy. "My own preference," Rangell stated, "is for what I call 'total composite psychoanalytic theory,' which contains all that is considered to have endured and all advances which are additive and contributory. Self and object each have as comfortable a theoretical niche within this umbrella theory as drives, ego, or superego. Self and object, oedipal and preoedipal, ego, id and superego, internal and external, all find their places within one total unitary psychoanalytic theory—from which derivative therapeutic procedures derive" (13).

To Rangell, this is the inclusive psychoanalytic "mainstream," firmly embedded in the ego psychology structural paradigm, yet he ruefully acknowledged that this may now no longer be main—may, in fact, well be a minority position worldwide. In 1989, Rangell amended and broadened his 1954 definition of psychoanalysis (chapter 5) to encompass "analysis of the transference neurosis *and/or any other areas displaced from the past*" (17); "to analyze the transference neurosis and the infantile and *childhood* neurosis from which it came"; to "give more substantial recognition" to the therapeutic alliance alongside the transference relationship. Finally he stated that "all of these changes apply both to psychoanalysis and psychoanalytic psychotherapy" (18).

Schlesinger (unpubl. ms) in his restatement drew a distinction between the "psychoanalytic situation" and the "psychotherapeutic situation" in terms of whether one tries to foster or to preclude the development of a regressive transference neurosis. He stated it thus: "My argument rests on the assertion that the major difference between the two 'situations,' and hence between the two forms of treatment, lies in the technical purpose of the psychoanalytic situation to facilitate the development of a transference neurosis. . . . To make the distinction as sharp as possible, I assert that it should be a major interim purpose of the analyst who aims to establish a therapeutic situation with his patient to preclude, in so far as it is possible, the development of a transference neurosis" (13–14).

In his panel report, Samuel Hoch (1992) highlighted the implementation of Schlesinger's distinction: "The definition of psychoanalysis is couched in terms internal to the process, and strives for internal goals, i.e., structural changes within the personality; it is an expectant treatment and its process is shaped primarily by what the patient does. Psychoanalytic psychotherapy is concerned more with external goals; it is an active treatment defined more by what the therapist does" (234–35). Schlesinger's pithy way of expressing this difference was that the (external) question that challenges psychoanalytic psychotherapy is, "Are we getting anywhere?" rather than the (internal) question posed to psychoanalysis, "Are we doing it right?" (13). (Clearly, neither of these questions should be taken quite literally as posed, yet clearly, also, the two lean toward the opposite ends of the spectrum of psychoanalytically based therapeutic modalities.)

Of all the participants in these 1989 panel discussions, Weinshel perhaps best epitomizes the current dilemmas in properly distinguishing psychoanalysis from the related psychoanalytic psychotherapies. Weinshel's conceptualizations are an inevitable by-product of his efforts (Weinshel 1990b, 1992; Weinshel and Renik 1991) to refine the nature of the psychoanalytic process—which he feels consists of the diligent and unremitting analysis of the resistances, a process of clarification that he initiated, actually, with a paper in 1984. In the 1990b paper, he expressed his own dilemma concerning this distinction between psychoanalysis and psychoanalytic psychotherapy in the following counterposed quotations: "When a resistance originating from either the analyst or the analysand arises, it poses an obstacle to the progress of the analytic work, and dealing with that obstacle becomes the central and necessary focus of the analysis. I suggest that it is our *special attitude and approach* to the resistances that serves to *organize* the analytic work and comprises the most significant and reliable distinction between psychoanalysis and so-called psychoanalytic psychotherapy or the even more vague 'psychoanalytically informed' psychotherapies" (635). However, in the same paper he also stated the practical clinical difficulty of making this distinction: "In an era of increasingly pluralistic conceptualizations of what defines psychoanalysis and what constitutes a clinical psychoanalysis, it is no longer feasible to insist that there is *one* 'standard psychoanalytic technique,' let alone a 'true analysis.' Nor can we differentiate, with any degree of assurance, true psychoanalysis from other psychotherapies, even when the latter are designated as 'psychoanalytic psychotherapy' " (631–32). (I would have said "especially when," not "even when").

In the 1991 paper with Renik, Weinshel stated this operational difficulty and the ensuing confusions even more starkly:

> In recent years it has become even more difficult to establish categorical differences between psychoanalytic psychotherapy and psychoanalysis proper. As psychoanalysis in the United States has become less homogeneous in its adherence to the ego-psychological structural-model approach, we have been presented with alternative conceptualizations of psychic structure, psychopathology, and the nature of psychoanalytic therapy; and these new concepts brought with them a considerably broadened base of indications for psychoanalytic treatment. As a result, many patients who traditionally were *not* considered appropriate for psychoanalysis were being found more and more frequently on psychoanalysts' couches. Additional confusion arose with the interest in the narcissistic and borderline patients, with some analysts insisting that many of these patients were analyzable and could be treated by traditional psychoanalysis and others arguing that these more disturbed patients could be treated only by psychotherapy or markedly modified psychoanalytic techniques. (19–20).

Such ambiguity about the nature of the treatment process inevitably leads to the same confusions about treatment results: "One aspect of that recognition is that patients who have been in several-times-a-week psychoanalytically informed psychotherapy sometimes achieve results that at least appear to approximate the goals we anticipate for carefully selected cases in psychoanalysis, while some of those carefully selected analytic cases do not seem to do as well after a long and apparently well-conducted psychoanalysis" (20)—an overall conclusion also arrived at, via a somewhat different route, by Rangell (1981b) and Wallerstein (1986a, 1988b) (see chapter 8).

In his 1992 paper (from the 1989 panels), Weinshel put the profound shifts on this issue into personal historic context and then tried to state how he would phrase these distinctions currently—as of 1989:

> Many years ago, when I was an advanced candidate [in the 1950s], I would have been quite comfortable and even certain about the similarities and

differences in technique between psychoanalytic psychotherapy and psychoanalysis. Those were the golden days of psychoanalysis in the United States, and I was convinced that once I achieved enough knowledge and experience to do "the right thing," I would have no trouble in distinguishing the two modalities, applying them appropriately, or in being clear about the impact my therapeutic interventions might have on my patients, analytic or psychotherapeutic . . . although I recognized that there was some sort of spectrum between pure psychoanalysis and a somewhat less admirable psychoanalytic psychotherapy, I was reasonably confident that in good time any problems related to those distinctions would yield to the burgeoning development of my psychoanalytic skills. (327–28)

In 1989—for the reasons adumbrated in the quotation above—the situation was altogether different: "Today my certainty is limited to the recognition that those distinctions are not as clear or unequivocal as many of us once believed. . . . It was surprising that in conducting a psychoanalysis or in doing psychotherapy, we would utilize ostensibly similar technical tools and speak of ostensibly comparable concepts in ostensibly identical terms. It has become increasingly evident, however, that those tools and concepts and terms do not have the same meaning and significance for all of the people who have been using them" (328).

I have quoted extensively from Weinshel's recent papers because they portray so graphically the sea change that has occurred in American psychoanalysis since the 1954 crystallization of the consensus, through the symposium of 1979, which marked the fragmenting of the consensus, to the present situation described in this chapter, a world without consensus. Weinshel did try in this article to lay out how he *would* attempt nonetheless to distinguish today between psychoanalysis and psychoanalytic psychotherapies, and he (inevitably?) did so in terms of more and less (just as Dewald did in the same panel series). Weinshel listed these considerations under eleven headings (343–45), summarized in Morris's (1992) report of the panel as follows:

In psychotherapy, . . . there is less focus on developing an internalized psychoanalytic process and more focus on symptoms, specific goals, and time limits. In psychotherapy there is likely to be more activity on the part of the therapist, with less neutrality and systematic exploration of transference and resistance with the therapist taking the lead and using more suggestion to focus on topics. In psychotherapy there tends to be less exploration before interpretation, more focus on dream content than associations and resistances and, as a result, more construction rather than reconstruction via transference understanding. Also, in psychotherapy the

analyst tends to be less abstinent and more tolerant of transference gratifications. With regard to the central role of transference interpretation in
psychoanalysis, he finds that in psychotherapy there is a tendency to make
earlier transference interpretations and to make more use of extra-analytic
transference interpretations rather than to explore systematically the developing transference configurations. Termination in psychotherapy is
more arbitrary and more linked to subjective improvement than to attainment of an internalized process no longer requiring input from the
analyst. (217)

Given the more/less nature of these distinctions, it follows that the determination can rarely be based on a single session or even a small sample of sessions,
as Weinshel acknowledged; one needs to follow the treatment process over some
sweep of time. In conclusion Weinshel quoted the distinction once made by
Helen Ross: "Psychoanalysis lasted longer, went deeper, and came up dirtier"—
calling it, admiringly, an "exemplar of directness and brevity" (345).

From the cluster of other recent papers dealing with these issues I will highlight only the following additional considerations: David Sachs (unpubl. ms) said
that the essence of the differentiation should be the degree of suggestion (in the
sense of unresolved transference) that characterizes the therapy ("in my view,
the central importance of the relationship of therapy to the use of suggestion
will remain a fixed star by which psychoanalytic therapists orient themselves"
[11–12])—a restatement of the original position of Freud, Ferenczi, Jones, and
Glover).[3] Owen Renik (1993a), in a paper on the inherent and inevitable countertransference enactments that characterize psychoanalytic work and that occur
prior to and as prerequisite to an achieved countertransference awareness, saw
the distinction in the degree to which these enactments are rendered explicitly
conscious—that is, converted into insights as against serving merely as corrective
emotional experiences.[4] To Jacobs (in Rothstein 1988) the differentiation was
in the way psychotherapy, via its method, limits the interpretive uncovering of

3. In a much earlier paper, Sachs (1979) had stated that the essence of the distinction between
the treatment modalities lay in the difference of method, the method of free association in
analysis as against "investigative procedures [which] . . . refers to all the methods of obtaining
associations that Freud used prior to psychoanalysis" (120) that characterize the psychotherapies. These two presentations are of course compatible with each other.
4. Renik put this as follows: "Since transference-countertransference awareness follows enactment, we can conceptualize a successful *psychoanalytic process* as one in which a series of un-
premeditated corrective emotional experiences come to be examined and understood
retrospectively . . . and a successful *psychotherapeutic process,* on the other hand, as one in which
corrective emotional experiences take place, but remain largely outside the patient's and perhaps the therapist's conscious awareness" (155).

the therapist's role as an essential stabilizing object ("In analysis with the neurotic patient, the object, though vitally important, remains in the background and the patient can explore freely the psychological terrain of his own mind. . . . In the case of the more disturbed patient in whom the unfolding may be limited or blocked by ancient and tenacious defenses, by rigidities of character, or by defects in the laying down of structure, the role of the object as stabilizer, introject, superego modifier, or model for identification assumes greater importance. This often happens in psychotherapy, too, although for other reasons" [67]—i.e., the psychotherapeutic method itself precluding or blocking the interpretive rendering into consciousness). Finally, Gray (in Rothstein 1988) stated the distinction to be the degree of *unanalyzed* reexternalization and modification of the authority images of early childhood with the subjection to a more benign superego—but without insight into this "transference cure" based on the "power of suggestion." Nonetheless, in such instances, "the therapeutic gains may be profound and extremely, even vitally, valuable . . . depend[ing] particularly on the influence of the way in which the patient perceives or experiences the therapist. . . . The most effective element empowering therapeutic action is the reexternalization and transference of those images of authority acquired in early childhood. Here I would expect the therapeutic actions to accompany the patient's use of strengthening identification, and/or relief through certain gratifications which, by relieving frustrations, lower the potential for anxiety otherwise provoked by conflicted yearnings" (43).

Helen Gediman (1990), Sander Abend (1990), and Kenneth Frank (1992) each brought a distinctive emphasis to these discussions not yet specifically focused by the others. Gediman made a plea to remove the pejorative cast from these distinctions, widely experienced—in fact, since Freud's day—but not often explicitly acknowledged (except in some of the 1954 publications and in PRP [Wallerstein 1986a, 1988b]). Gediman said, "Teaching psychotherapy and requiring supervision of a psychotherapy case deserve an emphasis on their inherent values, and not, as formerly, on their values as fallbacks from psychoanalysis. We would think in terms of mining the pure gold of psychoanalysis *and* of mining the pure gold of psychotherapy, eliminating the pejorative cast of the 'copper of direct suggestion,' yet retaining Freud's non-pejorative view that the most effective ingredients of psychotherapy are those borrowed from psychoanalysis." She quoted Sachs's view that "one way to remove the pejorative connotation of psychoanalytic psychotherapy is to expand its definition while narrowing the scope and defining characteristics of psychoanalysis" (9). And "It is . . . the widespread misnaming of psychoanalytic therapy as 'psychoanalysis' that artificially widens the scope and 'has had destructive consequences both for the appropriate selection of therapy and for the science of psychoanalysis. . . .

To restore a proper balance among different forms of psychotherapies, the stigma under which psychoanalytic therapies have suffered must be removed.' . . . We should think, rather, of a broadening range of patients treated by a broadened armamentarium of techniques, equally valued in their own right, derived from a unified psychoanalytic theory" (10).

Abend cast the issues, not in value terms, but in political terms (or are they the same?). As he put it, "Controversy about the theoretical shifts that were introduced as alternative or evolutionary forms of psychoanalysis promoted the tendency of analytic traditionalists to relegate these trends to the class of psychotherapies, while reserving the term psychoanalysis exclusively for their own version of Freud's methodology. Many proponents of emerging theories cling just as vehemently and tenaciously to the term psychoanalysis for their methods, even including some who wanted to set Freud aside as hopelessly outmoded" (542).

And Frank talked most broadly of integrating psychoanalytic and cognitive-behavioral techniques into a distinctive psychotherapeutic approach. The modus operandi and intent were expressed as follows:

Although the introduction of action techniques may be inappropriate in the analytic treatment of many patients, with certain others, especially those with whom a full analysis is not undertaken, integrative action techniques can often be useful. When they are introduced, they need not necessarily play an extensive role; yet even a sparing role can be highly significant. They may be used to promote adaptive action at two possible levels that interact productively with the analytic process: (1) They may serve to enhance psychological and social skills and personal competence, and (2) they may contribute directly to the modification of extra-analytic enactments, sometimes reducing symptoms. Integrated through the analytic process in a way that may modify psychic structure, and operating together with insight and the crucial, new and positive experience with the analyst, action techniques are thus seen as operating compatibly and effectively within a psychoanalytic approach. (70)

Frank protected his psychoanalytic bona fides by cautioning that, of course, the transferential meanings of such "action interventions" must be explored psychoanalytically (71) and that one must also consider possible countertransferential meanings whenever the introduction of "action techniques" is under consideration (72). For justification in terms of psychoanalytic proprieties, he called on recent writings, particularly those of Gill:

Compared to a strict blank-screen view, an interactional model conceptualizes the psychoanalytic situation in a way more compatible with psychotherapy integration. From the blank-screen perspective, the therapist's increased activity associated with action techniques inevitably is thought to constrain the analysis of transference by contaminating and narrowing the range of spontaneous fantasies the patient may have about the therapist. But from an interactional view, the analyst's influence is always present in the transference: *"whatever* the analyst does plays a role in determining the transference"* (Gill, 1982, p. 89). In the latter view, a therapist's level of activity and its contents, like his/her qualities and other behaviors, are incorporated into transferential elaborations based on determinants from the past. Accordingly, within limits that must be established empirically on the basis of further clinical experience, the interactional view can be extended to create a potential for the kind of deliberate therapist activity involved in the introduction of structured action-oriented techniques—provided that transferential elements of the patient's experience of the introduction of those techniques are taken into consideration and are analyzed. (61)

In an article addressed to psychiatric residents, Peter Novalis (1989) declared, almost as a codicil to Frank's argument, that supportive psychotherapy is after all "primarily a behavioral therapy. To draw an analogy, if you want to call psychodynamic [expressive] therapy a 'watered down' version of psychoanalysis, then you might as well call supportive therapy a watered down version of purely behavioral therapy, such as aversive or desensitization therapy. . . . In Winston's classification, for example, supportive therapy includes much of cognitive and behavioral therapy and certainly such specific techniques as assertiveness training and social skills training" (26).

Friedman's kaleidoscopic and truly monumental *Anatomy of Psychotherapy* (1988) touched only tangentially on the differentiation of psychoanalytic psychotherapy from psychoanalysis. The central thesis—expressed in more than six hundred criss crossing pages—is, rather, that theory is neat whereas therapy, being of the real world, is messy. Theory calms the therapist's anxieties while it expresses his desires—his worldview, value systems, and theoretic allegiances. It normalizes our really quite unnatural work. By contrast, therapy (and this is why it needs anchoring and shaping) is—more than we willingly admit—an ambiguous and seat-of-the-pants process that is entirely different from the expectable social situation when two human beings interact, while at every point it can be construed and reacted to as if it were an ordinary social relationship. The problem in all this is the eternal dialectic and disjunction between theory and therapy. The unremitting problem shared by therapist and patient is that each has to interact both with a theory (that gives meaning to their shared work) and with a person (the other), and the two tasks are not necessarily congruent.[5]

Germane to our interest here is that Friedman's book is almost entirely about a unitary psychoanalytic therapy; that is, essentially it conflates psychoanalysis and psychoanalytic psychotherapy—surprising indeed in so vast a book on this specific subject. Only in the last two pages of this sprawling opus does Friedman offer his views on psychoanalysis vis-à-vis the psychotherapy derived from it:

> Obviously the fate of the psychotherapy profession is more uncertain than it seemed 30 years ago. Yet in some ways it is better off. Thirty years ago no profession was as ragged or questionable as general psychotherapy. Psychoanalysis was more fortunate. It had a theory and a procedure. It had a curriculum, standards of performance, and a *lingua franca*. It was adorned with learned journals and subtle spokesmen. Psychotherapy had none of these. A handful of illustrious figures spoke seriously for psycho-therapy. But its periodicals were filled with recipes, practical hints, and shared experience. Detailed and subtle reflection about what, after all, is a matter of detail and subtlety, was confined to the analytic literature. Psychotherapy was taught in a make-do fashion with whatever scraps of theory and procedure it could snatch from psychoanalysis, therapists being too grateful for the scraps to worry about their place in a non-analytic setting, or to fuss about the mutual compatibility of random items carried over from a systematic psychoanalysis. The general rule was that a therapist should try to think and act like a psychoanalyst whenever possible, never mind the specific momentary rationale. (562)

Skipping ahead thirty years to the mid-1980s, Friedman said,

> Almost nothing has changed. But the "almost" is important. Today fewer people want a full psychoanalysis, whether because their troubles are dif-ferent, or their means fewer, or their interest less. And there has been a shift in psychoanalytic theorizing, partly the result of its wider application, but probably also to the intratheory tensions I have discussed. This has changed the relationship between psychotherapy and psychoanalysis. . . . The analytic literature is now concerned with treatment processes and meaning change in general. Thirty years ago theorists did not feel the need to enlarge their vocabulary, as is necessary to deal seriously with "parametric" problems. Nowadays psychoanalysts concern themselves

5. I have expressed my appreciation of Friedman's work in a book review (Wallerstein 1990c) and my detailed disagreement with much of his central argument in a longer critique (*Psy-choanal. Ing.*, forthcoming).

with issues that are properly psychotherapeutic because they are fundamental to all talking therapies. The tradition and habits of reflection cultivated by psychoanalysis are now available to psychotherapy. (562–63)

The quotation can of course be looked at as a capsule summary of this whole
book to this point. (Friedman's denigration and even trivializing of specifically
supportive psychoanalytic psychotherapy have already been cited in chapter 6,
note 11.)

In quite the opposite direction from Friedman's book, Oremland's *Interpretation and Interaction: Psychoanalysis or Psychotherapy?* (1991) represents a major
effort to reframe the dialogue on the similarities and differences between psychoanalysis and the psychoanalytic psychotherapies, in a manner strongly influenced by the newer views of Gill (who contributed a chapter of commentary)
on the nature of the therapeutic interaction, but also with very significant differences. Oremland's guiding assumption—and here he is indebted to Gill—is
that all therapy is interactive. The central distinction is whether it is interaction
with or *without* interpretation of the interaction; interpretation is what makes the
therapy distinctly psychoanalytic. Hence the book's title, and hence also the
new nomenclature Oremland introduced. He maintained the tripartite division
of 1954 (the spectrum from supportive psychotherapy to expressive psychotherapy to psychoanalysis) but renamed the components interactive psychotherapy (i.e., without interpretation, therefore supportive), psychoanalytically
oriented psychotherapy (expressive, interpretive, but not psychoanalysis proper),
and psychoanalysis (here, of course, without a suggested name change).[6]

Most of Oremland's book is devoted to the relationship between psychoanalytically oriented psychotherapy and psychoanalysis proper, leaving aside interactive psychotherapy for the most part as warranting less focused attention,
either because it is of lesser import or because its precepts and techniques might
be more self-evident and less in need of specification. Of his two central foci
of interest, he said, "The essential commonality between psychoanalytically oriented psychotherapy and psychoanalysis resides in the intervention employed,
that is, interpretation. The essential difference lies in the primary area of psychotherapeutic interplay. In broad sweep, the *operational* difference between

6. Oremland also rejected the term "transference neurosis," which he said stems from the superseded topographic model of the mind, and suggested replacing it with "regressive transference enactment," which he declared was more consonant with the structural model of the
mind—but seemingly without significant imputed technical implications (see 35–36). He also
felt that the use of the concept of the therapeutic alliance was fraught with risk, the risk of
heightening the uninterpreted, unanalyzed components of the therapeutic process, hence making the therapy more interactive than it need be.

psychoanalytically oriented psychotherapy and psychoanalysis is the training of the practitioner, the range of patients treated, the frequency of sessions, and the use of the couch. Simply put, the mode (interpretation) is the same; the modalities and what eventuates as the process unfolds is different" (112).

Oremland then laid out the distinctions in terms of what Gill called the (nonvital) external criteria. Psychoanalytically oriented psychotherapy should be at least twice a week but not less, because once-a-week sessions are just "a weekly request to bear witness to, or to correct, the events of his or her life," whereas twice-weekly sessions become "a beginning effort at introspection." ("Once-a-week psychotherapy frequently becomes interactive regardless of the psychotherapist's orientation or the nature of the psychotherapist's interventions.") But psychoanalytically oriented psychotherapy can also be "as frequent as seven times or more a week when the patient's object constancy is so impaired that transference *continuities* cannot be maintained" (115). Psychoanalysis is kept to the standard four or five times a week (seldom three times a week). Similarly, the couch is reserved for patients in psychoanalysis. Oremland said of this, "The role of the couch in psychoanalytically oriented psychotherapy requires special discussion. Unfortunately, often the unstated reason for using the couch in psychotherapies is the status afforded the practitioner and the patient by the patient's being 'on the couch.' Stated reasons include relaxing the patient, making the patient less aware of the psychotherapist's responses, and encouraging free association. Using the couch for these reasons is interactive and not psychoanalytic" (117).

In addition to these distinctions in external criteria, Oremland also held to internal differences in what he called the "Area of Interplay" (118):

> Although there is *marked overlap* between them, the two modalities move the patient's interests in different directions.... In psychoanalytically oriented psychotherapy the actualities of the interaction dominate, and there is exquisite dissection of the transference in the interaction. In psychoanalysis, the actualities of the interaction are less immediate.... The interpretations in psychoanalytically oriented psychotherapy progressively reveal ... the transferences within the actualities of the interplay. In psychoanalysis, as the internal soliloquy intensifies through interpretation of the resistances, the *historical aspects of the life experience* predominate. Essentially each modality explores different areas of the interplay. Yet in both a past is located that enriches the present. (118–19, italics added)

Each modality is therefore less complete in the central area of the other. But depending on the fit with the needs of the patient, neither is inherently superior or more complete. They are "complementary . . . modalities with different quantitative emphases" (120).

And there is no empirical evidence that one is a more effective therapy than the other: "Generally, existing studies and most clinical experience do not give psychoanalysis, even for equally suitable cases, a clear-cut therapeutic supremacy over the psychotherapies. Most investigations, echoing the experiences of clinicians, attest to broader sustained personality change from psychotherapy than traditionally espoused (Wallerstein, 1986a)" (122). This last statement led Oremland to his position on differential indications, already detailed in chapter 6— that he begins with *all* patients in psychoanalytically oriented psychotherapy and then sees which way it goes: "For the patient who is equally suitable for either modality, I equally favor continuing the psychoanalytically oriented psychotherapy or increasing frequency and beginning psychoanalysis" (127–28)—with most mental health professionals who are patients opting for psychoanalysis proper, and most other patients opting for therapy. This also makes conversion back and forth quite simple, assuring the essential "compatibility of psychotherapy with subsequent psychoanalysis by the same practitioner when the psychotherapy was not overly interactive or manipulative" (129–30).

In light of this exposition of differences and similarities, what stand does Oremland take on the interrelationships of the three main treatment modalities? He writes,

Currently, most theoreticians and clinicians use a continuum model within the tripartite division, a position championed by no less a theoretician and researcher than Robert Wallerstein (1986a). . . . [But] building on Gill's later (1982) paradigm, I propose a bimodal model regarding predominant intervention (mode), interactive versus interpretive modes, while maintaining a tripartite division of procedure (modality). . . . In my tripartite division, the modalities become *interactive psychotherapy,* and the two interpretive psychotherapies, *psychoanalytically oriented psychotherapy* and *psychoanalysis.* In this model, the three modalities are not on a continuum nor are they equidistant from each other. . . . Although all three share commonalities, the distance between interactive psychotherapy [i.e., supportive psychotherapy] and the two interpretive psychotherapies, psychoanalytically oriented psychotherapy and psychoanalysis, is greater for critical variables than is the distance between psychoanalytically oriented psychotherapy and psychoanalysis. When viewed as processes, interactive psychotherapy also stands relatively alone, whereas psychoanalytically oriented psychotherapy and psychoanalysis are intrinsically and complexly interrelated. Visually, psychoanalytically oriented psychotherapy and psychoanalysis become a double helix, entwined yet distinct. (130–31)

Then in summary,

Interactive psychotherapy is psychotherapy whose mode uses transference in directive, suggestive, and manipulative interventions, with modeling and *selective* transference interpretations, to produce changes largely according to the psychotherapist's evaluation. If the psychotherapist is psychoanalytically oriented, the interventions will be psychoanalytically guided. The prototype of the interactive psychotherapist is the seer/hypnotist. Although broadly effective therapeutically, interactive psychotherapy essentially directs, and therefore limits, understanding. . . . [By contrast] psychoanalytically oriented psychotherapy and psychoanalysis are interpretive in mode. Although interpretation is an interaction, as an intervention it is qualitatively different from any other intervention in that interpretation attempts to add explicit knowledge and when transferential makes the interaction itself the object of analysis. . . .

Both psychoanalytically oriented psychotherapy and psychoanalysis have extensive aims. Yet each modality explores different areas of the interplay. Both provide Freud's "after-education"—new perspectives gained through emotional reevaluation, reliving, and vitalized insight—with different potentials and limitations. In broad sweeps, the after-education of psychoanalytically oriented psychotherapy is cross-sectional; that is, the interplay emphasizes the psychodynamics of interpersonal functioning with correspondingly less detailed, genetic detailing. The after-education of psychoanalysis carries a longitudinal emphasis; that is, the interplay is heavily laced with genetically detailed reconstruction and less detailing of the psychodynamics of the ongoing interpersonal functioning. The prototype of the psychoanalytically oriented psychotherapist and the psychoanalyst is the teacher in its broadest meaning. (133–34)

And finally, Oremland stated, "Experience suggests that, from the clinically therapeutic perspective, the procedures roughly are equally effective" (135).

My own positions on these issues have already been stated in detail (PRP, Wallerstein 1986a, 1988b) but perhaps should be briefly summarized here in relation to Oremland's theses. Basically, I feel that Oremland's altered nomenclature is unnecessary because it inevitably introduces an element of confusion; I think there is more heuristic value in keeping the rubric "supportive" than in substituting "interactive," with its narrowed focus on a single determining element of the modality. I do believe in a spectrum of the psychotherapies with nodal crystallizations along that continuum of the three distinctive modalities; this allows for gradation and infiltration of techniques across unclear boundaries in contrast to the much sharper dichotomization that Oremland (along with Gill) conceptualizes, which creates more sharply distinguishable entities than clinical experience supports. I agree with Oremland, however, that the threefold distinction should be maintained, as against Gill's collapse of what Oremland calls psychoanalytically oriented psychotherapy into psychoanalysis, as simply more or less analysis.

In his invited chapter of commentary in Oremland's book, Gill agreed with Oremland that "the distinction is between interaction with analysis of the interaction and interaction without analysis of the interaction" (138). And "Oremland and I likewise agree that this latter distinction is a key factor in differentiating psychotherapy [Gill is clearly referring here to Oremland's "interactive psychotherapy," not to "psychoanalytically oriented psychotherapy," though Gill did not make this explicit] from psychoanalysis as an ideal, psychoanalysis being characterized aphoristically as interaction with analysis of interaction and psychotherapy as interaction without analysis of interaction." He adds, "The interactive effect of the analysis of an interaction can be more important than the effect of the original interaction," and, in further clarification, "the distinction we are making is more usually cast as the manipulation of the transference versus the analysis of the transference. Manipulation of the transference is often called suggestion" (139).

There is a further concordance: "Another important aspect of the aforementioned distinction is whether the interaction in question is witting or not. Since every intervention, indeed the therapy situation itself, is an interaction, it is always witting in that sense. But an important distinction must be drawn between an interaction that is designed to have an interpersonal effect and an interaction that has such an effect but was not intended to do so" (139).

Regarding Gill's areas of disagreement with Oremland, the first had to do with an epistemological distinction between psychotherapy and psychoanalysis. Gill agreed with Oremland's statement that interpretation as an intervention is qualitatively different from other interactions in that its aim is *solely* to add explicit knowledge whereas interactive interventions remain largely experiential. But he added that a central aim of *all* psychological therapy, *including* psychoanalysis, is to bring about an interpersonal effect. He declared that the dichotomy of change by way of insight and change by way of the relationship was a false separation of what can only be conceptually separated: He stated his belief that "Oremland's view is a remnant of the classical idea that lasting change comes about only through understanding; I believe, furthermore, that this view is part of a 'one-person' conception of psychoanalysis, which is mistaken, because . . . the psychoanalytic situation is inherently interpersonal" (140). Here he was saying that despite Oremland's basic assumption (shared with Gill) that all interventions, including the purest interpretations, also exert an interpersonal effect and that all therapy is therefore interactive—differing only in the extent to which the interaction is interpreted—Oremland was still captive to some extent of a "one-body" conception of psychoanalysis. Oremland might well disagree on this point. I regard it as a less substantial distinction than Gill does.

Gill then went on to indicate what to me is a more substantial difference with Oremland: "Oremland is convinced that the couch and the greater frequency of visits in analysis necessarily result in a major emphasis on reconstruction whereas the face-to-face posture and lesser frequency of visits in therapy necessarily result in a major emphasis on the patient-therapist interaction, although he grants that there is a major overlap in the two therapy situations" (140). This to me is the heart of their disagreement, and the issue on which my agreement is with Oremland. Gill also objects to the term "psychoanalytically oriented psychotherapy" "because it implies too great a gap between psychoanalysis and the modality he describes" (143) and suggests a change in nomenclature more in accord with *his* conceptions:

> With some hesitancy I would like to suggest a name for both what Oremland calls "psychoanalytically oriented psychotherapy" and what I clumsily called "psychoanalytic technique." It is a revival of a term that Alexander and French (1946) used for their manipulative psychotherapy, which employed psychoanalytic understanding of psychodynamics. The term has so fallen into disuse that I believe it is available for a new purpose. I refer to the term "psychoanalytic therapy." I suggest that the term be used for a therapy in which the analysis of interaction is a primary goal, regardless of how ambitious or lengthy the therapy is, and in which the couch is not used and sessions are less frequent than in psychoanalysis proper. I am not sanguine about the prospects for my suggestion. (158–59)

Gill also tried to draw Oremland's "psychoanalytically oriented psychotherapy" closer to proper psychoanalysis: "That both his 'psychoanalytically oriented psychotherapy' and my 'psychoanalytic technique' analyze interaction is far more important than that they differ in ambitiousness of goal and duration. And that they share the analysis of interaction in common with psychoanalysis proper is far more important than that they differ from the latter in the extrinsic factors of couch and frequency of sessions. Furthermore, as I said, the use of the term psychoanalytically oriented psychotherapy is so entrenched as a term for the continuum from exploratory psychotherapy to psychoanalysis that I do not see how it can be changed" (158). Here the conceptual tug is quite clear between

Gill's wish to diminish the distinction (to the point of actual amalgamation?) and Oremland's to maintain it, with its more than quantitative differences; these, in Oremland's terms, are in the selected and preferred "area of interplay."

One last quotation from Gill has to do with the sharp difference both he and Oremland expressed with the views of Eissler on what constitutes the analytic process: "For Eissler, a parameter was usually a simple, gross suggestion, like advising the analysand against getting married; whereas for Oremland and me the entire analytic situation is shot through with suggestion, whether witting or unwitting, that should be made as explicit as possible. We speak of the 'ubiquity of interaction' " (145). This states as well as anyone has the great arc from Eissler's austere conception of a proper psychoanalysis with the "ideal patient," consisting only of interpretation leading to insight and devoid of any hint of suggestion, to this more modern conception of the "ubiquity of interaction" in all interpersonal encounters, the most classical of psychoanalyses included.

This brings us to the present-day position on the line of development of the psychoanalytic psychotherapies. But from early on there were alternative visions of how to conceptualize the relationship of psychoanalytic psychotherapy to psychoanalysis. Subsequent chapters will deal with these in turn.

III. *The Transference, Transference Interpretation,*
and the Transference Neurosis

10 Interpretation, Insight, Working Through, and Action: I

In this section I trace out the meanings and usages, as they have evolved and diversified over time, of certain pivotal psychoanalytic concepts—most importantly, transference, transference interpretation, and the transference neurosis. In doing this, I will focus less on the more familiar historical conceptions than on the modern-day divergences. But first, in this chapter and the next I consider the concepts of interpretation, insight, working through, and action, which together define the essence of the expressive, exploratory, uncovering therapeutic approaches and the distinguishing line of demarcation between these modalities and the supportive, suppressive psychotherapies.

In an elegant review of the literature on interpretation, Jim Dimon (1992) began with the statement that "the varied psychoanalytic understandings of interpretation are foreshadowed by the diverse preanalytic meanings of the term. An interpreter, for example, is a translator from one language to another, an artist who gives creative meaning to a work of art, a scientist who accounts for a body of data, or a religious figure who reveals the will of God. Each of these usages is analogous to a psychoanalytic theory of interpretation." He went on to develop Freud's initial conception: "Freud . . . first used the word we translate as 'interpretation' in a title, *The Interpretation of Dreams* (1900).[1] He chose the German word *Deutung,* which in common usage referred to seers who read the future from signs—including dreams. He conspicuously did not choose the word *Erklaeren,* used by scientific contemporaries to describe their explanations of things. . . . In *The Interpretation of Dreams,* Freud describes the first psychoanalytic model of interpretation: interpretation as translation" (182–83). Using the Irma dream as his specimen, Freud "translated" the conscious manifest dream into its complex of unconscious latent dream thoughts; that is, the conception of interpretation as translation was fully in accord with the working of Freud's original topographic model of the mind.[2]

1. Though conceptually true and historically valid, this is not literally accurate. At least in the Guttman, Jones, and Parrish, *Freud Concordance* (1980) of Strachey's *English language* Standard Edition, the English word "interpretation" is given 1,012 listings and more than a dozen of these are in papers prior to 1900, at times in a quite colloquial usage, but at other times in the psychoanalytic technical sense of conveying the inferred meaning of a constellation of symptoms and behavior.

2. In his 1983 report of a panel on the topic of interpretation, Rothstein quoted Arlow that in its beginnings, "interpretation [was] in its most limited, restricted sense, a translation from one

However, as Freud developed the concepts of transference and resistance, both emanating from the unconscious, he encountered the failures of the interpreter as simple translator. The task now became to elucidate the meanings and functions of resistance and transference, and the concept of interpretation was launched on its journey of broadening and deepening. It was Strachey (1934) who, after Freud, made the most enduring contribution to the theory of interpretation. Strachey took as his starting point Alexander's earlier conception that the proper aim of psychoanalysis "must be the complete demolition of the superego" (134), modified that to the more realistic and appropriate goal of mitigating the improperly harsh and often sadistic superego of the suffering neurotic,[3] and then presented his ideas on how to achieve that desired end through the "mutative interpretation" (one that brings about psychic change).

Basically, Strachey described what he called "the neurotic vicious circle" (137), in which the patient, terrified of the sadistically aggressive superego, adopts an even more aggressive and destructive attitude toward the object in self-defense. If the patient could only be made less frightened of his superego or introjected object, he would in turn project less terrifying images upon the outer object and feel less need to be hostile to it—in effect, setting up a benign circle to replace the vicious one. In psychoanalysis, the patient projects onto the new object (the analyst) the introjected archaic objects (theory of transference). The analyst then becomes the "bad" (harsh) introjected object—the "auxiliary superego"—which gives the analyst the opportunity to make a mutative interpretation via a two-step process: "First . . . there is the phase in which the patient becomes conscious of a particular quality of id-energy as being directed towards the analyst; and secondly there is the phase in which the patient becomes aware that the id-energy is directed towards an archaic phantasy object and not towards a real one" (143). What makes the critical second phase possible is that the neurotic patient's sense of reality is sufficiently intact, and what makes the interpretation mutative is its immediacy, in that the urgent impulse or affect and its displacement from elsewhere (prior life experience and expectation) are immediately evident and felt in the here and now of the analytic setting. All this, of course, takes place in a multitude of small steps, with "working through" all along the way.

From this 1934 paper of Strachey's emerged the dictum that has prevailed in

---

language to another, from the language of the primary process to the language of the secondary process" (238).

3. Of this Strachey said, "This [Alexander's] wholesale attack upon the superego seems to be of questionable validity. It seems probable that its abolition, even if that were practical politics, would involve the abolition of a large number of highly desirable mental activities" (135).

psychoanalysis ever since: only interpretation in the transference is saliently mutative, and no other kind of interpretation (e.g., extratransference interpretations, explanations) could play such a role. Strachey put it thus: "Is it to be understood that no extra-transference interpretation can set in motion the chain of events which I have suggested as being the essence of psycho-analytical therapy? That is indeed my opinion" (154). This is because extratransference interpretations are far less likely to be given at the point of urgency (i.e., would be less affectively charged);[4] but also, at least equally important, if the object of the impulse is not present in the consulting room, it is much harder for the patient to become directly aware of the distinction between the real object and the fantasy object.

But Strachey's rejection of the place of extratransference interpretation was not as complete or as categorical as subsequent analytic generations took it to be. This was underscored by Harold Blum (1983), one of the few who has stressed the need to rehabilitate the extratransference interpretation as having a worthwhile place in therapy in its own right. He quoted Strachey's (1934) surprisingly little known concluding comments concerning extratransference interpretation:

"It must not be supposed that because I am attributing these special qualities to transference interpretations, I am therefore maintaining that no others should be made. On the contrary, it is possible that a large majority of our interpretations are outside the transference—though it should be added that it often happens that when one is ostensibly giving an extra-transference interpretation one is implicitly giving a transference one. A cake cannot be made of nothing but currants; and though it is true that extra-transference interpretations are not for the most part mutative, and do not themselves bring about the crucial results that involve a permanent change in the patient's mind, they are none the less essential. If I may take an analogy from trench warfare, the acceptance of a transference interpretation corresponds to the capture of a key position, while extra-transference interpretations correspond to the general advance. . . . An oscillation of this kind between transference and extra-transference interpretations will represent the normal course of events in an analysis (p. 158)."

4. Strachey put this as follows: "Extra-transference interpretations tend to be concerned with impulses which are distant both in time and space and are thus likely to be devoid of immediate energy. In extreme instances, indeed, they may approach very closely to what I have already described as the handing-over to the patient of a German-English dictionary" (154).

Three years after Strachey's paper, Bibring (1937) published "The Theory of the Therapeutic Results of Psycho-Analysis," in which he broadened the goals of psychoanalysis—and hence of interpretation—beyond those set by Strachey, to encompass changes not only in the superego but also in the ego and even the id and, consequently, in the relations of these psychic agencies to one another. This broadened focus has been a given of interpretive work ever since.[5] And in 1951, the major architects of American ego psychology, Rudolph Loewenstein, Ernst Kris, and Heinz Hartmann, each published a paper on interpretation in the same issue of *The Psychoanalytic Quarterly*. Loewenstein talked chiefly to the technique of interpretation in light of the new ego psychology. Though he acknowledged that there were a great many other methods of intervention by the analyst (e.g., the rule of abstinence, creating an "analytic atmosphere," offering explanations as to procedures or realities, even silences), Loewenstein focused on the cardinal role of interpretation in leading to insight: "In psychoanalysis this term is applied to those explanations, given to patients by the analyst, which add to their knowledge of themselves" (4). Like most others writing at the time, he felt he had to take Alexander to task for the devaluation of interpretation and insight that Loewenstein felt was inherent in the technical principle of the corrective emotional experience: "Some limited dynamic changes may occur independently of insight, and some limited insight may be gained without interpretations or even without analysis. In analysis, some insight may be gained from the very fact of talking frankly. The gain of insight, however, is limited if the patient is merely left to associate and is not given any interpretations" (3)—anchoring the essential connection between interpretation and insight and (in Loewenstein's view) also change.[6] For the rest, Loewenstein talked technically of "preparations for interpretation," of interpretation as a process that proceeds in "installments" (4) until it is ultimately complete, of interpreting from the surface down, from the known to the unknown, of optimal emotional distance for interpretation, of the concept of a "hierarchy of interpretations" (6), of issues of timing, repetition, working through, tact, and dosage, of matters of wording (in the patient's idiom and avoiding technical

5. For comprehensive discussions of the goals of psychoanalysis as they have been conceptualized over time, see Wallerstein (1965), "The Goals of Psychoanalysis: A Survey of Analytic Viewpoints," and an update a quarter-century later (Wallerstein 1992b), "The Goals of Psychoanalysis Reconsidered."

6. Bibring (1954) in his contribution to the series of panels published in 1954 on the similarities and differences between the dynamic psychotherapies and psychoanalysis proper also spoke to this specific issue of Alexander's devaluation of the roles of interpretation and insight in therapeutic processes. See footnote 5 in chapter 5 for Bibring's specific statement to that effect.

jargon), of Freud's concept of reconstruction (a certain type of interpretation), and of his own concept of reconstruction or interpretation "upwards" (10).

Finally, Loewenstein spoke to the dynamic impact of interpretations and their ultimate efficacy: "Interpretations bring forth new material, either in the form of resistance or in the form of additional details, memories, the flow of associations, information, and various changes in the intensity and in the form of symptoms, etc., revealing the dynamic effect of the interpretations. . . . The therapeutic effect of the analysis is due to a psychic process in which each part— the overcoming of resistances, the working through, as well as the remembering and reliving of repressed material and the effect of analytic reconstructions— has its respective place" (12).

In their articles, Kris (1951) and Hartmann (1951) added to these technical descriptions and prescriptions a focus on the array of meanings that could attend, and be invoked by, the interpretive act and interpretive process, each referring to Hartmann's "principle of multiple appeal." Hartmann first explicitly broadened Freud's original conception of interpretation as translation: "Soon Freud found that just to give the patient a translation of the derivatives of his unconscious was not enough. The next step was characterized by a more exact insight into the dynamic and economic problems of resistance" (37). This led Hartmann to state, "The necessity for scrutinizing our patients' material as to its derivations from all the psychic systems, without bias in favor of one or the other, is nowadays generally accepted as a technical principle" (39). And this led in turn to: "I return to the problem of the incidental effects of interpretation, which frequently transcend our immediate concern with the drive-defense setup under consideration, and which are not always predictable. . . . What I have in mind could be designated briefly as the 'principle of multiple appeal' " (41–42).

The next group of papers I turn to centers around the nature of insight and its relation to change, and then on the place of action as a necessary component between insight and change. Gregory Zilboorg, in a 1952 paper, declared that the term "insight" was the cause of the "utmost confusion." He said, "It came from nowhere, so to speak. No one knows who employed it first, and in what sense. . . . Moreover, in the course of the last thirty or forty years it has undergone so many changes and shifts that the concept has become even less clear" (2). And R. Horacio Etchegoyen (1991) reminds us,

"Insight" is not, in fact, a Freudian term. It comes from the English language,[7] not only as a word but also as a concept, since English-speaking

7. There is, in fact, no word for insight in the Romance languages, and French-, Spanish- (and I would expect, also, Portuguese- and Italian-) speaking analysts use the English word, "in-

analysts in Europe and America coined it. However, I think that those who employed this word did not do so with the idea of introducing a new concept; they thought, rather, that they had found an elegant and precise word to express something that belongs entirely to Freud. Analysis aims to offer the analysand a better knowledge of himself; what is meant by insight is that privileged moment of awareness. However, . . . the word *Einsicht,* corresponding to the English word *insight,* rarely appears in Freud's work, and certainly not with the theoretical significance currently accorded to it. (654)

Jerome Richfield (1954), a psychoanalytically informed philosopher, made a major effort—in a curiously unremarked paper—to clarify the psychoanalytic meanings and usages of "insight" and its various aspects—intellectual insight and emotional insight, pseudo-insight, empathic insight, dynamic insight, and so on. Through a process of logical analysis, he clarified the conceptual unclarities in the designations "intellectual" and "emotional" insight. For example, he elucidated two widely different possible usages of "emotional insight": (1) that a relevant emotion is a part of the content or connection grasped by the patient, and (2) that the insight evokes an emotional response, though an emotion may not be part of the content or connection. Richfield then approached the whole problem freshly by referring to two fundamentally different ways of knowing formulated by Bertrand Russell, *knowledge by acquaintance* and *knowledge by description.* For example, he said,

> I have knowledge of both morphine and alcohol. I know that one is a bitter, white crystalline, narcotic base, and is the principal alkaloid of opium; the other, I know to be a colorless, volatile, inflammable liquid which is the intoxicating principle in fermented and distilled liquor. I know, further, that the use of the one tends to inhibit aggressive impulses, while the other releases repressed impulses. At this point my knowledge of the two substances is no longer comparable. Of alcohol I have actually experienced the effects; I have knowledge of alcohol by *direct acquaintance* with the euphoric affective tone produced by its function of release. This is specific knowledge which no amount of discourse on the subject of the effects of alcohol could produce. I have no such direct cognitive experience of the effects of morphine. This quietude or freedom from pathological tensions induced by this opiate is known to me indirectly, if at all, by *analogy* and by *inference.* (400, italics added)

---

sight," in their discourse, because nowadays one can hardly think analytically without using the word.

This is as graphic a description as I have encountered of what we grope to convey when we talk about emotional and intellectual insights, though, as I have indicated, it has never caught on in the psychoanalytic literature.

Richfield went on to say, "The essential point for our purpose is that any cognition of a subject which is derived by description is knowledge *about* that subject and may be independent of any acquaintance with the same subject. . . . Only when knowledge takes this form [acquaintance] is it possible for the cognitive object to receive the necessary integration into the ego . . . the awareness must have the need itself as its object, and not merely facts about it, before changes in the distribution of cathexes are to be brought about" (401–02). Richfield then proposed the new nomenclature of ostensive and descriptive insights based on ostensive and nominal definitions:

> Something is said to be defined "ostensively" when the thing defined is actually exhibited. . . . This is in contrast to a "nominal" definition. For example, a systolic cardiac murmur may be defined nominally in terms which describe its area, pitch, volume, duration, and timing in the cardiac cycle, or it may be dealt with ostensively with a stethoscope. . . . Insights which incorporate the actual conscious experience of their referents can be termed "ostensive" insights. These are obtained through the direct cognitive relations involved in the acquisition of knowledge by acquaintance. The names "descriptive insight" and "ostensive insight" are stipulated as terminological conveniences. (404–05)

Richfield ended with a statement about why he considered both kinds of insight necessary to a proper therapeutic process, to support and consolidate each other. This same necessary conjunction of the two kinds of insight was put very persuasively (but in the familiar language of "emotional" and "intellectual") by Valenstein (1962): "Interpretations, as meaningful explanatory interventions, appeal to an ego which is actively experiential in the sense of emotional participation in, and acquaintanceship with, current and past events; as well as to an ego which is introspective, self-observant, and responsive in terms of intellectual recognition and explanation. . . . With proper timing and appropriate blending of the intellectual and emotional, the material which is brought to consciousness is dynamically accessible to interpretations, and the insights which follow feel authentic and immediately applicable to inner and outer life" (322).

A much more clinically focused article on insight was published by E. Kris (1956) two years after Richfield's and quickly achieved the status of a classic. Kris focused on the differences in the roles that insight, its achievement and its persistence or gradual erosion can play in the analytic process and in the relationship (or lack of relationship) of these differing fates of insight to analytic outcomes and their stability over time. "The closer study of the function of insight in analytic therapy," he wrote, "leads to an additional impression: We are faced with an extraordinarily wide range of individual differences. It is as if in every case the function of insight was differently determined, and its impact differently embedded in the balance of the personality. . . . I should like to refer to three functions of the ego which are intimately involved in the gaining of analytic insight by integrative comprehension. I refer to the control of temporary and partial regression, to the ability of the ego to view the self and to observe its own functions with some measure of objectivity, and to the ego's control over the discharge of affects" (450)—and individual egos vary widely, of course, in these capacities.

Kris then noted the startling differences among analysands in the role of insight in their treatment processes, in the ultimate achievement of insight as a treatment outcome, and in the postanalytic persistence of insight. About its variable and inconstant role in the treatment process he said,

> It concerns the degree to which insight reaches awareness. Interpretation naturally need not lead to insight; much or most of analytic therapy is carried out in darkness, with here and there a flash of insight to lighten the path. A connexion has been established, but before insight has reached awareness (or, if it does, only for flickering moments), new areas of anxiety and conflict emerge, new material comes, and the process drives on: thus far-reaching changes may and must be achieved, without the pathway by which they have come about becoming part of the patient's awareness. . . . As analytic work proceeds, the short-circuit type of reaction to interpretation decreases, that more and more the flickering light stays on for a while; some continuity from one insightful experience to the other is maintained, though naturally what was comprehension and insight at one point may be obliterated at another. But by and large, even these phases seem to become shorter, and the areas of insight may expand. (452)

Kris believed, of course, that insight was essential to the treatment process: "It has been said that insight is not a curative factor, but evidence of cure. The statement is, I believe, fallacious, since it overlooks the circularity of the process. Without other dynamic changes insight would not come about, but without insight and the ego's achievement which lead to insight, therapy itself remains limited and does not retain the character of psycho-analysis." But again, there are very wide variations in the impact of insight in individual cases:

> With some individuals the result of analysis seems to be connected with a lasting awareness of their own problems, a higher degree of ability to

view themselves; with others this is not so—and yet the two groups of patients cannot be distinguished according to the range of therapeutic effects. This possibility finds a parallel in the study of what patients retain in memory of the course of analysis, a problem frequently accessible in repeated analyses. It is well known that the variations are extraordinarily wide. It seems that insight with some individuals remains only a transient experience, one to be obliterated again in the course of life by one of the defences they are wont to use. And it is not my impression that these individuals are more predisposed to future illness than others. This might well remind us how much remains unknown about the conditions under which the ego does its silent work. (453)

(This paper is even better known for its graphic descriptions of the "good analytic hour" and its imitator, the "deceptively good hour.")

Just as, in Kris's words, "interpretation naturally need not lead to insight," so insight need not necessarily lead to change, and this too is a continuing puzzle to the psychoanalytic theory of change and cure. One additional ingredient to which attention was turning during this period was the role of will and action as essentials to be interposed between insight and change. This was first remarked in two papers by Allen Wheelis. In 1950 he said, "Therapy can bring about personality change only in so far as it leads a patient to adopt a new mode of behavior. A real change occurring in the absence of action is a practical and theoretical impossibility" (145), and he asserted that true personality change eventuates only out of repeated (new) behaviors. In 1956, Wheelis added a volitional connotation: "For just as surely as will alone is ineffective, so insight alone is ineffective. No one link can constitute itself into a chain, and no uncoupled link can mediate energy transformations" (298). By a linked chain, Wheelis indicated he meant the sequence from conflict to insight to will to action and finally to character change.

This theme was further developed in the next decade by Valenstein (1962): "However vital and veritable it may become, there is nothing magical about insight; in and of itself, it is not equivalent to a change in behavior, nor does it *directly* produce the relatively conflict-free readaptation which is the hoped-for outcome of a successful psycho-analysis. For there to be final adaptive change, alterations in behaviour, whether subtle or obvious must somehow come about as a result of modifications of action patterns" (323). Two decades later (1983), Valenstein put the word "action" into the title and developed this theme even further. He stated that the traditional premise of classical analysis encompassed the concept of action: "The implication was that once infantile memories, fantasies, and conflicts had become conscious, there would be an opportunity to compare reliving the *past* in the present, with living the *present* in the present, and for action consonant with the reality principle" (361). Therefore, "the ultimate working through of insight is pivotally related to the function of action and to definitive changes in action patterns" (354).

This very capacity to act (differently) or, put better, the presence or absence of an effective "will to act" is a distinct dividing line between the psychoanalytically amenable neurotic patient and the "sicker" narcissistic, borderline patient. As Valenstein put it, "For the so-called 'good neurotic,' with a strong ego who is motivated by suffering and disposed to change, the 'will to act' for the most part can be expected to exert an effect in a relatively silent, ego-syntonic way. For other patients, with so-called narcissistic neuroses, including borderline disturbances, the not-so-strong, ego-deficit patients anchored in a regressed position with a firmly entrenched passive orientation, it is quite different. It is not so silent a matter, this issue of the 'lack of will' to change, to exert oneself toward action in keeping with insight and reality" (366).

Rangell moved the theme of action as a vital component of the change process conceptually the furthest. A whole section of the two-volume collection of his papers (Rangell 1990) is entitled "Choice and Responsibility." One paper in this group, published originally in 1981 (1981a), "From Insight to Change," is emblematic of Rangell's thinking in this arena. In it, he introduced the concept of "the responsibility *of* insight" (129). The sequential thread can be telescoped as follows: "After exposure and amelioration of the etiologic anxiety, the patient has an expanded choice. What follows, however, does not take place automatically, contrary to perhaps one of the most prevalent fallacies in psychoanalytic practice" (127–28). Choice leads to the possibility of action: "What happens next depends mostly on the executive functions of the ego, the patient himself directing his next moves in life" (128); and "With the knowledge it has acquired, the ego is now confronted with the possibility of action which presents an opportunity but also a responsibility" (120). This brings up the responsibility of insight, for the analyst has contributed insights, but "these lead in turn to the role of the patient which follows each increment of insight but which becomes cumulative as the analysis proceeds" (129). Rangell declared, "The patient is ambivalent toward being assigned—and accepting—responsibility. Resistances to progress at this stage are as tenacious as to the original uncovering of the repressed drives—and are to be as vigorously analyzed to the end" (132).

In another paper on this subject, "The Psychoanalytic Theory of Change" (1992), Rangell surveyed his conception of the place of action in the sequence of events leading to change: "Psychoanalytic technique sets up the psychoanalytic situation, in which the psychoanalytic process can take place, by which psychoanalytic goals may be achieved . . . the present paper examines a central aspect of the fourth link, that of psychic change as the major psychoanalytic goal. The psychoanalytic process does not overlap with the process of change. The former may be present without the latter. The analytic process can indeed be operative and even fruitful in some respects, while inner or adventitious factors conspire to delay or thwart basic or significant psychic change" (416). To the patient who, after achieving insights, asks, " 'What then?' Or, as some patients ask explicitly, and all think subliminally, 'So what? What happens now? How does anything change?' " (417), Rangell answers, "Nothing 'happens' by itself" (421). What makes something happen, bringing about change, is the patient's burgeoning capacity to take responsibility for action: "the active necessity, and gradually the responsibility of the patient whose life it is to live" (419–20). He summarized the process by which this comes about: "Insights deriving from specific interpretations, besides having to be imbued and reacted to with the appropriate accompanying affect, need to take their place as examples within a wider ongoing process in which the patient's ego is being trained to oversee and direct the intrapsychic forces which impinge upon it with greater mastery and adaptedness than it did before analysis began" (419). This he called "the intrapsychic agent of action or behaviour," and to make it crystal clear, Rangell invoked the nonpsychoanalytic word "will": "I have added as indispensable to this functioning the factor of ego will. More specifically psychoanalytic, I have pointed to unconscious ego will, the force in the ego which actively chooses and then executes the behaviour chosen" (421). In short, what must be confronted interpretatively is that "with the amelioration of neurotic anxiety, 'I can't' comes to mean 'I won't' " (422). Rangell felt that misunderstanding at this point was responsible for many failed analyses and disillusioned analysts: "The automatic connexion between interpretation and change, which has become a formula for many analysts, led to failure and disappointment on a widespread basis, which led in its turn to a disillusionment with the effectiveness of psychoanalysis itself" (418).

Arnold Cooper (1989), in a historical review of the concepts of therapeutic effectiveness in analysis, commented on the role of action and introduced an interactional emphasis: "The experience of behavioral therapies has shown that the capacity to engage in new actions is not only a result of changing psychic structure but may, under certain conditions, contribute to changes of self-image and self-esteem, with secondary effects in psychic structure" (21). The role of action, which Cooper feels is an essential ingredient of the therapeutic change process, he finds is often an "unmentioned factor": "for example, an 'insight' not leading to new experiences, i.e., new actions, is worth little therapeutically and probably represents an intellectualizing defense. Analysts today tend to appreciate the need for actions, often initially tentative, and for 'practicing' new roles both within the transference and outside the analytic setting" (21). In a subsequent paper (1992), Cooper to all intents and purposes equated insight with its consequent action: "We could describe insight as the emotional and useful, i.e. leading to action, change of one's conscious and preconscious sense of oneself and the world that occurs in the course of actual experience" (248).

Articles by Jacob Arlow,[8] Harold Blum, Peter Neubauer, and Wallerstein, all but the last published in 1979, represent both a stocktaking as of that time and the platform for the next phase of conceptualizing in this realm. Arlow's (1979) paper, "The Genesis of Interpretation," added some distinctive emphases: (1) the function of interpretation in "disturbing the dynamic equilibrium between impulse and defense" (194), with interpretation of defense serving (in terms of Lewin's [1955] analogy to the wake-sleep cycle) to ask the patient to be less wakeful and vigilant, to let himself fall into reverie and produce derivatives of unconscious impulse, and interpretation of impulse serving to rouse the patient to observe the implications of what he has been verbalizing (194–95); (2) the ever-shifting role of the patient in the interpretive process from *passive reporter* of his thought processes to *active reflecter* on the analyst's interventions (195); (3) an elaboration in quite different terms of Strachey's concept of a two-step interpretive process:

> The insight that comes from introspection, intuition, and empathy constitutes only the first part of the interpretive work. This is the subjective or aesthetic phase of the analyst's response. As intriguing and dramatic as it may be it has to give way to a second phase of the interpretive process, one that is based on cognition and the exercise of reason. In order to validate his intuitive understanding of what the patient has been saying, the analyst must now turn to the data of the analytic situation. He must put his insight to the test of objective criteria in conformity with the data at hand. Most of the time the intuitive work has been so efficient that the sense of conviction is immediate, gratifying, and accompanied instantly

8. In between the three papers of 1951 on interpretation by Loewenstein, Kris, and Hartmann, already discussed, and that by Arlow in 1979, Louis Paul (1965) published a paper on interpretation "modified" to constitute a parameter in Eissler's sense. This was a recommendation with severely compulsive character neurosis and schizoid personalities with strong defenses of avoidance and denial, to counter these character defenses with forceful reiterated intrusions via affectively charged interpretations that had to be attended to and could not be ignored. He recommended these more intense interpretive efforts only when the customary more dispassionate tone proved repeatedly fruitless and then only until the desired impact in eliciting attention and response was achieved. In this sense, Paul defined such effort as a true, self-limited parameter.

by recollection of the supporting evidence from the patient's productions. (202–203)

The three articles on insight from the same period all grappled with the (problematic) relationship of insight to change and the twin observable clinical phenomena, change without insight and insight without change. Blum (1979) stated his central thesis at the start: "In analysis, insight is the one element that is never in excess and yet is never complete. I shall maintain that insight propels the psychoanalytic process forward and is a *condition, catalyst, and consequence* of the psychoanalytic process. There is a circular interaction between the development of insight and productive analytic work leading to structural change" (41, italics added). In psychoanalytic psychotherapies, Blum said, "Insight may also be achieved . . . but is more limited, circumscribed, and superficial, often confined to current derivatives of unconscious conflict in one sector of the personality. In supportive or suppressive psychotherapy as opposed to expressive or uncovering psychotherapy, the therapist may deliberately eschew insight as a goal" (42). In fact, Blum declared that this was a prime dividing marker between these modalities: "Correct interpretation and reconstruction depends upon and conveys insight, so that insight may be stated to be a *sine qua non* of psychoanalysis. Indeed, the psychoanalytic process can be differentiated from psychotherapies because it is a definable process requiring free association and interpretation and leads to insight" (43–44). Blum also raised some of the puzzling questions around these issues: "How much analytic ego growth might occur preceding, permitting, and perhaps by-passing the effects of insight? Can the analytic method really stimulate ego growth without benefit of insight and conflict resolution?" (47)—but he did not address them systematically.

Neubauer, in his companion paper (1979), also dealt with the relationship of insight to change, whether cause or effect:

It is not certain whether and under what circumstances insight produces a therapeutic effect. Some think it an instrument by which an analytic result is achieved, while others maintain that insight is the result of—a by-product of—an analytic process that is therapeutic in itself. Actually, the attainment of insight does not guarantee therapeutic improvement. There are many patients whose knowledge of themselves has markedly increased without consequent conflict resolution. Indeed, at times we observe therapeutic results without a significant increase in self-understanding. . . . The relative paucity of papers on the subject of insight indicates that we take its role for granted and have not bothered to explore fully the relation of insight and clinical improvement. (29–30)

Neubauer amplified Kris's earlier observation on the inconstant maintenance of insight: "It is striking that after analysis insight may not be maintained, particularly if we mean by it the memories of conscious retention of events, ideas, and affects which entered awareness during the course of the analysis. It is not what has been recovered that is retained, but rather new structure and function. A new *Gestalt* is established, a reorganized ego structure. Normal repression may occur concomitant with processes of integration and lead to forgetting of the conscious insights even though there is a new personality organization" (34). And like Blum, he raised some of the still puzzling questions, albeit somewhat different ones: "Is the insight gained during analysis by reconstruction, by re-experiencing in the transference, and by interpretation, by the slow building of connections between psychic elements, the past and the present, different from the intuitive insights of artists and poets or the insights of the normal man in everyday life?" (35). Neubauer then listed eight additional (and comparably refractory) questions.

It was this unsettled state of affairs in our understandings of insight that I tried to review in 1983. I spoke in that article of two "contrapuntal perspectives": "the near analytic unanimity of the to-be-taken-for-granted centrality of insight as both the essential vehicle and the curative mechanism of the psychoanalytic treatment process—indeed the purpose to which all else in the analytic process is bent" (34), and "the persistence over the same time span, of certain naggingly stubborn unresolved questions about the phenomenon of insight, its mechanism, its role, its relationship to change" (34–35). What I said about the *mechanism* of insight was paraphrased from the statement made in setting up the Psychotherapy Research Project in 1956 (Wallerstein and Robbins, 258–61). In response to the question of whether insight is "a precondition of change or a result of change, or an accompaniment of change, with either crucial or only incidental value" I wrote,

> In psychoanalytic psychotherapy, an "appropriate" degree of insight is a requisite ingredient; rather than being either a precondition of change or a direct consequence of change, it can better be viewed as the *ideational representation* of the change in ego functioning; this will be articulated more clearly by some patients and only with difficulty by others; the insights achieved need not bear an obvious or manifest relationship to the behavioral or structural change . . . in this sense, the insights might be . . . the means to explain and justify the change; and lastly . . . while the newly acquired more adaptive pattern of behaving and relating might become quite automatic and quite routine, the acquired insights might themselves sink back into the (descriptive) unconscious. (Wallerstein 1983b, 35–36)

The question of "the *role* or the contribution or the relative weighting of insight in the determination of change" is, of course, part of the larger question of interpretation leading to insight as *the* essential vehicle carrying the psychoanalytic change process (the basic premise of most of the literature considered in this book to this point, Alexander and, to some extent, Ferenczi excepted) or as *one* major vehicle, alongside "the *analytic relationship*," as being "of coordinate importance in inducing or promoting change either alongside of insight, or in intimate interaction with it, or as the necessary base or framework that renders useful insight possible and achievable" (36). (That literature is covered in detail in chapters 16 and 17.)

The third question I discussed was "the question of insight without change and also of change without insight" (41). Here, too, I reviewed the continuing inconclusive literature around this issue, concluding, "Perhaps this clinical-theoretical pathway cannot, in theory, ever lead us to definitive resolutions of such recurring questions—no matter what increasing theoretical sophistication is brought to bear upon them over time—or ever definitively help us towards the more precise parceling out of the relative contributions of complementary influences" (42)—and here I offered another, less congenial or less familiar pathway to the ultimate resolution of such questions, by more formal and systematic research into the clinical psychoanalytic situation. I say "such questions" because these are to me eminently researchable questions. Gill ended one of his clinical-theoretical articles (1979) with a plea for empirical research into the matters addressed (albeit in relation to issues other than insight):

> The points I have made are not new. They are present in varying degrees of clarity and emphasis throughout our literature. But like so many other aspects of psychoanalytic theory and practice, they fade in and out of prominence and are rediscovered again and again, possibly occasionally with some modest conceptual advance, but often with a newness attributable only to ignorance of past contributions. There are doubtless many reasons for this phenomenon. But not the least, in my opinion, is the almost total absence of systematic and controlled research in the psychoanalytic situation. I mean such research in contrast to the customary clinical research. I believe that only with such systematic and controlled research will analytic findings become solid and secure knowledge instead of being subject to erosion again and again by waves of fashion and what Ernst Lewy (1941) long ago called the "return of the repression" to designate the retreat by psychoanalysts from insights they had once reached. (286)

At about the same time as this cluster of articles on insight (1979–83), another group of four articles was published resurrecting the extratransference interpretation from the limbo into which Strachey (1934) had seemed to cast it—this despite Strachey's qualifying disclaimer at the end of his article. Two of these articles were rejoinders to Gill's contention in the 1979 Atlanta Symposium that the essence of what qualified to be called psychoanalytic was unremitting attention to the interpretation of the transference (and allusions to the transference) in the here and now.

Rangell (1981b) put this most vigorously (directly vis-à-vis Gill): "I offer the opinion that transference is . . . being thought of and pursued and interpreted too exclusively. An indispensable element can become hypertrophied in psychological as in somatic processes. Waelder (1967) pointed out that history is an alternation of excesses. This occurs in the history of science, psychoanalysis included, as it does in social processes" (671). He went on to assert that overvaluation of the transference interpretation as the be-all of psychoanalysis was a common failing of Kleinian and object-relations theorists but was gaining ground within American ego psychology as well. Gill, he said, was primarily responsible for promoting this trend.

Rangell then said, "While I do not minimize the universality of transference, transference is a necessary but not sufficient condition to see an analysis through to its goal. . . . To the generally accepted formulation that transference recapitulates the developmental history and brings the neurosis into the eye of analysis, I offer the proposition that the transference itself is not sufficient to contain and yield up the crucial events in the complex development of an individual neurosis. I . . . think of any number of instances . . . where I would understand the patients only incompletely and have a very inadequate concept of their neurosis from listening for and confronting the transference alone" (675–77). And even more sharply: "If all I knew about this patient's aggression was what comes out towards me, I do not feel I could know about his aggression. . . . The reason for this, in my opinion, is that the analyst is too kind, dependable, and rational within his neutrality to deserve the patient's load of aggression, and the patient is not without judgment or control at all, even at the unconscious level. Lest I be misunderstood, aggression, of course, invades the transference, subtle and overt, and is never absent. But the degree of aggressive conflict in life, I believe, cannot come out sufficiently to the analyst to routinely convey all that is there" (676–77). Summarizing his viewpoint, Rangell said, "The analyst hovers, *equidistant* not only from the three psychic structures but between intrapsychic and interpersonal, the internal and external world, past and present, transference and original objects (678, italics added).

Stone (1981b) characteristically put his response to Gill's position in a more nuanced though equally compelling way. He first gently mused about Gill's here and now: "It is as if all significant emotional experiences, including extra-analytic experiences, could be viewed as displacements or mechanisms of concealed expression of the transference. . . . That the preponderant emphasis on concealed transference may ultimately, in itself, constitute a 'de facto' change in technique and process, with its own intrinsic momentum, is, I believe, true" (715). Acknowledging that resort to the past or to the outside world could be evasive retreats from the discomfort of the transference affectivity in the present, Stone nonetheless said, "At the risk of slight—very slight!—exaggeration, I must say that, excepting instances of pathological neurotic submissiveness, I have not yet seen a patient who wholeheartedly accepted the significance of his neurotic or transference-motivated attitudes or behavior if he felt that 'his reality' was not given just due" (720).

Stone then began to develop his own complexly tempered perspective: "Granted the power and challenge of cumulative developmental and experiential personality changes, and the undeniable impact of current factors, it remains true that the uniquely personal, decisive elements in neurosis, apart from constitution, originate in early individual experience" (721). And more comprehensively, "The emphasis on the 'here and now' remains not only consistent with, but ultimately indispensable for genuine access to the critical dynamisms deriving from the individual's early development. Nor is this, reflexively—assuming adequate technical sophistication—inconsistent with the understanding and analysis of continuing developmental problems, character crystallizations, and the influence of current stresses as such. Adequate attention to the latter as a complex interrelated group permits the clear and useful emergence into the analytic field of significant early material, as defined by the transference neurosis" (722).

And just as there is past along with present, so there is extratransference along with transference:

Even if one agrees that transference interpretations have a uniquely mutative impact, how exclusively must we concentrate on them? And further: to what degree, and when, are extra-analytic occurrences and relationships of everyday life to be brought into the scope of transference interpretation? With regard to the concentration of transference interpretation alone: it is obvious that a large, complex, and richly informative world of psychological experience is lost, if the patient's extratherapeutic life is ignored. Further, if the transference situation is unique in an affirmative sense, it is also unique by deficit. To rail at the analyst, for example, is a different experience from railing at an employer who might "fire" the patient, or from being snide with a co-worker who might punch him. . . . Certain complex reaction patterns cannot become accessible in the transference context alone. . . .

Finally, there are incidents, attitudes, and relationships to persons in the patient's life experience who are not demonstrably involved in the transference neurosis, yet evoke important and characteristic responses, whose clarification and interpretation may contribute importantly to the patient's self-knowledge as to defenses, character structure, and allied matters. Furthermore, such data may occasionally show a vitalizing direct relationship to historical material. (727–28).

Stone, in overall perspective, reaffirmed the centrality of the "beyond here and now":

First, does the legitimate technical emphasis on the "here and now" devaluate the importance of the past in pathogenesis or in analytic process? With due regard for difficulties which may occur in the adequate recollection or reconstruction of the past and for the fact that changes in methods of approach have occurred, the opinion is offered that, despite special attention to the "here and now," the essential importance of the past remains unquestionable, not only in psychogenesis, but in the need for its technical reinstatement, to the degree reasonably and effectively possible. Second, is analytic work conceivable without resort to the influences and impacts of infancy and early childhood? It is thought that while such efforts might provide productive experiment and be capable of certain useful therapeutic effects, it would be severely (and unnecessarily) limited by its omission of ultimately decisive factors in the understanding of current distortions.[9] (730)

The papers by Nathan Leites (1977) and Blum (1983) differ from those by Rangell and Stone in that they were not such direct responses to Gill's advocacy

9. Like Rangell and Stone, Joseph and Anne-Marie Sandler (1983) responded to Gill's (over)emphases on the transference interpretation in the here and now, but less from the point of view of the also valuable focus on the extratransference current life and more from the point of view of the continued value of the temporal genetic dimension in the interpretive process. They put it as follows: "The analyst must listen for the dominant current conflict or preoccupation that is being censored (i.e., being resisted) and interpret it in a way that the patient experiences relief, and for this purpose he should make use of appropriate interpretations, preferably in the context of the transference, of the pain and discomfort the patient is suffering. . . . However, once that patient has been able to accept the reality of the here-and-now thoughts and feelings . . . particularly the thoughts and fantasies that arise in the transference, and his (second censorship) resistance has fallen away in that particular context, it is appropriate to reconstruct what has happened in the past, to take a genetic perspective in the knowledge that such reconstructions have as their main function the provision of a temporal dimension to the patient's image of himself in relation to his world, and help him to become more tolerant of the previously unacceptable aspects of the 'child within himself' " (423–24).

of exclusive focus on the here and now. Leites focused on the intensification of
the affective and immediate transference experience as a conceptual trend that
had in his view gotten out of hand and had even grown to reverse the original
understanding of the transference: "In the classical conception of transference
the patient was really concerned with the major persons in his childhood when
addressing the analyst. More recently, the patient has come to be viewed as apt
to be unconsciously engaged with the analyst while ostensibly absorbed with
someone else" (275). Or, "In classical transference—displacement from childhood persons to the analyst—the idea of sexual relations with mother evoked
more anxiety than that of intercourse with the analyst. In more recent times,
the opposite seems implied" (276). This is what Leites calls the transference
having "to a certain extent, reversed its direction" (275–76). And this reversal
is carried through consistently: "In the earlier belief, the patient repeated so as
not to remember in the hour; now he remembers so as not to repeat there"
(278). All this appeared to Leites as an unfortunate distortion of our understanding of the analytic process, initiated by Strachey's seminal paper of 1934 and
brought to its logical extreme in Gill's current position (along with others')—
though he does not refer specifically to Gill's work (Gill's signal paper marking
his new directions was not published till 1979, two years after Leites's paper).
Thus, Leites said ruefully, "The earlier belief in the power of the analytic situation to conjure up the past in strength has by now, to a substantial extent,
been tacitly abandoned" (284).

Blum (1983) addressed the whole scope of the extratransference in a paper
forthrightly entitled "The Position and Value of Extratransference Interpretation": "Nontransference interpretation might seem to be a poor relation and
preparatory, subordinate, and supplementary to transference interpretation. . . .
However, the analytic process deals with the patient's unconscious intrapsychic
conflicts and neurotic problems as they manifest themselves anew in the transference neuroses, but also in extratransference phenomena. Derivatives of unconscious conflict (and their interpretation) are not limited to transference.
Transference analysis can become exclusive, all-inclusive and overidealized"
(588). And though, of course, there is a transference dimension to everything
psychic, and though everything psychic is subject to the principle of multiple
function, nonetheless there is a principled place for the extratransference interpretation: "Extratransference interpretation may include transference to objects
other than the analyst, the real relationship to the analyst or other objects, or
may refer to the sphere of external reality rather than the psychic reality of
transference fantasy" (591–92). Further, the two interpenetrate and are mutually
enriching: "The extratransference interpretation not only drives home transference interpretation, but often the two are organically connected and deal with

different manifestations and localizations of the same unconscious conflict constellations. . . . The adult neurosis is never entirely within the transference; conflict derivatives and important compromise formations also appear outside the transference" (593).

For these reasons Blum could say, "It is, in essence, impossible to do analysis purely on the basis of transference without attention to current conflicts and realities and without reconstruction of the past in which the transference is rooted. Transference analysis only is an ideal fiction like the normal ego and would leave the analysis quite isolated from reality" (594).

In fact, avoidance of the nontransference realm could be (would be) analytically counterproductive: "Not all conflicts are represented solely, wholly, or primarily at any one point in the transference; and the transference representation may be diminished in intensity and fragmented when one of the important parts of the configuration is lived out" (599). And, in the same vein, "It is true that attention away from the transference may serve resistance, but exclusive transference interpretation will also serve resistance" (601). Extratransference interpretation may also help to better illuminate past traumata: "Extratransference interpretation also concerns the repression of real traumatic experiences often seen in anniversary reactions. Traumatic experience tends to be repeated not only in transference, but in dreams, screen memories, symptoms, and neurotic behavior. . . . If a crucial part of a pathological constellation is acted out, the complete pattern may not be available for analysis" (601–02).

Finally, Blum raised an interesting and logical question: "It would be interesting to know if child analysts are more comfortable, more at ease with extratransference interpretations and if this technical position complements or competes with essential analysis of the transference" (608). In light of all the foregoing, Blum's conclusion comes as no surprise: "I conclude there is no royal road to analytic interpretation. The transference is the main road but not the only road to mutative interpretation, and we do not analyze just transference or dreams, we analyze the patient" (614). It is this perspective on "the position and value of extratransference interpretation" that should be kept clearly in mind as a periodically needed counterweight to the far more weighty focus through the years on the unfolding of the transference (s) and of the transference neurosis as the central dynamic of the psychoanalytic treatment process.

As a final note in this chapter, a panel on interpretation ("toward a contemporary understanding of the term") was reported by Rothstein (1983). He gave most weight to the special emphases of Arlow, John Gedo, and Roy Schafer. Arlow's views were quoted as follows: The analyst "interprets a narrative fabrication created by each patient along the lines of what Kris called the personal myth, or what I would consider as more accurate, the *derivatives of the persistent unconscious fantasies* that developed out of the interaction between events and development" (238, italics added). And Gedo's views were quoted as "correcting [the] exclusive emphasis on its cognitive component and insight by stressing the 'paraverbal' and *identificatory aspects* of the analytic process, seeming to give them at least equal emphasis in the mode of therapeutic action of psychoanalysis . . . [and] stressing the *matrix of the object relationship* in influencing the therapeutic efficacy of an interpretation" (239, italics added). Last, "Schafer conceives of the analysand engaged in narrative and the analyst formulating interpretations . . . to be engaged in acts of *retelling or narrative revision*. Schafer's presentation emphasized the creative, subjective, inexact and inevitably incomplete and imperfect nature of the interpretive process" (239–40, italics added).

11 Interpretation, Insight, Working Through, and Action: II

The Past Decade

In the past decade the literature on interpretation, insight, working through, and action has burgeoned, but with only a few substantial conceptual advances. I will first review seven papers published between 1984 and 1988 on the nature and direction of interpretation; then four papers published between 1988 and 1990 on the mechanism and role of insight; then two recent efforts at review and integration in these related areas; and finally eight articles from 1992, most of them from an issue of *Psychoanalytic Inquiry* entitled "Interpretation and Its Consequences."

Within the first cluster, on interpretation, Joseph and Anne-Marie Sandler (1984) sought to recast the traditional interplay (and controversy) between interpreting within the here and now of the immediate transference and the there and then of the past prototypes of the transference within their proposed new nomenclature of "past and present unconscious": "The *past unconscious* can be conceived of as containing the whole gamut of immediate, preemptory wishes, impulses, and responses of the individual that have been formed early in his life . . . ; more than instinctual wishes . . . they also include the immediate and spontaneous modes of reacting in any given psychological situation" (369). That is, they "may be instinctual but need not necessarily be so. Thus, for example, solutions to conflict devised or elaborated in early childhood acquire a preemptory quality, as do all sorts of responses aimed at avoiding dangerous situations and preserving safety." In sum, the past unconscious represents the "child within the adult," the totality of the mental life roughly "corresponding, from a developmental point of view, to the first four to six years of life" (370–71). This is essentially sealed off by the repression barrier that covers the infantile amnesia and "is for the most part only reconstructed in analysis, reconstruction which is usually reinforced by those scattered memories that are available from the first years of life, but which memories can only be understood in the light of later reconstructions" (371).

Granted that this "past unconscious is active in the present, and is stimulated by internal or external events occurring in the here-and-now, what . . . we have termed the *present unconscious* is conceived of as a very different organization . . . Whereas the past unconscious acts and reacts according to the past, the present unconscious is concerned with maintaining equilibrium in the present and regards the impulse from the past unconscious as intrusive and upsetting" (372). And "While it is itself . . . the product of the past development of the individual, it [the present unconscious] is orientated, *not to the past, but to the present,* in order to prevent the individual from being overwhelmed by painful and uncontrollable experiences. It constantly creates conflict-solving compromises and adaptations that help to keep an inner balance. Foremost among these is the continual creation or recreation of current *unconscious fantasies and thoughts.* These have a function in the present, are constantly being modified and orientated to the present, although they will, of course, reflect their history in the past" (J. Sandler 1986, 188). In the clinical situation the prime example of such fantasies is the unconscious transference fantasies about the analyst.

It follows that the central interpretive work in the analytic situation is with the unconscious transference fantasies that are the direct representations of the activities of the present unconscious. And since "the *present unconscious* contains present-day, here-and-now fantasies and thoughts that are after all current adaptations to the conflicts and anxieties evoked by the contents of the *past unconscious*" (191), it is clear that via analysis of the fantasies of the present unconscious—centrally the transference fantasies—we can and do reach an understanding of the originating infantile past, which the Sandlers call the past unconscious. What the Sandlers have provided through these conceptualizations is an updated way of encompassing the there and then of the past with the here and now of the present in the interpretive understanding of the transference.

Pine's (1984) paper "The Interpretive Moment," which was referred to briefly in chapter 8, is considered here in the context of his views on the interpretive process. Pine's effort was to extend the applicability of properly interpretive work beyond the classically neurotic patients toward those sicker patients increasingly seen (or, better, recognized) in modern-day consulting rooms. For these sicker patients, "the moment of potential influenceability is simultaneously a moment of vulnerability [with proneness to various disruptive and disorganizing responses]. Is there a way out of this dilemma?" (56).

Pine proposed with such sicker patients "efforts to minimize the shock of the interventions and/or to emphasize the therapist's benevolent presence. . . . The style of intervention is gentle and supportive but its *aim* is to make difficult interpretive work possible" (58). He suggested four strategies to effect these aims: (1) "close off the implicit expectation of patient responsibility for associative response to the interpretation" by assiduously interpreting *both* arms of the conflict in "an explanatory and sympathetic tone" (58–59); (2) "strike while the iron is cold" (60)—that is, when the patient has more distance and control over affectivity, which is exactly the opposite from the strategy recommended with the typical "normal neurotic" ("Some fragile patients . . . need an increase in control capacity and a decrease in emotional force to be able to hold, and perhaps use, the difficult interpretive material"); (3) "increase the patient's relative degree of activity vis-à-vis the interpretive content" by preparing him for the coming interpretation, rendering it tentatively, and *explicitly* giving him the option of accepting, rejecting, or modifying it ("the activation of readiness/ control and the resulting dilution of the force of the interpretation may be precisely what makes it possible for poorly controlled patients to receive the interpretation") (61–63); (4) "increase the 'holding' . . . aspects of the therapeutic environment" (64)—in Donald Winnicott's sense. These are all variations of interpretation, not simply nonspecific support: the patients "feel themselves *supported in hard work* and not just 'taken care of by a kindly doctor' " (66). Further, "In contrast to the interpretive moment with a more analyzable patient, where the therapist might want to heighten the affective impact of interpretation, here the effort is to soften that impact" (69).

"Overall," Pine concluded, "I suggest that the distinction between interpretive (insight) therapy on the one hand and supportive therapy on the other is not the most useful one. A better distinction would be between *interpretation given in the context of abstinence* (i.e., classical psychoanalysis) and *interpretation given in the context of support* (the work described herein)" (70).

Each of the other papers from this group dealing with interpretation made a simple major point. Donald Spence (1986), for example, pointed out the sharp conceptual distinction between scientific explanations and clinical (psychoanalytic) interpretations. "In its typical form the latter provides us with what *might* be true, not necessarily with what *is* true. It provides us with reasons that are not necessarily causes. . . . It rarely suggests alternative explanations. Its principal goal is to persuade, convince, and bring about insight and change *in the patient,* rather than present a reasoned argument that relies on public data and shared rules of evidence and logic. When the clinical account is transposed to the public domain and presented as a form of explanation, it is no longer designed for the benefit of one individual, tailor-made to the needs of the patient, but must now be accessible to all" (5). That is, to put the interpretive act or process into a scientifically explanatory context would require that rules of transformation (canons of inference) be explicated, that data be presented in such a form that refutation and disconfirmation are possible, and so forth—all processes that the plausible and heuristically useful clinical narrative simply does not allow for.

Arlow (1987) emphasized the widening context of interpretation as a multisided process proceeding over time:

Interpretation is not a 'one-shot' experience. It is a process that unfolds in logical sequence, a process that involves the contingent relationships of various expressions of wish and defense. Between the manifest symptom or character trait and the underlying unconscious fantasy of which these are derivative expressions, there is interposed in the mind a whole series of compromise formations, reflecting the vicissitudes of the ego's attempts, over the course of time, to effect an acceptable and stable resolution of the unconscious conflict. The analyst interprets the dynamic effect of each contributor to the patient's unconscious conflicts. . . . The process of interpretation, therefore, may extend over a considerable period of time, as the analyst proceeds in a measured fashion, responsive to the dynamic interplay between wish, defense and guilt at each level of interpretation. (75–76).

In this sense, transference itself is not just a resistance but a complex compromise formation to be unravelled through the interpretive process.

Schlesinger (1988) underlined this conception of a "broader meaning" of the interpretive process. "Interpretation originally implied a kind of process of translation, expressing in ordinary language the meaning of a symptom cast originally in the language of the unconscious. It may still be used in that sense, of course. But interpretation has taken on a broader meaning, implying less the sense of the accurate translation from one language to another, and even less the reduction of superficial complexity to underlying simplicity, and more a broadening and enhancement of meaning" (20).

Brenner (1987) devoted his entire paper to a reconsideration of the concept of working through. He began with Freud's "Remembering, Repeating, and Working Through" (1914). By working through Freud meant helping the patient overcome resistances. Freud had found that merely calling a patient's attention to resistance was not sufficient to make it disappear: "One must allow the patient time to . . . *work through* it. . . . Only when the resistance is at its height can the analyst, working in common with his patient, discover the repressed instinctual impulses which are feeding the resistance" (Freud 1914a, 155). Brenner said that in developing this concept, "it is clear that Freud . . . was attempting to answer the question, 'Why does analysis take so long? Why doesn't a patient get well as soon as the analyst has understood correctly the nature and origins of the patient's unconscious wishes and correctly interpreted them to the patient?' It was in answer to this question that Freud first introduced the notion of working through" (92). Brenner added that in introducing the concept Freud "meant to counsel his colleagues to be patient in analyzing a patient's transference, then seen as resistance, and to urge the view that a neurosis is to be taken seriously, rather than looked upon as a piece of nonsense that can be expected to disappear as soon as one has shown a patient its irrational nature"

(93–94). Brenner added, "In 1914 Freud had a twofold view of working through. On the one hand he conceived of it as a bother and a nuisance—a regrettable delay in the process of cure. It was something that had to be done to overcome resistance, specifically, the resistance caused by transference. On the other hand, he viewed working through as therapeutically the most valuable part of psychoanalysis. Only working through leads to real insight and to dependable, lasting change in a patient, was his belief" (102).

After reviewing the significant literature on this topic over the seventy-year span since Freud's paper, Brenner stated his own position: "Working through is not a regrettable delay in the process of analytic cure. It *is* analysis. It is the interpretive work which, as Freud wrote in 1914, leads to truly valuable insight and to dependable, lasting therapeutic change. . . . The analysis of psychic conflict in all of its aspects is what should properly be called working through" (103). To make his point even more strongly, Brenner ended with, "To repeat, working through is not a special kind of analysis. It is ordinary, run-of-the-mill analysis, as we know it today. Nor is it the analysis of one or another component of psychic conflict. It is the analysis of psychic conflict in all its aspects, now one and now another" (106–07). In effect, Brenner was implicitly calling for abandonment of the term as a redundancy in describing analytic work. I have not seen any subsequent papers challenging his argument.

Of the four papers published between 1988 and 1990 on the mechanism and role of insight, Warren Poland's (1988) tried to open new ground. He first offered a comprehensive definition of insight: "In analysis we tend to make a division between the process, which we call introspection, and the knowledge acquired, the content, which we then call insight. But . . . we know . . . that what one knows and the act of knowing are not fully separable. Moreover, when we say someone values insight, we mean he values the knowing of himself, not simply some specific piece of knowledge. I shall use the word *insight,* therefore, in its broad sense of referring both to looking within and to what is learned by that search" (342). From this Poland covered some familiar ground (Blum, Neubauer): "Insight has . . . come to involve a continuum of ever-expanding stages, not a final point of perfect knowledge" (347); it "can be more or less, but it can never be complete" (348). Therefore, "Psychic truth is partial but cumulative. As a result, reconstructions may hold true and be of use in opening new possibilities of understanding beyond the question of their external historical validity" (353–54). His main point, and his new emphasis, is that insight is not *given* by the analyst or *achieved* by the patient; it is rather a *joint* construction of the analytic dyad. In answer to the question, "Does interpretation only expose meaning that already exists or does it create new meaning? Where in the dyad does an insight arise?" (359), Poland responded, "I believe that it would be wrong to follow the extreme path that the unconscious of one person is created by the unconscious of the other, and also wrong to adopt the view that the analyst offers nothing new, that all is already present in the patient's mind. The patient somewhere knew what it was that had to be repressed, or there would have been no repression. But he did not know why he was obliged to maintain repression. The labor of analytic work, of exposing and resolving resistance, belies the view that the analyst does no more than put into words what the patient already knew and was almost ready to acknowledge" (359–60).

The papers by Theodore Jacobs (1990) and Jule Miller (1990) came from the same issue of *Psychoanalytic Inquiry,* devoted to a reconsideration of the Alexandrian notion of the corrective emotional experience. They were among the papers giving the reconsideration (and to some extent the original consideration) a positive context. Jacobs said, "In our attunements we go beyond strict neutrality. Inevitably we act in 'corrective' ways, and in my view every good analysis includes a measure of this ingredient in its therapeutic mix" (446); of "corrective" experiences vis-à-vis insight he wrote, "Regarded not long ago as the oddest of bedfellows, insight and 'corrective' experiences in treatment have in fact turned out to be rather intimate partners. They are not, as we were once taught, mutually exclusive processes technically and theoretically worlds apart. They are, rather, synergistic forces in treatment, in continued interaction, one paving the way for the other, each important, each contributing in essential ways to the therapeutic action of psychoanalysis" (454). Similarly, Miller, while acknowledging Alexander's view that insight and genetic understanding, though important, had a secondary and supportive role in relation to the corrective emotional experience, also underlined his feeling that "the corrective emotional experience complements the therapeutic effects of insight gained through the analysis of a particular issue; often, the direct corrective experience has wider and deeper ramifications and stronger therapeutic effect" (384).

Rockland (1989), in his book on supportive psychotherapy, dealt with working through, insight, and mode of therapeutic action, each specifically in relation to the supportive psychotherapeutic approach. With regard to working through, in contrast to its operation in psychoanalysis, Rockland stated, "in supportive therapy, because there is no uncovering of unconscious conflict, working through refers to the repetitive pointing out of pathological and maladaptive defenses, the need to forgo certain maladaptive behaviors, the attenuation of negative transferences, the repetitive praise of positive change, and the time necessary for identification with the therapist to take place; in short, consistent reiteration of the techniques of supportive therapy" (159).

With regard to insight and the supportive approaches, Rockland said, "Both interaction and insight are crucial to therapeutic and structural change, and they cannot be separated from each other. They represent cognitive and experiential aspects of the same treatment process. These issues are relevant to the discussion because they take the exclusive focus off of interpretation and insight as the only mutative factor in psychoanalytic treatment. They furnish a theoretical background against which to understand how supportive therapy can also be mutative and can lead to structural change (Wallerstein, 1986a), without using interpretation and without making unconscious mental content conscious" (244). And with regard to (comparative) modes of therapeutic action, Rockland devoted major segments of his book to specifying the differences between expressive and supportive approaches: "Both types of treatment offer the opportunity for new introjections and identifications—psychoanalysis by interpretation of transference distortions, supportive therapy by directly expressing and modeling new values, perceptions, and modes of functioning. Both have the potential for the building of new mental structures, through either correcting old ones [psychoanalysis] or diluting them with newer ones [supportive therapy]" (245).

I turn now to two efforts to review and integrate these related areas, written from the other two major regions of psychoanalysis worldwide, Europe and Latin America, and from theoretical frameworks different from the ego-psychological structural theory so long dominant in North America. Harold Stewart (1990), a member of the British Independent group, with a basically object-relational theoretical perspective, entitled his article "Interpretation and Other Agents for Psychic Change." He began his historical overview, as almost every such presentation does, with Strachey's 1934 paper on the mutative interpretation, summarizing it as follows: "In this process, the analyst interprets the patient's impulses toward the analyst in the here-and-now together with the analyst's fantasized behaviour; for the interpretation to be successful, the patient will recognize the difference between the analyst's fantasized behaviour and his actual real behaviour from the patient's experience of the analyst over the course of the analysis. It means that the patient will recognize the difference between the archaic fantasy object and the real external object of the environment" (61–62). He added, "It needs saying here that the efficacy of the mutative transference interpretation relies heavily on the patient's capacity for reality testing to recognize this difference" (62).

Stewart then introduced what he called "two main varieties of transference interpretation. The first is the type . . . where the interpretation is aimed at understanding a drive-anxiety-defence conflict between patient and analyst in an anaclitic, dependent type of object relationship. The second is aimed at understanding the sensibilities and vulnerability of patients in a narcissistic type of object relationship, of understanding the patient's great potential for experiencing shame, humiliation and resentment of the analytic relationship" (62).[1] And this led Stewart to call on the concepts of Winnicott and Balint, two of the major formative influences in the development of the object-relational perspective, to further widen the parameters involved in assessing the change process. In relation to Winnicott's views, Stewart said, "The analytic setting in its reliability invited regression to a state of dependence on the setting with the possibility of a re-experiencing of the environmental failure situations in the past, together with the anger relating to such failure both in the past and in the present setting. This is repeated in different ways many times and ultimately it leads to a healing of the trauma of the failure situation and the resumption of healthy emotional growth and development" (64). And in relation to Balint's very similar views, Stewart said, "The analytic setting allows regression to the level of the basic fault with a re-experiencing of these early deficient object

1. Actually, these "two main varieties" are condensed from the six "types of transference interpretations . . . from the object-relations viewpoint" described by Stewart in a 1987 paper as: "(i) Interpretations aimed at understanding a drive-anxiety-defence conflict between a patient and analyst in an anaclitic type of object relationship. (ii) An extension of (i) having two simultaneous conflicts of a similar or complementary nature. (iii) Interpretations aimed at understanding the sensibility and vulnerability of patient and analyst in a narcissistic type of object relationship. (iv) An extension of (iii) to include the interpretation of failure to achieve such understanding. (v) Interpretations aimed at understanding the atmosphere or mood between patient and analyst which might be in either type of object relationship. (vi) Interpretations aimed at understanding the patient's unconscious response to the analyst's interpretations" (204). In a parenthetical remark about the third (and fourth) of these six types, Stewart noted, "This particular type of interpretation, together with the analyst's awareness of his failure to be sufficiently sensitive to his patients, is one that Kohut (1971) has written on extensively, but he has done this at the expense of interpreting the patient's conflictual anxieties. He believes that only this type of interpretation is truly empathic and reconstructive, yet this does not accord with clinical experience. The example of the use of my countertransference to understand the dilemma of my patient with her simultaneous conflicting anxieties, in my opinion, needs every bit as much of my empathy and intuition as any understanding of her narcissistic vulnerabilities which were certainly much in evidence in that patient" (201–02).

Treurniet (1993) has strongly supported Stewart's conception of two main kinds of mutative interpretations in almost identical language: "Besides the 'classical' mutative type of transference interpretation in a drive-anxiety conflict there is another type, no less mutative, aiming at understanding the vulnerability of narcissistic patients and their great potential for shame, humiliation, and resentment in the analytic situation, while recognizing our own reality as analysts-with-limited-empathy. From the reliving of the early infant environment, the analyst can interpret the past as it is regressively recreated in the present through the transference, reexperiencing the trauma within a new context, and providing a chance for repair and restoration with the analyst as a new object. In this sense transference can be hypothesized both as a repeatable configuration and as something created anew" (219).

relationships and, after this has been repeated in different ways, the basic fault can heal over and healthy growth recommence" (64–65). Stewart made the point that these regressions need to be reexperienced without interpretation, in contradistinction to the Kleinians, who would vigorously interpret the underlying archaic fantasies. And in consequence, "today, in view of the greater stress laid upon transference work in the here-and-now of the defensive manoeuvres of the ego, reconstruction has lost some of its therapeutic significance" (64).

These considerations on the analytic relationship as a primary (and mutative) factor in the therapeutic change process are developed at length in chapters 15, 16, and 17. Here I want to call attention to Stewart's categorization of the array of "agents necessary to produce psychic changes" (68)—that is, change agents beyond the single dimension described by Strachey in 1934 as the mutative transference interpretation. Stewart listed them as follows: (1) the various types of transference interpretations that he had cited; 2) extratransference interpretations (here he leaned heavily on Blum's 1983 paper on the extratransference interpretation, from which he quoted a whole paragraph); (3) reconstructions; (4) therapeutic regressions (à la Winnicott and Balint); and (5) techniques other than interpretation, to overcome analytic impasses, and Stewart gave some clinical instances of such extreme situations—for example, in the case of sicker patients, in whom transference interpretations "addressed to the rational aspects of the self . . . are no longer heard as such by the patient" (67) and in situations in which Stewart said he felt called on to yell at the patient, to threaten to stop the treatment, and even to physically restrain the patient: "One could say that in these situations where the analyst finds the patient's behaviour is becoming intolerable, the analyst has to behave as a sane rational person towards the rather insane irrational patient. The analyst's is the only voice of sanity and control and on the patient's ability to hear, listen to and identify with this voice depends the future of the analysis" (68). That is, the spectrum of recognized change agents in Stewart's lexicon has become far broader than was envisaged initially by Strachey and adhered to by analysts so singlemindedly for so long.

"The panoramic and virtuoso sweep" of Etchegoyen's (1991) lengthy book *The Fundamentals of Psychoanalytic Technique*—"his encompassing literally almost the entire world's literature in his topic area, together with the sober and unpolemical and undogmatic comparing and contrasting of differing regional and theoretical viewpoints" (Wallerstein, Foreword, xxxi)—cannot be assessed from the perspective of this book in just a few paragraphs. Its table of contents, listing sixty chapters, each with ten or twelve major subdivisions, is itself a rich survey of all the intersecting conceptual and technical areas involved the theory of psychoanalytic technique. I can perhaps best give some sense of how the book fits with my conceptual scheme by quoting a brief illustrative passage from Etchegoyen's statements on just one topic, curative factors in psychoanalysis.

Etchegoyen's intent was to look at diverse criteria for cure proposed within radically different theoretical perspectives and to search for their areas of convergence:

> Let us take as an example Hartmann's criterion of cure—that is, the reinforcement of the area free of conflicts and, consequently, a better adaptation to reality—and let us compare them with what Klein proposes when she affirms that paranoid and depressive anxieties have to be worked through. Put thus, the difference is evident and irreducible. Klein always said, however—following Freud . . . —that one of the fundamental elements of the depressive position is the contact with the object, that is, with reality. Mourning, Freud says, consists in that reality painfully reveals to us that the object is no longer there. And mourning, for Klein, consists in being able to accept psychic reality and external reality just as they are. Although Hartmann does not speak of mourning, his concept of adaptation to reality comes from Freud. Hartmann and Klein, then, have to agree that an analysand should end his analysis better in contact with reality than he was before he began.
>
> Let us take another criterion, such as Lacan's access to the symbolic order. Lacan always becomes angry with Hartmann; he has his reasons, but I do not know if they are justified. Considered in a pedestrian manner, Hartmann's criterion of adaptation sounds sociological and is repugnant to Lacan. Personally, I have many points of disagreement with Hartmann, but I do not believe he is superficial or a simple (simplistic) representative of "the American way of life." If one judges dispassionately what Lacan says, one realizes that it is necessary to abandon the imaginary order, which is the order of dual and narcissistic relations, to elaborate a conceptual or abstract type of thought, which he rightly calls symbolic. This thought is what allows access to the order of the real. (622–23).

Etchegoyen ended this small section with, "While the subject of curative factors leads us inexorably to the most complicated theoretical problems of our discipline and to the point possibly of a major confrontation of the schools, it is also true that in the practice of the consulting room there is a broad enough agreement, which is surprising, as to the evaluation of the analysand's progress" (623)—that is, a convergence at the technical and clinical level of what in theoretical (metapsychological) terms represents wide and seemingly almost unreconcilable divergence. And of course this last (programmatic) thought is very congenial to my own thinking (Wallerstein 1988a, 1990a, 1992a).

I turn now to eight papers from 1992, two of them—from opposite perspectives—dealing with reconstruction in analysis, five adding some nuances to consideration of the topic of interpretation, and one far-ranging paper encompassing considerations of the analytic process, structural change, noninterpretive supportive elements, and interpretation as a "transactional act."

Poland (1992), in a paper dealing centrally with the transference (as a mutual, and original, creation of analyst and analysand), refers quite briefly to reconstruction (as distinct from interpretation proper) in what seems a dismissive way, making it almost redundant and epiphenomenal as an activity. I cite this because I think it represents the broad consensus today on the declining significance of the process of reconstruction in the face of the current emphasis on the centrality of the here and now in interpretation, on the transference as an expression of the interactive, dyadic analytic relationship, on the intersubjectivity of the analytic process, and on the current hermeneutic emphases even within the ego psychology paradigm (Spence 1982, 1987).

Poland put this as follows: "An interpretation . . . refers to a statement which extends to a new level the understanding of dynamics, or genetics as based on an affective experience within the analytic moment. . . . A reconstruction, in contrast, hypothesizes a historical past which could explain with plausibility and probability the formation and shape of the patient's unconscious fantasies. . . . In short, interpretation links immediate experience with unconscious fantasies; reconstructions offer links between unconscious fantasies and possible or probable historical pasts. . . . Interpretations can come very close to approximating psychic truth. In contrast, reconstructions, useful as they are, are unavoidably more speculative" (201). I think this statement is a fair reflection of the currently low regard for the concept of reconstruction, which Freud (1937b) accorded a vital status, almost coequal with that of interpretation, in the psychoanalytic search for the veridical truth of the life story of the suffering patient.[2]

Gail Reed (1993), however, offers a ringing espousal of the distinctive continuing value of reconstruction in the analytic process. She states that though the psychoanalytic method may impose limits on the degree to which specific reconstruction of past events and the fantasies connected to them is possible, "it is my contention that specific reconstruction of memories and/or fantasies is sometimes the crucial therapeutic element in a treatment . . . when disavowed memories have become the nidus of organizing unconscious fantasies. Such combinations of memory and fantasy may represent the core of a patient's dif-

---

2. In Strachey's introductory note to Freud's 1937 paper, he reminded us that the whole of the Wolf-Man case (1918) as well as a large part in the case history of the Rat-Man (1909b) and of the homosexual woman (1920b) revolve around constructions in analysis.

ficulties and continue actively in patients' minds to affect their behavior, character and present perception while remaining sequestered from conscious awareness" (54).

Reed then specifies her method of approach:

> Reconstruction is an ongoing series of partial restatements in more and more precise language of memories and/or fantasies which have been disguised by specific, demonstrable mental operations. It is a reasoned technical procedure utilizing general principles of interpretation of verbal derivatives . . . which reverses these mental operations. Reconstruction is also an act of the analyst which becomes part of the transference and must be analyzed as such. *However, the purpose of reconstruction is not, to my mind, the isolated delineation of these fantasy/memory organizations. The point is to specify the way they have been fashioned by the patient, including, as far as possible, the specific materials he or she has used in their creation. The reason for such specificity is that the way they have been constructed explains how they organize meaning for the patient.* (54–55)

Reed goes on to give a very plausible clinical illustration of the sequence in a span of psychoanalytic work: transference interpretation followed by a dream report, which led to a recurrent dream from childhood and a related screen memory, followed by the reconstruction of a very specific childhood fantasy, which led directly to the recovery of a very conflicted and specific childhood memory that served as the initiator and organizer of the subsequently unfolding neurotogenic impulses, behaviors, and perceptions. Perhaps this and similar efforts presage a revival of interest in the place of reconstruction in the therapeutic process—an example of Rangell's tapping the dial needle that has gotten stuck at one point in its arc.

Of the five papers from the sequence on "Interpretation and Its Consequences," I will quote only efforts at fresh or idiosyncratic formulations. Samuel Abrams (1992) outlined three descriptive categories that he stated together comprised interpretation: context or climate, the how or the interpersonal aspect of interpretation; content, the what; and aim, the why of interpretation. These factors have both independent and interlocking roles in shaping the interpretation and in leading to an understanding of both its impact and the response to it. Abrams also distinguished between interpretation of character resistance and interpretation of transference resistance. He stated that character resistances come to the fore first and that "the resistance of the transference occurs later, once past images and past developmental organizations are revived. When you interpret traits of character you focus on the imagined advantages and disadvantages of the patient's approach to here-and-now situations; when you interpret the transference, you explain that a past has been revived and is being replayed in the present" (203). This is, of course, a particular way to allocate the emphases in interpretive work, now to the past, now to the transference, in accord with Abrams's categorization of resistances.

Joseph Lichtenberg's (1992) emphasis was on the aim or function of interpretations: "A shared belief in a *series* of interventions building toward a coherent aggregate effect may often (certainly not always) transcend theoretical differences as to what that effect should be" (273). And of aim or function he said, "As a working analyst I do not think of myself as concerned at all with encouraging destabilization of the status quo, . . . , finding chinks in the defensive armor . . . , or applying optimal frustration. . . . Rather, I am guided by an attempt to maintain optimal responsiveness . . . to the patient's inner state of mind, especially her affects and her intentions as *she* would recognize them to be. In so doing, I hope to encourage her exploratory-assertive motivation to remain active" (270).

Judith Chused (1992) focused on the interactive, transactional, back and forth nature of the interpretive process, carrying intended and also inadvertent meanings and conveying information both ways. To begin with, interpretations "are *the analyst's* interpretations. And this the patient knows. They do not just convey information about the patient's psychic functioning. They also provide information about *what* the *analyst* thinks and *how* he thinks, information which will be duly noted by the patient, albeit distorted by the transference. An analyst can not circumvent this" (276). This makes for "the multiple meanings the act of interpreting acquires during the course of analysis" (277). Chused amplified this as follows: "The *content of an interpretation* communicates to the patient an understanding of the *why* of his behavior; the *act of interpreting* conveys that the analyst can tolerate the behavior and the *why* without reacting adversely to it. When the act of interpreting, being a verbal action that is different from what is anticipated, disrupts the patient's psychic set, the content of the interpretation can provide a focus around which the perception of the analytic experience is reorganized." That is, "the act of interpreting is an experience that adventitiously provides more for the patient than just insight. An effective interpretation made from a position of neutrality and abstinence is a nonparticipation in the patient's attempt at transference gratification, and a nonverbal clarification that the analyst's expectation of the analytic relationship is different from the patient's. This is not a corrective emotional experience. It is an *informative experience* but like the corrective emotional experience, it provides an opportunity for the patient to learn something new about reality" (291). Overall, "the phenomenon of transference exerts its influence in how the interpretation is heard—even after the interpretation is heard. . . . With every interpretation an inequality in the analytic dyad is made evident. That the interpretation also conveys (hopefully) important information to the patient justifies but does not diminish this. Inevitably, how the patient utilizes the content of the interpretation will depend in part on the meaning he ascribes to the inequality" (292). As a final note, "Relevant interpretations are made about the meanings of the interpretive process for the patient" (294).

Joseph Weiss (1992) directed his article to the deployment of interpretations in relation to his particular perspective on the fundamental nature of the therapeutic process: "The patient suffers from his pathogenic beliefs and is highly motivated unconsciously to disprove them. They constrict him; they prevent him from pursuing highly desirable goals; they give rise to painful affects; and they limit his control over his mental life. In psychoanalysis or in psychoanalytic psychotherapy, the patient seeks the analyst's help in his efforts to disconfirm his pathogenic beliefs" (298). This conception shapes the intent of the interpretive process: "Interpretation is useful to the extent that it contributes to the patient's working to disprove the unconscious beliefs that underlie his psychopathology" (296). Interpretation works this way when its content exposes or "disconfirms" a false pathogenic belief. This is called "passing the test" (i.e., the patient's test of the therapist) and is therefore "pro-plan"; that is, it supports the patient's unconscious plan to utilize the therapy to disconfirm his pathogenic beliefs and thereby to overcome his neurosis.

However, it is explicit in this "control-mastery theory" that the therapist can also "pass the test" by other than interpretive means; for example, by behaviors that run counter to the patient's expectations based on his grim, unconscious pathogenic beliefs: "If the analyst passes his tests by noninterpretive means, the patient may be helped to disprove these beliefs. Moreover, as our research has demonstrated . . . a patient may develop insights on his own, unassisted by interpretation. This is because if the analyst passes his tests by noninterpretive means, the patient may feel safe enough to bring certain previously repressed mental contents to consciousness." But "Nonetheless, interpretation is an essential technique. The insight a patient acquires from the analyst's passing his tests by noninterpretive means is likely to be partial, incomplete, and less than explicit" (301). However, he also then said, in circumscribing interpretation, "In general, interpretation is effective *only* if it is pro-plan; that is, if the patient can use it in his struggle to carry out his plans. Indeed, if an interpretation is anti-plan, that is, if it tends to confirm the patient's pathogenic beliefs, the patient may be set back by it" (302).

To underscore his theoretical perspective in psychoanalysis and his radically different understanding of the function of interpretation within it, Weiss directly compared his control-mastery theory with "traditional theory," meaning all other views of psychoanalysis generally, not just traditional (American) ego psychology:

> Whereas the traditional theory recommends that the analyst be neutral or impartial when confronting an unconscious conflict, my approach recommends that in general he take sides. . . . in traditional theory, no one impulse is necessarily more pertinent to the patient's progress than another, and the analyst has no reason to favor one impulse over the other. Moreover, the analyst has good reason not to do this: he is strongly opposed to imposing his views on the patient.
>
> According to the theory proposed here, however, unconscious conflict is typically between certain of the patient's normal desirable goals and the expectation arising from his pathogenic beliefs that by pursuing his goals he will put himself in danger. Since the analyst's main task is to help the patient disconfirm his pathogenic beliefs and pursue the goals they warn him against, the analyst should, in general, take sides. He should help the patient realize that the dangers foretold by the beliefs are not real and that he may safely pursue the goals.
>
> In contrast to the traditional theory, which assumes that the analyst should rely as much as possible on interpretation, the theory proposed here assumes that in some instances the analyst's passing the patient's tests by noninterpretive means contributes considerably to the patient's progress. By so doing, the analyst may help the patient feel secure enough with him to face the dangers foretold by his pathogenic beliefs. (306–07)

This all amounts, of course, to a distinct and quite idiosyncratic position on the role, scope, and function of interpretation, set within and stemming from a distinct and idiosyncratic theoretical perspective in psychoanalysis.[3]

Renik (1992), the editor of the issue of *Psychoanalytic Inquiry* devoted to interpretation, wrote both a prologue and an epilogue for it. In the brief epilogue, he noted the striking lack of consensus in regard to the two questions posed to each of the eight authors, "What is interpretation?" and "What are its consequences?" This caused Renik to wonder, perhaps ruefully, "Perhaps the term *interpretation* itself has become something of a burden. It certainly originated in a conception of the analytic enterprise that is now obsolete—one that viewed the analyst as a decoder of encrypted messages from the unconscious—and brings with it a confusing legacy. *Intervention,* used by most non-English-

---

3. For a full development and explication of this new theoretical perspective, "control-mastery theory," see the full-length book by Weiss, Sampson, and their collaborators (1986). For a critique of it in relation to what Weiss calls "traditional theory," see my book review (1987).

speaking analysts, seems much more to the point" (368). To me, such a change in nomenclature would bring more confusion than it would resolve, since in the English-language literature currently, the word "intervention" is not an alternative to "interpretation" but a more encompassing word to describe the totality of the analyst's verbal and nonverbal ways of responding to the patient, interpretation among them but also many others, including silence.

Nikolaas Treurniet's paper (1993) is far-ranging, encompassing many considerations of the analytic process, structural change, noninterpretive supportive elements, and interpretation as a "transactional act," all under the synthesizing rubrics of "Noninterpretive Elements in Support of the Process" and "Interpretive Elements in Support of the Process." Here I want to comment especially on Treurniet's conceptualization of the interactive and mutually supporting nature of the elements within that dichotomization. After thoroughly reviewing the conceptions of the British object-relational theorists, especially Winnicott, Balint, Christopher Bollas, and Stewart, and their concepts of holding, of setting and safety, of frame and space, and of play and rules, Treurniet summarized,

> Support of the process is divided into noninterpretive and interpretive elements. The analytic setting, functioning as a protective environment preserving the analysand's private construction of reality, is currently considered to be a major element in the curative process. It is assumed that, besides drive-satisfaction and the wish to possess the object, there is a special object need which is indispensable for ego development: the need for "holding" in time and space. The holding function of the analyst has as its essential task the maintenance and preservation of the analytic potential space, its playground, while surviving the analysand's attacks in a non-retaliatory way. An essential feature of support of the analytic process is the analyst's survival and his protection of psychoanalytic technique while providing space for freedom of association and regression. (217)

Treurniet did not hesitate to align his conception of the meaning of the supportive aspects of treatment with the conceptions of the Menninger Psychotherapy Research Project, although he expressed it in very different language.

Turning to the interpretive elements, Treurniet emphasized that: "making an interpretation is a transactional act that cannot be separated from the state of relatedness between analyst and patient. Interpretations not only uncover hidden meanings but also create additional ones. It remains an open question if the analyst's acts and attitude are inferior to verbal interpretations. . . . The act of interpretation is a transactional process in which both partners have interwoven participations. What is interpreted often acquires additional meaning also by what is not interpreted" (219). Then, bringing the noninterpretive and the interpretive together in yet another way, Treurniet said, "If we define the analytical process as a course of events in which the intrapsychic reappears in the interactional, that is, the transference, then we can define support of the process as pertaining to all those interactional factors which advance this reappearance" (220).

After presenting detailed clinical material in support of the various concepts he advanced, Treurniet concluded that he had illustrated a number of key ideas, among them the notion of change without interpretation and without the kinds of insights generated in the interpretive process: "Re-experiencing early deficient object relationships repeatedly and in different ways can 'repair' the basic fault and restore growth; the importance of the regressive space becomes clear when considering the difference of the agencies of interpretation and of object relationships in the process of psychic change; there are apparently roads to psychic change other than the mutative transference interpretation; the symbolically experienced actions of the analyst can function as an equivalent to interpretation like the symbolic enactments of the patient can be an equivalent of free association" (228).

I can perhaps best end this sequence of chapters on interpretation, insight, working through, and action with a quotation from Stewart (1987) on the transference value, on appropriate occasions, of not interpreting:

> Apart from the necessity of not over-interpreting and of giving the patient the necessary psychic space to develop his own thoughts and feelings in his own way, there are times, usually late in the analysis, when the patient is recovering contact with his lost original objects. This is an experience associated with mixed feelings, a bittersweet remembrance of sadness, regret and love, free of paranoid hate and self-pity. These feelings of wholeness are extremely meaningful and moving for both patient and analyst and it is imperative for the analyst, in Balint's phrase (1968) "the unobtrusive analyst," to be there, to listen and to share, but above all, not to intrude with any interpretation, no matter how profound the analyst may think it to be. (204).

This moving statement about the useful place of appropriate (and tactful) silences during the course of analytic work is far removed from what Gill has correctly decried as the fetish of "the essentially silent analyst" (see chapter 12) as the logical extension of the doctrine of the utmost restraint in the interpretation of transference, especially in the early stages of analysis.

Just as the dynamic unconscious and psychic continuity have long been acknowledged as the most fundamental organizing concepts of Freud's theory of mental functioning (see, for example, Rapaport 1960), so has transference and the closely related concept of resistance been equally long recognized as the most fundamental organizing conception of psychoanalysis as a therapy, distinguishing it from all the varieties of nonpsychoanalytic psychotherapies. Yet, like just about every other critical psychoanalytic concept, transference has altered significantly since Freud's original statements and elaborations. Freud's own references to it are certainly among the most numerous in the *Freud Concordance* (Guttman, Jones, and Parrish 1980).

Though his first use of the term in a psychoanalytic sense occurred in *Studies on Hysteria* (Freud and Breuer 1893–95),[1] most writers agree that the first extended discussion was in Freud's write-up of the Dora case (1905a). There he defined transferences as "new editions or facsimiles of the impulses and phantasies which are aroused and made conscious during the progress of the analysis; but they have this peculiarity . . . that they replace some earlier person by the person of the physician. To put it another way: a whole series of psychological experiences are revived, not as belonging to the past, but as applying to the person of the physician at the present moment . . . by cleverly taking advantage of some real peculiarity in the physician's person or circumstances and attaching themselves to that. These, then, will no longer be new impressions, but revised editions." Further on he called transference "an inevitable necessity," and there are "no means of avoiding it" (116), adding that "psycho-analytic treatment does not *create* transferences, it merely brings them to light" and, in his most pivotal and consequential insight, that, "transference, which seems ordained to be the greatest obstacle to psycho-analysis, becomes its most powerful ally, if its presence can be detected each time and explained to the patient" (117). In that same paper, Freud acknowledged that his failure to detect the burgeoning (negative) transference in this case played the central role in Dora's abruptly breaking off the still quite incomplete treatment. Aside from its other meanings, this paper

1. There, Freud stated a number of reasons why resistance arises to the psychical work. The third one is listed as follows: "If the patient is frightened at finding that she is transferring on to the figure of the physician the distressing ideas which arise from the content of the analysis. This is a frequent, and indeed in some analyses a regular, occurrence. Transference on to the physician takes place through a *false connection*" (302).

became known as one about the possible deleterious consequences of such a failure of recognition.

In "The Dynamics of Transference" (1912a), Freud set forth his conceptions of the transference most comprehensively. Calling it *"the most powerful resistance to the treatment"* (101), he then expanded:

> We find in the end that we cannot understand the employment of transference as resistance so long as we think simply of "transference." We must make up our minds to distinguish a "positive" transference from a "negative" one, the transference of affectionate feelings from that of hostile ones, and to treat the two sorts of transference to the doctor separately. Positive transference is then further divisible into transference of friendly or affectionate feelings which are admissible to consciousness and transference of prolongation of those feelings into the unconscious. As regards the latter, analysis shows that they invariably go back to erotic sources. . . . Thus the solution of the puzzle is that transference to the doctor is suitable for resistance to the treatment only in so far as it is a negative transference or a positive transference of repressed erotic impulses. If we "remove" the transference by making it conscious, we are detaching only these two components of the emotional act from the person of the doctor; the other component, which is admissible to consciousness and unobjectionable, persists and is the vehicle of success in psychoanalysis exactly as it is in other methods of treatment. (105)

Freud ended this paper with perhaps his single best-known statement on transference: "This struggle between the doctor and the patient . . . between understanding and seeking to act, is played out almost exclusively in the phenomena of transference. It is on that field that the victory must be won—the victory whose expression is the permanent cure of the neurosis. It cannot be disputed that controlling the phenomena of transference presents the psychoanalyst with the greatest difficulties. But it should not be forgotten that it is precisely they that do us the inestimable service of making the patient's hidden and forgotten erotic impulses immediate and manifest. For when all is said and done, it is impossible to destroy anyone *in absentia,* or *in effigie"* (108).[2]

In "Observations on Transference-Love" (1915), Freud discussed the special countertransference hazards posed for analysts by importunate female patients caught up in erotic transferences, with the risks for the analyst that he will either reject the pleas because of moral repugnance or succumb to them as an accept-

2. A very similar, but far less often quoted, remark, appears in Freud's 1914a paper, "Remembering, Repeating and Working Through" (152).

able reality perception, rather than see them, as he should, as (erotic) transferences to be psychoanalytically comprehended and resolved.[3]

In his "Autobiographical Study" (1925b) Freud gave a comprehensive and succinct overview of the nature and role of the transference and of two differing, and subsequently problematic, conceptions about it:

> In every analytic treatment there arises, without the physician's agency, an intense emotional relationship between the patient and the analyst which is not to be accounted for by the actual situation. It can be of a positive or of a negative character and can vary between the extremes of a passionate, completely sensual love and the unbridled expression of an embittered defiance and hatred. This *transference*—to give it its short name—soon replaces in the patient's mind the desire to be cured, and, so long as it is affectionate and moderate, becomes the agent of the physician's influence and neither more nor less than the mainspring of the joint work of analysis. Later on, when it has become passionate or has been converted into hostility, it becomes the principal tool of the resistance. It may then happen that it will paralyse the patient's powers of associating and endanger the success of the treatment. Yet it would be senseless to try to evade it; for an analysis without transference is an impossibility. It must not be supposed, however, that transference is created by analysis. It is a universal phenomenon of the human mind, it decides the success of all medical influence, and in fact dominates the whole of each person's relations to his human environment.[4] (42)

Freud's more problematic conceptions, advanced in this same article, had to do with the treatability of psychotics and the uncertain relationship between transference and suggestion: "When there is no inclination to a transference of emotion such as this, or when it has become entirely negative, as happens in dementia praecox or paranoia, then there is also no possibility of influencing the patient by psychological means" (42). Freud had made a comparable statement in his paper "On Narcissism" (1914c), in which he talked of two fundamental characteristics of psychotic patients: "megalomania and diversion of their interest from the external world—from people and things. In consequence of the latter change, they become inaccessible to the influence of psycho-analysis

3. For a full discussion of the evolution of the concept of transference love, see the review by Wallerstein (1993) titled "On Transference Love: Revisiting Freud."
4. Freud had given a comparable (but far less succinct) overview of the nature and role of transference in the *Introductory Lectures on Psycho-Analysis* (1916–17, Lecture 27 on Transference, especially pages 440–45) and gave a final such overview in the posthumous *Outline of Psycho-Analysis* (1940, chapter 6, especially pages 174–77).

and cannot be cured by our efforts" (74). It was statements such as these that for so long discouraged psychoanalysts from treating the openly psychotic.[5]

On the relationship of transference to suggestion, Freud vacillated over his entire professional lifetime. On the one hand, as we saw in chapter 1, because of the origination of psychoanalysis out of suggestion and hypnosis, Freud took pains to differentiate between them sharply, constantly emphasizing that unlike hypnosis, which was effective by virtue of suggestion, psychoanalysis always strove to eliminate any suggestive influence by thorough "analysis" of all transference phenomena. On the other hand, in many places Freud indicated his awareness of the role of suggestion and suggestive influence as an underpinning of the affectionate or "unobjectionable" positive transference that he called an essential facilitator of the analytic progress.

In the "Autobiographical Study," he carried this view to the extreme of practically equating transference with suggestion:[6]

> We can easily recognize it [transference] as the same dynamic factor which the hypnotists have named "suggestibility", which is the agent of hypnotic *rapport* and whose incalculable behavior led to difficulties with the cathartic method as well. . . . It is [therefore] perfectly true that psychoanalysis, like other psychotherapeutic methods, employs the instrument of suggestion (or transference). But the difference is this: that in analysis it is not allowed to play the decisive part in determining the therapeutic results. It is used instead to induce the patient to perform a piece of psychical work—the overcoming of his transference-resistances. . . . The transference is made conscious to the patient by the analyst, and it is resolved by convincing him that in his transference-attitude he is *re-experiencing* emotional relations which had their origin in his earliest object-attachments during the repressed period of his childhood. In this way the transference is changed from the strongest weapon of the resistance into the best instrument of the analytic treatment. Nevertheless its handling remains the most difficult as well as the most important part of the technique of analysis. (42–43)

This issue—whether the proper aim of analysis is to thoroughly analyze and thereby "resolve" the transference as completely as possible, *including* the sug-

5. See in this connection comments on Frieda Fromm-Reichmann in chapter 5 indicative of contrary views on the accessibility of psychotics to analytic treatment, and Gill's comments, supportive of Fromm-Reichmann, in footnote 3 in that chapter.
6. This quotation has already been cited in part in chapter 1. It is cited here much more extensively because it is even more apposite in this context.

gestive component, or to *use* the suggestive power inherent in the transference to *induce* the patient to do the psychical work of overcoming the resistances (as Freud indicated)—has been the subject of discussion ever since (see, e.g., the discussion on Paul Gray in chapter 21).

The next significant contribution to transference theory, after Freud, was Anna Freud's (1936) delineation of three kinds of transference impulses. These are (1) "transference of libidinal impulses," which she called "extremely simple," being just a statement of the transference as originally elaborated by Freud; of this she said, "Generally he [the patient] is quite willing to co-operate with us in our interpretation, for he himself feels that the transferred affective impulse is an intrusive foreign body" (19); (2) "transference of defence," in which "the interpretation of the second type of transference is more fruitful than that of the first type but . . . is responsible for most of the technical difficulties which arise between analyst and patient. The latter does not feel the second kind of transference-reaction to be a foreign body, and this is not surprising when we reflect how great a part the ego plays—even though it be the ego of earlier years—in its production" (21–22); and (3) "acting in the transference," which is the most difficult for the analyst to deal with, so that, "It is natural that he should try to restrict it as far as possible by means of the analytical interpretations which he gives and the non-analytical prohibitions which he imposes" (25).

Fenichel, in his pioneering monograph summarizing the state of the field in regard to psychoanalytic technique (1941a), including the analysis of the transference, put it very simply: "In what is called 'handling of the transference,' 'not joining in the game' is the principal task. Only thus is it possible subsequently to make interpretations. The interpreting of transference reactions, it seems to me, presents no special problem; everything that has been said about interpretation in general holds true for analysis of the transference: the surface first of all, the defense before the instinct—the interpretation must be timely, not too deep and not too superficial; particularly necessary, preceding the interpretation, is 'isolation' from the critical ego" (73).

This was indeed the established psychoanalytic consensus on the nature of the transference until Macalpine's revisionary article of 1950. She began with a historical survey, emphasizing her view that Freud and the early analysts made such efforts to sharply differentiate psychoanalysis as a therapy from the hypnosis and suggestion out of which it came that they overlooked or at least minimized the many similarities that nonetheless continue to exist and play a role in the *development* of the transference in analysis. Though Macalpine cited several statements by Freud acknowledging the link between suggestive influence and transference analysis including the one I have quoted from the *Autobiographical Study*,[7] she also pointed out that he (and those who came after him) consistently tried to repudiate suggestion as a part of the analytic process by repeatedly implying, if not always explicitly stating, that in psychoanalysis the effects of suggestion are systematically undone by interpretive resolution of the transference and that suggestion is used at most "*only* to induce the analysand to realize that he can be helped and that he can remember" (507, italics added). According to the conventional analytic wisdom, "transference manifestations . . . arise within the analysand spontaneously" (516); treatment does not conduce to transference formations, it only unmasks them—and again she cited several statements of Freud to that effect.

Macalpine then asserted a squarely different emphasis: Psychoanalysis did develop, after all, out of hypnosis: "When one compares hypnosis and transference it appears that hypnotic 'rapport' contains the element of transference condensed or superimposed. . . . The analogy of course ends when transference is not resolved in hypnosis as it is in analysis, but is allowed to persist. To look upon it from another angle, analytic transference manifestations are a slow motion picture of hypnotic transference manifestations; they take some time to develop, unfold slowly and gradually, and not all at once as in hypnosis" (519). After thus asserting the common roots and nature of analytic and hypnotic transferences, Macalpine took on the other analytic truism, that transference unfolds spontaneously in psychoanalysis: "Freud . . . was taken completely by surprise when he first encountered transference in his new technique" (520) and in response was quick to stress that these demonstrations of love and hate emanated from the patient unaided—in fact represented psychic tendencies immanent in everyone: "historically, the onus of responsibility for the appearance of transference was shifted imperceptibly from the hysteric to the psychoneurotic, and then to the normal personality" (521).

All this, Macalpine felt, shifted attention away from the manner in which the very structure of the analytic situation and the analytic process powerfully conduced to the unfolding of the transference:

> If transference is an example of a universal mental mechanism . . . why does it invariably occur with such great intensity in every analysis? The answer to this question appears to be that transference is *induced* from

---

7. Another such citation by Macalpine was from the *Introductory Lectures* (1916–17). After a discussion of the universality of the phenomenon of suggestibility, declared by Freud to rest on sexuality, "on the activity of the libido," he went on to say, "And it must dawn on us that in our technique we have abandoned hypnosis only to rediscover suggestion in the shape of transference" (446).

without in a manner comparable to the production of hypnosis. The analysand brings, in varying degrees, an inherent capacity, a readiness to form transferences, and the readiness is met by something which converts it into an actuality. . . . Psychoanalytic technique creates an infantile setting. . . . To this infantile setting the analysand—if he is analyzable—has to adapt, albeit by *regression*. In their aggregate, these factors, which go to constitute this infantile setting, amount to a reduction of the analysand's object world and denial of object relations in the analytic room. To this deprivation of object relations he responds by curtailing conscious ego functions and giving himself over to the pleasure principle; and following his free associations, he is thereby sent along the trek into infantile reactions and attitudes. (522, italics added)

Macalpine then enumerated the factors that constitute this infantile setting to which the analysand had to adapt: the curtailment of the object world, the constancy of the environment, the fixed analytic routines, the factor of not receiving regular replies from the analyst, the timelessness, the infantile level of the interpretations, the reduction in ego functions to a state between sleep and waking, the diminution of personal responsibility, the perceived element of magic, the process of free association, the authority of the analyst, the full sympathetic attention of another human being, the illusion of complete freedom, the frustration of gratifications, and the shift from the reality principle to the pleasure principle (523–25).

Given all this, "the analysand . . . responds to the frustrating infantile setting by regressing and by developing a transference neurosis . . . [and therefore] it can no longer be maintained that the analysand's reactions in analysis occur spontaneously. His behavior is a response to the rigid infantile setting to which he is exposed" (526). This led to Macalpine's conclusion: "To respond to the classical analytic techniques, analysands must have some object relations intact, and must have at their disposal enough adaptability to meet the infantile analytic setting by further regression" (531). Finally, "Transference cannot be regarded as a spontaneous neurotic reaction. It can be said to be the resultant of two sets of forces: the analysand's inherent readiness for transference, and the external stimulus of the infantile setting" (533).

It is safe to say that ever since Macalpine's important paper, all subsequent discourse on transference has had to take her views into account.

In 1954 Douglass Orr undertook a comprehensive historical survey of the literature to that date on transference and countertransference. His own working definition of transference was as follows: "We all know that transference in its widest sense is regarded as a universal phenomenon in interpersonal relationships. In its most restricted sense, however, transference implies a specific relationship of patient to psychoanalyst, especially as revealed in the so-called transference neurosis" (621). In that same year, Greenacre (1954) undertook the next significant enlargement of the transference concept. Like all those before her, she stated that the transference is inherent in the human experience: "If two people are repeatedly alone together some sort of emotional bond will develop between them" (671). And "This need for sensory contact . . . probably comes from the long period of care which the human infant must have before he is able to sustain himself. Lonely infants fed and cared for regularly and with sterile impersonal efficiency do not live to childhood." This led to her conception of the special nature of the transference: "I believe the matrix of this [the emotional bonding between two people alone together] *is* a veritable matrix— i.e., [that it] comes largely from the original mother-infant quasi-union of the first months of life. This I consider the basic transference; or one might call it the primary transference, or some part of primitive social instinct" (672).[8]

The balance of Greenacre's article elaborated on this conception that the prototypical transference is rooted in the earliest mother-infant interactions. She then offered a detailed description of the various accoutrements of the analytic situation and the technical implementations of the analytic process from the standpoint of how they could enhance or impede the unfolding of the transference. Implicitly in full accord with Macalpine, Greenacre put it as follows: "The nonparticipation of the analyst in a personal way in the relationship creates a 'tilted' emotional relationship, a kind of psychic suction in which many of the past attitudes, specific experiences and fantasies of the patient are re-enacted in fragments or sometimes in surprisingly well-organized dramas with the analyst as the main figure of significance to the patient" (674). And because of the power of this emotional tug, evoking all the intensity of the earliest mother-child bond, the analyst must be especially cautious in the countertransference not to try to become (reenact the role of) the nurturing mother of infancy: "The . . . analyst . . . may be drawn unconsciously into an overly protective, essen-

8. Actually, Ferenczi was the very explicit forerunner to Greenacre in emphasizing the mother-infant matrix within which all object-relatednesses (and subsequent analytic transferences) originate. (See chapter 2 for an accounting of this.) But Greenacre cited no references in her 1954 article and, in a subsequent article on the transference (1959), cited only six, and Ferenczi was not one of them. Actually, Greenacre's articles were published during a period of real neglect of Ferenczi's contributions within American psychoanalysis; his work and his various original contributions to later psychoanalytic developments were, at that time, much better known in Great Britain owing to the influence there of Balint, his student and his interpreter (see chapter 2 for this as well). Ferenczi's work is today much more widely acknowledged and appreciated in America and around the world (again see chapter 2).

tially maternal nursing attitude toward the suffering patient. . . . One must remember in considering the effects of such transgressions that the analytic
situation *is* an artificial, tilted one. . . . It is one which more nearly reproduces
the demand of the child for a perfectly understanding parent, than any parent-
child relationship can possibly approach, and it is the only one in life in which
no emotional counterdemand is to be expected" (684).

Greenacre's views, like Macalpine's, have colored all subsequent considerations of the transference. For example, Stone (1961) had this to say: "Without
the support of this component of latent transference, I am skeptical that the adult
rational clinical need, supported by unconscious irrational transference expectations and fantasies . . . could sustain many analytic situations against the clamor
of ambivalent and vulnerable instinctual demands and disappointments. In gratifying this 'mature' wish of childhood, there is also in the analytic situation, as
in childhood, an acceptable form of love which, in an economic sense, may
well contribute importantly to the incentive for mastery of unneutralized and
unelaborated erotic and destructive drives" (50). And again, "the general latent
craving for an omnipotent parent, renewed and specifically colored with, indeed
given form by, the conflicts and vicissitudes of each phase of development. . . .
I shall refer to this dynamism, for clarity of statement, as the 'primal transference' " (70–71). This is, of course, exactly Greenacre's "basic transference" or
"primary transference."

Three additional articles from the 1960s and 1970s deal in whole or in part
with issues of transference. Hans Loewald (1960), in a landmark contribution
on the nature of the therapeutic action of psychoanalysis (discussed in detail in
chapter 16), identified three distinct conceptions of transference in Freud's corpus. First was "the transfer of libido, contained in the 'ego,' to objects in the
transference neuroses" (27)—the basis of Freud's nosological distinctions between transference neuroses amenable to psychoanalysis by virtue of their transference capacities and the so-called narcissistic neuroses (the psychoses), in which
the libido was retained in the ego and in which therefore transferences to the
analyst presumably could not take place, the basis for Freud's declaring these
patients unanalyzable. "The second meaning of transference, when distinguishing transference neuroses from narcissistic neuroses, is that of transfer of relations
with infantile objects on to later objects, and especially to the analyst in the
analytic situation. This second meaning of the term is today the one most frequently referred to, to the exclusion of other meanings" (27). This meaning of
transference is central to its conception as the major vehicle of, and also the
chief resistance to, the analytic process. The third meaning of transference Loewald quoted from chapter 7 of Freud's *The Interpretation of Dreams* (1900): "We
learn . . . that an unconscious idea is as such quite incapable of entering the

preconscious and that it can only exercise any effect there by establishing a connection with an idea which already belongs to the preconscious, by transferring its intensity on to it and by getting itself 'covered' by it. Here we have the fact of 'transference,' which provides an explanation of so many striking phenomena in the mental life of neurotics" (562–63). This is, of course, also Freud's very early conception of transference as simply a "false connection," a displacement (see note 1, this chapter).

All this leads to Loewald's conclusion about transference: "It should be apparent that a view of transference which stresses the need of the unconscious for transference, for a point of attachment for a transference in the preconscious, by which primary process is transformed into secondary process—implies the notion that psychic health has to do with an optimal, though by no means necessarily conscious, communication between unconscious and preconscious, between the infantile, archaic stages and structures of the psychic apparatus and its later stages and structures of organization" (32). This universality of transference as a phenomenon (or, in Loewald's words, a "need") in health and normality as well as in illness and its treatment is a main theme of Brian Bird's (1972) article. In Bird's view this central idea had been insufficiently appreciated: "I am particularly taken with the as yet unexplored idea that transference is a universal mental function which may well be the basis of all human relationships. I even suspect it of being one of the mind's main agencies for giving birth to new ideas and new life to old ones" (267). Bird went on to document what he felt was the paucity of Freud's writings on the transference, given its acknowledged centrality to the entire psychoanalytic process.

Arlow (1975) was the first to seriously challenge Macalpine's emphases— established a quarter century earlier and to try to correct the skewed picture he felt she had created. He put it this way: That psychoanalytic technique induces regression in the patient . . . is a principle which has been quoted and circulated without challenge for a long time. It seems to me what the psychoanalytic situation does is to create an atmosphere, a set of conditions, which permit regressive aspects of the patient's mental functioning, long present, to reemerge in forms that are clearer and easier to observe" (73). The issue thus joined, of whether the analytic situation and process fosters and induces or simply allows the unfolding of the (regressive) transference, has been debated ever since.

The next major shift in conceptualizing the transference was inaugurated in an article by Gill and Hyman Muslin (1976), though two other very signal contributions to this subject were also made in the same year. Arnold Modell in many articles (1976, 1988a,c, 1989) and in three books (1968, 1984, 1990), has become the most significant American exponent and interpreter of the concepts of Winnicott, most particularly the object-relational perspective, psychoanalysis as a two-person psychology, and the conception of the "holding environment" and its implications for our understanding of the therapeutic action of psychoanalysis. I want to draw first on Modell's 1976 article detailing his conception(s) of the transference. His focus was on the narcissistic character disorders and the transferences that mark their therapies. The first phase of the therapy, that of essential "nonrelatedness," with its illusions of self-sufficiency and the countertransference hazards of boredom and sleepiness, is characterized by what Modell calls the "cocoon" transference (294). The patients display a disdainful aloofness while enveloping themselves in a magical belief based on their contiguity to the powerful analyst. This should not be mistaken for a true therapeutic alliance; the analyst must supply a proper holding environment[9] while patiently waiting out this often quite long first phase.

In the middle phase of the treatment, the positively toned transference gradually changes into its opposite. The patient's grandiose aspirations and demands escalate and, as the analyst in turn becomes more *confront*ational (so different from Kohut's technique, to be described in chapter 20), the patient's unrelatedness gives way, and his narcissistic rage is mobilized and then becomes the focus of interpretive activity. Modell feels that individuation begins in the patient's growing awareness of his dependency and demandingness and with it the formation of a true "therapeutic alliance" (see chapter 15): "We believe that the holding environment of the first phase has led to sufficient ego consolidation to permit a shift in the focus of therapeutic action of psychoanalysis in the second phase. And we believe that the motive force for the therapeutic action of psychoanalysis in the second phase is interpretation" (298). Interpretation has also effected the dissolution of the cocoon transference and permitted the establishment of a therapeutic alliance. The third, or end, phase of treatment then proceeds like a classically neurotic case, with the predominant transferences to the whole objects of the oedipal triangulation, though the patient is always vulnerable under stress to regressive activation of the cocoon transference with its affect blockade.

To Modell, it is vitally important to maintain these distinctions between the narcissistic (or cocoon) transference and the object transferences of the classical transference neurosis. Many agree with this distinction. I would guess that there is far less agreement with another distinction he drew in this paper: "The transference neurosis . . . is fluid, changeable, and different in every patient. This is in

9. Modell defined "holding environment" as follows: "Winnicott introduced the term 'holding environment' as a metaphor for certain aspects of the analytic situation and the analytic process. The term derives from the maternal function of holding the infant, but, taken as a metaphor, it has a much broader application" (289). But in a later paper (1988a), Modell separated his conception from Winnicott's: "Unlike Winnicott, I do not consider this 'holding environment' to represent a regression but rather a process of symbolic actualization" (582).

marked contrast to the narcissistic transferences, which are *uniform* to the extent that they can be said to form an operational basis for defining the syndrome" (301, italics added). But most would agree, I think, with his final distinction between the two types of patients in the course of events under discussion: "In so-called classical cases, the analytic setting functions as a 'holding environment' silently; it is something that is taken for granted and can be described as part of the 'confident' transference. Where there is ego distortion, the analytic setting as a holding environment is central to the therapeutic action" (304–05).

In his later development of these ideas, Modell (1988a) shifted his nomenclature and further elaborated the distinctions between the two types of transferences. He now spoke of the "dependent/containing transference" rather than the cocoon transference, and of the "iconic transference" rather than the more familiar object-transference (or classical transference neurosis): "The dependent/containing transference, when it functions as we would wish, creates and *contains* the iconic transference. This term *iconic* connotes a visual portrait but may be used to express a representation, a similitude, that is not restricted to the visual sphere. . . . the term *iconic* embraces both what has been called in the older literature *imagoes* (that is to say, whole, subjectively created persons, father, mother, etc.), as well as projection of internalized objects that are part of the self" (588–89). Modell put the contrast between these two forms of transference as follows: "The Dependent/Containing Transference is continually present, represents the symbolic actualization of developmental conflicts, does not re-create the nuclear family (Oedipal) imagoes, and is enhanced and strengthened by mutative interpretations. By contrast the Iconic Transference is episodic (and may be absent), does not represent the symbolic actualization of developmental conflicts, but does re-create the nuclear family (Oedipal) imagoes, and is resolved or diminished by mutative interpretations" (590).

In another article published in the same year (1988c), Modell restated his 1976 and 1988a view of the *constancy* of what he was now calling the dependent/containing transference as against the *changeability* of the transference neurosis or iconic transference and also his position on the relative importance of these differing transference manifestations to the treatment process. In regard to the former he said: "I describe the holding environment and the object tie that is created by the analytic setting as part of what I have come to call the dependent/containing transference in contrast to the specific and idiosyncratic nature of the transference neurosis. Further, the dependent/containing transference is a constant while the transference neurosis may be present for varying periods of time or may be absent altogether" (98). In regard to the relative weight of these different kinds of transferences in relation to the therapeutic process, Modell now said quite explicitly, "I have come to believe that the patient's experience within the analytic setting itself is for many if not most of our current patients of *greater significance* in effecting a cure than is the creation and resolution of the transference neurosis" (103–04, italics added).

In an article the following year, Modell (1989) took up the issue of the "real" or "illusory" nature of the transference: "The dependent transference of the psychoanalytic setting becomes the medium in which developmental conflicts such as the conflict between merging and autonomy are reevoked; this is in contrast to the recreation in the transference of the idiosyncratic portrait of the analysand's internal imagos that we call the transference neurosis. We cannot say that the dependent transference is more or less 'real' as compared to the transference neurosis, or more or less real as compared to a dependency experienced in ordinary life, for that line of thinking will soon become absurd. *It is clarifying to think that the psychoanalytic setting, the 'frame' of the analysis, is the container of other levels of reality such as the transference neurosis*" (76–77). Therefore, "transference is both 'real' and 'illusory'; transference is both in the here-and-now and a repetition of the past so that the object tie to the analyst is both a repetition and a new beginning; it is both a 'real' object relationship and also symbolically recreates elements of the earliest mother-child interactions. As I have indicated, the controversies concerning the reality or illusory nature of the analytic setting, whether it is a 'real' relationship or transference, whether transference is in the here-and-now or whether it is a repetition of the past, reflect an emphasis on one or another wing of this paradox or, as I would now say, an emphasis on one or another level of reality" (84–85).

In his latest book (1990), Modell summarized his overall perspectives on these issues and their relation to the curative or "mutative" factors in psychoanalysis by linking them to both past controversy (Freud-Ferenczi) and current controversy (drive/conflict-developmental/arrest):

> If we accept the fact that psychoanalytic theories of treatment are not clearly demarcated from one another, we can, nevertheless, still discern two broad differentiating assumptions, which can be viewed as a continuation of the Freud-Ferenczi controversy. These theoretical differences have been described by Mitchell (1988) as the *drive-conflict model* and the *developmental-arrest model*. The drive-conflict model, the classical position, emphasizes that the primary therapeutic motor is interpretation and that the resulting insight is curative. The developmental-arrest model, on the other hand, which encompasses those theories that emphasize object relations, considers the goal of treatment to be the amelioration of trauma through a new object relation, a new self object, or a new protective environment. Here insight is not the goal of treatment, and interpretation

may be depreciated (Kohut), may be used sparingly (Balint, Winnicott), or, as I have suggested, may have a multiplicity of functions.[10] (147–48)

Sandler's (1976a) article, though focused ostensibly on countertransference issues and hazards, actually can and I think should be read as a statement about characteristic transference enactments and the pulls for complicity they normatively exert on the analyst. Sandler's central thesis was developed as follows:

> Transference need not be restricted to the illusory apperception of another person . . . but can be taken to include the unconscious (and often subtle) attempts to manipulate or to provoke situations with others which are concealed repetition of earlier experiences and relationships . . . when such transference manipulations or provocations occur in ordinary life, the person towards whom they are directed may either show that he does not accept the role, or may, if he is unconsciously disposed in that direction, in fact accept it and act accordingly. . . . I believe such "manipulations" to be an important part of object relationships in general and to enter in "trial" form into the "scanning" of objects in the process of object choice. In the transference, in many subtle ways, the patient attempts to prod the analyst into behaving in a particular way and unconsciously scans and adapts to his perception of the analyst's reaction (43–44)

All this is highly germane to the analytic task and also highlights the concomitant countertransference hazard: "From the side of the *patient* we may see a whole variety of very specific role-relationships emerge. What I want to emphasize is that the role-relationship of the patient in analysis at any particular time consists of a role in which he casts himself, and a *complementary* role in which he casts the analyst. . . . The patient's transference would thus represent an attempt by him to impose an interaction, an interrelationship (in the broadest sense of the word) between himself and the analyst." That is, "the patient, in the transference, attempts to *actualize these* [transference fantasies in which self and object in interaction have come to be represented in particular roles] *in a disguised way*, within the framework and limits of the analytic situation. In doing so, he resists becoming aware of any infantile relationship which he might be attempting to impose" (44–45). And this effort to actualize imposed role representations applies "to the whole gamut of unconscious (including preconscious) wishes related to all sorts of needs, gratifications and defences" (45).

Sandler then said,

10. This other "developmental-arrest" perspective, in all its dimensions and under a variety of rubrics, is the subject matter of chapters 15 to 20.

I want to suggest that very often the irrational response of the analyst, which his professional conscience leads him to see entirely as a blind spot of his own, may sometimes be usefully regarded as a compromise-formation between his own tendencies [countertransference based] and his *reflexive acceptance of the role which the patient is forcing on him.* . . . Within the limits set by the analytical situation he [the analyst] will, unless he becomes aware of it, tend to comply with the role demanded of him, to integrate it into his mode of responding and relating to the patient. Normally, of course, he can catch this counter-response in himself, particularly if it appears to be in the direction of being inappropriate. However, he may only become aware of it through observing his own behaviour, responses and attitudes, *after these have been carried over into action.* (46–47)

This paper of Sandler's has indeed played a signal role in relation to a whole recent body of psychoanalytic literature dealing with the interactive and imbricated nature of the transference-countertransference dialogue and the enactments on both sides of that dialogue. But despite these very significant contributions by Modell and by Sandler, it was Gill and Muslin's 1976 paper (already presented to some extent in chapter 8) that inaugurated what became ultimately a far-reaching reconsideration of the entire nature and conceptual basis of the transference. The paper began by taking exception to Freud's technical dictum of 1913: "So long as the patient's communications and ideas run on without any obstruction, the theme of transference should be left untouched. One must wait until the transference, which is the most delicate of all procedures, has become a resistance" (139). This precept of restraint in transference interpretation, certainly in the early stages of analysis, has been widely followed ever since, especially by those within the ego psychology paradigm, and, in its practical extension, has given rise to the common model of "the essentially silent analyst" again, especially in the earlier stages. Gill and Muslin's contrary view was that the analyst "should be governed by the intent to interpret transference and resistance whenever these phenomena appear and . . . they are commonly present in a variety of forms early in an analysis" (Gill and Muslin, 780). The crux of their argument was that transference, ubiquitous in human relationships, is always present, from the start, as a component in the analyst-patient relationship and is therefore amenable to interpretation from the start, and that this is what will make the analysis go best.

In building their argument, Gill and Muslin first disclaimed any similarity to the well-known Kleinian technical stance favoring early interpretation of the transference: "Because adherents to Kleinian technique regularly advocate early transference interpretation, we must state that by early transference analysis we refer not to 'deep' transference interpretations, which seem to constitute so much of Kleinian transference interpretation, whether early or late, but to transference interpretations that are related to the presenting psychic surface in the here-and-now relation between analyst and patient" (781). They then averred that Freud's early dictum that if the patient appears to be communicating freely, the analyst need not attend to analyzing the transference was simply a conceptual hangover from the preanalytic days of hypnotic therapy and its apparent ability to circumvent the resistances. They stated that this idea was certainly at odds with Freud's later conception that transference not only emerges as a resistance but is always present as the essential vehicle that makes therapy (and, in fact, all human relationships) possible.

This then led to the statement "though the recognition that, whatever else the patient's associations refer to, they also always refer, whether directly or indirectly, to the transference, is implied throughout Freud's technical writings, it rarely becomes explicit" (786). But Gill and Muslin pointed out that it did become explicit in the "Autobiographical Study": "We must, however, bear in mind that free association is not really free. The patient remains under the influence of the analytic situation even though he is not directing his mental activities on to a particular subject. We shall be justified in assuming that nothing will occur to him that has not some reference to that situation" (Freud 1925b, 40–41).

Gill and Muslin nonetheless opined that in most of his statements on the subject Freud "was assuming that if the patient's communications and ideas were running on without any obstruction, the transference had not yet become a resistance, or at any rate had not become a resistance that should be interpreted. That conclusion is incorrect. The patient may be talking freely, and there may nevertheless be important evidence of transference resistance which it would be desirable to interpret. There may *seem* to be no obstruction, but there nevertheless is one—the obstruction of transference resistance, as is demonstrated by the fact that the apparent progress is an illusion" (786–87). Thus, the first building block in the conceptual edifice Gill was to go on to erect, the need for transference interpretation from the start, despite Freud's advice to the contrary.

The authors then capped their argument: "One can still say that the formula that one should not interpret the transference until it becomes a resistance is correct, but that, in most if not all analyses, there are resistances relating to the transference from the beginning, and they may well require interpretation from the beginning. . . . While the usual argument runs that too early interpretation of the transference resistance will distort the transference, we consider it more likely that the failure to interpret leads to a distorted transference" (788).

A paper by Gill alone in 1979 marked a considerable expansion from this 1976 "first building block." This paper in turn was subsequently elaborated in a 1982 theoretical exposition by Gill alone and then in the clinical application of these ideas in a study of nine audio-recorded psychoanalytic sessions, written by Gill and Hoffman (1982). The essence of that whole development (1979–82) was already contained in the 1979 article, which I will therefore cite in extenso.

Gill began this article by distinguishing interpretation of resistance to *awareness* of transference and interpretation of resistance to *resolution* of transference: "With some oversimplification, one might say that in resistance to the awareness of transference, the transference is what is resisted, whereas in resistance to the resolution of transference, the transference is what does the resisting. Another more descriptive way of stating this distinction . . . is between implicit or indirect references to the transference and explicit or direct references to the transference. The interpretation of resistance to awareness of the transference is intended to make the implicit transference explicit, while the interpretation of resistance to the resolution of transference is intended to make the patient realize that the already explicit transference does indeed include a determinant from the past" (264). He then stated his central argument: "Not only is not enough emphasis being given to interpretation of the transference in the here and now, that is, to the interpretation of implicit manifestations of the transference, but also . . . interpretations intended to resolve the transference as manifested in explicit references to the transference should be primarily in the here and now, rather than genetic transference interpretations" (265).

Gill set out a five-part scheme that conveyed his technical recommendations in detail as well as their conceptual basis:

1. The principle that the transference should be *encouraged to expand* as much as possible within the analytic situation because analytic work is best done within the transference: "It is not that the transference is forced into the treatment, but that it is spontaneously but implicitly present [all the time], and is encouraged to expand there and become explicit" (270). And "To emphasize the transference meaning [of real life events] is not to deny or belittle other meanings, but to focus on the one of several meanings of the content that is the most important for the analytic process" (271).

2. The interpretation of disguised allusions to the transference is the main technique for encouraging the expansion of the transference within the analytic situation: "The analyst must be especially alert to the attitude the patient believes he [the analyst] has, not only to the attitudes the patient does have toward him," for "the investigation of the attitudes ascribed to the analyst makes easier the subsequent investigation

of the intrinsic factors in the patient that played a role in such ascription." And disguises (displacements) must be assiduously pursued: "In
the case of displacement the interpretation will be allusions to the
transference in associations not manifestly about the transference"
(272–73). (This has become an amplification of Gill's call with Muslin
in 1976 to replace Freud's dictum that the transference should not be
interpreted as long as the patient is apparently associating freely.)

3. The principle that all transference manifestations have some discernible
connection with something (some trigger) in the present actual analytic
situation. In analogy to the structure of the dream, the patient's transferences attach to some "analytic-situation residue" (276). What Gill
was asserting is that the analyst and the analytic situation are real and
provide clues and do not go away no matter how silent or unobtrusive
the analyst tries to be.

4. This connection between the transference and the actual analytic situation is then used in interpreting resistance to the awareness of transference. The analyst has to "find the presenting and plausible
interpretations of resistance to the awareness of transference he should
make" by capturing "how the patient is experiencing the situation"
(278). More concisely, "If the analyst interprets the patient's attitudes
in a spirit of seeing their possible *plausibility* in the light of what information the patient does have, rather than in the spirit of either affirm-
ing or denying the patient's views, the way is open for their further
expression and elucidation" (279, italics added).

5. Finally, to the relative roles of resolution of the transference within the
here and now of the analytic situation, and by genetic transference
interpretation: "The reserve and ambiguity of the analyst's behavior is
what increases the ranges of apparently plausible conclusions the patient may draw. If an examination of the basis for the conclusion makes
clear that the actual situation to which the patient responds is subject
to other meanings than the one the patient has reached, he will more
readily consider his pre-existing bias, that is, his transference" (281–
82). Gill did, however, concede that systematic interpretation of the
transference in the here and now of the analytic situation was not the
totality of the analytic work: "I agree that extratransference and genetic
transference interpretations and, of course, working through are important too. The matter is one of emphasis" (283).

Finally, Gill again disclaimed any relation to the Kleinian interpretive technique (as he and Muslin had done in 1976) since, to Gill's taste, the Kleinians

interpret too deeply; that is, they interpret genetic material "without adequate connection to the current features of the present analytic situation" (284). As his last major point in this article, he spoke to the "new experience" the patient was afforded in this properly carried-out analysis, in the very interpretation of the transference. "The patient . . . is being treated differently from how he expected to be. . . . Not only is the new experience not to be confused with the interpersonal influence of a transference gratification, but the new experience occurs together with insight into both the patient's biased expectation and the new experience. . . . What is unique about the transference interpretation is that insight and the new experience take place in relation to the very person who was expected to behave differently, and it is this which gives the work in the transference its immediacy and effectiveness" (282–83).

In his contribution to the 1979 Atlanta Symposium reconsidering the relationship between psychoanalysis and the psychoanalytic psychotherapies twenty-five years after the crystallization of 1954, Gill (1984a) published his radically altered views on this issue, as described in chapter 8. I have indicated there how Gill predicated his new perspectives on the nature of psychotherapy vis-à-vis psychoanalysis on his new views on the transference and the primacy of transference interpretations in the here and now as the central mutative factor in analytic work. In that same 1984 paper, Gill also advanced his evolving conceptions (already stated in the 1982 monographs) of the interpersonal context and perspectival framework of the interacting transferential reactions: "The implication that, whether advertent or inadvertent, the therapist's influence on the transference is avoidable, is carried in the concept of neutrality" (168). But this recommendation for a strict neutrality "cannot accomplish that aim because the patient inevitably interprets the analyst's behaviour in ways other than those the analyst had intended. . . . Because analysis takes place in an interpersonal context there is no such thing as non-interaction" (168)—that is, no such thing as the analyst's not influencing the patient's transference perceptions.

This means that the notion of an uncontaminated transference is simply a sedulously cultivated myth: "The usual view is that the patient *distorts* the situation by constructing it in terms of his intrapsychic patterns. I say instead that the therapist's behaviour lends plausibility to the patient's experience." And this requires a truly perspectival framework: "While the usual psychoanalytic perspective on the interpersonal aspect of the analytic situation is how the patient's view of it is *distorted* by his intrapsychic organization, I suggest instead that the integrate arising from the patient's intrapsychic organization and his experience of the interpersonal interaction should initially be treated as a rational formulation in a relativistic, perspectival framework of interpersonal reality" (164).

Because transference and transference resistance are ubiquitous, it is the analyst's task, according to Gill, to carefully clarify awareness of transference, by systematic interpretation of resistance to the nature of the patient's experience of the analyst (i.e., his transference perception); to focus on what factors make the patient's experience plausible to him (i.e., the search for the "analytic-situation residue"); to help the patient realize that his experience and interpretation, though plausible, are not unequivocal and that other equally plausible constructions exist; and finally to help the patient see that *his* particular plausible construction is derived from his own previous life experience with its built-in assumptions and expectations in new interpersonal encounters (i.e., his transference out of his past).

Again, Gill tried not to totally disregard the genetic and the recovery of repressed memories: "While I am not discounting the value of remembering, I believe that an analysis in which priority of attention goes to the transference expressed in the here-and-now, including the analyst's contribution, will be much freer of lasting effects of inadvertent suggestion than one in which priority of attention goes to genetic interpretation which may bypass transference" (165). And still on the issue of the relentless search to extirpate all vestiges of suggestion to the extent possible, Gill reversed his earlier (1954) judgment and entered the lists in relation to the continuing discussion generated by Macalpine's 1950 article. This time he argued counter to Macalpine's thrust: "In 1954 I emphasized not only Macalpine's demonstration that regression is wittingly induced in the usual analytic situation but I also wrote approvingly of how the analytic situation exerts a steady pressure toward regression. What I failed to see is how this unacknowledged manipulation of the transference constitutes a major unanalyzed suggestive influence" (169–70).

And Gill brought this thinking to its fullest expression in the two 1982 monographs already mentioned (Gill 1982; Gill and Hoffman 1982). Like so many of Gill's previous writings, these monographs won instant status as obligatory reading by the analytically informed, albeit in this instance with great controversy as to their newness, importance, and value as modifications or reformulations of theory and technique. These monographs set out, in Gill's characteristic style of logical system-building and exegetical development, the entire structure of the theory described in the 1976, 1979, and 1984 papers (in the first monograph), with clinical illustrations from the nine audiotaped hours (in the second monograph).

In a lengthy critique of these monographs for an issue of *Psychoanalytic Inquiry* devoted to critical responses to Gill, by eight analysts of varying theoretical persuasion, I devoted ten pages to a summary of Gill's fully developed "system" of analysis of the transference (Wallerstein, 1984). From that, I will simply cite one statement that I feel captures Gill's central message as of that time: "Gill is advocating two (he considers major) 'shifts in emphasis' in psychoanalytic work. The first is 'giving priority to the analysis of resistance to the awareness of transference'; the second is 'assessment of the transference attitudes in the light of the features of the actual analytic situation which serve as their point of departure' [Gill 1982, 120]; Both operate centrally in the here-and-now" (337).

I summarized my critique of Gill's total position as follows:

> I think that fundamentally Gill is correct that the transference is, in theory and in the technique appropriate to its proper elucidation and ultimate (to the best of our ability) resolution, more interactional than we customarily think, and that more explicit awareness of this and focus upon it can lead to improved psychoanalytic work. At the same time, I do not think that this emphasis is all that new with Gill; nor do I think that in reasserting both this interactional character of the transference as well as the total primacy of the analysis of the transference as forcefully as he does with us, Gill is fully aware of how he carries the concept of transference from its pivotal and central position to becoming the everything, the be-all and end-all of analysis, with all the risks to the Aristotelian notion of balance that is to me the linchpin of the psychoanalytic perspective on the human condition. (349)

In answer to the question as to whether Gill's views were just a matter of emphasis or major theory reformulation, I opted for assessing it as "just" (but a very important just) a matter of emphasis. But I ended with a caveat:

> Properly intense emphases can readily become overemphases, and I think that Gill has lent himself to them: the overemphases of overzealous intrusiveness, of overzealous interpretation which risks overlooking the impact upon the transference of such an active interpretation of the transference (despite Gill's repeated caveat that *that* in turn needs to be analyzed—which leads to the theoretical possibility of an infinite regress), and of an overzealous reading of co-equal contributions to the transference unfolding. The fact that analytic circumstances facilitate the *propensity* to overlook the analyst's contribution to the transference does not at all mean that that contribution is, except in unusual and unfortunate circumstances, an equal one. (353)

It should, however, also be said of Gill's new views on the transference, as I have said of Macalpine's paper, that all subsequent discourse on transference has had to take them into account.

Gill should be allowed a final response to the debate on his views in *Psychoanalytic Inquiry*. In reply to his critics' claim that he had overemphasized the centrality of the transference in the psychoanalytic treatment process, he said, "Since bias is inevitable, I prefer bias toward the transference, accompanied by openness to the content involved, to a bias toward particular contents, accompanied by openness with regard to whether the content is most approachable in the transference or elsewhere" (494). He then reaffirmed and elaborated what he regarded as his central argument: "There is a basic difference in position between the conception of transference which I espouse and the usual one. It is not merely that both patient and analyst contribute to the *relationship* but that both contribute to the *transference*. Further, the social conception of transference is based on a relativistic view of interpersonal reality in contrast to the usual absolutistic one. Transference is not only always contributed to by both participants, but each participant also has a valid, albeit different, perspective on it. . . . We see interpersonal experience . . . as always having a degree of plausibility" (498–99). And to underline what he meant, he added, "Since construal and construction are always operative and always based on past as well as present, all interpersonal experience is transferential"—and he explicitly stated that he equated the phrases interpersonal, interactive, intersubjective, and social conceptions of the transference (509).[11]

Gill also explicitly restated the change in his views since his 1954 paper; for example: "These distinctions between realistic and transference are the dichotomy between the veridical and the distorted, which I now disavow" (512). And in amplification: "I do not distinguish between transference and nontransference but between pathological and nonpathological transference, although transference not further qualified is assumed to mean pathological transference. Pathological transference is characterized by the stereotyped rigidity with which the patient construes situations, by his compulsive efforts to make people behave as he expects them to [cf. Sandler's 1976 paper on role responsiveness], and by his inability to envisage participating in a different kind of human relationship" (513). As a final riposte on the nature of interpretation (of the transference), Gill stated, "That principle lies in the recognition that an interpretation is an interpersonal interaction in which the interactive implication can take precedence over its cognitive significance. The analytic interaction is not only one directed toward insight but inevitably an interpersonal experience as well" (619)—with all the possibilities here, as Gill acknowledged, for an infinite regress in the interpretive pursuit.

11. In a 1988 paper with Hoffman (Hoffman and Gill 1988) on an empirical psychoanalytic research study of transference phenomena, the authors stated, "We will use the term 'transference' and the term 'the patient's experience of the relationship' interchangeably" (55).

13 Our Understandings of the Transference: II The Past Decade

As in chapter 11, one can say that the literature on the transference has grown considerably in the past decade, but with only a few substantial conceptual advances. Actually, the first two authors I cite in this chapter, James McLaughlin and Charles Brenner, have each put a distinctive imprint upon considerations of the transference. McLaughlin (1981) attempted to remove the countertransference from its separated position as the analyst's (untoward) response to the patient's transference and bring it within the orbit of the transference, as another manifestation of the ubiquity of *transferences* in human affairs. He stated at the very beginning of his article that "transference is a matter of equal rights, both on and behind the couch" and "all that we were/see ourselves as/wish to be is caught up in the analytic relationship, *as it is for the patient*" (639, italics added). This leads ineluctably to his conclusion that we should talk simply of the analyst's transferences, not of his "countertransferences"; the latter is a gratuitously skewed term, implying almost that a different psychology is operative for psychoanalysts.

In a significant sense, this argument is a logical extension of Sandler's (1976a) description of the analyst's "role-responsiveness" in relation to the analysand's pull to actualize desired role-relationships. It is also a conceptual and heuristic collapsing into one of the three strands of countertransference that Orr (1954) tried to distinguish in his historical survey of the literature: the analyst's untoward or enactive responses to the patient's specific analytic transferences (which Orr called countertransference proper); the analyst's motivated responses to the patient as a person caught in a relationship with him (called the analyst's transferences to the patient); and the analyst's motivated responses to the task of analyzing, as a sadistic, exhibitionistic, masochistic, indoctrinating, or whatever kind of act (called the analyst's transferences to the analytic process) (646–57).

McLaughlin began with a statement of "two conflicting concepts about the analytic relationship and the contribution of the analyst. The first is the objectifying ideal of the analyst hyperbolized in Freud's surgeon-mirror imagery and in the therapeutic power attributed to the verbal-interpretive function of the analyst; the other is the subjectifying ideal of the emotionally involved and responsive analyst asserting *his* analytic powers through all aspects of his affectively intense relationship to the patient, including, yet going far beyond in order to support and actualize, the interpretive mode" (644). By the 1960s, McLaughlin felt, the image of the analyst at work had begun its decisive shift into the second, subjectifying, conception: there was "no longer a removed and consistently objective 'catalyst' whose occasional perturbations were largely epiphenomena occasioned by the magnitude or special qualities of the behavior of certain patients under very particular circumstances; instead, a resonant and affectively immersed participant observer in a powerfully evocative intimacy touching on all issues of the developmental past of both parties, from the earliest preoedipal through adolescence to current adulthood" (647). This builds to "I wish to build the strongest possible case for asserting the relativism, on both sides of the couch, of a perceived reality (psychic reality) and the ubiquity of transference processes on which these perceptions are organized" (649).

The logical conclusion of this argument is that the term "countertransference" should be dropped as a special designation altogether. (For reasons of long usage and familiarity this has, of course, not happened.) "Unlike transference, which could be applied to any behavior anywhere, countertransference as term and concept has consistently reflected its base in the psychoanalytic situation" (653). More importantly, "The compound term, countertransference, itself fostered the skewing and differential attitude. 'Counter-' helped to anchor the analyst's phenomena both to the analytic situation and to the patient. It took on enduring connotations of 'reacting to,' a comfort to the analyst claiming rationality, detachment, and imperturbability in the presence of the all-too-humanness of his patient; he could more easily take a pejorative set toward the untoward behaviors of his patient and an I-was-pushed stance toward his own" (655). McLaughlin ended with an assertion of the ubiquity of affectively charged and historically rooted *transferences,* in every human relationship and interaction: "From this broader view of transference it is logical, and perhaps more fruitful, to see that the analyst's transferences, while importantly different in degree, are, as they are for the patient, involved in everything he does. This especially includes the functioning of his work ego. . . . More important than what we call it is the concept of an unbroken continuum of transference in the workings of the analyst, from his infantile beginnings to his best working behind the couch, a hierarchy of transferential states over which he ranges in empathic resonance with his patient" (657).

What I wish to take from Brenner's far-ranging book, *The Mind in Conflict* (1982), in this context is the bearing of his conceptions of psychic conflict and compromise-formations on this view of transference. Brenner's central concern was "the theory of psychic conflict" (5)[1] and its management by compromise-

---

1. Brenner is the most thoroughgoing modern exponent of and comprehensive developer of the definitional remark made by Ernst Kris in 1947 that psychoanalysis can be considered as *nothing but* human behavior considered from the point of view of conflict (Kris 1947).

formations: "My understanding of what conflict is: its components, their inter-action, and its consequences in mental life. Its components are several. They include drive derivatives, anxiety and depressive affect, defense, and various manifestations of superego functioning. These components interact in ways gov-erned by the pleasure-unpleasure principle. The consequences of conflict are compromise-formations" (7). Further, "It is compromise formations one observes when one studies psychic functioning. Compromise formations are the data of observation when one applies the psychoanalytic method and observes and/or infers a patient's wishes, fantasies, moods, plans, dreams, and symptoms. Each of these is a compromise formation, as are, indeed, the entire range of psychic phenomena subsumed under the heading of material for analysis" (109). And "the phenomena of our daily mental life, our fantasies, our thoughts, our plans, and our actions, are compromises among the forces and tendencies of id and ego and, later, of the superego as well. . . . I wish to emphasize that this holds true of psychic functioning in general. It is not true only for those relatively atypical phenomena called neurotic symptoms. Compromise formation is a gen-eral tendency of the mind, not an exceptional one" (113). In summary, "conflict and compromise formation are not hallmarks of pathological mental function-ing. They are equally important in normal functioning" (115).

It is no surprise, then, that when Brenner wished to "call attention to what is new in my evaluation of the role conflict plays in psychic life," he stated, "Wherever we look, what we see is a compromise formation" (119). When Brenner looked at transference, he naturally said that "1. Transference in psy-choanalysis is but one example of an object relation. Like every object relation, it is a compromise formation. 2. What is unique about transference in psycho-analysis is not its presence. It is the fact that it is analyzed. . . . 5. Erotic trans-ference is . . . a tautologous concept. Every transference manifestation is, among other things, erotic. 6. Transference is never positive or negative. It is always both. It is always ambivalent. . . . 10. To assert that a patient does not or cannot develop a transference is to assert the impossible" (211). Brenner's conceptu-alizations, stated so simply and flatly, seem so straightforward and unquestionable that they have become quite taken-for-granted and noncontroversial.

I next take up three articles from a 1984 panel of the American, reprinted in a single 1986 issue of the *Journal of the American*. All of these ostensibly deal with the countertransference, yet all in one way or another shed light on our con-ceptions of the transference. Robert Tyson (1986) does so in the most indirect manner. He set this survey article in the frame of what he called a fivefold expansion in our conceptualization of the countertransference over time: (1) from comprising the unconscious reactions of analyst to patient to also encom-passing the conscious responses; (2) from the analyst's reactions to the patient's transferences to the totality of his responses to the situation; (3) from concern with the analyst's unresolved neurotic conflicts to concern with his overall psychic functioning; (4) from recognizing and dealing with countertransference when its unhappy consequences perceptibly impact the analytic situation to a continued and continuous analytic self-monitoring; and (5) from experiencing countertransference as an unnecessary obstacle to the analytic work to experiencing it as an aid and contributor to better understanding. One can readily see this development as the almost exact counterpart of the temporally earlier comparable expansion of our understandings of the transference[2]—therefore a buttressing of McLaughlin's (1981) thesis of transference and countertransference as simply the same phenomenon viewed from opposite sides of the couch.

Loewald (1986) carried McLaughlin's conception of the equality of transference and countertransference further. He stated, "I believe it is ill-advised, indeed impossible, to treat transference and countertransference as separate issues. They are the two faces of the same dynamic" (276). He elaborated as follows: "Transference and countertransference are, to begin with, unconscious dynamics. By analytic work, an important share of them may become conscious. The analyst has achieved a significant degree of awareness of their operations in himself and in others. His awareness, and his experience-based conviction that awareness may lead to better integration and mastery of their workings, enable him to help the patient toward greater awareness and mastery. Be it noted that the impulse to help his patient in this particular analytic mode is itself a manifestation of the analyst's countertransference" (278). To underline this essential equality (with the analyst's advantage and expertise in the analytic process residing solely in his earlier immersion in the study of these processes in his personal analysis and training as well as all his intervening clinical experience), Loewald went on to state, "I have implied that both analyst and patient are subject to countertransference" (279)—the patient's countertransference, that is, to the analyst's transference to him.

This implies not only the coequal ubiquity of transference and countertransference but their coequal indispensability for the analytic work—again a statement of the heuristic gain if the terminology were collapsed in accord with

2. The comparable fivefold expansion of our understanding of the (patient's) transferences not only took place much earlier but was actually covered completely by Freud in his lifetime of work. In regard to the temporally later development of conceptualizations in the realm of countertransference, we should note that Freud did not introduce the term "countertransference" until 1910a, in his paper "The Future Prospects of Psycho-Analytic Therapy" (144), went through the comparable fivefold progression in regard to the countertransference only rudimentarily, and never came to the fifth step; this was introduced as late as 1950, by Paula Heimann, and 1951, by Margaret Little.

McLaughlin's prescription. Loewald put it this way: "Countertransference is the indispensable means for understanding the patient's transference. When its phenomena become conscious, they can provide valuable clues" (282). And "One runs the risk of arriving at incorrect interpretations when . . . countertransference mirroring is distorted by the analyst's own transference distortions. It takes his knowledge of himself and his overall knowledge of the patient to keep the differences in mind and make the necessary corrections" (283). Again, "If a capacity for transference, from its most primitive to its most developed form, is a measure of the patient's analyzability, the capacity for countertransference is a measure of the analyst's ability to analyze" (285–86).

Loewald's closing remarks put all this in developmental context:

> Countertransference, in this general sense, is a technical term for the analyst's responsiveness to the patient's love-hate for the analyst. This love-hate is a new edition of the patient's original love life as it was formed in interaction with early libidinal objects. The patient's transference to the analyst is a new rendition, shaped by these origins, by later experiences and growth, and increasingly modified by the libidinally based transactions in the analytic encounter between patient and that special new object— the analyst. On the analyst's side, his responsiveness to each patient is a new rendition, shaped by the patient's transference, of his specially trained ability to use his own love-hate in the service of analyzing. (286)

Jacobs (1986), in an article replete with revealing and illuminating clinical vignettes drawn from his own (counter) transference experiences, showed how both transference and countertransference can be embedded in customary or ordinary behaviors and thus escape notice; in the analyst's case, embedded in customary aspects of ordinary technique: "The analyst's countertransference reactions, however—and I am using the term here to refer to influences on his understanding and technique that stem both from his transferences and from his emotional responses to the patient's transferences—may be expressed in ways that are even more covert, as aspects of his well-accepted methods and procedures. When they take this form countertransference reactions are intricately intertwined with and embedded within customary—and often unexamined— analytic techniques and the attitudes and values that inform them" (290). Jacobs went on to talk of "the way in which countertransference elements may be concealed within our standard, well-accepted, and quite correct procedures" (294); and he wanted it understood that "in citing case examples . . . my focus will not be on the severely traumatized patient or the more disturbed one, but on patients whose symptoms and character problems make psychoanalysis carried out in an unmodified way clearly the treatment of choice" (294).

Jacobs then illustrated exactly what he meant via a number of clinical, very workaday examples. In his summary, he stated, "Often well camouflaged within the framework of traditional, time-tested techniques, this aspect of countertransference may attach itself to our way of listening and thinking about patients, to our efforts at interpretation, to the process of working through, or to the complex issue of termination. . . . For it is precisely those subtle, often scarcely usable countertransference reactions, so easily rationalized as parts of our standard operating procedures and so easily overlooked, that may in the end have the greatest impact on our analytic work" (289).

Certainly this whole trio of articles, by Tyson, Loewald, and Jacobs, has gone far to fulfill McLaughlin's agenda of establishing the essential identity of transference and countertransference—the same landscape perceived from opposite directions.

In 1987, Arnold Cooper (1987a) published an article synthesizing the literature on transference and transference interpretation, arranged under two organizing conceptions, which he called the historical and the modernist models. He began with an assessment of Freud's understanding of the transference: "He believed that the transference represents a *true* reconstruction of the past, a vivid reliving of earlier desires and fears that distort the patient's capacity to perceive the 'true nature' of the present reality . . . the task of the transference interpretation is cognitive 'enlightenment' that carries the emotional conviction of lived experience" (80). Cooper then counterposed the two major conceptions of the transference that had developed since Freud's time:

> The first idea, close to Freud, is that the transference is an enactment of
> an earlier relationship, and the task of transference interpretation is to gain
> insight into the ways that the early infantile relationships are distorting or
> disturbing the relationship to the analyst, a relationship which is, in turn,
> a model for the patient's life relationships. I shall refer to this as the *historical*
> model of transference, implying both that it is older and that it is based
> on an idea of the centrality of history. The second view regards the trans-
> ference as a new experience rather than as an enactment of an old one.
> The purpose of transference interpretation is to bring to consciousness all
> aspects of this new experience including its colorings from the past. I shall
> refer to this as the *modernist* model of the transference, implying both that
> it is newer, in fact still at an early stage of evolution, and that it is based
> on an idea of the immediacy of experience. (90–91)

Cooper then contrasted these two views, their consequences, and their implications. This will be quoted in extenso for its summarizing treatment of so much of the literature on transference):

In the first, historical view, the importance of transference interpretation lies in the opportunity it provides in the transference neurosis for the patient to reexperience and undo the partially encapsulated, one might say "toxic," neurosogenic early history. In the second, modernist view, the purpose of transference interpretation is to help the patient to see, in the intensity of the transference, the aims, character, and mode of his current wishes and expectations as influenced by the past. The historical view is more likely to regard the infantile neurosis as a "fact" of central importance for the analytic work, to be uncovered and undone. The modernist view regards the infantile neurosis, if acknowledged at all, as an unprivileged set of current fantasies rather than historical fact. From this modernist perspective, the transference resistance is the core of the analysis, to be worked through primarily because of the rigidity it imposes on the patient, not because of an important secret that it conceals. Similarly, it is a corollary of the historical conception to view the transference neurosis as a distinct phenomenon that develops during the analysis as a consequence of the expression of resistance to drive-derived aims that are aroused toward the analyst. Those holding the modernist view, much more influenced by the object-relational ideas of development, are likely to blur the idea of a specific transference neurosis in favor of viewing all transference responses as reflecting shifting self- and object representations as they are affected by the changing analytic relationship, and significant transferences may be available for interpretation very early in the analysis. . . .

The historical view is more likely to see the analyst as a more or less neutral screen upon which drive-derived needs will enact themselves. He is observer and interpreter, not co-participant in the process of change. The person of the analyst is of lesser importance. Those taking the modernist view hold that the analyst is an active participant, a regulator of the analytic process, whose personal characteristics powerfully influence the content and shape of the transference behaviors, and who will himself be changed in the course of the treatment. The historical view emphasizes the content and precision of the transference interpretation, especially as it reconstructs the past. The modernist view, at least in some hands, is likely to deemphasize reconstructive content and see the transference interpretation as one aspect of the interpersonal relationship in the present, acting as a new emotional and behavioral regulator, when past relationships have been inadequate or absent. (81–82)

In its furthest extension, the modernist conception states that, "while there is a past of 'there and then' it is knowable only through the filter of the present, of 'here and now.' There is no other past than the one we construct, and there is no way of understanding the past except through its relation to the present" (83)—which is the extreme of this view, underpinning the increasingly prevalent hermeneutic conception of psychoanalysis. Here Cooper mentioned Paul Ricoeur (1970), Schafer (1981), Gill (1982), and Spence (1982).

Cooper's overview assessment of this dialectic as of the time of his writing was, "Although the historical definitions of transference and transference interpretation have the merit of seeming precision and limited scope, they are based on a psychoanalytic theory that no longer stands alone and has lost ground to competing theories. Of necessity, the historical definition is being replaced, or at least subsumed, by modernist conceptions that are more attuned to the theories that abound today" (88)—an allusion to the widespread current acceptance of psychoanalytic theoretical diversity. Cooper did, however, indicate that Gill had gone further in positioning himself vis-à-vis this modernist conception of the transference than Cooper would accept: "The purpose of the analyst's alertness to distortion is not to correct his patient, but to allow him to understand the needs that are dictating the patient's construction" (95). Contra Gill, Cooper insisted that "the concept of distortion neither demeans the patient nor implies a single correct truth" (97). Cooper also sided with Schafer's criticism of Gill's apparent assumption of practical equality in contributions to the transference from on the couch and behind it. Cooper stated it as follows: "Schafer (1985) criticizes Gill's view as removing the gradients of expertise, of need for help, of closeness to conflict, etc., that characterize the different responsibilities of therapist and patient in the analytic situation" (94–95).

In his recent monograph on the epistemology of psychoanalysis, Strenger (1991) reinforced Cooper's perspectives on our changed "modernist" perceptions of the transference and carried their implications even further. First Strenger made clear that the modernist conception applies not just to the transference but to the totality of the analysis and the analytic work:

> It is [now] the patient as historian, as the writer of his own biography, who is the focus of the analyst's attention, rather than the actual events that patient is talking about. The shift in perspective away from the historical conception of psychoanalysis is that in the latter the past is the center of interest and the patient's present is seen as a function of that past. As opposed to this, the modernist conception focuses on the patient's present versions of his autobiography. All topics brought up by the patient are taken to be at the same level, and facts about the past do not have special explanatory status. Whatever the chronological location of the events related, it is the patient's perspective of them, more than the actual

events, which matters. Correspondingly, the question of the historical truth of the patient's stories matters only insofar as very unlikely versions of purportedly actual events serve as indications of some defensive distortion: i.e., they show us the patient's biases as narrator of his own biography. (88)

Another consequence of this modernist perspective is that it "weakens the link between clinical description and genetic speculation. As we saw, recent authors tend to emphasize the aspect of analytic work which is centered in the present. The reconstruction of the historical truth about the patient's past and the establishment of causal links between the past and the patient's present problems have lost their centrality in the modernist's conception of what the analyst does" (104).[3]

Richard Fox (1989) undertook to account retrospectively for the differences between Freud's original conceptions of technique, interpretation, and transference and today's modernist conceptions. His basic thesis was that Freud never conceived of the transference-countertransference interplay in interactional and experiential terms because his concepts of transference were powerfully formed in his self-analysis, primarily as a one-sided focus on dream analysis, without a living transference relationship with Fliess, the transferential surrogate. In Freud's self-analysis there was basically a text, not a dialogue; Fliess served as a day-residue, not as an interlocutor or interacter. For instance, "In the displacement model of transference drawn from Freud's description of the dream work, Fliess' person would provide merely a 'day residue' for the displaced representation. This intrapsychic model does not do justice to the importance of the participatory and experiential aspects of a transference actualization" (480–81).

3. Fosshage (1994) most recently has offered a revised two-model reconceptualization of the transference. The traditional, or classical, model he now calls the "Displacement model: through displacement, the patient inappropriately transfers feelings, wishes and attitudes that belong to past figures to the analyst. . . . through displacements, the patient *distorts* the *reality* of the analyst, based on the proposition that there is an objective reality" (268). Counterposed to this is the more current conception of the transference based on the evolution of the concepts of co-participation, a two-body psychology, and interacting subjectivities. This is called the "Organization model: through the use of primary organizing principles, established through past experiences, the patient perceptually and cognitively shapes . . . the experience of the analytic relationship. . . . through organizing principles, the patient (as well as the analyst) perceives and organizes the experience of the analytic relationship that becomes his/her *subjective reality* based on the proposition that 'reality' is relative and always partially determined by the perceiver" (268). This is akin to, if not completely identical with, the historical vs. modernist models of Cooper and Strenger. With both of these paired versions of transference conceptions there are similar implications for transference illumination and interpretation.

Further, Freud "tended to highlight the results of his self-interpretive work and to *minimize* the importance of the experiential dimension of the process which, I suggest, unfolded in his ongoing relationship with Fliess" (474). And finally: "To the degree that his self-analysis was carried out through the medium of dream interpretation this objectivization of the data was further strengthened by the fact that what was to be interpreted was a text, that is a dream narrative, rather than a dialogue or two person interaction. When he came to offer his recommendations for technique [in the six technical papers, 1911–15], Freud transferred aspects of this model drawn from his self-analysis and based upon his method of dream interpretation on to the two-person psychoanalytic situation" (476). This is certainly an interesting and a plausible accounting. Whether it actually corresponded to Freud's psychological processes we can never really know.

I come now to nine recent papers dealing with transference and transference interpretation. First among them is a pair of papers by Abend, one surveying the literature and present conceptions of the countertransference (1989), the other pursuing the same task with the transference (unpubl. ms). In the paper on countertransference, Abend spoke to the same expansion of countertransference considerations that has already been presented in the discussion of Tyson's (1986) paper. Abend ascribed this progressive expansion to two main developments, one internal to psychoanalysis, the other external. The internal development was the increasing effort to apply psychoanalytic techniques to patients with "deeper and wider ego disorders," paradigmatically the severely narcissistic and the borderline. These therapeutic endeavors are associated centrally with the names of Kohut (1971, 1977, 1984) and Kernberg (1975, 1976, 1980). The external development Abend pointed to was the sociohistorical context, the profound disillusionment following World War II and the de-idealization of traditional authority that has characterized the current American social and intellectual climate—a world in which authority structures have become suspect, in which the intellectual climate is actively revisionist, skeptical, even cynical, and in which the view of the countertransference (and transference) as actively interactional fits with a less elitist, less rigidly authoritarian perspective. A main consequence of these shifts—and this is what I wish to draw from Abend's paper—is that "countertransference can be said to have emerged from its former place in the dark, burdened by connotations of sin and shame, into the bright light of revelation. Acknowledgment of its impact has become a mark of one's analytic professionalism" (388).

Of course, "just how to transform countertransference into empathy and understanding, or how to distinguish the hindering from the helpful emotional reactions to patients continues to be the quintessential skill, even perhaps the ultimate test of the gifted analytic clinician." But at least we need no longer worry about the "connotation of countertransference as error resulting from analysts' own difficulties, which emphasizes it as a source of shame and guilt, and encourages defensiveness and polemics" (389). If true, this marks finally the full conceptual and emotional equalization of countertransference and transference. And Abend, an ego-psychology exponent, offered here a nod of appreciation to the Kleinians: "The original Kleinian proposition that analysts' emotional reactions to patients can become an important source of increased understanding of patients' material has become accepted in all quarters" (391).

Abend's (1993) counterpart article reviewing the conceptions of transference has a comparable structure. Here he also talks of a fivefold expansion of considerations encompassed by the transference (as compared with Freud's original conceptions), as follows: (1) the dimension of interpersonal experiencing in addition to and alongside interpretation and insight; (2) the transferences of defenses and superego structures in addition to drives (Anna Freud's early contribution); (3) the broadening of drive to encompass the vicissitudes of aggression along with sexuality—in fact, the broadening to all affective aspects of the interpersonal relationship; (4) the extensions to the preoedipal and onto the earliest basic matrix (Greenacre, Stone, etc.); and (5) the reactions to the present behaviors of the analyst and all the stimuli of the analytic situation (Gill's "analytic situation residue") as well as in terms of expectations derived from the past. As for current analytic preoccupations with the subject of transference, Abend cited four aspects: (1) the focus on the influence of the relationship, on a more interactive stance, on what is called "empathic immersion"; (2) the focus on the analyst's omnipresent subjectivity, a far cry from the early conception of countertransference as a (pejorative) label for the unconsciously determined limitations on the analyst's objectivity; (3) the dialectical tensions between an intrapsychic and an interpersonal reading of the transference, a dichotomy, a specious dichotomy, or an integrate; and (4) the widening of the domain of transference content to the oedipal and preoedipal, object- and self-object-related issues of aggression, envy, guilt, separation, and so on.

Papers by Stewart (1990) and Hayley (1990), two analysts from the British Middle or Independent Group, have already been presented in large part. I return to them here to focus on the interplay between them. Stewart's paper stressed the evolution of two kinds of transference interpretation, that aimed at the drive-anxiety-defense conflict in a classical (ego-psychological) conception of the anaclitic transference relationship and the other aimed at understanding the sensibilities and vulnerabilities of patients in narcissistic types of transference relationship. Stewart went on to lay out five types of change mechanisms in analytic work, transference interpretation (of either or both kinds) being only one of the five: (1) the varieties of transference interpretations, (2) extratransference interpretations, (3) reconstructions, (4) therapeutic regressions, and (5) more active interventions than interpretations. (For more detail, see chapter 11.)

Hayley's paper, from the same theoretical position and perspective, focused on the continuing role of charisma and suggestion. This never has been and never can be extirpated from analytic work. And, from his perspective, even if it were possible to do so, it never should be. Hayley took Stewart to task for his failure to mention suggestion as among his postulated psychoanalytic change factors—to Hayley, a surprising oversight for someone from the object-relational theoretical perspective. Hayley explained it thus:

> This is no doubt due to the fact that psychoanalysts fight the idea that suggestion is involved in our therapy. I would like to postulate that charismatic influence or suggestion is a factor inherent in Stewart's five agents. I doubt if it causes psychic change on its own. We know it has short-term effects as in hypnotism and other suggestive technique, but in my opinion it also has the power to aid in the conveying of a psychic truth to the patient and so helps to effect lasting change, perhaps, as Freud (1925b, p. 42) said, by overcoming a transference resistance. This would be important for unsophisticated patients in our society and primitive societies, where the effect is further heightened by enacted metaphors—the ceremonies. (7)

Actually, in returning to the way in which Freud (at times) emphasized the suggestive aspects of the transference authority and transference effects, Hayley has drawn a circle around much of the intervening literature—preeminently Gill's work, which was designed to reverse Freud's position and his example in this regard. And so the dialectic continues.

A final cluster of five papers deserves mention. Two of these attempt to break new conceptual ground: Poland's (1992) extension of ideas on the "jointness" of the transference unfolding within the two-party and interpersonal psychoanalytic situation, and Renik's (1993a) extension of the concomitant "equalization" of transference and countertransference, both chronicled in this and the preceding chapter. Poland subtitled his paper on transference "An Original Creation," a phrase from Proust's *Remembrance of Things Past* that Poland used to epitomize his central theme: "The past clearly and undoubtedly influences the present, but, Proust adds, the present shapes our views of the past. Speaking of our early ghosts, Proust says, 'erasing their former image, we recast them in an original creation'" (190). Poland began his article with the by-now familiar conception of the transference operating in the immediacy of the here and now. He put this evocatively as follows: "In essence, transference exists in the immediacy of the now. Dazzled by the past, in analysis we have at times lost our bearings in the present, as if we could reach for the past without putting our full weight on the present. Only the past that is alive in the present, even if buried, can we ever grasp in our hands. That is the past alive as it is recalled into present feelings by present sensations or as it is revived in present associations and enactments. The untouchable past is that which we can only reconstruct, inferring its shape by its imprint on the unconscious fantasies we come to know through present experience" (186).

This is amplified even more poetically a little further on: "Behind the present lies the past. But in analysis the border between the past and the present is not something temporal, not something in the linear actuality of time. When we speak of the psychoanalytic past, it is, rather, something present now, something within the deep structure of the mind but currently present, an enduring piece of the mind alive. We refer to reverberations of the past as they are alive in the present framework of the patient's mind whether or not they are accessible in the conscious tales of memory" (187). This leads ineluctably to "The past is not directly alive in the present as the past incarnate. The past is alive as it has shaped unconscious fantasies, and it is the set of unconscious fantasies that are alive in the present. . . . Recognition of the meaningfulness of organizing fantasies alive in the present is the doorway to the relevance of the past" (189).

At this point we have arrived at the conception embodied in the quotation from Proust: Through lifting our fantasies to consciousness as discourse within the analytic dialogue, we (our patients) shape and express the past via our wishes and fears in the present. In that sense we create the past or, in Proust's words, recast it in an original creation. This conception has now been stated quite matter-of-factly by Treurniet (1993) as a consensually accepted understanding of the transference: "The contemporary interest as to whether the transference is a repetition of the past or a newly formed creation emphasizes the point of the complex cyclic relation between affective memories and fantasies that are evoked by current reality. Transference, then, can be hypothesized, both as a repeatable configuration and as something created anew" (21). Corollary to this conception is Poland's definition of memory: "Memories are alive as present emotional experience. Their actuality is in the present even as their subject is the past. . . . The past is alive and can be known only in its continuity to the emotions and sensations experienced in the present" (202–03).

This, then, is the fullest actualization of the major shift in the conceptualization of the transference. In chapter 1, I indicated that I would not focus on the debate over the status of psychoanalysis as science, natural science, social science, "unique" science, hermeneutic science, or no science at all, but rather a hermeneutic discipline, kin to the world of the humanities and not to the world of science. (I have discussed these issues elsewhere [Wallerstein 1976, 1986b.]) Clearly, however, the whole hermeneutic movement within psychoanalysis has given powerful impetus to the position on transference expressed so clearly by Poland and reflective of so much (probably the majority of) contemporary psychoanalytic thinking. I can illustrate this hermeneutic influence by quoting from a paper in which I summarized the position of Spence, one of the leading advocates of the hermeneutic viewpoint within psychoanalysis (Wallerstein 1986b). There I summarized Spence's position in relationship to the entirety of psychoanalytic work, not just the conception of the transference, as follows: "The logic of all this can lead us—according to Spence—to a whole series of transformations of our usual analytic thought conventions: of reconstruction into new construction, of acts of discovery into acts of creation, of historical truth into (only) narrative fit, of pattern finding into pattern making, of veridical interpretation into creative interpretation, of all interpretation into a species of (more or less) inexact interpretation, of analysis as a science of recovery of the past into merely a dialogue of choice and creation in the present and future, and of psychoanalyst as historical scientist, into psychoanalyst as only poet and aestheticist" (423–24). The direct fit of Poland's paper into this context is immediately apparent.

Another of the five papers in this final cluster, by Norbert Freedman and Michael Berzofsky (unpubl. ms), is quoted here only as a definitional statement of what the modern day concept of transference does (can) encompass: "It is deemed to be one of the major agents of change, and yet we know that the conception of the transference varies greatly among psychoanalytic theorists and observers. Transference may involve the reactivation of the biographical past, the reactivation of an unconscious fantasy, the activation of a disavowed affect, or the play and the scenario of the relationship in the here and now, or a combination of all those factors" (3). The reader by this time will no doubt have established his or her resonances with each of these views, singly or in combination.

The other significant theme throughout this chapter is what I have called the equalization of the transference and countertransference. Renik's (1993a) specific focus was on "countertransference enactments," and his central point was that they are inevitable and necessary to the proper carrying out of the analytic task, not an unhappy and mischievous interference that a more experienced or better-analyzed analyst would somehow have avoided—the exact counterpart to the place of transference enactments, which are the very bread and butter of analytic work.

Renik's argument was that the analyst's countertransference enactment precedes his countertransference awareness and is in fact a necessary prelude to it:

"How does an analyst become aware of his countertransference?. . . . it is commonplace for an analyst first to become aware of some way that he has, in fact, been behaving in the clinical situation, and then, through consideration of what he has been doing to become conscious of a countertransference motivation. The sequence of events in which awareness follows enactment is generally conceptualized as less than optimal—though, of course, perfectly expectable, given human limitations" (137). This reasoning, Renik felt, was based on Freud's conception that thought and action are mutually exclusive activities, that drive impulses can be expressed in thought (fantasy) *or* in action. But the evidence is to the contrary, that thought and action are on a continuum, that thought is (as Freud also declared) a trial action, a highly attenuated motor activity.

Given this conception of continuity, Renik could state, "It seems likely to me that if we could always closely examine the sequence of events by which an analyst becomes aware of his countertransference motivations, we would find that it *invariably* begins with his noting how he has put them, sometimes almost imperceptibly, into action. We are familiar with finding ourselves able to profit in the clinical situation from post facto investigation of our countertransferentially motivated errors. We might ask ourselves whether such instances show us with unusual vividness what is regularly the case" (137–38). And here Renik drew the explicit equation with the transferential counterpart, with the equivalent implications for the therapeutic process: "We have little difficulty regarding transference enactment as a necessary prelude to transference awareness for an analysand. We expect an analysand to begin by playing out his transferences within the treatment relationship, and eventually to become aware of what he is doing; it seems we find it difficult to suppose that the same is true for an analyst with respect to his countertransferences. At the same time, we regularly observe that successful analytic work unfolds via a process of continuous mutually active embroilment between analyst and analysand, and continuous effort on the part of both to become aware of and clarify the nature of the embroilment" (138).

Thus we have the completed argument for the equivalency of transference and countertransference enactments and of their potential usefulness for (as well as risk to) the treatment process.[4] Toward the end of his article, Renik tried to

---

4. In their 1988 paper on their empirical research on the transference, Hoffman and Gill asserted this same position: "The shift in emphasis in our thinking that we want to describe here is one that moves from thinking that it is *not necessarily bad* for the analyst to participate in certain ways that are consistent with the patient's transference-based expectations, to thinking that it may be *desirable and useful* for the process for the analyst to participate partially in various kinds of transference-countertransference enactments which have important meanings for the patient" (57).

draw a distinction between psychoanalysis and psychotherapy along these lines, claiming that in psychoanalysis, the analyst and patient work insistently to make these enactments conscious while in psychoanalytic psychotherapy they are more often allowed to remain outside the patient's—and perhaps the therapist's—conscious awareness (see 238).[5]

Treurniet's article (1993) is set within a far broader context of explicating the essential and inevitable supportive elements in the psychoanalytic process. He called them "non-interpretive elements in support of the process" (191). With regard to the "supportive elements," Treurniet reviewed the conceptions of the setting as providing a background of safety, of the frame and space as creating an intermediate area of experiencing, of Freud's unobjectionable (or tender) positive transference, and of holding and the distinction experienced between the "environment-mother" and the "object-mother"; he traced the influences of Winnicott, Balint, Bollas, and Stewart (all from the British Independent or object-relational group) in the generation of these concepts. Treurniet's conception of the intertwining roles of noninterpretive (supportive) and interpretive components in the properly progressing psychoanalytic process, as well as the important supportive elements in *both* the noninterpretive and the interpretive aspects of the process, has already been presented in chapter 11.

After thus defining what he considered the vital supportive element (or supportive matrix) as it interacts continuously with the ongoing interpretive effort, Treurniet indicated how transference and/or countertransference enactments pose the threat of "disruptions" or "empathic failures" and, at the same time, the opportunity for insight and analytic progress: "Disruptions of the background are a most essential part of any analysis and to my idea determinative for psychic change. . . . partial acting out of countertransference is inevitable. Besides being impossible complete containment of it is also undesirable. Partial acting out means that the patient is able to see that the analyst is being affected by what is projected, is struggling to tolerate it, and is managing sufficiently to

5. Renik's position of the inevitability of mutual enactments in the transference-countertransference interplay that can be known and disentangled only in retrospect is gaining increasing currency. It is strongly supported in most recent contributions by Howard Levine (1994) and Alan Skolnikoff (1993). For example, Levine: "I have proposed replacing the possibility of an objective analyst safeguarding the analytic process with that of an inevitably subjective analyst operating within a wide range of possible analytic processes, the value and nature of which can only be known in retrospect" (675); and Skolnikoff: "What I wish to emphasize is my belief that most, if not all, analyses contain important enactments and trans-ference-countertransference reactions that, at the time of their occurrence, are not completely understood. It is the continuing *attempt* to understand these interactions by both members of the analytic pair that may be related to positive changes in outcome" (308).

maintain his analytic stance ('good enough' is better than perfect here). . . . Like the baby . . . the patient needs to feel that he can elicit real emotions in his analyst" (206–08).

Even more explicitly: "There are apparently roads to psychic change other than the mutative transference interpretation; the symbolically experienced actions of the analyst can function as an equivalent to interpretation like the symbolic enactments of the patient can be an equivalent of free association" (228). This last statement is clearly the same conceptualization as Renik's, the full equivalency of enactments across the whole of the transference-countertransference interplay.

Weinshel and Renik (1991), surveying changes in psychoanalysis in the United States over the 1980s, addressed two major themes: greater tolerance for uncertainty and more modest and tentative approaches and increasing acceptance of diverse viewpoints, theoretical and clinical. Within the frame of those themes, they then dealt with a range of specific issues. For example, "Previous decades saw much consideration given to whether a narrow or an expanded definition of *countertransference* would be more advantageous. This concern has faded into the background lately, inasmuch as most of us assume that the entire array of an analyst's emotional responses—those specifically induced by an analysand's transferences as well as those brought by the analyst a priori—must be taken into account in studying psychoanalytic technique and process." And in regard to the nature of the transference: "Whatever label one applies to psychoanalysis, hermeneutic or scientific, the conception that psychoanalytic investigation takes place and psychoanalytic reality is established within a two-person field—something that provoked heated debate not too long ago—is by now a consensual view" (15). These statements capture well the shifting conceptualizations over time and the newly converging views that I have traced in this chapter and the preceding one.

It remains to call attention to some views brought together in Etchegoyen's (1991) magisterial book, in which the section on transference and countertransference (broadly considered) comprises 17 chapters and 230 pages. Etchegoyen's overall posture—and this as a self-styled "fanatic" Kleinian analyst—is that "a reaction is never 100-percent transferential, nor an action entirely just and balanced. . . . We should consider, therefore, the transference as the irrational, the unconscious, the infantile in human conduct, co-existing with the rational, the conscious, and the adult in a complementary series. Certainly as analysts we should not think that everything is transference; we should discover the portion of it that exists in every mental act. Not everything is transference, but transference exists in everything, which is not the same thing" (83)—a viewpoint much more consonant with Rangell's prescription of "balance" than with Gill's single-minded focus on the ubiquity and overriding primacy of transference, to locate Etchegoyen's position in relation to well known American authors.

Most of Etchegoyen's consideration of the transference and countertransference will be quite familiar to American analysts. I want here only to direct attention to a few distinctions made that—even if quite unfamiliar conceptualizations—will nonetheless, I think, resonate congenially with generally accepted views. The first is his distinction between "transference at times as a function of *memory* and at others as a function of *desire*" (90). This is explicated as follows:

> With regard to remembering, the best resistance will be transference, because it transforms a memory into something present. . . . From the point of view of desire, on the other hand, its actuality will be what awakens the strongest resistance. At no time does Freud distinguish between resistance to memory and resistance to desire, and, therefore, in my view, he allows a contradiction to remain. . . . To repeat: that which most adjusts itself to the resistance to memory is transference, without doubt, where by means of it the patient does not remember. What could be better for not remembering than exchanging the memory for actuality, the present? . . . To avoid the memory, there is nothing better than the occurrence of transference: as an example, just when I was about to remember my rivalry with my father, I began to feel rivalry with my analyst, and this transference served me marvelously well in eluding the memory. . . . When we assert, instead, that it is the transferential event that conditions the strongest resistance, this is because we are no longer thinking about memory but about wishful impulses. What situation could be more embarrassing for us than recognizing a desire if its object is present? (90)

I also wish to note Etchegoyen's demarcation of "transference perversions" and "transference addictions" alongside the more familiar conceptions of transference neurosis and transference psychosis. He considers transference perversion to be "a technical concept with the same range as transference neurosis," the "special type of relation that, perforce, the pervert will develop in the analysis so that the *transference perversion* may be created and resolved" (189). His basic conception is that "the pervert does not feel the call of instinct; he has communication with his body only through the intellect. I suppose that it is mainly envy joined to guilt feelings that leads the pervert to feel his instinct not as desire but as ideology. These are reflections that may contribute to clarify the enormous creative potential of the perverse structure. Equally it can be understood why for the pervert, enclosed in a world of ideologies, polemics are so vital"

(191). From there, Etchegoyen delineated the implications for the technical handling of the transference perversion by way of clinical vignettes.

Etchegoyen developed a comparable line of thinking in regard to what he felt to be the even more difficult situation of the transference addiction, which "has attracted less attention than neurosis, psychosis, and perversion, perhaps because few analysts treat addicts (despite the fact that the scourge is so widespread nowadays), and because it is not easy to define a special type of transference link in patients like these, in whom psychological mechanisms are combined with the physiopathological effect of the drug. A peculiar difficulty with the addict is that if the taking of drugs is not checked, analysis becomes difficult, and if it is interfered with, analytical neutrality suffers" (198). "In my opinion," Etchegoyen said,

> a great obstacle to the definition of "transference addiction" lies in the imprecise limits of the psychopathological picture within which it must be located. Firstly both the classic authors . . . and those of our day . . . consider that addiction exists *with* drugs and *without* drugs. Food, the cinema, reading (unfortunately less than previously!), sport, games of chance, work, television, in fact any human activity can bear the stamp of addiction, and we must not forget that in his letter 79 (22 December 1897), Freud tells Fliess that masturbation is the primal addiction, for which all the others are substitutes. It must be added that it is not the same thing to be addicted to alcohol or morphine as to marijuana, tobacco, coffee, tea, or yerba mate. I am inclined to think that the mental structure is the same in every case, but the clinical consequences are different.

As for treatment implications, Etchegoyen said, "We consider as an addict the patient who turns to alcohol and/or drugs as his main recourse in order to maintain a psychological balance and gain relief from anxiety, and a feeling of pleasure and well-being. When the drug is used to counteract the negative effect that appears as its action ends, a vicious circle is formed, which is very important in the establishment of addiction. The addict's craving is by definition impossible to satisfy in so far as it *does not arise from necessity, but from greed*" (198, italics added)—the italicized phrase being the key to analytical understanding and treatment. Etchegoyen added a cautionary note: "Even transference love can take on an addictive character. We may add now that the analytical situation itself can turn into addiction, which is all the more difficult to resolve when the addictive urge is masked by a manifest desire to be analysed 'for as long as necessary' " (201). Finally on the understanding of any behavior or mental process: "There is always a bit of unreality (transference) in it and a bit of reality.

And the past is always utilized to understand the present (experience) and to misunderstand it (transference)" (251).

Perhaps I can best end these two chapters on transference and transference interpretation with three quotations. The first is from an effort by Sandler et al. (1973) to define transference in a way that would encompass both the earlier connotation of a repetition of the past in the present and the more contemporary connotation of a (new) relationship in the present, colored, it is true, by past experiences and expectations:

> We concluded that a useful statement of the transference concept would be to regard it as: "a specific illusion which develops in regard to the other person, one which, unbeknown to the subject, represents, in *some* of its features, a repetition of a relationship towards an important figure in the person's past. It should be emphasized that this is felt by the subject, not as a repetition of the past, but as strictly appropriate to the present and to the particular person involved . . . transference need not be restricted to the illusory apperception of another person . . . but can be taken to include the unconscious (and often subtle) attempts to manipulate or to provoke situations with others which are a concealed repetition of earlier experiences and relationships" [an allusion to the concept elaborated in Sandler's (1976) paper on role responsiveness]. (49–50, italics added)

In commenting on this quotation, Stewart (1987) said, "I would just add that these unconscious, or sometimes not so unconscious, manipulations are directed towards making the analyst behave in a way that would justify the patient in concluding that his apperception of the analyst was not illusory but real" (197–98).

The second quotation defining transference interpretation comes from the same 1987 article by Stewart: "A transference interpretation will involve two aspects of the patient-analyst relationship; one of the immediacy of that relationship, often called the here-and-now, and the other derived from the relationships of the past, called the there-and-then. The major part of the analytic work is devoted to the elucidation of these two aspects, i.e. to transference analysis" (198). The various authors cited in these chapters on transference and transference interpretation would, of course, accord different weightings to Stewart's "two aspects."

The third and most terse definition of transference is from an unpublished paper by Max Hernandez: "Transference, in so far as it is a repetition, refers us to a sort of *amnesic memory* that lodges events which cannot be recalled but only repeated" (3, italics added).

14 The Rise and Fall of the Transference Neurosis

In a 1967 paper on "transference psychosis,"[1] I began as follows: "On both clinical and theoretical grounds the transference neurosis has long been established as the central technical and conceptual vehicle of psychoanalysis as a therapy. The usual course of psychoanalysis and of the development of this regressive transference reaction is characterized by the familiar reactivation within the analysis of earlier (i.e., infantile) experiences and also of earlier (i.e., infantile) modes of reacting to and mastering those experiences" (551). This represented the received wisdom of the time, accepted as a noncontroversial platform from which to clarify deviations such as the transference psychosis. Currently the same two sentences would be very controversial and would need an explication of just how they were intended. The purpose of this chapter is to chronicle the vicissitudes of this concept in psychoanalytic discourse.

Like almost everything else central to psychoanalysis, the concept of the transference neurosis originated with Freud, who regarded it as pivotal to the psychoanalytic process. In one of his six technical papers (1914a), he wrote,

> We regularly succeed [in proper psychoanalytic work] in giving all the symptoms of the illness a new transference meaning and in replacing his [the patient's] ordinary neurosis by a "transference neurosis" of which he can be cured by the therapeutic work. The transference thus creates an intermediate region between illness and real life through which the transition from the one to the other is made. The new condition has taken over all the features of the illness; but it represents an artificial illness which is at every point accessible to our intervention. It is a piece of real experience, but one which has been made possible by especially favourable conditions, and it is of a provisional nature. From the repetitive reactions

1. By "transference psychosis" I did not mean the activation of psychotic ideation and behaviors in the psychoanalytic treatment of overtly borderline or psychotic patients, a meaning which was used by Herbert Rosenfeld (1954) and Little (1958), the latter actually entitling her article *On Delusional Transference (Transference Psychosis)*. I excluded those instances from my categorization and said instead, "In this presentation I am rather confining my usage and examples, like Reider, to patients deemed wholly within the neurotic range in terms of character structure and adjudged appropriate for classical analysis, in whom nevertheless a disorganizing reaction of psychotic intensity occurred within the transference. Examples of such in the analytic literature are rare" (Wallerstein 1967, 553). In that paper I reviewed the sparse literature and added detailed descriptions of two cases of mine, together with an effort to elucidate the mechanisms and the responsible conditions. I do not discuss the transference psychosis specifically in this book, either in terms of my usage or that of H. Rosenfeld and Little.

which are exhibited in the transference we are led along the familiar paths
to the awakening of the memories, which appear without difficulty, as it
were, after the resistance is overcome. (154–55)

Here the emphasis is on the *artificial* nature of the transference neurosis, unique
to and a product of the therapeutic work of the analysis, in contrast to the
ubiquity of the transferences, which are an essential underpinning of all affectivity and all interpersonal behavior.

In his "Introductory Lectures" (1916–17), Freud gave a similar definition of
transference but emphasized even more strongly how the transference neurosis
focused everything to a "single point": the patient's relation to the doctor. "We
are no longer concerned with the patient's earlier illness but with a newly created
and transformed neurosis which has taken the former's place. . . . All the patient's symptoms have abandoned their original meaning and have taken on a
new sense which lies in a relation to the transference; or only such symptoms
have persisted as are capable of undergoing such a transformation. But the mastering of this new, artificial neurosis coincides with getting rid of the illness
which was originally brought to the treatment—with the accomplishment of
our therapeutic task" (444). In *Beyond the Pleasure Principle* (1920a), Freud emphasized the transference neurosis as the essence and concentrate of the transference, seen as a repetition (an expression of the repetition compulsion) in the
service of warding off remembering:

> He is obliged to *repeat* the repressed material as a contemporary experience
> instead of, as the physician would prefer to see, *remembering* it as something
> of the past. These reproductions, which emerge with such unwished-for
> exactitude, always have as their subject some portion of the infantile sexual
> life . . . and they are invariably acted out in the sphere of the transference,
> of the patient's relation to the physician. When things have reached this
> stage, it may be said that the earlier neurosis has now been replaced by a
> fresh, "transference neurosis." It has been the physician's endeavor to keep
> this transference neurosis within the narrowest limits: to force as much as
> possible into the channel of memory and to allow as little as possible to
> emerge as repetition. (18–19)

In this emphasis on the repetition of the infantile past in the transference neurosis, Freud underscored his conception of its regressive nature, and the convention soon arose of referring to the unfolding of the "regressive transference
neurosis."

Thus established, the regressive transference neurosis soon rose to a position
of primacy in thinking about the therapeutic action of psychoanalysis as the

taken-for-granted, conventional wisdom. The first significant emendation of Freud's concept was in Macalpine's 1950 paper, in which she asserted that the unfolding of the transference neurosis, far from being a spontaneous evolution in the course of psychoanalytic work, was an *induced* response to the artificial "infantile setting" created by the conditions of the psychoanalytic situation: "To this infantile setting the analysand—if he is analyzable—has to adapt, albeit by regression" (522). This process of adaptation by regression brings about what we call the transference neurosis: "the stage in analysis when the analysand has so far adapted to the infantile analytic setting—the main features of which are the denial of object relations and continual libidinal frustration—that his regressive trend is well established, and the various developmental levels [are] reached, relived, and worked through" (529).

It was no surprise, then, that when Gill (1954) undertook to discuss the similarities and differences between psychoanalysis and psychoanalytic psychotherapy, he first defined psychoanalysis as "that technique which, employed by a neutral analyst, results in the development of a *regressive transference neurosis* and the ultimate resolution of this neurosis by techniques of interpretation alone" (775, italics added). Stone (1954), in his "widening scope" paper, echoed this position: "I would think that the mobilization of as full and undistorted a transference neurosis as may be possible, and its ultimate dissolution (or minimization) by interpretative means, would be regarded as essential to a genuinely analytic outcome" (574). As usual, Stone's statements were more nuanced and cautious than Gill's on the same issues.

Alexander (1956), who took a quite different position, nonetheless acknowledged "there are a great many practitioners [Gill, Stone, for example] who do not consider it difficult to separate psychoanalysis and psychoanalytically oriented therapy on the basis of the essential nature of the two procedures. One of the common propositions is that while psychotherapy may uncover unconscious factors, it never revives the genetically important neurotic conflicts in their totality and therefore, it can never thoroughly reconstruct the personality structure. In other words, the absence of a full-fledged transference neurosis in psychotherapy is the differential criterion which sharply separates psychoanalysis from all other therapeutic procedures" (160–61). Karl Menninger (1958) underlined the prevailing equation of "regression" and "transference neurosis": "In psychoanalytic treatment, *for one hour a day,* the regression is there, to be heard and seen and utilized and ultimately resolved. It is sometimes called the 'transference neurosis,' but whatever it is called, this phenomenon of regression and its technical exploitation are of the very essence of psychoanalytic treatment" (50). And "The process of recovery is always an other-sided view of the disease process: and this applies to the artificial induction of a therapeutic illness, which is what the regression of 'transference neurosis' really is. The psychoan-alytic patient must get 'worse' in order to get 'better,' and both changes require effort against opposition" (122–23).

But during that same time period, Glover (1955), in one of the earliest com-pendiums of psychoanalytic technique, was already raising questions about the universality and the essentiality of this concept in pproper psychoanalysis: "The analytic transference-neurosis is seen in characteristic form only in the transfer-ence neuroses, the hysterias, conversions, and obsessions. . . . The view that a typical transference-neurosis develops in all cases is not only theoretically im-probable but contrary to actual experience. Some cases that show uneventful transference may suddenly develop a transference-psychosis, still others manifest no transference-neurosis at any time in the analysis. This is observed in . . . [he mentions psychosomatic states, character cases, delinquent psychopaths] and in the training analysis of such candidates as are symptom-free" (114). A. Cooper (1987b), in his review article on the transference neurosis, summarized Glover's views as follows: "He emphasized the transference neurosis as a phase of the analysis in which the transference focus on the analyst was the predominant analytic work; this work aimed at uncovering and resolving infantile Oedipus conflicts, but this aim essentially confined its usefulness to the transference neu-roses, rarely seen even in Glover's time. . . . In summary, Glover, reluctantly, on the basis of his clinical experience, relaxed or relinquished each of the ele-ments that Freud regarded as central to the concept" (573–74).

In a 1956 article, Zetzel, an American trained in Britain, compared the Amer-ican ego psychological and British perspectives on the concept of the therapeutic alliance and in that context referred to the issue of regression and the transference neurosis. Basically her stance (elaborated more fully in chapter 15) was that within the American ego-psychological framework an important distinction was made between the therapeutic alliance and the regressive transference neurosis, both developing in complementary fashion vis-à-vis each other, while within the British object-relational framework, where the concept of a distinct and separate therapeutic alliance has not been regarded as useful, the whole of the transferences are seen as a revival or repetition of early struggles with objects, and "no sharp differentiation is made between the early manifestations of trans-ference and the transference neurosis" (372). More pointedly, in 1959, Green-acre found the conception of a distinctive regressive transference neurosis as something that evolved under the pressures of the psychoanalytic situation to be not very useful: "Usually, except in certain cases of severe disturbances, the transference-neurotic manifestations do not form a fabric of consistent pattern and thickness. . . . there is a *constant panoramic procession of transference pictures* merging into each other or momentarily separating out with special clarity, in

a way which is frequently less constant than the symptoms and other manifestations of the neurosis itself. The degree to which the transference attitudes are
played out in current relationships (other than the analytic relationship) also
varies considerably. For this reason, I have myself been a little questioning of
the blanket term 'transference neurosis' which may sometimes be misleading. I
would prefer to speak of *active transference-neurotic manifestations*" (485–86, italics
added)—making simply a gradient of more or less intense transferences.

Despite these cautionary voices (Glover, Zetzel, Greenacre), the conception
of the transference neurosis as the fulcrum of the therapeutic effort in psychoanalysis and as the differentiating criterion of psychoanalysis from the psychoanalytically based psychotherapies seemed firmly in place, certainly through the
1960s. A good example is Dewald's pioneering book (1964) on psychodynamic
psychotherapy as a distinctive but closely related offshoot of psychoanalysis (discussed in chapter 6). Though most of that book is devoted to a comparison and
contrast between supportive psychotherapy and expressive psychotherapy, the
entire underlying psychoanalytic theory, as well as, specifically, the chapter on
the relationship between psychoanalysis and "insight-oriented psychotherapy"
(Dewald's preferred phrase for expressive psychoanalytic psychotherapy), is governed by the notion that the evolving regressive transference neurosis is the
distinctive line of demarcation between psychoanalysis and all its derivative and
related psychotherapies: "The strategy of psychotherapy . . . involves the establishment of a *transference relationship* (as opposed to a *regressive transference neurosis*)
in which there is an emotionally meaningful experience of the *derivatives* of the
infantile and early childhood conflicts, with an attempt to resolve or modify
patterns of integration, structural organization and behaviour at the level of these
derivative conflicts. A deeply regressive transference neurosis is not only unnecessary in the psychotherapy situation, but is actually unwise, and if it does
occur, it frequently complicates and disrupts the treatment effort. . . . Regression for its own sake has little therapeutic value. . . . The resolution of a regressive transference neurosis in psychotherapy is extremely difficult and most
frequently is unsatisfactory" (289, italics added). Similarly, "It is through the
exploration and analysis of this regressive transference neurosis that the infantile
and earlier childhood experiences and conflicts can return to the patient's awareness. In the forms of insight-directed psychotherapy being discussed here, the
intensity and extent of the regression in the transference is much more limited.
The therapeutic situation does not lend itself as completely to regression. Furthermore, one tactical goal is to avoid deeply regressive transference experiences,
since it is less likely that they can be successfully resolved in this type of treatment" (203–04).

Despite this confident assertion of the enduring value of the conception of the *regressive* transference neurosis, the sense of disquiet about its usefulness that had been voiced by Glover, Zetzel, and Greenacre persisted and led to a major reevaluation panel on the subject at the American Psychoanalytic Association. Three papers from that panel, published together in 1971, will be discussed here. Blum undertook to review the entire concept, offering the following definition: "In the transference neurosis, the analyst is perceived and reacted to in terms of the crucial infantile object representations, allowing a living redramatization of the distorting influence of the past. . . . I would retain the designation of transference neurosis, bearing in mind a modern concept of neurosis which takes into account structure and character" (43–44). Here Blum reminded us that Freud originally described the transference neurosis before introducing structural theory and ego psychology.

Blum then outlined certain features of this transference neurosis:

1. It does not necessarily bar the extra-analytic ("I do not believe that transference neurosis literally precludes extra-analytic symptoms or pathological behavior. . . . Aspects of the pre-treatment neurosis and transference neurosis coexist in a complicated and often reciprocal relationship" [45])

2. It is not an exact reenactment or repetition of the past ("Infantile reactions . . . are rarely seen in adult transference *neurosis* in their original form, but in attenuated homologues. Ego growth and verbalization favor transference illusion rather than literal repetition-in-action")

3. It is not necessarily a universal requirement in analysis ("In the adult, a transference neurosis has been considered a prerequisite for analysis. This is not a requirement for child analysis, and it is a moot question whether it is either obtainable or essential in the analysis of various character disorders" [47])

4. It *is* fostered by the regression in psychoanalysis ("The analytic situation . . . fosters regression which is necessary for intense transference formation. Endogenous tendencies to regression in the patient are supported, but also regulated, by the analytic progress. Upon the regression inherent in the patient's illness, there is superimposed a regression fostered by psychoanalysis" [49])

Loewald, in his contribution to the 1971 panel, reconceptualized the transference neurosis in the context of his theory about the nature of the therapeutic action of psychoanalysis, as presented in his turning-point paper of 1960 (see chapter 16): It has become with Loewald a very broadened (and less distinct?) concept: "We are here in the area of character problems and problems of character analysis, and it is in this area, it seems to me, that the question frequently arises: where is the transference neurosis? . . . In contrast to the old-fashioned symptom-neurosis, one might say that the neurosis is spread over much of the whole personality. No well-defined symptomatology, no well-defined infantile neurosis, and thus no transference neurosis, in that sense, can be detected" (58). It follows that "transference neurosis is not so much an entity to be found in the patient, but an operational concept. We may regard it as denoting the re-transformation of a psychic illness which originates in pathogenic interactions with the important persons in the child's environment, into an interactional process with a new person, the analyst, in which the pathological infantile interactions and their intrapsychic consequences may become transparent and accessible to change by virtue of the analyst's objectivity and of the emergence of novel interaction possibilities" (61).

To Loewald the transference neurosis was a still-useful concept but significantly transformed from its original version:

> As I see it, the concept of transference neurosis has not lost its value. But it is true that the picture and consequently our concept of neurosis have changed so as to include most prominently what we call character neurosis, a form of neurosis which is more formless and more hidden; and the same can be said for the transference neurosis. Furthermore, the prominence of preoedipal problems and of deviations and distortions of ego formation at early stages, in many patients seen nowadays, tends to obscure the clear delineation of a transference neurosis. As distinguished from the character neuroses, here the specifically neurotogenic problems of the oedipal period are intertwined with early developmental problems and colored by them. (60)

Loewald then turned positively to his conception of the transference neurosis construct. First he labeled it an "ideal construct," which "structures, and thus always oversimplifies, a complex aggregation of events, brings some order into an at first chaotic constellation and sequence of events; it functions as an organizing principle which is gradually distilled out of the events when investigated in a certain perspective; it is neither arbitrarily imposed on them nor can it be found in them as an entity in pure culture" (64). Seen this way, the transference neurosis is what creates the possibility for changes in previously indurated neurotic structures: "The difference between such transference manifestations and transference neurosis or transference illness, then, would be that the former are essentially automatic responses, signs and symptoms of the old illness, whereas the transference neurosis is a creation of the analytic work done by analyst and patient, in which the old illness loses its autonomous and automatic character and becomes reactivated and comprehensible as a live responsive process and, as such, changing and changeable" (62). This is effected by the creation of an "intermediate region" between illness and life: "The intrapsychic process we call illness, by entering, and then being actively engaged in, the new interactional context of the analytic field of forces, becomes transformed into the transference neurosis. The transference neurosis represents 'an intermediate region between illness and real life' as well as a transitional stage between disease process and healing process" (65)—a signal restatement and reaffirmation, within a quite transformed conception of the psychoanalytic process, of Freud's original delineation of the role of the transference neurosis in the psychoanalytic treatment process.

In summary, Loewald said, "The main enduring value of the concept of transference neurosis, then, to my mind, lies in its defining the nature, scope, and point of impact of psychoanalysis as mental therapy. The issue is that the patient's illness, neurosis, maladjustment, character disorder, regarded as originating in his life experiences from early on, is drawn into a new context, the analytic relationship developing between patient and analyst. In this new context the crucial pathogenic experiences, and the patient's ways of assimilating them, of defending against them, and of letting himself be defeated by them, gain new intensity and urgency. This makes them available for fresh psychic work" (64).

Edward Weinshel, in his contribution to the panel, undertook a review of the literature on the transference neurosis conception within the framework of three questions posed originally by Willie Hoffer (1956):[2] about the concept: What does it mean? How does it develop? What role does it play in the therapeutic process? To the question, What does it mean? Weinshel articulated the consensus view that had come to emphasize the transference neurosis not as a simple repetition or replication of the past but rather as a new creation and transformation (as expressed, for example, in the passages just cited from Loewald). To the question How does it develop? the formulated consensus was that the capacity for transference investment is universal, that it is intensified in the neurotic because of the frustrations inherent in the illness, and that it is facilitated

2. Hoffer (1956) wrote one of the first articles on transference and transference neurosis, essaying to differentiate the two. Of transference, he said that people " 'transfer' their *memories* of significant previous experiences and thus '*change the reality*' of their objects, invest them with qualities from the past, judge them and try to make use of them in accordance with their own past" (377). By contrast, in a crystallized, "transference neurotic revival of an infantile conflict, the realization . . . interferes in the patient's mind with the continuity of his relationship with the analyst. As if the patient were to know; it cannot be done, I cannot be analysed, and at the same time have this urge towards the analyst, libidinal and aggressive, saturated" (378–79). That is, "a need transferred to the analyst has assumed the significance of a threat to the analytic relationship" (379).

by the favorable conditions (opportunities) of the analytic process and situation. Weinshel of course noted Macalpine's strong advocacy of the position that the transference neurosis is actively induced by the pressures of the analytic setting, and he also called attention to the literature on the transference neurosis as a manifestation of the repetition compulsion and on its relationship to regression. In regard to the subsidiary question of when the transference neurosis develops, Weinshel took exception to the usual view that it develops over time, fully emerging in midcourse in an established analytic process: "I would submit that such a 'timetable' concept is misleading, that the transference neurosis and its manifestations can be observed at virtually any stage of the analytic work, and that its presence is dictated by a complex of dynamic-economic considerations rather than temporal ones" (76).

In regard to the third question, Weinshel spoke of the role of the transference neurosis as both the central vehicle of and the central resistance to analytic progress. Weinshel summarized by endorsing a statement by Orr: "The development, interpretation, and resolution of the transference neurosis in the transference relationship is still the hallmark of psychoanalysis for perhaps a majority of analysts today, but for a considerable minority this is by no means the case, or at least not without considerable attenuation and modification" (Orr 1954, 646). Part of that minority, of course, consisted of Alexander and his followers, who cautioned against the hazards of the unfolded transference neurosis in the unduly dependent patient, recommended that the analyst control and limit the transference regression, and insisted that not all transference manifestations need to be analyzed and resolved; some could be better utilized in the service of the corrective emotional experience. Weinshel again expressed the consensus view in demurring from these Alexandrian notions: "I would suggest that the failure of most analysts to adopt these new techniques represents neither a captious insistence on or an adherence to psychoanalytic orthodoxy nor a stubborn refusal to change with the times; it represents, rather, a response to a realistic appraisal of psychoanalysis and what it can offer" (86). And in a short encyclopedia article written with Victor Calef a few years later, Weinshel reaffirmed these positions (Calef and Weinshel 1977), essentially arguing that although the concept of the transference neurosis continued to be under attack from diverse quarters and for various reasons, it was still necessary "in order to obtain an adequate therapeutic and analytic result" (260).

Another widely remarked paper on the transference from the same period, Bird's "Notes on Transference: Universal Phenomenon and Hardest Part of Analysis" (1972), warrants consideration along with the (re)formulations of Blum, Loewald, and Weinshel. Bird emphasized the analyst's position at the center of the transference neurosis as its most important element: "We forget sometimes that a neurosis is based upon conflict and that what is specific about a transference neurosis is the active involvement of the analyst in the central crunch of this conflict" (278); and even more tersely: "A transference neurosis is merely a new edition of the patient's original neurosis, but with me in it" (281). And, "For me, the transference neurosis is essential to the analytic situation. . . . Sharing a place with the transference neurosis are at least two other kinds of relationships: one based on ordinary transference feelings and the other on reality considerations—those of a patient to his doctor" (28). But "The only force powerful enough to bring the constituents of the encapsulated structure [the neurosis] back into the main stream of the patient's mental functioning seems to be the transference neurosis" (279). Bird then offered his own, perhaps idiosyncratic, perspective on the distinctions between the ("ordinary") transferences and the transference neurosis: "The transference neurosis is not always available to work with. Being an on-and-off thing, as I believe it to be, there may be long periods when it is not in evidence. This means that the bulk of the bread-and-butter work of analysis is carried on largely in a transference relationship that is broader and less specific than a transference neurosis" (283). Consistent work with these transferences is necessary to bring on "episodes of transference neurosis." According to Bird, "This can happen [reaching all the way to the center of the patient], in my experience, only if the persistent and effective handling of the daily transference reactions, along with everything else it does, sets the stage for the appearance of episodes of transference neurosis" (284).

This reestablished and (re)secured place for the transference neurosis did not rest unchallenged for long. In a discussion on the nature of the therapeutic alliance, Arlow (1975) explicitly challenged the conventional view that the analytic process is inherently regressive—which assumption is of course the required underpinning to the conception of a transference neurosis in the first place. This passage from Arlow (quoted in another context in chapter 12) represents a clarion call, arousing opposition to the necessity—or the usefulness—of the transference neurosis concept: "The oft-repeated statement that psychoanalytic technique induces regression in the patient. . . . is a principle which has been quoted and circulated without challenge for a long time. It seems to me what the psychoanalytic situation does is to create an atmosphere, a set of conditions, which permit regressive aspects of the patient's mental functioning, long present, to reemerge in forms that are clearer and easier to observe" (73).

And Gill, in the 1980s, in a complete reversal of his 1954 position, carried

Arlow's argument[3] to its logical extensions. He said (1984a), "The argument that regression is a necessary part of the analytic method is based on the idea that an earlier infantile neurosis has to be revived and resolved. I believe that the very idea that an earlier state can be reinstated as such is an illusion. Furthermore in the sense in which the infantile neurosis is still alive in the present it will be manifested in the present and does not require special measures to bring it to life. . . . I consider that a well conducted analysis is marked by a transference, not necessarily by a regressive transference" (170). Therefore, the transference neurosis becomes a superfluous conception: "I suggest that to some extent at least the distinction between transferences and a transference neurosis is artificially induced by the manner in which analysis is ordinarily practiced. I mean that if the analyst refrains from the early analysis of transferences he creates an unnecessary distinction between a beginning phase in which the transference remains implicit and a later phase in which it can no longer be ignored. In prevailing practice the later phase is considered to be the appearance of the true transference, but in my opinion that presumed observation of the appearance of the transference is heavily influenced by the fact that it has been ignored until then" (168–69).

In 1988, Gill added a redefinition of his widely quoted definition of psychoanalysis of 1954 (see chapter 5). The new definition was as follows:

> A transference neurosis, but not a regressive transference neurosis, and its resolution by both insight and new interpersonal experience are defining criteria of a successful analysis and. . . . while those results are most readily achieved by optimal frequency, the couch being a significantly less important adjuvant, such results are also achievable in a broader, yet to be determined, range of circumstances. . . . I believe that a regression beyond what the patient brings to treatment is iatrogenic . . . , that what is required is a confrontation of the regression which is present but denied, and that the patient's increasing capacity to participate in confronting what is present but denied is more aptly labeled progressive rather than regressive. (267–68)

Incidentally, I think that any apparent inconsistency in Gill's position—that he seems to allow a continuing place for the transference neurosis but not for the regressive transference neurosis—is dispelled by the fact that he has simply

3. Gill said of Arlow's statement, "I would differ only in that I would say that what Arlow describes is what analysis *should* aim for but that the usual analytic setting and practice may well often induce an unnecessary, if not harmful, iatrogenic regression" (1984a, 170).

equated the concept of transference neurosis with the interpretive conversion of implicit transference manifestations into explicit ones.

Brenner (1982) carried the positions of Arlow and Gill to their logical extreme, calling simply for the abandonment of the concept of the transference neurosis. In discussing still-unsettled differences of opinion about various aspects of transference, Brenner said, "One of them has to do with transference neurosis, i.e., with the 'true transference neurosis,' which, it is said, is the hallmark of a good or successful analysis and which, allegedly, must develop if an analysis is to qualify as genuine. Are these assertions correct? Is a transference neurosis present in every successful analysis? Is analysis, in the true sense of the word, possible without a transference neurosis?" (202–03). Brenner answered these questions unequivocally: "The term transference neurosis is a tautology. The concept is an anachronism. Analysts define neurosis as a symptom, or a group of symptoms, which are compromise formations arising out of conflicts over childhood drive derivatives . . . transference manifestations are also compromise formations arising from conflicts over childhood drive derivatives. A transference manifestation is dynamically indistinguishable from a neurotic symptom. To call it neurotic, or to call the totality of the transference a neurosis is to add a word without adding meaning. Transference is enough. Nothing is gained by expanding the term to transference neurosis" (202–03). For good measure Brenner added, "I believe they [those who use the term] mean by it no more than that the patient has intense transference manifestations which can be satisfactorily analyzed. 'True transference neurosis,' it has often seemed to me, is customarily used as a synonym for 'analyzable transference' " (205).

Yet the concept has clearly not fallen into disuse. In 1987 an issue of *Psychoanalytic Inquiry* was devoted to its reconsideration, seemingly a cyclically recurring process. Of the nine articles in that issue I will quote from three. Reed's (1987b) paper was a measured defense of the continued utility of the concept. She pointed to the close linkage of the transference neurosis concept to the concept of cure and curative action: "It is scientifically permissible to advance, examine, even adopt—given sufficient clinical evidence—the *hypothesis* that the resolution of the transference neurosis is the essence of psychoanalysis, that it is the only way in which the conflicts around infantile sexuality may be reached and resolved, and that it indeed differentiates psychoanalysis from psychotherapy. . . . It is another thing to use that hypothesis to give a mode of treatment an identity, to declare by fiat: unless a patient has a transference neurosis no psychoanalysis can be said to have taken place" (468). Reed then called for an attitude of open-ended inquiry into this question and stated Freud's position that "unlike [other] . . . procedures, psychoanalysis annihilates suggestion by annihilating the transference. Thus only with the annihilation of the new transference illness was a patient truly freed from suggestion. . . . Through its annihilation, the analyst became the victor over disease and liberator of the patient from its clutches. . . . The transference neurosis was thus central. It was the sign of the transformation of disease into something accessible to interpretative intervention; it allowed the patient to experience and understand in the present what had been experienced and misunderstood in the past; it facilitated the analyst's mastery of disease and the patient's liberation from it; it liberated psychoanalysis from suggestion and by doing so, confirmed for psychoanalysis its claims to science. (470)

After surveying the literature since Freud, Reed concluded, "Our personal psychoanalysis, our clinical experiences, and our theory prepare us to begin each analysis anticipating a transference neurosis . . . which we hope will be accessible to analysis and which will include among its elements infantile sexual conflicts. . . . To create the atmosphere in which a transference neurosis or regressive transference can evolve and be analyzed we need the freedom, paradoxically, to feel that the treatment need not live up to a theory of cure. That is, a successful analysis may indeed depend on the resolution of the transference neurosis—in its broadest definition—but it also depends on our willing suspension of disbelief that this is so" (482). To underline the intellectual danger of any other attitude, Reed had stated earlier, "If the necessity for a transference neurosis to occur in psychoanalysis is held by fiat and the definition of that transference neurosis consists of the patient's *conscious* preoccupation with the analyst and the cessation of all symptoms not concerned with the analyst, there is a danger that such givens may prevent contrary observations from modifying the definition of the transference neurosis" (477). Clearly a defense of the continued usefulness of the concept, but a qualified and uncertain defense, and ever open to contrary observations.

Arnold Cooper's (1987b) paper, a comparable survey of the literature on the concept, turned out to be a measured denial of its continued utility. Cooper laid special stress on the contributions of Glover, Loewald, and Brenner. He summarized Glover's views as follow: "He did not support the clear distinction that Freud claimed for the transference neurosis as a new construction that included the entirety of the patient's neurosis. Furthermore, the analysis of the character disorders may proceed without a transference neurosis, and he is of two minds about the need for a transference neurosis for the understanding of the genesis of neurosis. In summary, Glover reluctantly, on the basis of clinical experience, relaxed or relinquished each of the elements that Freud regarded as central to the concept" (574). As for Loewald, "He stresses, in a way that Freud did not, that the new creation of the transference neurosis, while providing opportunities for the understanding of the past, is therapeutically significant primarily for providing the opportunity for *new* forms of object relations, rather than for its elucidation of the infantile neurosis . . . [and] he emphasized that a transference neurosis need not be present during a well-conducted analysis" (576). In fact, "Clinical experience seems to have led to rejecting each of the defining aspects of the concept of transference neurosis that Freud suggested; and what remains, as Loewald suggested, is an ideal construct that describes psychoanalysis generally" (578).

Cooper noted Brenner's views by quoting the same passage cited in this chapter, calling for abandonment of the term and the concept transference neurosis. Cooper added that its putative basis was in the reactivation and repetition of the infantile neurosis, a concept that is itself dubious at best, "a holdover from an earlier time of psychoanalysis" (582). What, then, is the distinctive motor power of psychoanalysis? "It seems clear that analysis derives its power and perhaps its distinctiveness as a form of therapy through its focus on the intensification of the transference brought about by the intensity of the treatment, by the new experience with a new object, and by the focus on transference interpretation" (578). As for the concept of the transference neurosis, it has at least—and maybe at most—had a heuristic value: "The repeated efforts over half a century to clarify the term have, however, resulted in a rich yield for psychoanalysis. We now have a greatly refined understanding of the analytic process, and of the transference as a new construction of the patient and the analyst in a new and unique relationship that provides the deepest opportunity for altering, reorganizing, and reintegrating psychic representations and modes of conflict resolution" (583).

Nathaniel London, co-editor of the journal issue on the transference neurosis, wrote both a prologue (1987a) and a final discussion (1987b) for it. In the prologue he summarized the issues to be explored: "The clinical evidence for a transference neurosis is hard to define and is frequently elusive. The salient questions are whether a transference neurosis can be distinguished from other forms of transference, whether such a distinction is useful, and, if it is useful, whether it refers to clinically observable events in the course of an analysis or is a theoretical construct serving to organize complex events in the course of an analysis. There is also a question whether the concept can serve to define analysis" (462). London's discussion of the responses to these questions is labeled a defense of the concept, but it is a very tempered defense indeed. After reviewing the arguments of the six invited contributors, London concluded, "The distinction between transference and transference neurosis is more complex and

significant" (592) than the detractors of the concept have allowed. He continued, "Psychoanalysis is separable from psychotherapy because it is specifically
designed to elicit a transference neurosis. There are analyses that fail to realize
their potential because a transference neurosis was not developed, recognized,
or analyzed. In addition, those psychotherapies which lead to aspects of a transference neurosis, however abbreviated, are different from other psychotherapies" (596). In apparent response to Brenner's nihilistic view, London added,
"Transference neurosis includes both transference and neurosis, although it involves more than transference (extratransference experiences) and more than
neurosis (the 'new' feature emphasized by Loewald)" (597). Implicit in London's formulation is the fear that if we drop the concept of transference neurosis
we will have no agreed way (or perhaps any way) of distinguishing psychoanalysis from psychoanalytic psychotherapy.

Allen Rosenblatt (1987) also made the point that we need to retain the
concept of the transference neurosis and the concomitant regression in order to
maintain a meaningful distinction between psychoanalysis and psychotherapy:

> The significant difference between psychoanalysis and insight-directed
> psychoanalytic psychotherapy (even if the two are considered as aspects
> of a continuum) is that in psychoanalysis a strategy that induces regression
> is employed, while in psychoanalytic psychotherapy regression, for the
> most part, is not encouraged and, in fact, is sometimes actively discour-
> aged. As a consequence, more primitive motivational systems are not fully
> reactivated and do not then receive new informational input. Therefore,
> although interpretation remains a major vehicle of conveying information
> in analytic psychotherapy, *other ways* of introducing new information to
> motivational systems assume greater importance, especially in modalities
> such as supportive therapy (181)

—and here Rosenblatt spoke of fostering more mature identifications and, with
patients functioning at lower levels of integration, of aiding the introjection of
aspects of the magically and omnipotently endowed therapist.

These are not quite the last words on the present status of the transference
neurosis concept. Dale Boesky, in an unpublished paper devoted to countertransference and resistance, offered his redefinition of the transference neurosis:
"It is the transference as resistance which is the unique and indispensable core
of the psychoanalytic treatment situation. So I am speaking of the transference
resistances in toto as the updated equivalent of the transference neurosis" (25).
Oremland (1991), in his book on psychoanalysis and psychotherapy, opted to
drop the term (but not really the concept) altogether: "It is the increasingly
regressive, usually intermittent enactment in the sessions—the transference

neurosis—that gives transference its iatrogenic quality. Such a view regards transference and transference neurosis as a continuum reflecting shifting predominance of covert aspects of the relationship. A more useful term than transference neurosis is the generic term regressive transference enactment. Regressive transference enactments encompass a broader range of transference manifestations, reflecting many developmentally related psychopathologies that can be treated psychoanalytically." He supplied a footnote presenting an additional rationale for the change in nomenclature: "The term transference neurosis comes from the early psychoanalytic topographical model of conscious, preconscious, and unconscious. The transference neurosis was seen as a reexperiencing and reenacting of early childhood conflicts, the repressed childhood neurosis 'erupting,' so to speak, into consciousness. This scheme emphasizes oedipal achievement and well-established repression barriers. . . . The term regressive transference enactment is derived from the structural metapsychological model (id, ego, and superego) with emphasis on integrated structuralization, intra- and intersystemic conflicts, and multiple substructures and developmentally related distortions in self- and object presentations" (35–36). And of course the structural model is more "advanced," conceptually as well as temporally, than the topographic model.

Weinshel (1990b), in an article on the psychoanalytic process, had some comments on the transference neurosis, hardly altered in tenor from his review two decades earlier (1971): "The transference neurosis is still viewed by some as a simple replication of the infantile neurosis. What Freud suggested was that the transference neurosis was a repetition in a different setting (within the psychoanalytic situation and process) with a new object (the analyst) of certain psychic conflicts (predominantly oedipal). Furthermore the transference neurosis does not just happen, and it does not emerge suddenly or magically as a full-blown entity. It is invariably the product of a good deal of prolonged analytic labor (working through), with many transferences and the resistances associated with them" (641). Weinshel then offered his own modification of Freud's conception: "Freud stated that analysts 'regularly succeed in . . . replacing [the patient's] ordinary neurosis by a 'transference neurosis' of which he can be cured by the therapeutic work' (Freud, 1914a, p. 154). Today we would probably say that appropriate psychoanalytic work with a patient manifesting a transference neurosis will result in a more effective 're-solution' of crucial intrapsychic conflicts, with less pathological, more adaptive compromise solutions than had been possible in childhood" (642). This perhaps states as well as anyone has the current view on the transference neurosis of those inclined to accept the continued usefulness of the concept for the theoretical and clinical understanding of psychoanalytic work.

In the most recent panel of the American Psychoanalytic Association on the subject of transference neurosis, the three main presentations were by Tyson, Renik, and A. Cooper. Tyson offered a fourfold schematic classification of "transference forms" (Shaw 1991, 229):

1. "*Habitual modes of relating* refers to ways of establishing personal ties or patterns of interaction which are part of character"
2. "*Transference predominantly of current relationships* refers to instances when the patient is intensely involved in a response to someone in his current life which 'spills over,' i.e., is defensively displaced or projected onto the analyst"
3. "*Transference predominantly of revived past experiences* occurs when the patient's feelings about and attitudes toward the analyst have undergone significant changes in relation to the analytic material. At these times there is a revival, reenactment, or redramatization of past experiences in a new and different format, one in which the analyst plays a special part for the patient"
4. "*Transference neurosis* refers to a merging of episodic transference manifestations into a complex fabric of related, intertwining, and overlapping ones. The 'merging' and 'special clarity' as perceived by the analyst, have no inherent durability and may come and go" (229–30)

What Tyson has done is to separate out what most current writers on the subject condense into one stream, whether or not they conceive of a distinctive transference neurosis.

Renik, in the same panel (Shaw 1991), stressed the problematic nature of the concept. He referred to the "unfolding sequence of interrelated transferences, culminating in the exposure of the patient's oedipal struggles, as the transference neurosis. Inasmuch as what we do when we identify transference is to construct an inference, a transference neurosis is an *inference about a series of inferences*" (231, italics added). And Cooper called, even more directly than in his 1987 paper, for giving up the term altogether: "Cooper feels that the uniqueness and power of the transference is at the heart of all psychodynamic thinking. However, when our tradition describes the transference neurosis and its companion, the infantile neurosis, as the distinguishing hallmark of psychoanalysis and our researches do not bear this out, it is time to relinquish the term" (Shaw 1991, 234).

It remains only to refer once again to Etchegoyen's (1991) massive compendium on technique. Etchegoyen defines the transference neurosis, with his own distinctive emphasis, as follows: "Transference neurosis in its technical sense . . . is the psychopathological correlate of the analytical situation. I mean that the analytical situation is established when transference neurosis appears, and vice versa, when transference neurosis is divided from the therapeutic alliance, the analytical situation takes shape" (149). Is this then a living reality of a properly progressing analysis? "The situation of a transference neurosis that establishes itself slowly while the relaxed analyst fulfils Freud's mandate to clear up the resistances while not touching the difficult theme of the transference is an ideal in our practice (and of our transference neurosis with Freud), which is only permitted to us when we face a case of neurosis that is not too severe. In other cases, which are now the most frequent ones, transference phenomena soon present themselves; and the same always happens with children and adolescents" (607). Clearly, to Etchegoyen, the transference neurosis is not an everyday occurrence but an ideal construct, describing the events in the ideal analysis with the ideal patient.

Etchegoyen laid the related conception of therapeutic regression at the door of the (American) ego psychologists: "It is well known that many ego psychologists state firmly that the analytic process is of a regressive nature, that this regression is produced as a response to the setting and is the necessary condition to constitute an analysable transference neurosis. With other nuances this opinion is found among most ego psychologists of Europe and the New World" (541). In fact, "the ego psychologists think that the setting was designed by Freud precisely to provoke the patient's regression and so that it can be regulated by the analyst." And as part of the regression-inducing process, there is an emphasis on sensory deprivation in both the auditory and visual spheres: "The analyst's silence, like his temporary invisibility, continues to be for many analysts an indispensable feature of the analytic process" (543)—another link between interpretive restraint all the way to silence (idealized in the depiction of classical technique within the American ego-psychological model), regression, and the evocation of a full-fledged transference neurosis.

To these statements, Etchegoyen counterposed his own (Kleinian) view: "I will go resolutely to the point and say that regression in the psychoanalytic process has to do with the illness and not with the setting. The patient *comes* with his regression, his illness *is* the regression. The setting does not cause it; the regression is already there. What the setting does is to detect and contain it" (546). And a little further on, Etchegoyen gave a pointed example of just how he meant this: "There is also much emphasis on the fact that the analytic couch, the asymmetrical dialogue and the analyst's reserve can only foment regression. Here objective reality is again confused with the patient's infantile desires and fantasies. The confusion between object and psychic reality (fantasy) is perhaps the weakest point in Macalpine's article. If I tell a person that she has to lie down on a couch in order that a particular task (analysis, auscultation, massage, etc.) can be accomplished, then if that person thinks of a rape scene, that is her affair" (548).

It should be evident now why I have entitled this chapter "The Rise and Fall of the Transference Neurosis," and why quite a few among us, I am sure, would insert a question mark after the word 'fall.'

IV. *The Psychoanalytic — and Psychotherapeutic —*
Relationships

15 The Therapeutic Alliance and the Working Alliance

The proponents of what came to be called the classical technique during the 1950s and 1960s took as their point of departure Freud's technique of interpreting his patients' free associations as the key to resolving their neurotic conflicts and unraveling the unconscious meanings of their symptoms. But almost from the beginning there was a concomitant emphasis, given enormous impetus by Ferenczi, on the important curative role also played by the affective relationship between analyst and analysand. Though this component of the therapeutic process played a lesser role in Freud's thinking than did the interpretive process (especially the transference interpretation) leading to insight, working through, and change, nevertheless, clear forerunners of the focus on the psychoanalytic relationship can also be found in Freud's technical writings. I will point to two succinct statements to illustrate. In 1913, Freud spoke of *rapport*, seemingly equating it with the transference itself: "It remains the first aim of the treatment to attach him [the patient] to it and to the person of the doctor. To ensure this, nothing need be done but to give him time. If one exhibits a serious interest in him, carefully clears away the resistances that crop up at the beginning and avoids making certain mistakes, he will of himself form such an attachment and link the doctor up with one of the imagoes of the people by whom he was accustomed to be treated with affection. It is certainly possible to forfeit this first success if from the start one takes up any standpoint other than one of sympathetic understanding, such as a moralizing one, or if one behaves like a representative or advocate of some contending party" (139–40). And in the other statement (already cited in chapter 12), Freud (1912a) tried more carefully to disentangle this concept of rapport, under the rubric of "unobjectionable positive transference," from the "negative transference or [the] . . . positive transference of repressed erotic impulses." The former by definition need not be analyzed and is in fact "the vehicle of success in psychoanalysis" (105); the latter, of course, required thorough analysis.

Richard Sterba (1934), however, is generally credited with providing the conceptual basis for one of the unfolding lines of development of the role of the analytic relationship in the therapeutic change process, that which became the important focus (mostly in America) on the therapeutic alliance and/or the working alliance, two theoretically distinguishable but closely related concepts, often used interchangeably. Sterba attempted to explain how the analyst could enlist the analysand's participation in the task of experiencing the revivified past via the unfolding transference (neurosis) and at the same time maintain the objectivity needed to analyze the meaning of that past. He proposed that in the course of the analytic work there is a necessary therapeutic (and nonpathological) "dissociation within the ego" of the analysand between the experiencing part, engaged in the process of free-associating, and the observing part, which can look at or be brought to look at the pattern of free associations in the effort to divine their meanings.[1] "This capacity of the ego for dissociation," Sterba wrote,

> gives the analyst the chance, by means of his interpretations, to effect an *alliance* with the ego [of the patient] against the powerful forces of instinct and repression and, with the help of one part of it [the patient's observing ego], to try to vanquish the opposing forces. Hence, when we begin an analysis which can be carried to completion, the fate that *inevitably* awaits the ego is that of *dissociation*. A permanently unified ego, such as we meet with in cases of excessive narcissisms or in certain psychotic states where ego and id have become fused, is not susceptible of analysis. The therapeutic dissociation of the ego is a necessity if the analyst is to have the chance of winning over part of it to his side, conquering it, strengthening it by means of identification with himself and opposing it in the transference to those parts which have a cathexis of instinctual and defensive energy. (120, italics added)

How is this split in the ego brought about? Sterba declared that the process of interpreting the transference brings about in the patient

> *a new point of view of intellectual contemplation.* In order that this new standpoint may be effectually reached there must be a certain amount of positive transference,[2] on the basis of which a transitory strengthening of the ego takes place through identification with the analyst. This identification is induced by the analyst. From the outset the patient is called upon to "cooperate" with the analyst against something in himself. Each separate

1. Though Sterba's explicit focus was on the necessary split in the patient's ego, his article can be read as also encompassing at least implicit awareness of a necessary counterpart split in the analyst's ego, so that both parties can be united in empathically sharing the experiencing while simultaneously taking distance, coolly comprehending, and understanding via the analyst's proffered interpretations. The distinction between patient and analyst, of course—and on this the successful progression of the analysis depends—is that in the patient's case, the experiencing part is much the larger of the two, while in the analyst's case the reverse holds true.

2. This is the source of the conceptual derivation of the alliance concept from Freud's "unobjectionable positive transference," which over subsequent decades has become the focus of fierce debate.

session gives the analyst various opportunities of employing the term "we," in referring to himself and to the part of the patient's ego which is consonant with reality. The use of the word "we," always means that the analyst is trying to draw that part of the ego over to his side and to place it in opposition to the other part which in the transference is cathected or influenced from the side of the unconscious. We might say that this "we" is the instrument by means of which the therapeutic dissociation of the ego is effected. (121)

The prototype for this therapeutic ego dissociation in the patient, Sterba averred, is

the process of *superego formation*. By means of an identification . . . judgments and valuations from the outside world are admitted into the ego and become operative within it. . . . The result of superego-formation is the powerful establishment of moral demands; in therapeutic ego-dissociation the demand which has been accepted is a demand for a revised attitude appropriate to the situation of an adult personality. . . . There is constituted, as it were, a standing relation between that part of the ego which is cathected with instinctual or defensive energy and that part which is focussed on reality and identified with the analyst, and this relation is the filter through which all the transference-material in the analysis must pass. Each separate interpretation reduces the instinctual and defensive cathexis of the ego in favour of intellectual contemplation, reflection and correction by the standard of reality.[3] (121–22)

Zetzel (1956) referred to an article by Bibring (1937) as an additional precursor to the development of the alliance concept. The relevant passage from Bibring's paper is, "There are thus two parts of the ego which we set over against each other: the methods of working over of the conscious, uniform and rational ego against the unconscious, defending ego and its mechanisms. . . . Through making the unconscious ego-reactions conscious, the defending part of the ego becomes the object of the observing, conscious ego" (184). The analyst is aided in this task by the patient's wish to be cured, which, of course,

3. A seldom remarked conceptual forerunner of Sterba's concept of the necessary and inevitable split or dissociation of the patient's ego in a going analysis is Ferenczi's (1928) comment on the corresponding task demanded of the analyst: "He has to let the patient's free associations play upon him; simultaneously he lets his own fantasy get to work with the association material; from time to time he compares the new connexions that arise with earlier results of the analysis; and not for a moment must he relax the vigilance and criticism made necessary by his own subjective trends" (96).

contains rational and irrational components; the ego's "synthetic function" (Nunberg 1931); and an admixture of "pedagogical" (suggestive?) influences: "What is the attitude of the patient that enables us in analysis to appeal continually to him in a pedagogic way? Apart from factors of transference, which need not be discussed here . . . a natural tendency towards recovery. . . . a tendency to recognize the requirements of reality, a capacity for experience, a sense of what is expedient, a higher valuation of the object-relationships as compared to other relationships of the libido, an inclination towards a social environment, etc." (188).

It is, however, Zetzel and Ralph Greenson who are most centrally associated with the concepts, respectively, of the therapeutic alliance and the working alliance. Zetzel's crucial article (1956) "Current Concepts of Transference" contrasted American ego-psychological and British object-relational (including Kleinian) notions of the transference, a task for which Zetzel, an American psychoanalytically trained at the London Institute, was particularly qualified. She put it this way:

> From one point of view [the American ego-psychological], the role of ego is central and crucial at every phase of analysis. A differentiation is made between transference as therapeutic alliance and the transference neurosis, which on the whole, is considered a manifestation of resistance. Effective analysis depends on a sound therapeutic alliance, a prerequisite for which is the existence, before analysis, of a degree of mature ego functions, the absence of which in certain severely disturbed patients and in young children may preclude traditional psycho-analytic procedure.[4]

4. This conception is a main basis for the major revision of Freud's dictum that the psychotic patient whose libido is theoretically totally withdrawn into his ego and is therefore suffering from a "narcissistic neurosis" and is unable to establish object-related transferences is necessarily inaccessible to psychoanalytic influence. As indicated in a number of footnotes in this book, clinical experience by Fromm-Reichmann (1950) and a host of others has been clearly to the contrary. The metapsychological explanation is as follows. Rather than being unable to effect transferences, clinical experience has repeatedly demonstrated that psychotic patients are disposed toward wildly fluctuating and abruptly unpredictable transference manifestations. The difficulty in treating them analytically resides not in their inability to form transferences but in the inability of their weak and fragmented ego (based on developmental failures stemming from the earliest traumatic experiences within the mother-infant interactions) to forge a strong enough therapeutic alliance to contain the transference vicissitudes and to guard therefore against the various transference-induced disruptive pressures upon the treatment. By contrast, the much better put together ego of the typically neurotic patient (who has more successfully traversed the vicissitudes of the earliest developmental stages within the mother-child matrix) is capable of a much stronger therapeutic alliance which can, more assuredly, contain the much

. . . Those, in contrast, who stress the importance of early object relations emphasize the crucial role of transference as an object relationship, distorted though this may be by a variety of defenses against primitive unresolved conflicts. . . . Less differentiation is made between transference as therapeutic alliance and the transference neurosis as a manifestation of resistance. Therapeutic progress depends almost exclusively on transference interpretation. (370)

In this British object-relational (and Kleinian) view the pre-analytic maturity of the ego is not stressed in the same way as a prerequisite to successful engagement in the analytic process, and, pari passu, children and more disturbed adult patients are seen as potentially more amenable to analytic treatment than in the American ego-psychological world. Also, we can see here the basis for the greater acceptance of the therapeutic alliance concept in America (and in other places influenced by the ego-psychology paradigm) than elsewhere in the psychoanalytic world.

Zetzel continued to draw the contrasts:

First . . . those who emphasize the analysis of defence tend to make a definite differentiation between transference as therapeutic alliance and the transference neurosis as a compromise formation which serves the purposes of resistance. In contrast, those who emphasize the importance of early object relations view the transference primarily as a revival or repetition, sometimes attributed to symbolic processes of early struggles in respect to objects. Here, no sharp differentiation is made between the early manifestations of transference and the transference neurosis. . . . In the second place, the role of regression in the transference situation is subject to wide differences of opinion. . . . Those who emphasize defence analysis . . . tend to view regression as a manifestation of resistance; as a primitive mechanism of defence employed by the ego in the setting of the transference neurosis. Analysis of these regressive manifestations with their potential dangers depends on the existing and continued functioning of adequate ego strength to maintain therapeutic alliance at an adult level. Those, in contrast, who stress the significance of transference as a revival of the early mother-child relationship do not emphasize regression as an indication of resistance or defence. (371–72)

---

more moderate and less abruptly reversible, typically neurotic transference fluctuations. Zetzel (1965) made this point as follows: "It must be emphasized . . . that no patient will be capable of tolerating the added stress roused by the emergence of the transference neurosis unless the therapeutic alliance is not only established but maintained at all times" (49).

It was clear in everything Zetzel said that for those who found the thera- peutic-alliance concept useful, even vital, to an understanding of the therapeutic mechanism in psychoanalysis, the necessary underpinning to this, and therefore to amenability to psychoanalysis, was the successful navigation of the early dy- adic, mother–child-focused developmental phases, manifest in the evidences of adequate "ego strength" in the (neurotic) adult seeking analysis. With more "primitive" personalities, those with lesser ego strength, "the relative failure of ego development . . . not only precludes the development of a genuine thera- peutic alliance, but also raises the risk of a serious regressive, often predominantly hostile transference situation. . . . Instead, a therapeutic approach based on an- alytic understanding which, in essence, utilizes an essentially implicit positive transference as a means of reinforcing, rather than analysing the precarious de- fences of the individual is advocated" (373). In other words, Zetzel was calling for the application of the techniques of supportive psychoanalytic psychotherapy in cases in which an effective therapeutic alliance cannot be forged because of the weakness of the ego. And, as if to anticipate later severe attacks on the alliance concept (see Brenner 1979 and Stein 1981), Zetzel acknowledged that the alliance itself was not immune to appropriately timed and directed inter- pretation: "Those . . . who make a definite differentiation between transference and the transference neurosis stress the importance of analysis and resolution of the transference neurosis as a main prerequisite for successful termination. The identification based on therapeutic alliance must be interpreted and understood, particularly with reference to the reality aspects of the analyst's personality" (372).

Zetzel carried her thinking even further in a later article (1965), discussed in chapter 18. Here I will cite only one summarizing passage from that paper: "Successful analysis thus demands a dual approach to the therapeutic process. This highlights the intimate relationship and the crucial differences between the transference neurosis, which is subject to infinite changeability, and the thera- peutic alliance, which as a real relationship requires a consistent, stable nucleus. Such a dual approach implies a developmental differentiation between the de- fensive ego which must regress, and the autonomous ego which must maintain the capacity for consistent object relations" (50).

Greenson's hallmark statement was in "The Working Alliance and the Trans- ference Neurosis" (1965). He started with "It is the contention of this paper that the working alliance is as essential for psychoanalytic therapy as the trans- ference neurosis. For successful psychoanalytic treatment a patient must be able to develop a full-blown transference neurosis and also to establish and maintain a reliable working alliance. The working alliance deserves to be recognized as a full and equal partner in the patient–therapist relationship" (156).

In regard to his choice of nomenclature, Greenson said,

> The term *working alliance* is used in preference to diverse terms others have employed for designating the relatively non-neurotic, rational rapport which the patient has with his analyst. It is this reasonable and purposeful part of the feelings the patient has for the analyst that makes for the working alliance. . . . The designation, working alliance . . . has the advantage of stressing the vital elements: the patient's capacity to work purposefully in the treatment situation. It can be seen at its clearest when a patient, in the throes of an intense transference neurosis, can yet maintain an effective working relationship with the analyst. The reliable core of the working alliance is formed by the patient's motivation to overcome his illness, the conscious and rational willingness to cooperate, and his ability to follow the instructions and insights of his analyst. The actual alliance is formed essentially between the patient's reasonable ego and the analyst's analyzing ego. (157)

Here the distinctions from Zetzel's conceptualization are very explicit: to Zetzel, the capacity for the therapeutic alliance is grounded in the successful management of the earliest stages of infantile development within the dyadic mother-child matrix; to Greenson, the capacity for the working alliance is based on the highest levels of mature, secondary-process, logical, and consciously directed ego functioning. Obviously the second depends upon the first; the "alliance" is thus a compound of a consolidated ego emerging from a reasonably successful outcome of the earliest developmental stages as now expressed in the mature capacity to cooperate with the analyst in the service of restoring mental health and well-being.

Greenson gave four case vignettes illustrating various conditions of interaction between the transference neurosis and the working alliance and noted a number of consequences of his overall frame: (1) the transference neurosis and the working alliance often interpenetrate in complex ways "This differentiation between transference neurosis and working alliance, however, is not absolute since the working alliance may contain elements of the infantile neurosis which eventually will require analysis. . . . Not only can the transference neurosis invade the working alliance but the working alliance itself can be misused defensively to ward off the more regressive transference phenomena" (158); (2) with sicker patients and more "fragile" egos, the working alliance needs to be specifically fostered, whereas "in the classical analytic patient the working alliance develops almost imperceptibly, relatively silently, and seemingly independently of any special activity on the part of the analyst" (160); and (3) the working alliance can itself be used as a powerful resistance in the service of the transference neurosis ("Those patients who cling tenaciously to the working alliance because they are terrified of the regressive features of the transference neurosis . . . develop a reasonable relation to the analyst and do not allow themselves to feel anything irrational, be it sexual, aggressive, or both. Prolonged reasonableness in an analysis is a pseudo-reasonableness for a variety of unconscious neurotic motives" [168]).

The patient's contribution to the working alliance "depends on two antithetical properties: his capacity to maintain contact with the analytical situation and also his willingness to risk regressing into his fantasy world. It is the oscillation between these two positions that is essential for analytic work" (174). And from the standpoint of the analyst, "All analysts recognize the need for deprivations in psychoanalysis; they would also agree in principle on the analyst's need to be human. The problem arises, however, in determining what is meant by humanness in the analytic situation and how does one reconcile this with the principle of deprivation. Essentially the humanness of the analyst is expressed in his compassion, concern, and therapeutic intent toward the patient" (178)[5]— manifested in his concern with the working alliance. Greenson ended his article on the same note with which it began: "The transference neurosis and the working alliance are parallel antithetical forces in transference phenomena; each is of equal importance" (179).

Greenson developed his conception more fully in an article with Milton Wexler (Greenson and Wexler 1969):

To facilitate the full flowering and ultimate resolution of the patient's transference reactions, it is essential in all cases to recognize, acknowledge, clarify, differentiate, and even nurture the non-transference or relatively transference-free reactions between patient and analyst. The technique of "only analysing" or "only interpreting" transference phenomena may stifle the development and clarification of the transference neurosis and act as an obstacle to the maturation of the transference-free or "real" reactions of the patient . . . it is also important to deal with the non-transference interactions between patient and analyst. This may require non-interpretive or non-analytic interventions but these approaches are vastly different from anti-analytic procedures. (27–28).

Here, Greenson has proceeded further in separating off the alliance as real and therefore no longer even to be considered within the transference orbit.

5. Which is to say that Greenson did not take Freud's surgeon-mirror metaphors literally, as the intended total expression of the analyst's proper stance in the therapeutic relationship and therefore a vital underpinning of classical technique, any more than did Lipton (1977)—see chapter 7.

The authors called on Anna Freud (in a personal communication) in support of their position: "I have always learned to consider transference in the light of a distortion of the real relationship of the patient to the analyst, and, of course, that the type and manner of distortion showed up the contributions from the past. If there were no real relationship this idea of the distorting influences would make no sense" (28).[6]

The authors then elaborated the positive considerations of the working alliance, which will be cited in extenso:

1. The working alliance is to be distinguished from the positive transference: "The *working alliance* is the non-neurotic, rational, reasonable rapport which the patient has with his analyst and which enables him to work purposefully in the analytic situation despite his transference impulses. . . . The patient's awareness of his neurotic suffering and the possibility of help from the analyst impel him to seek out, and work in, the analytic situation. The positive transference, the overestimation and overevaluation of the psychoanalyst, may also be a powerful ally, but it is treacherous. Above all, the reliable core of the working alliance is to be found in the 'real' or non-transference relationship between patient and analyst" (29)

2. The working alliance is adaptive and realistic: "All object relations consist of some elements of repetition from the past, but the so-called 'real,' the non-transference relationship differs from transference in the degree of relevance, appropriateness, accuracy, and immediacy of what is expressed. Furthermore, non-transference responses are basically readily modifiable by both internal and external reality. They are adaptive and 'realistic' " (28)

3. The working alliance is a relative, not an absolute, concept: "The terms transference, non-transference, transference-free, and 'real' relationships must be considered as relative and overlapping. All transference contains some germ of 'reality' and all 'real' relationships have some transference elements" (28)

4. The capacity for a working alliance defines analyzability: "All patients, whether neurotic, borderline, or psychotic, have transference reactions in and out of the therapeutic situation. It is our belief that only those patients are *analyzable* who have the capacity for transference-free re-

6. See in this connection the quotation in chapter 7 from Anna Freud's "widening scope" discussion of 1954, in which she talked of the "real personal relationship" between analyst and analysand, which should not be neglected or ascribed to "true transference." She called these thoughts "technically subversive," to be "handled with care."

lationships as well. . . . Patients who lack this capacity . . . require *pre-paratory psychotherapy*. This means they need to be helped to build an object relationship based on reliable and predictable perceptions, judgements, and responses. They require more than interpretation and insights" (36)

5. By the same token, the working alliance is antecedent to and preparatory to effective interpretation: "The analyst's acknowledging, accepting, and working with the patient's 'realistic' responses and bringing them into a coherent relationship with the rest of the analysis . . . forms the avenue for increasing his capacity to accept and utilize new interpretations and insights into his unconscious" (29)

6. This is not anti-analytic: "Anti-analytic procedures are those which block or lessen the patient's capacity for insight and understanding. Any measure which diminishes the ego's function or capacity for observing, thinking, remembering, and judging would fall into this category" (29)

7. It is indeed the analyst's job to confirm the patient's healthy functioning—that is, his working alliance: "If part of our therapeutic aim is to increase the patient's healthy ego functions and capacity for object relations, it is important that we confirm those aspects of his behaviour which indicate healthy functioning. By ignoring those undistorted aspects of the patient's productions we unwittingly imply that his realistic reactions are unimportant, hardly worthy of comment and that all that matters is understanding the unconscious meaning of his behaviour" (37)

8. Along this line, we should willingly acknowledge technical mistakes: "An important rule of thumb we have found useful in promoting the non-transference reactions is the frank admission of any and all errors of technique, whether they be due to countertransference reactions, faulty interpretations, or shortcomings in the analyst's personality or character" (37). "Technical errors may cause pain and confusion but they are usually repairable; failure of humanness is much harder to remedy.[7] The overemphasis on transference interpretation and the neglect of the 'real' relationship tend to reduce all life to explanation, which is not life and not living: (34)

9. All these considerations are more so with borderline and psychotic patients: "The suggested difference from the ordinary analytic situation

---

7. My colleague Edward Weinshel has often quoted a comparable aphorism: "Patients will always forgive mistakes of the head; what they don't forgive are mistakes of the heart."

lies in the fact that frequently psychotic patients seem to require an early introduction to a reality beyond their capacities at the moment, an opportunity to make even the most primitive identification with the analyst, and to borrow aspects of reality from his perceptions or behaviour and utilize them as their own. It is as if the internal 'road map' . . . had been fragmented or partially destroyed and had to be filled in by the analyst's understanding in order that external reality may be 'rediscovered" (35). In regard to how this is accomplished, "With borderline and psychotic patients the focus is so largely on reality and 'real' relationships that the technical recommendations are both more extensive and more flexible. They include, among a host of other procedures, maintaining a face-to-face relationship, concrete assistance with reality adaptations, control of instinctual outbursts where called for, education, fostering compulsive tasks, keeping appropriate psychological and even physical distance, and a wide variety of other actions, attitudes, and communications which are designed to facilitate the development of reparative object relations and restore internal object representation" (37)—indeed, for these sicker patients a prescription that in other contexts (see chapters 3 and 5) has been called supportive psychoanalytic psychotherapy. All in all, these considerations add up to "some blending of restrained humanitarian concern with scientific discipline"; they were not intended as a formula for "attempting painless or cheerful psychoanalysis" (38), for which there is no warrant.[8]

In a discussion of this paper at the 1969 Congress of the International Psychoanalytical Association (Gumbel 1970), Greenson remarked, "Our emphasis on the non-transference relationship between patient and analyst is a result of our dissatisfaction with the current one-sided stress on transference interpretations as the main, if not the only, therapeutic tool." On "necessary reservations," he commented: "There is always the danger of misrepresenting our position to

8. Hanly (1992b) gave a most succinct comparison of the related but different alliance conceptions: "Zetzel (1966) recommends maternalistic reassurances to allay a primitive fear of object loss due to regression in any patient whose original mothering was not adequate enough to foster a basic confidence, even in reliable and trustworthy objects, sufficient to sustain a therapeutic alliance. Greenson (1965) stresses the importance of sustaining the patient's reality testing, especially with respect to the analyst and the analytic situation, by various communications to the patient of the analyst's humanity, e.g. by confirming to a patient that a criticism he has made of the analyst is correct when it is, rather than by focusing upon the patient's need to criticize the analyst" (2).

imply overprotective acting out as a teacher, parent or leader, misusing the 'real' as a basis for seductive gratifications and unnecessary support. We are making no plea for role-playing or for attempting painless or cheerful psychoanalyses" (145). In trying to summarize the discussion, Paula Heimann, the moderator, said, "It appeared that greater clarity is needed to arrive at an understanding of the way in which 'reality' and 'humanness' (as posited in the paper) affect the way in which the analyst as a worker in the analytic situation listens to his patient, perceives what happens in him, and, as Freud put it, bends his own unconscious to that of the patient so as to gauge correctly the lines to be taken in the journey from the patient's conscious thoughts and feelings to his unconscious processes" (147).

These formulations of Zetzel and Greenson struck a widely responsive chord in American psychoanalysis, and very rapidly the "alliance" concept (in almost all instances as the therapeutic alliance) was propelled into an almost coequal conceptual place with the (vicissitudes of the) transference neurosis in explaining the therapeutic action of psychoanalysis. This acceptance was especially marked among psychoanalytic or dynamic psychotherapists, reaching its apogee in the psychotherapy research literature—including the nonspecifically psychoanalytic—where it has become virtually reified as the almost all-explanatory basis for therapeutic change. For example, Lester Luborsky (1984), in a book intended as a manual for supportive-expressive treatment, adduced two major "curative factors" in analytic psychotherapy—understanding and a "helping relationship" (he called the therapeutic alliance the 'helping alliance'). On the 'relative power' of these factors, Luborsky said, "The pursuit of greater understanding . . . cannot be of much use unless an adequately supportive relationship is present. . . . Even though the two curative factors work in tandem, when they are isolated for the sake of comparison, the power of the relationship may prove to be the more potent of the two" (28). Leonard Horwitz (1974) carried this even further, making the therapeutic alliance virtually the centerpiece of the explanation for all therapeutic change: "The therapeutic alliance is a necessary, but by no means sufficient, condition for the success of the therapeutic process in psychoanalysis. It provides the framework within which the main work of the treatment, the development and analysis of a regressive transference neurosis, occurs. To the extent that a psychotherapy is supportive, the therapeutic alliance, with its various by-products, becomes both an end in itself and the major vehicle of the treatment. Thus, in a primarily supportive treatment the alliance is not only necessary, but often sufficient, for the therapeutic change to occur" (157).[9]

---

9. In *Forty-Two Lives in Treatment* (1986), I specifically demurred from the flatfootedness of Horwitz's accounting and, concerning the understanding of the treatment and change processes

During this period of burgeoning acceptance of the therapeutic alliance con-cept, a variety of supporting, somewhat modifying, and critical perspectives was advanced. Anna Freud (1962), a staunch supporter of the therapeutic alliance, leaned more to Greenson's than to Zetzel's concept: "I think you will not misunderstand me if I say that the therapeutic alliance between analyst and patient is *not* carried by any of these earlier stages of object-relationship, although all these earlier stages are 'material.' The therapeutic alliance is based, I believe, on ego-attitudes that go with later stages, namely, on self-observation, insight, give-and-take in object-relationships, the willingness to make sacrifices" (241–42). Greenacre (1959), in her cautious espousal of the concept, spoke of the dangers of the "insidious dilution" of the therapeutic alliance by "ingredients of a narcissistic alliance" (487), where *undue* active support or intervention un-intendedly weakened the critical functioning and autonomy of the patient's own ego. She warned that correcting the patient's reality perceptions through the coercive pressures of the analysis inevitably inherent in the patient's wish for approval or protection from the analyst "again risks a narcissistic rather than a therapeutic alliance with a transference alleviation rather than an analytic one" (489).

And Friedman (1969), in a critical survey of the implications of the thera-peutic-alliance concept within the differing perspectives offered by Sterba (1934) and Nunberg (1926, 1928, 1932) on the basis for therapeutic change (opposed views that will not be discussed here), wrote that the alliance concept arose in the first place in the need to explain a paradox in the theory of thera-peutic action: "There is the emphasis on the need for a strong emotional tie to the physician to increase his persuasiveness, and there is the emphasis on the use of that persuasiveness to diminish the insistence of the drives" (141). In Freud's view, to begin with, the "therapeutic alliance was largely a libidinal attachment of patient to physician. . . . After all, Freud . . . regarded a hypnotic type of re-sponse by the analysand as ideal in analytic work . . . and that can hardly be described as an alliance with an autonomous, independent ego!" For Sterba, on the other hand, "The suspicion arises that we have been able to establish a drive-

---

in this *same* cohort of research patients offered an "alternative conceptualization of the *varieties* of change mechanisms operative in successful supportive psychotherapies. Put succinctly, my thesis is that a consolidated and successful 'therapeutic alliance' is a necessary but by itself insufficient condition (or vehicle) for change in both expressive *and* supportive psychotherapies; in both types of therapies, there are *additional* specific operative mechanisms that account for the varieties of change and the varieties of bases for change, and these mechanisms differ in the supportive therapies and the expressive therapies" (24). I considered Horwitz's thesis an "oversimplified synthesis."

free ally possessed of great motivating energy only by attributing to it drive properties" (143)—i.e., the paradox. Further, "Sterba's view provides the illusion of escaping our paradox: how are we to draw from the patient the interest and energy necessary for analysis while subduing the impulses which seem to provide that interest and energy?" (144). Friedman offered no resolution of this paradox, only a constant awareness and effort at integration: "The analyst's attitude must combine a kind of acceptance with a kind of non-acceptance in the sense of not settling for the way things are" (151). And finally, "In very general terms, the paradoxes we have examined relate to the obligation of the analyst to find some kind of concordance in the midst of apparent discordance between the patient's direction and his own" (152).[10]

Blum (1971), reviewing the concept of the transference neurosis, had this to say about the therapeutic alliance: "Transference analysis is, I believe, inextricably dependent upon the therapeutic alliance. This relatively autonomous alliance preserves the realistic doctor-patient relation alongside revived infantile object relations of the transference neurosis. . . . The therapeutic or working alliance. . . . , however, incorporates transference elements. Primal transference love, basic trust, and receptive dependency are all essential to the analytic com-

---

10. In subsequent years Friedman made two additional quite striking and quite idiosyncratic comments on the therapeutic alliance. In his 1988 book *The Anatomy of Psychotherapy,* he defined it very unconventionally: "It is useless to instruct a patient in a theory of the mind. No one has been much helped with his personal problems by reading a book on the psychoanalytic theory of the mind. Nor can a person be persuaded to understand himself psychoanalytically by an argument based on that theory. But when, because of personal involvement with his psychoanalyst, a patient is inclined to accept the analyst's view of his mind, then he begins to look for problems relevant to analysis, starts to see questions and answers of an analytic sort, and practices them in many examples (called working through). And at that point he may be said to have grasped the analytic paradigm. That could be one way of defining the therapeutic alliance" (239). And in a 1992 article comparing the perspectives on therapeutic action of Sterba and Strachey published in the same 1934 issue of the *International Journal,* Friedman offered this, again, quite singular view of the alliance concept as it took its start in Sterba's "dissociation of the ego": "It is noteworthy that for Sterba the alliance is at once more ephemeral and more universal than the alliance imagined by later writers. We first note its transience. Like Strachey's mutative interpretation at the 'point of urgency,' Sterba's alliance, although requiring continuous preparation, is not a working contract but a happening—an immediate dissociation within the patient who experiences himself simultaneously in (resistant) disguise and as seeing through his disguise. Furthermore, it is a genuine dissociative state, not merely an act of reflection or the flexing of a perspective" (2). How different this is from the essential reification of the alliance concept as a stable entity both predictive of therapeutic outcome and the principal vehicle of that outcome that characterizes so much of the literature, most particularly the psychoanalytic psychotherapy and the psychotherapy research literature that I have made some reference to.

pact. Transference distortion, realistic perception of the analyst, therapeutic alliance, and the analyst as new object and developmental reorganizer are over-lapping dimensions of analytic relationship" (47).

If this was the prevailing sense of the American psychoanalytic world on the place of the therapeutic alliance concept at the beginning of the 1970s, and I think it was, it did not go unchallenged for long. As early as 1975, from within the favorably disposed American ego-psychological theoretical perspective, Mark Kanzer offered a far more critical view. To Kanzer, the problem that begged for solution (Friedman had called it the "paradox") arose because Freud had recommended two discrepant technical stances for the analyst at work: on the one hand "sympathetic understanding" and "serious interest" (see citation from Freud 1913, at the start of this chapter), and on the other hand the famous mirror and surgical metaphors (Freud, 1912b). Kanzer wrote, "If he [Freud] saw contradictions in these precepts, he never indicated as much" (51). Re-viewing the development of the alliance concepts (particularly by Zetzel and Greenson) as efforts to deal with this issue, and in light of the supporting clinical material those authors had adduced, Kanzer was severely critical. For example, in assessing one of Zetzel's clinical examples, Kanzer said, "The kindly 'ac-knowledgement' of the patient's 'infantile' anxiety, after long delay, seems con-descending and gratuitously assumes that a display of motherliness will be an adequate substitute for correct procedures" (60). Kanzer's overarching objection was that "Zetzel came to see the entire course of analysis as closely paralleling stages of maturation, with different phase-specific types of support necessary to maintain the alliance"; Kanzer, to the contrary, rejected "the notion that there were any simple analogies to be drawn between stages of treatment and of normal maturation—indeed, there is much to suggest the opposite trend" (57). Greenson's views and his examples were reviewed in comparably critical fash-ion, though Kanzer felt that Zetzel's therapeutic alliance concept and Greenson's working alliance concept were "very different in a remarkably complementary way," with the focus of the one on roots in the primal aspects of the mother-child relationship and of the other on the most advanced secondary-process levels of relationship—"though many (including the principals) have used the terms interchangeably" (60).

Kanzer summarized: "Whereas, in earlier days, the resistances received fore-most consideration and the areas of collaboration were much taken for granted, the therapeutic and working alliances have come to focus on the latter. Con-comitantly, however, they often seem to seek autonomy in their own right rather than recognize their inherent connections with the substratum of past analytic experience." And he spoke of the sharp danger that such confusion could become "synonymous with a self-conscious 'humane viewpoint,' with injudicious experiments that give free rein to 'intuition' and with loosely conceived exercises in 'reality-testing' " (67).

Arlow (1975), in his discussion remarks, strongly supported Kanzer's stance: "Both Greenson and Zetzel establish an artificial dichotomy between external reality and internal fantasy life. Each one sees the need to breach this dichotomy with a bridge of reassurance and interpretation of the so-called 'real relationship.' Both de-emphasize thereby the dynamic interplay of the mutual influence of perception and fantasy, memory and reality, past and present. . . . The logical endpoint of . . . [this] approach is a corrective therapeutic experience—not the single, dramatic, circumscribed type of corrective experience advocated by Alexander, but a whole atmosphere of corrective influences modifying the 'mistakes' of the parents" (72).

A few years later, another group of critiques of the alliance concepts was published, and these effectively unsettled completely the hitherto strong consensus on the utility, even the indispensability, of these concepts. Brenner (1979) began by calling himself a "member of an unconvinced minority" on this issue, because "I believe it is neither correct nor useful to distinguish between transference and therapeutic or working alliance" (137). After a detailed review of the clinical material adduced by Zetzel and Greenson in support of their views, Brenner concluded, "One cannot judge from the printed record what data persuaded Zetzel that more than correct transference interpretations are necessary for analytic progress, that therapeutic alliance is distinct from transference neurosis, and that it is no less important to foster the alliance than to interpret the transference" (144). He made a similar comment about Greenson's case material: "In my opinion, it is not being more or less 'human' that is most important. What is most important, I believe, is to understand correctly the nature and origin of one's patients' transference reactions, however one behaves" (148). "In short," Brenner stated, "I am convinced by all the available evidence that the concepts of therapeutic alliance and working alliance that have been current in psychoanalytic literature since 1956 [reference to Zetzel] are neither valid nor useful. In analysis, resistances are best analyzed, not overcome by suggestion [the old bugaboo of Jones and Glover; see chapter 1] or by some corrective emotional experience [Alexander, of course; see chapter 4]. That is to say, their nature and origin are to be understood and, when understood, interpreted to the patient" (149). And, most emphatically, "Whether at the beginning, in the midst, or in the final stages of analysis, timely, accurate interpretations that are based on correct understanding are far more useful in promoting a patient's ability to do his part than is any behavior, however well intentioned, humane, and intuitively compassionate, that is intended to make him feel less withdrawn, uncomfortable, or antagonistic. In analysis, it is best for the patient if one approaches *everything* analytically" (150). This of course leaves no room at all for an alliance concept; in spirit it is most akin to Eissler's (1953) statement of the fundaments of "classical technique."[11]

Homer Curtis's (1979) article had a comparable cautionary thrust but used far more nuanced language, which allowed for a possible reconciliation of the opposed viewpoints (around the sicker, more-than-neurotic patients, for example). To illustrate, Curtis stated,

> In her later paper (1966) Zetzel appears to move closer to the Kleinian position by postulating that even neurotic patients in analysis cannot maintain their mature ego functions on a sufficiently stable level to form a therapeutic alliance without the help of early, nurturing, supportive interventions and a diatrophic relationship with the analyst. This implies an instability and relative lack of autonomy in the ego structures of reality testing, capacity to maintain self-object differentiation, impulse control, and tension tolerance, which are essential for a therapeutic alliance. From a clinical point of view, such a tenuous ego integration is at the mercy of real and fantasy object vicissitudes, and most analysts agree that patients of this type require supportive psychotherapy or analytic parameters (Eissler, 1953).[12] While the "widening scope of psychoanalysis" has brought many such patients to the analyst, there is no question that there are also many patients whose ego functions and capacity for object relations permit them to comprehend and utilize a psychoanalytic situation without the need for supportive interventions, which, while aimed at cementing a therapeutic alliance, are likely to provide regressive transference gratifications to the detriment of transference analysis. (171–72)

In regard to Greenson's formulations, Curtis stressed a somewhat different caution: "The obvious danger in attempting to foster the patient's collaboration

11. Criticizing Brenner's critique, Stone (1981a), after first agreeing that Brenner had offered "many cogent observations, and a correct linear . . . presentation of the essential classical view of the psychoanalytic relationship and process" (112), said that, nonetheless, "no weight is given to the responses of the two participant adults as such, to the sometimes ineffable modes of expression and perception of attitude, intention, interest, and allied matters, which exist between them. And it is overlooked that a real grievance, even though germane to individual personality structure (as are all responses), cannot be equated with a pure transference response and similarly reduced. The admission and correction of the analyst's error or of his failure of prior adequate explanation of a deprivation might, in some instances, render such interpretation effective, or at least restore such possibility for the future" (112).

12. Though from what has just been quoted it appears unlikely that Brenner, with his more austere conception of psychoanalytic proprieties, would agree.

is the possibility that some aspects of the relationship may be labelled 'realistic' and therefore not to be analyzed. This would be similar to taking a rationalization at face value, recognizing the realistic element, but stopping short of revealing the conflictual motivation which uses the rational aspect as a disguise, either primarily or after the fact" (176). In the same vein: "What I am stressing is the necessity of keeping open the possibility, or better, the likelihood of a transference element in even the most apparently realistic interaction between patient and analyst" (177).

Putting these critiques of Zetzel and Greenson together, Curtis *has* left room for an alliance concept, but one circumscribed by a cautious skepticism, the suspicion that for many patients it can serve as a convenient hiding place for analyzable transferences, and by a conviction that it is a more salient consideration and more useful as a technical conception with sicker patients. Given these caveats, he could say positively, "Among the qualities and characteristics the analyst contributes to the setting up of an optimal analytic situation are, first of all, his competence and experience, which give coherence and direction to his free empathic responses. These capacities of the analyst, which the patient deserves, in turn deserve and elicit the patient's realistic trust and cooperation, and combine with the analyst's physicianly dedication and respect for the patient's individuality and goals to match the patient's mature object-related capacities. It is this mutually respectful and adult partnership that forms the solid and reliable nucleus of the therapeutic alliance" (183). The greater applicability of these considerations with sicker patients was propounded as follows: "It is the experience of many analysts that the need for such actively supporting measures is in *inverse proportion* to the strength and stability of the patient's mature ego capacities. . . . It is in the psychoanalytic psychotherapy of sicker patients that, following the model of child analysis, the ego insufficiencies require the analyst to undertake extra measures to supplement the immature or deformed ego's capacities. The provision of supportive nurturing words and attitudes not only makes possible some degree of insight, but offers a new object relationship for identification and structure formation and modification" (184–85, italics added).

Stein's (1981) article in opposition to the alliance concept was essentially in agreement with Brenner's uncompromising position but, unlike Brenner and Curtis, he took his point of departure not from Zetzel and Greenson but from Freud's famous statement on the "unobjectionable positive transference." (cited in chapter 12). He illustrated his concerns about the potential limitation to the analytic treatment process that could be posed by uncritical acceptance of this conception of Freud's by reference to a "special group of patients" (871), described as intelligent, articulate, motivated for analysis, highly cooperative, rational and reasonable. Their symptoms are moderate, they have generally good relationships, and are adequately self-supporting. Their transference feelings are predominantly positive, respectful, sometimes affectionate, often with some teasing and traces of irony. Whatever transference passions of love and hate exist are concealed within this seemingly unobjectionable positive transference—and the analyst is readily tempted into becoming a pleasant, appreciative parent surrogate to his "good analysand." The patient in fact can readily become the favorite child. Stein's contention was that all this rationality, intelligence, and capacity for cooperative effort can be (usually is) in the service of maintaining a powerful resistance. He warned, "In what is admittedly a highly simplified fashion, we might consider the case of these patients who treat their analysts as if they were kindly, intelligent, benign, well-trained and disciplined, very interested and even fond of them, but not a danger in any erotic sense. It seems a reasonable enough description of the actual situation so long as one does not examine its unconscious components" (883).

Stein offered then his own contrary stance: "But in spite of the fact that it [the therapeutic alliance] is necessary and useful for initiating and maintaining the analysis, we are hardly justified in concluding that it is altogether accessible to consciousness, nor that it is by its nature unobjectionable. In fact, it carries a particularly heavy load of unconscious conflict, much of which has to be repressed in order for the treatment to begin, and its long-term effects are often *highly objectionable*" (879, italics added). A successful treatment outcome requires that ultimately it be analyzed: "There is a vast difference in accepting a phenomenon as reality-based, conflict-free, representing only itself, and, on the other hand, treating it more properly as the surface manifestation of a complex set of opposing forces, most of which operate outside of conscious awareness, and which require explanation sooner or later in the course of analysis" (886). Failure to so treat it can lead to a failed analysis or at least a severely limited one: "Undoubtedly some conflicts are so heavily defended during the period of analysis that even as we suspect their presence, we are baffled in our efforts to uncover them, much less to analyze them. . . . It is possible to achieve some comfort by convincing ourselves that conditions had not been propitious, for example . . . a difficult marriage or some other situation that favored stubborn resistances. No doubt this is often the case—I have used the excuse myself—but still, was that the only reason? Could we and should we have done more?" (878).[13]

---

13. Gill (1982) too entered the alliance debate, taking a position as negative as Brenner's and Stein's on its utility. Gill's, however, was a more peripheral argument, ancillary to the thrust of his monograph *Analysis of Transference*. He stated, "I shall argue that the various alliance concepts suffer from the same failure to distinguish clearly between present and past deter-

With these statements of 1979–81, the debate over the place of the alliance concept within psychoanalytic theory and practice was fully joined, and it has continued almost unchanged; some are committed to the heuristic values in the use of the concept (perhaps the majority among American psychoanalysts and certainly the majority of psychodynamic psychotherapists and psychotherapy researchers) and others find it divisive, potentially hurtful (a significant but influential minority in American ranks), or simply irrelevant and therefore not useful (the majority internationally who subscribe to other psychoanalytic theoretical perspectives than the ego-psychological).

In the past decade, a number of additional contributions have been made to this literature. Moss Rawn's (1991) perspective is basically positive: "I would say that patients hear us with two ears, as it were: one conflict and the other nonconflict, one transference and the other working alliance, respectively. If we did not really believe this, then we would not take such pains to offer correct, well-timed, dosed interpretation. If all is transference, then our interpretations are *merely* stimuli for misunderstanding triggered by wishes, defenses, and unconscious guilt" (382–83). But this working alliance is the patient's observing ego making contact with the analyst's *work ego,* as the patient is able to work constructively with the analyst. When, however, both analyst and patient are under the influence of anxiety- and guilt-triggered defense and a transference-countertransference bind develops, this state is called a *misalliance,* following Langs' (1976) apt usage" (384).

Charles Hanly's (1992b) perspective, on the other hand, is much less positive and poses a very limited and circumscribed use of the concept. Though he began by acknowledging the growing concern with the "human influence" in psy-

---

minants of the patient's attitudes as does the concept of the unobjectionable positive transference. The alliance concepts simply emphasize the present and cognitive determinants, whereas the unobjectionable positive transference emphasizes the past and affective determinants. In taking realistically appropriate behavior on the analyst's part for granted, both deemphasize any examination of the actual situation" (96). Gill put his counterconception as follows: "A genuinely integrated view would recognize that behavior is a resultant of both kinds of determinants [present and past]. The individual sees the world not only as his intrapsychic patterns dictate, but also as he veridically assesses it. Furthermore, the two kinds of determinants mutually influence each other. The intrapsychic patterns not only determine selective attention to those aspects of the external world which conform to them, but the individual behaves in such a way as to enhance the likelihood that the responses he meets will indeed confirm the views with which he sets out. This external validation in turn is necessary for the maintenance of those patterns" (92). Given this, Gill's central point again emerges: any distinction between rational and irrational transference components, however they are named, is neither feasible nor desirable, whether the effort be to segregate off the therapeutic alliance, or the transference neurosis, or whatever.

choanalysis, he said, " 'Human influence' is, in a certain respect, a seriously misleading expression because it is used to denote the non-interpretive aspects of the analyst's relation to his patient. But, of course, interpreting itself is a form of 'human influence.' And there can sometimes be the hidden implication in the use of the expression 'human influence' that the work of interpreting in psychoanalysis is in some subtle way coldly scientific, indifferent, unempathic and de-humanizing and that it needs to be softened and ameliorated by demonstrations to the patient of the analyst's caring attitude, especially if the patient's conflicts are preoedipal, narcissistic or 'borderline' " (1). Hanly then stated his own thesis: "I shall argue that the therapeutic alliance is a necessary but not a sufficient condition of therapeutic change, whereas interpretation is a sufficient condition" (3).

Hanly then warned of two major technical risks in the conception of the therapeutic or working alliance as formulated originally by Zetzel and Greenson. The first risk consists of an exaggeration of its importance and its formative role: "But is it [the usual description of the working of the alliance] a true description or is it an idealization? If it involves idealization may not the concept of the working alliance be a defensive exaggeration of the part played by the conscious ego and a diminution of the part played by the unconscious in analytic work?" (3). He added that even "an advocate of a separable working alliance, such as Greenson, recognizes that elements of the working alliance can be enlisted in the service of defence and that they can be infiltrated by the transference" (4). "A second risk inherent in the overemphasis upon the working alliance," Hanly went on, "is a failure in the analyst to sufficiently appreciate the fundamental importance of the *involuntary* aspects of the engagement of the patient with the analyst. This engagement is neither conscious nor rational. It will seek to secure satisfaction from the analyst that could be neither obtained nor abandoned in the past. . . . Thus, insofar as the concept of the working alliance implies an independence from transference, it lends itself to a defensive rationalization of a failure in the analyst to carry out the self analysis of interfering countertransferences and the recourse to the 'human influence' of the analyst as a substitute for the search for interpretations. This could be captured in the formula 'Even if I cannot understand the patient, the relation I can offer him is enough to bring about improvement' " (4).

What, then, in Hanly's view, was the proper place for the alliance conception? It is, he stated, in the "*implicit* meanings" of the proffered interpretations, through which "the analyst inadvertently conveys to the patient something of the affective attitudes in himself which helped to lead him to this understanding and something of his response to the patient thus understood" (5). Again, "Interventions aimed at creating a working alliance are less likely to be effective than the implicit meanings of well-timed, correct interpretations" (6). And finally, "Psychoanalysis can proceed by interpretation alone so long as it is understood that the therapeutic work of interpretation depends upon a working alliance. . . . nothing could possibly foster a working alliance more than a correct interpretation which is mutative" (7).

Earlier in the article, Hanly listed four possible positions on the place of the conception of the therapeutic or working alliance:

> 1. a treatment alliance is not necessary for psychoanalysis, let alone special interventions inside or outside the analytic frame to foster it; transference neurosis is sufficient [a position imputed particularly to the Kleinians] . . . 2. a treatment alliance is necessary for psychoanalysis but it may be sufficiently sustained by means of interpretation [stated to be Freud's original position] . . . 3. a treatment alliance is causally equal to and relatively independent of the transference neurosis and requires specific non-interpretive interventions within the analytic frame [Zetzel, Greenson, and others] . . . 4. a treatment alliance is causally equal to and relatively independent of transference neurosis and requires specific non-interpretive interventions outside the analytic frame at least for more seriously ill patients [the most extreme position]. (2)

Hanly is without doubt solidly aligned with the second position.[14]

Morton and Estelle Shane (1992), in an appreciative overview of Greenson's contributions, defended Greenson against the more extreme charges of his critics (like Brenner and Stein) but pointed nonetheless to a difficulty that besets all those concerned with these issues: "In Greenson's defense, it should be obvious from our review . . . that Greenson himself was aware of both neurotic intrusions into the alliance and the danger of the patient's using the alliance for defensive purposes" (296). But "it seems that there is a genuine problem . . . with the alliance concept; those who find it valuable and, in fact, irreplaceable, and those who find it problematic and, in fact, dismissable, are alike in the difficulty they identify of distilling it from the transference" (298). Is this unclarity, even perhaps ambiguity, that the Shanes point to the source of at least some of the failure to resolve the contentious clamor that seems to beset the alliance concepts, with so little apparent progression toward shared understanding and harmonization of sharply opposed views?

Tahka (1993) has put forth a quite novel view of the *separateness* of the

---

14. In 1994, Hanly published essentially the same article, updated, in a more readily accessible journal.

therapeutic and working alliance concepts and the sequential and consequential nature of their potential relationship. He stated this position as follows:

> I propose to restrict the term working alliance to refer primarily to the contemporary aspects of the analytic relationship that are based on the patient's preexisting capacity for emotionally meaningful age-appropriate collaboration between individuals. Once the developing transference has given the analyst the position and authority of a developmental object, it depends on the patient's remaining developmental urges, as well as on the analyst's ability and willingness to present himself as a new developmental object for the patient, whether a newly motivated and reactivated developmental interaction will ensue. Provided that this will be the case, and that the established relationship between the patient and the analyst as a new developmental object will be adequately allied with the contemporary aspects of the relationship, the *working* relationship has been expanded to a *therapeutic alliance*. (230, italics added)

In this conception, the therapeutic alliance is a "higher" form that, as a consequence of proper analytic work, has evolved out of the working alliance.

What, finally, Etchegoyen (1991) added to the concept of therapeutic alliance in his book is another form of sequential progression, not from working to therapeutic alliance (as Tahka proposed), but more fundamentally from transference neurosis to therapeutic alliance. He stated this in the context of his elaborate explication of Zetzel's conceptions of the therapeutic alliance vis-à-vis the transference: "Analytic treatment consists in the gradual integration of certain areas, as they are analyzed—and which originally belonged to the transference neurosis—into the ego structure, thus becoming part of the therapeutic alliance. The essence of analytic therapy is founded, in fact, on this change—if a particular conflict is analysed in the transference neurosis and made conscious, it becomes the property of the ego, a new facet of the ego that establishes a real relationship with the analyst, since if the therapeutic alliance can be defined at all, it is as a real type of relation with the analyst. . . . The curative process consists in the transformation of the transference neurosis into the therapeutic alliance, and this continues to be valid" (503–04). Here, the therapeutic alliance, rather than being the essential counterpart structure to the transference neurosis, which provides the matrix and context within which the transference neurosis can be analyzed, has been transformed into the successfully analyzed (and renamed) transference neurosis, the proper outcome of successful analysis, not its necessary facilitator. If Etchegoyen sees this as a wrenching reformulation of Zetzel's emphases, he does not so indicate.

It is clear that this latest group of contributors—Rawn, Hanly, Shane and

Shane, Tahka, and Etchegoyen—has not helped sway the argument in one direction or the other as to whether the alliance concept is useful and even indispensable or useless and even mischievous. It is still both widely used (for explanatory and heuristic purposes alike) and subject to vigorous criticism within American ego-psychological ranks and is considered tangential or even irrelevant by most of those whose allegiances are to other theoretical perspectives in psychoanalysis.

16 The Psychoanalytic Relationship and the Role of New Experience: Leo Stone and Hans Loewald

During the period when the writings of Zetzel and Greenson on the therapeutic and working alliances were making so deep a mark upon the American psychoanalytic world, another expression of the growing interest in the affective analyst-patient relationship as an essential factor in understanding the psychoanalytic change process was emerging into prominence. This new perspective focused more explicitly on the nature of the dyadic interpersonal therapeutic relationship and, like the alliance concept, can be traced back to the original impetus given to this line of concern by Ferenczi, whose influence was duly acknowledged in the two central publications that signified the crystallizing of this trend, Loewald's "On the Therapeutic Action of Psychoanalysis" (1960) and Stone's *The Psychoanalytic Situation* (1961). These contributions made a less dramatic initial impression than the alliance concepts and were not fully recognized at the time as the far-ranging reconceptualizations of the therapeutic action of psychoanalytic therapy that they were. They have, however, won increasing acceptance over time and today form the underpinnings of a virtually universal consensus in our understandings of the therapeutic process and change mechanisms. Unlike the alliance concepts, with their particular American rootedness, the considerations advanced by Loewald and Stone are congenial to object-relational thinking in the British Independent group (see chapter 19); they also provide a bridge to the conceptions of interpersonal psychiatry pioneered in America by Harry Stack Sullivan, which now, as the interpersonal theoretical perspective, are approaching a closer meeting ground, if not a full rapprochement, with the American psychoanalytic mainstream.

Before considering Stone's and Loewald's approaches, I will draw attention to two precursory statements. Rene Spitz (1956), in his comments on the analytic situation, had stated, "The patient is helpless, while the analyst's role is to be helpful. The situational stimulus in the analytic setting which acts on the analyst is, therefore, the patient's helplessness. It evokes in the analyst fantasies derived from the ego ideal which he formed in identification with his parents. We have postulated that the analytic setting places the patient into an anaclitic relationship. I may be permitted to suggest a distinctive role of the analyst's in this setting. *Anaclitic* means leaning onto; I recommend for the analyst's attitude the term *diatrophic* [from the Greek, to maintain or support], which means supporting" (260). Spitz then indicated how he intended these concepts to be taken:

"In the analytic setting, in the ideal case, both anaclitic and diatrophic relations have to operate on the level of fantasies, conscious and unconscious, triggered by the condition of the setting itself. Neither of them should be translated into action. The patient, in acting out, attempts to achieve reality fulfillment. The aim of the rule of abstinence is to frustrate this fulfillment. The analyst becomes able to impose this frustration on the patient only if he himself does not act out the diatrophic attitude. He has to understand the origin of his diatrophic fantasies sufficiently to be able to accept as a matter of course that *the rule of abstinence operates for himself as much as it does for the patient*" (261).

Gitelson, in a 1951 paper, took a developmental approach to the psychoanalytic therapeutic process: "One of the as yet unsolved problems of psychoanalysis is concerned with the essential nature of psychoanalytic cure. It is not insight; it is not the recall of infantile memories; it is not catharsis or abreaction; it is not the relationship to the analyst. Still, it is all of these in some synthesis which it has not yet been possible to formulate explicitly. Somehow, in a successful analysis the patient matures as a total personality. Somehow, a developmental process which has been halted or sidetracked, resumes its course. It is as though the person, reexperiencing his past in the transference, finds in the new condition a second chance and 'redevelops' while he is reliving" (285).[1] In his later 1962 paper, Gitelson specifically enlarged on Spitz's anaclitic-diatrophic conception. He began with a declaration of intent: "The paper concerns itself with what the author concludes to be the largely non-verbal *givens* which operate in the initiation of the psycho-analytic process. These are *necessary but by themselves not sufficient precursor conditions* for the establishment of an effective psycho-analytic situation" (194). Such considerations have come to the fore because "since the 1936 Symposium on the Theory of Therapeutic Results there has been expanding concern with the nature of the *interpersonal* relationship of patient and analyst" (195).

These "necessary precursor conditions," according to Gitelson, are, first, *inherent* in the properly conducted analysis: "I think that in the existing form of the analytic situation, without benefit of the corrections and additions which it has received in recent years, there reside all the 'curative factors' which neo-

1. Gitelson's phrase "second chance" goes back to Balint's (1932) conception of the "new beginning" Balint had put it as: "By this I mean a change in his behaviour, more exactly in the libido structure, of the patient. . . . This enables us to understand why the tracing back of the libido development, either through remembering or through repetition, is absolutely necessary. To be able to begin something anew, one must go back to the point of interruption. The return itself, that is, the remembering, the disclosure of the repression, means no change as yet, it is however an absolutely necessary prelude to the change—to the new beginning" (165).

analysis in its various forms presumes to have discovered." And "The thesis is that what happens 'normally' in the psychoanalytic situation is comparable to the course of events under more or less normal circumstances in the developmental situation in which the child finds himself on the road to more or less non-neurotic autonomous adulthood" (196). This developmental analogue brought Gitelson to the necessary precursor conditions, the expression, particularly in the opening phase of analysis, of "primitive rapport," the meeting of the anaclitic needs of the patient by the (quoting Spitz) "diatrophic function of the analyst—his healing intention to 'maintain and support' the patient" (198), which Gitelson called countertransference in its affirmative sense: "The diatrophic attitude arises as a response to the patient's need for help even as the parent responds to the anaclitic situation of the child." This becomes the basis for analytic empathy, a convergence with the patient's need for ego-support, and a context in which the analyst, like the mother, functions as an auxiliary ego, providing direction and purpose to the patient's mobilization of psychoanalytic effort and response. The patient, in turn, discovers the "dosed appropriateness" (199) of the analyst's response.

The "rapport" thus created elicits the patient's feelings of hope for (and expectation of) the diatrophic response, and this, Gitelson contended, was more than suggestion; it was, rather, a meeting of the patient's desire for cure with the analyst's professional commitment to cure, setting up the anaclitic-diatrophic equation and creating the conditions that would make the new development and new beginning possible. Gitelson insisted that the diatrophic intention is *not* explicitly enacted: "The implicitness of the diatrophic attitude in the person qualified to be an analyst is all that is required. Of course, that 'all' is quite a lot, as those who have studied the pathology of the counter-transference can testify" (202). Rather, "these [implicit diatrophic attitudes] are the full extent of the 'interpersonal' and the 'supportive' which the abiding developmental impulse requires for its revival" (203). Secondly, Gitelson emphasized that all these considerations apply particularly to the opening phase of the analysis and become less germane as the analytic situation becomes well established and the analytic process unfolds with the evolution of the transference neurosis.

Finally, Gitelson felt it necessary to defend these conceptions against the charge that they were reversions to suggestion (Jones and Glover) or to active therapy (Ferenczi) or new instances of the corrective emotional experience (Alexander). "In the classical view," he wrote, "this role has been considered an *unfortunate* contamination of analysis by 'the power of suggestion,' " and, as indicated, he entered his vigorous dissent. "The difference from 'active therapy' is found in the fact that the latter, in its various interventions, provides direct libidinal gratification and, as in hypnosis, takes over the functions of the patient's superego.' And in regard to the corrective emotional experience: "I certainly am not supporting the view that the essential nature of the analytic procedure is found in its provision of a 'corrective emotional experience' aided by marginal suggestion and representational gratification. My intention is to extend the classical view that *only the ego can be influenced therapeutically,* and that to this end accurate interpretation is the prime curative factor" (203). Gitelson ended with a restatement of just how pivotal these considerations could be to the possibilities for success in analytic work: "In the transference neurosis we are confronted by projections and displacements of the 'closed system' psychology which has eventuated from the development of psychic structure. As such it is inaccessible. But the 'open system' of the infant and young child, recapitulated in the anaclitic regression of the patient in the first phase of analysis, provides channels of affective communication which make interpretation possible" (204).

Within this evolving climate represented by the contributions of Spitz and Gitelson, Stone (1961) undertook a far-ranging reconsideration of the nature, meanings, and conditions of "the psychoanalytic situation." This was widely seen as a measured but critical response to Eissler's effort to enunciate classical technique in psychoanalysis, and this was in fact made quite explicit early in the monograph. Stone listed the components of Eissler's generally accepted model of the classical analytic situation: "the analytic (perceptual and emotional) 'vacuum'; the total or relative nonvisibility of the analyst during the hours; the relative confinement of his responses to interpretation, clarification, or other 'neutral' maneuvers; the stereotypy of schedules and fees; the relative lack of even conventional emotional responses to the patient's personality and career; the lack of intervention in the patient's everyday life, whether through advice or persuasion, or purposive extra-analytic contact; the general 'blanketing' of the analyst's personality, actively, and passively, except as it appears inevitably or inadvertently" (20). Of the extreme of this position, the noninvolvement of the analyst with the patient except to interpret, Stone said, " 'Only to analyze' or an equivalent phrase became a sort of catchword or slogan for the definition and circumscription of the analyst's function, and often, by implication, of his personal attitude" (29).

Stone understood this attitude as a reaction to the deviations in technique so strongly advocated by Alexander and his followers in that period: "There is also a historical factor, which deserves consideration. If what were felt to be an overintellectualization of the analytic process and excessive aloofness of the analyst contributed to the reaction of Ferenczi and certain of his followers, it is also probable that the pressures toward radical modifications of the psychoanalytic situation and techniques in a more recent period (conspicuously those of Alexander and his co-workers, 1946) have occasioned intellectual and scientific reactions in those convinced of the greater soundness and value of classical methods" (30). Eissler was indeed central to both the counterattack against the Alexander position and the articulation of the so-called classical position, to which Stone's monograph took exception: "One may see this tendency in its extreme current development in Eissler's designation as a 'parameter' of any technical action of the analyst except interpretation" (18). The intent of course was "to permit the transference to develop as a discrete and 'uncontaminated' phenomenon" (20), but this Stone declared to be an unrealizable and undesirably extreme ideal: "This theoretical conceptual structure of the analytic situation does undeniably exist as a sort of ideal which many analysts actually try to embody in their clinical work, the 'human' element appearing as a sort of conscious *detente,* or reservation, or minimal forced concession" (19).

By contrast, Stone's own vision of the ideal analytic situation, first of all, is *explicitly therapeutic* (physicianly) in intent: "Psychoanalysis, as a genuine process, finds its only adequate motivation in the suffering and the needs for help of the patient, however primitive or subtle the specific disturbance may be. In other words, as genuine process, psychoanalysis can never be *purely* and *primarily* investigative or exploratory" (16). It is also in a very real sense *educational:* "Only the conception 'teacher' . . . would seem to me to be a valuable and germane secondary conceptualization of the analyst's role, in terms which have a general meaning to human beings, even though the 'teaching' be confined almost exclusively to the elucidation of the patient's unconscious psychic life. The idea of the teacher derives its underlying power from its resemblance to the secondary function of the parent, just as the idea of the physician derives its unique power from its resemblance to certain primary functions of the parent in earliest infancy" (117–18). "The common element," Stone stated, "is the frank and evidently therapeutic (i.e., physicianly) commitment" (119). "I assert my conviction regarding the unique transference valence of the physician" (17).[2]

Stone then systematically asserted his modifications of Eissler's austere ideal: "My conviction that a nuance of the analyst's attitude can determine the difference between a lonely vacuum and a controlled but warm human situation, which does indeed offer . . . gratifications along with its undoubted rigors. . . . It is one of the burdens of this presentation to suggest that the intrinsic formal stringencies of the situation are sufficient to contraindicate superfluous deprivations in the analyst's personal attitude" (21–22). In keeping with these views, Stone pointed out that Freud had himself tempered his pronouncement of the

2. As noted in chapter 4, Stone intended the words "physician" and "physicianly" in these contexts to mean therapeutic or healing and not to be limited to those with medical qualifications.

principle of abstinence in his "Transference Love" paper (1915); although Freud said, "The treatment must be carried out in abstinence," he followed this immediately with, "By this I do not mean physical abstinence alone, nor yet the deprivation of everything that the patient desires, *for perhaps no sick person could tolerate this*" (165, italics added). Stone extended this remark: "Beginning with the type of reservation introduced by Freud himself, writers who deal with the psychoanalytic situation . . . quite regularly introduce qualifications which indicate the necessity for a basically friendly or 'human' quality in the analyst, apart from the now long-standing and general recognition of the part of personal attitude in the considerable technical variations required by severe illness or other exceptional conditions" (27). Within this frame, Stone referred approvingly to a paper by Leo Berman (1949). Regarding how one could be both properly "analytic" and properly "human" at the same time, Stone said that in Berman's view, "the quandary finds simple expression and resolution: 'The answer could simply be that the analyst is always both the cool detached surgeon-like operator on the patient's psychic tissues, and the warm, human, friendly, helpful physician' " (Stone 1961, 128).

Stone illustrated what he had in mind: "There are occasions when, for example, it is insufficient to interpret why a patient does not go for physical examination, or for contraceptive advice. I must also note in this connection that mature and intelligent patients—not 'borderline'—under the stress of clinical neurosis and life vicissitudes, often suffer impairments of reality testing, judgment, and indeed strange and equivalent hiatuses in their fund of knowledge, in relation to which the analyst cannot shirk his responsibility for the minimal, sometimes indirect, but often decisive help *beyond interpretation* for which the patient often cannot turn elsewhere" (32, italics added). Of course there are (reasonable and self-evident) limits to this: "It is likely that limits of a sort appropriate to the complexity and subtlety of our work can be set, with reasonable allowance for individual variation. . . . Our basic technical method excludes purposive social contacts or any other physical, emotional, or communicative relationship which is judged to be significantly stimulating or gratifying to the patient's primitive transferences" (39). It is rather that "the suffering child in the patient can probably always be loved (in a sense) by the parental component, which is an inevitably important affirmative factor in the physician's identity. But it is an inescapable fact that there is [also] more in the patient, and more in the doctor respectively, than patient and doctor or child and parent" (44). All this "brings me to the general question of *legitimate* 'transference gratification.' The very phrase, I realize, may stimulate initial protest. Nevertheless, it comprehends an indisputable system of facts" (49). And "there is an element in analytic technique, however strictly interpreted, which does inevitably and legitimately provide transference gratification" (51–52).

Stone then summarized his thinking as follows: "In oversimple terms there are three discernible patterns of relationship between analyst and analysand, no one of them ever obliterated (although it may be ignored), coexisting and intimately interrelated in contrapuntal fashion: the real and actual integrated personal relationship, which includes the basic vocational (essentially physician-patient) relationship; the transference-countertransference relationship, and finally the unique system of routinized activities, deprivations, and prohibitions which find origin in the requirements of analytic technique" (55). In this context, Stone circumscribed the definition of transference: "Clarity . . . is best served by confining the unqualified term 'transference' to that aspect or fraction of a relationship which is motivated by persistent unmodified wishes (or other attitudes) toward an actual important personage of the past, which tend to invest a current individual in a sort of misidentification . . . with the unconscious image of the past personage" (66).[3] Stone then returned to his starting point, the conditions necessary to establish analysis as a therapy: "This historic process, i.e., the affirmative establishment of the analyst in human cultural consciousness, will occur only in so far as the element of therapeutic commitment in analysis is restored to its full dignity . . . via recognition of the impulse to help, to relieve suffering, with the primary caretaking attitudes which gave all early teaching its affirmative infantile significance" (63).

Stone then offered a final plea for the human element in psychoanalysis: "An important question: may not the trend toward a schematic perfection in carrying out the principle of abstinence and allied technical precepts have overwhelmed awareness of the reservations supplied by common sense and intuitive wisdom from the beginning, and thus subtly and inadvertently produced superfluous technical difficulties of paradoxical character? The tendencies I have in mind are the withholding or undue limitation of certain legitimate and well-controlled gratifications, which can provide a palpably human context for the transmission of understanding, which is, by general agreement, the central function of the analyst." He added, "What I have in mind in this presentation is a subtle shift

3. He related this analytic transference to the "transferences of everyday life" as follows: "The initial [analytic] transference . . . is a relatively integrated phenomenon, allied to character traits, an amalgam or compromise of conflicting forces, which has become established as a habitual attitude, the best resultant of 'multiple function' of which the personality is capable, in the general type of relationship which now confronts it. It differs from its everyday counterpart only in its relative separation from its usual everyday context, in the relative lack of tangible provocation, justification, or substantiation, and—sooner or later—in the failure of elicitation of the gratifications or adaptive goals to which it is devoted" (74–75).

in the general base line of the classical psychoanalytic situation, applicable throughout treatment, to *any* patient" (107–08); "What I have recommended, in effect, is that the patient be permitted to experience his analyst's physicianly vocation (an integrated reality-syntonic representation of parental functions) as a stable and active reality of the relationship, to whatever degree may be necessary, without yielding any of the crucial issues of nongratification, in the sense of primitive transference wishes" (110).

In a subsequent paper, "Noninterpretive Elements in the Psychoanalytic Situation and Process," Stone (1981a) reviewed the entire span of psychoanalytic literature on the nature of the psychoanalytic situation and process in the context of the views advanced so comprehensively in his 1961 monograph. Here he renewed his incisive critique of the stringent viewpoint on technique identified with Eissler: "Perhaps the most elegant codification of what I would call the neoclassical point of view is that of Eissler (1953), in which the hypothetical (or fictive) 'normal ego' is susceptible to favorable change by interpretation alone; any variant is regarded as a 'parameter,' subject to strict rules for its employment and dissolution. Apart from the fact that this is a structure of metapsychological assumptions, there would be doubt in mind that even a 'hypothetical normal ego' would respond to interpretation alone, except, of course, as the response is a required fiction of definition" (102). Stone again differentiated his recommendations from what he called Ferenczi's failed experiment in giving the patients the demonstratively accepting or responsive love of which they had been deprived as children, from Alexander's corrective emotional experience, which he likewise considered to be unsoundly based, and from Kohut's efforts to provide the empathy not provided originally by the maternal self-object of infancy. Of all these Stone said, "One cannot give to the elaborately organized personality of an adult what he missed as an infant or young child, in the original form in which the lack occurred, and expect it to repair the defective structuralized developments occasioned by its lack" (103). He did concede, à propos Kohut's work, "While I do not believe that the analyst's mirroring empathy can make up for the mother's empathic deficits, it can make for a much better analysis" (108). And in reference to Winnicott's "holding environment" and Modell's stress on the handling of the "cocoon transference" within the "holding environment," Stone said, "Whether or not the postulated infantile prototype of the holding process is actually intrinsic in the analytic experience, the concept does express an analytic attitude, however conveyed to the patient, which may, after a time, permit him to go ahead with analytic work and to sustain its rigors" (107).

Stone thus carefully repositioned himself (along with Winnicott and Modell?) between Eissler and his followers on the one side and Ferenczi, Alexander, and

Kohut on the other, but clearly, he was temperamentally and technically more sympathetic to the latter. He restated his convictions on the centrality of contributing elements to the change process that are beyond simply interpretive method and content, dwelling particularly on a reassessment of the place of abstinence in the analytic process:

> To the extent that it [the classical attitude] does not become equated with coldness, aloofness, arbitrary withholding, callousness, detachment, ritualization, or panicky adherence to rules for their own sake, it is an integral, indeed central element in the rule of abstinence, without which there is no analysis. However, it must be of a character which the ego of an intelligent adult can understand as rational and appropriate. Where the deprivation goes beyond the intelligibly rational or becomes merged with aversive, rejective, or clearly detached qualities, it can stimulate iatrogenic regressions in the transference which present a remarkable resistance to interpretive reduction. . . . It was in relation to this contingency that I proposed in 1961 a reasoned and measured reduction in the rigors of abstinence in all spheres and—above all—their restriction to spheres essential and relevant in the development of the transference neurosis. For ultra-simple example, if a patient asks, 'Are you seeing patients on Christmas Day?' I do not believe that failing to answer will further the analytic purposes. Nor will wishing him well on the eve of a major surgical operation hinder these purposes. I realize that these examples will seem absurd to some; yet I know that there are others to whom my view is unacceptable. (100–01)

Stone concluded, "The 'love' implicit in empathy, listening and trying to understand, in nonseductive devotion to the task, the sense of full acceptance, respect, and sometimes the homely phenomenon of sheer dependable patience, extending over long periods of time, may take their place as equal or nearly equal in importance to sheer interpretive skill" (114)—though assuredly these factors are not curative in and of themselves; they merely foster and facilitate the curative process. They are manifest mainly via "the relative naturalness of the analyst's attitude (within well-defined professional boundaries) and the considered relaxation of superfluous nonrational deprivations, cognitive and affective" (116)—a succinct statement of his overall position.

Though, as I have indicated, Stone's views are generally considered today to be relatively noncontroversial, there have been those who have demurred, at least to some extent. Among them, Brenner is widely perceived as the current major exponent of the position espoused earlier by Eissler. Brenner (1979) stated,

I thoroughly agree with Stone's major emphases [in his 1961 monograph]: that analysis is a form of therapy, that a patient should be able to count on his analyst's professional commitment to him as a "doctor," that the business of analysis is to analyze *that* case, that technical rules are not commandments, and that in every instance one should be guided by one's analytic understanding of the entire analytic situation. Moreover, the examples of analytic reserve that Stone cites with disapproval seem as unwarranted to me as they do to Stone. It seems to me, however, that what Stone recommends with respect to what wishes are permissibly and usefully gratified in analysis is likely not to be in the best interests of analytic progress. Nor do I agree that . . . analysts, as good doctors, should aim at keeping to an irreducible minimum the suffering they must impose on their patients by subjecting them to analysis. . . .

Provided his analyst is competent . . . it is a patient's own illness that determines whether he experiences the analytic situation in and of itself as a source of pain, as essentially neutral, as a welcome anodyne, or as a positive source of pleasure. . . . Whatever an analytic patient feels about the analytic situation, whether it be suffering, indifference, or gratification, is analytic material. It should in principle be treated like any other material: understood if possible and interpreted if appropriate. It is neither inhumane nor inhuman for an analyst to be guided by this principle in his attitude and behavior toward his patient. If, for example, a patient suffers a catastrophe or a success in life, it is not the best for him and his analysis for his analyst to express sympathy or congratulations before "going on to analyze." It is true enough that it often does no harm for an analyst to be thus conventionally "human." Still, there are times when his being "human" under such circumstances can be harmful, and one cannot always know in advance when those times will be. As an example, for his analyst to express sympathy for a patient who has just lost a close relative may make it more difficult than it would otherwise be for the patient to express pleasure or spite or exhibitionistic satisfaction over the loss. As another example, it is difficult for me to imagine instructing an adult patient to have a physical examination or to go for contraceptive information. I can easily imagine saying to a patient that there must be a reason why he is neglecting his health and that I wonder what his thoughts are about it, or to another that there must be some reason why she is inviting or risking pregnancy and that I wonder what she thinks about it. (152–54)

Loewald is the other pillar of our more current conceptualization of the role of the analyst–patient relationship in furthering the analytic process. The title of his seminal paper on this subject "On the Therapeutic Action of Psycho-Analysis" (1960), is almost identical to Strachey's "The Nature of the Therapeutic Action of Psycho-Analysis" (1934), and the Loewald paper has been comparably influential in redefining psychoanalytic perspectives on this topic. In contrast to Stone's emphasis on the "humanness" in the analyst-patient relationship, Loewald's was on the analyst's role as a "new object" in the patient's life, with whom therapeutically productive "integrative experiences" could be (should be) achieved: "If 'structural changes in the patient's personality' means anything, it must mean that we assume that ego development is resumed in the therapeutic process in psycho-analysis. And this resumption of ego-development is contingent on the relationship with a new object, the analyst." Loewald added, "While the fact of an object-relationship between patient and analyst is taken for granted, classical formulations concerning therapeutic action and concerning the role of the analyst in the analytic relationship do not reflect our present understanding of the dynamic organization of the psychic apparatus" (16).

Loewald then presented his conception of this understanding: "In an analysis, I believe, we have opportunities to observe and investigate primitive as well as more advanced interaction-processes, that is, interactions between patient and analyst which lead to or form steps in ego-integration and disintegration . . . which I shall call integrative (and disintegrative) experiences." Such interactions often go unnoticed and/or are frequently denied: "The theoretical bias [in this failure of attention] is the view of the psychic apparatus as a closed system. Thus the analyst is seen, not as a co-actor on the analytic stage on which the childhood development, culminating in the infantile neurosis, is restaged and reactivated in the development, crystallization and resolution of the transference neurosis, but as a reflecting mirror, albeit of the unconscious, and characterized by scrupulous neutrality" (17). This postulated neutrality theoretically helps the analyst to avoid falling into the role assigned to the transference figure and thus to remain sufficiently objective to reflect back to the patient the roles that he has assigned to the analyst and himself in the transference drama. But Loewald asked us to "take a fresh look at the analytic situation. Ego-development is a process of increasingly higher integration and differentiation of the psychic apparatus and does not stop at any given point except in neurosis and psychosis." Throughout growth and development there is a to-and-fro of processes of relative ego-regression followed by new reorganizations and consolidations:

> Erikson has described certain types of such periods of ego-regression with subsequent new consolidations as identity crises. An analysis can be characterized, from this standpoint, as a period or periods of induced ego-disorganization and reorganization. . . . The transference neurosis in the

sense of reactivation of the childhood neurosis is set in motion not simply by the technical skill of the analyst, but by the fact that the analyst makes himself available for the development of a new "object-relationship" between the patient and the analyst. . . . The patient can dare to take the plunge into the regressive crisis of the transference neurosis which brings him face to face again with his childhood anxieties and conflicts, if he can hold on to the potentiality of a new object-relationship, represented by the analyst. (17–18).

This Loewald called a "new discovery of objects, not the discovery of new objects, because the essence of such new object-relationships is the opportunity they offer for rediscovery of the early paths of the development of object-relations, leading to a new way of relating to objects as well as of being and relating to oneself. . . . Such a new object-relationship for which the analyst holds himself available to the patient and to which the patient has to hold on throughout the analysis is one meaning of the term 'positive transference' "— and also, we could add, of the terms "therapeutic" and "working" alliance. One of the qualifications the analyst must possess in this encounter is reasonable objectivity. But "this objectivity cannot mean the avoidance of being available to the patient as an object. The objectivity of the analyst has reference to the patient's transference distortions. Increasingly, through the objective analysis of them, the analyst becomes not only potentially but actually available as a new object, by eliminating step by step impediments, represented by these transferences, to a new object relationship." The analyst, however, not only reflects the transference distortions: "In his interpretations he implies aspects of undistorted reality which the patient begins to grasp step by step as transferences are interpreted. . . . In analysis, we bring out the true form by taking away the neurotic distortions. However . . . we must have, if only in rudiments, an image of that which needs to be brought into its own. The patient, by revealing himself to the analyst, provides rudiments of such an image through all the distortions— an image which the analyst has to focus in his mind, thus holding it in safekeeping for the patient to whom it is mainly lost. It is this tenuous reciprocal tie which represents the germ of a new object-relationship" (18).

This objectivity with which the analyst should observe and interpret the patient and himself in interaction "should not be confused with the 'neutral' attitude of the pure scientist towards his subject of study. . . . the analyst may become a scientific observer to the extent to which he is able to observe objectively the patient and himself in interaction. The interaction itself, however, cannot be adequately represented by the model of scientific neutrality. . . . [Rather], the patient and the analyst identify to an increasing degree, if the analysis proceeds, in their ego–activity of scientifically guided self-scrutiny" (18–19). This "requires an objectivity and neutrality the essence of which is love and respect for the individual and individual development." The model for all this Loewald found in the parent-child relationship: "The parent ideally is in an empathic relationship of understanding the child's particular stage in development, yet ahead in his vision of the child's future and mediating this vision to the child in his dealing with him. This vision, informed by the parent's own experience and knowledge of growth and future, is ideally, a more articulate and more integrated version of the core of being which the child presents to the parent. This 'more' that the parent sees and knows, he mediates to the child so that the child in identification with it can grow." The analyst thus always relates to the patient, or should relate to the patient, "from the viewpoint of potential growth, that is, from the future" (20). Of course, "the more intact the ego of the patient, the more of this integration taking place in the analytic process occurs without being noticed or at least without being considered and conceptualized as an essential element in the analytic process" (21).

In this context Loewald further developed the conception of a necessary developmental gradient between analyst and patient just as between parent and child: "The mother recognizes and fulfills the need of the infant. Both recognition and fulfillment of a need are at first beyond the ability of the infant. . . . the organization of the psychic apparatus beyond the discernible potentialities at birth . . . proceeds by way of mediation of higher organization on the part of the environment to the infantile organism. . . . The higher organizational stage of the environment is indispensable for the development of the psychic apparatus and, in early stages, has to be brought to it actively. Without such a 'differential' between organism and environment no development takes place." Translating this to the therapeutic context: "The patient, who comes to the analyst for help through increased self-understanding, is led to this self-understanding by the understanding he finds in the analyst. . . . the analyst structures and articulates, or works towards structuring and articulating, the material and productions offered by the patient. . . . A higher stage of organization, of both himself and his environment, is thus reached, by way of the organizing understanding which the analyst provides. The analyst functions as a representative of a higher stage of organization and mediates this to the patient" (24).

Within this framework, analytic progression and "analytic interpretations represent, on higher levels of interaction, the mutual recognition involved in the creation of identity of experience in two individuals of different levels of ego-organization. Insight gained in such an interaction is an integrative experience" (25)—and this is one of only four uses of the word "insight" in this article on the therapeutic action of psychoanalysis, in such sharp contrast to the central and essential position of the sequence interpretation → insight → change as the primary (only) explanatory vehicle of analytic progress and cure in Eissler's model. Another instance is on the following page: "Once the patient is able to speak, non-defensively, from the true level of regression which he has been helped to reach by analysis of defences, he himself, by putting his experience into words, begins to use language creatively, that is, begins to create insight" (26).

Overall, then, in Loewald's conception, "The analytic process . . . consists in certain integrative experiences between patient and analyst as the foundation for the internalized version of such experiences: reorganization of ego, 'structural change' " (25). "By an interpretation," he continued, "both the unconscious experience and a higher organizational level of that experience are made available to the patient: unconscious and preconscious are joined together in the act of interpretation. In a well-going analysis the patient increasingly becomes enabled to perform this joining himself" so that "the patient, being recognized by the analyst as something more than he is at present, can attempt to reach this something more by his communications to the analyst which may establish a new identity with reality." Finally, "We call analysis that kind of organizing, restructuring interaction between patient and therapist which is predominantly performed on the level of language communication" (26–27).

Loewald reiterated and extended these conceptions in a number of papers over the following decades. In a 1970 paper, he restated the analogy of the psychoanalytic process to the process of normal growth and development and to the educational role of good parents: "We have become increasingly aware of the fact that this [psychoanalytic] process, although on quite a novel level of operation and organization, repeats and reveals essential features of the formative stages of psychic development" (61). He went on,

> I do not labor under the illusion that a therapeutic analysis consists, or could consist, only of strictly psychoanalytic procedures and interventions. This is decidedly not the case. An actual analysis, as an undertaking extending over a number of years, contains, apart from the attempts to enforce the rules of the procedure, many elements which in themselves are not psychoanalytic, but which are intended to underline, bring back to mind, and promote the specific task of analysis or to prevent the patient from engaging in activities that interfere with the analysis or from self-destructive moves in his life. The less mature the patient is, the more are such interventions at times necessary. While ideally and ultimately such moves are to be understood as resistances and analyzed, these and other types of resistance, especially during earlier phases of analysis, often cannot

be dealt with analytically. . . . We would go along with this as long as it serves the analysis. We utilize this lever . . . by not analyzing such "transference love" prematurely and by relying on it in our educative interventions. These often are similar to educative measures employed by sensible and affectionate parents. (64)

Here, much more explicitly than in his 1960 paper, Loewald called some of the interventions designed to promote the unfolding of "integrative experiences" in themselves *not* psychoanalytic, albeit essential to the facilitation of the analytic process, and therefore decidedly not anti-analytic. In declaring such interventions educative or growth-promoting and in pointing to their kinship to the ministrations of the good parent, is he more clearly indicating his closeness to Stone's formulations?

In 1979, Loewald added a strong caution against taking these analogies too literally or too far. First, on the kinds of intervention he had in mind:

A therapeutic analysis, as a treatment process extending over a long period of time, is a blend consisting, even in the hands of the most purist analyst, not only of verbal interpretations . . . in terms of transference and resistance. . . . Clarifications and confrontations are used, historical discrepancies are pointed out, comments and interpretations are made that are not or only indirectly related to the analytic transference itself. Tact, basic rapport and its fluctuations, the analyst's breadth of life experience and imagination, the manner in which intercurrent events in the patient's life, incidents before, during, and after the analytic hour, are handled—all these and other factors are significant ingredients of the therapeutic action. They constitute the actual medium without which the most correct interpretations are likely to remain unconvincing and ineffective. So-called educational measures, at times encouragement and reassurance, are used. If used judiciously, they often make possible and enhance the more strictly psychoanalytic interventions, and this not only in the initial phases of an analysis. Psychoanalysis . . . in actual practice makes use, if sparingly, of therapeutic measures that are in themselves not analytic, while inspired and guided constantly by the model of the psychoanalytic method. A clinical analysis and the nature of its therapeutic action are more complex, more lifelike than any theory or model. Attempts at conceptualizing the therapeutic action always will stress certain aspects at the expense of others. (158)

At the same time, Loewald asserted a strong caveat regarding the misunderstandings that could arise "when the analytic situation is compared with the early parent-child dyadic relationship, as illuminating as this comparison is in many respects. When all is said and done, the widening scope of analysis notwithstanding, the analytic situation, in contradistinction to other, often related psychotherapeutic settings, presupposes or is encompassed in an adult overall setting—at least as far as work with adults is concerned. . . . The analysis of adults, no matter how much given to regression or immature they are in significant areas of their functioning, is a venture in which the analysand not only is in fact, chronologically, a grownup, but which makes sense only if his or her adult potential, as manifested in certain significant areas of life, is in evidence (163–64).[4]

In his most recent (1988) comments on these issues, Loewald reasserted once again his vision of the analyst as parent/educator and pointedly dissented from Gitelson's (1962) view that such an approach should be limited to the opening phase of analysis: "Psychotherapists, if they are worth their salt, have certain characteristics in common with professions of a different cast, with priests, rabbis, ministers, the old-fashioned doctor, who at their best function also as significant models of steady convictions, whatever their content, and of compassionate concern and dedication. Therapists blend in with aspects of the conduct of a good parent, teacher, educator, or lover. . . . The patient's placing the therapist in some such position is not simply a matter of 'transference' to be 'resolved' but of deeply felt needs and hopes for loving guidance, which in a good treatment situation may be met by means and in ways the patient had not known or anticipated." To Loewald, it was clear that "such irrational meanings of psychotherapy play a significant part in the totality of therapeutic action modes. Ignoring them does not make psychotherapy any more rational; it only con-

4. Mayes and Spence (1994) in a current article that draws upon the findings of developmental research underline strongly this caution about using the "developmental metaphor" too literally, since it "can all too often evoke a false sense of exactly how therapeutic change takes place" (793). After strongly *contrasting* the analytic situation conducted almost exclusively in the auditory sphere with the multimodal richness of the mother-infant interactions (visual, tactile, etc. as well as auditory), they point to the limitations of the developmental metaphor, especially with the sicker patients with whom it is so often invoked: "In the early phase of treatment with the patient who is deprived of the necessary internal structures and is therefore unable to 'fill in' the missing information when faced only with auditory cues, it would seem as if the analyst is handicapped by the fact that language is his only means of influencing the patient. He has no ready equivalent for such indicators as eye contact, facial expression, body language, touching, and all the other means by which mothers influence their offspring and upon which functions such as contingency and social referencing are based. For these patients, the classic analytic situation is quite different from the early relationship between parent and infant in its very absence of visual cues and for some patients this is experienced as a confusing and marked deprivation" (808).

demns these elements to remain hidden, repressed, without depriving them of their power" (55–56). To make his point most emphatically, Loewald stated his difference with Gitelson: "I believe that the diatrophic therapeutic attitude and activity he so tellingly describes does not apply only to the first phase of analysis but remains instrumental throughout the whole process, pervades the total course—granted that it needs to be less and less explicit when basic rapport is established. Spelling out these factors does not mean that they are the whole story even in the beginning of treatment. If one asks how treatment helps, one must nevertheless recognize that they are indispensable elements" (58).

As Loewald's views have become more widely accepted, they have evoked an array of commentaries, almost all favorable, seeking to fix his increasingly acknowledged position in the evolution, or rather the transformation, of (American) ego-psychology into what is currently designated the post-ego-psychology era. Friedman's article (1978) was a comprehensive overview of evolving trends in the psychoanalytic theory of treatment. The two major turning points he marked were the Marienbad Symposium in 1936 on the "Theory of Therapeutic Results in Psychoanalysis" (1937), with contributions by Glover, Fenichel, Strachey, Bergler, Nunberg, and Bibring, and the Edinburgh Symposium in 1961 on "The Curative Factors in Psycho-Analysis," with contributions by Gitelson, Nacht, and Segal. Friedman properly singled out Gitelson's 1962 paper on the diatrophic-anaclitic relationship as having initiated the modern emphasis on the therapeutic force of relationship factors in the psychoanalytic situation. But, Friedman said, "the Edinburgh Conference took a dim view of Gitelson's project" (540); he had "disturbed the conference by treating attachment factors as curative. . . . Gitelson implied that valid understanding is built into these affective factors" (538).

Friedman credited Loewald (1960) and Stone (1961) with bringing these concepts within the accepted conventions of the American ego-psychological mainstream. Loewald, Friedman said, "traces the origin of the [patient's] identification to earliest relationships and thus relates attachment and understanding. He suggests that the patient's work in translating between his experience and the analyst's more integrated perception is itself internalized and serves as a model to bridge the gap from unconscious to preconscious." In other words, Loewald has finally implicated the central importance of the analytic relationship ("attachment"), along with insight ("understanding"), in explaining therapeutic change—the culmination and vindication of a line of thinking that had originated in Ferenczi's restless struggles to increase his understanding and mastery of the therapeutic change process. Friedman accorded equal importance to Stone for establishing the modern-day legitimation of this focus, calling attention to

Stone's description of "a 'primal transference' to the omnipotent parent as a useful and appropriate vehicle for analytic work. He regards transference as a quest for the original maternal object who both nurtured the child and fostered independence. . . . And Stone feels that it is beneficial to the analysis that these affective structures envelop the analyst, because the patient's structures correspond to what the analyst actually offers as a physician" (544).

A. Cooper's (1988) article was a comparison of the views of Strachey (1934) and Loewald (1960) on the theory of technique, based on the decisive, almost mutative, impact each had on the psychoanalytic thinking of its time. Cooper adumbrated what he regarded as the central conceptions in Loewald's 1960 paper: (1) the centrality of interactional processes in every aspect of human existence; (2) the constitutive nature of object relations, viewed as internalizations of interactional processes between individuals and their significant human objects—with this relatedness being the psychic matrix out of which id and ego, inner and outer reality, differentiate; (3) the real environment as a vital ingredient in the development of mental health; (4) structure-building through increasingly complex interactions on developmentally more advanced levels; and (5) psychoanalysis as the therapeutic road to the resumption of the normal developmental process (22–23). Cooper summarized this aphoristically by stating that in Loewald's hands the benignly neutral analytic mirror had become interactive (20) and that Loewald had in effect used "new ideas of interpersonal interaction and communication as his inspiration for a new description of the method of analytic therapy" (19). Further, "This different concept of motivation, having interaction of subject and object as the creator of motivational processes, and assuming a basically adaptive and cooperative, rather than intrinsically antagonistic, relationship of infant and environment is key to understanding Loewald's view of therapeutic action" (21).

In effect, Cooper hailed Loewald as the "revolutionary" agent who succeeded—quietly and without stirring angry opposition—in transforming the generally accepted theory of technique, based on the primacy of interpretation leading to insight, into the current wide acceptance of the coequal status of the affectively loaded interactive psychoanalytic relationship in bringing about change: "Hans Loewald is one of those rare figures in psychoanalysis who have managed to be intellectual revolutionaries with none of the trappings that usually accompany a revolution. . . . It is likely that his conservative style of revolution has disguised the full depth of his disagreements with traditional analysis" (15).

Fogel (1989), in his overview of Loewald's work, took a similar stance. He too listed what he saw as Loewald's basic contributions to the generally accepted theory of technique:

1. That "internalization is the organizing activity that is the very essence of, that defines and constructs, the human mind"; that it is "a growth principle, an inherent developmental tendency" and is "the integrative experience longed for"
2. That "the mind contains no static entities, no reified structures . . . [and] is always dynamic, always process"
3. That everything mental "takes place in a context, within a 'force field' *codetermined,* fatefully, by human objects"
4. That everything, "the therapeutic relationship, the therapeutic process, insight and change, the normal mind, human development and human individuation," is isomorphic
5. that "psychic reality . . . has inherent values, is not morally neutral. This goes beyond superego morality. It is rather an extension of the potential inherent tendencies for self-reflection, personal responsibility, and integration" (428–32).

(This listing, though couched in somewhat different language and with somewhat different emphases than Cooper's, substantially overlaps it.) To Fogel, the core concept advocated by Loewald in regard to analytic technique was of "the analyst as a new object; this is the *first so-called classical paper* to place interaction with the analyst and resumption of ego development at the center of the therapeutic process" (424, italics added).

But although Loewald has transformed central conceptions of the nature of the therapeutic process, he has never abandoned them. For example, Fogel wrote, "The transference neurosis remains his central process concept. Loewald does not replace it with his new emphasis on object relations and intersubjective phenomena. Far from abandoning it, he gives it new life, as an intrapsychic event that takes place inevitably—developmentally and analytically—in an interpersonal and intersubjective field. The term is transformed and enriched by the new and the old. His metaphor resonates in both the intrapsychic and the interpersonal realms while his theoretical range helps us separate these realms where it is important and possible to do so" (444). All this led Fogel ineluctably to the same overall judgment as Cooper's: "I will argue that he [Loewald] is both revisionist and traditionalist, . . . that he creates a theory that is at once new and old" (420). Fogel stopped short of calling Loewald revolutionary, although he did speculate about some early influences in Loewald's work: "Undoubtedly, Loewald derived some of . . . his interpersonal sensibilities from his exposure to Sullivan and Fromm-Reichmann during the years of his analytic training in Baltimore in the 'forties. . . . Despite their clinical and therapeutic richness, however, these interpersonal schools virtually exclude any intrapsychic emphasis, and perhaps this accounts for the lack of their tangible presence in Loewald's writings and possible lack of usefulness to him in his theory building" (424).

Before closing this chapter, I would like to briefly bring the contributions of Modell, the American carrier of Winnicott's views, into conjunction with this focus on the affective analyst-patient relationship as a vital explanatory factor in therapeutic change. For Modell has served as the conceptual bridge between the relationship focus, articulated in America so centrally by Stone and Loewald, and the comparable focus on the analyst-patient relationship as a central explanatory vehicle of therapeutic change articulated by the British object-relational school, especially by Winnicott (and by Balint). In his 1976 paper, Modell discussed the psychoanalytic relationship as the reactivation (or more conservatively, the contemporary therapeutic analogue) of the "idealized maternal holding environment": "There are actual elements in the analyst's technique that are reminiscent of an idealized maternal holding environment, and these can be enumerated: the analyst is constant and reliable; he responds to the patient's affects; he accepts the patient, and his judgment is less critical and more benign; he is there primarily for the patient's needs and not for his own; he does not retaliate; and he does at times have a better grasp of the patient's inner psychic reality than does the patient himself and therefore may clarify what is bewildering and confusing." This was all put under the heading "The Holding Environment and the Analytic Setting as an *Object Relationship*" (291, italics added).

A recent commentary on Modell's place in this scheme of things is Kenneth Newman's (1991) review of Modell's most recent (1990) book. Modell, Newman stated, "brings all of his previous efforts together to attempt his most comprehensive examination of the role of analytic setting and relationship in the curative process" (739). From his very sympathetic overview of Modell's contributions, I just cite two statements bearing on the centrality of the therapeutic relationship to the mutative process. First, "Among the major questions arising from positioning the setting and the relationship as central in the therapeutic action is whether the 'real bond' that exists between analyst and analysand is identical [to] or different from that experienced in other relationships. This question, in turn, activates a series of ambiguities which involve shifting levels of reality as well as the interplay between time past and present" (740). And "It is the interaction of the past with current reality—including 'real failures' in the current situation—which gives rise to the transference . . . [which in turn inevitably arouses the affect-laden countertransference and] the ability to manage these powerful countertransference states is a vital part of the holding environment and is, possibly, the core of the mutative action required to alter and disconfirm the toxic introjects. . . . his point that ultimately the crucial capacity of the analyst to survive inevitable countertransference feelings is the usable 'holding' environment" (741)—a perspective on Modell that is consistent with the position of Stone and Loewald on the power of the relationship and of its management (only in part by direct interpretation) in effecting psychoanalytic change.

17 The Psychoanalytic Relationship and the Role of New Experience: The Past Decade

In his contribution to the 1979 Atlanta Symposium, Gill (1984a) offered what he felt was the accepted view of the factors leading to therapeutic change: *"persisting transference effects, new experience and insight. . . . They all play a role in both psychotherapy and psychoanalysis.* But psychoanalytic technique aims towards as complete an exposure of the transference as possible while the new experience is not deliberately engaged in as such but is an inherent accompaniment of the treatment as a whole and particularly of the technique of analyzing the transference. In prevailing practice inadvertent transference effects are inadequately recognized and dealt with while in prevailing theory the role of new experience in bringing about change is understated" (171–72, italics added). In a somewhat more conservative vein, Valenstein (1983) wrote, "Insight remains the paramount aim of analysis in the classical tradition, notwithstanding that current shift in practice which assigns therapeutic priority to the experiential recapitulation in the transference of early object relations, with an emphasis on attachment to early objects and separation from them, and their further vicissitudes and normative significance for the emergent sense of self. However, if insight is not enough, if insight *in itself* does not quite do it, does not lead to definitive change, then we must consider other factors" (354).

Valenstein went on to state these other factors: "I [have] felt that affect and experience in the form of emotional reliving were possibly understated in the theory of psychoanalytic therapy, and in those descriptions and advices which, insofar as they have suggested the ritualization of technique, gave a warped picture of the psychoanalytic situation and process" (354). He stated this even more strongly further on: "At least through the initial and middle phases of treatment, the more interactive and experiential therapeutic features *of necessity* assume a temporal hierarchical priority over cognitive aspects, over the explanatory content of interpretive interventions" (362, italics added).

Valenstein then distinguished psychoanalytic work with individuals suffering from what he called "structural neuroses (formerly termed 'transference neuroses')"—that is, the classically neurotic—and work with individuals suffering from what he called "developmental neuroses"—that is, the sicker patients, the preoedipally disordered, the narcissistic, and the borderline. "Both in practice and in the theory of psychotherapies," he wrote, "I favor the making of a distinction . . . between psychoanalysis as such, in the classical or standard sense, where insight and change through insight are the paramount goal, and the widened scope, widened variety of psychoanalytic psychotherapies which are predominantly interpersonal and mutually experiential in their intention and therapeutic effect. Not that the latter are second best (the copper rather than the pure gold of analysis [Freud, 1919]); indeed they may require just as much or more of the therapist in intuitively perceptive improvisation than analysis, but they are not paramountly insight-oriented, and perforce are more appropriate to different clinical circumstances and a different sector of conditions" (363). That is, for the classically neurotic patient, Valenstein was still adhering to the classical conception of the primacy of interpretation and insight as change factors in analytic therapy, while for the widening scope or sicker patients, those anyway treated more "psychotherapeutically," he accorded at least equal valence to affect and experiential reliving within the therapeutic relationship.

These quotations I think state clearly both the *degree of change* in the (American) psychoanalytic conceptualization of the mutative forces in analytic therapy as a consequence of the emphases on the therapeutic and working alliances and on the related concepts of the role of the psychoanalytic relationship and of new experiences within it; and also the varying *degrees of acceptance* of these changed perspectives within the psychoanalytic community—that is, the wholehearted acceptance of Gill and the far more qualified acceptance of Valenstein. Most contemporary psychoanalysts would align themselves with at least one of these statements. Since they were written, there has been a consolidation of this (varying) degree of acceptance into a virtual consensus, and some recent contributions have widened still further the arc of distinguishable and relevant relationship factors.

In *How Does Treatment Help? On the Modes of Therapeutic Action of Psychoanalytic Psychotherapy* (Rothstein 1988)—in which, incidentally, very few of the authors differentiated psychoanalysis proper from psychoanalytic psychotherapy—at least three chapters in addition to those by Loewald, Modell, and Werman, already cited, dealt centrally with the role of relationship factors in the change process. Jacobs focused on the analyst-patient relationship as a "corrective influence" and asserted that "in psychoanalysis, as in other forms of therapy, the corrective influences that one personality exerts upon another are an *integral part* of the healing process"—adding that it was because of the need to separate psychoanalysis as completely as possible from suggestion and hypnosis that this fact was so long denied. Jacobs went on, "The result, I believe, was an overidealization and reification of insight as the primary, if not the sole, curative factor" (64). One of the "noteworthy contributions of object relations theory," he said, was that "it has put the *relationship of psychoanalysis* on a more *scientific footing*. One can speak of a holding environment, of the analyst's role in containing and metabolizing certain affects and projections emanating from the patient, of opportunities for the resumption of development with a new object, of transmuting internalizations and of the therapeutic potential of the analyst's countertransference responses without inevitably being regarded (and regarding oneself) as an *ersatz analyst* or a *supportive psychotherapist* masquerading as the genuine article." He continued, "We would be naive . . . not to recognize the power of the supportive aspects of analysis" (65, italics added) and then listed some of these in by-now-familiar terms.

Last, Jacobs underlined the basic continuity in purpose, spirit, and *technique* of psychoanalysis and the psychotherapy that not infrequently follows it:

> Psychotherapy following analysis [after an interval, and with the same analyst] is not a subject much discussed, but it deserves some attention as a rather special situation. In most patients I have worked with in this way following analysis, the therapy is carried on essentially as a less frequent and less intense analysis, but as an analysis all the same. The patient draws on his former experience to help sustain the continuity. Transference feelings and resistances quickly arise and can be worked with in ways not much different from what occurs in a formal analysis. While in some respects the work is slower, it may also benefit from the patient's strong motivation to gain what he can from the more limited treatment. Also, factors of age and a more advanced stage of life, with a strong wish to solve certain pressing life problems, may enhance motivation. (78)

Here, at least in these special circumstances, Jacobs has moved close to Gill's view on the continuities of psychoanalysis proper and analytic therapies. This point of view is especially congenial to those who emphasize the salience of relationship factors to the analytic process (though of course not limited to them).

Edgar Levenson's (1988) contribution to the Rothstein volume was from the perspective of a contemporary exponent of the Sullivanian school of interpersonal psychiatry—the once-dissident group in American psychoanalysis that focused from its beginnings (in the 1930s and 1940s) on mental disorder and its treatment as fundamentally interpersonal processes. In keeping with this perspective, Levenson wrote that the medium (the relationship) *is* the message (the interpreted content): "It is not an issue of 'insight versus relationship,' but rather the isomorphism, the similarity of form, between the two that defines psychoanalysis and distinguishes it from other psychotherapies . . . it is *recursive,* isomorphic patterning of analytic content and transferential relationship that makes psychoanalysis work" (137); and "Perhaps the genuine therapeutic effect is neither insight into his [the patient's] dynamics alone, nor awareness of experience with the therapist, but the striking recursion of theme in both parameters; that what we are talking about is simultaneously happening between us" (139). This seems to me an effort to say something more than that the transference experience, the impinging present, and the reawakened past active at any moment are alternative expressions of the same themes. It is, rather, an effort to say that the experienced analytic relationship is itself the insight we are seeking—not just the partner or co-actor with the achieved insights on the analytic stage. In accord with this view, "the intent of the exchange is not to show him [the patient] that he is distorting the relationship with the therapist or, conversely, that he is really accurate. Rather . . . [it is] elucidating a recursive pattern of experience" (140).

Pine (1988a) discusses the therapeutic relationship as a major change agent in analytic treatment within the frame of his conceptualization of psychoanalysis as comprising four basic "psychologies"—those of drive, of ego, of object, and of self, each a relevant perspective upon the analytic material, and any of them, at any given point, the most salient focus for the analytic work. The theoretical conceptualization of these four psychologies and their clinical application are elaborated in Pine's book *Drive, Ego, Object, and Self* (1990). In his article for the Rothstein volume, Pine related these four perspectives specifically to the issue of interpretation vis-à-vis the relationship. He accorded interpretation in its traditional sense a greater role in regard to the elucidation of drive pressures and of object relationships. In relation to the psychology of ego function, especially in areas of so-called ego defect, and in relation to deficiencies in the self experience, he felt that traditional interpretation was less effective (more resisted) and that though "verbalization has a significant mutative potential . . . it is verbalization more in the form of description, explanation, and reconstruction—especially if voiced in a 'holding' tone" (151).

Pine then counterposed the role(s) of the relationship in the mutative process in terms of the four psychologies: (1) from the standpoint of the psychology of drive he spoke of the absence of condemnation or judgment that can gradually lead to a modification of conscience (as Strachey [1934] had long before pointed out) and of the fact that the analyst survives and does not retaliate with rage or rejection; (2) from the standpoint of the psychology of object relations, a new, "corrective" relationship is provided with the possibility for new integrative experiences (Loewald's conception of 1960); (3) from the standpoint of the psychology of the self, experiences of mirroring and idealizing are provided and/or allowed (Kohut's formulations of 1971, 1977, and 1984); and (4) from the standpoint of the psychology of the ego, Pine again drew on Loewald (1960) and the reaching of higher levels of ego organization via the new integrative experiences (152–55). (It is clear here how Pine has tried to synthesize the perspectives of various theorists concerning the analytic relationship into a more comprehensive composite.)

Like Loewald (1960), Stone (1961), and others, Pine emphasized that these relational effects for the most part do not require specific or formal interventions but "are largely inherent in the process. . . . They simply happen between people and, in analysis, they happen in ways that are functional (and malfunctional) in multiple ways for the patient. As the malfunctional, the pathological, uses of the relationship that the patient makes are pared away by interpretation, more functional aspects of the relationship remain, often not noticed because they are conflict-free and not verbalized. In summary, I have suggested that, in the context of an intense and intimate relationship where things matter for the patient, both interpretation (and other verbal interventions) and relational factors have important mutative effects" (155). (In another article published in the same year, Pine [1988b] expanded on these notions, again emphasizing the efficacy of "traditional" interpretations in relation to issues of drive, and of object relations, and different kinds of verbal interventions more in the form of "description, explanation, and reconstruction" [586] in relation to issues of [defective] ego and of impaired self-esteem, and emphasizing as well the relational aspects of the therapeutic encounter in their mutative function.)

In an earlier (1984) article, Pine said, "A patient may 'hear' an interpretation . . . as a gratification or deprivation (from the standpoint of drive); as a condemnation or permission (from the standpoint of conscience); as an access to a new view of reality or as a stimulus to cling to one's old defenses (from the standpoint of adaptation); as a repeated or a reparative object-relation experience (from the standpoint of internalized object relationships); and as a humiliation or a sign of special attention (from the standpoint of self-esteem)" (57).

In a 1993 article, Pine brought relational factors and interpretation together as "inseparably intertwined" (195) aspects of proper psychoanalytic process: "These relationship factors are . . . universal, not idiosyncratic parts of a psychoanalysis, and my aim in connection with them will be to highlight their role in the change process and to contrast them to idiosyncratic, nonspecific, and iatrogenic relational characteristics" (188). Pine placed the origin of this conception in Strachey's 1934 article: "It is the co-occurrence of the cognitive clarification with an *experience* in the analyst-patient relationship—the actualized contrast of the patient's fantasy and the analyst's noncondemning stance—that produces the maximum therapeutic effect. . . . In the moment of which Strachey writes, the interpretive factor and the relationship factor are inseparably linked. And each requires the other. The interpretation can have its maximum effect because the relationship (noncondemning) belies the patient's inner world" (192). And again, "The two are inseparably intertwined, interpretation able to be effective because of the context of safety, and the context of safety mattering especially in the moment of anxiety" (195). Pine summed this up as follows: "Certain specific relational factors of the psychoanalytic situation have an essential and general role to play in relation to interpretation. By contradicting the patient's wish, fantasy, or expectation at the moment of interpretation . . . they add a direct experiential impact to the already affectively laden cognitive impact of interpretation. And by producing a reliable context of safety, they permit the patient, at the moment of destabilization (Arlow and Brenner [chapter 22]) or mini–disintegration (Loewald [chapter 16]), to reintegrate in progressive ways" (196).

Another cluster of three articles worthy of mention appeared in 1989. N. Gregory Hamilton's article was addressed to a psychoanalytically informed general psychiatric audience. The author declared, "The object relations emphasis on external as well as internal relationships has contributed to our understanding of the importance of providing a holding environment, containment, empathic attunement, and sustaining relatedness in therapy. These relationship aspects of psychotherapy have been reintegrated with the technical aspects of treatment, largely *overcoming the previous polarization* between corrective emotional experience and interpretation as the legitimate agents of change" (1557, italics added)—a synthesis perhaps somewhat prematurely proclaimed.

Rangell (1989) sought to simplify the terms of the dialectic between interpretation and relationship by trying to collapse the various ways in which different theorists have described relationship factors into alternative synonyms for familiar concepts:

> Whether the therapeutic alliance as described in its maternal, caring aspects by Zetzel (1956), the primary transference of Greenacre (1954), the basic trust of Erikson (1950), the positive transference of Freud (1912a), the diatrophic relationship of Spitz (1956), the anaclitic relation felt necessary by Gitelson (1962), the holding environment of Winnicott (1958, 1965), the real relationship of Greenson and Wexler (1969) or the listening with empathic immersion described by Kohut (1971, 1977) and the followers of self psychology, all of these fall under the rubric of the *necessary empathy* and *basic humanity* of personal relationships which cannot be excluded from the analytic bond without harsh consequences and self-defeating results. (56, italics added)

Whether Rangell served the field well in drawing attention to the common elements of empathy and basic humanity in these various efforts to conceptualize the nature and effect of the therapeutic relationship, and in then reducing them to nothing but that, is, of course, an arguable matter.

Rangell then did the same with descriptions of another aspect of the analyst-patient relationship, which, he proclaimed, "is what makes the emergence of transference phenomena possible. These are the ego alliance of Sterba (1934), the equidistant stance described by Anna Freud (1936), the rational transference of Fenichel (1941a), the mature transference of Stone (1961), the basic transference of Bibring (1954), the therapeutic alliance in its more analytic sense described by Zetzel (1956), the working alliance of Greenson (1972), all of which I feel are best subsumed under the *analytic alliance* between patient and analyst" (56, italics added). Whereas the first list named empathy and humanity as the analytic attitude embodied by the analyst, Rangell here grouped another array of concepts as a therapeutic (or, in his words, "analytic") alliance without making clear the basis for these separate categories of assignment, which, to me at least, are not self-evident. What does emerge from this attempt is just how diverse the domain of conceptualizations of the therapeutic relationship has become.

A. Cooper (1989) essayed a more ambitious overview of the history of alliance and relationship conceptions, giving greater attention to the positions of the British object-relational school and of Loewald and Kohut. The object-relational perspective he presented as follows:

In order to achieve a change in inner attitudes towards aspects of oneself or one's desires there has to be a change in mental representations of self and object, and in the mental representation of the affective relationship between self and objects. These changes in mental representations were brought about by the special characteristics of patient and analyst in the analytic situation. These special characteristics included the analyst's steadfast interest in the patient, his benign neutrality, his capacity to forgo expected retaliations, his ability to maintain his integrity despite attacks or seductions from the patient, and his consistent and persistent curiosity about and attempt to interpret the meanings of the patient's neurotic behaviors, both outside the treatment and in the transference. But perhaps most important, through these means he provides the patient with the experience of living in a different kind of emotional and relational "space"; a "holding" or "facilitating" environment, newly safe and potentially comforting. The analyst, in fact, provides a new emotional experience with another human being, different in essence from the traumatic relationships that were developmentally and genetically at the core of the developing psychopathology. It is of prime significance that the analytic situation is not only a new relational affective experience, but that the transferential meaning of the patient's response to this encounter is constantly being interpreted. (12)

He described Loewald's quite similar position more succinctly: "Loewald, dedicated to an interactional, object-relational view of the psyche for understanding both development and current psychic functioning, thought that the therapeutic action of analysis depends upon the new experience with the analyst that induces a resumption of development by permitting transference regression, and by providing the patient with a new opportunity for the experience of appropriate parenting. This appropriate parenting includes the therapist's modeling or communicating to the patient, though not in so many words, the therapist's sense of the patient as an integrated human being with a past and an expected future. Loewald emphasized the humanity of the analyst and the humanistic terms of the transaction between analyst and patient" (14).

Cooper then set Kohut's central contribution (see chapter 20) within this same framework: "He [Kohut] said 'psychoanalysis cures by the laying down of psychic structure. And how does this accretion of psychological structure take place? The most general self psychological answer to this second question is also simple: psychological structure is laid down (a) via optimal frustration and (b) in consequence of optimal frustration, via transmuting internalization.' He says, 'a good analysis, we believe, leads to a cure only by employment in countless repetitions, of the basic therapeutic unit of understanding and explaining, that is, the interpretations, the analyst's only active function in the analytic process' " (17).

Citing an overall perspective with which he seemed clearly to identify, Cooper wrote,

> Michels (1986) has described that change is usually attributed to one of three elements—insight, intensity of emotional experience, or a new relationship. Those who emphasize insight stress the centrality of interpretation. . . . the analytic situation provides a setting of safety and regression in which interpretations can be made and tolerated. Those emphasizing the intensity of experience believe that psychological change is a crisis event occurring when rigidly established psychic structures are shaken by powerful affects, particularly those aroused in the here-and-now of the transference. . . . From this viewpoint the crucial points of the therapy will be those severe affective ordeals, often referred to as the transference neurosis, that promote regression and subsequent new growth. Analysts believing in the crucial nature of the relationship stress the new experience that the patient has in the analytic relationship. . . . All of these emphases—insight, affect, relationship—are compatible with each other and with a variety of theoretical points of view concerning the nature of change. (20)

Three current contributions attempt to bring all these issues to new conceptual ground or to significantly revise older conventional conceptual ground. Milton Viederman (1991) made an effort to revise long-standing notions about the meaning of traditional analytic conceptions of abstinence, anonymity, and neutrality, conceptual revisions that have been tacit in all the literature on the analytic alliance and the analytic relationship. Within the context of warmth, encouragement, and what he called "the wishful good-parent transference" (476), Viederman argued, "I contend that in many situations . . . a climate of warmth that the patient experiences as supportive offers the possibility of an easier examination of issues . . . and in itself does not prevent the development of angry negative transferences that require analysis" (453); And "The analyst's particular stance in relating the change encourages the patient to overcome inhibitions and to confront the world in a new way. This encouragement may involve suggestion as the analyst questions inhibitions with implicit valuation and support for new behaviors" (454). This is all carried out via "the unconscious desire to find the wished-for ideal parent who eluded them in childhood. . . . a background and a facilitator of the analytic process. I separate this transference phenomenon from ordinary transference that involves the reenactment of experienced old self- and object constellations, the everyday substance of psychoanalytic process" (476). This special, separate transference phenomenon is "analogous to good parenting. I would add that this is generated not only by the interpretive stance of the analyst, but that it represents the coming together of the patient's wish and the real behavior of the analyst as a benevolent and growth-promoting figure in the analytic situation, and as such represents the analytic response to developmental failure" (477).

All this is described as "a background phenomenon that operates unconsciously and, although it involves some gratification, is a support for the analysis, ultimately to be analyzed . . . this is quite distinct from the immediate clamor and demand for gratification implicit in the everyday behavior of the analytic patient as manifested in usual transference. It is important to distinguish between an ideal transference (the wished-for good parent) and an idealized one rooted in defense and conflict, subject to ongoing interpretation or awareness by the patient as the analysis proceeds" (477). The object of all this is evident: "to place the *real person* of the analyst at center-stage as it relates to the curative process of psychoanalysis" (487, italics added). This was followed by the perhaps obligatory disclaimer: "It is not my intent to espouse wild analysis, to propose that analysis is a cure by love, or to view it as a manipulative process designed by the analyst to change the patient's behavior. However, one must take seriously the powerful effect of the real person of the analyst, the intensity of his emotional involvement with the patient over many years, the special qualities that inevitably evolve in each individual analytic situation, and the use of noninterpretive interventions" (487).

Viederman began his reassessment of our conceptions of analytic abstinence, anonymity, and neutrality with Freud: "Freud's (1912b) surgical metaphor coupled with the notions of neutrality, anonymity, and abstinence to create a field for transference in which conflict is played out and interpreted has clarity, conceptual elegance, and a purity that identifies its origins in nineteenth-century positivism" (458–59). He added that any "emphasis on the personal element in the analytic process threatens to blur the boundary between psychoanalysis and psychotherapy. Psychoanalysts therefore have been hesitant to recognize the importance of personal influence lest it cloud the definition of transference, countertransference, resistance, defense, interpretation" (459). But this hesitation should be discarded, and with it traditional conceptions of abstinence, anonymity, and neutrality. After citing Gill's (1982) newer views, Viederman added, "I would go further [than Gill] in suggesting that in a properly conducted analysis, strict abstinence and anonymity as a goal do not adequately describe the most effective analytic stance.[1] As a model of analytic behavior, it constricts

1. Gill's revisionist views on the concepts of abstinence and anonymity were laid out most systematically in his 1982 monograph *Analysis of Transference*, as an inherent consequence of his revised conceptions of the nature of transference as an interpersonal reflection of a "two-body psychology" (see especially 87–88). In my discussion of Gill's views on the analysis of transference (Wallerstein 1984), I summarized his position as follows: "The analytic transference . . . is not a one-way street. It is rather an interactional effect unavoidably arising within the analytic situation, in significant part out of the real impact of that situation upon the patient and the reality cues that the situation (and the analyst's conduct within it) make available as rationale for the transference responses. . . .

"Therefore, complete anonymity and total abstinence become impossible analytic ideals, leading only to withdrawn or silent analysts who do not see that behavior in itself as an analytic message that the patient interprets in accord with his predispositions. . . . In fact, the analyst simply cannot avoid inadvertent effects on the patient's experience of the relationship and it is part of proper analytic neutrality to include 'persistent attention to the inadvertent effects of the therapeutic setting on the patient's experience of the relationship' " (335–36).

The counterposed view, which seeks to maintain a more traditional conception of the role of abstinence in psychoanalysis within a classical ego-psychological position, while at the same time acknowledging the altered modern-day conceptions of the importance of the analytic relationship, has been articulated by Dewald (1992), who has stated, "Abstinence by the analyst is not synonymous with stiffness, rigidity, emotional coldness, or punitiveness toward the patient nor . . . with long periods of silence or inactivity by the analyst. It relates instead to an attitude of curiosity about motivations and meanings, a recognition of the multidetermined nature of human behavior, acceptance of the concept of all behavior (whether 'normal' or 'neurotic') as representing a compromise formation of conflicting tendencies, and a willingness to place the overall goals of analysis ahead of immediate relief or reduction of distress. The most effective way of maintaining abstinence is through appropriately conveyed interpretation

the analyst in such a way as to encourage formality and rigidity in his work" (464). Viederman went on to discuss the facts of a more appropriately modified analytic stance and ambience.[2]

The contributions by Petruska Clarkson (1990), from Great Britain, and by a trio from Holland (Frans de Jonghe, Piet Rijnierse, and Rob Janssen 1991, 1992) tried to lay out a comprehensive typology of therapeutic relationships based on the totality of the world literature on the subject to that point. Clarkson's grouping was fivefold. The first was the working alliance in terms of Greenson's conception, which Clarkson considered akin to a relationship with family, though not parents or children: "In kinship terms the relationship of working together can be likened to that between cousins (or uncle, aunt, niece, nephew). . . . The notion is meant to convey a metaphoric distance from the family of origin (different parents) but kindred loyalties to each other's welfare" (151). The second was the transferential-countertransferential relationship in accord with the definition of Jean Laplanche and J-B. Pontalis (1973). This Clarkson analogized to the relationship with a stepparent or godparent, with, of course, both negative and positive transferential images. The third, the "Reparative/Developmentally Needed Relationship," is close to the positions described in this chapter and the preceding one: "This is the intentional provision by the psychotherapist of a corrective/reparative or replenishing relationship (or action) where the original parenting was deficient, abusive or over-protective" (153). Historically, "Sandor Ferenczi . . . attempted this early in the history of psychoanalysis. He departed from neutrality and impassivity in favour of giving nursery care, friendly hugs or management of regression to very sick patients, including one whom he saw any time, day or night, and took with him on holidays. Ferenczi held that there needed to be a contrast between the original trauma in infancy and the analytic situation so that remembering can be facilitated instead of a renewed trauma for the patient." (153) Here, "the metaphoric kinship relationship being established is clearly closer to a real parent-child re-

---

which demonstrates understanding and at the same time shows respect for the patient's conflicts and distress" (156–57). Clearly this is much modified from Eissler's (1953) model of the psychoanalytic process but is also at some remove from the modified conception that derives from the fully interactional and two-body psychology propounded by Gill (1982).

2. For a less revisionist perspective on analytic neutrality, but still mindful of the shifts in analytic perspectives since Freud (1912b) presented the surgical and mirror metaphors, see J. and A-M. Sandler 1992. While more or less upholding the traditional concept of "the neutral stance," they say, for example, "What is grossly countertherapeutic is an attitude of aloofness or detachment on the part of the analyst masquerading as analytic neutrality. This is usually either the analyst's defense against his own anxiety, or an attitude of omnipotence on his part coupled with a belief in the 'magic' of interpretation, or both" (41).

lationship than any of the other forms of bonding in psychotherapy." And "It is certainly true that this depth of long-standing psychotherapeutic relationship as the primary therapeutic relationship modality is more frequently reported between psychotherapists and more severely damaged patients" (154).

The fourth relationship pattern Clarkson described in Martin Buber's terms, the I-You relationship, "the ordinary relationships which human beings have experienced as particularly healing over the ages." "The emotional involvement in this relationship between psychotherapist and patient is that between *person and person* in the existential dilemma where both stand in a kind of mutuality to each other. . . . Genuine well-judged use of the I-You relationship is probably one of the most difficult forms of therapeutic relating. Doubtless this was the very good reason behind the early analysts regarding it with extreme suspicion. Also, of course, it is in the name of the I-You relationship that many personal relationships have been destructive. It probably requires the most skill, the most self-knowledge and the greatest care because its potential for careless or destructive use is so great" (155). It is "characterized by the *here-and-now existential encounter* between the two people. . . . Its field is not object relations but subject relations" (156). In kinship terms this was analogized to the relation between siblings because of "the shared empathetic understanding from a similar inherited frame of reference. Although they are different, they are of more or less equal standing and share the ambiguous and ambivalent legacy of existence" (157).

Fifth, and most difficult to characterize, is what Clarkson called "the Transpersonal or Kinship Relationship": "This refers to the spiritual dimension of relationship in psychotherapy" (158), and Jung is declared to be one of the intellectual forebears. It is analogized in kinship terms to the marital relationship and is "characterized paradoxically by a kind of intimacy and by an 'emptying of the ego' at the same time. . . . The essence of the communication is in the heart of the shared silence of being together in a dimension which is impossible to articulate exactly, too delicate to analyse, and yet too pervasively present in psychotherapy to ignore" (159).

In conclusion, Clarkson stated, "Different psychotherapies stress different relationships for different reasons. It is perhaps time that psychotherapists acknowledged explicitly that these five forms of relationship are intentionally or unintentionally present in most approaches to psychotherapy. How explicitly and purposefully which of these modes of psychotherapeutic relationships are used may be one of the major ways in which some approaches resemble each other more and differ most from other approaches" (160).

By contrast, the typology of relationship patterns advanced by de Jonghe, Rijnierse, and Janssen was more pragmatic and less spiritual/existential. They

listed four fundamental aspects of the analytic relationship: transferential, working, realistic, and primary. In what they called the period of the Classical Approach—from the 1920s to roughly the 1960s, the heyday of American
ego-psychology—only the first three of these were systematically delineated and
explored. First is the transference or oedipal-object (infantile-object) relationship, which the authors defined as follows: "Transference is an actual reaction.
It may be said to be provoked, triggered, elicited or occasioned by the present.
It is, however, rooted in the past. It is a reactivated and intensified past which
is present in actuality" (694); "in adults, it expresses regression from the mature
to the infantile level of functioning, but not full, massive and uncontrolled
regression." Misconceptions about the transference need to be cleared up:
"Transference and countertransference are often called 'unrealistic' and 'irrational', and neither 'real' nor 'actual.' We think there is some confusion here:
transference and countertransference are phenomena occurring in the present
and in that sense they are real (authentic, sincere, not artificial); they may be
triggered by but are not determined by present reality and in that sense they
indeed are unrealistic (one may say 'fantastic'); they are mainly emotional, not
rational phenomena and in that sense they indeed are irrational. All genuine
feelings, thoughts and actions of the patient and the analyst are actual and real
but they are not always realistic or rational" (695).

"The working relationship," the authors continued, "certainly presupposes
an 'object relationship' but not on an 'infantile level.' We therefore consider it
a concept referring to the post-oedipal level of psychic functioning, as the transference concept refers to an oedipal level. . . . The working relationship is often
emphatically said to deal with the rational (i.e., intellectual, cognitive) capacities
of the patient and the analyst. As we see it, this aspect of the analytic relationship
is real and realistic, but certainly not exclusively rational, as emotional aspects
too are an important part of it" (696). Under this rubric, the authors encompassed the ego alliance of Sterba (1934), the rational transference of Fenichel
(1941b), the therapeutic alliance of Zetzel (1956), the mature transference of
Stone (1961), the working alliance of Greenson (1965), the treatment alliance
of Joseph Sandler, Christopher Dare, and Alex Holder (1973), and the helping
alliance type II of Luborsky (1976).

Alongside these two the authors placed the "realistic relationship": the "mature, realistic and healthy aspects of the relationship other than the working
relationship. These aspects relate to the other person in his own right, not as a
parent substitute nor as a working partner" (696). And, "Where the transference
relationship is an here-and-now phenomenon determined by the past, the
working and the realistic relationships are here-and-now phenomena determined by the present" (697). That is, all three are stated to be characterized by

object relatedness—in the case of the transference, to an infantile object, and in the case of the working and the realistic relationships, to a mature object.

This situation is different, however, with the fourth kind of relationship, which came to the fore in what the authors call the current "Post-Classical Period," characterized by the spreading acceptance of the developmental approach (see chapter 18), the object-relational approach (see chapter 19), and self psychology (chapter 20), and with Ferenczi and Balint as precursors. This "primary" relationship is characterized not by object relatedness, as the other three are, but by "narcissistic relatedness" (700):

> The post-classical view emphasizes the critical role of early childhood and the vicissitudes of the early infant-mother relation. . . . It may be seen, not as a psychology of conflict but as a psychology of developmental arrest. . . . It offers, not a neurotic-mind model but an archaic-mind model, which is a model of ego malformation due to developmental arrests. This model stresses the pathogenic role of the "maternal environment" when a lack of parent-infant fit results in a traumatic reality. To some extent it revives Freud's initial trauma theory. As far as the causation of pathology is concerned, it may shift the emphasis from the almost exclusive role of the phallic-oedipal phase (as is contended in the classical view) to the almost exclusive role of the pre-oedipal events. (697)

This fourth fundamental aspect of the analytic relationship "is essentially a recapitulation of the very early relationship between mother and infant, the experience of the undifferentiated self-object representation of the mother-child symbiotic phase and the separation-individuation phase. . . . It is a tie or bond of a pre-oedipal nature, not a relationship between separate individuals" (698–99). Encompassed here are such concepts as the rapport of Freud (1925b) and Glover (1955), the anaclitic relationship of Spitz (1956), the narcissistic alliance of Greenacre (1959), the corrective object relation of Augusta Alpert (1959), the basic transference of Bibring (1954), the basic or primary transference of Greenacre (1954), the primal transference of Stone (1961), the narcissistic tie of Jeanne Lampl-de Groot (1975), the narcissistic transference of Kohut (1971, 1977), the therapeutic alliance of Zetzel (1966), the helping alliance type I of Luborsky (1976), and the dependent-containing transference of Modell (1990).

Putting all these together, the authors declared that "the primary relationship excludes the existence of an object-relationship. We therefore consider the primary relationship a concept referring to the pre-oedipal level of psychic functioning, as the transference relationship refers to the oedipal and as the working and realistic relationships refer to the post-oedipal level" (700). "In the analytic relationship," they went on, "the analyst may loosely be called a 'new' object.

Actually, he is a new pre-object in the primary relationship, a new surrogate infantile object in the transference relationship, and a new mature object in the working and the realistic relationship" (701).

Their final point assessed the therapeutic role and significance of the primary relationship brought to such prominence in this postclassical period: Although "it could be argued that this refers to the therapeutic relationship of psychotherapy, perhaps also to that of modified analysis, but certainly not to that of 'ordinary' psychoanalysis" (703), their contention is exactly the opposite: "Even in ordinary psychoanalysis, with patients with an essentially neurotic structure, the primary relationship plays an important though often underestimated role" (703).[3] In fact, "to us it is beyond dispute that the primary relationship is an important aspect of *any* analytic relationship. We consider it an error to think that the primary relationship is important in some but not all cases of psychoanalysis or in some but not in all phases of an ordinary, unmodified psychoanalysis" (704).

They ended the article on a comparative historical note:

> There seem to be some similarities in the history of the concepts "transference relationship" and "primary relationship." The phenomena concerned were first seen not at all. After their discovery: (a) they were first seen as pathological and only afterwards as normal, natural, inevitable; (b) they were first seen as a hindrance or disturbance of the analytic process and only afterwards as rich in potential for understanding, even as necessary for analysis to proceed, although they may interfere with it when they are inflexible, fixed or unworkable; (c) they were first seen as specific for the analytic relationship and only afterwards as ubiquitous and underpinning every relationship; (d) they were first seen as incidental acute events and only afterwards as chronic, part and parcel of the continuing relation.[4] (704)

3. The authors cite Bibring as an early advocate of their view. Bibring (1937) wrote, "In my opinion the analyst's attitude, and the analytical atmosphere which he creates, are fundamentally a reality-correction which adjusts the patient's anxieties about loss of love and punishment, the origin of which lies in childhood. Even if these anxieties later undergo analytical resolution I still believe that the patient's relationship to the analyst from which a sense of security emanates is not only a pre-condition of the procedure but also effects an immediate (apart from an analytical) consolidation of his sense of identity which he has not successfully acquired or consolidated in childhood" (182–83).

4. Still more recently, Meissner (1992), without reference to the work of either Clarkson or de Jonghe, Rijnierse, and Janssen, revived a threefold differentiation of the analytic relationship— the transference, the alliance, and the real relationship—that had earlier been given some tentative conceptual space in the ego-psychology literature but had never really taken hold.

The following year de Jonghe, Rijnierse, and Janssen (1992) published an article grounded in the same fourfold conceptualization of relationship modes but focused specifically on the role of support in analytic treatments. They stated their thesis as follows: "It is generally agreed that the most important . . . [factor in] the analytic process . . . is the interpretation of the analyst leading to the insight of the patient (the interpretation-insight factor). However, another factor, the analyst's support leading to a specific experience by the patient (the support-experience factor) has long been a controversial issue" (475–76). The support factor, they argued, is equally important (albeit as a silent force usually working unnoticed) in all analytic treatments, not only in modified analysis with sicker patients (and they quoted the findings of the Menninger Psychotherapy Research Project [Wallerstein 1986a] in their support). They then tried to specify what they meant by support: "We do not mean merely ordinary support, but the specific type of psychoanalytic, adequate support which, inspired by Strachey (who would certainly disagree), we would call mutative support." This "external support can either consist of need gratification, thus reducing drive tension, or of defense strengthening, thus enhancing drive control. . . . It may belatedly reactivate arrested development in the deficiently structuralized adult,

---

"Part of the difficulty in these [prior] formulations," he stated, "was that a clear line was not drawn between alliance factors and transference on the one hand, and between alliance and the real relation on the other. . . . The therapeutic relationship actually involves three discriminable components that can be adequately distinguished, but that occur simultaneously and concurrently within the therapeutic relationship. The three components are the therapeutic alliance, the transference, and the real relationship" (1062). Meissner's article is an attempt to delineate these distinctions: "While the distinction between these real aspects of the therapeutic interaction and elements of transference is easily drawn, the related distinction between such real factors and the therapeutic alliance is more difficult. The alliance concerns itself with specific negotiations and forms of interaction between therapist and patient that are required for effective and meaningful therapeutic interaction. The element of basic trust, for example, is not part of the real relation, but entails a quality of the interaction within the object relation that must be engendered by specific behaviors that aim at the establishing and sustaining of such trust" (1070). What characterizes the real relation if it is separated from such elements of the alliance? Meissner's (partial) answer is, "Reality pervades the analytic relationship. There are realities of time, place, and circumstance. The realities of the location of the analyst's office, the physical surroundings, the furniture and decorations in the room, the geographic location itself, and even how the analyst dresses, affect the analytic relation and influence how the patient experiences the person of the analyst. The surrounding circumstances set the conditions for the analytic effort—the patient's financial situation, job demands, arrangements for payment of the fee, whether the patient has insurance or not and what kind, what kinds of pressures are pushing the patient into treatment—all reality factors extrinsic to the analysis, but exercising significant influence on the analytic relation and how it becomes established and maintained" (1068–69).

and is then a prominent curative factor. This is why some authors, usually disapprovingly, call it a corrective or educational experience" (482). This the authors saw differently: "Support that deserves to be called psychoanalytic means the providing of adequate gratification of preoedipal (archaic) needs and/or the fostering of their repression. The patient's experience of this kind of support . . . is a mutative factor, actually a 'corrective' and thus a curative one" (483), and "the supportive aspect of analytic technique activates the second curative factor of psychoanalysis: experience. . . . It is clearly not the support in itself that is mutative, but the experience it provokes. Therefore (again inspired by Strachey, who again would definitely disagree) we would call support mutative insofar as it achieves mutative experience" (484). The authors asserted that both mutative interpretations leading to mutative insights and mutative supports leading to mutative experiences can bring about comparable structural changes in personality organization. And here there must be a sense of coming full circle to the kinds of conclusions arrived at in the Psychotherapy Research Project, as described in chapter 8.

The authors then tackled the issue of the psychoanalytic as against the psychotherapeutic provenance of their assertions about "supportive factors": "Most analysts agree that support is crucial to the psychotherapy of severely disturbed patients. It involves, however, a psychotherapeutic and not an analytic technique, they argue. The controversy arises when support is claimed to be a crucial aspect of ordinary analytic technique" (485–86). In light of their 1991 paper on the supportive role of the primary relationship in "ordinary" as well as "modified" analyses, it is clear that they disagree that the supportive factor should be eliminated from proper psychoanalysis. It is true that "support and experience are phenomena often occurring on the nonverbal level. In contrast to interpretation and insight . . . they are the silent power of psychoanalysis" (488). They are important, however, because "apart from growth by insight, the analytic process is also characterized by growth by experience. This view holds not only when severely disturbed patients are treated by modified analysis, but also in the case of ordinary neurosis treated by ordinary analysis" (491). The mix may of course be different from case to case given that "the developmental achievements of the patient determine to what extent insight is possible and to what extent support is necessary" (489). This must again give a sense of coming full circle to the debates and the crystallizations of prevailing viewpoints of the early 1950s.[5]

5. In their most recent article (1994), de Jonghe, Rijnierse, and Janssen focus specifically on what they call "Psychoanalytic supportive psychotherapy" (PSP) and the "paradoxical situation that PSP is practiced by so many and studied by so few" (422). They divide psychoanalytic psy-

I close this chapter with a brief reference to a group of recent articles on the role of new experience in the psychoanalytic relationship as a major change factor in treatment. Sydney Pulver (1992), addressing the issue of insight versus relationship as the principal vehicle of psychic change, tried to surmount the ostensible dichotomy by conjoining these terms—and this is a stand of many: "The problem that has divided the exponents of these two viewpoints is the failure to realize that an understanding relationship cannot be maintained without insight into the dynamics of the relationship itself" (204). Blum (1992) focused more on the different emphases on this issue as regards the classically normal-neurotic patients and those with wider and deeper ego disorders. Though he began by asserting that "insight is the unique, critical agent of psychic change in clinical psychoanalysis" (257), he went on to state that "with some very disturbed, regressed patients, interpretation really turns out to . . . have a secondary, synergistic role to that of the analytic relationship. The analyst as a supportive, nurturing, primary object and as an auxiliary ego may be crucial to the maintenance of an integrated personality and narcissistic equilibrium" (258). And "the affective reliving in an atmosphere of safety, empathy, and objectivity and the long exposure to and identification with a consistently mature new 'object' may result in profound facilitation of treatment goals" (259). Again, with "very ill patients . . . the predictability, reliability, stability of the analytic situation and process, the corrective experience provided by understanding and being understood, the protracted contact with a mature object who demonstrates empathy, concern, on-going therapeutic interest, and respect for the patient and his developmental achievements may be an important condition for eventual utilization of interpretation and insight" (261).

To Pulver's (1992) view that the relationship is as integral to therapeutic change as is interpretation leading to insight, and Blum's (1992) view that this is especially so with sicker patients (and, by implication, either less so or more

chotherapies into the modalities "psychoanalysis proper, interpretive psychotherapy, and psychoanalytic supportive psychotherapy" (442) and say that as opposed to its early days, "psychoanalysis now has become a multimodal discipline" (443). In regard to the therapeutic process in PSP, they say, "In the classical view there is hardly any process in PSP. If there is any therapeutic factor operating, it is suggestive, which is an ill-defined term. Following the postclassical view, we would say that in PSP the therapeutic process mainly . . . consists of structure building. The process relies essentially on the operation of the support/experience factor, due to the therapist's supportive technique. That does not take away the fact that restructuring due to the operation of the interpretation/insight factor may play a role, though often a minor one" (435). And they define what they mean by supportive technique: "Support can only be called psychoanalytic when, inspired by psychoanalytic theory, it gratifies some preoedipal (archaic) needs or fosters their repression" (429).

to be taken for granted with more traditionally neurotic patients), Oremland (1991) supplied a cautionary note: "If the psychotherapist adopts the view . . . [that] to initiate psychotherapy, the psychotherapeutic alliance must be induced through condoning attitudes and facilitating comments, the psychotherapy from the beginning develops an underlying interactive quality. Rather than early identification and interpretation of the transference resistance that reveals and intensifies the transference, such inducing interventions impede and obfuscate the transference and increase the potential for identification and certain lower-order internalizations of the psychotherapist" (40).

Janine Chasseguet-Smirgel (1992), in an article on the psychoanalytic situation, offers a French perspective on these issues. "[I] view the analytic situation as an enclave where the basic human wish to return to the maternal matrix can develop asymptotically, precise limits being set to contain this wish. The subject is thus able to regress knowing he will not be engulfed forever within the mother's body. In other words, the paternal dimension that draws in the contours—the frame—of the analytic situation makes intrauterine regression in the session possible, supplying a canvas of sorts onto which contents in varying degrees of development pertaining to the totality of the patient's drives may be projected without the danger of loss of reality" (14). Lest this be received too literally by an English-speaking audience, Chasseguet-Smirgel added the qualification, "In speaking of the father as a separation principle and as representing reality, I do not mean that men are closer to reality than women . . . I am speaking of a *function* that the presence of an obstacle between mother and infant fulfills, this being of fundamental importance in the early development of the human mind" (23). In all, a characteristically French way of speaking to what de Jonghe, Rijnierse, and Janssen have called the primary relationship.

Jacobson (1994) has stated as well as anyone the degree of contemporary consensus on the analytic relationship as a major dimension of the analytic process:

> The often remarked unseating of humankind from the center of our universe, by Copernicus, then Darwin, then Freud, did not yet, in the early decades of psychoanalysis, apply to quite everyone. The analyst in the analytic situation was visualized as being motionless at the center of the action, observing, presenting as a target for loving and hating, holding up a mirror to the patient by means of interpretations, but, if properly analyzed, not influencing the course of the analytic process. This oversimplified view was necessary to allow us to make a beginning without being swamped by data. . . . The growing recognition over the years of the interactional nature of the analytic process, and the consequent appreciation

of the importance of the analyst's personality to the process, reflects one dimension of the maturation of our field from its beginnings. We no longer have to maintain the fiction that a properly analyzed analyst does not contribute significantly to the psychoanalytic process. Some analysts have made this shift within a framework they consider essentially classical; others identify the shift with a particular post-Freudian view, be it self psychology or one of the object relations theories. (29)

Somewhat further on, in talking of the kinds of noninterpretive interventions that carry the therapeutic influence, Jacobson turned Eissler's conception of parameters around completely: "In other words, we can [now] see such non-interpretive interventions as integral aspects of the analytic work, rather than being restricted to viewing them as gratifications, as suggestions, as distractions from the optimal emergence of the instinctual drive derivatives, or as merely incidental or supportive. By the same token, this view can help us see the *withholding* of a needed response at its proper time as a countertransference, or as a *parameter of omission,* a complex issue to which we probably have not paid enough attention" (31, italics added). An ironic reversal indeed of Eissler's (1953) concept of parameters—a striking statement of how far the field has come.[6]

---

6. To show how thinking of the psychoanalytic process in relationship terms has become practically universal, I cite a recent statement by Harold Sampson (1992), the cocreator with Joseph
Weiss of the "control-mastery" perspective in psychoanalysis—an essentially cognitive view
of both psychopathology and its psychoanalytic treatment—claiming a very specific *relationship
attitude* as central to the mutative process within the control-mastery paradigm: "The relationship itself is a crucial factor in treatment, including analytic treatment. Weiss' theory,
however, adds a great deal of specificity to this notion: The attitude of the analyst is important
to therapeutic progress *to the extent that it disconfirms a pathogenic belief* of the patient. For
example, Mr. A was not helped by some generalized 'relationship' or 'closeness' or 'warmth'
or 'empathy'—but by a specific attitude in a relationship that disconfirmed his particular pathogenic belief. . . . There is a lawful relationship in treatment between *specific experiences* that
tend to disconfirm a pathogenic belief and *specific changes* in the patient that follow from the
disconfirmation of the belief" (522). (Some, of course, would see a great deal of semantic
elasticity in the use of the word "relationship" in the sense here indicated, as if that put it on
a conceptual par with the usage throughout this chapter.)

18 A Hierarchical and Developmental Model of the Psychoanalytic Therapies: John Gedo and Veikko Tahka

Concomitant with the focus on the affective analyst-patient relationship as a central component of the change process in psychoanalytic therapy has been the emergence of a developmentally grounded hierarchical model of the psychoanalytic therapies, in which the optimal technical approach to the patient and the most salient relationship mode at each level are geared to the developmental progression of the patient and the psychopathology reflective of that stage of progression or fixation.

John Gedo has been a central figure in the elaboration of this way of categorizing the psychoanalytic therapeutic approaches and their stage-specific rationales. His 1964 article on "concepts for a classification of the psychotherapies" (530) was one of the very first papers to articulate—in embryonic form—this conceptual approach to psychopathology and psychotherapeutics. He started with a basic differentiation between therapies for the treatment of *current* developmental crises (e.g., the typical crisis of ego identity in the adolescent or the common acute situational reactions which can be regarded as the developmental counterpart crises of adult life) and therapies for the treatment of *late sequelae* of earlier developmental arrest or distortion. In the first group, the solutions of previous developmental tasks are basically sound; the problem is principally a current one and is age-appropriate. The therapist enters the patient's life as a reality figure who furnishes an essential age-appropriate relationship, centered around the reality of the therapeutic alliance and confronted vigorously with every transference irrationality. Where appropriate (prototypically, but of course not only, in adolescent crises), this kind of therapy was declared to be "the only one which can produce emotional growth in a relatively brief period of work." But Gedo warned that it should not be *called* "brief psychotherapy": "treatment may have modest goals, but how long the attainment of its goals may take can never be predetermined. A brief therapy . . . is a retrospective measurement of duration, not a treatment plan" (535).

As against such focal, reality-oriented, present-centered therapy for current developmental crises Gedo placed all therapies that treat in the present the late sequelae of unfavorable resolutions of the crises of the past (of childhood), including "psycho-analysis, supportive therapy, and a heterogeneous group of

therapies with poorly defined criteria and indications" (536). Gedo then spelled
out the differential indications for them in terms of the life crises that had been
surmounted or alternatively had become points of arrest and fixation. At one
end of this spectrum Gedo placed psychoanalysis as the therapy that "presupposes a capacity on the part of the patient to tolerate the frustration of his wish
for an infantile object in external reality . . . some adult identity must have been
attained; however shakily, the psychosocial crisis of adolescence must have been
passed through; the problem must be principally related to sequelae of the crisis
of initiative and industry (corresponding to the Oedipus complex)" (535). At
the other end of the scale Gedo placed supportive psychotherapy, which consisted, in his view, essentially of complementary relationships, systems of need
gratification and fulfillment. This is the therapy said to be indicated for those
who have been unsuccessful in mastering the infantile crisis of autonomy (anal
phase). And if there are still earlier (oral phase) failures of resolution, such as "an
excess of basic mistrust, *any* therapeutic attempt will be perceived in terms of
magic from the potential malevolence of which the patient may flee at any
moment. Any attempt to deal with the central conflicts of such patients must
produce degrees of anxiety which exceed their integrative capacities. Consequently, such attempts usually necessitate the use of [supportive psychotherapy
in] a hospital setting" (535–36).

It is in the cases intermediate between those suited for psychoanalysis and
those suited for supportive psychotherapy, those Gedo calls a "heterogeneous
group" (in the literature usually called cases suitable for expressive psychotherapy), that Gedo was vaguest about definitions, psychogenetic bases, criteria, and
indications. For these cases he called for "ego-building techniques which help
patients to progress within the hierarchy of psychosocial maturation, either to
spontaneous growth by resumption of an interrupted developmental crisis or to
analysability" (538). At its best this seems to be a "preparation for analysis"
(536). Into the same conceptual basket Gedo seemed to place Aichhorn's (1935)
special preparatory techniques with wayward adolescents and Felix Deutsch's
(1949) "sector therapy" ("In connection with uncovering measures, sector therapy, in leading the patient as quickly as possible into the past, exposes the ego
to the original conflicts which the child's ego could not handle and aids their
resolution in terms of the present" [537]). In this otherwise admirable effort,
Gedo avoided that earlier literature (cf. Gill 1954) which attempted to focus
specifically on just these "intermediate types of psychotherapy."

Gedo spelled out his concepts of the psychotherapy of developmental arrests
even more fully in a 1966 paper. He made the same twofold division of therapies
and noted that for those in the first group—individuals with "arrests in development" (25) or "fixation to a particular developmental task" (27)—"the tech-

nique of this treatment . . . [is] to fill a real need in the patient's life, that of a reasonable model for identification which permitted some gratification without guilt-producing impulsivity and then encouraged the seeking out of autonomous solutions" (29). "Favourable therapeutic results," he continued,". . . can be achieved only when a more-or-less healthy personality is prevented from mastering a developmental task by a real deficit in his environment" (31). Further, "This goal and the treatment procedures designed to accomplish it are appropriate whenever the interruption in development is primarily an outcome of a deficit in essential object relations, caused by the absence of one or both parents or by certain limitations of the parents' capacity to provide ego-building experiences for their child. . . . The outcome of these successful treatments may be compared to that type of 'transference cure' which is based on identification with the therapist" (32).

Gedo described the other group of therapies in much more familiar terms (as in the 1964 paper): "Therapies which deal with the results of unfavorable resolution of earlier developmental crises comprise psychoanalysis proper, supportive psychotherapy . . . , techniques of preparation for psychoanalysis" (25), and so on.

A corollary to Gedo's classification was the distinction introduced by Wolfgang Lederer (1964) between "anabolic" and "analytic" therapies (68). Anabolic therapies (roughly equivalent to what Gedo called therapies of current developmental crises) Lederer called "paternal"—that is, "essentially demanding, . . . competent in those cases where the paternal model, for one reason or another, was inadequate (as in delinquents and in patients without identity). . . . Anabolic therapy deals with conditions that arise typically during adolescence—when the need for paternal guidance is greatest" (71). By contrast, analytic therapy (essentially what Gedo brought together as the range of therapies dealing with the late sequelae of failures of resolution of life crises in the past) Lederer called "maternal" (71), "essentially accepting and uncritical . . . it has its competence . . . where proper maternal acceptance was lacking (as may be the case in some of the schizophrenias and psychosomatic conditions) or where an excessively harsh father/superego needs to be maternally mitigated (as in the classical neuroses) [cf. Strachey 1934]. . . . analytic therapy thus deals with conditions that have their root in childhood—the age-period when maternal acceptance and security are paramount" (71).

It was, however, Zetzel (1965) who first explicitly linked a "theory of therapy" to a "developmental model of the psychic apparatus" (39). Her effort was to create a bridge linking the perspectives of the British object-relations school with those of American ego psychology, around the issues of development, psychopathology, and therapy. She analogized the developmental process and the psychoanalytic process, both characterized by alternating progressive thrusts and (one hopes temporary) regressive retreats. The latter, if too severe, could of course seriously threaten treatment: "Regression affecting ego capacities . . . may obliterate the capacity to differentiate therapeutic alliance from the transference neurosis [and] . . . It has become increasingly evident that one of the most important prerequisites concerns the pre-existence of a degree of secondary autonomy which will substantially mitigate against the regression of basic ego functions" (41).

The goal of psychoanalysis was also set in developmental terms: "a partial but adaptively modified revival and repetition of major aspects of the original developmental process" (45). Developmental difficulties or deviations would pari passu create later therapeutic difficulty: "failure in basic trust has not only affected the original developmental process, but also presents serious problems in the establishment of a therapeutic alliance" (47). But this does not mean that the analytic process is a simple repetition of the developmental process: "It is too often assumed that references to the primitive source of the doctor-patient relationship in psycho-analysis imply that the analytic situation represents a repetition of the early mother-child relationship. Such assumptions have stimulated strong objections on the part of those who, following Sterba (1934), . . . stress the mature features of that part of the patient's ego which allies itself with the analyst" (48). Rather, it means that "the initial stages of analysis concern the . . . achievement of a new and special object relationship in a two-person situation. This initiates a new ego identification which, it is proposed, determines the nature, quality, and stability of the therapeutic alliance which may thus be defined as both an object relationship and an ego identification. . . . The first and most significant object relationship leading to an ego identification occurs in the early mother-child relationship." This led to Zetzel's central thesis: "I am neither suggesting that the analytic patient resembles a new-born infant nor that the analyst's role is explicitly maternal. I am, however, proposing that the analytic situation demands from the outset maximal mobilization of those ego attributes which remain for the most part contingent on the success achieved at a relatively early stage of psychic development. . . . Though regression is an inevitable concomitant of the analytic process, the patient must retain and reinforce his capacity for basic trust and positive ego identification" (48–49).

Despite this explicit modeling of the therapeutic process after the unfolding developmental process and the explicit characterization of the therapeutic tasks and requirements of the initial stages of analytic treatment, Zetzel did not carry her developmental schematization to the point of delineating different tasks and different technical approaches to the psychopathologies deriving from the failures of the various developmental stages.[1] That task was to be undertaken by Gedo and Arnold Goldberg in *Models of the Mind: A Psychoanalytic Theory* (1973).

Gedo and Goldberg essayed an ambitious hierarchical organization of therapeutic approaches built around the array of clinical theories (or models of the mind) that best characterized the different levels of developmental achievement. Their aim was "to show that different behaviors can be observed from different vantage points, that these behaviors can be understood using a variety of clinical theories or models of the mind, and that these concepts can be organized according to a hierarchical overall arrangement" (7). Further, "We hope to demonstrate that the concept of epigenetic schemata, that is, the interaction of the organism with the environment in a sequence of specific phases, is the most useful theoretical conception of the development of human mental functioning" (8).

Accomplishing these aims required, in the authors' opinion, the deployment of *different* models of the mind: "A different model may be most useful and theoretically valid for the study of each of the various phases of an individual's life history" (11). But, they cautioned, "in any model of the mind the successive stages of development are artificially represented as discontinuities. In real life, discontinuity of functions does not occur, and developmental stages unfold in a manner that allows for the assimilation of new structures. There are always regulating functions at work, for example; this is implicit in the concept of lines of development" (14).

The authors then presented five successive models of the mind. Three were drawn explicitly from Freud. First was the Topographic Model as developed most explicitly in *The Interpretation of Dreams* (1900). This model of the three mental systems, unconscious, preconscious, and conscious, served well for the understanding of dreams, neurotic symptoms, parapraxes, jokes, and so forth. It was designed to illustrate the idea of "psychical locality" (23), hence the designation topographic; it facilitated a "dynamic" explanation of disturbances in mental functioning; and it made the concepts of "censorship" and "repression barrier" central to the understanding of the mind in conflict.

Freud's second model was the Tripartite (or Structural) Model, articulated first in *The Ego and the Id* (1923) and further developed in *Inhibitions, Symptoms,*

1. Zetzel's formulations of the developmental model of the psychoanalytic treatment process are quite comparable to those of Modell, who was also strongly influenced by the British object-relational school, especially Winnicott, (see chapter 12), and of Loewald, whose work in Baltimore brought him into close contact with the American interpersonal school centered around the teaching of Harry Stack Sullivan (see chapter 16).

and Anxiety (1926). This model was designed to cope with the problem of the unconscious aspects of the ego (especially the defense mechanisms) and of the superego (the unconscious sense of guilt and need for punishment that played such a crucial role in the negative therapeutic reaction). It dealt with the unconscious self-regulating forces within the psyche. Freud's third model, the model of the Reflex Arc or the Unstructured Psyche, propounded in chapter 7 of *The Interpretation of Dreams* (1900), was a "picket-fence" model built on a stimulus-response base and dealt (economically) with issues of overstimulation and its avoidance through effective discharge, in both the motor and affective realms. These three models explicitly drawn by Freud to illustrate his various conceptualizations of mental functioning, Gedo and Goldberg stated, "fall into two types: one is applicable to the state of the psyche at the hypothetical inception of its functioning; the other two are applicable to psychic functioning at the stage of full structural differentiation. The former is the reflex arc model; the latter are the topographic and tripartite ones" (51).

To Freud's three models Gedo and Goldberg added the model of the nuclei of Self and Object and the model of the Self and Object, both based on the emerging formulations of Heinz Kohut, with whom both authors were closely identified at the time. They called Kohut's emerging "psychology of self" a vital (though difficult) effort to comprehend the representational world of intrapsychic objects and self-representations: "The utilization of the construct 'self' has been hampered not only by the inherent difficulty of grasping the subtle idea that the organization of the personality as a whole may be an important developmental achievement of early childhood but also by the semantic problems created by attempts to superimpose this concept on the tripartite model of the mind" (64). They elaborated the following developmental sequence for the stages of selfhood: "that of the self in formation, capped by a state of cohesiveness; that of the self in conflict among its drives, its internalized standards, and its reality sense; and that of the self beyond conflict, the expansion of permanent capacities which make themselves felt in behavior through internal harmony" (66).

With these conceptualizations in place, Gedo and Goldberg then offered their own epigenetic series of developmental lines in interaction:

1. The stage of the reflex arc model (of primary narcissism) with its danger of traumatic overstimulation
2. The stage of the self-object model (after differentiation of self from object) with its danger of loss of the object or of the object's love, its conception of the grandiose self and idealized parent, and its characteristic separation anxiety

3. The second self-object stage with its danger of castration, its central "phallic narcissism," and its characteristic castration anxiety
4. The tripartite model (after established superego formation) with its moral anxiety danger, its established ego ideal, and its characteristic moral (superego) anxiety
5. The topographic model with the mature transformation of the evolved psychic apparatus, with its characteristic signal anxieties, and with its danger being realistic threats.

Comparable developmental lines were drawn for narcissism (following Kohut), for the sense of reality, for the elaboration of the typical defense mechanisms, and so forth. For example, for the developmental hierarchy of defenses the authors proposed the sequence instinctual vicissitudes, primal repression (the stage of the reflex arc), projection and introjection, disavowal, repression proper, and finally, renunciation: "After it has been succeeded as the characteristic mode of defense, every mechanism may undergo a change of function so that it may begin to operate in the service of nondefensive, adaptive tasks. Concurrently, in case of greater than expectable stress, regression may occur to the earlier mode of organization once more reinstating the defensive function of the mechanism" (94).

This was then built into a "Hierarchy of Modes of Psychic Functioning" (101): the five stages, each with characteristic dangers, defenses, and anxieties, and all complexly—hierarchically—layered. The authors wrote, "Because successively acquired functions do not replace each other but are added cumulatively to the repertoire of behavioral potentialities, mental life and its portrayal in this type of model becomes progressively more elaborate with maturation" (105–06). Gedo and Goldberg then went on to construct a psychoanalytic nosology of psychopathological syndromes and their implications for therapeutic approach. They designated (in ascending order) the five characteristic states of psychological (dys)function: (1) the traumatic state, (2) psychotic disintegration, (3) narcissistic personality disorders, (4) neurotic character disorders, and (5) expectable adult functioning—and reiterated that "early functional capacities always persist, both in their original 'primitive' forms and in the various progressively more 'mature' forms they may attain" (156). They then elaborated (also in ascending order) the hierarchy of central treatment strategies to deal with these five states: (1) pacification, (2) unification, (3) optimal disillusionment, (4) interpretation, and (5) introspection—each in turn defined, specified, and illustrated.

Unlike those who define efforts 'beyond interpretation' as psychotherapeutic, supportive, etc., this hierarchical organization is based on the thesis that these modes represent a progressive broadening of psychoanalysis to encompass an ever-wider array of intervention modes, directed to the phase-specific developmental needs of the patient. Gedo and Goldberg acknowledged that "this progressive broadening of the scope of psychoanalysis as a therapy beyond its utilization for the treatment of the psychoneuroses has created controversies about the appropriate limits of its application" (159) and also that the conceptual rationale for such a broadened scope of interventions had not previously been clearly articulated *psychoanalytically:* "Parameters [departures from strict interpretation] have thus far been described for the most part in behavioral terms alone, by listing various actions on the part of the analyst that have gone beyond interpretation. There has been no attempt to classify the infinite variety of these possible behaviors into a rational ordering of noninterpretive therapeutic modalities" (159–60). This of course is exactly what Gedo and Goldberg set out to do.

For the disorders of "traumatic states" with the dangers of massive overstimulation, they prescribed *pacification* "through utilizable avenues of discharge [regularity of sessions, catharsis in any 'talking cure']. . . . However, in many instances more radical measures may have to be employed to provide adequate pacification. The use of medication, the provision of protective environments [hospital settings], or even the use of judicious strategies of relative isolation may help to pacify the overstimulated patient" (161). For the threats of psychotic disintegration, they prescribed *unification* "based on the ability of the therapist to serve as a focus around whom the cluster of unintegrated nuclei may coalesce into an integrated, cohesive self. . . . This can be provided through the continued availability of a reliable object, that is, the presence of a real person or even of a reliable setting. In other words, in this mode of organization it is no longer necessary to provide the need gratifications that lead to pacification: it is enough to establish an uninterrupted relationship" (162). And "this experience is usually not the reliving of any past relationship . . . but a real experience in the present which may have had no precedent. This is why it would be erroneous to think of it as the transference of a repressed past onto the present" (163).

For the narcissistic personality disorders, they prescribed *optimal disillusionment:* "confrontation with reality as the principal therapeutic tool for the difficulties of disillusionment . . . the realities which must be faced are those that have been disavowed through narcissistically motivated illusions. Therefore we prefer to think of the therapeutic aim of confrontations as *optimal disillusion.*" Kohut introduced specific technical modifications into analytic technique with such patients: "He advocates the acceptance of the patient's idealization of the analyst without interpretation for a long period," which leads to optimal disillusion "very gradually through interpretation of the genuine need for idealized parental imagoes." For classically neurotic disorders, the prescription is for *interpretation:* "Here the principal aim of treatment . . . must be the resolution of intrapsychic conflict through interpretation" (165). And last, for those with "expectable adult functioning," treatment as such is unnecessary: "*Introspection* is sufficient for the understanding of the psychopathology of everyday life, dreaming, and such creative products as jokes, artistic works, and others" (166).

Gedo and Goldberg concluded with an optimistic portrayal of treatability (albeit not "classical" analyzability) within their expanded hierarchical organization of models of mental functioning: "Successful therapeutic interventions in patients with relatively archaic organization of the psyche is indeed possible. We have emphasized that success in such efforts depends primarily on the use of technical modalities of treatment different from that of psychoanalysis proper, that is, on interventions other than interpretation. If the treatment goal is that of attaining the level of functioning expectable in adults . . . , it is necessary first to master the developmental tasks of earlier phases of psychic organization" (167).

Both Gedo and Goldberg went on separately to each write a number of subsequent books. Gedo's *Beyond Interpretation: Toward a Revised Theory for Psychoanalysis* (1979) represented a significant clarification, modification, and extension of his 1973 book with Goldberg. First he proposed a revision of psychoanalytic psychology, no longer, in his view, to be conceived as either a psychology of drives or a psychology of object relations but rather as a psychological hierarchy of personal aims: "The central concept around which my tentative revision of psychoanalytic psychology is built is that of human personality as a hierarchy of personal *aims.* The infant's biological *needs* constitute the earliest of these goals; by the end of the second year of life, these have been supplemented by a variety of subjective *wishes;* the entire hierarchy, in both conscious and unconscious aspects, will form the person's primary identity, or, as I would prefer to call it, the 'self-organization.' The formation of the self-organization and its later transformations, especially through the acquisition of systems of *values,* should be viewed in epigenetic terms as the core of personality development (xi, italics added). He added,

> The personality as a whole is most fruitfully understood as a hierarchy of potentials for action, i.e., of both organismic and subjective goals, as modified by a system of values. . . . In my proposed theory, I distinguish two sets of human aims, which I have named 'goals' and 'values.' I have chosen these terms as extensions of the familiar concepts of ambitions and ideals, which have long been used to refer to personal aims within the realm of human intentionality. The range of psychoanalytic clinical material re-

quires that we also take into account the effects of prepsychological infantile experience on the patterning of later motivations. In other words, the hierarchy of personal aims must integrate the realm of subjectivity with a nonexperiential one involving organismic needs. (11–12)

The revision of the psychoanalytic theory of the mind into a self-organization created by an increasingly differentiated hierarchy of personal aims led Gedo to a revised schema of the five successive modes of mental organization: (1) the prepsychological or sensori-motor organization, an "archaic state of unthinking reliance on the milieu" (204) with its central danger of traumatization via overstimulation; (2) the transition to the experiential and the subjective, with evolving personal aims, but totally uncoordinated, coexisting with many "nuclei of the self" (206), beset by threats to self-cohesion and the dangers of separation; (3) the stage of subjective wishes, with the dangers of parental sanctions; (4) the stage of internalized morality, with the dangers of conflict and moral anxiety; and (5) the stage of renunciation, with only reality dangers (195).

Gedo did not alter his array of technical approaches (pacification, unification, optimal disillusionment, interpretation, and introspection) to suit the malfunctionings at each developmental level; rather, he claimed that all of them were present and salient in all analytic treatments, though of course with differing emphases depending on the predominant developmental level, fixations, and regressions of each patient. He stated that this position was also inherent in his 1973 book with Goldberg: "We believed each of these modalities to be absolutely necessary to *every* psychoanalytic effort, even if in varying proportions, depending on how often the analysand functions in which mode. In other words, the use of the various modalities should be a routine feature of psychoanalytic treatment technique; it is *not* a departure from classical procedures, as Eissler (1953) seemed to suggest when he called any intervention on the part of the analyst other than verbal interpretation a 'parameter' " (6). Gedo now made this idea the centerpiece of his therapeutic strategy:

a theory of technique based on a contemporary understanding of the epigenesis of mental life and the pathologies potentially produced by its developmental vicissitudes. Most relevant to my thesis here is our conclusion that the appropriate interventions of the analyst do not consist of interpretation alone. . . . [Rather,] depending on the degree of regression, various interventions may be needed; in *Models of the Mind,* we devised the terms pacification, unification, and optimal disillusionment to characterize the interventions appropriate to the three archaic modes within the hierarchy. . . . [Modell designates all three of these via Winnicott's term, 'holding environment']. . . . What is under discussion here involves no actual departure from the usual analytic *procedures:* the issue is one of explicitly recognizing certain aspects of the psychoanalytic situation as legitimate and even essential factors in the process of treatment. (17–18)

That is, "the provision of a holding environment, interpretive assistance, and witnessing the analysand's introspective efforts are unavoidable concurrent tasks in *every* analysis" (21, italics added).

Gedo reiterated this theme in yet another sequence. He conceded that "it is perfectly true, of course, as Eissler stated in his work on technical parameters, that establishing better adaptation through a symbiotic relationship, which is what the provision of a holding environment amounts to, does not constitute an analytic end-result, or any kind of therapeutic success, for that matter" (22). Nonetheless, "every psychoanalytic encounter presents us with episodes of overstimulation, with temporary disruptions of a cohesive self, and with a multiplicity of behaviors based on a variety of illusions. Yet the traditional theory of treatment addresses itself only to the problems typical of the more advanced modes of psychic functioning, the conflicts typical of Mode IV, and the frustration experienced in Mode V" (26–27). Gedo continued, "During the first half-century of the history of psychoanalysis, only personalities organized in this manner [around nuclear Oedipal conflicts] were thought to be analyzable. With the growth of the epigenetic viewpoint in recent years, most of us have come to regard such an ideal developmental course during the preoedipal years as a theoretical fiction" (28). Rather, we ("most of us") now believe that the psychoanalytic treatment of disturbed minds is subtended by a hierarchically organized "natural history of the self-organization [that] could be divided into three major periods: that of the self-in-formation, completed with the establishment of a single hierarchy of potentials for action; later, that of the self-in-conflict among its repudiated wishes, its morality, and its sense of reality; and finally, that of the self-in-internal-harmony beyond conflict" (252).[2]

Michael Franz Basch, a colleague of Gedo and Goldberg, published three books directly on psychotherapy (not specifically psychoanalysis). *Doing Psychotherapy* (1980), *Understanding Psychotherapy* (1988a), and *Practicing Psychotherapy* (1992) that were influenced strongly by the formulations of Kohut and of Gedo and Goldberg. Basch's books were much more clinically focused, however, built around extended verbatim presentations from a range of psychotherapies and supervisions. His first book (1980), anchored in the hierarchical developmental

2. An entire issue of *Psychoanalytic Inquiry* (Grand and Hill, 1994) has been devoted to a critical discussion of the possibilities and the dangers of the multiple model approach of Gedo by four authors, with a response by Gedo, as well as a comparable critical discussion by four other authors of the multiple model approach of Pine, with a response by Pine.

schema of Gedo and Goldberg, made two incisive points that extended the logic inherent in their formulations. The first was the explicit narrowing of the indications for psychoanalysis proper, classically conceived: "It is only when I believe that I am dealing with an unconsciously motivated pattern of self-defeating behavior that is clearly repetitive, not related to particular external circumstances, and not accounted for by lack of either experience or developmental opportunities that I would rule out comparatively short-term and less intensive psychotherapies and think of psychoanalysis as not only desirable but necessary. In my experience, the need to establish and work through a transference neurosis—that is, to mobilize and resolve the Oedipus complex—is one of the absolute indicators for psychoanalysis, though it is not the only one" (109).

The other, complementary point is that the psychoanalytic therapy offered to those deemed not amenable to classical psychoanalysis should not, in Basch's view, be confused with what is called "supportive therapy" in the literature:

> Any patient is most likely to benefit from treatment and to tolerate its difficult moments successfully and productively if he knows that the therapist respects him and finds good in him, even if he cannot yet do either one for himself. It is important to understand that reassurance, guidance, and gratification of the patient's psychological demands may well be essential ingredients in the therapy of an individual who has not had sufficient opportunity in the relationship with his parents to learn how his own actions can influence the treatment he receives, and how that treatment then influences his self-concept. This approach to . . . therapy should not be confused with so-called supportive psychotherapy which is aimed at strengthening extant defenses and at covering rather than uncovering a patient's problems. The ultimate goal in [this] case . . . remains the promotion of cure through helping her gain insight into her characteristic behavior patterns; but first the therapist must lay the groundwork necessary to permit the patient to face herself. (78)

Of course, it is precisely at the point of Basch's disavowal that the conceptual controversy is evoked; in terms of conventional usages, most people would designate what Basch describes as precisely what he disclaims, "supportive psychotherapy" or the "supportive aspects" of all psychoanalytic therapy, and might similarly see Gedo's hierarchy of psychoanalytic therapeutic approaches in exactly the same way, as variant ways of describing the expressive-supportive psychotherapeutic continuum.

In his second book, Basch (1988a) tried, ecumenically, to encompass the range of explicitly nonpsychoanalytically based psychotherapies within the context of psychoanalytic theoretical meaningfulness. For example, he described "the three basic types of psychotherapy: the dynamic [meaning psychoanalytically based], which deals with the often-hidden or unconscious influence of development on a patient's character and motivation; the behavioral, which focuses on a patient's capacity to change in action; and the cognitive, which seeks to ameliorate or eliminate a patient's difficulties by examining and altering the manner of that patient's reasoning about his or her problems. While these approaches are often presented as disparate, even irreconcilable, in practice the seasoned therapist, whether acknowledging it or not, develops a technique that disregards the boundaries that supposedly separate one from the other" (54). For example,

> If the therapist finds that the transference either cannot be or, because of the limited nature of the patient's problem, need not be promoted and explored, he or she may employ basically cognitive and behavioral techniques to help the patient. . . . Behavioral strategies can sometimes be employed to circumvent the defenses, and cognitive techniques can help some patients to alter the manner in which they employ their defenses so that they become more effective and/or less disruptive of a patient's life style. However, in insight or dynamic therapy, though the therapist continues to employ cognitive and behavioral techniques as ancillary maneuvers when indicated, the primary focus is on the overt and covert goals of behavior, especially when these are in conflict. These dynamics can be most effectively studied and resolved within the therapeutic transference. (138–39)

Again, what Basch here calls an admixture of the behavioral and cognitive techniques into dynamic or analytic therapies others would simply call the supportive psychotherapeutic techniques inevitably present in even the most expressive of therapies.

Basch's third (1992) book was again built around detailed case material from therapies and supervisions organized around his explicit developmental approach. In his introduction, he spoke of the recurring problems brought to him for discussion by novices and experienced therapists alike: "I have concluded that the difficulty is not that the therapists lack either insight or empathy but that they are following a symptom-oriented approach rather than a developmental one. Our training and our literature tend to focus on the effects of patients' difficulties and the accompanying signs and symptoms . . . rather than on the underlying developmental disturbance that first brought about the problems. Freud's discovery notwithstanding, it is too often forgotten that . . . what our patients complain of represents not the problem but, rather, an unsuccessful attempt at its resolution" (xvi).

Last, in a chapter in the Rothstein volume, Basch (1988b) emphasized the contribution of the developmental perspective that he, following Gedo and Goldberg, was advocating: "I have tried to sketch in broad strokes the idea that the effective factors in therapy are the same ones Freud taught us, interpretation based on empathic understanding. What we today can bring to therapy that our predecessors could not is a knowledge of development that will let us gauge more accurately both the significance of what our patients are telling us and the sort of interventions we need to make in order to help them, in other words, what constitutes an appropriate interpretation for that patient at that particular time" (133).

A thought-provoking addendum to the work of Gedo, Goldberg, and Basch was provided by Paul Holinger (1989), also a colleague of these authors. Holinger's goal was to separate what is specifically psychoanalytic from what is specifically psychotherapeutic in this developmental approach to therapy. He located this difference in the *context* rather than the *content* of the described interventions: "Goldberg (1980–81) suggested that in discriminating psychoanalysis from psychotherapy, the difference may lie less in the method than in the goal (the goals being reorganization [psychoanalysis] or repair [psychotherapy] of the self). . . . Or, as Basch (1988a) stated, the goal of psychoanalysis is cure through the formation and resolution of the transference, whereas the goal of psychotherapy is the resolution of particular problems" (1404). Holinger then counterposed his distinction between these modes, based solely on the developmental perspective:

I suggest that difficulties arise in efforts to distinguish psychoanalysis from psychotherapy because the content or type of intervention is evaluated rather than the developmental phase of the patient at the time the interventions are made and the results of such interventions. The understanding of dyadic transferences, based on the early mother–infant relationship, is beginning to catch up with what is known about triadic or triangular oedipal transferences. Interventions that seem to be supportive psychotherapy and may inhibit the unfolding of the transference in a patient with triadic oedipal issues may be precisely what is necessary to facilitate the working through of the transference of a patient with psychopathology on an earlier and/or different level. That is, it is the developmental context of the intervention and not merely the type of intervention itself which determines whether or not the process and ultimate goal are those of psychoanalysis or psychotherapy. (1405)

Holinger developed his argument in even more detail: "Historically, . . . , at least two trends are discernible. First, there has been a trend toward recognizing the analyzability of patients where primary pathology exists at developmental levels prior to the phase of concrete operations. Second, there has been increased use, or at least increased understanding of such use, of interventions other than transference interpretations in the analysis of patients with pathology at varying levels. To further explore the idea that such interventions can best be termed psychotherapeutic or psychoanalytic only on the basis of context and not content, it is now necessary to explore more fully the issue of interpretation and transference in light of recent advances" (1407). And in considering interpretation and transference, Holinger said, "There appears to be an unstated equation between interpretation and analysis; yet, . . . various interventions (such as pacification, unification, optimal disillusionment, or Kohut's confirmatory interventions) are not only appropriate but necessary in the mobilization of analytic transferences . . . [and] in the analysis of patients with earlier developmental problems. . . . Even at various phases of the analysis of psychoneurotic patients, interventions other than interpretation are necessary and lead to the mobilization of analyzable transference" (1409). Holinger's conclusion was that "interventions within the earlier types of transferences may have seemed, from their content, to be supportive psychotherapy if they were incorrectly perceived to be occurring within a psychoneurotic framework; however, interventions with the same content can be shown to be psychoanalytic when the context is correctly understood as a narcissistic transference or earlier psychological mode" (1411). Obviously, given that the predominant transference position is neither always clear nor stable, there is great room for ambiguity as to when any particular kind of intervention constitutes a psychotherapeutic or psychoanalytic maneuver.

Over the same time period as the Chicago workers, Tahka (1979), in Finland, was also elaborating a developmental approach to psychoanalytic therapy, fully articulated in his book *Mind and Its Treatment* (1993). Tahka's key concept is that of "psychotherapy as a phase-specific interaction in which the curative factors change in accordance with the changes in the level of the patient's relatedness to his therapist. What in the classical analysis are defined as 'parameters' of the technique appear to be curative factors of prime importance when dealing with patients whose disturbances are more severe than neurosis" (1979, 113). To put this a little differently, he wrote, "There are therapeutic applications of the psychoanalytic theory not only for the treatment of neurosis but also for the more severe levels of pathology. This does not mean 'widening' the scope of application of the classical *technique* to the treatment of personality disturbances for which it has not been developed. What it does mean is the application of analytic *knowledge* to patients who represent earlier and more extensive disturbances of personality development than neurotic patients do and who therefore also benefit from other aspects of the therapeutic interaction" (115–16).

In this context Tahka advanced his concept that repetition is not always transference; this concept in turn undergirded all his recommendations for technique: "Pathogenic object relations from the past regularly repeat themselves in the patient's relationship to his therapist. . . . It is important to realize that this repetition is not always that which we call transference . . . that the term transference is also used to describe repetitions of disturbed developmental interactions from levels other than neurotic easily leads to erroneous conclusions about the nature of these repetitions and a tendency towards treating them as neurotic transferences" (118). And here, unlike Gedo and Basch, Tahka clearly distinguished the psychotherapeutic from the psychoanalytic process: "Prestructural disturbances in object relations may be treatable but it is very questionable whether they are analyzable" (119).

Tahka made his developmental distinctions in terms of three levels, not the five specified by Gedo and Goldberg, corresponding to the familiar psychopathological categories of the psychotic, the borderline, and the neurotic. In the overtly psychotic, "the patient's regression has then reached an objectless period, and this makes it impossible for the interactional disturbance to repeat itself in transference which, by definition, is an object relationship" (119). In this sense, he adhered to Freud's original conception that psychotics do not form transferences in the true sense. Then what is the nature of the therapist-patient relationship in such cases? "If our basic assumption is . . . that this pathogenic disturbance repeats itself in a phase-specific way in the patient's relationship to his therapist, then the therapist, at least to some extent, has a position analogous to that of the primary object at the time of the original disturbance. The therapist's becoming a phase-specific object to the patient also gives him an opportunity in a new interaction to try to repair or ameliorate the consequences of the once disturbed interaction between the patient and his primary objects" (121). This proffered interaction with the psychotic Tahka called the "experiences of gratification":

> The analysts who have studied the early development of personality quite unanimously emphasize the importance of the *experiences of gratification* as the central precondition for those early internalizations which lead to differentiation of self and object. . . . The therapist should, therefore, act in a way which leads to the formation of a good object image in the patient's representational world. . . . The key word is *gratification* and a kind of gratification in which the therapist has, by the help of his complementary reactions, correctly grasped the patient's need and an accept-

able form and time for its gratification. . . . A central problem in offering gratification to psychotic patients is that the infant-mother analogy cannot be carried too far. . . . The experiences of gratification should therefore usually be offered in indirect and symbolic ways, for which the therapist's phase-specifically tuned presence provides the foundation.[3] (123–24)

Next are the borderline states, defined more broadly than usual:

> Borderline states represent that level of pathology which, in addition to the "regular" borderline states, includes the so-called narcissistic personality disorders (Kohut), most addictions and perversions, and a considerable fraction of various character disorders (Kernberg). . . . The specific developmental disturbance of the borderline pathology is thought to consist of disturbances of those internalization processes which normally create the basic structure of the ego. Differentiation between the self and the object has been sufficiently reached, which protects the patient against psychotic breakdown, but the interaction between his primary objects and himself has failed in its phase-specific task of promoting internalization and structuralization of the personality. . . . The individual's ability to secure drive satisfaction, control anxiety and maintain an inner balance remains deficient and dependent on outside sources. (126)

Therefore, "the . . . goal with a borderline patient seems to be to help him build that inner equipment which is the precondition of his autonomy, identity, and ability to love and hate real people. This goal can also be expressed in Mahler's terminology as the resolution of the separation-individuation crisis, in Hartmann's as the attainment of object-constancy, in Kohut's as the transformation of a prestructural object into a poststructural one, or in Kernberg's terminology as the integration of the good and bad representations." And finally, "As the key word in the treatment of the psychoses is gratification, in the case of the borderline states it seems to be *identification*" (127).

With the neurotic the key words are "interpretation" and "insight." Interpretation, it is understood, means different things at the different phase-levels: "If interpretations mean to a psychotic patient oral gifts from the therapist, to a

---

3. Sometimes such a need-gratifying therapeutic approach has to become endless: "A progressive process of internalization, which presupposes certain frustration tolerance, often cannot with psychotic patients be brought farther than to the formation of a good inner object, which must then be sustained with maintenance therapy. A continuous 'psychic presence' of the therapist will then be a necessary condition for the patient's nonpsychotic existence" (125). These are among the patients whom I called "therapeutic lifers" (1986a, 631–41).

borderline patient their effects seem to depend primarily on their suitability for identification models." Insight, too, is qualified: "Insight does not create structures—it mainly changes the economic and dynamic relationships between already established structures" (128). Further, "The analyst's task in this phase-specific repetition [of the transference neurosis] is to liberate the patient from his unconscious ties to his parents, whom he no longer needs as developmental adjuvants. The analyst refuses to assume the role offered to him by the patient and, instead, reveals to the patient the existence and origins of his transference. There is little doubt that the analyst's main instrument in this work is interpretation, and that *insight* is the specifically curative factor in the treatment of neurotic pathology" (129).

Tahka concluded;

> If *psychosis* is considered a condition in which the differentiation between self- and object-representations has been lost, the therapist's phase-specific task is to become a good object in the patient's inner world by adequately providing him with experiences of *gratification*. If *borderline states* are thought to be conditions in which the disturbance in the formation of ego structures is specific, the therapist's function, analogous to that of the primary object, is to provide the patient with useful *identification models* for a belated ego building. If *neurosis* is regarded as the pathology of an already structured personality, in which repressed oedipal love and hate problems are specific, the therapist's task is to help the patient to become conscious of them and resolve them by providing him with *insights* through interpretation and working through. (130)

And then, even more tersely, "For the psychotic patient we have to become an object, for the borderline patient we have to act as an object and, finally, the neurotic patient we have to liberate from an object which has become superfluous" (131).

In his 1993 book, Tahka expanded on these basic formulations, with very significant refinements. First, in regard to the meaning and place of gratifications vis-à-vis interpretations in the therapy of the overtly psychotic Tahka stated, "It seems to be of the utmost importance to realize that providing experiences of gratification is the only way to approach an undifferentiated mind, in order to enter into it as a structure-building and thus development-promoting element. Gratification is the only language received and accepted prior to the emergence of a self experience. . . . Thus, adequate gratification of a patient reiterating his symbiotic failure in a regression to undifferentiation seems to be very different from if not diametrically opposite to gratification of a neurotic patient's transference expectations" (275).⁴ Of so-called interpretations with the psychotic, Tahka said, "It seems inevitable that as long as interpretations are offered to a patient who has regressively lost his self experience, any signs indicating that the analyst's words have reached and influenced the patient's structure-building representational processes are due to the positive affective attributes of the analyst's words as 'things,' instead of being results of a new 'insight' due to the abstract content of the interpretation. What was meant to be effective as an increase of self-knowledge may thus turn out to be effective more in the manner of a lullaby" (281).⁵

Then how best to describe the gratifications that are stated to be the proper therapeutic approach to the psychotic? "Since the useful introjects represent soothing, tension-regulating, and security-inducing functional presences in the mind of a developing individual, the creation and maintenance of a generally safe 'holding' atmosphere in the interaction between him and his developmental

4. And therefore the concept of analytic abstinence must be understood very differently with the psychotic and the psychoneurotic. Tahka put it this way: "The problem of the analyst, trained to work with neurotic patients, is that he has been taught never to satisfy a patient's infantile needs. Analytic abstinence as one of the cornerstones of the classical technique seems to be seriously threatened by any suggestion that the analyst might, or even should, gratify an undifferentiated patient's symbiotic needs. However, as I hope to show, this is a misunderstanding, based on an erroneous equation of the psychotic patient's developmental arrest with that of a neurotic patient" (272).

5. For a diametrically opposed view on the nature of the psychotic process and its amenability to an essentially unmodified psychoanalytic approach, I quote Arlow and Brenner (1969): "Transferences can and do occur in schizophrenia. These transferences may be transient, volatile, unstable and fraught with aggression, but they represent, nonetheless, the same fundamental process which can be recognized in the transference of neurotic patients, i.e., the displacement onto the image of the analyst of instinctual cathexes originally vested in infantile objects. The difficulties inherent in the management of the transference in psychosis reside in the inability of the ego of the psychotic patient to cope with the massive instinctual danger and with the anxiety which it engenders" (8). In terms of a theory of etiology and of therapy, Arlow and Brenner stated that they were "applying to the psychoses Freud's later views of mental functioning as conceptualized in the structural theory. . . . We propose to apply to the formation of symptoms in the psychoses the same principles which Freud applied after 1926 to the formation of symptoms in the neuroses." For, "To be sure, there are significant differences between the neuroses and the psychoses. These differences, however, appear to be variations in the degree of severity of certain processes. The processes themselves, e.g., fixation, trauma, conflict, regression, etc., are *qualitatively* the same in both categories of mental illness" (10)—with the clear implication that the therapeutic approach would also be qualitatively the same. This starkly opposed, and incidentally quite influential, position is presented here only to illustrate the strong antidevelopmental view on psychopathology and its therapy of which Arlow and Brenner are such conspicuous spokesmen; as I have indicated in my preface, I make no effort in this book to disentangle the vast literature specifically on the therapy of the psychoses.

object is necessary for offering such experiential models for introjection. In the treatment of newly differentiated schizophrenic patients this includes the stability and relative unchangeability of the therapeutic setting, regular and predictable treatment sessions, as well as full availability and interest from the analyst, whose demeanor could ideally be kind but not intrusive, genuine but not courting, firm but not disciplinary" (288). Where this is reasonably successful, "when there has developed an analyst-derived, quantitatively and qualitatively sufficient, security-inducing introjective structure in the patient's mind to ensure differentiation and to counteract 'all-bad' introjects that become mobilized by frustrations, the schizophrenic patient may feel safe enough to attempt the first functionally selective identification with some of the analyst's introjected functions" (294)—that is, he has advanced to the borderline level of functioning.

With the borderline, "I have . . . tried to demonstrate that the decisive and essential structure-building process, and thus the crucial curative factor, . . . is . . . the patient's *functionally selective identifications* with his analyst" (313, italics added). Accomplishing this is a very different task than with the psychotic: "The analyst tends to become accepted and idealized as a new developmental object for a borderline patient specifically through his function as a provider of interest in the patient's subjective way of experiencing, rather than a provider of concern for his staying mentally alive, as is just as specifically the case with psychotic patients" (341). Further, "The specific way for the analyst to enter into a borderline patient's world of experience as a new developmental object, as well as to provide the latter with models for functionally selective identifications, is for the analyst to catch the patient's subjective way of experiencing through *transient informative identifications,* and to *forward the resulting empathic understanding to the patient*" (349, italics added). Again, where it is reasonably successful, "structure building through identification in the treatment of borderline patients . . . means a gradual loss of the experiential presence of a functional object" (395).

And last, with the neurotic,

> transference interpretations will be the communications of the analyst that specifically confront the patient with the illusory and anachronistic nature of his analyst-directed expectations, thus building a bridge between past and present, and initiating a gradual replacement of the transferential images by real or fantasied images of the oedipal parents, correctly located in space and time. This gradual giving up the images of oedipal objects as existing in the present, with simultaneously emerging recollections of them as belonging in the past, is analogous to the "classical" sector of mourning work (Freud, 1917) that comprises the gradual "letting die" of the lost object as an individual, through a painful comparison of the re-

called and actual realities, accompanied by a simultaneous rebuilding of the object's image in the mourner's mind as a remembrance of a past object. (426–27)

Tahka concluded,

> As a rule, the content and form of interpretations do not correspond with the experiencing and receiving conditions of a borderline or psychotic patient. Functional experiencing, as well as a partly or fully undifferentiated world of experience, cannot be understood, and that understanding communicated in the form of an interpretation. Instead the functional experiencing, characteristic of borderline patients, can be understood as something that can be empathically described to the patient. The psychotic experiencing, with its partial or total loss of differentiation, will be phase-specifically understood mostly as an unarticulated and thwarted neediness. This understanding can only be communicated by the analyst's letting himself and the treatment setting become a holding atmosphere, impregnated by generative complementarity, that it is hoped will be accepted by the patient as a new developmental agency, leading to a resumed dialogue between him and the object world. Thus, the nature of understanding and its conveyance depend entirely on the respective level of the patient's mental structuralization and relatedness. While an *interpretative* understanding mostly seems to be phase-specifically appropriate for a neurotic patient, a *describing* understanding appears to be similarly adequate for a borderline patient. Finally, the analyst's complementarily tuned-in *presence* understanding seems to represent the most elementary and basic form of phase-specific understanding, necessary in the work with psychotic patients (372)

Put succinctly, the ameliorative agents are "symbolic gratification of a psychotic patient's symbiotic needs, empathic descriptions of a borderline patient's inner experience, or empathically caught and formulated interpretations of a neurotic patient's dissociated mental contents" (352).

Tahka considers *all* these treatment approaches psychoanalytic (and does not designate any of them as "only" psychotherapeutic):

> If by psychoanalytic treatment is meant those applications of established psychoanalytic knowledge that strive to promote maximally a belated growth of the patient's personality, it is obvious that techniques founded in psychoanalytic developmental psychology and proved as phase-specifically adequate and effective should be included under the general heading of psychoanalytic treatment. . . . Many therapeutic interactions

and techniques discussed may customarily be regarded as belonging to psychotherapy and not to psychoanalysis. I do propose, however, that when used in cases in which they have proved to be growth-promoting and phase-specifically founded in the developmental theory of psychoanalysis, they should be regarded as important elements of the entirety of psychoanalytic treatment, in which the classical technique stands as an advanced and well-established segment for the treatment of predominantly neurotic patients. (165)

A few other major contributors in recent years have given explicit attention to a developmental perspective on the therapeutic process. Of those whose work I have already described, Pine (very explicitly as a developmental-psychologist psychoanalyst) and Loewald (as the central figure imbricating a developmentally focused perspective into American ego-psychological understanding of the psychoanalytic process) should especially be noted in this context. In his paper on the four psychologies of psychoanalysis, Pine (1988b) declared that interpretations in what he called the classical manner are most useful in understanding the vicissitudes of the drives and the fate of internalized object-relations, but that with defects in ego functions or deficiencies of the self-experience (presumably anchored in developmentally more archaic mental stages) an "interpretation" "does not in itself lead to a useful 'now I see' experience" because it can "pose the danger of rubbing salt in wounds or of eliminating hope and merely causing pain"; instead, "verbalization may have a significant mutative potential when it comes in the form of description, explanation, and reconstruction—especially within the overall 'holding' context of the analytic relationship" (586)—a formulation quite the same as Tähkä's for dealing with the borderline.

In a paper on theory in relation to technique, Pine (1992) stated his distinction between conflict pathology (presumably the oedipal) and developmental pathology (presumably the preoedipal): "I further propose that interpretation (in the transference or outside it) is a *relatively* more effective tool in dealing with conflict pathology than with developmental pathology" (252).[6] In another paper (1994), he added, "Interpretation may be more fully suited to work in areas of conflict, though we well know that there is no one-to-one correlation between interpretation and insight or between insight and change. What I have tried to do in this paper is to suggest that much interpretive work must also be carried out in the developmentally faulted areas of deficit and defect as well. . . .

6. He defined "developmental pathology" as "Unreliability of object contact or object constancy, failure to tame drives or to develop stable defences, deficiencies in self-esteem, in frustration tolerance, in affect modulation, blurring of self and object boundaries—these and innumerable others" (1992, 252).

But work in these areas may also involve something more, something that includes description and explanatory reconstruction as well as the patient-specific kind of things that I have illustrated at points in this paper" (238).

To place Loewald's profoundly influential developmental views of the psychoanalytic process into appropriate context here, I need only remind the reader of my previous citations from his seminal paper "On the Therapeutic Action of Psychoanalysis" (1960) and of his central theses that a thwarted ego development will be resumed in the psychoanalytic therapeutic process, that this resumption of development is contingent on the relationship with a new object, the analyst, that this (resumed) ego development is a process of increasingly higher integrations and differentiations, that the analyst helps accomplish this task by holding before the patient (and safeguarding for the patient) an image of what the patient could be, and that a proper template for this process—though clearly not a veridical forerunner—is the good enough mother-child or parent-child relationship. The subsequent papers by Loewald also cited in this book (1970, 1979, 1986, 1988) served to extend and deepen the implications of this developmental perspective.

That acceptance of this developmental perspective within the psychoanalytic world is by no means unanimous can be seen from almost diametrically opposed recent statements by two prominent contributors to both the adult and the child psychoanalytic literature. Abrams (1990) posed two differing views of the psychoanalytic process. The integrative view, to which he subscribes (together with a cited list of very illustrious colleagues), essentially sees psychoanalysis as "a treatment that focuses on intrapsychic events and activates integrative tendencies to promote insights" (650), and this works by resulting in the patient's " 'knowing' something in a different way. This different 'knowing' induces changes" (662). By contrast, the developmental perspective, he stated, tried to "activate . . . inherent developmental processes by facilitating . . . stage consolidation and thereby enabling new integrations and structural reorganization to take place" (657). Abrams's strong objection to this perspective is that a supportive focus on helping to propel and consolidate a developmental process, while perhaps *psychotherapeutically* useful at various treatment junctures, may run counter to the *psychoanalytic* intent to uncover the deformative pressures on current functioning emanating from the past. He feels that this stems from confounding the meaning of the word "developmental" when applied in the same (undifferentiated) way to growth processes in children and to their presumed analogues in adults (the latter over even the entire life cycle).[7] The developmental concept,

7. Abrams took sharp exception, for example, to a colleague's paper in which "an elderly widower is described who learns to cook and entertain in his own home after mourning his dead

he stated, properly applies to childhood growth and progressive development powered by a biologically determined, maturationally unfolding timetable that gives rise to progressive transformations (not just endless reworkings on higher integrative levels) of earlier achievements, for example, the successful childhood negotiation of the separation-individuation process. To Abrams, what is called "development" and "developmental" throughout the life process *and* the treatment process should not be so cavalierly equated and confused with this clear childhood growth process, and his article was intended to illustrate the intellectual mischief that such confusion can produce.

The contrary (prodevelopmental perspective) view of the psychoanalytic process has been articulated by Lichtenberg (1988) in his contribution to the Rothstein (1988) volume. Lichtenberg put this perspective as follows:

> I suggest that pathological developments may be corrected or reversed by two processes innately preprogrammed as emergent capacities—the tendency for self righting and the capacity to form and reorganize symbolic gratifications. Exploratory psychotherapy and psychoanalysis are fashioned to promote both self righting and symbolic reorganization. By self righting I mean an inherent tendency to respond to a positive change in an external condition [like the impact of the relationship with the "new" object, the therapist]. In self righting, a normal developmental step that has not been taken or a normal experience that has been absent becomes possible. . . . symbolic representation is the result of information processing in . . . cognitive-affective modes [the role of interpretation and insight]. . . . I would place all the factors we have been offered to explain how treatment works into these two inherent potentials for recovery that each human has.[8] (186–87)

---

wife. This new adaptation is explained as due to *developmental* processes . . . without much regard as to what intrapsychic activities were mobilized to effect such changes" (1990, 667).

8. The workers at the Anna Freud Centre in London expectedly weigh in on the prodevelopmental side in this debate. Peter Fonagy and George Moran (1991), in an article on the nature of psychic change in child analysis, divided the domain of inquiry with children into neurotic disturbances and developmental disturbances. In neurotic disturbances we work with a representational conceptual model with conflict amongst organized mental structures and interpretation is the central therapeutic tool. In developmental disturbances (borderline, narcissistic, atypical, etc.) we work with a mental process conceptual model, i.e. a pathology of a maldeveloped ego and inhibited mental processes. Here 'developmental help'—not very clearly specified—needs to be offered to the child-patient." The authors concluded, "We take the view that the concept of structural change . . . encompasses both psychic changes achieved through modification of [distorted] mental representations and the re-establishment of inhibited mental processes. Both representation and process are subject to dynamic factors and interpretation in

It can be readily seen from these counterposed views of Abrams and Lichtenberg that acceptance of the developmental perspective on the psychoanalytic treatment process is far from being a settled matter in psychoanalytic thinking.

---

the psychoanalytic situation" (21). Earlier in the article the authors had grounded their whole line of thinking in Anna Freud's conceptions: "In her studies of child psychopathology she came to distinguish primary developmental disturbances which were due to an imbalance in the unfolding of development on the one hand, from true neurotic disturbances which were initiated by frustrations at a higher level of development, leading to a regressive search for drive satisfaction at an earlier mental level, on the other" (16).

While psychoanalytic contributors from around the world have figured prominently throughout this book, I have also emphasized that the special circumstances peculiar to the American scene made it the logical locus for the development of psychotherapies based on the theory of psychoanalysis but with techniques adapted to the clinical needs of the wider array of patients not amenable to classical analysis. In this chapter, I trace the growth of a dynamic psychotherapy in Great Britain, making itself felt independently of the American development (at least in the first decades), with actually an even earlier onset, albeit, at least in the earlier days, with less conceptual and theoretical clarification. It is also fair to say that the impact of this development in Britain was always more circumscribed than the comparable development in America and, for the most part, was on the periphery of the medical-psychiatric world of medical schools and hospitals. In a review article on the relationship between psychoanalysis and psychotherapy, Glover (1960b) made this same point: "Apart from . . . [its] firm integration with psychiatry, psychoanalysis in the U.S. has established much closer relations with general medicine, general psychology and social work than is the case in England. . . . Non-analytical psychiatrists make more extensive use of analytical concepts in treatment than do their opposite numbers in England. . . . Social workers in the U.S. are also more analytical in orientation than they are in this country" (76).

Glover placed the beginning development of "general psychotherapy" (73) in Britain in the immediate post–World War I period and especially mentioned in this connection the establishment of the Tavistock Clinic in 1920. But, he said, "down almost to the Second World War the main body of psychiatrists remained aloof from and usually hostile to medical psychology. In fact the solitary forum for the interchange of ideas on the subject was provided by the Medical Section of the British Psychological Society." This situation changed after World War II, however: "As far as general psychotherapy is concerned, the outstanding feature of the last fifteen years [1945–1960] has been the increasing involvement of psychiatry in psychotherapeutic method, a development which proceeded apace during and after the Second World War, and [which] in spite of a moratorium brought about by the introduction of neuro-psychiatric methods (shock, drug therapies and neuro-surgery) has retained some of its original impetus." Glover called this "general psychotherapy" partly psychoanalytic and partly a "hotch-potch" (74). He offered his own demarcation: "The difference between psychoanalysis and general psychotherapy is the difference between a mainly dynamic and a mainly structural approach, in the one case reducing pathogenic charges and in the other reinforcing the ego-defences against pathogenic charges" (82). And he also offered his misgivings: "There seems no reason to suppose that in course of time, the sharp distinction between psychoanalysis and rapport therapies will not become blurred in this country also [as in the U.S.]" (81–82)—a trend he clearly deplored.

Malcolm Pines (1990, 1991a, 1991b), a historian of dynamic psychotherapy in Britain, has characterized "psychodynamic psychiatry" as "not identical to, though closely linked with the psychoanalytic school." Turning into virtue what Glover scorned as merely "hotch-potch," he said it had "the character-istically British features of eclecticism, empiricism, and individualism" (1991a, 31). The formal beginnings of this development, Pines said, were W. H. B. Stoddart's 1915 lectures entitled "The New Psychiatry" at the Royal College of Physicians in Edinburgh. He also spoke of the early involvement of Ernest Jones, David Eder, and Bernard Hart. Hart's book *The Psychology of Insanity* (1913), Pines declared, "was probably the most widely read and influential work on a psychoanalytic approach to psychiatry for more than two decades" (1991b, 210). It was the combined endeavors of these men and a good many others that, in the context of the neuropsychiatric disorders in the military in World War I, succeeded in wresting British psychiatry from its domination by neurology and making it more receptive to a psychological approach to mental illness.

Until then, as Pines stated, there was "a very highly developed neurological science in England, but psychiatry was almost non-existent—much below the level recorded . . . in France and Italy; it was thus entirely subordinate to neu-rology and took its cue from the latter" (1991b, 207). Hughlings Jackson, the dominant figure in British neurology, was staunchly opposed to psychoanalysis. During World War I the struggle between a neurological and a psychological approach to mental casualties, battle hysteria, neurasthenia, shell shock, and the like was joined within the British army. Pines wrote, "The war saw much suffering, many brave men broken down by the stress of warfare, and many left cruelly and stupidly treated by neurologists, who saw it as their task to force distressed soldiers, by whatever means they chose to apply, to give up their symptoms" (1991b, 218). But the organically trained psychiatrists seemed no better equipped. Pines quoted a 1917 article from *Lancet,* the prestigious British medical journal: "We do not misrepresent the situation when we state that the average neurologist has, as a rule, been preoccupied with the organic nervous disease to the exclusion of functional disease; while the psychiatrist, attached to an institution, has little or no chance of studying, and no incitement to study, mental disease in its early manifestations" (1991b, 213).

Into this therapeutic vacuum stepped the first generation of British analysts, led by Jones, together with psychoanalytically interested psychiatrists, followers of Jung and Adler, and diverse allies ranging from members of the Society for Psychical Research (students of spiritualism and psychic phenomena), followers of Havelock Ellis, the "philosopher of love," and all the intellectual and literary supporters of the psychoanalytic idea in the Bloomsbury Group, including Bertrand Russell, Maynard Keynes, Lytton Strachey, Roger Fry, Clive Bell, Leonard and Virginia Woolf,[1] James and Alix Strachey, and Adrian and Karin Stephens (1985). (The last four of these became well-known psychoanalysts.) It was in this ferment in the immediate aftermath of World War I that the Tavistock Clinic and the Cassel Hospital were established for the psychological treatment of mental illness. One can say that with these developments the New Psychiatry and the New Psychology took root in Britain.[2]

At the Tavistock, an outpatient psychotherapy facility, the New Psychiatry was represented by J. R. Rees, Henry Dicks, Ian Suttie (whose book *The Origins of Love and Hate* [1935] can be viewed as the beginnings of the British object-relational school), Wilfred Bion, John Bowlby, Michael Balint, and a host of others; its work was given major impetus by concern with the war neuroses and their sequelae and with issues of loss, separation, bereavement, and mourning in the wake of the war. "The 'New Psychologists,' " Pines said, "were prepared to work with all psychotherapeutic techniques, suggestion, persuasion, and to

1. Virginia Woolf, as is well known, was less friendly to psychoanalysis than most other members of the Bloomsbury Group. Pines wrote, "Virginia Woolf . . . avoided reading Freud for many years. Her early attitude to psychoanalysis was that it represented an unbearable intrusion into personal privacy, for even the private realm of illness should remain veiled" (1991b, 228). Yet her husband, Leonard Woolf, founded and managed the Hogarth Press, which, among other things, published the monographs of the International Psycho-Analytical Library as well as Freud's five-volume Collected Papers and later the twenty-volume Standard Edition. For a full account of this fascinating story, see Perry Meisel and Walter Kendrick, eds., *Bloomsbury/ Freud: The Letters of James and Alix Strachey, 1924–1925.*

2. Actually, the Brunswick Square Clinic and an associated training center for psychotherapy had been established several years earlier (1913–15) and were soon joined by James Glover, brother of Edward. However, in 1920, Glover went to Berlin for analysis with Abraham, with "the consequence . . . that Glover became a convert to a more disciplined form of psychoanalysis, and therefore opposed the eclectic therapy that was practised at the clinic" (Pines 1991b, 212). And he influenced a whole group of pioneer psychoanalysts away from it. Within a few years the clinic, its society, and the training center were all liquidated, some members going to the newly established British Psycho-Analytical Society, some to the Tavistock Clinic.

some extent hypnosis, and to apply psychoanalysis in full or modified form when these methods did not succeed" (1990, 6).

In the same period the British Psycho-Analytical Society was established by Jones and others (1920) to replace the earlier London Psycho-Analytical Society, which Jones had disbanded because it had been heavily infiltrated by Jungians. The official journal of the British Society, the *International Journal of Psycho-Analysis,* was founded in 1920, as was the *British Journal of Psychology: Medical Section,* (two years later renamed the *British Journal of Medical Psychology*) with Jones among its editors and articles by Pierre Janet, William McDougall, Jones, Jung, Morton Prince, Theodor Reik, and J. C. Flugel in early issues. All this built up to Jones's great triumph in 1926, when, after fierce discussion, an official committee of inquiry of the British Medical Association "acknowledged that psychoanalysis was an authentic form of treatment and that the term should not be used for any other technique or theory, apart from those described by Freud." This imprimatur was not given to psychotherapy. Pines added drily, "This result was very welcome to the British Psychoanalytical Society" (1991b, 221).

Jones clearly played a central role in all these developments, and yet in regard to psychotherapy other than "strict and untendentious psychoanalysis" his attitude was always markedly ambivalent and in many ways very oppositional. Pines strongly faults Jones for his obstructive positions: "In the 1930s, the eclectic school, partly represented by the Tavistock Clinic, and psychoanalysts within the Psychoanalytic Society both emphasized object relationships. This British school followed a largely separate developmental line from that of the Viennese. However, there was a definite cleavage between the Tavistock and the Psychoanalytical Society, which seems to have been largely the work of Ernest Jones. He felt the need to maintain strict control of psychoanalysis, and therefore forbade members of the Psychoanalytical Society to work at the Tavistock—a ban only removed after World War II" (1991b, 224). Elsewhere, Pines had said that the ban was levied because Jones "saw this [the work at the Tavistock] as a dilution of the pure gold of psychoanalysis" (1991a, 39). And in reference to the work of W. H. R. Rivers, an English psychiatrist interested in spreading psychoanalytic ideas into mental treatment (and who, Pines said, "probably more than anyone else, made psychoanalytic thinking acceptable to a wide circle of influential persons—psychiatrists, psychologists and anthropologists" [1991b, 217]), Pines charged, "Jones, Edward Glover, John Rickman and other pioneer analysts vehemently opposed the work of people such as Rivers, who they saw as purloiners of Freud's ideas without being true disciples. It was this intransigent view . . . that helped maintain the longstanding isolation of psychoanalysis from the mainstream of British psychiatry" (1991a, 36)[3]—along, of course, with the equally intransigent positions of many in the British academic psychiatry establishment on the other side of this great divide. The implication is clear: these entrenched hostilities significantly delayed the development of a solid psychoanalytic psychotherapy in Britain as compared with America.

And yet ultimately the enterprise flourished, and Pines's (recent) judgment is both prideful and upbeat: "British empiricism, and the tendency to seek compromises, led to the creation of a native school of psychotherapy that was original in its synthesis but not in its origins. Outside of psychoanalysis proper, confined to the Psycho-Analytical Society, there was steady progress towards the recognition of family dynamics, the importance of the maternal and sibling relationships in emotional development and of a need to apply psychodynamic understanding to problems of disturbed children and of delinquency. A movement that can produce the Tavistock Clinic and the Cassel Hospital, the Institute for Scientific Treatment of Delinquency and the Portman Clinic, that can promote the work of Winnicott and Bowlby and the Independent Group [the official designation of those who espouse the object-relational perspective] of the Psychoanalytic Movement has much to its credit" (1990, 8).

Of these many achievements between the two world wars, pride of place goes to the Tavistock Clinic. In 1970, Henry Dicks, one of its senior long-term clinicians, wrote a loving history of its first fifty years, that, together with the articles by Pines, richly portrayed the singular position of the "Tavi" in the evolution of psychodynamic *psychotherapy* in Britain. In 1920, in the wake of World War I, Hugh Crichton-Miller, "impressed by these [wartime] experiences, . . . decided to found a clinic for the treatment of functional nervous disorders, and soon attracted to it a number of like-minded persons. . . . Crichton-Miller was always an eclectic, both a supporter of psychoanalysis and an advocate of holistic medicine" (Pines 1991b, 221)—and the Tavistock soon became "the main centre of psychodynamic psychiatry in Britain" (Pines 1991b, 221–22). The Tavistock's main goal, "to provide systematic major psychotherapy on the basis of concepts inspired by psychoanalytic theory for outpatients

3. In that same article, Pines tried to give a balanced portrayal of Jones's overall role in British psychoanalysis, psychiatry, and psychotherapy, but clearly his biases tipped the scales of judgment negatively: "Jones likes to portray himself as the father figure of British psychoanalysis and, with his combative nature and intellectual brilliance, he did indeed play the most significant part in the British psychoanalytical movement for many years. However, there were negative aspects to his contributions. He drew tight boundaries around the Psycho-Analytic Society, more or less dictated who would be accepted as a psychoanalyst and excluded from the Society many people who had contributed significantly to the widening knowledge and acceptance of Freud's ideas before, during and after the First World War" (Pines 1991a, 33).

suffering from psychoneurosis and allied disorders who were unable to afford private fees" (Dicks 1970, 1), soon expanded from the shell-shocked or the battle neuroses of World War I to all the "educated poor" (17).

The Tavistock was created with a multidisciplinary and a multitheoretical team, including Freudians, Jungians, Adlerians, McDougallians, self-styled eclectics, and followers of Janet and the French suggestionist school. According to Dicks, "The Clinic from the first had a curiously independent, indeed isolated, position somewhere between official psychiatry and medicine on the one hand and 'orthodox' psychoanalysis on the other." It was a "meeting ground of psychotherapists of several schools or of none" and therefore "not wholly committed to the then still much feared and suspect psychoanalytic school (to whom nonetheless the Tavistock staff group owed much of its conceptual basis)" (1970, p. 2) This particular position as self-conscious bridge between the psychiatric establishment and the psychoanalytic establishment helped explain the peculiar fate of the Tavi. Though its roster over the years included almost all of the major Middle Group (or Independent) analysts and in later years many of the most influential Kleinians as well as analysts from abroad who were training and studying in England,[4] it was at the same time regarded with suspicion by the "orthodox" British Psychoanalytical Society under the leadership of Jones. The Tavistock's range of therapeutic offerings was as diverse as its staff: "The analytic procedure could be carried out under conditions resembling the orthodox method; indeed, some patients received full [psycho]analytic therapy from those who themselves had been analysed. Others received treatment more nearly resembling the Jungian technique, or the kind of therapy which can be summed up as analytic counselling with liberal doses of suggestion or persuasion" (Dicks 1970, 29).

World War II and its aftermath gave the Tavistock additional impetus. A cadre of individuals with Tavistock connections—Bion, S. H. Foulkes, John Rickman, John D. Sutherland, Harold Bridger, Eric Trist, and Tom Main among them—were drawn together in the British army as part of the Northfield Experiment, working on problems of officer selection, personnel placement, military morale, and the rehabilitation of battle casualties and returned prisoners of war. They came back as the "invisible college" of Tavistock people, effectively taking over the Tavistock Clinic, with Sutherland as the newly named

---

4. At the invidious risk of omitting equally noteworthy names, I will mention only Bion, Rickman, Suttie, Little, Malan, Wittkower, Fordham, Trist, Sutherland, Main, Foulkes, Bowlby, Jacques, Ezriel, Caplan, Menzies, Bridger, Dicks, Robertson, Ainsworth, Sandler, Rice, Turquet, Heinecke, Hinde, Laing, Balint, Rycroft, Joffe, and from abroad, Sanford, Janis, Newcomb, Shakow, Jahoda, Mitscherlisch, and Teruel.

medical director. Pines wrote, "The post-war history of the Tavistock represents the end of the period of eclectic psychotherapy and the full dominance of psychoanalysis [as the theory underpinning all the psychotherapy]. The 'invisible college' of Tavistock staff who had been active and successful in wartime psychiatry came together . . . and, under the chairmanship of Bion, made a successful take-over bid. Long-standing members of the pre-war Tavistock staff eventually resigned, and the new clinic began to take shape" (1991b, 224)—at last, thoroughly psychoanalytic in the theoretic basis underlying its psychotherapy, with a gradual shift in theoretical perspective from the object-relational (the Middle or Independent Group) toward the Kleinian. In 1948, the Tavistock opted to affiliate with the newly established National Health Service (NHS); the burgeoning Tavistock Institute of Human Relations (TIHR), its nonclinical social science research and application arm, was separately incorporated outside the NHS.

Programs diversified into the realms of group analytic study and therapy (Bion, Foulkes), out of which developed the Leicester Conferences on Group Relations (A. K. Rice), work with general practitioner groups on the applications of psychoanalytic understanding to the problems of general medical practice (Balint and the Balint Group movement), research into brief psychodynamic therapy (David Malan, inspired by Balint) and the psychological understanding of industrial relations (Elliott Jacques, Trist), and, probably best known and ultimately most widely influential—especially within developmental psychology and also ethology—Bowlby's work on attachment, separation, and maternal deprivation. Taken together, these undertakings reflected a self-conscious effort to broaden the influence of psychoanalytic thinking into all the spheres of preventive and social psychiatry, including the community mental health emphasis of the NHS. The role of the Tavistock in these developments was summarized by Jonathan Pedder (1990a): "Since . . . [Freud], psychoanalytic ideas have been applied in individual, group, family and marital therapy, brief therapy and child psychotherapy. The Tavistock has been central in these developments and applications, and particularly the three B's . . . : Bion, Bowlby and Balint" (208). It is part of the glory of the Tavistock that many of the seminal contributions by these three major figures were made from within their base at the Tavi.

The Cassel Hospital, a psychotherapeutically oriented inpatient psychiatric facility, was founded in 1920, the same year as the Tavistock outpatient clinic, but did not become a dominant force in British psychoanalytic psychotherapy until the arrival of Tom Main as medical director in 1946. Main, along with Rickman, Jacques, Dicks, Bridger, Isobel Menzies Lyth, Trist, and Bion, was part of the invisible college of the Tavistock at Northfield Hospital during the war, and his goal at the Cassel Hospital was to create a thoroughly psychoanalytic "therapeutic community" of interdependent and mutually supporting systems geared to the psychological rehabilitation of the severely mentally ill. Like the Tavistock, the Cassel came into the NHS in 1948. Over the thirty years of Main's directorship, about one-quarter of the members of the British Psycho-analytical Society worked for some period at the Cassel; Main's own theoretical allegiance was to the Independent Group. Under his guidance the Cassel pio-neered such ventures as admitting whole families for conjoint treatment and creating a special unit where ill mothers could have their babies with them in the hospital.

Eric Rayner, in his introduction to Main's collected papers (1989), said, "Main wanted to create a model hospital community that was self-examining in all its systems" (xix) and felt that this must be securely rooted in a psycho-analytic base. Rayner continued, "Tom Main's therapeutic community, with its basis resting upon individual psychotherapy, has always been thought to de-mand a high concentration of therapists who are analytically trained" (xxviii). And Jennifer Johns, in the same volume, summarized Main's impact as follows: "Tom Main describes his life's work as having two strands. One is that of training others, beginning in the Army and continuing at the Cassel. . . . He is very aware of the numbers of psychoanalysts, doctors, nurses, community work-ers and so on who have passed through the Cassel and spread its influence widely, as well as their more direct experience of being trained by him. His second perspective is that of the application of psychoanalysis, which he believes enriches and fertilizes many other fields, and can be enriched in turn, while maintaining clinical experience in the consulting room as an essential to avoid dilution of psychoanalysis itself" (4). Hayley (1991), in his obituary of Main, said, "He was essentially a psychoanalytically oriented social psychiatrist" (722). These comments could just as well have been made of Jock Sutherland, Main's psychoanalytic confrere, also of the Independent (object-relational) group. As medical director of the Tavistock, Sutherland too was devoted to the two realms of intensive clinical training and the applications of psychoanalysis to realms of human endeavor beyond the individual—families, groups, culture.

The evolution of psychotherapy at the Maudsley, the most renowned aca-demic and research psychiatric hospital in England, was different from that of the Tavistock and the Cassel, which had a psychoanalytic frame and purpose almost from the beginning as well as an increasingly psychoanalytic leadership and programing. Henry Maudsley, after whom the hospital was subsequently named, wrote in the late nineteenth century, "It is not our business, it is not in our power to explain *psychologically* the origin and nature of any of the depraved instincts manifested in typical cases of insanity. . . . The explanation, when it comes, will not come from a mental, but from a physical side" (quoted in Pines

1991b, 207). The physician for the mentally ill in this frame carried a moral/ pastoral responsibility, authoritarian, patriarchal, benign, and well intentioned; in this context, "the new methods of psychological analysis were perceived as being incompatible with the traditional professional conceptions of the doctor's moral/pastoral responsibilities" (208). This spirit has been well represented by Sir Aubrey Lewis and Hans Eysenck, the figures identified most closely with the post–World War II Maudsley.

Nonetheless, there has also been another, less prominent conceptual current at the Maudsley. As early as 1923, in his annual report, Edward Mapother wrote, "All forms of this [psychotherapy at the Maudsley] have been practised here— ordinary suggestion, persuasion and re-education, superficial analysis, explora- tion under light hypnosis and complete psychoanalysis. Though I find myself incapable of accepting all the alleged facts of any school of psychoanalysis, or all the concepts proposed by them, yet there is no doubt of the great advance which the intensive methods introduced by these schools have made in their understanding of cases, nor is there any doubt that in certain cases results are achieved by psychoanalysis which cannot be otherwise obtained, whatever the exact explanation may be" (Pines 1991b, 225).

Pedder (1990b) pointed to the continuing presence of psychoanalysts at the Maudsley almost since the beginnings of British psychoanalysis. In 1994, fifty- seven of the members of the British Psychoanalytical Society and ten of the candidates worked at the Maudsley, and "the majority of our senior registrars over the years have been also engaged in psychoanalytic training and moved on to occupy important consultant psychotherapy posts" (15). Nonetheless, Pedder has said (personal communication) that "the Maudsley is chronically ambivalent about psychoanalysis" and has only recently filled (by an analyst) a senior lecturer post in psychotherapy. "At the Maudsley," Pedder wrote, "we have often ar- gued about whether we should be content to remain part of the underculture, available to those who find our psychoanalytic way of thinking valuable, or whether we should strive toward greater integration into the total life of the Joint Hospital and Institute of Psychiatry, where the emphasis is on research" (15).

Another signal institution, also psychoanalytically inspired, was the Psycho- pathic Clinic, founded in 1933 and renamed the Portman Clinic when it moved to Portman Street in 1937. The Portman was created by the Institute for the Scientific Study of Delinquency to be a "model delinquency clinic" (Rumney 1992), with the aim, in Edward Glover's words (quoted by Rumney), of con- ducting "diagnosis, treatment, and, where possible, research." The treatment offered was psychotherapy based on psychodynamic principles. Glover was in- strumental in the creation of the clinic and was one of its early medical directors, later an emeritus consultant; and psychoanalysts have continued to play central roles into the 1990s (Mervin Glasser, Adam Limentani). There was always a large caseload, mostly referred from the courts and probation officers and encompassing individuals found guilty of robbery, fraud, sexual deviancy, arson, vandalism, delinquency, and so on. Glover called it "the only specialised clinic dealing under ambivalent conditions with offenders of all ages." Most of the therapy was only once weekly and much of it under court order; this "led to interesting and valuable adaptations of the 'classical' psychoanalytic treatment framework." Like the Tavistock and the Cassel, the Portman was taken into the NHS in 1948. In 1950, the *British Journal of Delinquency* (renamed the *British Journal of Criminology* ten years later) appeared under its auspices.

Last in this description of psychoanalytically based psychotherapy settings is the Brent Consultation Centre, recently renamed Johnston House, for the treatment of disturbed adolescents. Unlike the others, Johnston House was started after World War II and was never incorporated into the NHS. The original impetus in the early 1960s was from Anna Freud; the first effort failed, but a few years later the clinic was revived under the auspices of the Borough of Brent in London, which subsidized its work for twenty years. In addition to offering consultation and many workshops for educators, police, youth leaders, and community workers, the Brent Centre has sustained about a dozen adolescents in full-scale, five-times-weekly psychoanalysis, plus a somewhat larger number in once- or twice-weekly psychotherapy. The work done there and its theoretical base have been described in *Adolescence and Developmental Breakdown,* by Moses and Egle Laufer (1984). Recently, financial exigencies led to the termination of the funding by the Borough of Brent, and M. Laufer wrote (personal communication), "Although we certainly intend to maintain our service and research, the present atmosphere is not in our favour, partly because of extreme lack of funds and the general atmosphere in the country to find cheaper ways of working, quicker results, and efforts to dismiss psychoanalytic work."

This chapter does not describe the work of the Hampstead Clinic (now called the Anna Freud Centre), developed in the immediate wake of World War II out of the Hampstead War Nurseries. This is because, though there has always been substantial work with parents, much consultation activity, and a nursery school (with both normal and problematic or disturbed children), its main focus has been on training and clinical work, specifically in *child psychoanalysis.* I do, however, discuss the *British Journal of Medical Psychology,* which for a long time was the central carrier of the accumulating literature on this psychotherapy that stood uneasily between the "orthodox" psychoanalytic establishment and the "orthodox" psychiatric establishment. Founded in 1920, with Jones a major figure on the first editorial board, within the first decade it published almost all the major figures in British (and world) psychoanalysis, including Karl Abraham, Marjorie Brierley, Rickman, Edward and James Glover, Sylvia Payne, Melanie Klein, Ferenczi, Roger Money-Kyrle, Susan Isaacs, Trigant Burrow, and Georg Groddeck. In 1926, with volume 6, Rickman joined the editorial board, and in 1935 (volume 15) he became editor in chief. After World War II, Sutherland succeeded to the editorship, and in 1957 he in turn was succeeded by Main and Sandler as co–editors in chief. The psychoanalytic dominance in this journal was indeed well established.

I will mention only a few of the articles that appeared in the journal, especially in the earlier formative years for the journal and for the psychoanalytic psychotherapy enterprise. James Glover (1926), in his Presidential Address to the Medical Section of the British Psychological Society, spoke to the effort to establish a *scientific* psychotherapy. He dismissed the environmental manipulations much in vogue at the time: "The treatment of neurotic disorders by modifications of environment is a 'hit or miss' therapy, in accordance with whether or not it meets certain psychological needs, which escape ordinary methods of observation, and even at best it is a therapy of palliation and not of cure" (101–02). He then posed the contrasting visions of a pure psychoanalysis versus a modified psychoanalytic psychotherapy: The relationship, or rapport, or the transference "can be exploited along one of two directions. . . . Now the choice he has to make is between using the Transference to influence the patient directly and using it as a technical means of bringing into consciousness his forgotten infantile past, and the dilemma arises from the fact that in order to achieve this second technical result he must scrupulously refrain from the first" (107); again, "we may add ourselves to a recurring unrealized series of parent representatives, or we may free our patient from this fated repetition and endless re-enacting of attitudes responsible for his neurosis, but we cannot do both" (108)—a dichotomization of psychoanalysis from (suggestive, or transferential) psychotherapy in the spirit of Jones and Edward Glover, quite distinct from what would become the American differentiation of a continuum of psychotherapies, from the most supportive to the most expressive, psychoanalysis itself.

A series of five articles in 1930 discussed the *psychotherapy* of the psychoses. Here, too, the discussion dichotomized, between H. Devine, who called himself an "institution psychiatrist" (220), and Edward Glover, R. D. Gillespie, Melanie Klein, and Sylvia Payne, all psychoanalysts. Devine's stand was that psychotherapy could be therapeutically useful to the psychotic while psychoanalysis could not: "It will probably be generally admitted that the therapeutic possibilities of psycho-analysis are definitely limited in their scope, and that, as far as the psychoses are concerned, they are practically negligible. Similar limitations would appear to exist in respect to the therapeutic methods associated with the names of Jung and Adler" (217). But Devine saw a definite place for the psychotherapy of psychotics: "It might be maintained that if the psychoses are related to definite physiological disturbances or changes, as I personally believe them to be, psychotherapy could scarcely be expected to be efficacious as a curative remedy. Certainly I would not suggest that psychotherapy could cure a psychotic, but would assert with confidence that it helps to do so. . . . Though the psychotherapeutic methods utilized in psychotic patients cannot be considered causal or specific in their aims, this does not mean that they are haphazard and unsystematized, though it must be admitted that, like much medical treatment, art as well as science is called for in these cases" (221). Devine went on to indicate his approaches: "To develop what is normal in the psychotic patient, as he is unable to dissipate what is abnormal . . . ; to exercise the function of consciousness in the hope that the narrow, isolated, morbid psychic content . . . may melt away, or at least be relegated to the background, as wider social relations become established. . . . It is essentially an active therapy, and because of this it is evident that the psychiatrist cannot be after the manner of the analyst, a shadowy figure in the background, for he has to intervene in the life of his patient, advise, stimulate, and be a friend as well as a doctor" (222–23). But Devine nonetheless found a place for psychoanalysis: "Possibly its discoveries may do something in the way of prevention of the psychoses, and the emphases it has given to the significance of family situations and sexual difficulties give precision and direction to the advice given to the psychotic patient at a stage when he is sufficiently receptive to respond intelligently to psychotherapy" (224).

Expectedly, the psychoanalysts took an opposed position and spoke for the efficacy of a (modified) psychoanalytic approach. Glover was the most comprehensive. In disagreement with Freud's dictum, he said, "The main difficulty in such analysis [of psychotics] is not the absence of positive transference but the heavy bias of concealed negative transference which is performing a protective function" (1930, 229–30). He then commented on "the most ticklish problem in analytic treatment": "It is essential that the analysis should be maintained as long as is possible, or rather advisable, wrapped in the cotton-wool of a narcissistic identification. One steps out from time to time for the specific purpose of reducing guilt and retires at once to passivity. . . . But ultimately the delusional system must be drawn into the analysis and examined directly" (230). Finally, "the modifications necessary in treating different conditions do not imply modifications in analytic principle, but are simply adaptations of a method of mental approach in accordance with the variety of mechanisms encountered" (232). In the discussion period after the five papers, Glover, in reference to Devine, dismissed "the so-called organic methods [of treatment as] . . . simply 'hit or miss' systems of psychotherapy . . . in that sense [they] deserve to be called the 'wild' psychotherapy of the psychoses" (249). What was so characteristic of the British experience in this saga (in contrast to the American) was that psychoanalysts and traditional psychiatrists, whatever their differences, were discussing issues of shared concern face-to-face.

Five years later, Clifford Allen (1935), talking of the "early psychotic" and the "prepsychotic," those whom we would today probably call borderline, contrasted the psychoanalytically informed approach to these cases with the more classical approach to the usual neurotic:

> A totally different technique is essential with psychotics [read, borderline] in contradistinction to, let us say, hysterics. Somewhat crudely, it may be stated that with hysterics it is the *past* traumatic events and phantasies which are deeply buried under a barrier of repression that must be broken down to unearth them, whereas with psychotics it is found that the phantasies are quite conscious, or at any rate near consciousness, but that they are *present* phantasies, although of course rooted in infantile wishes. The meaning of these phantasies must be discovered and attacked by continuous interpretation, which is a wearisome business, but it seems the most effectual way. There is a curious resemblance to Melanie Klein's analyses of children and of course, psychologically, the psychotic is an infant. (151)

Except for the simplistic final sentence, this whole quotation could have come from our present-day discourse on the modifications of psychoanalytic techniques with borderlines (see discussion of Kernberg, chapter 20).

Payne (1936) once again conflated all psychotherapy other than psychoanalysis with suggestion, indicative of the continuing power of this viewpoint in Britain:

> Apart from the employment of suggestion with hypnosis, analytical treatment which is adulterated by suggestion is likely to figure largely amongst methods of psychotherapy for practical reasons. The main drawback to superficial forms of analysis combined with direct or indirect methods of suggestion is that the most dynamic instrument in the technique of psycho-analysis cannot be employed in a way which will give most benefit to the patient. The transference between the patient and doctor is always of paramount importance whether it is recognized or not. If it is not analyzed and the patient is helped by the treatment, it means that an allegiance to the doctor of a varying degree remains and a disturbance to the positive aspect of the transference may mean relapse. The persisting

transference situation does not necessarily cause trouble, but it is liable to do so in certain cases. (9)

The opposite tack was taken by Crichton-Miller (1937), the nonpsychoanalyst founder and first director of the Tavistock: "The Freudian School will make a notable step forward, if I may venture to say so, when it admits openly that objectivity, as a condition of therapy, however desirable, is unattainable; that suggestion infiltrates every analysis, and that, even without the phenomena of the transference, no analysis can conform to scientific criteria" (182). Again, an exchange of views that could well reflect a very contemporary dialogue on the role of suggestion, or "relationship factors," or "supportive mechanisms" in psychoanalytic work.

Finally, from the pre–World War II period, in 1938 this journal published another noteworthy sequence of articles, from a symposium on the treatment of the unwilling patient, led by Denis Carroll, director of the Institute for the Scientific Treatment of Delinquency. The methods described were reminiscent of Ferenczi's active therapy and August Aichhorn's (1935) approaches to the treatment of the delinquent. The symposium ended on an optimistic note: "Detailed [psycho]analysis is out of the question in the circumstances [once-weekly treatment], but many successes are promised even from the methods which are possible" (Woodcock 1938, 75).

As in the United States, psychoanalytic psychotherapy in Britain after World War II has greatly diversified. There has been a succession of official and institutional landmarks:

1. The institution of the NHS in 1948; as has been mentioned, the Tavistock Clinic, the Cassel Hospital, and the Portman Clinic, all psychoanalytic bulwarks, soon joined it, whereas the British Psycho-Analytical Society and Anna Freud's Hampstead Clinic opted to remain outside
2. The founding of the Association of Child Psychotherapists in 1949, with two major centers training for entry to it, the Hampstead Clinic outside the NHS and the Tavistock Clinic within the NHS
3. The organization in 1951 of the British Association of Psychotherapists, with parallel Freudian and Jungian training tracks
4. The formal recognition of psychotherapy as a separate specialty by the Departments of Health and Social Security in 1975
5. The organization of the Association of Psychoanalytic Psychotherapists in the NHS and the founding of two journals, *Psychoanalytic Psychotherapy* and the *British Journal of Psychotherapy*
6. The recent creation of an umbrella organization, the United Kingdom

Standing Conference for Psychotherapy (UKSCP), which is playing a major role in current planning for an all-European Federation of Psychoanalytic Psychotherapy (EFPP).

Pedder, who has been chronicling these developments, sees the field of dynamic psychotherapy in Britain today as "a separate specialty of psychotherapy, both separate from psychiatry and within it" (1989, 44); further, "Tensions between the pure gold of analysis and its applications have always been a problem. . . . I see psychoanalysis as the central lighthouse that illuminates and informs all other forms of analytic psychotherapy, and by the light of which dynamic psychotherapists in varying craft navigate at varying distances from the rock on which the lighthouse stands. We need both devoted lighthouse keepers and rough-and-ready sailors prepared to explore into strange waters. Too often they tend to polarise and scorn each other, failing to recognise that each depends on and needs the other" (1990a, 210). In terms of theoretic conceptualization, Pedder first quoted Guntrip that "the position that seems to be emerging is that at all stages psychotherapy has to be an appropriate mixture of mothering (management) and analysis (giving insight)" and then, "As I would see it, it is a mixture of feminine and masculine elements, both of which the analytic psychotherapist has to combine in him- or herself" (1989, 48).

It should be clear from the material presented to this point that it is the object-relational perspective (the former Middle, now Independent, Group within the British Psychoanalytical Society) that has been most concerned with the evolving relationships of psychoanalysis and the psychoanalytic psychotherapies.[5] Chapters 16 and 17 have emphasized how congenial this object-relational theoretical perspective, associated with the names of such pioneer British analysts as Suttie, Fairbairn, Guntrip, Balint, Winnicott, and Bowlby, and the many who have come after, has been with the psychoanalytic viewpoints of Stone, Loewald, and many of the others cited in those chapters.[6]

5. This concern has, however, not been exclusive to the Independent Group. I have mentioned several contributions to the dialogue around these issues from within the Contemporary Freudian Group, from Anna Freud (1954), and, even earlier, Edward Glover (1931, 1954, and 1960b particularly), through to Joseph Sandler (1976a, and with Anne-Marie Sandler, 1984 particularly), though the Sandlers can be viewed as having moved toward a synthesized incorporation of much of the object-relational theory into ego psychology structural theory. For reasons inherent in their theoretical framework, the Kleinians have paid much less attention to the conceptual distinctions between psychoanalysis and the psychoanalytic psychotherapies, dealing rather with the application of psychoanalysis per se, in as unmodified a form as possible, to the whole spectrum of psychopathological formations, all the way to the overtly psychotic, and to the whole span of ages, all the way to very young children.

6. For whatever reason, the alliance formulations described in chapter 15, associated with the

The theoretical viewpoints of the Independent Group have been comprehensively presented in a book edited by Gregorio Kohon (1986), with contributions from nineteen members; in Rayner's 1990 book, a historic overview of the contributions of individual members of this group to the major issues in psychoanalytic theory and practice; and in three books by Christopher Bollas (1987, 1991, 1992), perhaps the best known of the contemporary members of this group in America. For purposes of theoretical exposition, however, I will focus on two books by Patrick Casement (1985, 1990a) and an article (1990b) he contributed to *Psychoanalytic Inquiry,* "The Corrective Emotional Experience." Though not written with a specific focus on psychoanalytic psychotherapy vis-à-vis psychoanalysis, these works lend themselves well to such consideration and in that sense convey the essence of British Independent perspectives on the theme of this book.

Casement's basic thesis is that proper psychoanalytic therapy consists of a combination of interpretation and "containment," to which concepts he gives a distinctively personal emphasis: "Therapists have to be able to interpret as well as contain. Passive containment is not enough, as it feeds a phantasy of the therapist being made unable to continue functioning as therapist. Interpretation alone is not enough, particularly if it can be experienced as the therapist maintaining a protective distance from what the patient is needing to communicate. Psychotherapeutic technique has to be able to bring together these two functions, in such a way that the patient can experience a real feeling-contact with the therapist and yet find that the therapist is able to continue functioning" (1985, 154)—that is, that the patient's passions have not destroyed the therapist, that the therapist has survived and has continued functioning therapeutically, that is, has neither collapsed nor retaliated.[7] "Containment" is Casement's designation (taken from Bion) for the appropriate therapeutic relationship. He underscored its high importance as follows: "The nature of a patient's experience of the therapeutic relationship is at least as important a therapeutic factor as any gain in cognitive insight. It is within this relationship that there can be new opportunities for dealing with old conflicts, for recovering what had been lost, for finding what had been missing in earlier relationships" (168).

---

names of Zetzel, herself psychoanalytically trained in the London Institute, Greenson, and their colleagues, have not seemed useful to British colleagues within either the Independent or the Kleinian Group.

7. In a quite comparable statement, Treurniet (1993), a Dutch psychoanalyst close theoretically to the American ego-psychological perspective, wrote, "Patients need to recreate the experience of the externality of the analyst who is beyond omnipotent control and survives the patient's maximum destructiveness" (198).

This opportunity is created by a relationship that provides "the necessary 'period of hesitation' . . . [Winnicott's phrase]. Without the space created by this hesitation there can be no room for analytic discovery or play. With it there is room, in every analysis and therapy treatment, for theory to be re-discovered and renewed" (1985, 220). This can be blocked by what Casement calls "premature interpretation . . . implicitly directing the patient to proceed along the anticipated lines of regression, or transference, etc." (1985, 219) or by the analyst's attempt to "mastermind the analytic process rather than follow it. As with infants, the process of analytic growth has its own impetus" (220). To the contrary, the therapist should be willing "to be led by the patient: he has to recognize when he is being prompted and cued, unconsciously supervised or having aspects of himself mirrored by the patient. In ways like this, the therapist . . . discovers how to follow the analytic process" (217).

The chief way to accomplish this is for the interpretive effort to be always tentative, often to consist of what Casement calls "half-way interpretations": "When a patient is ready to recognize the unconscious implications of what is being communicated, or being experienced in the session, the therapist can begin to draw the patient's attention to the evidence that points to possible unconscious meaning. For this reason, I prefer to speak more in terms of 'maybe' or 'perhaps' which I believe to be the natural language of potential space. I have also suggested that therapists should develop the art of finding a half-way step toward insight. This does not foreclose on the patient's options, and it allows mental space for him to play with the therapist's comments when these are offered tentatively. They can then be altered, added to or dismissed—by patient or therapist. Instead of insight being *given* to the patient it can be *discovered* by patient and therapist together. Interpretation does not then become an impingement" (218–19).[8]

In chapter 4, I quoted from Casement's 1985 book and the 1990 paper in which he commented specifically on his view, within the British object-

8. Indicative of this converging understanding of the therapeutic process from many originally theoretically diverse sources is the following quotation from an American ego-psychologist, Ralph Roughton (unpubl. ms) on the values of a tentative approach to the interpretive process: "Like literary texts, the verbal and non-verbal productions of our patients are rich with multiple meanings, with ambiguity and irony; and our interpretations are tentative understandings seeking validation, not revealed truth. Literature understands this better than psychoanalysis, perhaps because a literary text may have hundreds of 'analysts' who disagree and argue publicly over their interpretations, whereas a psychoanalytic patient has one analyst (or at least only one at the time) whose interpretations are given in private" (3–4). The literary analogy reflects the fact that this paper was given at an international conference on Psychoanalysis and Literature.

relational tradition, of the rationale and clinical implications of Alexander's position. Here, within the broader context of British perspectives on psychotherapy overall, I contrast these British views more generally with Alexander's conceptions, in both their original and their more modern "revisited" forms.

Casement distinguished diagnostically "between 'libidinal demands,' which cannot be gratified in any analytic psychotherapy without risking a serious disturbance of the analytic process, and 'needs,' which cannot be frustrated without preventing growth" (1990b, 325). But, unlike Alexander, he said that the meeting of needs is found by the patient: "The meeting of needs is not *provided* by the analyst: it is in this fact that it [Casement's concept of the corrective experience] is most singularly different from Alexander's use of the corrective emotional experience. But the meeting of needs can be *found* by the patient. It then becomes possible for development and growth, which had been retarded through early environmental failure, to be resumed" (1990b, 345). "It is a seductive idea," Casement continued, "that what our patients might be needing, for recovery from past bad experience, is an analyst willing to provide opportunities for good experiences as a substitute for those that had been lacking in childhood. But things are not so easily changed in the internal world of the patient. The analytic 'good object' is not someone better than the original object: it is someone who survives being treated as a 'bad object.' But surviving it means neither collapsing under that experience nor retaliating because of it" (1990a, 269–70). Put most tersely, "The point . . . is that any attempt at 'being the better parent' has the effect of deflecting, even seducing, a patient from using the analyst or therapist in a negative transference" (264).

This then circles back to what Casement means by containment and the kind of relationship it connotes: "The analyst does not attempt *actively* to fulfill any of those parental functions. But, in my opinion, the analyst should not hold back from being used by the patient to represent them" (347). The congruences between Casement's view on the therapeutic process, as an exemplar of the Independent or object-relational perspective, and the conceptions of Stone and Loewald as developed in chapter 16 are I think quite clear; in Casement's conceptions of the therapist's allowing himself to be led and refraining from "masterminding" the process there are equally striking congruences with the views of Evelyne Schwaber and, to some extent, of Gill and Hoffman, to be presented in chapter 21.[9]

9. Implicit in everything Casement has stated is the conception that in psychoanalytic work patients plumb the depths of their most archaic and regressive experiences in their reliving within the transference their need to re-create these earliest experiences *as they had been* in order to experience (find) a new relationship in which the analyst neither collapses nor retal-

The most recent expression of British perspectives on these issues may be found in two papers presented at a Conference on Psychoanalysis and Psychoanalytic Psychotherapy held at University College London in 1988. The presentation by Sandler (1988) drew from a talk he had given a decade earlier at the

---

iates, so that the patient can both survive and begin to transcend the childhood traumata. This is the conception of the therapeutic value of psychoanalytic regression formulated by Balint (1968) and Winnicott (1958, 1965). Anthony Bass (1992), in his review of Margaret Little's account of her analysis with Winnicott, succinctly stated this (British object-relational) position of the values and the meanings of therapeutic regression. Quoting from Little: "From the analyst's point of view the value of regression can be stated very simply: it is a means by which areas where psychotic anxieties predominate can be explored, early experiences uncovered, and underlying delusional ideas recognized and resolved, via the transference/countertransference partnership of analyst and analysand, in both positive and negative phases. In practice, of course it is not so simple." The issues of the meanings (or functions) of regression, Bass stated, are "far from simple in practice, nor are they less complex in theory. In fact, questions surrounding the use of regression in psychoanalysis are part of a long-standing controversy that goes back to some of the earliest divergences in the field. Should regression be regarded as dangerous and pathological or regenerative and integrative? Is it a powerful form of resistance, an acting out in the face of disorganizing anxiety, or a hopeful if stubborn demand for what the patient knows he needs to resume growth? Should the analyst inhibit it, make interpretations about it, facilitate it, or simply make room for it?" (119).

The *positive* view of the therapeutic usefulness of the regressive experience Bass traced back to Ferenczi (see chapter 2), and found its staunchest advocates in the British object-relational perspective: "The analysts from the British Psychoanalytic Society's Independent Group (Winnicott, Balint, Rickman, Heimann, Milner, Rycroft, Kahn, Little, and, most recently, Bollas) most clearly and cohesively extended and developed Ferenczi's plea for a psychoanalysis that made room for experiences of deep regression and that could be therapeutically responsive to patients who could not benefit from classical analysis. These analysts have written extensively about the necessity of an opportunity for deep regression for these patients. Because work with such patients often placed special demands on the analyst and challenged his psychic and physical resources in ways that a more standard psychoanalysis did not, this group became increasingly interested, as well, in the analysis and use of countertransference in the treatment, not simply as pathological distortions needing to be cleared away but as a potential resource and source of crucial psychoanalytic data. They were in agreement with Freud in the sense that they acknowledged that for such patients interpretation alone was an inadequate procedure. But rather than suggest that such patients were unsuitable for analysis, they sought to extend the parameters of the clinical psychoanalytic situation" (122).

Treurniet (1993), in Holland, writing from within a position close to the American ego-psychology paradigm, nonetheless strongly endorsed this point of view for these "sicker" patients: "The reliability and atmosphere of the analytic setting invite regression to a state of dependence on the setting, which promotes the possibility of reexperiencing environmental failure situations of the past at the level of the 'basic fault' (Balint, 1968). Reexperiencing these early deficient object relationships repeatedly and in different ways can repair the basic fault and restore growth. Both Winnicott and Balint stress the fact that in regressed states, inter-

8th Pre-Congress on Training of the International Psychoanalytical Association in New York in 1979 (Sandler 1982). There Sandler had spoken of the conceptual difficulties in distinguishing proper psychoanalysis from those psychotherapies that are close to it in form and orientation on the basis of any of what Gill has called the extrinsic and/or intrinsic criteria (see chapter 8), though Sandler did not use Gill's terminology. However, Sandler said, "many factors *contribute* to the differentiation of psychoanalysis from psychotherapy, even if a large gray area, in which differentiation is difficult, remains. Perhaps the most critical differentiating factors include the analyst's attitude to his patient, his willingness to listen and wait, his attitude of research into the vicissitudes of the patient's unconscious impulses and conflicts as relived in the analysis, his analytic detachment, and the maintenance of a setting in which regression and transference manifestations can develop" (1982, 43–44). This cautious distinction is based on differences (of more or less) in matters of *attitude,* and indeed the word "attitude" occurs twice in the brief passage I have quoted.

Having said that, Sandler withdrew to an even more conservative (and, I think, regressive) position:

> The difficulties in the way of finding formal differentiating criteria prompt one to turn to formulations rather like "psychoanalysis is what is practiced by psychoanalysts." A view of this sort, which does away with the need for *formal* criteria . . . has much to commend it, for it could be said, quite correctly, that a good psychoanalyst has in any case to modify his technique to suit each of his patients, because what is appropriate differs from one patient to another. Similarly (the argument would run), if the patient can only attend (or afford to come) once or twice a week, then the analyst's technique would be adapted to the patient and his special circumstances. It would still, from this point of view, be regarded as psychoanalysis, because the analyst could maintain that he had internalized a "psychoanalytic attitude," and that it is this which counts. (44)

Clearly Sandler did not really embrace the position that it is simply an "internalized psychoanalytic attitude" that marks a treatment as fully analytic, but it also seems clear from this quotation that such a position is held by a sizable portion of British psychoanalysis (and also no doubt by analysts in other regions),

---

pretation is not what is needed, that speech or movement can ruin the process, and that only after the patient has emerged from regression may interpretive work become essential" (208). This is in sharp contrast to the widely accepted view in America, articulated so clearly by Arlow (1975) and Gill (1988), that therapeutic regression, when it occurs, is artifactual (usually iatrogenic), unnecessary, and often enough, detrimental to the treatment course.

though the preeminence of the object-relational perspective in British lends itself
to a readier eliding of psychoanalysis and psychoanalytic psychotherapy as an
almost indistinguishable continuum of techniques.

Sandler (1982) made an additional point about the way the teaching of analytic work via supervision could add to the possibilities for confusion between
psychoanalysis and the other psychoanalytic therapies. The dilemma is that

> [the supervising] analyst will certainly find himself in the situation of pre-
> senting and maintaining, of necessity, a relatively "orthodox" or "analyt-
> ically proper" stance which may not correspond to what he actually does
> in his own practice. However, what as an experienced analyst he might
> permit himself to do, or even feel to be indicated in a particular case,
> *might be quite inappropriate in an analysis conducted by a candidate.* He is in a
> position of being tempted to say "*I* may do it, but you are not permitted
> to." While he may not actually say this, it reflects a position which he
> may be forced to adopt in attempting to get the candidate he is teaching
> to "unlearn" elements of psychotherapeutic skill which would interfere
> with analytic work (but which may resemble measures which might ju-
> diciously be used in certain cases by the experienced analyst). (46–47)

As cogent a statement as any of what seems to be the increasing ambiguity of
the central subject of this book!

In the 1988 panel paper, besides reaffirming these positions, Sandler asserted
that (1) there are no decisive, but only partial, differentiating criteria between
these two modalities; (2) that the production of so-called structural change, so
often claimed to be the hallmark of proper differentiation, is no better a differentiating criterion than others—in fact, probably less so—and (3) that often one
cannot readily distinguish which patients are more suitable for and amenable to
the one than to the other. After listing the "criteria that can be drawn upon in
the attempt to differentiate psychoanalysis from psychoanalytic psychotherapy . . . the conclusion is inevitable that *all* are partial criteria only, applicable
for purposes of differentiation in some instances and not at all in others. Certainly
no single criterion is suitable" (175); he went on to say, "There is little doubt
that both psychoanalysis and psychoanalytic psychotherapy have the capacity for
bringing about structural change, and that not all such change is a consequence
of interpretation. There is no complete agreement on the mechanisms of psychic
change in either psychoanalysis or psychotherapy, and we certainly lack a psychoanalytic theory of technique which would encompass both psychoanalysis
and psychotherapy" (177); and "The view has been put forward in the past that
the suitable analytic patient should be relatively well-integrated, with less well
put-together and more disturbed patients being seen as appropriately treated by

psychotherapy. I do not think that nowadays this criterion is at all valid—at least in this country" (174). And as a final confusing fillip: "The problem is complicated by the fact that we cannot readily equate one psychoanalysis with another, nor one psychotherapy with another" (173).

Heinz Wolff (1988), a senior psychotherapist at the same conference, gave somewhat more emphasis to the conceptual *distinctions* between psychoanalysis and psychoanalytic psychotherapy, albeit acknowledging the practical difficulties in making these distinctions: "The fact is that they have a great deal in common and could be seen as two ends of a continuous spectrum," because after all, "psychoanalysis is the source of analytical psychotherapy. . . . In a sense psychoanalytic psychotherapy could be looked upon as the child of psychoanalysis with all the inevitable parent-child conflicts involved" (178). "I believe this conflict is inevitable," he wrote—and our job is only to manage it fruitfully for all. Perhaps Wolff felt that Freud had helped set it up that way: "Perhaps the term 'pure gold of analysis' expressed Freud's wish to emphasize the superior role of psychoanalysis in order to protect its professional identity when faced with the development of modified forms of psychoanalytic treatment, much though he himself invited such developments" (179).

To Wolff, the distinctions between psychoanalysis and psychoanalytic psychotherapy lay in the differences in the *experience* of the therapy, the transference, the reliving, the regression: the "task of getting the process under way and of maintaining continuity between sessions is usually *more difficult* for the therapist the less often he sees the patient. . . . the longer duration and open-endedness of an analysis provide a *more stable basis* for the ongoing therapeutic work. . . . It is also important to recognize that for some patients, e.g. those with borderline personality organization and psychotic features, and for some patients with psychosomatic disorders, psychoanalytic psychotherapy two or three times a week may be *safer* and more effective than five times a week analysis" (181–82, italics added). The words "more difficult," "more stable," "safer," of course, all describe aspects of the experience of the treatment, in some situations with the tilt in favor of psychoanalysis, and in others, in the opposite direction.

Wolff felt there were clear conceptual distinctions between the two modalities in goals and purposes; he designated the aim of psychoanalysis as personal growth and that of psychotherapy as symptom relief. But, he added, "in practice this distinction . . . is far less clear cut than is often assumed. . . . In my view it would be wrong to equate the aim of the psychoanalyst with the developmental and that of the analytical psychotherapist with the therapeutic function. . . . Both need to learn how to integrate these two functions" (182–83). Nonetheless, Wolff insisted that this was a real distinction, with real consequences, and expanded further in terms borrowed from Winnicott, who had distinguished "being with," a receptive "female" function, from "doing to," an active "male" function. According to Wolff, "In any kind of psychotherapeutic work it is helpful to think of being with the patient as essential to promote the development of a sense of Self by providing space and time which frees and facilitates the patient's own potential for growth, whilst doing something to the patient, such as commenting on his communications or behaviour, or making interpretations, relates more to the therapeutic function. . . . When one applies these considerations to the relationship between psychoanalysis and psychoanalytic psychotherapy it is probably true to say that there is a tendency for *being with* to play the major role in long-term psychoanalytic work whilst in short-term analytical psychotherapy *doing to* may take a more prominent place" (183).

In the end, Wolff, though not a psychoanalyst, circled back to the centrality of psychoanalysis to the entire psychoanalytically oriented psychotherapy enterprise: "Psychoanalysis . . . remains the theoretical and clinical source of all forms of psychoanalytic psychotherapy. Its continued practice remains essential for further progress and discoveries to be made, and it remains the most thorough form of training as an analytical psychotherapist or psychoanalyst known to us so far" (184–85). These statements of Sandler and Wolff, with their shades of difference as well as their similarities, express as well as any the converging consensus within Great Britain today over the issues of psychoanalysis and psychotherapy, as well as their likeness to formulations within the American psychoanalytic community, despite, again, the differing, more object-relation-molded psychoanalytic theoretical context in Great Britain as compared with America.

20 The Narcissistic Personality Disorders and the Borderline Personality Organizations: Heinz Kohut and Otto Kernberg

No American analysts have had more impact on psychoanalytic thinking over the past quarter century than Heinz Kohut, with his concerns for the problem of narcissism and its particular expression in the narcissistic personality disorders, and Otto Kernberg, with his concerns for the problem of the borderline personality organization. Neither of them focused centrally on the issues of the psychoanalytic psychotherapies vis-à-vis psychoanalysis, yet each has played a major role in defining the parameters of application of psychoanalysis (though in both instances with considerable controversy) and thereby marking—each somewhat differently—the boundaries between psychoanalysis and the psychoanalytic psychotherapies.

Kohut's concerns, which evolved over time into the full theoretical structure of self psychology, emerged somewhat earlier than Kernberg's. The nodal forerunner papers by Kohut were "Introspection, Empathy, and Psychoanalysis" (1959) and "Forms and Transformations of Narcissism" (1966). By now a vast literature by Kohut and his followers has accumulated, including his own three books *The Analysis of the Self* (1971), *The Restoration of the Self* (1977), and the posthumously published *How Does Analysis Cure?* (1984). I will not review the clinical and theoretical corpus of Kohut's self psychology; rather I will focus specifically on its implications for the central themes of this book, drawing considerably on three of my own essays that critique the structure of self psychology and its place in the psychoanalytic scheme of things (Wallerstein 1981, 1983a, 1985).[1]

Kohut's clinical point of departure had to do with the treatment difficulties

1. For a full explication of Kohut's clinical and theoretical edifice as it evolved over time, the reader is referred of course to Kohut's three books, the first (1971) setting forth his views on the developmental lines of narcissism, the understanding and treatment of the narcissistic personality disorders, and the psychology of the self in the narrower sense; the second (1977) elaborating on the psychology of the self in the broader sense as an alternative (and supraordinate) theoretical system within psychoanalysis; and the third (1984) focusing specifically on the mechanisms of change and cure postulated by self psychology as distinct from the traditional conception of these processes. For a friendly, albeit critical, assessment of Kohut's contributions, see Wallerstein 1981, 1983a, and 1985. My first essay is a clinical appraisal, the second a theoretical appraisal, and the third an overview dealing especially with the self psychological

posed by patients designated narcissistic personality disorders, patients with profound problems in maintaining a realistic and healthy self-esteem and with character configurations marked by inflated, grandiose propensities and a simultaneous exquisite sensitivity to slights and other narcissistic hurts. Kohut broadened this perspective by focusing our psychoanalytic awareness on the (normal) psychological as well as the psychopathological phenomena of narcissism as representing a salient aspect of the psychological functioning, normal and abnormal, of all people. This aspect of personality functioning, which previously had not been so regularly and systematically conceptualized and explicated, is of overriding clinical and technical importance, particularly as regards the so-called narcissistic personalities or characters, the prototypical individuals of Christopher Lasch's (1978) new age or "Culture of Narcissism," individuals ever more visible in our psychoanalytic consulting rooms.

Kohut's central clinical contribution to psychoanalysis (in my view) has been his unswerving focus on the characteristic transferences these narcissistic patients present in analysis and the countertransferences they typically evoke.[2] In his first book (1971) he designated them narcissistic transferences and countertransferences, renaming them in his second book (1977) selfobject transferences and countertransferences. This nomenclature was taken from his conception of the characteristic relationship of such patients to their objects, not as separate individuals ("individual centers of initiative," in Kohut's phrase), but as extended parts of the patients themselves, existing in order to meet the requirements and

---

vs. the more traditional views on mechanisms of change and cure. These essays also draw on the critiques of others, some hospitable to Kohut's views and some not.

2. I bypass here any discussion of Kohut's many other self psychology clinical perspectives, all of them more controversial and problematic, including (1) his proposal of a separate developmental line for narcissism as distinct from object-relatedness; (2) the putative distinction between a so-called normal oedipal *phase* and the classical Oedipus *complex* as a set of "pathologically altered experiences of the child" (Kohut 1984, 214); (3) the primacy of the libidinal over the aggressive component in emotional interaction and development (with aggressive manifestations, prototypically "narcissistic rage" reactions, representing untoward responses to defective parental [and other] empathy); (4) the concomitant concept of drives and defenses as but "breakdown products" emerging under fragmenting psychic pressures stemming from improper and "disempathic" interactions, rather than as primary component manifestations of the malfunctioning psyche whose unconscious meanings are surfacing for exploration and elucidation; (5) the consequently sharply diminished role of the drives and of object-related origins in the development of the superego; and (6) the overvaluation of maternal empathy (and with it, of real experience) in the development of pathology (in the extreme, a reductionistic simplification of all subsequent psychopathology to but a single, all-encompassing etiological base). My assessment of each of these propositions is developed in Wallerstein 1981 and 1983a.

expectations projected into them. Kohut at first delineated two varieties of such selfobject transferences: the mirror transference, in which the individual's damaged pole of ambitions attempts to elicit the confirming-approving responses of the selfobject (in developmental terms, the admiring "gleam in the mother's eye" in response to the child's developmental thrusts), and the idealizing transference, in which the individual's damaged pole of dedicated values and ideals searches for a selfobject that will accept and carry the idealization (in developmental terms, the parent's protection and nurturing of the child from the idealized vantage point of their omnipotence and beneficence). In his last book (1984), Kohut added the twinship or alter ego transference to this schema, "those in which the damaged intermediate area of talents and skills seeks a selfobject that will make itself available for the reassuring experience of essential alikeness" (193). Kohut's careful delineation of these interactional modes as well as of the counteractive and countertransference responses they characteristically evoke, allowed our interpretive work, previously done more intuitively or haphazardly, to be now much more precisely focused, in the light of the clinical formulations of self psychology. Because of this, many commentators (myself included) agree that in this clinical and technical realm Kohut and his collaborators have made an enduring and major contribution to the psychoanalytic endeavor.

But Kohut went far beyond this contribution to the understanding and treatment of these especially characteristic (preoedipal) transferences of the narcissistic personality disorders—transferences that also play varyingly important roles across the whole gamut of psychopathological formations into the most classically neurotic character organizations. In his first two books, he developed an elaborated (meta)psychology of the self, starting with the narrower sense of content of the agencies of the mind—that is, as mental representations within the ego, id, and superego (1971)—and developing into the psychology of the self in the broader sense, as a supraordinate unified and coherent constellation, the wholeness of the personality as active agent, with the drives and the defenses (the classic ingredients of psychic functioning within the traditional ego-psychological framework) subsumed as breakdown constituents of this self (1977). This is the view of what Kohut called the bipolar self, with, in its maturation, the crystallization of normally self-assertive ambitions as one pole and of attained ideals and values as the other pole. The two poles are connected by a tension arc of talents and skills, which, with the three arenas of ambitions, ideals and values, and talents and skills, give rise to the three targets of focused selfobject transferences: mirroring, idealizing, and alter ego or twinship. It is this evolution in theorizing that was hailed by Paul Ornstein in his statement that psychoanalysis has come through three successive paradigms, that of drive psychology and then ego psychology (both created by Freud), and now the new paradigm of self psychology (the addition of Kohut).

Linked to this new metapsychology of the bipolar self is Kohut's concept of Tragic Man, beset by developmental failures and deficits in the evolution of a coherent, integrated self that would be proof against the fragmenting and disorganizing pressures of life's average expectable vicissitudes. Kohut opposed this new prototypical man of our time to the traditional concept of Guilty Man, victim of the anxieties and other dysphoric affects arising within a developed self beset by conflicts among its component aspects deriving from maladaptive solutions to earlier, stage-specific developmental tasks and dilemmas. This is the distinction Kohut constantly drew—and it is probably the most crucial distinguishing mark of self psychology, according to its proponents.

In contradistinction to the neurotic problems stemming from the intrapsychic conflicts of the developmentally more structured and integrated personalities, in which attention to the opposition of drive and defense—that is, to *conflict*—and to the attendant regressive neurotic transference or transference neurosis is the key to analytic amelioration and restoration, the key to resolution of the narcissistic problems of unintegrated selves vulnerable to fragmenting pressures under stress is attention to the unfolding of selfobject transferences stemming from earlier and more archaic (more undifferentiated) experiences of failures of maternal (or parental) empathy—that is, experiences of emotional *deficit*. In this conceptualization, self psychology is centrally a psychology of deficit and its reparation, as against classical psychoanalysis, a psychology of conflict and its resolution. This is posed somewhat inconsistently by Kohut and in the self psychology literature generally as either a complementary (alternative) theoretical conceptualization particularly applicable to the typical problems of the narcissistic personality disorders or an overarching theory providing a technically superior understanding of the therapeutic issues with all patients, including the best-integrated neurotic. In Kohut's final book, the latter view seems to have prevailed.[3]

3. My own contrary argument is twofold: (1) On *clinical grounds*, I see no need to dichotomize as Kohut did. Kohut's central clinical contribution can be viewed as seeing so many aspects of the psychopathology of pregenital development not as regressive defense against the emergences of oedipal transferences *alone*, but *also* as re-creations of deficient childhood constellations within mirroring, idealizing, and alter ego transferences. This is simply a restatement of Kohut's either/or into a both/and. For in the flow and flux of analytic clinical material, we deal constantly, and in turn, with both the oedipal, where there is a coherent self, and the preoedipal, where there may not yet be; with defensive regressions and with developmental arrests; with defense transferences and defensive resistances, and with recreations of earlier traumatic and traumatized psychic states, etc. (2) From this follows my position on *theoretical*

Given this statement of the essence of Kohut's (and self psychology's) clinical and theoretical propositions, what can be said about self psychology's position on mechanisms of change and cure and on the issues of psychoanalytic psychotherapy vis-à-vis psychoanalysis? According to Kohut, because the essence of the normal developmental process is declared to reside in the progressive differentiation and maturation of (but never independence from) selfobject relationships, cure comes not through interpretation ("It is not the interpretation that cures the patient" [1977, 31]) or through the achievement of insight[4] but

---

grounds, that there is no need to posit a separate psychology of deficit and of Tragic Man. The very significant clinical contributions of self psychology can be incorporated into the main fabric of classical or traditional psychoanalysis.

If we follow Sandler (1974, 1976b) in his broadened conceptualization of conflict as any situation in which there is opposition between any kind of peremptory urge and any impulse to delay, involving any aspect of psychic functioning in any form ("We can regard all conflict as being a conflict of wishes of one sort of another," 1976b, 61), or similarly, Theodore Dorpat (1976) in his conceptions of "Structural Conflicts" between the psychic instances in the developed, structurally differentiated personality, and "Object Relations Conflicts" "between the subject's wishes and the ideals, injunctions, and prohibitions that are not experienced as his own, but rather as represented in primary or secondary process representations of some (usually parental) authority" (856), then the dichotomy between deficit and conflict falls away, and the whole of the self psychological theoretical corpus can be translated into the familiar (traditional) language of conflict.

In this vein I wrote (1981), "I . . . see the life course or the life cycle as one of the successive facing and the adequate resolution—or not—of a sequence of phase-specific developmental tasks . . . in each phase and in each instance, a task created by the unique conjunction of the innate maturational developmental unfolding of capacities and readinesses, together with the phase-linked normative societal expectations within that culture at that historic moment, and added to by the happenstance and timing of more or less traumatic and adventitious life experiences. . . . At . . . [all] levels, that of the earlier arena of primary development of the self and that of the later structuring of the personality under the impact of the emergence and resolution of the Oedipus complex, severe anxieties and other attendant dysphorias can arise that must be coped with to the best of the ability of the immature ego, or self, of that stage, given the resources, defenses and coping mechanisms available to it within, as well as the empathic supports and material and psychological nutriments available to it without. This coping will then have a more or less healthy *vis-à-vis* a more or less pathological outcome in specific character formation or deformation. I do not really see how it is therefore any more or any less a matter of developmental task or dilemma, of attendant anxiety and of its management, in short of psychic conflict, and its more or less healthy or pathological resolution, in either case" (389–90).

4. In fact, the quest for insight is viewed as a misguided commitment to a constraining and not so subtly detrimental "truth morality" (1984, 54) championed by Freud. For Freud (and presumably for classical analysts since Freud), "To have knowledge withheld from him was experienced as an intolerable narcissistic injury" (1984, 54). In terms of the so-called classical conception of therapy, "the acquisition of verbalizable knowledge (often referred to as insight)

through "the establishment of empathic in-tuneness between self and selfobject on mature adult levels . . . [which] supplants the bondage that formerly tied the archaic self to the archaic selfobject. . . . The gradual acquisition of empathic contact with mature selfobjects is the *essence of the psychoanalytic cure*" (1984, 66).

Kohut summarized,

A successful analysis is one in which the analysand's formerly archaic needs for the responses of archaic selfobjects are superseded by the experience of the availability of empathic resonance, the major constituent of the sense of security in adult life. Increased ability to verbalize, broadened insight, greater autonomy of ego functions, and increased control over impulsiveness may accompany these gains, but they are not the essence of cure. A treatment will be successful because . . . an analysand was able to reactivate, in a selfobject transference, the needs of a self that had been thwarted in childhood. In the analytic situation, these reactivated needs were kept alive and exposed, time and again, to the vicissitudes of optimal frustrations until the patient ultimately acquired the reliable ability to sustain his self with the aid of selfobject resources available in his adult surroundings. According to self psychology, then, the essence of the psychoanalytic cure resides in a patient's newly acquired ability to identify and seek out appropriate selfobjects . . . as they present themselves in his realistic surroundings and to be sustained by them. (1984, 77)[5]

---

constitutes the essence of the psychoanalytic cure—'the talking cure' " (56). Kohut insisted that in speaking this way, "I am not demeaning knowledge and truth values" (58), just removing them from their "disproportionately exalted position—alone at the pinnacle of his [Freud's] value hierarchy" (58).

5. This focus on the central role of empathy is neither that unique or that new with self psychology. It has in fact been part of psychological (or human) understanding even before Freud and psychoanalysis. Ralph Roughton (unpubl. ms), in a paper on Hawthorne's *Scarlet Letter*, described Hawthorne's character Dr. Chillingworth via a quotation that can be read as a description of the establishment of a psychoanalytic situation by a process of empathic immersion: "The kind and friendly physician strove to go deep into his patient's bosom . . . prying into his recollections, and probing everything with a cautious touch, like a treasure-seeker in a dark cavern. . . . If [a physician possesses native wisdom] and a nameless something more,—let us call it intention; if he shows no intrusive egotism, nor disagreeably prominent characteristics of his own; if he have the power, which must be born with him, to bring his mind into such affinity with his patient's, that [the patient] shall unawares have spoken what he imagines himself only to have thought; if such revelations be received without tumult, and acknowledged not so often by an uttered sympathy, as by silence, an inarticulate breath, and here and there a word, to indicate that all is understood; if, to these qualifications of a confidant be joined the advantages afforded by his recognized character as a physician;—then, at some inevitable moment, will the soul of the sufferer be dissolved, and flow forth in a dark, but

Lest all this sound too different from our usual conceptions of the *method* of psychoanalysis, Kohut and his followers have insisted that the chief vehicle for accomplishing these changes is the same unalloyed interpretive process that has always characterized psychoanalysis. This was highlighted in the casebook edited by Arnold Goldberg (1978), which contained descriptions of six patients treated according to the tenets of self psychology under Kohut's influence or his direct supervision. In the introductory section, Goldberg stated, "The activity of a psychoanalyst is *interpretation*. Analyses of narcissistic personality disorders are no different in this respect from those of the more familiar neurotic syndromes" (9). And this was amplified in the concluding section as follows: "The principles determining the use of the interpretive process in narcissistic personality disorders are no different from those involved in the oedipal neuroses. The analyst listens with even-hovering attention, which is his counterpart of the analysand's free associations. By virtue of his own analysis, training, and experience, the analyst is acutely sensitive to his inner experiences and thus becomes consciously aware of mental states evoked in him through empathic contact with the analysand. Such empathically derived data then become the raw material for processing into the hypotheses that are tested by interpretation" (446). Goldberg added,

> This is the essence of the analytic treatment: interpretation without gratification per se . . . an analytic ambience gratifies neither narcissism nor sexuality, but is equivalent to the average expectable emotional environment that facilitates the analytic process. . . . The analyst does not actively soothe; he interprets the analysand's yearning to be soothed. . . . The analyst does not actively mirror; he interprets the need for conforming responses. The analyst does not actively admire or approve grandiose expectations; he explains their role in the psychic economy. The analyst does not fall into passive silence; he explains why his interventions are felt to be intrusive. Of course, the analyst's mere presence, the fact that he talks, and especially the fact that he understands all have soothing and self-confirming effects on the patient, *and they are so interpreted*.[6] (447–48)

---

transparent stream, bringing all its mysteries into the daylight." This remarkable passage was published forty-five years before Freud's *Studies on Hysteria*.

6. This is all stated so categorically to counter the many psychoanalytic critics of self psychology who have declared that its theoretical and technical modifications do not constitute a new variant theoretical perspective within psychoanalysis but rather represent a "degradation" to psychotherapy. Frederic Levine (1979), for example, charged that self psychology overlooks or suppresses conflict, that it lends spurious confirmation to patients' neurotic fantasies of defect or deficit, and that it gratifies rather than analyzes the selfobject transferences. Levine cited in

If self psychology is thus another theoretical perspective within our increasingly pluralistic psychoanalysis, how does it relate to psychoanalytic psychotherapy? Its literature has paid little attention to this issue. Basch (cited in Wallerstein 1981) declared that self psychology "made it possible once more to draw a definitive line between psychoanalysis and psychotherapy" (385), by bringing the narcissistic disorders technically to the side where proper and thorough analysis can also be done with them, as against their prior consignment to the domain of the unanalyzables, for whom less thoroughly reconstructive psychotherapies would have to suffice. Along these same lines, Kohut in the very first pages of his third (1984) book repeated his general interdiction of analysis for those diagnosed as borderline as well as for the overtly psychotic, while then describing rather generous criteria of analyzability for those within the range of what he called the narcissistic personality disturbances. In this sense, self psychology widened the arc of those deemed amenable to psychoanalysis, correspondingly diminishing the ranks of those beyond or not amenable to full-scale analysis, those to be treated by (psychoanalytic) psychotherapy.

Goldberg, one of the current leaders of the self psychology movement, sought to further clarify the distinction between psychoanalysis and psychoanalytic psychotherapy from a self-psychological perspective by talking of different *goals*—conceived in self psychological terms: "The difference between psychotherapy and psychoanalysis lies *less in the method than in the goal*" (1980–81, 62). He then elaborated:

---

support numerous examples from Goldberg's Casebook of interventions that he declared to be psychotherapeutic rather than psychoanalytic, ending with the statement, "Such [psychotherapeutic] methods perform important functions when appropriate, but they are not comparable to or interchangeable with psychoanalysis" (17). On this issue, I specifically differ with Levine and support the self psychology position that it is a variant form of psychoanalysis (though not the form most congenial to me). Certainly examples could indeed be found in the Casebook of every kind of supportive psychotherapeutic activity. But mainstream psychoanalysis, including the effort at even the purest kind of classical analysis, can be faulted (if that is the correct word) in exactly the same way, and perhaps to a similar extent. (In support of this, see the statement of the findings and conclusions from the Menninger Psychotherapy Research Project in chapter 8 above.)

Valenstein's critique (1979), less sweeping than Levine's, contended that self psychology does indeed downgrade the classical insistence on the centrality of the interpretation and analysis of conflict: "The heretofore familiar and useful clinical concept of unconscious intrapsychic conflict, both in the inter- and intrapsychic sense, would hardly seem to pertain. And presumably the theory of psychoanalytic technique as being primarily an articulate interpretive procedure which ultimately depends upon rational explanatory means of resolving psychic conflict, formerly unconscious but now made conscious, predominantly but not solely through the transference neurosis, would no longer be of cardinal importance" (129).

The essential distinction between psychotherapy and psychoanalysis involves a change or transformation within the latter that does not take place in the former. The essentials of psychotherapy involve the integration of a self-concept. The techniques of achieving this are quite variable and range from confrontation to interpretation. The results of the technique are in the direction of a new meaning about one's self arising vis-à-vis the therapist and others. In analysis we reorganize the self, or perhaps more often we restore a self to its more fundamental state from one of disorganization or faulty organization. At a certain point in every effort to line things up according to quantity, a qualitative change does take place. . . . we can distinguish psychoanalysis in its task of reorganizing the self from psychotherapy and its job of repairing a segment of the self. (67)

Whether the putative distinction between repair (psychotherapy) and reorganization (psychoanalysis) is merely a matter of enough change in quantity becoming a change in quality (since the method has been declared to be essentially the same) was not further clarified by Goldberg, though he did state, "The distinction between repair and reorganization also demands a break in the continuum theory of treatment" (69).

In a later book (1988), Goldberg seemed to bring psychoanalysis and psychotherapy closer: "Psychoanalysis is often seen as restrictive in its forms in order to allow a relatively uncontaminated transference to emerge, whereas psychotherapy seems burdened with all sorts of permissible parameters. Of late, however, I think we have witnessed the erosion of the analytic posture by a variety of allowances ranging from occasional phone calls, to shared coffee, to the full range of doing what comes naturally. Psychoanalysis seems to approach psychotherapy in its looseness and flexibility in some cases; in other cases, therapy seems to borrow heavily from analysis such as charging for missed hours" (179). And Paul and Anna Ornstein, also among the current leaders of the self psychology movement, made a statement on the distinction that is in no way specifically Kohutian in its provenance: "Psychoanalysis places the transference neurosis into the center of the therapeutic activity, whereas psychoanalytic psychotherapy focuses upon intra- and extratherapeutic transferences within the broader context of the therapist-patient relationship" (1977, 340). In a chapter in the Rothstein (1988) volume, Paul Ornstein wrote of the curative factors and processes in the psychoanalytic psychotherapies that in no way demonstrated clear distinctions or differences among differing modalities, though he did speak of a spectrum of focal psychotherapy, then intensive psychoanalytic psychotherapy, and then psychoanalysis. As with Goldberg, the distinctions seem to be matters of intensity and quantity that at some point presumably have become differences of quality.

As already indicated, self psychology has been subjected to intense critical review, especially in America, where it originated—in contrast to a more uniformly welcoming reception in Latin America and in much of Europe. The most incisive and thoughtful of the earlier critiques (by Morris Eagle, Charles Hanly and Jeffrey Masson, Jacob Jacobson, Kernberg, Frederic Levine, Loewald, Modell, Rangell, Rothstein, Lester Schwartz, Nathan Segel, Martin Stein, and Treurniet) are discussed in my own essays of critique (Wallerstein 1981, 1983a, 1985). Here I will mention four of the more recent additions. Friedman's assessment (1988) is the most directly in line with what has been stated here to this point: "The most important assignment this theory [self psychology] gives to interpretation is to cement a growth-promoting therapeutic relationship. And Kohut is finally bold enough to say that 'It is not the interpretation that cures the patient' (1977, 31). . . . His students seem especially anxious to hold on to . . . the intellectual, informational rationale. . . . In the end, Kohut (1984) relinquished the intellectual rationale for treatment and allowed the experiential spirit to triumph. He finally believed that it is the experience of the empathic bond that effects the cure" (383). It is this position that puts Kohut in a direct line with the spirit of Ferenczi rather than of Freud. Etchegoyen (1991) spoke to this same point but gave it a novel emphasis: "Kohut's great innovation: empathy ceases to be a necessary condition of the work of analysis (as we have all thought since Ferenczi), to become the very essence of the method, so that it is given a real *methodological blank cheque*" (275, italics added).[7]

The assertion about a methodological blank check has powered the whole critique of Leon Balter and James Spencer (1991), who argued that Kohut's shift to the primacy of introspection and empathy (vicarious introspection) as the avenue of access to the mind of the patient leads inevitably to a downplaying of the method of free association (and the corollary free-floating attention) as a guide to the observation of behaviors that can lead to inferences about the

---

7. See Wallerstein 1983a, 585–87, for a discussion of Kohut's redefinition of psychoanalysis as in its essence what is achieved by "empathic-introspective immersion" (Kohut 1977, 302)—i.e., the *method* of empathy, rather than, as in Freud's original definition (1914b), the dealing with the *phenomena* of transference and resistance. I quoted Kohut as follows: "I am not able to imagine how analysis could *at this time* do away with the two concepts—transference and resistance—that are the experience-distant distillate of these two [intra-analytic and interactive] activities. I would still insist that some future generation of psychoanalysts might discover psychological areas that require a novel conceptual approach—areas where even in the therapeutic realm these two now universally applicable concepts have become irrelevant" (Kohut 1977, 308, italics added).

unconscious workings of the mind. Kohut's method, they stated, indeed led to a fuller exploration of what is preconsciously available, what can be felt as experienced, what is "phenomenological." Inevitably, this bias in favor of the (preconscious) experiencing of the whole self (which they compared to Bibring's [1954] "clarification" as distinct from interpretation) leads to a diminished focus on the unconscious, on "analyzing" underlying structure and structural conflict: "Freud introduced free association to overcome the limitations of purely introspective self-observation. The latter is not effective in facilitating the inference of unconscious mental processes" (368); and "Evenly suspended attention treats the patient's associations as behavior that may not initially be understood. . . . Freud was recommending that we may not, and should not, try to 'understand before we explain' " (369). Further, "Freud recommended free association, a unique and new addition to observational method, to overcome the limitations in the process of introspection. He was equally concerned with the limitations on vicarious introspection (empathy), and to overcome them he recommended evenly suspended attention as a new and unique method for listening" (370).

By contrast, Balter and Spencer continued, "Kohut took the most consistent and recurrent findings of the analyst's vicarious introspection, the patient's self, to be an observed psychological phenomenon of fundamental importance, 'not-further-reducible' within the frame of reference operationally defined in the 1959 paper" (384). In this context, "Taking the patient's needs . . . at face value indicates that defensive, infantile, or other unconscious ('disguised') meanings are not seen by the analyst to be of primary importance for understanding the patient; and responding to a patient's conscious needs assumes no great value put by the analyst on the subsequent analysis of their unconscious, defensive, or infantile meanings, since the recommended response may actually preclude the appearance of clues to such meanings. Thus, the importance of the concept of unconscious mental content and process is diminished" (374). This led Balter and Spencer to state, "For *self psychology* what is meant by analysis of the self is *clarification* of self experience. . . . the distinction between clarification and interpretation sharply delineates from a technical point of view a crucial difference between self psychology and classical psychoanalysis. The latter does not see the self as a fundamental, irreducible psychological unit" (385).

In making this distinction, they stopped short of declaring self psychology a form of analytic psychotherapy (as Levine, for example, had done); they left it open to maintain it as a variant of psychoanalysis, distinguishable from other forms essentially by altered method: "In taking the patient's conscious self experience as an irreducible fundamental whole, rather than a 'constructed' mental product, Kohut's *theory followed* his observational *method*" (386, italics added).

Unlike Balter and Spencer (1991), who challenged Kohut's *method* of empathic immersion as representing a fundamental deviation from Freud's method of free association, Reed (1987a) challenged Kohut's *system of interpretation* as representing an equally fundamental deviation from the open-ended and "hermeneutic" system of interpretation in classical analysis. By this, she meant that Kohut's self psychology was declared to be an effort at *restoration of meaning,* one that would repair the disjunction between the signifier and the signified, between the manifest and the latent elements, but that would not alter the relations among the elements or the actions of the elements, which were simply taken as undisguised aspects of the theory of the self immanent in the presentation of the self in the consulting room (and in all other interpersonal encounters, for that matter). In Reed's words, "The relation explicitly described by self-theory is always manifest and awaiting revelation. Only its elements are disguised. . . . self-psychological interpretations . . . seem to assume that self-theory informs and is present in content. . . . Neither the relations among the elements nor the actions of the elements are assumed to have a hidden content. Only the elements *per se* are assumed to have a hidden content" (427). In that sense, proper interpretation restores the meaning of the elements (manifest to latent) and simultaneously reveals the theory of the self, thereby confirming it.

By contrast, Reed declared, "the hermeneutic system of classical analysis need not be seen as a system that restores meaning. . . . What separates interpretation in classical psychoanalysis from interpretation in self psychology is the possibility classical theory affords of a change in relations among the analyst-observer, the data to be interpreted, and the theory that helps organize the data. That this possibility is not always realized is not the fault of the theory but evidence of the human frailty of its practitioners" (434–35). "Classical theory," Reed goes on, "puts us in the humbling position of not knowing anything about the patient's meaning from the manifest content, including the manifest content of the transference. It requires, instead, that we rely on both the patient's free associations, and nonverbal communications such as reenactments. Thus, while the patient . . . was expressing her conscious, internal, subjective state, neither analyst nor patient would know in advance the reason for that state" (438). And finally, "Because the classical interpreter cannot rely on surface content for clues leading directly both to theory and to a revelation of the truth—that is, because surface content is mysterious—empathy and introspection are not enough" (439).

On the other hand, self psychology has had its defenders, including some from outside its ranks. Jule Miller (1987) spoke of the "purity" of Kohut's psychoanalytic vision. First he stressed the essentially psychoanalytic nature of Kohut's work: Kohut's discovery of "previously unrecognized forms of analyzable transferences, new editions of infantile situations that could be worked with by the *usual analytic techniques*" (541, italics added); and "This working through is accomplished primarily by interpreting, first in the transference, and then, by augmenting spontaneous memory recovery with reconstructions of crucial genetic experiences" (544). These selfobject transference formations "contain the core of the patient's psychopathology, and they can be worked through analytically with optimal resolution of that psychopathology. Kohut believed that, in principle, parameters were not necessary in analysis. With the recognition of selfobject transference formations, problems formerly requiring the adoption of parameters could now be resolved through transference analysis. Kohut believed that if an analysis is properly conducted from a self psychology point of view the need to resort to educative pressure, direction, confrontation, prohibition, arbitrary termination dates, or other nonanalytic techniques, is minimized" (546).

Anton Kris (1990a), who represents the traditional American ego-psychological perspective and is in no way an adherent of self psychology, leaned heavily on Kohut's formulations and techniques in his own contribution to the subject of helping patients by analyzing their self-critical and self-punitive attitudes. Kris began with a statement of what he felt was a frequent deficiency of customary analytic technique: "I believe that analysts have regularly, though unintentionally, sided with self-punitive attitudes of the patient. This failure of neutrality on the part of analysts is in large measure the result of a systematic error in psychoanalytic theory, overuse of the concept of unconscious guilt. I prefer to employ a distinction between punitive self-criticism and constructive self-criticism, both having conscious and unconscious components" (606). And "With the theoretical primacy of guilt . . . analysts failed to appreciate sufficiently the patient's inevitable view that the analyst—whose self-perception was one of neutrality—must actually agree with the self-punitive attitudes. Externalization of punitive self-critical attitudes onto the analyst in this way is virtually automatic, and the importance of shame reactions was regularly underestimated" (609).

It was this unfortunate but all too commonplace analytic interaction that Kris felt Kohut's technical stance avoided (and counteracted): "Kohut's orientation became *consistently* more tolerant of the patient's need to love the analyst and of regression and of acting out than was common in the 1950s and 1960s. He was far less committed to the authoritarian certainty of the analyst in the analytic situation and far more open to patient's judgments than most others" (611). Further, "he made it a central point of his new stance that the analyst's attitude to allegedly insatiable demands no longer be implicitly critical. . . . He no longer approached them as undesirable behavior to be *overcome* (by suggestion or other behavioral means smuggled into analytic technique) but, from the vantage point of an 'affirmative attitude' . . . he treated them as manifestations of mental life to be *understood* and mastered by way of an analytic process" (613).

This "affirmative attitude," Kris declared, specifically counteracted the patient's projection of his punitive self-criticism and made its analysis possible: "The question of importance, here, is whether Kohut and his followers have failed, as I believe, to take into account the significance of their stance for the neutralization of the patient's punitive unconscious self-criticism. I believe much of the success of their clinical work derives from the elements of their stance that reverse self-criticism, and from unrecognized analysis of conflicts in which punitive unconscious self-criticism represents one side" (614). Further,

> Attention to punitive unconscious self-criticism soon leads the analyst to recognize that neutrality requires more than *silent* acceptance, for in the presence of punitive unconscious self-criticism, the analyst's silence is experienced as confirmation of the self-critical attitude. Similarly, in making interventions the analyst must take into account the patient's tendency to hear criticism where none is intended. All this has led me to conclude that an attitude consciously directed to preventing such self-critical reactions is required, which is, I believe, the essence of Kohut's "affirmative attitude." This component of the revised analytic stance posed and continues to pose a great challenge to the classical stance, because it questions the assumptions that define where proper analytic clarification ends and allegedly unanalytic supportive measures begin. (615)

None of this meant that Kris accepted Kohut's new metapsychology: "The narcissistic vulnerability to shame dictates the use of an 'affirmative' attitude to provide *functional* neutrality—that is, neutrality defined by the patient's experience of the analyst—rather than a viewpoint of *externally descriptive* neutrality. The concept of punitive unconscious self-criticism accounts for this aspect of Kohut's stance of an affirmative attitude, but it does so—in contrast to Kohut's formulations—without abandoning either the concept of unconscious conflict or the important role of unconscious guilt" (615). Rather, this affirmative attitude is the vital underpinning of successful analytic work: "The affirmative attitude, far from being a substitute for resistance analysis, is the *sine qua non* when punitive self-critical attitudes run high" (619).[8]

8. In his most current paper (1994), Kris has applied these insights to a reconsideration of Freud's more successful treatment of Joan Riviere after Jones had failed with her: "The idea that the outcome may depend on the extent to which the personality of the analyst allows the patient to put him in the place of his ego ideal—that is, whether the analyst's more tolerant judgment can replace the patient's punitive self-criticism—may very well refer to the difference between Freud's relative success and Jones's impasse with Riviere" (658). Kris ended his article with a

Otto Kernberg's contributions, focused on the pathology and therapy of the so-called borderline personality organizations (with attention to what he calls "pathological narcissism" [1975] as a subset of these), also represent a prodigious theoretical and clinical body of work and have similarly attracted passionate discussion and debate. Since first marking out his selected terrain in "Structural Derivatives of Object Relationships" (1966), Kernberg has published six closely argued books (1975, 1976, 1980, 1984, 1989, 1992) on the borderline personality organization and pathological narcissism—their diagnosis, prognosis, and effective therapeutic management.[9]

Kernberg's contributions began with the clinical study of the sicker borderline patients in the Psychotherapy Research Project of the Menninger Foundation (Kernberg et al. 1972; Wallerstein 1986a, 1988b). This was soon elaborated into a full-fledged reconceptualization of the fundaments of psychoanalytic theory, which, he argued, could better account for the borderline phenomena and their etiological roots in the early (essentially preoedipal) parent-child interactions. This theoretical creation was an effort at an amalgamated object-relational ego-psychological theory for psychoanalysis (with Kleinian influences as well, in its strong emphasis on innate aggression, especially oral greed and envy). Kernberg's theory would construct Freud's tripartite structural mental world out of the building blocks of internalized object relations— that is, units of self- and object-representations and the affective valences and role relationships that bind them—and then would delineate the consequences

---

question that was in the back of his mind: "How is it possible that Freud's attitude of support in the treatment of Riviere failed to persist, particularly in North American psychoanalysis and required rediscovery?" (661)—by Kohut. His answer was, "I believe that Freud's commitment to his capacity for 'objective' evaluation played a most important role in his reluctance to endorse publicly the analyst's personal involvement. . . . Throughout his published writings, Freud attempted again and again to dismiss the criticism that suggestion played a significant role in psychoanalysis lest that allegation undermine its scientific standing. . . . I believe that Freud's failure to acknowledge his 'breaking the rules' should be understood . . . as a result of a divided allegiance between his sense of what was needed by his patients and his determination to promote and preserve the scientific standing of psychoanalysis" (661–62). The result Kris feels to be unfortunate: "Influenced more by Freud's published writings than by his conduct, Freud's colleagues slipped into a minimalist technique that failed to provide the support he had known was needed" (662).

9. As with Kohut, the reader is referred to Kernberg's books for a detailed accounting of the unfolding of his conceptions of the psychoanalytic understanding of these sicker patients. For critical assessments of Kernberg's contributions, all written from within the established classical psychoanalytic position, yet sharply divergent in their intellectual biases, see Calef and Weinshel (1979), Segel (1981a), and Wallerstein (1986c).

of this for technical and therapeutic application in clinical endeavors with borderline and narcissistic patients.

But, unlike Kohut, Kernberg has not encouraged a revisionist movement or a new (and different) overall metapsychology for psychoanalysis, and one has not developed in the sense that Kohut's self psychology has. Kernberg has unswervingly seen his contribution as falling squarely within the edifice of traditional psychoanalysis. His effort has been to integrate two of its major emphases, the American ego-psychological and the British object-relational, in one coherent schema; in that sense it is additive and synthesizing, not divisive or cultish.

In his study of the borderline condition, Kernberg had been struck by a phenomenon he was soon to conceptualize as the essential and pathognomonic defensive operation of these patients. This is the mechanism he called splitting, the parallel or alternating appearance of opposing ego states, an *active* process of keeping apart introjects and identifications of opposite affective quality (all-good and all-bad). This regularly recurring hallmark feature convinced him that the borderline personality, while often presenting a chaotic, wildly fluctuating, impulse-ridden picture, nonetheless represented on closer scrutiny "a specific, *stable,* pathological personality organization," unique and well demarcated from both neurosis and psychosis.

How did this specific character organization develop?[10] Because of the presence in some individuals of excessive amounts of aggressive drive—owing to some combination of constitutional instinctual forces, a weak ego unable to adequately tolerate anxiety, and intense external trauma from the childhood caretakers—they are unable to phase-specifically, appropriately integrate self- and object-representations linked by a positive emotional valence with those that are negatively linked; this leads to the persistence of all-good and all-bad self- and object-representations. The borderline condition is distinguished from psychosis in that some differentiation of self from object has been achieved, even though this does not yet extend to the integration of positive and negative self- and object-representations into more complex (and quintessentially ambivalent) self- and object-representations. If such integration occurred, it would lift the patient beyond the dominance of splitting to a (conflicted) neurotic structure. With the psychotic, on the other hand, the self- and object-representations are still fused or re-fused.

The splitting that thus began as a weakness of ego functioning comes to be used actively to protect the all-good self and objects from being destroyed by

---

10. The condensed statement of Kernberg's theorizing in the next four paragraphs is paraphrased—albeit with significant modifications—from Segel (1981a, 222–24), the most succinct and yet comprehensive summary I have seen.

the powerful oral aggression (greed and envy) of the all-bad self and objects. Splitting is fortified in this defensive work by what Kernberg calls other "low-level defensive operations," among them projection, projective identification, omnipotence and grandiosity, primitive idealization, denial and devaluation. These are in contrast to repression and its allied defensive operations (isolation, reaction-formation, and so on), which are "higher level" and characteristic of the neuroses. The low-level defenses of the borderline are associated with "non-specific ego weaknesses," for example, lack of impulse control, inability to tolerate anxiety, or to use sublimations as a significant channel for gratification and discharge. Because of the inability to integrate aggressive and libidinally colored object relations, there is interference with ego and superego development as well as perpetuation of primitive superego introjects of both sadistic and over-idealized types.

Building on these ideas, Kernberg took on the ambitious project of attempting to revise the classification of character pathology so that it would lend itself more readily to accurate diagnosis, prognosis, and therapy. To do this, he distinguished among pathology in the ego and superego structures, pathology of internalized object relations, and pathology in the development of libidinal and aggressive drive derivatives. Each of these was in turn subdivided into categories of higher-, intermediate-, and lower-level pathological functioning. They were then recombined so that instinctual development, superego development, defensive ego operations, and the vicissitudes of object relations could be compared at the three levels of character pathology. This methodical development, Segel stated, "gives the impression of a precise steplike march from one level of clinical pathological organization to the next. The precision, however, is more apparent than real, according to my own clinical experience. In a similar chapter in the book on object relations, I felt the implication of our being able to go from detailed structural formulations to normal and pathological hierarchies, which in turn lent themselves to computerlike diagnoses, prognoses, defensive operations, and then to matching and exact treatment modalities, was again an unrealistic projection of the current state of our theoretical and clinical knowledge" (1981a, 223–24).

Such misgivings aside, what are the implications of this theoretical structure for the treatment of borderline patients? Kernberg tried to carefully delineate where unmodified psychoanalysis should and should not be used (for the essentially neurotic and most borderlines, respectively); where his version of "modified psychoanalytic technique" is to be preferred (for the borderline); and where external "structuring," including periods of hospitalization and the use of psychoactive medication, is required (for some of the lower-level borderline). The early phases in the treatment of the borderline are seen to be loaded with chaotic,

primitive transferences heavily marked by projections and projective identifications. Here, Kernberg followed Heinrich Racker (1968) in describing how
the therapist experiences the feelings evoked and provoked by the patient. There
are both "complementary" and "concordant" identifications, depending on
whether the analyst experiences himself in the role of the patient's object, a
possibly sadistic, threatening parent-figure, or in the role of the patient as the
small and helpless child. The analyst, as the fantasied object, may be filled with
anger, disdain, and wishes to impose his will; as the proxy for the patient, he or
she can feel small, terrified, impotent, and worthless. Where Kernberg differs
significantly from Kohut in dealing with these somewhat overlapping patients
is in feeling that the patient's projections of aspects of his primitive self- or
object-representations may equally represent distorted amalgams of parts of the
self and parts of the object and early fantasized aspects of both that were never
actually true of either. He does not automatically assume that the markedly
sadistic part-object projections represent actual unempathic childhood objects
or experiences. In fact, the persistent separating out of these primitive transferences (centrally, orally aggressive greed and envy) and their appropriate constant
interpretation represents the core of Kernberg's modified psychoanalytic technique with the borderline and fosters the ultimate integration of self- and object-
representations, gradually enabling one to achieve a more accurate conception
of the patient's actual childhood experiences. This, of course, means an unremitting focus on the here and now aspects of the transference interactions,
leaving genetic reconstructions aside for a later phase, when the patient has
reached a more neurotic level of psychic functioning. Although during periods
of stress there may be regressions to actual psychotic transference manifestations,
these are usually limited to the therapeutic setting and are felt to be manageable
with the "treatable" borderlines.[11]

In a chapter entitled "A Theory of Psychoanalytic Psychotherapy" (1980,
181–208), Kernberg declared that the established formulations of 1954 regarding
the supportive and the expressive psychotherapies had been worked out in relation to the classical ego-psychological structural model, based on and appro-

---

11. Sander Abend, Michael Porder, and Martin Willick (1983) took specific exception to Kernberg's focused technical approach based on his conception of the specific underlying pathology
of the borderline. They said, "Since we could not agree with the phase-specific hypothesis,
we could not subscribe to a therapeutic approach geared to a single conflict. Such a suggestion
is at variance with our belief in the complexity and individuality of all psychopathology and
treatment. Consistent with these ideas, we could not offer any special technique for the analysis
of these patients. Defenses of all types, transference reactions, superego conflicts, genetic material, and anamnestic data from all stages of development were interpreted and worked
through as they emerged with sufficient clarity in the treatment" (205).

priate to consolidated and integrated neurotic character structures centering on oedipal pathology, and were inappropriate for patients with "wider and deeper ego disorders"—paradigmatically the borderline patients. Nor did he follow the British object-relations theorists (particularly the Kleinians but also the Middle or Independent Group), who tended to apply (their versions of) relatively unmodified psychoanalytic technique to these sicker patients. Rather, Kernberg called for a specifically modified psychoanalytic technique:

> Because primitive transferences are immediately available, predominate as resistances, and, in fact, determine the severity of intrapsychic and interpersonal disturbances, they can and need to be focused on immediately, starting with their interpretation in the "here and now" and leading into genetic reconstruction only at the late stages of the treatment (when primitive transferences determined by part-object relations have been transformed into advanced transferences or total object relations . . .). Interpretation of the transference requires maintaining a position of technical neutrality. For there can be no interpretation of primitive transferences without a firm, consistent, stable maintenance of reality boundaries in the therapeutic situation, and without an active caution on the part of the therapist not to be sucked into the reactivation of pathological primitive object relations by the patient. Insofar as both transference interpretation and a position of technical neutrality require the use of clarification and interpretation and contraindicate the use of suggestive and manipulative techniques, clarification and interpretation are maintained as principal techniques.
>
> However, in contrast to psychoanalysis proper, transference analysis is not systematic. Because of the need to focus on the severity of acting out and on the disturbance in the patient's external reality (which may threaten the continuity of the treatment as well as the patient's psychosocial survival) and also because the treatment, as part of the acting out of primitive transferences, easily comes to replace life, transference interpretation now has to be codetermined by (1) the predominant conflicts in immediate reality, (2) the overall specific goals of treatment . . . and (3) by what is immediately prevailing in the transference.
>
> In addition, technical neutrality is limited by the need to establish parameters of technique, including, in certain cases, the structuring of the patient's external life and establishing a teamwork approach with patients who cannot function autonomously during long stretches of their psychotherapy. Technical neutrality is therefore a theoretical base line from

which deviations occur again and again, to be reduced by interpretation. (191–92)

What is somewhat confusing about Kernberg's categorizations is that this quotation is from a chapter explicitly devoted to a theory of psychoanalytic psychotherapy as distinct from psychoanalysis, though throughout most of his writings this selfsame therapeutic approach is called "modified psychoanalysis," not (expressive) psychoanalytic psychotherapy. Also, though Kernberg takes exception to the customary view that these are precisely the patients for whom the more supportive approaches are indicated, and even in the quotation just cited states that "suggestive and manipulative techniques" are contraindicated, he nonetheless talks of the need with many of these patients to "structure their external life" or to bring "a teamwork approach." These are, of course, the very ingredients that are traditionally encompassed within the range of supportive techniques and mechanisms.

The conceptual and technical edifice created by Kernberg has been remarkably influential in (American) psychoanalytic and psychotherapeutic circles. On that, all the major critics have agreed, albeit with different valences. Calef and Weinshel (1979) acknowledged that Kernberg's writings "enjoy a popularity and currency in the psychoanalytic marketplace . . . [so that] the whole area of the 'borderline' has become ineluctably identified with . . . [his] name." But they added, in an implicitly pejorative footnote, "It may well be that no contribution by a psychoanalyst has been taken up so avidly and so happily by the nonpsychoanalytic segment of the mental health community, with the possible exception of Erikson's introduction of the identity concept a quarter of a century ago" (470). In that same vein they referred to its resemblance to "a cult movement within the scientific community" (471) and to "the cult-like atmosphere that has surrounded much of his work" (490).

Segel's (1981a) stance differed sharply: "It is not difficult to understand the vast following of anyone who seems to offer a solid and relatively straight road through this wilderness, beset as it is with fantastic transference manifestations . . . and the guilt-laden countertransferences that they so often evoke" (222). On the previous page he had said admiringly, "Those fortunate enough to possess the talent for integrative clarity are able to provide major theoretical and clinical insights to the rest of us" (221). In my own review essay (1986), I stated, "There is probably no psychoanalytic author more widely read or quoted in the world today both within specifically psychoanalytic circles and in the far wider arena of the psychoanalytically influenced world of mental health professionals" (711) and cited an informal survey of three leading English-language psychoanalytic journals from 1969 to 1982, in which fourteen authors accounted for thirty-six of the sixty most frequently cited articles. Kernberg was the author of six of these thirty-six articles, Margaret Mahler and John Bowlby of four each, and the other eleven most cited authors, two each.

Yet all three of these critiques pointed to the same difficulty in fully accepting what seems to be Kernberg's ultraprecise theoretical scheme. What Segel (1981a) called "the impression of a precise steplike march" and a "precision . . . [that] is more apparent than real" (223) was criticized much more strongly by Calef and Weinshel (1979): "We must ask whether the nature and quantity of the data available to us and to Kernberg is truly amenable to the kind of precise categorization and systematization which Kernberg has undertaken. . . . Our own reaction is that . . . Kernberg has been too intent on isolating too many psychopathological entities and making sure that each was securely placed in its appropriate diagnostic pigeonhole" (477). I think this shared conclusion of two otherwise quite divergent critiques of Kernberg's work reflects a consensus within specifically psychoanalytic ranks that the very nature of the continuously interacting fluid (and subjectivistic) phenomena of our field must defeat any psychoanalytic effort to achieve such precision in diagnosis, prognosis, and treatment planning. I should add, however, that the widespread uneasiness in specific psychoanalytic ranks about this effort to delineate and categorize these phenomena very precisely is not shared by the much wider group of mental health professionals; in fact, it may very well be part of the basis of Kernberg's great appeal to this audience.

An example of the problems created by the effort to achieve such precision is in the differentiating diagnostic maneuver Kernberg claimed distinguishes the psychotic from the borderline, namely, the differential response during the diagnostic process to the trial interpretation of the manifest primitive defensive operations. With the borderline, such interpretation is declared to have a positive and integrative effect, helping to strengthen the patient's ego functioning and reality testing; with the psychotic the same approach is declared to have a negative and regressive impact, uncovering even more the lack of differentiation between self and nonself. All this may often be true, but hardly to the degree that it can be lifted to the status of an ever-useful diagnostic measure. Calef and Weinshel, who took full measure of just this difficulty, said,

> Granting, however, that the interpretation framed by a given therapist is sensible and seemingly appropriate, how can one accurately predict, when dealing with patients at this level of disturbance, what the impact of such an interpretation might be? . . . All of us are quite aware how often in our clinical work we are quite surprised (both pleasantly and unpleasantly) at the impact a given intervention . . . may exert on even reasonably healthy

patients. What may seem to the therapist a bland and innocuous remark can bring about apparently devastating reactions. Conversely, what may seem to the therapist to be a potentially disruptive and threatening statement may well have a most salutary effect. We certainly do not know nearly as much as we should about these somewhat commonplace experiences, but we do recognize that the complexity of the psychic apparatus and the fluidity of that apparatus even in more stable patients make the accuracy of our "predictions" (which is what is involved in interpretations, after all) somewhat less than foolproof. With more disturbed individuals, at the moment we embark on an interpretive effort, we are simply not really sure what the exact state of the patient's mind may be; we are not certain how the patient will "hear" and experience that particular interpretation; and we can be even less confident of what will be the reverberations of the interchange. . . . We submit, therefore, that to depend on the reaction to what can at best be only a subjectively determined interpretation is hardly a dependable and convincing form of diagnosis. (479–80).

Calef and Weinshel have indeed identified a central weakness in Kernberg's theoretical and clinical structure—yet one that derives from his very success in developing an orderly conceptual framework within which the borderline and narcissistic phenomena are arrayed *and clarified*. This to me is the heart of a major dialectical dilemma posed by Kernberg's work.

Calef and Weinshel indicated other concerns about Kernberg's contributions to theory building and their implications for clinical practice, which will not be elaborated here.[12] I will, rather, focus on three significant themes in his 1984 book that are central to the subject of this book and that represented significant extensions and amplifications of Kernberg's thinking. These themes are (1) the interplay of the expressive and supportive psychotherapeutic modes in the treatment of the borderline; (2) the better delineation of the very refractory-to-treatment or essentially unanalyzable (and perhaps untreatable) patients; and (3) the psychoanalytic understanding of hospital treatment.

The heart of Kernberg's book is chapters 6 to 10, which directly apply the diagnostic considerations of the first five chapters to differential treatment indications for different kinds of patients, especially to the continuing debate over just how psychoanalytic, and with how much or how little modification of what is properly psychoanalytic, treatment can and should be in the face of progres-

12. For a full statement, see Calef and Weinshel (1979, particularly 487–89); for my summary of them, see Wallerstein (1986c, 714).

sively wider and deeper ego disorders. On this issue, Kernberg and I have long differed in our interpretation of the same clinical phenomena, originally stemming from our study of the same patients in the Psychotherapy Research Project of the Menninger Foundation (Kernberg et al. 1972; Wallerstein 1986a, 1988b). To capsulize this difference: Kernberg's view is that for these sicker borderline and narcissistic patients, the supportive psychotherapeutic approaches initially pioneered by Knight (see chapter 3) are contraindicated. For patients with this kind of "ego weakness" a specifically expressive "modified analytic" approach is indicated, with structure and support relegated to the concomitant hospitalization so often invoked at Menninger with these patients (for example, see Kernberg 1984, 98, 102, 103, 105, 122). Typically, Kernberg stated, "I cannot emphasize strongly enough that a heavy price is paid whenever the therapist yields to the temptation of introducing supportive techniques; immediate improvement is followed by the patient's later rationalizations of transference developments that cannot be resolved fully and thus limit the fundamental personality changes the treatment aims for" (122).

The opposed view, put forward initially by Knight (1945, 1949, 1952, 1953a) and developed in detail by Wallerstein (1986a, 1988b), is that explicitly supportive elements are vital components of the therapeutic approach to severely ill patients. The treatment owes a substantial amount of the success it achieves to the skillful deployment and blending of an array of psychoanalytically conceptualized supportive techniques. This is just as true of the very cases cited by Kernberg. I feel he has simply ignored the supportive elements inevitable in the interactions with the sanatorium support and structure, to which Kernberg tries to totally consign these influences—as if they thereby could be excluded from a role in the therapeutic interplay in the treatment hour itself. Actually, Kernberg has expressed a partial agreement with this view under more extreme circumstances—"supportive therapy is usually appropriate as a treatment of last resort—that is, when other modes must be ruled out" (1984, 151). Our difference is that I draw that line much more deeply into the borderline region of the pathology spectrum than he does, and I submit that those same supportive elements operate (but are not explicitly acknowledged) in the very patients with whom Kernberg claims to be working fully expressively and psychoanalytically. We do agree on the appropriateness of the working adage "Be as expressive as you can be; be as supportive as you have to be" (e.g., 1984, 168–69) but differ both on the proper placement of the demarcation line and on how to interpret the data of the treatment processes under study. And that, after all, is the central issue of this entire book.

Kernberg is known for the optimism he has contagiously brought to therapeutic work with the borderline, so it may be somewhat surprising to those who have oversimplistically assumed that he has offered us blueprints for the therapeutic modification of even the most refractory of character structures that his optimism has been tempered by a healthy respect for the kinds of patients and conditions in the face of which therapeutic endeavors, of whatever kind, may prove of little or no avail. Kernberg's constant stress on the role of primitive and pregenital aggressions of often unmanageable intensity as a fundamental source of psychopathology led him ineluctably—and reluctantly—to this position. Here I want particularly to mention Kernberg's delineation of the treatment stalemates that represent especially refractory negative therapeutic reactions, those that stem predominantly from an envious need to destroy, as in the borderline and over-the-border patients whose unconscious identifications with primitive sadistic objects require such torment as the price for maintaining any kind of object attachment at all (1984, chap. 15); those he described as suffering from "malignant narcissism" (chap. 19); the cold and guilt-repressed truly antisocial characters (chap. 18); and those for whom suicide is a "way of life" (chap. 16). In connection with all of these, Kernberg rightly decried the "dangerous tendency . . . to underestimate the many forms human aggression and aggression against the self can take." He cautioned that (all too frequently) the therapist's "unconscious tendency to 'play God' is counterpart to dangerous naivete in neglecting the severity of destructive tendencies in the patient and his family" (260). The minor cavil I have is with Kernberg's failure at times to make clear when he meant unanalyzable and when he meant totally untreatable (at least at this stage of our knowledge)—but that is, after all, part of my quarrel that he has failed to give proper professional due to the supportive psychotherapeutic components in the therapeutic scheme of things.

Though it is beyond the declared purview of this book, I will mention briefly Kernberg's conceptualization of psychiatric hospitalization as a structuring, "holding," and therapeutic environment because of the supportive role that recourse to hospitalization, when needed, can play in the treatment of borderline patients. In this context, Kernberg undertook to compare the internal psychological structure of the psychotherapy situation that is set within the hospital environment and the social-psychological structure of that milieu and to analyze how these variously reinforce or work at cross-purposes with each other. Along the way, he discussed the issue of the specious democratization advocated by some therapeutic community enthusiasts (1984, 332), such as Maxwell Jones and his followers, who "neglect the importance of intrapsychic determinants for psychopathology and support the illusion that a healthy social atmosphere in the hospital can replace psychotherapy and produce fundamental personality change" (338); the important distinction between ideological and technical convictions about a democratic versus an authoritative (but not authoritarian) hierarchical organization of hospital ward communities (334); and the various ways in which the development of a more egalitarian ward environment may only "sharpen the awareness of real social conflicts and contradictions [i.e., within the total administrative organization of the hospital community, within which the ward is set and necessarily has to operate] that are beyond the therapeutic community's ability to resolve satisfactorily" (336).

In a wise summary statement, Kernberg posed the conceptual organizational problem brought to light by these social-psychoanalytic considerations of hospital treatment: "A major task facing American psychiatry today is to disentangle the new technical knowledge obtained in the past 50 years from the ideological distortions and social extrapolations of that knowledge. In practice, optimal utilization of this knowledge requires that the psychiatric hospital permit the use of staff's emotional reactions to patients for therapeutic purposes and promote an atmosphere of openness and a functional—in contrast to an authoritarian—administrative structure. A functional administrative structure is not a democratic one. The distinction between functional administration and democratic political organization is one aspect of the new learning that is being integrated at this time" (328–29).

It remains now only to make some statement comparing Kohut and Kernberg in their profound impact on the climate and character of American psychoanalysis over recent decades and on the reference frame within which we conceptualize the many issues of psychotherapy vis-à-vis psychoanalysis. Segel (1981a), in his review essay, devoted several pages to just such comparison (226–29). He also, in a subsequent article published in the same year (1981b), made this comparison much more tersely: "Although Kernberg stresses the presence of libidinal as well as aggressive components in their [the borderlines'] psychopathology, it is the aggressive drive derivatives that lend this group its special flavour. Where Kohut fosters the positive transference, Kernberg insists the negative transference must be worked through. The pregenital conflicts are around an intense oral rage and envy that must be defended against lest the patients feel threatened both by their projected paranoid fears and by a total sense of worthlessness related to fear and guilt that their primitive rage will destroy any possibility of their being loved" (468). Within this juxtaposition one can place Kohut's development of the concepts of empathic in-tuneness and immersion within which to elicit the selfobject transferences that must ultimately be worked through in order to resolve narcissistic pathology and restore a damaged self to a healthy coherence and cohesiveness, as well as Kernberg's vigorous interpretation of the oral greed, envy, and rage needed in order to resolve borderline pathology and to promote the integration of split good and bad self- and object-representations.[13]

Yet what Segel calls "perhaps most striking and even surprising"—given the gross severity of the disorders that both men bring within our therapeutic orbits—"is the relative optimism of both Kohut and Kernberg with regard to the treatment of such patients" (1981b, 469), given, of course, Kernberg's caveats, just mentioned, about those he considers truly untreatable. Both have widened our psychotherapeutic horizons, albeit in Kohut's case it is a declared psychoanalysis (in accord with the tenets of self psychology) with the narcissistic, and in Kernberg's case it is a declared modified analysis (conceptualized within his object relational–ego psychological perspective) with the borderline.

13. In this context it is important to point out that the differences between Kohut's approach of "empathic immersion" and Kernberg's of "active confrontation" of negative transference do not stem from the differing requirements of narcissistic and borderline patients; indeed, there is very significant overlap of the clinical populations the two theorists are describing. Rather, their differences are a matter of differing conceptions of how to most effectively treat the "sicker than neurotic" patients. For an example of how another major worker with borderline patients advocates a therapeutic approach that seems much more akin in spirit to Kohut than to Kernberg, I quote from Adler's (1993) review of Kernberg et al. (1989): "The authors' treatment strategy can work with some patients and some therapists in some settings, but can also be seen as limiting the treatment potential of borderline patients who require something more. . . . Although it is intrinsically caring, their framework simultaneously minimizes the intense experience of affects between patient and therapist in both the real relationship and in the transference. . . . These patients instead may seek other therapists who are willing to engage them in a way that acknowledges the importance of the real relationship for both patient and therapist, valuing the caring and protecting experience as inevitable, not to be feared, and leading to the working through and ultimate internalization of needed structure" (296).

V. Contemporary Developments and Issues

21 Contemporary Emphases in Psychoanalytic Therapy: Anton Kris, Paul Gray, Evelyne Schwaber, and Irwin Hoffman and Merton Gill

There are various contemporary trends in the theory and technique of psychoanalytic therapy that, though not necessarily addressed specifically to the issues of psychoanalytic psychotherapy vis-à-vis psychoanalysis, nonetheless bear importantly on our understanding of those issues. The five writers whose work is presented in this chapter bring distinctly individual perspectives to these issues, yet each, from a micro-analytic point of view, focuses on the details and nuances of moment-to-moment therapeutic interactions. The logic of the sequence in which these writers are presented should become clear in the unfolding.

Anton Kris, the one who is the least microscopic in his focus, has published a sequence of papers (1977, 1984, 1985, 1988, 1990a, 1992) progressively elaborating a distinction that he has brought to our awareness, between two types of intrapsychic conflict: One had been part of the classical understanding of psychoanalysis from the beginning (typically drives versus defenses, or id pressures versus superego constraints) and one that he called "either-or dilemmas" (1977). The latter had been curiously unremarked—though Kris did point to earlier writings by Rangell (1963a, 1963b) and Kubie (1974) that had called specific attention to these dilemmas. Rangell (1963b), in an article on intrapsychic conflict, had stated that there are "two different types and meanings of conflict. These are (1) an opposition type, of forces battling against each other, in hostile encounter, and (2) a dilemma type, the need for a choice between competing alternatives. Traditionally, before the advent of the structural point of view, intrapsychic conflict referred always to the first of these meanings. . . . Although the second type of conflict came into play with the advent of the tripartite structural model, with the role of the ego as a mediator and integrator between the other two systems, this differentiation in forms of conflict was not explicitly spelled out" (104). In a preceding paper (1963a), Rangell had said, "This differentiation has not been pointed out or at least is usually neglected or insufficiently kept in mind in the psychoanalytic literature on intrapsychic conflict. Historically, it was the opposition-of-forces type which first held sway in our early theoretical formulations" (86).

Kubie (1974), in "The Drive to Become Both Sexes," made the same distinction in somewhat different language: "seriously pathogenic conflicts may arise not only between basic instinctual pressures on the one hand and the conscience processes (superego) on the other, but can also arise out of conflicting and irreconcilable identifications. . . . these in turn can give rise to irreconcilable distortions of body images and identity goals. This is an important addition to the earlier concept of intrapsychic conflicts as arising always between id processes and superego processes, but it is not irreconcilable with them. They are supplementary and in no sense mutually exclusive" (408). Earlier, Kubie had stated, "Yet he [Freud] seemed to underestimate another source of conflict, namely that which arose out of man's frequent struggle to achieve mutually irreconcilable and consequently unattainable identities. This study of the drive to become both sexes deals primarily with this second category of internal conflict" (352).

It is this "second category" of conflict that Kris has developed in his sequence of papers. In his 1977 paper, he said, "The either-or dilemmas are conflicts experienced as insoluble—that is, their solution appears to require intolerable loss on one side or the other. As psychoanalysts we encounter such conflicts frequently: either obedience or self-fulfillment; self-indulgence or self-denial; erotic love or affection; dominance or submission; rational thought or irrational feeling; action or reflection; and so on. Usually the patient shuttles unsatisfied between the horns of the dilemma" (91). And "Such cases illustrate the mutual frustration of active and passive libidinal wishes in the intrasystemic conflicts of a neurosis. No sooner does the patient express the wishes on one side than she must express those on the other, which have been threatened with frustration. The result is that neither side achieves satisfaction *because* of the danger of frustration to the other" (103). Further, "It is the antithetical nature of the paired instinctual wishes, produced by the tendency of one to bring the other into conflict, while they are yoked in obligatory condensation, that inevitably leads to mutual frustration when, for one reason or another, the balance gets tipped" (110).

In this same paper, Kris offered a first statement of the therapeutic implications of this dilemma: "The free associations must be permitted to swing back and forth between the sides, slowly lengthening the pendulum to permit longer periods on either side. In this way each side can receive its full and independent expression, permitting intersystemic conflicts associated with the instinctual wishes on each side to enter the analytic process" (114).

In his second (1984) paper in this sequence, Kris elaborated two kinds (or paradigms) of conflict, now named "conflicts of defense" and "conflicts of ambivalence." Conflicts of defense, the classical conflicts between drive and defense, the conflict of opposing forces, are resolved through the lifting of the repressions (and the other defenses) by interpretations, with working through leading to achieved insights. Contrariwise, in the conflicts of ambivalence, the opposing components diverge, pull away from each other rather than converge and push against each other. There is a painful tension when either side is pursued to the neglect of the other, a reluctance to proceed down one track in the free association process because of the anticipated loss of the other side. The resolution, Kris said, occurred via pendular alternations in the free associative process with incremental mourning of what was being given up and lost. Kris explicitly analogized this to the process of mourning, "alternation," and "painful detachment" described by Freud in "Mourning and Melancholia" (1917), adding that these conflicts of ambivalence are especially highlighted in adolescence and are a characteristic of borderline states, in which the patient is driven to deal with them by the extremes of splitting.

In the third (1985) paper, Kris altered his nomenclature to the more felicitous one of "convergent" and "divergent" conflicts and offered a very graphic metaphor, that of the football game versus the tug of war. Football is prototypically the convergent conflict of opposed hostile forces, grouped as offense and defense; the tug of war is the divergent conflict of (irreconcilable) forces pulling in opposite directions with no distinction between offense and defense. He abandoned his earlier term "conflicts of ambivalence" because these conflicts cover a much wider territory than the most common (and defining) usage of ambivalence: love and hate directed toward the same object.[1] In bringing the whole conceptual field of conflict (and resistance) within his orbit, Kris looked at the five categories of resistance designated by Freud in "Inhibitions, Symptoms and Anxiety" (1926). Three of them, the resistances of repression, of transference, and of the superego, were pictured in convergent opposition; the other two, resistances of secondary gain and of the id, were represented in terms of divergent conflict, although not so labeled. For example, Kris quoted Freud to the effect that the resistance of the secondary gain "is of quite a different nature. It proceeds from the *gain from illness* and is based upon an assimilation of the symptom into the ego. . . . It represents an unwillingness to renounce any satisfaction or relief that has been obtained" (1926, 160). Yet neither Freud nor the analytic writers who came after him made this distinction between kinds

1. "The antithetical pairs in conflicts of ambivalence, as I conceive of them, are not limited to love and hate. They are most easily recognized in the characteristic alternations in the free associations of the adolescent, between such formless opposites as activity and passivity, homosexual and heterosexual, pregenital and genital sexuality, old objects and new ones, independence and dependence, autonomy and loss of self, self-control and dissipation, altruism and egotism, spontaneity and regulation, mind and body, fantasy and reality. Each of these pairs may at times be the subject of a sense of either-or, conscious or unconscious" (1985, 539–40).

of conflict; rather, they continued to represent all evidence of intrasystemic and intersystemic conflict as convergent—that is, with neither arm of the conflict displacing, excluding, or warding off the other—rather than as divergent, with the two arms alternating and equally accessible to consciousness.

Nonetheless, Kris could demonstrate that Freud, as well as those who came after, had always *implicitly* encompassed the concept of divergent conflicts: "I have already illustrated this thesis by demonstrating the model of divergent conflict in the early concept of the pull component of repression, in the later concepts of adhesiveness of the libido, resistance of the id, resistance of secondary gain from illness, and resistance from relative immobility of cathectic attachment, and in the idea of oscillation between heterosexual and homosexual feelings" (546). He added that the concept of divergent conflicts was embedded in many other central psychoanalytic formulations: that of fixation, progression and regression, pregenital and genital, the rapprochement phase of separation-individuation, the pleasure principle and the reality principle, primary process and secondary process, and so on. In terms of therapeutic handling, Kris reaffirmed his conviction that Freud's conception of making the unconscious conscious via interpretation applied aptly to convergent but not to divergent conflicts, in which both elements in the conflict might well be conscious. Alleviation of the divergent conflict is in the process of successful mourning, the acknowledgement of loss and lost opportunity, the gradual dwindling of the painful poignancy of having to live with choice and compromise. In the same article Kris also gave many examples of the complex interaction between convergent and divergent conflicts and their often necessarily sequential therapeutic handling.

Kris's fourth and final paper in this sequence (1988) presented a long clinical case illustration of how the concept of two kinds of conflict could facilitate a uniform approach of resistance analysis in regard to preoedipal as well as oedipal issues. Here Kris elaborated a concept of conflict very much akin to what I quoted from Sandler (1974, 1976b) and Dorpat (1976) in chapter 20. Kris said,

> Conflict refers to incompatibility. It may be used to describe events or their inferred determinants at all levels of abstraction in psychoanalysis. It may refer to two tendencies that lead to a slip of the tongue or to a conflict between two functions, such as accurate perception and the avoidance of painful emotion, or to the hypothesized relationship between ego, id, and superego in neurosis. It may refer to the contradictory feelings and wishes of a little boy in the oedipal phase in his relationship to his father, or it may refer to any one of those wishes and the tendencies that oppose them. My current preference is to speak of two types of conflict, because that

highlights their differences, especially in regard to four characteristics, the *form of opposition,* the *resistances* encountered, the *patterns of resolution* required, and the kind of *insight* obtained in psychoanalysis. In practice, however, the two types are interwoven in the fabric of mental life. (431–32)

Within this expanded framework, Kris addressed the issue of oedipal versus preoedipal conflicts: "All the clinical experience of the past three decades with severely disturbed patients, however formulated, speaks to a requirement for some additional, very different process, beyond the lifting of repression, in the treatment of pre-oedipal disorders. This becomes increasingly apparent when more 'primitive' conflicts and less adequate ego development are involved; for example, when the wish for independence seems poised against a threat of annihilation . . . called the wish-fear dilemma" (433). These developmental conflicts (involving usually progression-regression) typically have the character of divergent conflicts, but Kris was wary of blanket correlations: "I hasten to add that I do not mean that pre-oedipal conflict is divergent only or that oedipal conflict is convergent only" (434).

In two more recent articles (1990a, 1992), neither addressed centrally to these specific issues, Kris elaborated his view of the two kinds of insight achieved in the resolution of the two kinds of conflict: "Each of the two patterns or types of conflict is associated with a characteristic form of resistance, patterns of resolution, and kind of insight. Resolution of the divergent conflicts requires alternating expression of the two sides. This process leads to a form of insight, a recognition that what seemed to be either-or no longer seems so. This is a different kind of insight from the insight that comes with lifting of repression. . . . Whereas the insight connected with lifting of repression develops at some relatively circumscribed moment (though some such insights may come and go several times before they become established), the insight connected with resolution of divergent conflict usually develops silently unnoticed by patient or analyst" (1992, 216). Earlier he had put this more succinctly: "The insight achieved in the resolution of convergent conflicts is relatively discrete, while the insight that develops in the resolution of divergent conflicts appears gradually and is usually little more than a change of opinion: what seemed to be either-or no longer seems so" (1990a, 623).

Paul Gray, in his sequence of articles on technique (1973, 1982, 1986, 1987, 1988, 1990, 1991),[2] also focused on issues of conflict, but in a much more

2. These articles have been brought together (along with additional materials) in Gray's recent book, *The Ego and the Analysis of Defense,* 1994.

microanalytic way than Kris, accenting what he called the proper "inside focus" for psychoanalytic therapy and in the process contrasting psychoanalytic work with psychotherapeutic work. In his first (1973) paper in this series he outlined what he called the intrapsychic and "inside focus" on the patient's mind and how it works, as distinguished from an "outside focus" on the patient's life outside the hour. He called the central task of psychoanalysis an unremitting focus on the ego's defensive processes as manifest in the transference expressions in the analytic hour—how unwanted impulses and affects (being defended against at that moment) are kept out of consciousness. Any, even momentary, focus on outside reality events in the patient's life (other than as displaced or metaphoric expressions of internal psychic processes) inevitably, in Gray's view, made the treatment more *psychotherapeutic* than psychoanalytic. At times, of course, as in instances of acute loss and bereavement, it may be necessary to pay attention to reality events, but this had a price: "The analysis of any defense against the patient's facing such a process [as grief and mourning] *may* provide a better understanding of the patient's traditional forms of resistance. However, the direct benefits that the stable presence of the analyst and the analysis provide for the patient during such times are probably to a considerable extent, and unavoidably so, rather psychotherapeutic ones" (486, italics added). In his exclusive focus on the detailed analysis of the ego's defensive processes, within the transference of the analytic hour, Gray is in effect (like Brenner with his focus on conflict, anxiety, and compromise formations), a modern-day exponent of Eissler's (1953) austere model of analysis. To Eissler, everything but well-timed veridical interpretation was a parameter, potentially anti-analytic in effect unless properly undone; to Gray, all else was psychotherapy, necessary at times, but not to be confused with (or permitted to contaminate) proper psychoanalysis.

In his second article in this arena, on "developmental lag" (1982), Gray expanded his conceptions considerably. He stated that "the therapeutic results of analytic treatment are lasting in proportion to the extent to which, during the analysis, the patient's *unbypassed ego functions* have become involved in a consciously and increasingly voluntary co-partnership with the analyst" (624, italics added). Yet Gray felt that psychoanalysts often gave only lip service to these universally acknowledged tenets: "I borrowed the phrase 'developmental lag' to characterize a puzzling reluctance to apply certain ego concepts to the method of psychoanalytic technique" (640). He called these reluctances "resistances" to progress in this area of making "ego analyzing" a constant part of analytic technique. He listed four such resistances: (1) Fascination with the id: "Analysts are often reluctant to give up or dilute the degree of gratification they so commonly experience when they seek, perceive, and name drive derivatives of another human being" (640); (2) Predilection for an Authoritative Analytic

Stance, called, "the authoritarianism inherent in a parental role—even a benign parental role" (642–43). Again, this may at times be *psychotherapeutic:* "The benignly authoritative roles which I believe are inimical to effective *analysis* of defenses may of course have useful, even essential, functions in the intensive treatment of many patients for whom consistent defense analysis would be too burdensome (i.e., many patients with narcissistic disorders, borderline conditions, some very severe neuroses, most children, and many adolescents)" (643). To Gray, such authoritative, parentlike functioning raised the specter of suggestion (as antithetic to proper *analysis*) and therefore was to be rigorously eschewed. Here we are again in the tradition of Jones and Glover in carrying out their conception of Freud's program.

Gray asked, "If one is to provide opportunity through psychoanalysis for therapeutic change not due primarily to internalizing processes [of benign parentlike introjects], what elements of change can we rely on?" The answer was, "This is cognitive process, in respect to the patient's *comprehension* of the analyst's observations concerning the ego and id aspects of the neurotic conflicts; and an experiential process, in respect to the patient's discovery that his ego can *tolerate and control* the increments of drive derivatives." Anything less (less rigorous) is lost opportunity: "To the extent that the analyst presents himself, through his remarks, in an authoritative or parentlike manner, the nonincorporative learning modes of acquiring insight are significantly compromised. The analyst who makes direct interpretations of id derivatives without approaching them through the defense relies primarily on the suggestive power of the positive transference to overcome resistance" (644–45). Then, "Those patients whose egos *are* suited to an approach that does not require interpersonal therapeutic ingredients should not have to be deprived of the opportunity for greater autonomy" (645)—and here Gray set himself squarely against the kinds of "softening" of Eissler's model represented, for example, by Loewald (1960) and Stone (1961).

There are still other reluctances to explain the developmental lag: (3) Preoccupation with External Reality, Including the Past as External Reality: Gray's central point here is that even memory should be seen (and analyzed) as an internal event of immediate intrapsychic importance rather than in its function as a reference to a past (external) reality. Yet, "after all these years, the universally preferred stereotypic view of psychoanalysis remains, that it is a procedure which consists of a search for memories of the past, rather than one devoted primarily to the gaining of voluntary controls over previously warded-off instinctual impulses" (648)— and here we see a kinship to Gill's (1979) zealous focus on the here and now of transference manifestations as the almost exclusive domain of the analytic work.

Last in the list of reluctances is (4) Countertransference to Transference Affects and Impulses: "Historically, it was not uncommon for the analyst to make genetic interpretations of observed unconscious material relating to the analyst, without providing the patient with an opportunity to work through the full awareness of those affects or impulses toward the analyst. The patient's resistance to this particularly advantageous experience was thus supported. This resistance-supporting tendency persists, although to a lesser degree" (650).

These tendencies have a noble lineage, for Freud never gave up the persisting hypnotic-suggestive influence in analytic technique; Gray quoted Freud (1916–17) as saying, "This [the analysis of the transference-resistance] is made possible by the alteration of the ego which is accomplished under the influence of the doctor's suggestion" (455). But Freud could be forgiven such faults, for "prior to a more detailed grasp of the ego's mechanisms in its defensive role [Freud 1923, 1926], the continued use of a partially hypnotic influence may well have been a necessary technical adjunct." But our persisting in it today is simply "further evidence of the lag in integrating knowledge of the ego into psychoanalytic technique" (Gray 1982, 631).

It is this fundamental stance, the effort (once again) to "purify" proper psychoanalysis by trying to expunge all traces of "suggestive" influence on the transference in favor of unremitting *analysis* of it (ego analysis, transference analysis)—all in an updated version of Eissler's efforts of a quarter-century earlier—that Gray expanded and refined in his later papers. The 1986 paper described the effort to "help" the analysand achieve this capacity to focus on his intrapsychic ego-defensive activities: "Here I explore specific techniques for helping the analysand make better use of those observing skills that are essential for systematic analysis of the resistances to free association, as well as valuable in the development of a self-analytic capacity" (245). This is "a primarily cognitive educative endeavor . . . [of] strengthening analysands' motivation for developing a capacity for intrapsychic observation" (246). This focus Gray felt was different from usual analytic practice: "Traditionally, motivation for the work of analyzing . . . relies heavily on response to or compliance with transferentially endowed authority; that is, it stems from a fear of punishment or need to express devotion and gain love. This use of aspects of the positive transference . . . is a form of suggestion that is still widely used to overcome resistance. It is usually more accepted in practice than acknowledged in theory" (247).

Gray's contrary approach is avowedly in the direction of making the analytic procedure fully rational: "The intention is to provide, as early as possible, a *rational basis* for the motivation to develop the ability for self-observation, rather than to depend on an *irrational basis* of working for the analyst, a motivation that sacrifices a fuller development of autonomous faculties" (249, italics added). And this "educational" process makes for the proper "objectification" of the ego's activities as the target of the analytic pair's scrutiny: "By gradually familiarizing analysands with the characteristics of those identifiable processes within their verbalized thinking that are responses to conflict, the properties of otherwise unconscious ego activities become 'objectified' and hence more accessible for repeated observation" (250). It is this consolidated process that Gray declared made for *effective* psychoanalytic work: "Even-hovering attention and skillful, id-resonating interpretations in a transferentially enhanced authoritative atmosphere are, by themselves, relatively *ineffective* in bringing into the patient's awareness the unconscious ego activities that carry out repetitive forms of defense as resistance" (245, italics added). Not only is all this an effort to counter the focus on the therapeutic aspects of the psychoanalytic relationship—represented, for example, by Loewald (1960) and Stone (1961); it also raises the nagging question of whether what Gray proposes is even possible theoretically in light of the strong suspicion of a potential infinite regress in his position: for does not the effort to "educate" the analysand to expunge suggestive influence, in favor of truly rational "objectification" of ego defensive activities, itself rest on the unanalyzed (suggestive) transferential authority of the analyst?

Gray's fourth (1987) paper in this sequence focused on the particular problems of the analysis of superego functioning. The starting point is by now familiar: "As a result of Freud's ambiguity (and that of later analysts) regarding the nature of the superego and how to treat it in clinical practice, it has taken many years and many theoreticians to move from Freud's predilection to use it for purposes of 'suggestion' in overcoming resistance, toward the concept of the superego as part of the ego's hierarchically mobilized defensive activities in the analytical process" (130). And even "Freud's three monumental additions and revisions of theory (1920a, 1923, 1926) had little effect on bringing about a shift away from *using the influence* of transferred superego, toward *analyzing* the superego as a defense activity" (140). The first step toward this goal was credited to Anna Freud's (1936) concept of "transference of defense" (142), which "provided a key to the eventual perception of the superego as an analyzable neurotic activity of the ego" (152). Gray explained, "By *analysis* of the superego, I mean: systematically making available to consciousness those repetitions of defensive formations in the analytic situation . . . which were earlier mobilized, especially in connection with the oedipal situation, to the end that the compromised ego function components can be progressively reclaimed, from the beginning of the analysis, by the relatively autonomous ego. . . . I take the position that optimal analysis of the superego, as of resistance generally, is best achieved by perceiving and interpreting superego manifestations primarily as part of the *ego's* hierarchical defensive activities, mobilized *during the analytic situation*" (145).

Gray's most recent paper in this sequence (1991) further developed the theme of proper superego analysis. Here Gray aligned himself squarely with Brenner

(1979), Curtis (1979), and Stein (1981) in opposing the acceptance and explicit use of "alliance" concepts in psychoanalysis, in favor of strict and unremitting *analysis* of the so-called unobjectionable positive transference or, in Gray's words, the "transferences of affectionate safety" (4), those "used to resist conflict-anxiety through a fantasy of the analyst as an *affectionate, approving, and protective authority*" (3). In aligning himself so directly against those who he declared would try to *use* these transferences therapeutically (a line going back to Ferenczi), Gray stated, "I shall . . . examine how important theoreticians and practitioners of wider-scope analytic methods, rather than regarding it [the fantasy of affectionate approval] as a resistance, have made therapeutic use of this . . . form of transference, often enhancing its influence by fulfilling certain of the patients' infantile needs for safety. I shall explore the argument that these trends, although sometimes clinically necessary with certain patients, both reflect and support professional inhibitions against improving our methodology for *essential* structural psychoanalysis" (3).

Gray then declared that his 1987 paper on superego issues had focused on the analysis of the reexternalized authority images as inhibitors (the moral constraints of the superego) as against those who "compromised precise conflict analysis by *using* the transferred authoritarian power in order to *persuade* the patient to respond to interpretation" (2). The 1991 paper, he said, would focus on the "transferential re-externalization of images of authority [that] the ego uses to protect against anxiety, this time by providing a defensive illusion of safety through fantasies of affectionate approval" (3). Gray continued,

> The greater difficulty in analyzing transferences of affectionate safety lies especially in the degree to which they blend in with the analyst's wish to be regarded as uncritical. One is often reluctant to recognize that the analysand's ability to acquire a viable sense of *objective safety* in allowing inner spontaneity and its disclosure is an incremental process through analysis of the inhibiting fantasies of danger. It takes a long time for most patients to risk emotionally (and often intellectually) accepting the analyst as *analyst* and as actually working with a *morally neutral* attitude. It is often safer for the patient to choose between the fantasy of a critically restraining image or an affectionately forgiving one. We are naturally reluctant to examine the supportive elements of transference. Beyond their virtually ubiquitous use for psychotherapeutic relief of human suffering, these aspects of transference contribute to the matrix of congenial relatedness among people generally. (4)

Therefore, "The influential transference images, although they may free the patient from some anxiety and resistances, are nevertheless clearly incompatible with an analytically earned, rational view of the analyst as neutral. *Whenever these transference images are allowed to remain influential, an important part of the patient's ego's superego activity and potential for neurosis remains unanalyzed*" (6). And here Gray found a significant distinction between psychoanalysis and psychotherapy: "Transferentially encouraging, anxiety-relieving images are, of course, capable of enormous influence. They, alternatively with the inhibiting images, are the essential backbone of the vast majority of psychotherapies" (7). But unhappily, Gray felt, this vital distinction has not been consistently maintained. In this regard he quoted from Schlesinger (1988): in the developing concern with the affective climate in which treatment takes place, "the therapeutic relationship began to be seen as the 'message' as well as the 'medium.' The empathic bond . . . was seen as equally important to the effectiveness of interpretation as the ideational content. In this way, 'suggestion,' implying the power of the relationship, which officially had been excluded from among the therapeutic factors relied upon by psychoanalysis, returned and was reembraced, though under a series of different names" (16). One of these rubrics is what Gray has called "wider-scope analysis," basically a conglomerate of the British object-relational perspective, the developmental perspective of Gedo and Tahka, and attention to the analyst as (new) object—that is, Loewald and Stone.

Of all these trends, Gray said, "To the extent that wider-scope theorists successfully teach analysts that there is a ubiquitous clinical *need to preserve* safety-seeking aspects of transferences of defense, they inadvertently detract from the possibility of effective analysis of the ego and superego activities for many patients who demonstrably do not need such limitations" (13). And "With highly narcissistically vulnerable analysands, *as long as the continuing unanalyzed influence of an internalized bonding fantasy . . . remains undisturbed,* I could envision general symptomatic relief comparable to a standard structural approach. On the other hand, what may be gained if such safety-seeking fantasies can be analyzed instead of used as a silent partner of the therapeutic 'medium' is achievement of a greater measure of capacity for exercising ego autonomy from unconsciously motivated superego activities" (14). Gray thus made his distinction (and took his stand) between two kinds of therapy: "By now it should be clear that I believe that analysis of the ego's superego activities is central to the analysis of resistance. The extent to which superego analysis is possible or desirable can provide a very practical dividing line or zone, dividing those patients who are clinically suitable for essential psychoanalysis from those who are not, or are less so, and who instead need to be permitted transferentially supportive elements, a concession that *naturally compromises resistance analysis.* . . . [Therefore,] I propose that *essential psychoanalysis* refer to an essentially uncompromised resistance analysis and that *wider-scope psychoanalysis,* including 'object relations' analysis, refer to methods that need to preserve certain transferences of defense in order to achieve their goals" (18–19). What Gray has called "wider-scope analysis" is what in the 1950s was declared to be (varyingly expressive and supportive) psychotherapy—Gray too at times calls it that.

Gray's intervening papers of 1988 and 1990 made the same points, with a few more specific references to psychotherapy vis-à-vis psychoanalysis. In the 1990 paper, on the nature of therapeutic action in psychoanalysis, Gray again spoke of "the short-changing role of suggestion" (1088) when used in the ways already adumbrated and then linked this to an interpretive activity geared more to drive than to ego defense: "The need for suggestion in order to face the resistance is more apt to be present when the analyst tries, through *an* interpretation, to confront a drive derivative not yet in consciousness but sensed to be not far below the surface. All too often the analyst uses authority *to overcome* the resistance sufficiently to bring the drive derivative into consciousness; as a result, the ego's often highly defended role in enforcing the repression is less likely to be subject to the important perception, examination, and exploration of its history" (1092). Gray's prescription was, of course, otherwise: "My working hypothesis, on which my technique depends, is that consistent, detailed analysis of the forms and motivations of the ego's surface-near manifestations of resistance against specific drive derivatives will *of itself* allow gradual, analytically sufficient ego assimilation of the warded-off mental contents as they are able to move less fearfully into consciousness" (1095).

Of course, there are (wider-scope) analysts who fear the disadvantages of a loss in this approach: "They are the ones who, in dealing with the resistance, have depended to a considerable extent on helping the patient to bring to the surface drive derivatives, not yet in consciousness, through timely and accurate interpretations of their hidden locations." But this id-analysis or analysis of drives, once the very model of psychoanalysis, is, to Gray, not "essential psychoanalysis" and in fact is now relegated in large part to a species of psychoanalytic psychotherapy: "The more direct, broader uses of interpretation of instinctual derivatives continues to be of value with patients who virtually cannot free their observing capacities from domination by the ego's superego functions, or for psychoanalytically oriented psychotherapy where one assumes that interpretive work is, of convenience, going to deal with resistance by means of considerable authoritative transference influence" (1095–96).

In the 1988 paper, Gray had made the distinction between psychoanalysis and psychotherapy in other words but along parallel lines: "I shall select for this occasion the by no means narrow therapeutic aim of attempting to reduce the patient's *potential* for anxiety [psychoanalysis] as differentiated from an aim that

merely seeks to reduce the patient's anxiety [psychotherapy]" (41). Expanding
the psychoanalytic end of this range, he added, "In moving on toward the other
end of my improvised spectrum, we phase into therapeutic approaches that
intend to provide, for those patients whose ego capacities are suitable, therapeutic actions that depend more and more on factors whose primary aim is to
achieve *conscious solutions* to those conflicts that, when they were unconscious,
threatened to mobilize anxiety. A variable in this part of the spectrum that needs
greater exploration is the difference in degree to which there is a reliance on
the persuasive powers of the transferentially endowed authority to overcome
the patient's resistances, as distinct from analyzing those resistances" (44)—thus
bringing the distinction back to his central clinical position, the issue of analyzing
transferential authority as against "riding" on it for its suggestive utility.[3]

Evelyne Schwaber shares with Paul Gray a concern for the most detailed
therapeutic interactions at the most micro-analytic level and also an effort to
focus on the internal (and intrapsychic), to the exclusion, as much as possible,
of the interpersonal and the external. Otherwise she represents a very different
approach, one based on empathic in-tuneness with the patient's experience of
the therapeutic relationship. The first of her sequence of papers on this topic
(1981, 1983a, 1983b, 1986, 1987, 1988, 1990, 1992a, 1992b) was on empathy,
called "a method of observation—of gathering depth-psychological information" (358), but a method "independent of the particular theory upon which
the clinician draws. I believe that the theory does not determine the nature of
its application" (358). Here Schwaber distinguished her stance from that of
Kohut, who embedded empathic in-tuneness in the whole technical and theoretical matrix of his self psychology.

From this simple beginning Schwaber drew far-ranging clinical and technical
implications:

> I offer this dialectic in consideration of the extent to which implicitly or
> explicitly analytic listening has employed the use of two realities—that of

---

3. Fred Busch (1994), in full support of Gray's views, has adduced an additional basis for what
Gray labeled the developmental lag in implementing the full possibilities for thorough analysis
of the ego's resistances. He attributed this to the way in which Freud (and those who came
after) implemented the method of free association, which was conceived when the prevailing
model of the mind was topographic, not structural: "His [Freud's] technical handling of resistances relied primarily on suggestion, education, and the influence accrued to the analyst,
via the positive transference, to overcome resistances. The method of free association as first
developed was geared to *overcoming* and not *understanding* the resistances" (366). Busch stated
that "instruction in the method of free association needs to be updated" (367); "In essence,
investigating the resistances to free association rather than circumventing them, has been shown
to be an ego-strengthening rather than weakening technique" (370).

the observer from the "outside" and that from within. . . . Concepts such as therapeutic alliance (which addresses that aspect of the patient's view which allies itself with "outside" reality), reality testing, magical thinking, reality principle, the "real" relationship, each is a further indicator of this "two-reality" outlook in our analytic listening and theorizing. The concept of transference, understood as "distortion," sharply illustrates this perspective; the analyst, given, of course, that he has paid careful heed to his countertransference responses, simultaneously maintains a view of himself as "objectively" different from the qualities which are "projected" into him by his patient. Thus, there are two realities—one internal, the other external; one that the patient experiences or perceives, the other that the analyst "knows." However we may choose to deal with this technically, analytic listening, embedded in this dual vantage point, must then ultimately imply that the aim is to help the patient gradually shift or "correct" his view as he attains more mature functioning. (364–66)

To this classical perspective on the analytic situation, Schwaber counterposed her stance based on her conception of empathy: "Empathy . . . attempts to maximize a *singular focus* on the patient's subjective reality, seeking all possible clues to ascertain it. Vigilantly guarding against the imposition of the analyst's point of view,[4] the role of the analyst and of the surround, as perceived and experienced by the patient, is recognized as intrinsic to that reality; the observer is part of the field observed" (379, italics added). Schwaber added a major caveat: "That we must rely on some echo of experiential alikeness does not mean,

4. This is where Schwaber parts company with Kohut's self psychology, which she felt is as guilty as any other theoretical perspective of imposing its theoretic preconceptions upon its understandings of clinical interactions. She said, "Empathy is not the domain of any one theoretical view; any theory, once elaborated, can again be used to impose its own view of reality from without" (Schwaber 1981, 374). A. Kris (1983), in a paper on the free association method, supported Schwaber's position from a different vantage point: "A further problem that confronts psychoanalysts in regard to the use of theory arises whenever theory is permitted to co-opt the method of psychoanalytic observation and deprive it of its independence. . . . The frequent criticism of circularity in the psychoanalytic method, which allegedly makes it 'unscientific,' applies correctly, I believe, only to the extent that the observational method is defined by the theory it purports to test. To demonstrate deficiencies of theory requires use of a method that is described and defined in terms that are independent of the theory" (408). And "The limitations [imposed by theory] increase when theory is externally imposed rather than evoked within the clinical context of partnership in the method of free association. Close attention to the sequences, patterns, and determinants of the free associations as the point of departure for theoretical formulations protects the analyst's observational and conceptual freedom" (410). That is, one should move from the observations to the theory, rather than in the reverse direction.

however, that we are to share the patient's experience as our own. To place ourselves in the other's shoes, into what he or she is feeling, is not the same process as considering what *we* would feel if *we*—who *we* are—were in those shoes. It requires a considerable degree of self-awareness to make this crucial distinction, to know what belongs to our own conceptual or perceptual frame of reference so as to reduce the risk of superimposing it. Empathy, then, is not equivalent to identification" (385).

In regard to transference, Schwaber stated the implications of her views as follows: first, "the transference, from the perspective of the analyst-observer standing outside the field of observation, did not include the analyst's contribution to the patient's perception as fundamental to its very nature" (369); and, second, "consistent with the notion that our listening stance attempts to minimize the introduction of an 'outside' view, there is a shift in the understanding of transference. Rather than being defined as a distortion to be modified, transference is here understood as a perception—interwoven with the emerging intrapsychic concerns—to be recognized and articulated. Such a perspective— of the observer from within—would hold as spurious the division of an 'inner' from a 'real' reality, and the notion that we must ultimately help the patient to disengage our real selves from the patient's psychic view of us" (389)—a view completely in line with Gill's current conceptions of the transference (see chapter 12), though arrived at differently.

In 1983, Schwaber published two papers expanding on these perspectives. The first one, clinically focused (1983a), presented a detailed account of a single analysis, bounded by two remarks: (1) "My effort was to maintain the listening perspective of the observer within the experiential world of the observed. I shall try to convey the sense of my own recurrent, groping, often failing attempts to locate my place within that world" (527); and (2) "The systematic search for one's own place in the context of another's psychic experience—even as I have made an active effort to pursue this—is a task most difficult to sustain" (536).

The second, more theoretical paper (1983b) enlarged on why Schwaber felt that this task was nonetheless worth pursuing. She declared her linkages to Gray in terms of the microanalytic intrapsychic focus, to Gill in terms of the relativity of the reality of the analytic situation, to which both participants contribute, and to James McLaughlin (1981) in placing the countertransference on the same conceptual level as the transference. Then, after acknowledging her resonance with Kohut's bringing into central focus the method of data-gathering by empathic immersion, she drew her own sharp line of difference with Kohut: "The analyst, making such an affirmative judgment regarding the patient's responses or perceptions [the self psychological affirmation of the patient's needs for comfort and admiration], is no less in the position of arbiter of the patient's truth than if he assesses them as distortions. Thus we begin to see, deeply embedded within our analytic listening—even with differing theoretical vantage points employed—a hierarchically ordered two-reality view in which the view of the analyst serves to objectify that of the patient" (383).

Contrasting the classical view of the analytic process with her own, Schwaber said, "Consistent with this scientific outlook [of nineteenth-century, classical physics], the psychoanalytic view similarly did not regard the impact of the analyst-observer as *intrusive* to the field of observation. There was then no systematic place assigned to this impact in the elucidation and understanding of transference. Viewed as a distortion created by the patient's projection of his inner strivings and defenses, the concept of transference, if optimal 'neutrality' were maintained, did not include the analyst's contribution—as perceived by the patient—as a fundamental and specific component of its evolution" (p. 386). Schwaber rested her opposed position on uncompromising acceptance of Freud's famous dictum "in the world of the neuroses it is psychical reality which is the decisive kind" (Freud 1916–17, 368). This of course refers to the patient's reality, not ours: "The challenge . . . for us as analysts and therapists is to find a way, from deeply within ourselves, to come to terms with the idea that . . . the patient's view, even about us, is as real as the one we believe about ourselves. We may then recognize how we are continually at risk of utilizing whatever theory we espouse . . . to protect us against acknowledging this very phenomenon—the relativity of each of our realities" (390). And from this position we can then acknowledge that from our patients' vantage point, "there is another way to experience my responses to them, and that I cannot be the arbiter of which is the more valid—theirs or mine" (390), and perhaps also acknowledge our "resistance to the acknowledgment that the truth we believe about ourselves is no more (though no less) 'real' than the patient's view of us—that all that we can 'know' of ourselves is *our own psychic reality*" (389, italics added). Our effort must be always (and only), according to Schwaber, "to elucidate the *patient's* experienced perspective" (380).

The other papers in this sequence expand and refine these same concepts. The 1986 paper focused on the "knowing" involved in the one reality–two reality perspective: "It would seem that our listening stance remains imbued with a hierarchical 'two-reality' outlook which allows for the analyst to be the arbiter of what is the more 'correct' reality—and has not caught up with the implications in Freud's shift to the fantasy theory" (921). But if we can make this shift wholeheartedly, there is everything to gain: "Suspending any notion that we already 'know,' leaps of inference on our part will be reduced, while the patient's capacity for self-observation [is] enhanced" (930).

In the 1988 paper, Schwaber elaborated on what she meant by "reality" and "real": "Real is how things are felt to be, and how they are perceived, how feelings and perceptions, wishes and defenses, interdigitate. Real is what each of us, therapist and patient, experiences as true, and the correctness of which we, as therapists, cannot be the arbiter. Real, as it is felt by another, must include ourselves, the observers, as its participants" (85).

The 1990 paper looked at the process of interpretation within this framework: "It is my central argument that an interpretive effort which has as its goal to help the patient recognize such a differentiation (between the 'real' nature of the analyst and the past internal object) [going all the way back to Strachey 1934 and to Freud before him], of the truth of which the analyst implicitly has antecedent knowledge, derives from an outlook on reality which can serve to foreclose rather than to further psychoanalytic inquiry." Put simply, "There is no room in this schema for the patient to attribute a meaning to the interpretation, as yet unknown to either—patient or analyst, and for that meaning to be the source of the mutative effect" (230)—that is, the "unknown" meaning arising from the fact that the patient is the true source of mutative effect. And also, "when I slip into the mode of arbiter, what is unconscious becomes a unilateral inference instead of a joint discovery. And my interpretation, skipping over data that do not fit and arising from my, and not the patient's vantage point, can serve to distance the patient from me" (232).

This, of course, will lead the patient to seek out and/or be wary of our "preferred agenda": "We may believe we have no preferred agenda, but the patient may feel we do. What is so difficult is to forgo being the final arbiter of even what we believe about our own behaviour, to regard the patient's experience of how we have intervened as our sole data to pursue" (237). The idea of a preferred agenda was pursued in still another article (1992a): "In assuming this stance of 'knowing'—even about ourselves—what is the 'correct' reality, we implicitly maintain an agenda for what we hope our patients will achieve. Thereby, we depart from the play of psychic possibility and *lose the psychoanalytic vantage point*" (359, italics added). The issue of agenda can be linked to the larger concern with accepted models and theories as providing ready-made agendas within which we work, often unreflectively. In an article on models of the mind (1987), Schwaber put it thus: "The choice of model profoundly influences what is interpreted; theory and technical stance go hand in hand. But a question may be raised: if the model determines how the material is understood and what is to be interpreted, is it not then assigned a primacy that goes beyond serving its purported function of organizing the data and broadening our perceptual scope? Is it not then given a use by which the analyst may render judgment about what is relevant, what is real, and what may be omitted in the patient's experience?" (262). Schwaber is of course aware that we can never be free of models or theories in our mental work: "The question may be raised: is it ever possible to forego our model as we listen and gather that data? Isn't any clinical material necessarily contaminated by the analyst's theoretical persuasion, much as we may try to remove it? Is it not similarly true that we can never really extricate our own view, our own values, life experiences, from our understandings of the patient's communications? What we can know of the world is by our own ways of seeing it" (273). Therefore, "I make no argument for an atheoretical orientation, even if that were possible. I argue, rather, for our recognition that no matter what theory we espouse, we run the risk of using it to foreclose rather than to continue inquiry, to provide an answer rather than to raise a new question" (274).

Schwaber also offered her perspectives on countertransference, the mode of therapeutic action, the epistemological base of psychoanalysis, and how she distinguished her perspectives from Gill's. On countertransference she said, "I have elsewhere (1992a) described such an inclination [to override the patient's reality by drawing upon theory-based inference] as marking the countertransference— that is, countertransference reflecting a retreat from the patient's vantage point toward an added certainty in the correctness of one's own. I have suggested such a definition of the concept of countertransference with its related potential for enactment, in keeping with the theoretical views expressed here about the centrality of focus on the patient's psychic reality" (1992b, 1051). On therapeutic action, she stated succinctly, "It is not the relinquishment or renunciation of childhood wishes that makes treatment effective, but their discovery and elucidation, the search for their meaning, and the reestablishment of their historical continuity" (1988, 91). And on epistemology: "It may be especially hard to relinquish the notion that ours is the more 'correct' truth when there is a difference between us and the patient about how we are perceived. Herein lies the essential epistemological implication in the theory of transference. Another's view—even of us—has a reality as real, as true as our own" (1992b, 1048). That is, the epistemological base of psychoanalysis is declared to reside in uncompromisingly making the psychic reality of the patient, as expressed via the transference, into the only reality of psychoanalysis.

Last, in comparing her views with the seemingly similar perspectives of Gill, Schwaber stated, "That we are participant observers does not make psychoanalysis a two-person psychology. To be sure, the impact of our participation . . . must be a fundamental aspect of our inquiry—*but as seen from and as data about the patient's point of view*. This position contrasts with those that argue for an interpersonal framework in elucidating the analyst's participation in the transference, as for example, in the work of Gill (1982). I highlight that it is the patient's vantage point, not that of the analyst or any other outside observer, that defines our investigative terrain. However similarly or differently we may perceive our own contribution, such a determination offers us only our perspective, and does not yet tell us how we are being experienced by the patient" (1992b, 1046).

Merton Gill's contributions have been presented in several places in this book. In his emerging reconceptualizations of the centrality of analysis of the transference as the overriding mark of the psychoanalytic process, presented in chapter 12, Gill was joined by Irwin Hoffman, who co-authored one of the two 1982 monographs referred to in that chapter. A further sequence of ten papers published in the past decade are devoted to the further development of the Gill-Hoffman position on the nature of psychoanalysis, the psychoanalytic relationship, and the transference.

Gill's 1980–81 paper was written as a critique of Fenichel's (1941) pioneering monograph *Problems of Psychoanalytic Technique,* which had been the first effort at a systematic exposition of issues of technique, that is, problems of interpretation, analysis of the transference, and working through. Gill faulted Fenichel for not insisting on the centrality of the analysis of transference in psychoanalytic work and in the course of his essay made a point of underscoring the importance of new experience as a mutative factor in analysis alongside the interpretation of the transference, a corrective worth keeping in mind in view of the easy temptation to see only what seems to be the extreme one-sidedness of Gill's views on analysis of the transference: "I believe the importance of new experience in analysis as a factor in change is often underestimated for fear that to grant it opens the gate to manipulation and corrective emotional experience in Alexander's sense (1946). I believe it should be possible to recognize that the experience of being treated otherwise than one expected provides the inestimable service of making immediate and manifest the fact that people can be different from what one has come to expect. One can grant experience its role without having to belittle the importance of insight into these experiences, both expected and new" (53).

In 1983, Gill and Hoffman separately published major (and complementary) statements on the dyadic psychoanalytic relationship in the journal *Contemporary Psychoanalysis,* directed particularly to the Sullivanian interpersonal school of psychoanalysis. Gill (1983) started with what he called two major cleavages in psychoanalytic thought: "One cleavage is between the interpersonal paradigm and the drive-discharge paradigm. The other cleavage is between those who believe the analyst inevitably participates in a major way in the analytic situation and those who do not" (201). Though these two distinctions are often confused, Gill concluded that they do not necessarily run parallel or even have any intrinsic connection. For example, among the (Freudian) followers of the drive-discharge model, analysts were ranged on both sides of the issue of the role of the analyst in the interactive analytic encounter, with McLaughlin and Bird cited on the side of major impact and Abrams and Leonard Shengold on the opposite side.

Freud's position on this issue has always been disputed. The surgical and mirror metaphors can certainly be read (as they were by Eissler) as advocating the utmost objectivity of the outside observer, upon whom the patient projects his internally generated transferences. We also know from the available accounts that Freud did not act like the opaque uninvolved mirror with his analysands. Yet it is true that Freud's major expressed concern about the analyst's participation was with the danger of becoming overinvolved. This evolved into the "official Freudian position": "Despite recent emphasis on the real relationship and the various alliances there is no doubt that insofar as there is an official Freudian position, it is to advocate a lesser participation by the analyst than Freud did. Freud is frequently criticized by Freudian analysts for having been as interactive with his patients as he was. Lipton (1977) argues that Freud was more manifestly interactive than contemporary Freudian technique would permit but he considers Freud's technique to be preferable" (208–09). Gill's sympathies are clearly with Lipton's perspective.

Gill described contemporary positions on this issue in terms of "*Prescription versus Description*. It is important to distinguish between the concepts of how much the analyst ought to be involved and how much he is inevitably involved. . . . The primary current Freudian position on the analyst's participation is in the prescriptive mode. The analyst is warned against too great participation. The Freudians believe it is important to struggle against involvement and to render it as minimal as possible. Tarachow's (1963) distinction between psychoanalysis and psychotherapy argues, for example, that both participants in the therapeutic situation are constantly tempted to engage in an interaction and that a therapy is psychoanalytic rather than psychotherapeutic only to the extent to which the analyst successfully resists this temptation" (212). Gill's thinking is the opposite: interaction is inevitable;[5] it should be forthrightly acknowledged, becoming the

5. Using a somewhat different language from Gill's—"emotional reaction" rather than "interaction"—H. Levine (1994) added an explanatory note that should of course be kept in mind: "Conceptually, our theory of the therapeutic action of psychoanalysis would be simpler if the impact of interpretation as a source of information was more clearly separable from its impact as action. . . . However, I am afraid that no such easy distinction can be drawn" (668). But we should bear in mind that "from the perspective of the analyst and the analyst's participation in the analytic process, one cannot distinguish an 'emotional reaction' from a 'proper interpretation,' because a proper interpretation *is* an emotional reaction. This is not to say that the opposite is equally true; not every emotional reaction of the analyst is also a proper interpretation" (671).

very focus of analytic scrutiny and interpretation; and it should not be considered important only with the sicker patients: "The emphasis on inevitable major participation in treating patients with sever pathology can be used to sidestep the question of the average expectable participation in treating the average expectable neurosis—the patient who meets the ordinary criteria for a classical analysis" (213).

What are the implications of this view of interaction as an inevitable feature of the (average expectable) analytic process for our understandings of the transference? Of transference (and countertransference), Gill stated, "We [he and Hoffman] have come to the conclusion that the concept of a dichotomy between transference as distortion and non-transference as realistic does violence to the actual nature of the relationship between patient and analyst." This is so because "we reject the argument that the analyst's view is necessarily the correct one because we reject the view that the analyst can be the arbiter of reality." Rather, "Our argument in effect rests on the ambiguity and relativity of interpersonal reality. We continue to distinguish between transference and non-transference but the distinction is not between realistic and distorted but rather between rigidity and flexibility of an interpersonal attitude, that is, whether it is susceptible to influence from the outside" (216–18).

This conceptualization in turn has implications for technique: "The first step in technique should be to clarify the patient's experience of the relationship, while the second should be to discover what is the patient's justification in the analyst's behavior or attitude or even just in a plausible conjecture as to the analyst's subjective feeling for the construction the patient makes of the field" (219–20). Gill then outlined his three principles of technique: (1) "Because the presenting manifestation of psychopathology lies in the immediate interpersonal interaction, the therapist should be ever ready to inquire into the patient's experience of the relationship" (222); (2) "The analyst should always be ready to consider that associations not explicitly about the relationship may nonetheless be disguised allusions to it" (224); and (3) "The analyst will inevitably to a greater or lesser degree fall in with the patient's prior expectations" (Sandler's role responsiveness, 1976a) (226). This then sets up the successful treatment process: "The therapeutic process is both participation and understanding, that is, . . . the therapist inevitably participates and works his way out of that participation by progressive understanding of the interaction, at the same time communicating that understanding to the patient, who of course plays a role in reaching that understanding too, at least in what he says in response to the therapist's effort to understand what the patient is experiencing and how he accounts for that experience" (227).

With all this go certain risks and caveats. Countertransference confession is not necessarily implied: "The position that the analyst makes a major contribution to the transaction does not necessarily mean that a mutual analysis is desirable or perhaps even possible" (229). And the role of the genetic past *can* be unintentionally slighted, since inevitably a focus on interactions in the here and now of the analytic encounter will result in underemphasis on past determinants (229–30). And clearly inadvertent interventions should be distinguished from those that are intended: "By an inadvertent interpersonal effect I mean, for example, an analyst making an interpretation which the patient experiences as a criticism when, so far as the analyst was aware, the analyst had no such intent. An advertent interpersonal intervention would be one in which he encouraged, reassured, scolded, or whatever knowing that he was doing something intended to have such an effect. Even then I would say that what is unanalytic would not be that the analyst engaged in such an intervention but only if he failed to look for and make explicit the interpersonal significance to the patient of his intervention" (232). Finally Gill circled back to the relationship of insight and new experience in the ultimate change process: "I believe that both insight and new experience play a role in bringing about change in psychoanalysis. . . . Most of all I believe that the insight into one's pattern of interpersonal relationship at the same time that one is being exposed to a new pattern of interpersonal relationship is the most mutative of all" (233). But the new experience should itself be subjected to analytic scrutiny: "The question as I have just put it must be differentiated into the role of new experience as such and the role of new experience which is examined and reflected upon" (230).[6]

Hoffman's (1983) companion article in the same journal was entitled provocatively "The *Patient* as Interpreter of the Analyst's Experience" and was bolder in its extension of the Gill-Hoffman perspective. He began by stating that the blank screen concept of the nonparticipating analyst had been under

6. In a final summarizing book (1994), Gill has chronicled the full sweep of his evolving views over his lifetime on the nature of psychoanalytic theory and the consequent altering implications for technique, and set these, as a "personal view," within the context of what he correctly describes as a sea change in our consensual understanding of the nature of the psychoanalytic enterprise itself over that same time span, a change or transition, of which he has been one of the significant architects. Gill's book is more measured and balanced in its formulations than some of his writings along the way have been. He acknowledges that every swing of the pendulum can go too far and takes pains to correct his reformulations on the nature of the transference (and the countertransference) which could readily be interpreted as abolishing any place for the traditional (including Freud's) formulation of mental functioning in terms of the intrapsychic and of a one-body psychology. In this book Gill finds place for both conceptualizations (one-body *and* two-body), in constant dialectic interaction, with one or the other to the explanatory fore at any moment in the understanding of mental functioning and of the therapeutic dialogue, depending on circumstance and context.

increasing attack from all sides and had even been pronounced dead many times: "The blank screen idea is probably not articulated as often or even as well by its proponents as it is by its opponents, a situation which leads inevitably to the suspicion that the proponents are straw men and that shooting them down has become a kind of popular psychoanalytic sport." But Hoffman felt that the blank screen concept, part of a broader "asocial conception of the patient's experience in psychotherapy" (390), with its corollary that transference represents a "distortion" of a current reality, had been more resilient than this would imply and indeed still implicitly undergirded much psychoanalytic thinking.

Hoffman then discussed critiques of the blank screen concept that had been articulated by various theorists, dividing them into conservative and radical. The conservative critique, from which he distanced himself, retains the concept but feels that it should be significantly qualified, first, by acknowledging an "unobjectionable positive transference" (Freud) or "alliance" (Zetzel, Greenson, and others) that is not part of the transferentially distorted blank screen, and second, by removing the patient's (proper) responses to the analyst's overt countertransference expressions from the arena of transference distortion. Among the conservative critics, Hoffman said that Strachey, Loewald, Stone, Kohut, Greenson, Robert Langs, and many others either "have in common some kind of amplification of the realistically benign and facilitating aspects of the therapist's influence" (396) or (as in Langs's case) emphasize the importance of the patient's objective perceptions of the analyst's countertransferences. He continued, "Perhaps the theorist who best exemplifies a conservative critique of the blank screen fallacy is Greenson. Greenson's 'real relationship' encompasses both the patient's accurate perceptions of the benign aspects of the analyst and his perceptions of the analyst's countertransference expressions, and Greenson's position is an emphatic objection to the tendency he sees to underestimate the inevitably important role of the real relationship in the analytic process" (404).

Hoffman, of course, aligned himself with the radical critiques, which "reject the dichotomy between transference as distortion and non-transference as reality based. They argue instead that transference itself *always* has a significant plausible basis in the here-and-now" (393, italics added). Furthermore,

> The radical critic is a relativist. From his point of view the perspective that the patient brings to bear in interpreting the therapist's inner attitudes is regarded as one among many perspectives that are relevant, each of which highlights different facets of the analyst's involvement. This amounts to a different paradigm, not simply an elaboration of the standard paradigm which is what the conservative critics propose. . . . For the radical critic the distinguishing features of the neurotic transference have to

do with the fact that the patient is selectively attentive to certain facets of
the therapist's behavior and personality; that he is compelled to choose
one set of interpretations rather than others; that his emotional life and
adaptation are unconsciously governed by and governing of the particular
viewpoint he has adopted; and perhaps most importantly, that he has
behaved in such a way as to actually elicit overt and covert responses that
are consistent with his viewpoint and expectations. The transference represents a way not only of *construing* but also of *constructing* or shaping interpersonal relations in general and the relationship with the analyst in
particular. (394, italics added)

Among the radical critics, Hoffman gave prominence to Racker (1968) but
included Sandler, some contemporary neo-Sullivanians, and Gill, whom he saw
as still struggling to move from the position of conservative to that of radical
critic. The radical critique, he said, rested on two basic propositions: "1. The
patient senses that the analyst's interpersonal *conduct* in the analytic situation, like
all interpersonal conduct, is always ambiguous as an indicator of the full nature
of the analyst's experience and is always amenable to a variety of plausible interpretations. 2. The patient senses that the analyst's personal *experience* in the
analytic situation is continuously affected by and responsive to the way in which
the patient relates and participates in the process." With this comes a different
perspective on reality, namely, that events are ambiguous and that consensus is
hard to come by, that reality is constructed as much as it is perceived or construed: "This view is simply that reality is not a preestablished given or absolute"
(407). And "What the patient's transference accounts for is not a distortion of
reality but a selective attention to and sensitivity to certain facets of the analyst's
highly ambiguous response to the patient in the analysis" (409). In this sense,
"it behooves the analyst . . . to regard the patient as a potentially astute interpreter of his own (the analyst's own) resisted internal motives" (410)—ergo, the
title of the article.

What are the stated implications of this new "social paradigm" of psychoanalysis for questions of technique? From the patient's side, "the patient, as interpreter of the therapist's experience, has good reason to think and fear that
the countertransference-evoking power of his transferences may be the decisive
factor in determining the course of the relationship. Or, to say the same thing
in another way, he has good reason to fear that the analyst's constant suscepti-
bility to a countertransference will doom the relationship to repeat, covertly if
not overtly, the very patterns of interpersonal interaction which he came to
analysis to change" (414). This is rectified by appropriate interpretation: "By
making it apparent that the countertransference experience that the patient has

attributed to the analyst occupies only a part of his response to the patient, the analyst makes it apparent that he is finding something more in the patient to respond to than the transference-driven provocateur" (415). And in doing this, "systematic use of the patient's associations as a guide to understanding the patient's resisted ideas about the countertransference is a critical element of the interpretive process in the social paradigm. Without it, there is a danger that the analyst will rely excessively on his own subjectivistic experience in constructing interpretations. The analyst then risks making the error of automatically assuming that what he feels corresponds with what the patient attributes to him" (416).

Hoffman ended the article by setting the place of the traditional psychoanalytic exploration of a life history within this new paradigm:

> An important weapon that the patient and the therapist have against prolonged deleterious forms of transference-countertransference enactment . . . is an evolving understanding of the patient's history. This understanding locates the transference-countertransference themes that are enacted in the analysis in a broader context which touches on their origins. Such explanation, because it demonstrates how the patient's way of shaping and perceiving the relationship comes out of his particular history, also adds considerably to the patient's sense of conviction that alternative ways of relating to people are open to him. Again, what is corrected is not a simple distortion of reality, but the investment that the patient has in shaping and perceiving his interpersonal experience in particular ways. (419)

Of the seven most recent papers by Hoffman in this sequence (1987, 1990, 1991, 1992a, 1992b, 1992c, 1993), that of 1991 represents—after the 1983 paper just cited—the next extension of Hoffman's thinking on this new "social-constructivist" paradigm. He began with a clarification: "An important source of inconsistency and confusion derives from the confounding of the two axes: drive-relational and positivist-constructivist. Many relational theorists who hold fast to the idea that analysts can grasp the truth of both their own experience and that of the patient are no closer to the constructivist point of view than was Freud" (74). For, after all, this is nothing less than the emergence of a new and revolutionary paradigm for psychoanalysis, and the new is always resisted: "My own conviction is that there is a new paradigm struggling to emerge in the field but that it has not yet fully 'arrived,' much less been firmly established" (76). Hoffman means not the shift from the drive model of psychoanalysis to the relational model, to which much of the psychoanalytic world has already subscribed, but rather a wrenching change in the epistemological base of the field, the shift from the positivist to the constructivist model: "The paradigm changes, in my view, only when the idea of the analyst's personal involvement is wedded to a constructivist or perspectivist epistemological position. Only in effecting that integration is the idea of the analyst's participation in the process taken fully into account. . . . what the analyst seems to understand about his or her own experience and behavior as well as the patient's is always suspect, always susceptible to the vicissitudes of the analyst's own resistance, and always prone to being superseded by another point of view that may emerge" (77). That is, "we have moved into a world of mutual influence and constructed meaning. Experience is understood to be continually in the process of being formulated or explicated. Although not amorphous, unformulated experience is understood to be intrinsically ambiguous and open to a range of compelling interpretations and explications" (78).

Hoffman credits Racker (1968) as being the only wholehearted forerunner of these concepts, quoting from a 1957 article reprinted in Racker's book: "The first distortion of truth in the myth of the analytic situation is that analysis is an interaction between a sick person and a healthy one. The truth is that it is an interaction between two personalities, in both of which the ego is under pressure from the id, the superego, and the external world; each personality has its internal and external dependencies, anxieties, and pathological defenses; each is also a child with his internal parents; and each of these whole personalities— that of the analysand and that of the analyst—responds to every event of the analytic situation" (203). Most others leaning in that direction have not fully understood and embraced its implications, and here Hoffman included even "Sullivan, Winnicott, and Kohut, [who] continue to suggest that analysts can somehow manage to keep their own subjective experience from 'contaminating' their patients' transferences. A corollary of this view is that analysts are in a position to assess accurately what they and their patients are doing and experiencing. . . . in the end, I am not sure that the gulf that separates Kohut, Winnicott, and Sullivan from the social–constructivist point of view is less wide than the gulf that separates Freud from that perspective" (84). And of Freud, Hoffman declared, "The swing of the pendulum in Freud's thought from literal seduction in childhood to drive-determined fantasy . . . in the etiology of the neuroses seems like a thesis and an antithesis that are just begging for the synthesis that constructivism could offer" (86).

Hoffman then cited the risks and responsibilities of the new model: "Both the process of explication and the moment of interpersonal influence entail creation of meaning, not merely its discovery. And whatever is explicated by the patient and the analyst about themselves or about each other, out loud or in their private thoughts, affects what happens next within and between the two people in ways that were not known before that moment." But there is a

(relatively) safe ground for the analyst: "The baseline to which the analyst continually returns remains that of critical reflection on the way the immediate
interaction is being shaped by the participants, but a deeper appreciation is
required of the fact that the unformulated aspects of the process necessarily and
continually elude analytic closure." For this reason, Hoffman feels that the word
"technique" itself is misleading in that it "suggests a degree of control that does
not fit the fluid movement of the process" (91–92).

Hoffman also addressed the issue of how to deal with the "asymmetrical"
character of the therapeutic situation, which after all must be maintained "as a
means of ensuring that the patient's experience remains the center of attention
and as a means of reducing the chances that the analyst's involvement could
become excessive and ultimately traumatic for the patient. . . . [But] I would
[also] argue that it is against the backdrop of idealization, promoted by the
ritualized asymmetry of the psychoanalytic situation, that the analyst's willingness to participate in the spirit of mutuality can become so meaningful for the
patient and so powerful" (92). His final point was that "psychoanalysis can be
viewed as a psychologically complex kind of relearning in which a major objective is to promote critical reflection on the way the patient's reality has been
constructed in the past and is being constructed interactively right now, with
whatever amalgam of repetition and new experience the current construction
entails" (97).

Five other papers by Hoffman in this group each elaborate a single point in
the edifice constructed by the 1983 and 1991 articles. Both the 1990 and 1992a
papers emphasize that the therapeutic interaction is always ambiguous and never
"transparent" to the therapist. Hoffman points to the major technical consequence of this state of affairs: "What is not possible is that the therapist . . . will
simply treat the patient with an appropriate intervention of some sort on the
basis of a correct diagnostic assessment of the patient's general condition or even
of his or her immediate state of mind" (1992a, 3). The following passage from
the 1990 paper spells out the implications of this position:

> A constructivist position would allow that the analyst's behavior is am-
> biguous and that there is room for the patient to interpret it plausibly
> according to his own lights. . . . Similarly, there is room for the analyst to
> read what the patient says in keeping with his/her own personal and
> theoretical biases. What is not acceptable in this model are the dichotomies
> of latent and manifest, intrapsychic and interpersonal, fantasy and reality,
> inner and outer, subjective and objective. In the idea of "construction"
> all of these polarities are blurred and none of them, as traditionally defined,
> retain the relevance that they had in a more positivist framework. A con-

structed world is not reducible to an intrapsychically determined fantasy nor to an interpersonally determined reality. This is not to say that one cannot describe certain experiences or attitudes in terms of their relation to a common sense view of reality . . . or that there is no acknowledgment of the experience of being caught up in fantasy or of trying to deal with something realistically. However, in terms of theory the baseline is still a socially constructed world which is neither imaginary nor externally given. In addition, the emotionally charged issues that are of central concern analytically are viewed as particularly ambiguous and amenable to a variety of plausible interpretations. (297)

At this point—the blurring or obliteration of all the stated "dichotomies"—Hoffman seems to have taken the social-constructivist position (or paradigm) to an extreme that few will follow, however widespread the appreciation of its corrective emphasis on the two-body psychology that more adequately explicates the psychoanalytic process. The 1987 paper emphasized the *value* of this ambiguity for the understanding of the therapeutic process and the appropriate stance of the therapist. First, "it is important for the analyst to acknowledge that at any given moment he *does not know* the full meaning of his own actions. Certainly, the analyst should not claim to know the meaning and probable impact of his own behavior before taking into account the patient's subsequent more or less disguised interpretation of it" (208); and "There is a uniqueness in the moment of interaction that makes it a mistake for the analyst to assume that he knows what he is doing because his actions conform to a prescribed procedure of some sort" (209). From this the main point follows: "At the heart of the psychoanalytic attitude there is a deep respect for the *value of uncertainty* about the implication of conscious ideas, affects, and intentions, along with the recognition that to live fully is to act despite this uncertainty. Consistent skepticism about what is manifest and curiosity about what is latent and resisted in experience, as well as the recognition that there is something truly interminable about the process by which the meaning of one's actions can be formulated are content-free principles that are more defining of psychoanalysis than any particular thesis about the origins of psychological disturbances" (213, italics added).

In his 1992b paper Hoffman outlines three potential (and competing) psychoanalytic paradigms, the positivist, the limited constructivist, and the full social-constructivist. In the positivist or objectivist paradigm, which is "implicitly diagnostic and prescriptive," analysts "can be confident, not only about their sense of what their patients are doing and experiencing, but also about the nature of their own participation at any moment" (289). In the limited constructivist view, "the patient's experience is thought to be more ambiguous and malleable.

Interpretations suggest ways of organizing the patient's experience among the many ways that are possible. Suggestion, that bugaboo of the process in a positivist framework, becomes an intrinsic aspect of any interpretation in the alternative framework. Indeed, in an important sense, within this framework interpretations *are* suggestions . . . there is more leeway for a range of interpretations that are persuasive, and it is understood that, inescapably, there is some influence coming from the side of the analyst in deciding what line of interpretation to pursue." The limitation of this model, according to Hoffman, is that "it does not challenge the notion that analysts can know the personal meaning of their own actions on a moment-to-moment basis in the process" (290).

With the full social-constructivist position, which Hoffman espouses, there are ever-present uncertainties, but also liberating rewards: "Working within this perspective confronts the analyst with a new sense of risk and personal responsibility regarding whatever he or she chooses to do from moment to moment." But "with the elimination of the standard of doing the 'right' thing according to some external criterion, there is more leeway for a spontaneous kind of expressiveness than there was before, and that spontaneity might well include expressing conviction about one's point of view." Additionally, "personal, emotional reactions can be utilized in the development of interpretations; in other words, they become incorporated into technique. What is not possible in this point of view is a total transcendence by analytic therapists of their own subjectivity" (292). For the many who do not accept all of Hoffman's views, these statements can represent simply an opening of Pandora's box: anything goes in psychoanalytic work, all disciplined and informed technical constraint is abrogated.

In the last paper of this cluster of five (1992c), Hoffman drops the word "perspectivist" as an acceptable synonym for "constructivist": "Whereas perspectivism merely promotes the idea that the patient's experience can be viewed in various plausible and compelling ways, none of which is comprehensive, constructivism also confronts the analyst and the patient with their responsibility for shaping the quality of their interaction through what they say and do, even through what interpretations they decide to pursue. The participants do not merely study the patient's history or the course of the transference; they also make new history in which the experience of each participant is partially constituted interactively" (569–70). And "To argue for the advantages of 'constructivism' over other ways of conceptualizing the process is not a contradiction in terms . . . unless, by definition, constructivism is said to mean that there are no criteria whatever for choosing one point of view over another, a claim that I reject. Good constructions are never creations devoid of recognition of multiple facets of reality" (570). Here perhaps are some of the safeguards against the unbridled expression of "spontaneity."

Finally, the recent paper by Hoffman (1993) recapitulates the evolution of our understanding of the analytic process from this constructivist perspective. It also explicitly reintroduces into that understanding a reconsideration of the inherent role of suggestion in that process, the suggestion that Gill had been striving so hard to fully explicate, and thereby minimize in impact, through interpretation. Hoffman begins by asserting,

> Whatever the analyst does is invariably saturated with suggestion (Gill, 1991). To follow whatever one decides is the patient's lead, to choose to pick up one or another of the patient's more or less ambiguous communications, is also to *lead the patient* in a particular direction (Hoffman, 1990). . . . Those of us who have been trying to work out a "constructivist" view of the analytic process are faced with the necessity of coming to grips with the full implications of that perspective for the role of the analyst in the patient's life. If we believe that the analyst is involved in the construction rather than merely the discovery of the patient's psychic reality, we are confronted with the fact that, according to that view, there is no way to reduce one's involvement to being merely that of a facilitator of self awareness or even integration. There is no objective interpretation and there is no affective attunement that is merely responsive to and reflective of what the patient brings to the situation. (16–17, italics added)

Even further, "the process of affirmation is never content-free. I do not think it's possible to locate and respond to a pure potentiality for experience and choice within the patient. Our affirmative attitude inevitably gravitates toward some of the patient's potentials at the expense of others" (22). And because the patient's life goes on during the analysis, and he often acts on the basis of potentials he has come to understand and value, it follows that he often acts in directions influenced by the analyst: "Analysis goes on in real time—time that really counts—and . . . the patient is continually making real choices under our influence, both within and outside the analytic situation. . . . Opportune moments for action come and go. They do not necessarily recur and they certainly do not last forever" (16). Overall, a statement in harmony with the modern rehabilitation of the lines of understanding initiated by Ferenczi, alongside the initiating understandings promulgated by Freud, concerning the nature of the therapeutic psychoanalytic process.

At the end of this article, Hoffman offered his capsule overview of how our understanding of the analytic process has evolved:

we can trace a movement—one that is decidedly nonlinear—from Freud's solitary reflection on his own dreams which set up self-analysis as the ideal, to the detached presence of the analyst as a scientific observer and facilitator of the transference and its interpretation, to a view of the analyst as responsive in a therapeutically corrective way to the patient's needs and deficits, to an appreciation of the usefulness of countertransference in the process, to an understanding that the analyst's interpretations do not simply map on to a prestructured reality but rather contribute something to the construction of that reality, to an appreciation of the extent and implications of our personal involvement with our patients as they struggle to make sense of and to modify their ways of experiencing and constructing their worlds. (23)[7]

In a recent commentary on the growing popularity of this constructivist perspective, Steven Cooper (1993) makes the cautionary point that just as Hoffman marshaled evidence of the untenability of the positivist ideal of the psychoanalytic process, wholehearted constructivism, an equally unrealizable ideal, can be approached only asymptotically:

> In my view, no analyst is able to live up to the theoretical and clinical ideals set forth in our new developments in theory, particularly theory which describes us as constructivists, attempting to understand and create new realities in the analytic situation. All analysts, even those who maintain the most "open" interpretive stance, with the least imaginable au-

---

7. In his most current extension of his views, Hoffman (1994) has described the momentum accumulated by the movement toward full appreciation of the inevitability and usefulness of the personal involvement of the analyst in the analytic process—and among analysts of diverse theoretical backgrounds, classical Freudian, Kleinian, object-relational, and interpersonal. And yet, "one of the commonalities among them that has struck me is the extent to which the clinical experiences that they report include, at some juncture, implicitly or explicitly, a *feeling of deviation* from a way of working which they view as more commonly accepted, more a part of their own training, more traditional in one sense or another" (188). Hoffman declares that this "sense of spontaneous deviation" can actually promote the analytic process: "When the patient senses that the analyst, in becoming more personally expressive and involved, is departing from an internalized convention of some kind, the patient has reason to *feel recognized* in a special way. The deviation . . . may reflect an emotional engagement on the analyst's part that is responsive in a unique way to this particular patient" (189). Hoffman is also mindful of the dangers of such a technical stance. Just cultivating spontaneity "won't do at all." Rather, "analysts . . . must try, in a relatively consistent way, to subordinate their own personal responsivity and immediate desires to the long-term interests of their patients. Such consistent subordination can be optimized only in the context of the analyst's ongoing critical scrutiny of his or her participation in the process" (193–94).

thoritarian predilections, cling to a mode of understanding or interpretive stance for their analytic bearings. Each practitioner holds his or her own epistemological beliefs, preferences, and burdens. . . . Thus despite our increasing attunement to the relativism of psychic reality, the complexities of transferences and countertransferences, the inevitability of enactments and the augmented recommendations regarding the usefulness of hypothetically stated interpretations, we never have and probably never will have had anything approaching free-floating or even-hovering attention. Not all avenues of understanding and interpretive tack are created equal. (98)

Cooper sees the constructivist trend as part of the general sociocultural deidealization of authority since World War II. He defines "deidealization" of the analyst as "increased emphasis on the analyst as participant-observer attempting to understand psychic and multiple realities rather than as the arbiter and dispenser of views of objective reality within the analytic situation; emphasis on psychoanalysis as a hermeneutic discipline, shifting, in Heidegger's terms, away from 'canonical' truth to the creation of a 'mutual' truth; transference as meaning and expression of psychic realities, not exclusively distortion; the inevitable arousal of the analyst's subjectivities (transference and countertransference); and enactment as a frequent prelude to the capacity to put into words the patient-analyst process" (109). And yet, the clear truths as well as the seductive allure of these considerations notwithstanding, Cooper tried to strike a more therapeutic balance in the dialectical tensions between this constructivist approach and the continuing values of the opposite stance: "The analyst need be prepared to regard the analysand's response to interpretation as *either or both* an accurate comment about the correctness or incorrectness of interpretation or one that is potentially defensively motivated or based on transference. The analyst is poised between the listening poles of respecting and according to the patient a discriminatory faculty to assess the validity of interpretation, or of considering the patient's views as manifestations of transference, defense, or resistance" (120, italics added). Like many of the other polarized issues discussed in this book, this balanced posture seems like a consensual meeting ground of intuitive broad appeal.

Other writers have also singled out the special contributions of the theorists discussed in this chapter for the importance (and popularity) of the technical approaches they advocate. Steven Levy and Lawrence Inderbitzin (1990), in their discussion of "analytic surface," note "four technical approaches that aim at more systematic interpretive efforts based on attention to specific aspects or 'surfaces' in the analytic material as points of departure for interventions. Gray's focus on opportunities for illustrating defensive ego operations, Gill's careful attention to here-and-now transference manifestations, Kris' search for discontinuities in the patient's free associative process,[8] and Schwaber's consistent efforts to clarify deficiencies in the analyst's understanding of the patient's subjective experiences all take off from various suggestions inherent in Freud's ideas about technique. They organize the analyst's listening and responding" (386).

Levy and Inderbitzin had earlier clarified, "By analytic surface we mean some aspect of the patient's verbal and nonverbal behavior to which the analyst *and the analysand* can direct their attention in order to gain access to important material that will be explored in a consistent, systematic manner" (374). They added, "Important in the above considerations is our conviction that, at least potentially, all of the material usually described as central and necessary for an analytic result can emerge for analytic interpretation via systematic attention to *any* of the surfaces described" (386). In a subsequent article on interpretation, Levy and Inderbitzin (1992) added that the analytic surface "is the beginning point of systematic exploration and interpretation, frequently recognized in dis-

8. Here Levy and Inderbitzin focus on Kris's studies of free association rather than his writings on convergent and divergent conflicts. In an article entitled "Support and Psychic Structural Change" (1993), Kris brought these two major themes into conjunction. For Kris's elucidations of the method and process of free association see his 1982 book and two recent articles (1990b and 1992). Here I quote from the 1992 article on the central element in Kris's conception of free associations: "In the method of free association, I see the aims of my interventions from the perspective of their influence on associative continuity and freedom of association, rather than from the narrower angle of their ultimate effect on understanding or insight, which I believe is the more usual way of viewing the analyst's aims. That is, while increased understanding is a crucial aim of analytic work, I believe that at any point in the course of this work, it is more fruitful to focus on the expression of freedom of association [by analyzing the resistances which serve as unconscious restrictions on freedom of association], irrespective of immediate gains in insight, symptom relief, or behavioral change" (1992, 213). Two citations from the 1982 book indicate how he sees the free association process to function differently in psychoanalysis and in (expressive) psychoanalytic psychotherapy: "In less frequent psychotherapy it is the rule rather than the exception that there is an interval of two days or more between sessions, in addition to the usual weekend break. While this repeated sense of interruption does not necessarily interfere with all components of the free association process, such as intensity of transference wishes, for example, it always affects the sense of continuity and rhythm. There is a strain, then, in the conflict between the need to continue free association induced by the free association method and the need to diminish tension in the interval between sessions. For the patient in less frequent psychotherapy this strain usually results in a tendency to diminish the significance of free association" (99). And "in psychotherapy the vis-à-vis position combined with less frequent sessions permits a greater sense of external organization in the treatment and the substitution of formulation for some actions of free association in the treatment process" (102).

turbance, discontinuities, or disequilibria in the analytic material and relationship that attract the analyst's attention, often with an element of surprise" (107).

Finally, the authors discussed in this chapter have taken a variety of stances on the central theme of this book, the relationship of psychoanalytic psychotherapies and psychoanalysis. Kris, with his focus on the two kinds of conflict, and Schwaber, with her focus on empathic immersion in the psychic reality of the patient as the only reality that counts in the therapeutic process, seem to take no position on this issue. Presumably their viewpoints hold equally in work with *both* therapeutic modalities, though Schwaber would concede, I think, that in practice there would be a greater tendency toward an outside rather than an intrapsychic focus in psychoanalytic psychotherapy. Paul Gray, with his focus on the effort to expunge as much as possible the (suggestive) reliance on the analyst's transferentially endowed authority in carrying on interpretive analytic work, more explicitly distinguishes between the two modalities: the more successful the effort he advocates, the more the outcome becomes "essential" psychoanalysis; the less successful, the more it becomes just a psychotherapy. Contrary to Gray, Gill and Hoffman work to blur rather than sharpen the distinction between psychoanalytic psychotherapy and psychoanalysis by amalgamating them in accord with the thinking already marked out in Gill's 1984a revision of the views on the subject that he expressed in the 1979 Atlanta Symposium (see chapter 8).

Along with the distinctive conceptual and technical contributions of the individuals highlighted in the preceding chapter, the past decade has been marked by a number of thematic emphases that bear importantly on the relationship between the psychoanalytic psychotherapies and psychoanalysis.

First, for issues of the nature of the therapeutic process. Many of those writing on this subject have called attention to the same quotation from Freud (1913) as introducing the concept to our technical lexicon: "The analyst is certainly able to do a great deal, but we cannot determine beforehand exactly what results he will effect. He sets in motion a process, that of the resolving of existing repressions. He can supervise this process, further it, remove obstacles in its way, and he can undoubtedly vitiate much of it. But on the whole, once begun, it goes its own way and does not allow either the direction it takes or the order in which it picks up its points to be prescribed for it" (130). Today, of course, we would not accord the analyst so little influence on that process.

Implicit in Freud's statement is his conception of the meaning of process. Yet, the word can have multiple meanings and is variously used by psychoanalysts, and this has perhaps been one of the major sources of confusion over time. For example, during the time when the Menninger Psychotherapy Research Project was grappling with this issue, Helen Sargent (1958) stated that the word and concept "process" could be applied to any phenomenon that shows a continuing change over time, for example, the process of growth, that is, a state of movement and change as opposed to a static state; or to a series of actions or operations conducing toward an end, such as the process of manufacture. Gerald Ehrenreich (1958) offered a distinction between an intrapsychic process, a pattern of change in intrapsychic structures and variables, that is, within the patient; and an interactional process between patient and therapist. In regard to this last distinction, there has been a gradual shift in recent decades paralleling the shift in emphasis away from the conception of a one-body psychology toward a two-body psychology in accounting for change in treatment—from the intrapsychic to the interpersonal focus in the study of process.[1]

---

1. This shift, however, has been far from universal. Abrams, in an article as recent as 1987, acknowledged that "other definitions are certainly plausible," but offered a closely reasoned

In the same context, Sargent offered an allegorical statement about the difficulties of studying process: "The processes of interest are difficult to observe because they are too slow, as in the formation of mountains, too rapid, as in a volcanic explosion or lightning, too hidden, as in the growth of a seed which one day suddenly sprouts a shoot visible to the eye, or too irregular in tempo, as in the differential growth of organ systems, or too complex, slow, rapid, hidden and irregular, as in therapeutic process."

In one of the first articles devoted specifically to the concept of the psychoanalytic process, Rangell (1968) presented the then-consensual understanding. "The specific and indispensable central core . . . the *sine qua non* of the psychoanalytic process" (20), he declared, resided in free association: "the analytic process can be said to begin when the patient really free associates. . . . The sum total of his free associations, memories, fantasies, dreams, etc., along with their contingent affects" (22) is then "tested" within the process: "Via material which comprises the analytic hour, derivatives of instinctual drive are brought forth within the analytic view, to be tested by the patient's ego in front of, and if necessary, with the help of, the analyst." And this testing function is in itself the object of scrutiny, "so that the observing segments of the ego examine not only the drives but the operations of other parts of the ego (the defensive functions) in relation to them" (23). All this takes place by way of the unfolding regressive transference neurosis: "Within the analytic arena the current psychic product by means of which the past of the patient is mainly exposed, with its intrapsychic conflicts and their sequelae, is the transference neurosis and its complex vicissitudes" (14). And last, the analyst's role in all this "is a limited and specialized one, to provide insight by furnishing interpretations" (25).

It is, however, a signal paper by Weinshel (1984) that first defined the contemporary concerns with the nature of the therapeutic process. After presenting Freud's definition, just cited, Weinshel offered his own: "The psychoanalytic process is a *special* interactive process between two individuals, the analysand and the analyst. There may have been a time when the 'process' was seen as something taking place only within the patient. The psychoanalytic process requires that there be two people working together, that there be object relationships, identifications, transferences" (67) (a marked shift from Rangell's intrapsychic, one-body presentation sixteen years earlier). Weinshel went on to designate the work with the treatment *resistances* as the centerpiece of that ongoing process: "The resistance, together with its successful negotiation by the analyst (most often by interpretation), is the clinical unit of the psychoanalytic

justification for having "chosen to define the process as psychological activities *within* the patient's mind" (443).

process" (69); and, "In relation to the psychoanalytic process, we view these [dynamic] forces as organized according to those elements which move in the direction of supporting and pursuing the analytic work and those elements which serve as obstacles to the work, the resistances" (70). Further: "This process, this clinically demonstrable interaction of resistance and interpretation, continues throughout the analysis. There are times when the force of resistance seems diminished and when the interval between the manifestations of resistance is increased, but neither the process nor the resistance ever entirely disappears. . . . The establishment of an effective analytic process in which the patient demonstrates the so-called working or therapeutic alliance—when the patient may be said to be 'in analysis'—is not a once-and-for-all achievement . . . [it is] constantly prone to impingement by conflict, regression, anxiety, sexualization, etc." (74–75).

This conjunction of considerations of process and of resistance has persisted, and considerations of the two have now become essentially intertwined. There are, of course, many precursors for this. As early as 1905, Freud made the very specific statement, "Psycho-analytic treatment may in general be conceived of as . . . a *re-education in overcoming internal resistances*" (1905b, 267). And in his paper on "wild analysis" Freud stated, "The task of the treatment lies in combating these resistances. Informing the patient of what he does not know because he has repressed it is only one of the necessary preliminaries to the treatment" (1910b, 225). He followed this with a statement on how this combating of resistances is accomplished: "Since, however, psycho-analysis cannot dispense with giving this information, it lays down that this shall not be done before two conditions have been fulfilled. First the patient must, through preparation, himself have reached the neighbourhood of what he has repressed, and secondly, he must have formed a sufficient attachment (transference) to the physician for his emotional relationship to him to make a fresh flight impossible. . . . Attempts to 'rush' him at first consultation, by brusquely telling him the secrets which have been discovered by the physician, are technically objectionable. And they mostly bring their own punishment by inspiring a hearty enmity towards the physician on the patient's part and cutting him off from having any further influence" (225–26). It should be noted that these citations predated Freud's papers of 1911–15 on technique (S.E. 12:83–173).[2]

2. Of the long intervening period between Freud's paper of 1910 and Weinshel's of 1984, I will mention only (in addition to Rangell's) Strachey's (1934) seminal paper on the mutative interpretation (i.e., on the transference interpretation as the vehicle for analysis of the resistance embedded in the superego) (see chapter 10) and Loewald's (1970) somewhat unclear statement explicitly linking therapeutic process and resistance: "Transference and its correlate, resistance,

Weinshel (1984) called attention to Siegfried Bernfeld's (1941) often over-looked paper "The Facts of Observation in Psychoanalysis" as the specific in-spiration for his thesis: "Bernfeld saw the removing of obstacles as the analyst's chief function" (79), and "The pattern of resistance and confession [Bernfeld's language] . . . constitutes . . . the basic unit of the psychoanalytic process as well as the basic fact of observation in psychoanalysis" (80). And, after successful enough treatment, "the enhanced capacity for a more objective and effective self-observing activity represents both the continuation of and the heir to the psychoanalytic process" (83). Weinshel also drew on Arnold Pfeffer's studies (1959, 1961, 1963), which provided evidence that the transferences are not definitively "resolved" (nor are conflicts "shattered" or "obliterated") even in the best of analyses; but rather, their salience and poignancy is attenuated, per-manent intrapsychic representations of the analyst remain in the psyche of the patient, and, under triggering circumstances, old transference patterns can be reactivated at least transitorily. In this sense, the ongoing (self-) analytic process (or at least, amenability) becomes lifelong for the ex-patient. "In these state-ments," Weinshel said, "Pfeffer indicated the ongoing viability and activity of the analysis, the transference, and the process, as well as the adaptive value of this 'residual' activity" (84).

With this focus on the repetitive work with the resistances as the center of the analytic process, Weinshel felt it appropriate to end (cf. E. Kris 1956) with a statement about the "not-so-good" analytic hour: "What I have in mind by 'The Elevation of the Not-So-Good-Hour' is an increased recognition of and attention to the less glamorous and exciting exchanges that take place daily at the interface of the analyst-analysand interaction, the more prosaic and 'quiet' ele-ments of that interaction, and the nuances of how the analyst and his interven-tions assist the patient's analytic efforts—instead of so much attention to those 'frames' in the analytic work which feature the analyst in a starring role" (90).

Gray (1986) offered his definition of resistance to this dialogue, a simple equation of resistance with aspects of defense "that are stimulated by the task of free association. I believe that such a theoretical perspective, though not ex-haustive, is practical in comprehending and observing resistance during the analytic process" (250).[3] Dale Boesky's (1988b) definition was within the frame-

---

however, not only are elements of what we intend to study, they also are the processes by which we study them" (55).

3. Others, of course, have seen the relationship of resistance to defense differently, not just as a simple equation. Gill (1982) stated his concept as follows: "The distinction I am proposing here is between 'defense' as connoting something intrapsychic and 'resistance' as connoting something interpersonal. In other words, character defense has concomitant expressions in the

work of Brenner's conceptualization of compromise formations as the essential activity of psychic life: "Resistances during the analytic treatment are usefully understood as structurally mediated compromise formations between drive derivations, defenses, painful affects, the need for punishment, and considerations of reality" (315)—thus widening the purview of the resistance concept far beyond just defense. And Weinshel (1988), in an article on structural change, reiterated his joining of resistance and process and then tried to specify how this works:

> I feel most comfortable in following the progress of my analytic work in terms of the vicissitudes of the resistances as they emerge, are recognized, interpreted, and analyzed in the course of the analysis; and this is why . . .
> I have suggested that the psychoanalytic process can be conceptualized most effectively in terms of the vicissitudes of those resistances. . . . It is reasonable that we can and do observe: (1) the clinical evidence of the obstacles/resistance to the analytic work; (2) the intervention/interpretation of the analysis of the resistance, even if the only intervention is silence; (3) the response of the patient to the analyst's interventions. When that response includes some change in the patient, especially in the way he approaches the analytic work, the analysis, the analyst, or himself (self-observation), it seems reasonable to assume that some kind of structural change has taken place. If that change . . . persists, that assumption seems more legitimate and convincing. (265–67)

In 1990, this discussion was broadened by the publication in a single issue of the *Psychoanalytic Quarterly* of nine articles on this subject. These articles are of special interest because five of them came from a single Study Group on Psychoanalytic Process established by the American. The members were all "analysts of substantially similar views [since] the choice was intended to minimize one variable that can complicate the study of psychoanalytic data and constructs: diverse and conflicting theoretical approaches"; yet, "Within that common perspective, the approaches to the concept of 'the psychoanalytic process' were quite varied" (Erle 1990, 527). I will illustrate these differences by quoting from six of the papers.

Abend (1990) emphasized the difficulty and complexity of the task: "The question of whether we have one psychoanalysis or many, of whether these are

---

transference; these are the *resistances*" (35). And Daniel Jaffe (1991) offered a third nuance on the relationship. "I believe that *resistance* is a generic entity consisting of all mental activity aimed at keeping intolerable wishes and affects (drive derivatives) unconscious, whereas *defense* refers to the specific mechanisms by which resistance is carried out" (510).

variations on a common ground or a disparate family with little in common but its ancestor, has never been more important, or more troublesome, than at the present time. That very pressure motivates our search for a definitive outline of the psychoanalytic process, while the conditions that prevail seem to assure that any description that is broad enough to embrace our diversity will fail to satisfy our desire for greater scientific and administrative clarity" (545). Such thinking led Abend to feel that "there is not much to be gained by speaking of psychoanalysis as a process; what we are really interested in doing is refining our understanding of what psychoanalysis is, of how it is best carried out, of what it brings about in the patient and how it does so, and what a successful analysis looks like. The better we can answer those questions, the better we can both practice psychoanalysis and teach others how to do it." Even after listing six "core features" of psychoanalysis, Abend found that "taken together, this combination of features distinguishes psychoanalytic treatment from many other kinds of therapy. However, it does not differentiate good psychoanalysis from not-so-good psychoanalysis, nor even from those treatments that would more properly be described as psychoanalytic psychotherapy" (540).

Boesky (1990) found similar difficulty with the concept of process: "The term 'psychoanalytic process' as used in this paper is intended to be roughly synonymous with the less rigorous term 'in analysis'. . . . The singular term 'process' should really be a plural term 'processes,' because the psychoanalytic process is actually an extremely complex hierarchy of sub-processes whose adequate description requires a diverse mixture of frames of reference, levels of abstraction, theoretic assumptions, and descriptive, observable phenomena. . . . [Instead of] the erroneous and simplistic view of a singular, conceptually unitary process we should . . . think of the psychoanalytic process as more akin to other heterogeneous multimodal processes, such as the learning process or the democratic process" (562–63).

But on the phenomenon of resistance (as it relates to process), Boesky was much more specific:

> I propose that we view resistance as the joint creation of patient and analyst [similar to Poland's emphasis on transference (1992) and on insight (1988) as joint creations] in a number of instances that are not necessarily a manifestation of a disadvantageous countertransference. I do not refer to all resistances, nor do I suggest that the analyst creates the transference. I am referring to certain forms of resistance to which the analyst inadvertently contributes in every successful analysis as an unavoidable expression of the essential emotional participation of the analyst in the interactional definition of the psychoanalytic process which I favor. I consider the "purity"

of a theoretic analytic treatment, in which all the resistances are created only by the patient, to be a fiction. If the analyst does not get emotionally involved sooner or later in a manner that he had not intended, the analysis will not proceed to a successful conclusion. Countertransference is too vague and abstract a concept to account for the myriad of interventions by the analyst which I am here indicating. . . . it makes little sense to refer to the ubiquitous minor intrusions of the analyst's unconscious as mere "lapses" of technique. There must be important reasons *why* these so-called minor lapses are universal and inevitable. It is time that they be removed from the category of forgivable but regrettable "countertransferences" and studied in careful and selective detail to see what light they shed on the nature of the psychoanalytic process as the expression of an interactional experience. (573–74)

Speaking to the centrality of resistance analysis, Boesky could say, "Just as history has been defined as one damned thing after another, so one can define the process of successful analysis as just one damned resistance after another" (557).

In concluding, Boesky tried to summarize the spirit of the whole group of contributors on the nature of the process: "At the conclusion of our study group discussions we agreed that the enormous complexity of the psychoanalytic treatment situation defies any effort we could make to achieve a satisfactory, systematic definition. We also felt that this was not surprising in light of the discoveries of recent decades, which have revealed the psychoanalytic treatment situation to be vastly more complex than had been realized by the early generations of psychoanalysts. At this point in the evolution of our science we are more aware of what we do not know, and we include in what we do not know any coherent or systematic definition of the psychoanalytic process" (582–83).

Both Abend and Boesky despaired of encompassing the complexity and elusiveness of the psychoanalytic process. Allan Compton (1990) went even further, offering four models of the process: (1) changes in the mind of the patient during the course of analysis, which he called the "natural emergence process model" (cf. Abrams 1987, Rangell 1968); (2) the interactive means by which these changes are brought about, which he called the "interactive process model" (cf. Dewald 1978; Weinshel 1984); (3) the "process model" (cf. Thoma and Kachele 1987); and (4) "all of the steps along the way from the start of a patient/analyst contact to its termination" (585–86). After considering the complexities and present status of other central technical concepts of psychoanalysis, especially the interactive play of transferences and countertransferences, Compton asserted, "If, then, there is no natural process which simply emerges unless vitiated; if there is no resolution of transference; if the analyst doing analysis is, like the patient, a conflicted human being who interactively shapes the course of treatment events on the basis of his or her process model, 'countertransference,' and other factors: then there is no 'right' or 'true' or 'real' or 'valid' psychoanalytic process. Such disputes refer to competing process models" (590). Compton concluded, "We have no justification for discarding any of the currently promulgated process models, even though there are, in my view, many cogent arguments for preferring one over others"—in other words, the search for a unitary and unifying conception of the treatment process is perhaps simply illusory. As corollary, I can cite another of Compton's conclusions: "No *essential* difference between psychoanalysis and other forms of dynamic psychotherapy has been demonstrated" (593).

Unlike the articles by Abend, Boesky, and Compton, Weinshel's contribution (1990b) was a (re)affirmation of the conviction that "persistent and effective work with the resistances (of both analysand and analyst) constitutes the core of the psychoanalytic work and process" (633). "Foremost," he continued, "is the conviction that *resistances are inevitable* in the psychoanalytic work, that they are not 'bad' or necessarily an indication of trouble within the analysis, and that the resistances will not 'go away' or be 'overcome' as Freud was wont to say" (635). Weinshel indicated that many analysts emphasize instead the analysis of the transference as the central element of the analytic work and process. "These preferences," he said, "may be a matter of personal style; but, in many ways, it is difficult to separate clearly the two concepts. We are, of course, mindful of Freud's dictum that the transference is '*the most powerful resistance* to the treatment' (Freud, 1912a, p. 101) as well as the treatment's most powerful tool" (640).

In this article, Weinshel added a clearer delineation of what he called "two forms of resistances": "When all is said and done (notwithstanding the efforts to classify various manifestations of resistances encountered in the analytic work), as psychoanalysts, we essentially deal with two forms of resistance: those that come from the analysand and those that come from the analyst. It is, however, the analyst who must serve as the 'conscience of the analysis' and the 'keeper of the analytic process who has the responsibility for maintaining the psychoanalytic work and process in the face of resistances which inevitably arise (in himself as well as in his analysand) in the case of such endeavor' (Calef and Weinshel 1980, 279)" (640).

Arlow and Brenner (1990) offered a broader conception of the therapeutic process as "synonymous with the progressive changes brought about by consistently applied technique in a standard analytic situation, exercised primarily through interpretive interventions by the analyst, though influenced, to be sure, by the vicissitudes of daily life and other extra-analytic factors. . . . There are many analysts who, like ourselves, . . . equate the two and make no distinction between process and technique, using the terms synonymously" (690). The way in which the analyst furthers this process Arlow and Brenner conceptualized as a succession of destabilizings of psychic equilibrium: "What the analyst communicates to the analysand serves to destabilize the equilibrium of forces in conflict within the patient's mind. This leads to growing awareness and understanding on the part of analysands of the nature of their conflicts, i.e., their forbidden wishes, self-punitive tendencies, irrational fears, and defenses used to contain them" (680)—that is, the familiar classical conception of correct interpretations leading, via working through, to insight and change as *the* mechanism of the process.

Dewald (1990) added a distinction between tactical and strategic resistances: "The tactical resistances are those mental operations which relate to facilitative change, and which oppose the further exploration of or change in the psychic operations that prevent access to consciousness or that are disruptive of progress in the analysis. The strategic resistances are the patient's continuing attempts to achieve re-enactment of infantile or childhood wishes and fantasies, or to achieve relationships with current versions of old or age-inappropriate objects. It is these strategic resistances which constitute the repetition compulsion, and the wish to reenact and repeat even painful or traumatic past experiences and/ or relationships" (703–04). Dewald also proposed an interesting test to demonstrate that the analytic process was a sequence of progressive changes over time: by selecting at random "detailed process notes, or nearly verbatim transcriptions" (707) of five sessions from different periods in a completed analysis to see whether one could arrange these undated sessions in correct chronological order with an explication of the criteria upon which the judgments of sequence were based.

In an article published in the same year, but not as part of the sequence in the *Psychoanalytic Quarterly,* A. Kris (1990b) added another distinction, that between "resistances" and "reluctances": "Where the method requires that the patient try to express his associations as freely as possible of *conscious* restriction, which is all that is free about free association, the first aim of the method is to help diminish through understanding the *unconscious* restrictions that limit the associations. These unconscious restrictions, the *resistances,* can be said to oppose *freedom* of association, and it is very useful to distinguish them from the conscious restrictions on free association, which I refer to as *reluctances*" (27).

Since this group of articles was published, a 1991 paper by Weinshel and Renik seemed to be responding to the view promoted by Arlow and Brenner in their 1990 contribution: process as embracing almost the totality of the work of analysis. Weinshel and Renik countered with, "Not all analysts . . . agree. . . . Some [analysts] conceptualize the process in very broad and all-inclusive terms and argue that it should contain *all* of the elements and activities that play some part in the ongoing course of a psychoanalysis. Others believe that an all-inclusive concept fails to separate those elements which are fundamental and relatively unique to psychoanalysis from those which are much more nonspecific or secondary. . . . Our own view is that a reasonable conceptualization of psychoanalytic process should include both specific and nonspecific components" (24). In a 1992 paper, Weinshel compared the psychoanalytic to the so-called psychotherapeutic process: "Elsewhere (Weinshel, 1984) I have suggested that the patient's resistance to the analytic work, the analyst's interpretation of that resistance, and the patient's response to that interpretation represented the basic 'unit' of the psychoanalytic process and the core of the analytic work." Imprecise as this may be, to Weinshel it is far better demarcated than its counterpart "psychotherapeutic process": "Because 'psychotherapy' is a more diffuse practice involving a much wider and heterogeneous array of psychopathology and therapeutic settings, I find it difficult to conceptualize a 'psychotherapeutic process' that would be comparable to a psychoanalytic process in terms of cohesiveness and usefulness" (334).

Boesky's most recent paper (unpubl.) is an ambitious effort to build on the themes advanced in his 1990 article on resistance as the joint creation of patient and analyst. He began with a statement that was both extension *and* qualification: "The interaction between patient and psychoanalyst is epitomized by the creation, observation, interpretation and lived in experience of resistance by both patient and analyst. My proposal is that in contrast to conventional wisdom the subjectivity of the psychoanalyst *inevitably* leads to iatrogenic elements in the creation of some resistances. Finally I will argue that the subjectivity of the analyst in this type of interaction with the patient often transcends any currently available definition of countertransference" (2). Boesky's emphasis on the word "inevitably" has, perhaps inadvertently, downplayed the important qualification he added here to the views expressed in his 1990 article by his use of the word "some" (resistances) toward the end of that sentence. It is this qualification that he developed further in this paper.

Boesky then outlined the changes that he felt had taken place in the concept of resistance over the developmental history of psychoanalysis, along three dimensions: (1) descriptively, the change from resistance to being hypnotized, then to remembering and catharsis, then to free association, and finally to change and cure; (2) technically, the change "from a view of the patient opposing the analyst to a view of the patient struggling with himself and attempting to embroil the analyst in such a manner that the resistive behavior will seem plausible to the patient" (3); and (3) theoretically, that resistance is a compromise formation, never only a defense, occurring "in the context of a psychoanalytic or psychoanalytically oriented treatment situation" (4). These resistances occur only in the context of a therapeutic process and are necessarily linked to the transference: "It is inconceivable to me that any important resistance can develop without transferential linkages. In that sense all resistance is really transference resistance" (18). But, Boesky added, on the basis of a long clinical case description, that *in this instance* he viewed "the intervention of the analyst as a direct and unintended iatrogenic contribution to the formation of the patient's resistance" (18).

This set the frame for Boesky's more measured assessment in this paper than in the 1990 paper of the analyst's contribution to the development of the resistance. He now specifically rejected the "totalist" conception of the countertransference as embracing the totality of the analyst's impact upon the analysis: "It is one thing to insist correctly that every fiber of the analyst's being is employed in the task of analyzing. It is very different to say that everything the analyst does is countertransference" (20). Neither does he agree that the countertransference, which is inevitable and universal, can always be "turned to good advantage" for the treatment; this "is a seductive and beguiling trap which can anaesthetize the unwary analyst" (22). In extension of this thought, Boesky added, "I agree with those who have questioned the entire idea of using the emotional reactions of the analyst as a *reliable* indicator of what the patient is feeling" (23–24, italics added).

Having said all this, Boesky turned to the role the analyst nonetheless *can* play in the creation of resistance: "What I propose is that an important aspect of the analyst's emotional interaction with the patient is his/her inadvertent contribution to the formation of a resistance which was *the only way that particular analyst could become aware of that particular transference configuration. . . .* We don't merely observe and interpret resistances, we inevitably join in creating some of them. . . . In my view only the patient creates the transference, but the transference expressed as a resistance is *sometimes* a joint creation" (24). This, Boesky declared, was "the embedded topic of my entire paper": "*the vast problem of how to account for the reality adaptive utilization of unconscious conflict in the functioning of the analyst.* [Yet] for all of that the analyst will for the most part interact with the patient more outside of his or her own conflicts than the patient will, and when he or she acts out, the analyst will recognize that he or she is doing so sooner than the patient."

Put even more directly, "I believe that at certain times in every analysis the resistance results as a more or less *unconsciously* 'negotiated' agreement between the patient and the analyst in accordance with the conflicted wishes of both participants. In my view one component of the so-called good fit between patient and analyst can be defined as the optimal balance between the type of transference wishes the patient wants to gratify and the type of resistance the analyst wishes to analyze and with which he or she prefers to work" (27). Boesky then spoke of "this paradoxical dialectic between the impossible task of the patient who must resist in order to be cured and the impossible task of the analyst who must become a bit irrational to help his patient to gain rationality. That is the view of the minimal joint creation of workable resistances as a universal feature of psychoanalytic treatment" (29).

And where, according to Boesky, is countertransference in all this? In the inevitable unconscious resistances of the analyst in their interplay with the patient's transferences, and the joint creation of (some) transference resistances: "The terms resistance and countertransference each designate a range of therapeutic and anti-therapeutic potential. Without resistance and countertransference there can be no successful analytic treatment. There would be nothing to analyze without resistance and no way to analyze it without 'countertransference.' But certain resistances and countertransferences can destroy any hope for a successful treatment outcome"—again, that essential qualification. And how can this countertransference involvement operate therapeutically? "It is one thing to act out with a patient and hope that it will never happen again. It is another thing altogether to be aware that sooner or later one is bound to act out with the patient as a prerequisite of the task, as something inherent in the nature of the interaction with the patient. It is a question not of justifying countertransference but of distinguishing what is possible from what is unattainable" (30). And finally,

> I am suggesting that the neglected component of the interaction with the analyst is not his understanding, but his inevitable misunderstanding and his necessary recovery from that misunderstanding. It is in the cycles of misunderstanding, the struggles to clarify, the unavoidable frustrations in a relationship which is at the same time characterized by the basic benevolence and therapeutic intent of the analyst that I see the role of the relationship rather than in the corrective emotional experience. The participations of the analyst which I have been describing are the opposite of the corrective emotional experience in which the analyst is supposed to manipulatively counteract the behavior of a pathologic parent. Instead the analyst is here described as temporarily failing to meet the therapeutic needs of the patient but he is doing so because of human limitations rather than pathologic motives. I suppose I could say that I am here describing the analyst of the *incorrect* emotional experience who is also more sincere

in his moments of misunderstanding than to pretend to play a role. The consequence might be described as a *benign* iatrogenic resistance.[4] (31)

A fair summary of Boesky's views would be that the analytic *process* consists of the analysis of the play of resistances on *both* sides of the therapeutic dialogue.

Renik, in his 1993b paper on the analyst's "irreducible subjectivity," took as his point of departure the thesis, elaborated at length in his 1993a paper on countertransference enactments, that "an analyst's awareness of his or her emotional responses as they arise in the course of an analysis *necessarily* follows translation of those responses into action, i.e., awareness of countertransference is always retrospective, preceded by countertransference enactment" (556). This leads directly to the statement, "If we accept that an analyst's activity . . . is constantly determined by his or her individual psychology of which the analyst can become aware only after the fact, then we acknowledge the necessary subjectivity of even ideal analytic technique" (559). In a telling commentary on the difficulty of accepting the full implications of this view, he added, "Just the fact that we still use the term *interpretation* would seem to indicate the extent to which we retain a conception of analytic technique as potentially objective, rather than inherently subjective—the extent to which we implicitly see the analyst trying to transcend his or her own psychology in order to deal with the patient's psyche 'out there' " (559–60).

Renik's own stance on this issue is clearly the opposite: "Instead of saying that it is *difficult* for an analyst to *maintain* a position in which his or her analytic activity objectively focuses on a patient's inner reality, I would say that it is *impossible* for an analyst to be in that position *even for an instant:* since we are constantly acting in the analytic situation on the basis of personal motivations of which we cannot be aware until after the fact, our technique, listening included, is *inescapably* subjective" (560). This is what he calls the analyst's "irreducible subjectivity" (562). If we fully accept this view of the analytic interaction, what are its practical implications? (1) "For one thing, it means we discard a widely accepted principle of technique which holds that countertransference enactment, so called, is to be avoided" (562); (2) "a second implication [is] . . . that *unconscious* personal motivations expressed in action by the analyst are not only unavoidable, but *necessary to the analytic process*" (564); (3) "a problematic third implication . . . Since an analyst acting on his or her personal mo-

---

4. Boesky's position is quite akin, though in a distinctly different idiom, to Casement's objections to the Alexandrian position from within the British object-relational perspective—that the patient needs to use the analyst in order to work through feelings about early experience as they had been, and that, within that context, the new experience has to be *found,* not provided or contrived (see chapters 4 and 19).

tivations is inherent in productive technique, how are we to say where analytic work leaves off and exploitation of the analytic situation by the analyst begins?" (564–65). This is indeed the crucial question, one that has no definitive answer. Renik says, "There is no avoiding this very disconcerting question. In struggling to answer it we cannot afford to deny the fact of an analyst's personal involvement. . . . We do not profit, ultimately, from the comforting but misconceived ideal of what is essentially an impersonal use of the self of the analyst in clinical analysis" (565). And (4) "Another implication of a conception of technique that accepts the analyst's subjectivity is that communication to the patient of even an implicit pretense of objectivity on the analyst's part is to be avoided" (566).

Once all this has been accepted, the analyst has acquired greater freedom and flexibility (as well as assumed greater risk) within the analytic situation,[5] being willing even—in marked contrast to Schwaber, for example—to present his or her viewpoint on an issue as persuasively as possible when it differs from that of the patient. Renik writes, "Sometimes the best way to facilitate a patient's self-exploration can be for an analyst to present his or her own different interpretation of reality for the patient's consideration—even to present it as persuasively as possible, in order to be sure that the patient has taken full account of it," for "it seems to me a fundamental principle of analytic collaboration that an analyst's aim in offering an interpretation is not to have it accepted by the patient, but rather to have the patient consider it in making up his or her own mind" (567). Along the way Renik offered remarks about interpretations, which "are considered more as stimuli to the patient's self investigation than as truths about the patient's mental life to be communicated to him or her" (569); about the analyst's belief that he or she can transcend the inherent subjectivity of the process—that this could simply promote an iatrogenic idealization of the analyst (569); and about suggestion: "Analysts [following Freud] have often felt the need to deny the role of suggestion in analytic technique, whereas the truly scientific approach is to study the role of suggestion in effective analytic technique" (570)—this last again a convergence of the current views of many workers arrived at by many different routes.[6]

Final perspectives may be gained from recent books by Casement (1990a) and Etchegoyen (1991). The brief quotation from Casement is meant to illustrate a typically British object-relational view. His main point is that the analytic

---

5. Compare the discussion of Hoffman's work (pp. 430-39), which has arrived at a position completely congruent with Renik's.
6. Skolnikoff in two recent articles (1993, 1995) strongly supports Renik's theses that enactments by the analyst in analysis are as inevitable as those of the patient and can only become fully known in retrospect, and that this is linked to, and is part of, the irreducible subjectivity of the analyst. Analysis takes place within these "interacting subjectivities."

process can develop only in a properly maintained "analytic space"—a Winnicottian conception—and that within that space, "contrary to the expectations of what common sense might suggest, the unconscious search here is not simply for better experience. . . . It is for a sufficient security within which it may eventually come to feel safe enough for the patient to risk feeling again unsafe—in order to work through the feelings that had been associated with earlier difficult experiences. And whether that security can be found in the presence of the analyst will depend, to a large extent, on his/her ability to preserve the analytic space from the disturbances that can arise from the analyst's way of being with the patient" (345)—this last is quite similar to Boesky's concept of benign iatrogenic resistances. In connection with Casement's emphasis on feeling safe, it is another British analyst, Sandler (1960), who introduced the notion of a "*safety-principle* which mediates the development of the reality-principle from the pleasure-principle" (351).

From Etchegoyen's (1991) compendium, I draw two main considerations: his distinction, taken from the work of Gregorio Klimovsky, an Argentine philosopher devoted to the epistemological issues of psychoanalysis, of four main ways to define the therapeutic process; and the to-and-fro argument on the nature or conditions of the treatment process. First, Etchegoyen proposed the following definitions: (1) process defined in terms of the passage of time (i.e., states or configurations changing over time); (2) process as occurrences in time that acquire a unity relative to a final determining state (i.e., the cathartic method constituting a process that ends in successful abreaction); (3) process as a causal chain with subsequent states somehow determined by preceding ones (i.e., the analytic process considered in terms of progressions and regressions); and (4) process "as a succession of events with their causal connexions plus the actions the therapist applies at certain moments for the sequence to be that one and no other" (530). Of these, Etchegoyen opted for the fourth as "the model best adapted to the psychoanalytic process" (531).

Etchegoyen then summarized two differing conceptions of the nature of the therapeutic process: "For one of these, the psychoanalytic process arises spontaneously and naturally from the analytic situation in which analysand and analyst are placed [a way of thinking that goes back to Freud, of course]. For the other, . . . the process is an artifice, an artifact or contrivance, of the rigorous conditions in which analysis develops and to which the patient must adapt (or 'submit') [a way of thinking that originated with Macalpine 1950]. Characterized in this way, both positions seem extreme and intemperate, seemingly without a point of contact or convergence" (531).

Etchegoyen then offered a way of reconciling these seemingly antithetic perspectives. First, he said, "When it is maintained that the psychoanalytic process is *natural* and any type of artifice is denied it, it is thought that the transference is basically a spontaneous process, that all of us have a natural tendency to repeat in the present the old ways of our remote infantile past, that it is in no way necessary to pressurize or induce that analysand for this to happen. . . . Certainly the fact is ignored that any process where the hand of man intervenes is artificial" (531–32). Then he took on the other side of the argument:

> Those who defend the alternative conception, on the other hand, and affirm that the analytic process is an *artificial* product of our technique begin by saying that the relation the analytic setting imposes on the two participants in the cure is excessively rigid and conventional, it lacks any spontaneity, and it is acknowledged to be asymmetrical. What sort of dialogue can this be where one of the participants lies down and the other sits, where one speaks without being allowed to take refuge in any of the rules of normal conversation and the other remains impenetrable, responding through interpretation? No, it is asserted, the analytic process runs its course along paths so rarely frequented that it has an ineluctable seal of artifice. Were it not so, were the analytic process to run its course naturally, the past would have to repeat itself without changes, and there would really be no process. (532)

Despite the apparent tilt to the second of the two positions, Etchegoyen, perhaps surprisingly, while looking for some accommodation of views, opted for a position closer to the first: "In general, all analysts admit that analysis is a process of growth and also a creative experience. Everything depends, then, on which of these two aspects we give preference to. I favour the first alternative and think that the essence of the process consists in removing the obstacles [Weinshel's analysis of the resistances], so the analysand can go his own way. The analyst's creation consists, for me, in the capacity to give the analysand the necessary instruments for him to orientate himself alone and become himself again. The analyst is creative more through what he reveals than by what he creates. . . . the psychoanalyst rescues rather than creates meanings that have been lost" (533). I feel that this is the proper (unsettled) point at which to leave this still ongoing debate.

23 Contemporary Emphases in Psychoanalytic Therapy: Structure, Structural Change, and Issues of Conversion

Integrally related to issues of process (and of resistance) discussed in the preceding chapter are the notions of psychic structure and structural change, which are at once among the most central and the most problematic concepts in psychoanalytic theory. They are also crucial to any effort to elaborate the theory of psychoanalytic therapy and, within that, to differentiate psychoanalysis as therapy from all the other psychoanalytic psychotherapies (and crucial as well to the differentiation of these psychoanalytically based psychotherapies from psychotherapies conducted within other theoretical paradigms). Set within the framework of the then-dominant (in America) ego-psychology paradigm, Rapaport's (1960) statements on structure were long widely regarded as the most definitive. He stated, "Controls and defenses are conceptualized as structures; *their rates of change are slow* in comparison with those of drive-energy accumulations and drive-discharge processes" (28–29, italics added). And "In contrast to the drive processes, whose rate of change is fast and whose course is paroxysmal, the factors which conflict with them and co-determine behavior appeared to be invariant or at least of a slower rate of change. The observation of these *relatively abiding determiners of behavior and symptom* seems to have been the foundation on which the concept of structure was built" (53, italics added).

I have detailed elsewhere (Wallerstein 1988d) the various ways in which Rapaport's seemingly clear-cut conceptualizations turned out to be increasingly problematic. At this point, I will take as the point of departure the indicators of structural change posited by Dewald (1972) as a full elaboration of Rapaport's conception by someone who has found it most useful in his own theorizing (see chapter 6). Dewald (1972), operating within the dimensions set by Rapaport's definition, studied structural change along the "distinctions between the *core* psychic structures established during the infantile and early childhood phases of development, and *derivative* psychic structural development which occurs in later psychological maturation. In keeping with the concept of genetic fallacy, some of these later-developing psychic structures may ultimately achieve various levels of functional autonomy and thus become independent of the earlier phases of psychic conflict from which they evolve" (303, italics added).

This distinction between core and derivative conflicts and structures was crucial to Dewald's conception of the differences between the characteristic course and outcome of psychoanalytic psychotherapy as distinct from psychoanalysis. Of psychoanalysis he stated, "To the degree that core structures are modified as a result of the working-through process in the transference neurosis, those functions which are derivatives of the core elements and which have not achieved autonomy will likewise undergo change. This is one of the significant reasons why resolution of the transference neurosis by working through will be accompanied by resolution of conflict and modification of previously structured behavior patterns in other relationships and situations outside the analysis" (305). By contrast, "in nonpsychoanalytic forms of psychotherapy [an awkward locution for psychoanalytic psychotherapy that is not proper psychoanalysis], this tends to be the level of derivative structural change that occurs. As mentioned above, these forms of treatment are not designed specifically to expose or explore the infantile neurosis, but rather, they focus upon the manifold behaviors by which the core neurosis and structures are repeated in derivative form. The establishment of new derivative behavior patterns can lead to more effective modes of adaptation, particularly if these provide increased satisfaction, or decreased conflict with reality, and thus become self-reinforcing and self-sustaining" (310).[1]

Within this context, Dewald then elaborated some fourteen criteria or indicators of structural change in psychoanalysis vis-à-vis psychotherapy (311–22):

1. Changes in the id, "the degree to which drive energies are mobilized, the extent to which genital primacy is established, the degree of fusion of libidinal and aggressive drives, and the fate of the pregenital strivings"

2. Changes in the superego, "the degree to which primitive and primary process introjects are replaced by secondary-process, reality-oriented, and personally developed systems of moral values"

3. Changes in the ego, "the progressive modification of some of the specific component microstructures (individual functions) . . . which include the degree to which the reality principle replaces the pleasure principle; the freeing of previously impaired ego functions from intrapsychic conflict; the stability of the sense of the self and of identity;

---

1. Without using Dewald's language of core and derivative conflicts, The Psychotherapy Research Project of the Menninger Foundation was conceived within the same ego-psychological framework of structure and structural change (see chapter 5), and its main findings and conclusions were brought to final clinical accounting in the post-ego-psychological era of fragmented consensus (see chapter 8).

the flexibility, appropriateness, and degree of consciousness of the defense systems; the stability of the sublimations that are developed; the age-appropriateness and the constancy of object choices; and the extent to which adaptive ego-processes assume direction and control of the patient's behavior and reactions"

4. The "overall psychological adaptation and reactions [which] . . . includes his (the patient's) ability to cope with new or more stressful situations"

5. The dwindling of the central organizing importance of the core fantasies

6. The "progressive acceptance into conscious awareness of the drives and their derivatives as being part of the self, without undue neurotic guilt or anxiety"

7. The derivative manifestations changing spontaneously without specific scrutiny or conscious effort, once the nuclear conflicts are resolved

8. The altered reaction to "previously traumatic or anxiety-provoking material, so that he (the patient) is now capable of remembering, accepting, and understanding the traumatic experiences that previously evoked intense affect"

9. "The increasing freedom and directness with which the underlying dream thoughts and wishes can be expressed, as well as the patient's increasing ability to interpret his own dreams"

10. "The changed nature of the patient's relationships with other people outside the analysis"

11. "The patient's growing dissatisfaction with previously gratifying infantile objects or relationships, and the replacement of these by age-appropriate, realistically satisfying objects"

12. The deepening of the patient's affective life with the overcoming of inhibitions and restrictions

13. The ability to "remain symptom-free without other neurotic substitutions while facing the conflicts or situations which previously had evoked the symptoms"

14. The decathexis of the analyst, "free from the distortions that signify the transference neurosis."

It is clear that all of these are quantitative shifts along continua, and Dewald leaves it completely unclear when we are dealing only with changes in derivative conflicts (the declared outcomes of psychoanalytic psychotherapies) and when with changes in core conflicts (achieved presumably only in full psychoanalyses).

Though the ego-psychology paradigm within which Dewald's conceptualizations were framed was modified over the 1970s and 1980s, it was not until 1988, with the publication of four successive panels at the American Psychoanalytic Association on the concept of structure in psychoanalysis, that there was a full-scale reconsideration of the implications of these shifts—toward the incorporation of object-relational perspectives, toward an increasing focus on the mutative role of the treatment relationship, what came to be called widening scope analysis, developmental considerations, and so on—for our notions of structure and structural change. (Four of the seventeen papers in those panels, those by Weinshel, Kernberg, Boesky, and myself, will be singled out, in that order, for their special relevance to the considerations of this chapter.) Actually, Weinshel heralded these reconsiderations in his 1984 article when he questioned the whole concept of structural change, which "has become not only a highly prized goal but also a kind of slogan and shibboleth; it is also difficult to demonstrate and explicate" (70). In his contribution to the panels, he offered a way out of this dilemma: "Since structural change in psychoanalysis may be difficult to demonstrate in a manner that is clear and open to consensual validation, and difficult to differentiate from changes brought about by unanalytic mechanisms or therapies, the term 'psychoanalytic change' may be more realistic and more useful" (264). (He underlined this further in a 1990 article, in which he stated, "Our long-held claim that 'structural change' is the sacrosanct province of psychoanalysis may be a somewhat solipsistic one" [636].)

Kernberg (1988) essayed to redefine structural change in the light of the theoretical advances of the several decades since the formalization of the ego-psychology paradigm by Hartmann and his collaborators in the 1940s and the 1950s and its systematization by Rapaport: "A definition of structural change in general terms of impulse-defense configurations, and in terms of modification in the mutual relations of ego, superego, and id impulses implies a well-differentiated tripartite structure as characteristic of mental functioning . . . [but] I think, based on findings regarding the psychopathology of borderline conditions indicating lack of integration of ego and superego structures, . . . that impulse and defense should be explored in relation to patterns of internalized object relations, which are the 'building blocks' of the tripartite structure. The dissociation or integration of these building blocks is reflected in predominant patterns of interpersonal relations, transference developments, and characterologic constellations" (316). These "changes in the internal organization of self-representations and object representations should be incorporated in the psychoanalytic concept of structural change" (317). And these in turn are built upon affects as motivators: "I view affects as the primary motivators of behavior. Affects are gradually organized into libidinal and aggressive drives, indissolubly linked to object relations from the onset of individuation. I view self-representations and object-representations, together with their affective charge, as the building blocks of id, ego, and superego" (p. 319).

These then all relate to structural change in the following way:

> The specific aspect of the relation between interpretation and structural change is the emergence of new information, spontaneously provided by the patient in the context of exploring the transference, information that indicates new understanding of the patient's present behavior as well as its linkages to the patient's other experiences, both present and past. . . . The unpredictability, the spontaneous emergence of new information, and the expansion of understanding as a precondition for changes in the transference, and the extension of such changes and understanding into other areas of the patient's behavior are what differentiate insight derived from interpretation from other, cognitively induced change in the patient's present understanding, and from direct instructions for behavioral change by the therapist that the patient complies with. (332)

But all this still left the question, "If lasting change that profoundly affects an individual's relations with himself, with others, with work and life in general, can be obtained in so many ways, is there any specific mechanism of stable change derived from psychoanalysis and psychoanalytic psychotherapy?" (318)—or distinguishing psychoanalysis from psychoanalytic psychotherapy? Kernberg did not attempt to formulate specific answers to these questions.

Boesky (1988a) essentially updated Dewald's "traditional" ego-psychological formulations in light of Brenner's contemporary reformulations of this paradigm, with the emphasis then on the shifts in compromise-formations and the essential interrelatedness of all the component elements: "An important difference between the tripartite model and modern structural theory is the better capacity to describe these multiple and complex interactions of compromise formations rather than only the more abstract interactions of id, ego, and superego" (127). And, in further amplification, "Another dimension . . . remains insufficiently appreciated. That is the interrelatedness of all elements in a structure. In this sense one refers to a sonnet, a symphony, or a government as a structure. A common quality of all structures, physical or mental, is the special relatedness of each part to all the other parts and to the whole, as well as the effect of the whole system on each of its components" (124). In another article the same year (1988c), Boesky defined structural change as "the alteration in the organization of the pathologic compromise formations in a manner that allows greater realistic gratifications, improvements in the capacity to work and to love, less interference in personal relationships by neurotic conflicts, an increased capacity for utilizing personal resources that had been previously inhibited, and less need for punishment" (173).

And in a third paper that year (1988b) Boesky considered structural change in relation to the mode of therapy—and came down on the side of restricting it to the changes brought about only in proper psychoanalysis: "For many years it seemed useful to make a sharp distinction between psychoanalysis and all other forms of psychotherapy by insisting that 'true' psychoanalytic change was structural in nature as compared to certain 'transference cures' achieved in other forms of psychotherapy. But areas of overlap between intensive, interpretive or 'analytically oriented' psychotherapy and classic psychoanalytic treatment were recognized and discussed extensively. . . . Nevertheless, 'structural change' still has prevailed as a distinguishing 'proprietary' criterion and as an almost semi-official proof that a patient had been 'in psychoanalysis' or that a successful psychoanalytic *process* had been established." (310). And, "For some time now we have simply tended to minimize the challenge of these questions [to this argument about the necessary conditions for structural change to eventuate] by insisting that the therapeutic changes induced by 'truly' psychoanalytic resolution of transference and resistance was different from what could be obtained in psychotherapy, normal development, or actual spontaneous remissions. The crucial difference according to this argument is that only 'genuine' psychoanalytic treatment can produce the essential 'structural change' which is supposedly the *cause* of the 'cure' " (310–11).

Boesky's view is at variance with the one I presented in the same sequence of papers (Wallerstein 1988d). My position, built on the findings and conclusions of the Menninger Psychotherapy Research Project (Wallerstein 1986a, 1988b), was simply that the changes reached via psychoanalytic psychotherapies "seemed often enough just as much 'structural change' as the changes reached in our most expressive-analytic cases" (chapter 8), and I questioned strongly the continued usefulness of the effort to link the *kind* of change achieved so tightly to the intervention mode, psychoanalytic or psychotherapeutic, by which it is brought about. My article in the 1988 panel series (1988d) was designed to take this discourse to the next level, and to do so in a research context. For, if one is to explore clinically *or* in research the proposition that the kinds of changes produced in psychoanalysis do or do not differ from those that occur in psychoanalytic psychotherapies, one needs to have (or create) independent, consensually agreed upon, and reliable indices of intrapsychic structures, (which do not yet exist), and also a consensually agreed upon and reliable metric along which structural change can be assessed—for example, some scale anchored to clear, concise descriptions of scale points, preferably illustrated by clinical vignettes.

In approaching this problem from a research standpoint, the first issue is to define "structure" and "structural change" in empirically meaningful ways. To begin with, psychic structures are only useful explanatory *constructs;* they have no tangible substance. Also, they are theory-bound and, even within an overarching psychoanalytic framework, depend for their form on the psychoanalytic theoretical allegiance of the investigator. That is, structure is conceptualized within an ego-psychological framework in terms of impulse-defense configurations; within a Kleinian framework in terms of good and bad part objects (in the paranoid position) and ambivalently held whole objects (in the depressive position); within an object-relational framework in terms of self- and object-representations and the affective valences that bind them; and within a self psychological framework in terms of a varyingly cohesive or vulnerable bipolar self. And this is not to speak of Kernberg's effort (1988) to define structure within an amalgamated ego psychological-object relational perspective. All this, despite the fact that the overarching theory within which these constructs have meaning is declared to be (the same) psychoanalysis. At this stage in the development of psychoanalysis, consensus on these concepts is not possible; in fact, it is probably the most salient dividing line among these presently alternative theoretical perspectives within psychoanalysis.

Therefore, rather than decide on dimensions of intrapsychic structure and structural change that reflect a particular theoretical position within psychoanalysis, our research group[2] has sought to formulate a list of assessable "psychological capacities" that adherents of all prevailing psychoanalytic perspectives could agree comprehensively describe personality functioning and that will necessarily shift if there is "underlying" change in intrapsychic structures. That is, sustained change in these psychological capacities should be consensually accepted as reflecting underlying structural change, which may then be formulated differently by adherents of different theoretical positions in analysis.

To this point, seventeen such psychological capacities have been elaborated to describe the array of personality attributes that in sum define an individual's characteristic modes of functioning. They are designed to be low-level (experience-near) constructs, readily and reliably inferred from observable behaviors (interview data, etc.). In this sense, they are in contrast to such abstract (experience-distant) concepts as the intrapsychic structures intended to represent the central elements of comprehensive personality theories. How these seventeen psychological capacities were developed, how scales to measure them were cre-

2. Based at the Langley-Porter Institute in San Francisco, this group has also included Daniel Weiss, Kathryn DeWitt, Saul Rosenberg, Nathan Zilberg, and Dianna Hartley, and most recently, also Connie Milbrath and Michael Windholz

ated, and how the issues of the reliability and validity of the scale assessments were approached are described in detail elsewhere (Wallerstein 1988d; DeWitt et al. 1991, Zilberg et al. 1991; Wallerstein, unpubl. ms d).

Here, I will mention only the central questions to which this research is addressed. Where symptom and behavior changes have occurred consequent to analytic therapy (psychoanalysis or psychoanalytically based psychotherapy), when does structural change, as assessed by changes on these scales of psychological capacities, also occur and under what conditions? Do such structural changes come about concomitant with the symptomatic and behavioral changes only in psychoanalysis per se, or perhaps additionally in expressive psychoanalytic psychotherapy? or do they also come about as a consequence of the more supportive therapeutic techniques, geared not to the interpretation of resistance and defense, but to the bolstering of defenses and the restoration of the ego's faltering adaptive and coping capacities? Last, with adequate follow-up, we should be able to discern the extent to which the instances of 'true' structural change that may be induced in the more supportive psychotherapies compare in stability, durability, and proof against future environmental vicissitude with the structural changes induced in the expressive and purely analytic modes.

Taken as a group, then, the articles from the 1988 panels did not forge a consensus on any of the outstanding issues around the concepts of structure and structural change: whether the concept is theoretically meaningful and clinically useful or should be replaced by something that promises less, like "psychoanalytic change" (Weinshel); whether, if useful, it should be redefined in terms of recent conceptual advances in formulating the theoretical structure of psychoanalysis (Kernberg); whether, if useful and maintained in updated but more traditional ego-psychological terms, it could serve as a reliable demarcation between the expectable outcomes of psychoanalysis and the psychoanalytic psychotherapies (Boesky); or whether, even if useful and maintained, it could at best serve only as a springboard to more intensive clinical and research study— that is, could reliable and independent measures of structure and structural change be devised to assess the conditions under which such changes do or do not eventuate as a consequence of psychoanalysis and varyingly expressive and supportive psychoanalytic psychotherapies. (Wallerstein).

Since the publication of those panel discussions, several other authors have dealt with these issues, but with neither new conceptual positions nor any discernible movement toward a convergence of views. Sandler, (1988), for example, stated, "There is little doubt that both psychoanalysis and psychoanalytic psychotherapy have the capacity for bringing about structural change [agreeing with Wallerstein, and not Boesky, on this issue], and that not all such change is a consequence of interpretations. There is no complete agreement on the mechanisms of psychic change in either psychoanalysis or psychotherapy, and we certainly lack a psychoanalytic theory of technique which would encompass both psychoanalysis and psychotherapy" (177). He added, "The problem is complicated by the fact that we cannot readily equate one psychoanalysis with another, nor one psychotherapy with another" (173). Werman (1989), on the other hand, in an article titled "The Idealization of Structural Change," called for abandoning the concept altogether: "I believe that the idea of structural change based on *metapsychological* concepts has outlived whatever usefulness it might ever have had" (120, italics added)—and for a retreat to clinical, experience-near conceptions to explain clinical interactions and their consequences. He implied that structural change is actually a mischievous concept because "to speak of structural change inflates the depth and permanence of the changes that seem to be typically obtained in analysis" (134), and he offered the opinion that the continuing popularity of the concept among clinicians and researchers owed much to the persuasive writings of Dewald.

Abend (1990) arrived at a position similar to Werman's on the basis of similar reasoning. Opting to speak of "change" ("The very notion of process implies change over a period of time" [537]), he nonetheless decried the implied *structuralization* of "structural change": "In my view, the term is unsatisfactory because it is seductively vague; it is employed as an article of faith in the superiority of analysis. Just which structures are involved in structural change are not self-evident, nor are they always spelled out by analysts when they make use of the term in writing or discussion. Neither are there clear explanations of what the metapsychology of other, presumably nonstructural types of change might be" (538). Of course, the wish to address just this ambiguity and possible confusion is just what motivates our San Francisco research group's efforts to reach consensus on discernible structural change by demonstrated shifts in clinically manifest (experience-near) psychological capacities.

In 1992 Betty Joseph, a leading Kleinian, speaking from a theoretical position that had never found the concept very meaningful or useful, proposed the notion of "psychic balance" to replace psychic change: "The main concern for the analyst will be to try to understand how his patient maintains his psychic balance. . . . This balance, which some might call his 'compromise formation,' is, in fact, a complex system of phantasies, anxieties and defences, which will inevitably express themselves in the relationship with the analyst in the transference, as well as the attitude that the ego takes towards the nature of his balance" (237). Therefore, "It follows naturally that the analyst will not be concerned about whether the change he has observed is good or regressive, perverse or hopeful; his only concern is that it is his patient's individual way of keeping his balance at that moment" (238). Rangell (1992), a continuing bulwark of the ego-psychology structural paradigm, offered a historical defense of the continued utility of the concept: "Change has changed from an effect on symptoms, to underlying etiologic conflicts, to background character, to the functioning of psychic structural systems. The psychoanalytic process does not overlap with the process of change. The former may be present without the latter" (426). And in relation to this, Rangell said, "It was from this gradual development and direction of psychoanalytic theory that psychoanalytic change came to be associated and eventually equated with structural change. This came in fact to be the hallmark of psychoanalytic treatment, and to be regularly regarded as the differentiating criterion between psychoanalytic and other forms of psychotherapeutic change" (416).

Of the group of publications in 1992, de Jonghe, Rijnierse, and Janssen proposed the freshest perspective. They attempted to bring together conceptually different roads to structural change in psychoanalysis and in psychoanalytic psychotherapy. They called it "Two-Factor Clinical Theory" (485) and presented it in diagrammatic form. One factor, or pathway, they called the classical or "neurotic mind model," the traditional ego-psychological paradigm, within which "mutative interpretations" lead to "mutative insights," which effect structural change. The other factor they called the "post-classical model" or the "archaic mind model," the major modification of the ego-psychological position under the combined impact of increasing clinical concern with sicker patients (narcissistic and borderline) and theoretical infusions from object-relational perspectives, a model in which "mutative support" leads to "mutative experience," which in turn converges on (the same?) structural change. ("Improvement brought about by mutative experience is not a 'transference cure' according to our definition for it is based on the primary aspect of the *analytic relationship*" [485, italics added].) This conception is only a schematic. The authors do attempt to explain how they mean the word "mutative" when it precedes "interpretation," "insight," "support," and "experience," but they do not specify the basis on which they can assume that the structural change reached by these two alternative pathways is truly the same. Conceptually, however, the Dutch proposal represents an integrative effort to accommodate otherwise seemingly divergent trends.

Another paper on this topic is Dewald's unpublished presentation from a 1989 panel on the similarities and differences between psychoanalysis and psychoanalytic psychotherapy. This is cited only to underline the persistence with which Dewald propounds and extends his positions. The paper is again cast in terms of therapeutic attention ultimately to core and derivative conflicts and to core and derivative elements of psychic structure and function. Again Dewald offers a list, somewhat similar to the fourteen points in his 1972 article, delineating the distinctions between psychoanalysis and the psychoanalytic psychotherapies. On the issue of "structural change" in the psychoanalytic psychotherapies, Dewald modified (or merely clarified?) his evolving position:

> The question has been raised as to whether psychoanalytic psychotherapy can and does produce lasting (and in that sense, structural) psychic change in the patient. The traditional view has been that unless there is exposure and resolution of core psychic conflict, derivative symptom substitution will occur and that more superficial forms of psychotherapy are predominantly supportive, and do not result in lasting change. Empirical observation contradicts the idea that only psychoanalysis produces significant and lasting change. . . . Other things being equal, the differences in the extent and depth of structural change between psychoanalysis and psychoanalytic psychotherapy are essentially relatable to how far proximal or distal to the core of psychic function the process is focused. In successful psychoanalysis, one would expect more diffuse, broader, as well as deeper, structural change as a result of the treatment process. In psychoanalytic psychotherapy such change would tend to be more focal, segmental, or specifically targeted, while other areas of personality and psychic function remain essentially unchanged. (10–13)

Recently, a book entitled *Psychic Structure and Psychic Change* (1993) brought together contributions on this subject by leading clinicians and theorists representing the three major psychoanalytic regions of the world—North and South America and Europe—and several of the major prevailing theoretical perspectives in psychoanalysis—the ego-psychological, the Kleinian, the object-relational, and the (non-Lacanian) French. All fourteen of the contributors have been cited previously in this book. Here I will single out six of this group, each essentially for a single central or unifying conception.

Chasseguet-Smirgel and Angela Goyena directly challenge, from a francophone perspective, the whole notion of structure and structural change. They opened their article with the arresting statement, "Let us imagine a world where Freud's first theory of the mental apparatus divided into three systems is known as the first topographical model and his second theory, the second topographical model. This world happens to be the psychoanalytic world in general, with some exceptions in English-speaking countries. There is no mention of a 'structural theory' anywhere in Freud's works. His division of the mental apparatus into three agencies is not considered more 'structural' or less so than the sequence of unconscious, preconscious, and conscious, and in a certain sense, is equally localized. . . . Who then named the second topographical model the 'structural theory'? Certainly not Freud. In all probability this is a term we owe to one of the founders of ego psychology in the United States" (1993, 233). In place of the concept of structure the authors offer that of a central organizing fantasy: "There is a fantasy or a series of interrelated fantasies . . . (one often capping all the others and containing them all) which represents an attempt to solve the central conflict. . . . Such fantasies have the stable, permanent characteristics of structure. . . . A true psychoanalytic change takes place when . . . the fantasy is abandoned around which the psyche is organized" (238).

Dewald, who previously lined the indicators or criteria of such changes along fourteen dimensions of change, in his 1993 article, also singled out changes in "primary process fantasies" as the most salient change indicator: "It is this process of voluntary renunciation of age-inappropriate expectations and behavioral demands or limitations . . . that results in the ultimate structural changes. Distorted and previously conflict-inducing primary process fantasies can be corrected, thereby changing them from previously active motivational organizations into conscious but relatively harmless memory systems of once powerful fantasies" (1993, 123). Kernberg focused his 1993 paper on changes in "dominant transference patterns": "In my view, structural intrapsychic change is represented first in the treatment situation, in significant changes in dominant transference patterns reflecting shifts in the organization of internalized object relations. These shifts differ from the usual repetitive alternations of different transference patterns in that the change appears in response to the psychoanalyst's interpretation of these patterns. Surprisingly new, previously repressed, split off, or projected internalized object relations are revealed that now can be accepted by the patient as part of his conscious repertoire of experience" (1993b, 330). He added, "Change . . . can be evaluated by establishing for each individual patient the dominant internalized object relations activated in the transference, their significant change resulting from interpretation, and the conscious awareness and understanding of previously repressed, split off, or projected aspects of the relevant conflicts. These are the primary indicators of structural intrapsychic change" (336).

Joseph and Anne-Marie Sandler (1993) in turn shifted the focus back to the analysis of resistance, the emphasis made so strongly by Weinshel:

> It has been said that analysis is essentially the analysis of resistance to the analytic work, and there is much truth in this. . . . What is countertherapeutic is to regard them [resistances] as willful obstructiveness on the part of the patient! Resistance in analysis reflects the organized solutions evolved by the patient during the course of development in order to hold himself together and to protect himself from overwhelmingly painful and threatening affective experiences. The giving up of such solutions, which

have worked in the past even though they may have caused suffering, must face the patient with the most painful and threatening feelings which he defended against in the first place. . . . Resistances occur in the here-and-now of the session and always relate to some conflict currently in the patient's mind. Thus resistance always has a transference aspect. (1993, 67)

They added a caveat about how to interpret conflict manifesting via resistance: "Interpretations must be phrased in a way that shows respect for the conflict in the patient, in particular respect for the forces that protect the patient and are in opposition to the current threatening, unconscious wishful fantasy pushing forward for expression in the here-and-now of the analysis. . . . Above all, we need to indicate in some way our appreciation of the fact that there *is* a conflict. Not to do so, to interpret the content of what is being warded off without indicating the analyst's understanding of why the particular impulse or fantasy is being defended against, is countertherapeutic" (69).

Rangell (1993) reemphasized his conception of the often missing link in the chain from interpretation and consequent working through and insight to change—that is, the place of action and ego decision making in effecting real and enduring change (see chapter 10): "The first agent to bring about the beginning and early stages of the psychoanalytic process is the combined effort under the analytic alliance. This bond, which is not there de novo but gradually builds, is between the analyzing function of the analyst . . . and the patient's rational ego, his capacities of observation, discrimination, judgment, and decision making. Every patient fulfilling the criteria for analyzability has a sufficient degree of rational ego available to undertake the task, however compromised his ego functioning is on other scores" (1993, 168). On this base the ego's capacity for "action" and "will" is built: "The ego [of the patient] pulls into a final psychic product the forces impinging upon it from instincts, superego, and the external world, and upon which it has exercised its powers of judgment and discrimination, and it is now ready to act. I have added as indispensable to this functioning the factor of ego will. More specifically psychoanalytic, I have pointed to unconscious ego will, the force in the ego which actively chooses and then executes the behavior chosen" (171). Rangell added that failure to recognize this sequence has created much of our troubles therapeutically: "The automatic connection between interpretation and change, which has become a formula for many analysts, led to failure and disappointment on a widespread basis, which led in its turn to a disillusionment with the effectiveness of psychoanalysis itself" (166).

One of the contributors to the 1993 volume, Kris, made perhaps the most ambitious effort, an attempt to reconceptualize my conceptions of support as elaborated in the write-up of the Menninger Project (Wallerstein 1986a, 1988b) by integrating his conceptions of the needed "affirmative attitude" in psychoanalytic work (see chapter 20) with his elucidations of convergent and divergent conflicts (see chapter 21), and in so doing redefining the notion of support. He began as follows: "I believe that the dichotomy between expressive-interpretive therapy and supportive therapy that was generally accepted by psychoanalysts at the beginning of the 1950s, when the Psychotherapy Research Project of the Menninger Foundation (Wallerstein, 1986a) was undertaken, is misleading. The distinction between expressive and suppressive therapy, on the other hand, seems to me clear and useful, but support may be part of either. Furthermore, interpretation is a powerful means to achieve support and, contrary to the views of the early 1950s, support may be the major focus of expressive therapy" (1993, 95–96). Kris then defined "support" as "a particular experience of patients: a sense of endorsement. Support refers, at the same time, to the interventions that produce this effect. I distinguish support, the patient's sense of endorsement or affirmation by the analyst, from what may be supportive, for, in my view, any helpful component of analytic technique, even if it is immediately stressful, will have its supportive aspects. Interpretation of punitive, unconscious self-criticism (Kris, 1990a), which is common to shame, guilt, humiliation, and depressive affect, necessarily produces the experience of support in the specific sense, when it is made from an affirmative stance (Kohut, 1972), which constitutes a position of *functional* neutrality" (96–97). He continued, "In every analytic instance in which I have tried to account for the occurrence of support, I have come upon the reversal of punitive, unconscious, self-criticism" (98).

Kris then linked this conception of "endorsement" or "affirmation" to his views on divergent conflict: "I shall try to show that the interpretation of punitive, unconscious self-criticism, from a position of functional neutrality, releases the associative process by which divergent conflict gains resolution" (98) and declared that "the reduction in punitive, unconscious self-criticism [also] through *noninterpretive* measures, in situations in which such self-criticism has blocked spontaneous association, may [also] release associative processes sufficiently to produce a therapeutic result" (99, italics added). This in turn leads directly to (structural) change: "I approach the question of change, including 'structural' change, from the perspective of increased freedom of association. . . . Freedom of association correlates with . . . identifiable behavioral changes, such as symptomatic improvement, resumption of interrupted development, and character change" (101). Kris summarized as follows: "I have tried to demonstrate the advantage of defining support as the patient's experience of endorsement and the analyst's intervention that produces it. Support may be produced by interpretation or by nonverbal means, in analysis or outside it. Distinguishing support in a specific sense from generally helpful (and, therefore, supportive) measures, I have tried to demonstrate that support can lead to enduring (structural) psychic change" (112).

The other topic to be discussed in this chapter, the possibilities and conditions of the "conversion" of psychotherapy to psychoanalysis, for a long time was not a focus of analytic interest. Though conversion of psychoanalysis to psychotherapy took place often enough, this was considered an attempt to rectify or rescue a failed or misguided effort at proper psychoanalysis; it was assumed that at least some therapeutic benefit could be garnered from the psychotherapy that was being settled for. However, within a psychoanalytic community still under the influence of Freud's position (solidified by Jones and Glover) that the world of mental treatment was sharply divided between proper psychoanalysis (with all traces of suggestion eschewed and/or expunged) and all the variants of suggestion, and a community subsequently under the sway of Eissler's (1953) directive on the austere (interpretation only) model of proper psychoanalysis, there was little room to think of the possibilities of converting a psychotherapy (inevitably drenched in suggestion and transferential authority, according to those views) into a rigorous, suggestion-free psychoanalysis. At best, when it appeared that a patient in psychotherapy was or had somehow become amenable to psychoanalysis, the conventional wisdom was that an appropriate referral should be made to (another) psychoanalyst for that treatment.

The first mention of this issue was in Gill's landmark paper of 1954. After discussing Eissler's stricture that any "parameter must be capable of being undone, of being drawn into the sphere of explicit transference with interpretation and resolution" (782), Gill wrote, almost as an aside, "Here is the area of problems concerning the possibility of converting a psychotherapy into an analysis" (782)—without any further elaboration. A decade later, Gedo (1964) made a similar point: "The theoretical implications of the possibility of transforming a given case from an unanalysable one to one amenable to psychoanalysis deserve extended scrutiny. The most pertinent point for my thesis is that non-analytic psychotherapeutic techniques are capable of producing permanent structural changes within the mental apparatus. . . . Such structural changes may be extensive enough to constitute an alteration in the resolution of one of the psychosocial crises of the past. In the case of 'preparation for analysis,' it is the crisis of identity which is solved in a new way—by acceptance of the adult identity of a neurotic patient" (536). Here Gedo linked the possibility of structural change *in psychotherapy* to the conversion of the patient from one refractory to one amenable to analysis—and with the implication at least that this could properly proceed with the same therapist (if there were no other disqualifying circumstances), a possibility not even hinted at by Gill a decade earlier.

However, it wasn't until 1983 that an entire paper was devoted to the topic of treatment preparatory to psychoanalysis. Stephen Bernstein defined his topic as follows: "a period of preparatory treatment of certain adult patients which may then progress to an unmodified psychoanalysis—one which proceeds along classical lines—conducted by the same analyst. This extension of technique is applied in the treatment of patients assessed to have unimpaired egos and who are considered classically analyzable except for certain potentially transient resistances to analysis which cause them to refuse psychoanalysis and to request psychotherapy. . . . The underlying problems that bring a patient to treatment often coincide with the issues that make him resistant to analysis" (363–64). He continued, "These patients' resistances are related to the meaning of analysis as it represents the facilitator of a feared regression and the rekindling and reactivation of warded-off libidinal and aggressive impulses and wishes, which are experienced as more controllable in psychotherapy" (366).

While so carefully circumscribing the circumstances in which this once taboo activity (conversion with the same analyst) was advocated, Bernstein described a patient seen for twenty-two once-weekly sessions who was then converted into an analytic patient who went on another four and a half years in a successful psychoanalysis. He concluded, "Increasingly . . . many analysts practicing in the classical tradition have found preparatory treatment compatible with progression to psychoanalysis with the same analyst"—without here marking off so narrowly the kind of patient being considered in this way. But he added, perhaps ruefully, "But neither this process nor the concerns about it have been described to any extent in the literature" (388).

What had transpired in the three decades between Gill's article (1954) and Bernstein's (1983) was not only the increasing prominence of the so-called widening scope patients—that is, the greater willingness to apply psychoanalysis more broadly to patients once thought not suitable for it—but also the diminishing availability of the classically neurotic patients, who once thronged to the available psychoanalytic consulting rooms. In this sense, Bernstein's article finally brought into the open a trend that had been gradually developing and increasing in strength in the everyday realities of clinical practice.

In 1987, Charles P. Fisher published the report of the first panel discussion of the American Psychoanalytic Association focused upon the still somewhat contentious issue of whether such conversion required a transfer of the patient to another analyst: "The more historical and conservative view was that a new analyst is required. The idea that a change in analysts is unnecessary is emerging in recent years as the result of significant conceptual shifts concerning the relation between psychotherapy and psychoanalysis" (713). The several panelists took a variety of stands. Horwitz (whose interest in this issue started with his participation in the Menninger Psychotherapy Research Project) was strongly positive. He traced the uneasiness on this subject to Freud's assumption that the only alternative to psychoanalysis was a therapy based on suggestion. Such a clear dichotomy would make conversion conceptually much less feasible, if possible at all. But, he said, in a psychotherapy "conducted in a nondirective manner by a neutral therapist in which transferences were resolved by interpretation . . . it has become possible to begin thinking about the same therapist converting such treatments to psychoanalysis proper with all the advantages inherent in such a procedure for both patient and analyst. Questions about the scientific validity of this technique may reflect at least in part a continuing failure to differentiate psychoanalytic psychotherapy from treatments based on suggestion, a blurring derived from the earlier decades of psychoanalysis" (1987, 716). There were, according to Horwitz, three classes of patients suitable for conversion: (1) those for whom psychoanalysis is contraindicated but who with psychotherapy can be rendered amenable to it (the patients Gedo seemed to refer to); (2) those for whom practical considerations (e.g., money, time, geographic distance—which may change—preclude daily analysis; and (3) those suitable but unable to make the commitment (the group Bernstein addressed). After describing three successful cases of conversion, "Horwitz commented that it is common to observe a surprisingly marked intensification of the process after conversion. This is reflected in the sudden emergence of regressive transference which 'show the earmarks of accumulated pent-up affects which had not been permitted expression in the prior treatment.' The setting of analysis allows the patient and analyst 'to fully observe and use the regressive developments which otherwise tend to remain latent' " (717)—a testament to the possibly beneficial impact of the prior psychotherapy upon the subsequent psychoanalysis.

E. Ticho (who had also participated in PRP) took a similarly positive stance: "Ticho stressed the need, when considering psychoanalysis with a patient who has previously had psychotherapy, to get a clear idea of the kind of treatment the patient had been exposed to. An advantage of conversion with the same analyst is that one at least knows what kind of therapy the patient had. Ticho's impression is that for those who know how to conduct systematic expressive therapy, there are few difficulties in changing the treatment to psychoanalysis with the same therapist/analyst" (718). Ticho referred to a study of twenty conversions in which he found that "when the expressive therapy was systematic in nature, it had comparatively little influence on the analysis" (719).

Kernberg (the third panel member who had participated in PRP) took a much more cautious and conservative position. He stated, "The abandonment of neutrality and the use of supportive techniques makes it difficult to establish a satisfactory psychoanalytic setting later on. Usually the analyst who has begun seeing a patient in expressive psychotherapy has departed from technical neutrality in significant ways which may distort the transference, making psychoanalysis difficult or impossible. The more neutral the position of the psychotherapist, the easier such a shift will be" (720). In keeping with this more reserved posture, Kernberg offered his prescriptions for carrying out a conversion, should it become desirable and be felt feasible. First, where the psychotherapy has been of some duration, "it may be preferable to terminate the psychotherapy and consider the possibility of starting psychoanalysis later on . . . with a different analyst, after an interval . . . to allow for a consolidation of the effects of the psychotherapy" (721). A second alternative, especially if it involves a shift with the same analyst is to make the shift as early as possible: "It is essential to analyze the patient's reactions to a proposed change, particularly the transference implications" (721). Third, if the analyst is convinced from the start that psychoanalysis is the treatment of choice, he should try to persuade the patient to that effect or, failing that, to suggest that it might be preferable for the patient to wait for more propitious circumstances rather than undertake a treatment that would be "second-best" (for him).

Gill, the fourth panelist, took the opposite position from that of Kernberg, pushing further than Horwitz and Ticho in calling for radical rethinking of traditional views: "The question of converting psychotherapy into psychoanalysis should rarely arise in the practice of a psychoanalyst because he should be almost always practicing psychoanalysis" (722). Gill emphasized that "psychoanalysis should be defined as 'movement in an analytic direction' and not as the achievement of an end point such as 'the development of a regressive transference neurosis and its resolution by techniques of interpretation alone.' A partial analysis is better than none, and one may 'set out to do as much analysis as one can in the given circumstances' " (723). Under what circumstances, then, should one consider a change, and how should any change in the dimensions of treatment be made? "Gill commented, 'it could be that an optimal balance between keeping the situation safe and increasing the pressure to change requires a change in the external circumstances.' It is important to remember that one cannot know how the patient will experience the consideration of such a change. Therefore, 'It is essential to analyze the transference meanings of such a move before making it and of the new transference meanings that appear if it is made.' We cannot take an external situation to have a universal meaning" (724).

In a subsequent paper, specifically on conversion, Gill (1988) offered a full-scale exposition of his familiar (reconceptualized) views on the essential oneness of psychoanalysis and proper psychotherapy, and on the transference as an "integrate of [the patient's] intrapsychic interpersonal schemata and the current situation [in which] the relativity of interpersonal reality is such that the patient's experience is not correctly construed as a distortion of current reality in any simple sense but is rather an idiosyncratic construction of that reality with its own kind of plausibility" (268–69). Within this framework, he reiterated that the analyst should always be trying to practice analysis, that this can be done under a great variety of less than optimal external conditions, and that he should "recognize that analysis is always successful only to a greater or lesser degree, that a partial analysis is better than none, and that even a failed analysis is still an analysis" (266). From this it follows that "my reply to the question of whether psychoanalytic psychotherapy can be converted to analysis is, therefore, that of course it can be, but that if one is practicing analysis [as Gill defines it] in the first place, it will not be necessary. . . . Analysts now behave differently in psychoanalysis and psychoanalytic psychotherapy as conventionally defined. I am advocating that they always do analysis. This doesn't mean that they will behave the same, whatever the circumstances. It does mean that their aim is to look for the transference meanings which can be made explicit to the patient, however much delay is required by considerations of tact and the patient's ability to accept and profit from the insight" (271).

Gill then ended with two vital "empirical questions," both unanswered, that in many ways represent the heart of the modern dilemma about the distinctions among therapeutic modes: "I grant, of course, that if some ill defined range of interactions is exceeded, the effect of the analyst's contribution cannot be significantly resolved by interpretation. The power of interpretation has limits, but what they are is still an empirical question and they may well differ from patient to patient" (269)—that is, that there are indeed influences and, therefore, change forces that are "beyond interpretation" and leave scope for noninterpretive intervention modes. Gill has, of course, tried to minimize these almost out of existence. His second question is, "whether in a particular instance more could have been accomplished in a therapy undertaken with the intent of doing psychoanalytic psychotherapy rather than with the intent of doing analysis which then failed" (272)—again the issue of greater suitability for psychotherapies other than psychoanalysis, even in Gill's sense.

Robert Stolorow's (1990) article on conversion (one of eight articles on this subject comprising an entire issue of *Psychoanalytic Inquiry*) took the same stand as Gill—that one should as much as possible be doing analysis and that conversion, when indicated, was not a very special issue—but came to this position in a quite different way. Stolorow spoke to four assumptions or, as he called them, myths about analysis; accepting and abiding by these myths has created artificial distinctions among therapeutic modes that would naturally lead to the spurious perception of wondering when and how to convert from one to another. These prevailing myths, according to Stolorow, are as follows:

1. "The Myth of the Neutral Analyst," an impossible ideal, striving for which could actually be countertherapeutic ("the so-called regressive transference neurosis, thought by many to be a *sine qua non* of an analytic process, may actually be iatrogenic reactions to the indiscriminate application of the principle of abstinence. Thus an attitude of abstinence not only may fail to facilitate the analytic process; it may be inherently inimical to it," 120)[3]

2. "The Myth of Interpretation Without Suggestion," which "creates a false dichotomy" because "each time the analyst offers an interpretation that goes beyond what the patient is consciously aware of, he invites the patient to see things, if ever so slightly, from the analyst's own theory-rooted perspective. To that extent, *interpretations are suggestions*" (123–24)

3. "The Myth of Uncontaminated Transference." "When transference is conceived not as displacement (or regression, or projection, or distortion), but as an expression of unconscious organizing activity . . . then it becomes apparent that the transference is shaped *both* by contributions from the analyst *and* the structures of meaning into which these are assimilated by the patient. . . . the countertransference (broadly conceptualized as a manifestation of the analyst's organizing activity) has a decisive impact in shaping the transference. Transference and countertransference together form an intersubjective system of reciprocal mutual influence" (125–26)

4. "The Myth of the Analyzable (or Unanalyzable) Patient." "Diagnoses and assessments of analyzability that are based on transference are, in a very profound sense, relative to the particular patient-analyst dyad— the specific intersubjective system—in which they take form" (128); therefore, "analyzability is a property not of the patient alone, but of the patient-analyst system. . . . —which can lead even to the extreme statement that, while there are doubtless some patients who could be analyzed only by the most gifted of analysts, I believe that, in principle, anyone with an intact nervous system is analyzable by *someone*" (129)[4]

3. For a less revisionist perspective on issues of analytic abstinence and neutrality, see J. and A-M. Sandler, 1992.
4. This last statement is quite different indeed from Weinshel's (1992) view that over the past few decades there has been "a relatively unobtrusive campaign to bring psychoanalysis within a more realistic—and modest—frame of reference . . . a corrective to the unrealistic goals and

Given these views, it follows that Stolorow sees the task of the analyst very differently from those who aspire to a blameless neutrality, and this impacts on how the issue of conversion is seen. According to Stolorow, "What the analyst can and should strive for in his self-reflective efforts is awareness of his own personal organizing principles—including those enshrined in his theories—and of how these principles are unconsciously shaping his analytic understandings and interpretations. . . . the analytic stance is best conceptualized as an attitude of sustained empathic inquiry—an attitude, that is, that consistently seeks to comprehend the meaning of the patient's expressions from a perspective within, rather than outside, the patient's own subjective frame of reference" (122–23). From this framework, "converting psychotherapy to psychoanalysis does not in principle pose technical problems that substantially differ from those arising from any other contribution of the analyst to the intersubjective system. The transference meanings of the previous nonanalytic procedures, of the newly assumed analytic stance, and of the change from the former to the latter should all be investigated in detail" (127). That is, the issue of conversion is not a special problem at all.

Arthur Malin (1990), in his epilogue to this sequence of papers in *Psychoanalytic Inquiry,* said, "The contributors accept the proposition that the conversion of psychotherapy to psychoanalysis is a legitimate endeavor, even with the same therapist, and is not necessarily doomed to failure. . . . Conversion of psychotherapy to psychoanalysis has clearly become a common procedure. . . . The change might well be based on economic considerations and the availability of cases, or perhaps on the widening scope; in any event, the overall direction seems to be toward approving conversion to analysis with the same therapist" (135). And Oremland (1991) took the same stand, of "strong support for the compatibility of psychotherapy with subsequent psychoanalysis by the same practitioner when the psychotherapy was not overly interactive and manipulative" (129–30). Perhaps the fitting last note on this major change in psychoanalytic views on conversion should be from Simons' (1990) paper on ideals and idealizations in our psychoanalytic heritage: "The earlier conviction that conversion from psychotherapy to psychoanalysis ideally and invariably required the transfer of the patient to another analyst may have been based on a series of idealizations of both theory and technique" (26).

---

expectations that characterized the early history of psychoanalysis in the United States" (330). For a fuller statement of these views, see Weinshel, 1990a.

The authors discussed in the preceding three chapters have all focused in one way or another on the ever more detailed elucidation of the therapeutic process and interaction. Over recent decades, and especially in the past ten years, there has been a concomitant development of systematic, formal *research* into the processes of psychoanalytic therapies, most of it based on audio- or videotapes of therapeutic hours, including some entire analyses—transcribed then to research standards and subjected to varieties of highly sophisticated, computer-assisted study. Most such formal research studies have been conducted in the United States and Germany and some in the United Kingdom, the Scandinavian countries, Holland, Switzerland, and Italy.[1] Alongside this vast clinical and now also research literature on the therapeutic process, a body of contributions has grown on the outcomes of psychoanalysis and, more recently, of psychoanalytic psychotherapies, as assessed primarily at treatment termination but also at planned follow-up. Though most of this literature has been conceived within an explicitly research framework, a continuing clinical and theoretical interest also exists in issues of outcome.

Before discussing these, I will first cite the interrelated definitional, conceptual, methodological, and practical considerations that necessarily interlock with any discussion of the efficacy (i.e., the outcomes) of psychoanalysis and of the linked psychoanalytic psychotherapies as treatment modalities. These include

1. The *goals* of these modalities, both ideal and practical (realizable) (see Wallerstein 1965, 1992b)
2. The issues of suitability or *treatability* as against *analyzability*, which are not the same thing, though the two are often conflated

1. See *Psychoanalytic Process Research Studies* (1988), edited by Hartvig Dahl, Horst Kachele, and Helmut Thoma from the proceedings of an American-German conference on psychoanalytic process research held in July 1985, as well as, for more particular focus on highly productive process research groups, the books by Luborsky et al. at the University of Pennsylvania (1984, 1988, 1990) and by Horowitz et al. at the University of California San Francisco (1979, 1984, 1991). For an overview of a plan to bring together a consortium of sixteen psychoanalytic process and outcome research groups (fifteen in the United States and one in the United Kingdom), each of which would apply its own concepts and instruments to a common data base of transcribed therapeutic hours, in order to contrast and compare their observations and findings in regard to the *same* clinical material, see the research proposal for funding support crafted by Wallerstein (unpubl. ms c).

3. *The indications and contraindications* for these treatments as they have evolved over time, including the issues of *widening or narrowing scope* for analytic treatment and of so-called heroic indications for analysis

4. The role of the initial *diagnostic and evaluation procedures* in *differential treatment planning* (as opposed to the view that only a trial of analysis or trial of treatment can lead to proper formulation and prognostication)

5. The place then of *prediction* (including the question of predictability) in relation to issues of outcome, expectable reach, and limitation (see Wallerstein 1964)

6. The *theory of technique,* how treatment works, by what procedures it achieves its goals—a statement, that is, of the relationship of means to ends

7. The *similarities and differences* between psychoanalysis and the dynamic psychotherapies from the viewpoint of the therapeutic goals projected for patients with differing illness pictures and character organizations

8. The *criteria* for satisfactory treatment termination

9. The *evaluation of results,* a conceptual as well as technical issue, involving assessment of *therapeutic benefit* as against *analytic completeness* in terms of the resolution of intrapsychic conflict and structural changes in the ego

10. What theoretically constitutes the *ideal state of mental health* and the unavoidable impingements on efforts to assess it empirically by value judgments as well as by the vantage point and partisan interests of the judge (see Wallerstein 1963)

11. The place of *follow-up* assessment as a desirable, feasible, and appropriate activity (or not) in relation to psychoanalytic therapies, for research and/or clinical purposes (see Wallerstein 1989b, 1992c)

12. The place of the continuing accretion of experience and knowledge in relation to all these areas by the traditional *case study method* innovated by Freud, as against the desirability of or need for more *formal, systematic clinical research* into these issues by methods that are responsive to the subtlety and complexity of the subjectivistic clinical phenomena, yet remain loyal to the canons of empirical science (see Wallerstein and Sampson 1971).

The first substantial reports on psychoanalytic outcomes were actually incidental to Freud's original case descriptions, particularly the Dora case (1905a), which he acknowledged to be unsuccessful owing to his failure to deal with the burgeoning negative transference; the Rat Man (1909b), a declared treatment success in a young Austrian army officer whose life was abruptly ended a few years later in World War I; and the Wolf-Man (1918), an equivocal and problematic outcome in a patient subsequently seen by Freud, by Ruth Mack Brunswick, and then by Muriel Gardiner (see *The Wolf-Man* by The Wolf-Man, edited by Gardiner [1971], and *The Wolf-Man, Sixty Years Later* by Karin Obholzer [1980]). Follow-up, however, except where adventitious, was for long not a matter of psychoanalytic attention or concern. In fact, the conventional wisdom of the field, justified on grounds of theory and supported by the practical considerations of the usual private practice setting, was that postanalytic contact between analyst and analysand was ideally to be avoided. As early as 1924, Ferenczi and Rank stated that, because the resolution of the transference was taken as the proper end point of analysis, "the 'ideal case' in analytic, in contrast to medical, practice is that of the patient who having once been treated is never seen again, best cured when one never hears from him again." They immediately added, however, "This result . . . presupposes a power of sublimation and renunciation on the part of the patient such as is not given to all people" (8).

Freud, however, never seemed bound by such rigid and absolute ideals, and there are some posttreatment data on all of his best-known case histories. In the case of Dora, who abruptly broke off her three-month-long treatment because of unrecognized negative transference identification of Freud with her would-be seducer, Herr K., Freud (1905a) wrote in a postscript, "It was not until fifteen months after the case was over and this paper composed that I had news of my patient's condition and the effects of my treatment . . . Dora came to see me again: to finish her story and to ask for help once more. One glance at her face, however, was enough to tell me that she was not in earnest over her request" (120–21). He then detailed the intervening events in Dora's life, including her subsequent contacts with Herr and Frau K., and ended by stating that years had gone by since that visit and that in the meantime Dora had married—he did not state how he had heard this.

Little Hans also paid a subsequent visit to Freud, who described it thus: "A few months ago—in the spring of 1922—a young man introduced himself to me and informed me that he was the 'little Hans' whose infantile neurosis had been the subject of the paper which I published in 1909[a]. I was very glad to see him again, for about two years after the end of his analysis I had lost sight of him and had heard nothing of him for more than ten years." Freud was glad to be able to publish an account of this follow-up interview, since he was clearly smarting under what he called the "great stir and even greater indignation" his original case report had aroused; "a most evil future . . . [had been] foretold for the poor little boy, because he had been 'robbed of his innocence' at such a tender age and had been made the victim of psychoanalysis" (148). Freud could now say that "none of these apprehensions had come true. Little Hans was now a strapping youth of nineteen. He declared that he was perfectly well, and suffered from no troubles or inhibitions." In fact, it was never made clear what need or wish had prompted this return visit. Freud did find one piece of information quite remarkable. When he had read his case history, Little Hans did not recognize himself and could remember nothing of his treatment; his amnesia for the analysis was complete, Freud said, "so the analysis had not preserved the events from amnesia, but had been overtaken by amnesia itself" (1922, 148–49).

The Wolf-Man had a far longer and more extensive follow-up study. The original course of treatment lasted from February 1910 to July 1914, and the retreatment by Freud from November 1919 to February 1920 (Freud 1918, 122). The subsequent treatment by Ruth Mack Brunswick (October 1926 to February 1927) and periodic quasi-therapeutic follow-up contacts through the whole course of the Wolf-Man's life, together with the Wolf-Man's memories, have all been brought together in a book edited by Muriel Gardiner (1971). Gardiner noted (1971) that this was the most fully documented of all psychoanalytic cases, "the only case which has been followed from infancy to old age" (v), and Anna Freud stated in her foreword, "We have before us the unique opportunity to see an analytic patient's inner as well as outer life unfold before our eyes, starting out from his own childhood memories and the picture of his childhood neurosis, taking us through the major and minor incidents of his adulthood, and leading from there, almost uninterruptedly, to a concluding period when 'The Wolf-Man Grows Older' " (xii). The Wolf-Man died in May 1979 at the age of ninety-two, and in 1983, Gardiner published her account, "The Wolf-Man's Last Years."

None of these postanalytic encounters between Freud and his patients was planned, however. This was characteristic of most other analysts as well, who at times had chance meetings with previous analysands and took the occasion to publish accounts of these cases. The best known is Helene Deutsch's 1959 report on two young female patients, both presumably successfully analyzed, who returned for interviews twenty-five and twenty-seven years after termination. According to Deutsch, although "the analytic literature is rich in case histories . . . there is . . . an evident lack of information about the postanalytic psychic state of patients whose treatment has been successfully terminated" (445). The first case was a twenty-year-old suicidal woman whose treatment had ended with a feeling of complete success. The posttermination interview, after twenty-five years during which there had been no contact between them, apparently was not held at the patient's wish but was, rather, "a coincidence" (452); Deutsch stated that from her own side she had anticipated this interview with some foreboding. Although the ex-patient was hostile and derogatory regarding her old analysis, it nonetheless appeared to have been a stable therapeutic success; the structures of the old neurosis were still visible, but they were now handled by "ego-syntonic" defenses, the "results of constructive sublimations" (454).

The other patient, also declared successfully analyzed, had maintained a different postanalytic relationship with Deutsch: "I was informed about all the important events in her life; she sent me photographs of her children and asked my advice whenever she needed it" (454). Then, "after an interval of twenty-seven years I received a letter containing complaints for the first time" (456). The original neurotic symptoms had first erupted around the patient's menarche with all its multidetermined meanings for her; the recrudescence was now around her menopause and her oldest daughter's menarche. Deutsch's conclusion after the follow-up interview was, "[The patient] could remain healthy as long as she could make use of her formerly neurotically distorted physiologic functions in a normal, active manner. However, when the menopause confronted her with the fact that her active functions as a woman must come to an end, the regressive forces were revived and created neurotic difficulties similar to those in her puberty. The achievement of the analysis could not withstand the biologic assault and proved reversible" (457).

It was Glover who, as recently as 1954, was the first to attack forthrightly the prevailing psychoanalytic view that *planned* follow-up would make resolution of the transference neurosis more difficult and thus would complicate both the termination phase of the analysis and the possibilities for maximal postanalytic consolidation; Glover pointed rather to the clinical opportunity and need for an adequate "after-history." "Like most psychotherapists," he wrote, "the psychoanalyst is a reluctant and inexpert statistician. No accurate records or after-histories of psychoanalytical treatment exist: such rough figures as can be obtained do not suggest that psychoanalysis is notably more successful than other forms of therapy: and in any case none of the figures is corrected for spontaneous remission or resolution of symptoms" (393). For adults, "an after-history of *at least five years* is essential. Unfortunately, it has to be admitted that satisfactory after-histories are seldom forthcoming; consequently our knowledge of the therapeutic range of psychoanalysis is vitiated by unchecked surmise which too often errs on the side of complacency . . . the success of a child analysis cannot be satisfactorily checked until an after-history of *15 years* has been secured" (398, italics added)—that is, until the developmental process has carried the child to adulthood.

In contrast to follow-up study, evaluation of the efficacy of psychoanalytic treatments has always been an accepted aspect of clinical practice and thinking, but because of its seeming (merely) behavioral or external frame it has usually been viewed as only a practical consideration, not a theoretically very interesting one. Actually, as early as 1917, within the first decade of the introduction of psychoanalysis in America, Isador Coriat reported on the therapeutic results achieved in ninety-three cases. Based on his "personal investigation and experience" (209), 73 percent were declared either recovered or much improved, and these rates were nearly equal across all his diagnostic categories, though the more severe cases required longer treatment. As in all the early statistical studies noted here (which I call the first-generation research studies), the judgments of improvement were made by the treating clinician according to (usually) unspecified criteria and with no clinical details or supporting evidence to enable the reader to comprehend the basis for the judgment or to form his own conclusion.

In the 1930s, several comparable (but larger scale) reports emerged from the collective experiences of the treatment clinics of some of the pioneering psychoanalytic training institutes. Fenichel (1930) reported on the experience of the Berlin Institute, the first formally organized psychoanalytic training institute in the world. During its first decade, 1,955 consultations were conducted and 721 patients were accepted for analysis; 60 percent of the psychoneurotic cases, but only 23 percent of those classified as psychotic, were judged to have received substantial therapeutic benefits.[2] Essentially the same proportions in these two major diagnostic groupings were declared to be unchanged or worse—22 percent and 24 percent, respectively. Six years later, Jones (1936) reported on 738 applicants to the London Psychoanalytic Clinic, of whom 74 were taken into psychoanalysis. Forty-seven percent of the neurotic cases were judged to have benefited substantially, with only 10 percent judged unimproved or worse. Of the 15 so-called psychotic cases, all but one were treatment failures. The year after that, Alexander (1937) reported on 157 cases from the Chicago Psychoanalytic Clinic. Here, 63 percent of the neurotic cases, 40 percent of the psychotic, and 77 percent of those designated psychosomatic were judged to have received substantial therapeutic benefit, with no more than 10 percent in any category judged unchanged or worse. During this same period, L. Kessel and H. Hyman (1933), two internists who followed up 29 cases whom they had referred for psychoanalysis, again reported the neurotic cases to have benefited (all but two) and the psychotic ones unchanged or worse.

In a 1941 review article evaluating the results of psychoanalysis, Knight combined the findings of the Berlin, London, Chicago, and Kessel and Hyman studies and added 100 cases treated at the Menninger Clinic between 1932 and

2. "Psychotic" here is to be taken as ambulatory and in some sense functioning in the community though considered psychotic from the standpoint of the quality of mental life.

1941, where the overall results were judged to be comparable to those of the other studies in the observed outcomes with neurotic and psychotic cases. The composite tabulation comprised 952 cases, classified as neurotic, psychotic, psychosomatic, and other by whatever (unspecified) criteria governed the original judgments. The combined substantial-benefit rate was approximately 60 percent for the neurotics, close to 80 percent for the psychosomatics, and only 25 percent for the psychotics, with about 20 percent unchanged or worse among both the neurotic and psychotic groups. Knight made particular reference to the pitfalls of these simple statistical summaries: the absence of consensually agreed upon definitions and criteria, the crudity of nomenclature and case classification, and the failure to consider the experience and skill of the therapists in relation to cases of varying degrees of severity.

The most ambitious of these first-generation studies was the report of the Ad Hoc Committee on Central Fact-Gathering Data of the American Psychoanalytic Association (Hamburg et al. 1967).[3] This committee, established in 1952, collected data over a five-year span and produced a report in 1958 (unpublished). The data consisted of 10,000 initial responses to detailed questionnaires submitted by the 350 then-members of the American and the 450 then-candidates in training, plus approximately 3,000 termination questionnaires submitted upon treatment completion. The criteria for both diagnosis and improvement were unspecified (as in all the previous studies), and numerous flaws in the original questionnaire construction led to many unintended confusions, ambiguities, and omissions in the responses, which led to the original decision against scientific publication of the findings.

In the early 1960s, a successor committee was formed to review the data in order to salvage what was still scientifically useful and publishable. The Hamburg committee ultimately produced an "experience survey" of American psychoanalysis circa the fifties comprising facts about the demographics and the sociology of analytic practice, analysts' opinions on their patients' diagnoses, and analysts' opinions on the therapeutic results achieved. Judgments were made about changes in symptoms, in the patients' feeling states, in their character structures, and in their total functioning. Not unexpectedly, the great majority were declared substantially improved.

And finally, in 1968 Fred Feldman reported on the results of the psychoanalysis of all 120 patients referred on the basis of 960 evaluations in the clinic

---

3. Though the span from Coriat (1917) to this study (1967) is a half-century, I call them all first generation in terms of the degree of conceptual and methodological sophistication they represent, rather than in temporal terms (though of course each generation was either initiated at a later point in time than its predecessor or spanned a later period of time).

of the Southern California Psychoanalytic Institute in its eleven-year history. The patients seemed to have been more comprehensively evaluated and studied than those in the earlier reports, having been chosen after four to five hours of group interviews and committee discussions, followed by a careful review of the detailed semiannual institute reports gathered as long as they were still clinic patients and their analysts not yet graduated. (Some of the patients could be followed into private practice status after the institute graduation of the analysts.) Efforts were made to specify improvement criteria in the poor, fair, good, and very good categories. Difficulties were experienced for the research owing to lack of clear and agreed-upon criteria, concepts, and language for diagnostic assessment, analyzability, and analytic results. Improvement rates reported were again comparable to those of all the preceding studies, two-thirds being in the good or very good categories.

Taken together, these first-generation outcome and efficacy studies, actually spanning a half-century, were scientifically simplistic and failed to command the interest of the psychoanalytic clinical world. Most apparently agreed with Glover's (1954) ironic and dour assessment: "Like most psychotherapists, the psychoanalyst is a reluctant and inexpert statistician" (393)—and, one could add, researcher. Such conclusions spurred what I call the second-generation studies, efforts at more formal and systematic outcome research, geared to overcome the glaring methodological simplicity that marked the studies described to this point.

The methodological flaws in the first-generation type statistical enumerations of psychoanalytic outcomes have been indicated. In addition to the lack of consensually agreed-upon criteria at almost every step—from initial diagnosis and assessment of analyzability to outcome judgments of therapeutic benefit and analytic result—and the use of these judgments by the (necessarily biased) therapist, usually as the sole evidential primary data source, there is the further methodologic difficulty that these studies were all retrospective, with all the potential that implies for bias, confounding, and contamination of judgments, *post hoc, ergo propter hoc* reasoning and justification, and so on. Efforts to address these issues, including the introduction of methods of prospective inquiry and even the fashioning of predictions to be validated or refuted by subsequent assessment, began in earnest in the 1950s and 1960s. Three major projects based on studies of clinic cases from the Boston, Columbia, and New York Psychoanalytic Institutes stand out as representatives of this second-generation research approach.

In 1960, Peter Knapp and his colleagues reported on 100 supervised psychoanalytic cases from the Boston Psychoanalytic Institute Clinic, rated initially (prospectively) for suitability for analysis. Twenty-seven of these were followed up a year later by questionnaires addressed to the treating analysts in order to ascertain how suitable the patient had turned out to be—as discernible at this relatively early treatment point. To avoid the dangers of *post hoc* reasoning and reconstructive rationalization, the evaluation procedures (initial committee judgments on suitability and subsequent judgments of the treating analysts' questionnaire responses) were blind and made by different judges in almost all instances. There turned out to be fair but limited success in assessing suitability for analysis at the initial evaluation. However, two significant limitations of this study should be noted. First, the testing of the predictions took place at only the one-year mark in treatment rather than more suitably at termination; clearly much can change—in both directions—later in the analysis. Second (and this is an issue in all research on this model), the cases selected by clinic committees for student analyses are already carefully screened and obviously unsuitable cases already rejected. The range of variability in the accepted cases is thus relatively narrow, making differential prediction within that group inherently less reliable.

Jerome Sashin and his colleagues (1975), inspired by this work, subsequently studied 183 cases treated at the same clinic over the years 1959–66. Final data were collected on 130 cases (72 percent) after an average of 675 treatment hours and at a point averaging 6 years after treatment termination. The authors' goal was to conduct a "quantitative systematic study . . . [of the] patient factor predictability of outcome" (345). Predictor variables were assessed by a 103-item questionnaire based on six major outcome criteria, first elaborated by Knight (1941): restriction of functioning by symptoms, subjective discomfort, work productivity, sexual adjustment, interpersonal relationships, and availability of insight, each criterion fashioned into a 5-point rating scale. Only 10 of the items demonstrated some predictive value in relation to assessed outcomes, and that with only modest (albeit statistically significant) correlations. These few relationships, which might have appeared on the basis of chance alone, were studied to determine if they could be meaningfully understood in clinical terms but the grouping "made little clinical sense." Overall, these two Boston Institute studies yielded only fair prediction to judgments of analyzability as assessed at the one-year mark in treatment, and no effective prediction to treatment outcomes from the patients' characteristics as judged at initial evaluation. Nor was any effort made to distinguish therapeutic benefit from the successful navigation of an analytic process over the treatment course.

The Columbia Psychoanalytic Center project, contemporaneous with the Boston studies, was written up in a sequence of publications in 1985 (Weber et al. 1985c, 1985a, 1985b, and Bachrach et al. 1985), reporting the characteristics of the patients, the outcome study from sample one (1,348 patients treated between 1945 and 1962), the outcome study—by somewhat altered and improved criteria—from sample two (237 patients treated between 1962 and

1971), and finally a clinical and methodological review with recommendations for future directions. These were geared to be prospective studies of large numbers of patients, with data collected from multiple perspectives over time (initially and upon treatment completion), with opportunities to compare findings from those in psychoanalysis (about 40 percent of the total sample) with the findings of those in psychoanalytic psychotherapy, all treated by the same body of therapists. The authors stated that all previous studies had been limited in at least one of the following ways: small sample size, inadequate range of information about outcomes, not based on terminated cases, or restricted by retrospective data. And no other study had permitted comparison between large numbers of terminated analyses and psychotherapies conducted by the same analysts. Also, this study established criteria for therapeutic benefit distinct from criteria for analyzability. Criteria of *therapeutic benefit* comprised the circumstances of treatment termination, clinical judgments of overall improvement, and change scores on various indices of improvement. Criteria of an evolved *analytic process* (analyzability) comprised judgments about patterns of handling psychological data, enhanced flexibility in use of ego resources, and transference manifestations during treatment.

A most striking finding from this project was that the therapeutic benefit measures across every category of patient substantially exceeded the analyzability measures. For example, only 40 percent of those who completed analyses with good therapeutic benefit were characterized as having been "analyzed" by the project criteria.[4] An equally striking finding was that the outcome of these treatments was only marginally predictable from the initial evaluation, whether employing the direct predictions by the clinic's admissions service chief or the various presumed research predictor variables. This was, of course, fully in keeping with the Boston Institute studies—and was presumably based on the same factors. As the authors cautiously stated (Weber et al. 1985a), "The prudent conclusion from these findings is *not* that therapeutic benefit or analyzability [is] *per se* unpredictable, but that once a case has been carefully selected as suitable for analysis by a candidate, its eventual fate remains relatively indeterminate" (135).

Another finding of interest was that "retrospective assessments of patient qualities by the treating analyst show a more substantial relationship to outcome than assessments made at the beginning of treatment" (136). This could be a result of the greater accuracy of the retrospective judgments at termination, their greater contamination by knowledge of outcome, or some undetermined ad-

---

4. See in this connection the very comparable findings from the Menninger Psychotherapy Research Project (chapter 8 above and Wallerstein 1986a, 1988b).

mixture of the two. More expected was the finding that those selected for psychoanalysis were assessed initially as functioning at higher levels than those selected for psychotherapy and achieved greater therapeutic benefit than the latter, especially when the analyses continued beyond the candidates' graduation and into their private practice. This positive correlation between therapeutic benefit and treatment length did not hold for the psychotherapies in the same way. The authors suggested that "treatment length and therapeutic benefit are . . . related for psychoanalysis, but perhaps not necessarily [related] for other psychotherapies where progression does not pivot upon a natural process requiring years to evolve" (136–37)—a conclusion to which many might take exception.

In conclusion, the authors noted that their sample was three times larger than any previously published and that it was the first to have a psychotherapy comparison group and one of the first to make the conceptual distinction between analyzability and therapeutic benefit. They did state as a major limitation that there could be only "the most rudimentary exploration of the contribution of the analyst's qualities to the treatment process" and that "there are also matters of changing life circumstances and the analyst-analysand match to be considered" (138)—omissions that can be major contributors to the poor level of prediction of treatment outcomes. Sample two was a smaller sample, gathered a decade later, with some refinements in methods of data collection and some differences in observational vantage points, but in almost every particular all the findings of sample one were replicated. Overall, the conclusion from both samples—over a more than twenty-five year span—was that "a substantially greater proportion of analysands derive therapeutic benefit than develop an analytic process, and that the development of an analytic process is associated with the highest levels of therapeutic benefit. Yet, what we do not yet know precisely is the nature and quality of therapeutic benefit associated with the development of an analytic process and without its development" (Weber et al. 1985b, 261).[5]

The final article by the Columbia authors in their series of four (Bachrach et al. 1985) was devoted to a review of clinical and methodological considerations. They stressed the advantages of their project over other comparable studies: (1) that the *N* was very large, (2) that it was a prospective study with preset hypotheses and with predictive evaluations done before outcomes were known, (3) that they used many (clinically meaningful) scales, (4) that in addition to evaluations by patients and therapists, they used independent judges, and (5) that psychoanalysis and psychotherapy were comparatively assessed. They ac-

5. This last issue is the central focus of PRP-II the current San Francisco research group described by Wallerstein (1988c), DeWitt et al. (1991), and Zilberg et al. (1991).

knowledged that their central evidential base consisted of the judgments of clinicians assessing cases in their customary ways and then expressing their judgments on quantitative dimensions—that is, trying to make their clinical opinions reliable and comparable through the use of standardized quantitative rating scales. This they felt made the work also clinically relevant: "It is precisely because our methodology pivoted upon a clinical survey of psychoanalysts about their own cases . . . and was consistently framed according to standard clinical precepts, that we believe our findings bear correspondence to the findings of psychoanalytic research proper" (381)—that is, the findings from the traditional psychoanalytic case study method.

The most important substantive conclusion from the project was that "some patients treated by psychoanalysis develop an analytic process and achieve therapeutic benefit, while others achieve therapeutic benefit while not apparently developing an analytic process. By analytic process we refer essentially to a collaborative endeavor between analyst and analysand in which increasingly intense and cyclic analysis of resistance and transference in free association evolves into the development of a transference neurosis and transference phenomena, and where continued analysis leads towards enhanced awareness and mastery of intrapsychic conflict which we conceptualize as structural change. . . . By therapeutic benefit we refer to the non-specific amelioration of symptoms and the general improvement in the mental economy of patients" (382). Almost equally important was the finding that the predictability of these developments "remains relatively indeterminate *among carefully selected cases*" (381) or, stated alternatively, that "most suitably selected patients treated by psychoanalysis achieved substantial gains; though the level of these gains is no more than marginally predictable from the perspective of initial evaluation" (386).

The New York Psychoanalytic Institute studies (Erle 1979; Erle and Goldberg 1979, 1984) were very similarly constituted, though with more focus on the study of treatments carried out by more experienced analysts. They began (Erle and Goldberg 1979) with a comprehensive and sophisticated discussion of the conceptual and methodological issues involved in proper outcome research, which at the end they summarized as follows: "In a review and discussion of the problems in the assessment of analyzability . . . we noted: (a) a lack of consistency in the definition of terms; (b) difficulty developing and validating criteria for patient selection; (c) the assumption that prediction of analyzability is, or might be, reliably made at the outset of treatment; (d) failure to differentiate between analyzability and therapeutic benefit; (e) the need for a prospective study which would assess all phases of an analysis: selection, prediction, analytic process, and outcome" (Erle and Goldberg 1984, 315).

The first of their two studies (Erle 1979) consisted of a sample of 40 supervised analytic cases selected from 870 applicants to the Treatment Center of the New York Psychoanalytic Institute over a two-and-a-half-year span in the late 1960s. The results were comparable to those of the Boston and Columbia centers. Twenty-five of the patients terminated satisfactorily, but only 11 of these were considered complete; 24 of the patients were judged to have benefited substantially, but only 17 were judged to have been involved in a proper psychoanalytic process. Those who stayed in treatment for longer periods were judged to be more suitable and had better outcomes, though 3 of the 9 who were in treatment for more than six years were declared to have benefited substantially in an intensive psychotherapeutic sense, but were judged to be not analyzed or analyzable. A sample of 42 *private patients* from seven analyst colleagues who started in the same calendar period and were assessed in the same manner as the Treatment Center patients showed substantially comparable results.

The second study (Erle and Goldberg 1984) extended the work to a sample of 160 private patients gathered over a subsequent five-year span from 16 cooperating experienced analysts. The treating analysts' evaluations ranged from patients "made for analysis" to those taken into analysis on the basis of "heroic" indications (722). The outcomes were completely comparable to results of earlier studies of clinic patients treated by candidates.

Over a time span parallel to these relatively large sample outcome studies, which were assessed by pre- and/or posttreatment rating scales and statistically aggregated, Pfeffer at the same New York Treatment Center initiated a quite different kind of outcome and follow-up study of terminated psychoanalysis by intensive individual case studies of a small research-procured population (Pfeffer 1959, 1961, 1963). His first report was of nine patients who had completed analyses under the auspices of the New York Treatment Center and who agreed to a series of weekly follow-up interviews by a "follow-up analyst" who had not conducted the treatment. The interviews were open-ended and were considered analytic in the sense that they were "structured around the issue of results, but remain[ed] unstructured within this framework in that the patient . . . [took] the lead in introducing and elaborating various themes relating to results" (1959, 420). The interviews ranged from two to seven in number before the participants agreed upon a natural close. The chief finding, in *all* instances, was that characteristic analytic transferences were rapidly reactivated, including even acute and transitory symptom flare-ups, as if in relation to the original treating analyst, and rapidly subsided, at times with the aid of pertinent interpretations, and in a manner that indicated the new ways of neurotic conflict management achieved in the analysis. And therefore, "those aspects of the transference neurosis that are unanalyzed remain organized as transference residues which are available for neurotic reactions in certain life situations" (437).

In the last of his three reports (1963), Pfeffer essayed a metapsychological explanation of these "follow-up study transference phenomena": "The recurrence in the follow-up study of the major preanalytic symptomatology in the context of a revived transference neurosis as well as the quick subsidence of symptoms appear to support the idea that conflicts underlying symptoms are not actually shattered or obliterated by analysis but rather are only better mastered with new and more adequate solutions" (234). The neurotic conflicts thus "lose their poignancy" (237). The metapsychological explanation offered was that "in the regression of the analytic process the person of the analyst initially becomes the present-day representative of the oedipal father of the past. Then with the resolution of the transference the analyst becomes, in addition, the father in relation to whom the oedipus complex is resolved. In the course of the analysis, the person of the analyst becomes, and after the analysis remains, it is here suggested, a permanent intrapsychic image intimately connected with both the regressively experienced conflicts and the resolution of these conflicts in the progression achieved" (238).

Two other research groups, one in San Francisco and one in Chicago, replicated the Pfeffer studies with slight alterations in method and confirmed what has come to be called "the Pfeffer phenomenon." In the San Francisco studies (Oremland et al. 1975 and Norman et al. 1976) the subjects were chosen from among individuals who, it was agreed, had been successfully analyzed; yet "specific areas of incompleteness were discovered" when these cases were called back for restudy (Oremland et al., 820). The group concluded that "the transference neurosis is not obliterated during analysis. Rather, the patient experiences, understands, and senses varying degrees of control over it—i.e., it becomes a structure that comes under the control of the unconscious ego" (Norman et al., 491). "The infantile neurosis had not disappeared. What had changed was the degree to which it affected [the patient's] everyday life" (492). The Chicago study (Schlessinger and Robbins 1974, 1975, 1983), with a more developmental focus, more specified and focused change criteria, and a larger sample, also confirmed the Pfeffer findings: "Psychic conflicts were not eliminated in the analytic process. The clinical material of the follow-ups demonstrated a repetitive pattern of conflicts. Accretions of insight were evident but the more significant outcome of the analysis appeared to be the development of a preconsciously active self-analytic function, in identification with the analyzing function of the analyst, as a learned mode of coping with conflicts. . . . The resources gained in the analytic process persisted, and their vitality was evident in response to renewed stress" (Schlessinger and Robbins 1983, 9). This focus on the development of the self-analytic function (at least to some degree) as a proper and expectable outcome in successful analysis has also been highlighted by Maria Kramer (1959) and Gertrude Ticho (1967). The overall finding from all three research studies, that even in analyses considered highly successful neurotic conflicts are not obliterated or shattered but are tamed or muted or lose their poignancy, is echoed in the well-known analytic quip that we all still recognize our good friends after their analyses.

Characteristic of all these second-generation studies, whether broad, group-aggregated statistical accountings or individually focused, in-depth research studies, is the failure to conceptually or practically separate outcome results discerned at treatment termination from the fate of those results as revealed at some established follow-up point—whether consolidation and further enhancement of treatment gains, the simple maintenance of treatment achievements, or regression toward the pretreatment state. Conceptually, this was a failure to accord specific theoretical status to what Rangell (1966) has called the "postanalytic phase." Rangell (1990, 718–25) described several possible courses that can characterize this phase. Some analyses are finished with no returns by the former patient. In other cases the door is clearly left open for any returns that might be indicated. For example, "It is frequently the case that a patient with an optimum ending will call again, even years later, for a specific and localized need to which he is immediately accessible. The path between the analyst and the patient's unconscious can remain surprisingly open, so that a 'deep interpretation' may be made almost at once [in a single interview] with convincing receptivity and effective results" (719). If this is not possible, if there is too rigid an avoidance of further contact, there may have been a flaw and a major incompleteness in the termination. In still other cases the analytic relationship is succeeded by a social or interprofessional relationship of greater or lesser constancy and intensity. Again, this can be problematic:

> At one extreme there is an undue retention of 'the analytic attitude' when it is not only no longer indicated, but is actually inhibitory and harmful. . . .
>
> At the other extreme, in an effort to avoid or undo such an outcome, there is sometimes a gratification or stimulation of the patient by a premature and excessive social intimacy which is reacted to as a threatened seduction. . . . In contrast to both of these, the desired goal should be a transition to a normal interchange in which the analyst can be seen and reacted to as a normal figure and no longer as an object for continued transference displacement. (722)

Actually, in the third-generation studies, where the distinction between results at termination and at a subsequent follow-up from two to five years later is a clearly demarcated research focus, many more variants of posttermination therapist-patient contact or interaction have been delineated.

What I am calling the third-generation studies have been actually contemporaneous with the (conceptually) second-generation studies. These are systematic and formal psychoanalytic therapy research projects that have tried to assess psychoanalytic outcomes across a significant array of cases and at the same time to consider the processes through which these outcomes have been reached via intensive longitudinal study of each of the cases, thus combining the methodological approaches of the group-aggregated studies with those of the individually focused studies. Like the best of the second-generation studies, they have crafted careful definitions of terms, have constructed rating scales, and have tried to operationalize their criteria at each assessment point. These have been prospectively constructed studies starting with pretreatment assessment of the patients. Unlike the second-generation studies, they have carefully separated outcomes at termination from functioning at a specified follow-up point with an effort to account for changes that took place during this postanalytic phase. Henry Bachrach and his colleagues (1991), in their comprehensive survey of research on the efficacy of psychoanalysis, singled out the newer studies of the Boston Psychoanalytic Society and Institute (Kantrowitz 1986, Kantrowitz et al. 1986, 1987a,b, 1989, 1990a,b,c) and the Psychotherapy Research Project of the Menninger Foundation (Wallerstein 1986a, 1988b) as the only ones that met these specifications (903–11).

In these newer Boston studies, undertaken in the 1970s, twenty-two supervised psychoanalytic cases at the clinic of the Institute were selected for prospective study. The initial assessment was based on a psychological projective test battery. Measures were constructed of variables salient to therapeutic change, in alteration of; affect availability, tolerance, complexity, and modulation; level and quality of object relations; adequacy of reality testing; and the nature and level of motivation for change. Seven-point rating scales were constructed for each variable. The analyses were all conducted at a frequency of four or five sessions weekly and lasted from two and a half to nine years. Approximately a year after termination the initial projective test battery was repeated, and both the patient and the treating analyst were interviewed.

The results were described in a series of three papers (Kantrowitz et al. 1986, 1987a, 1987b). Nine of the twenty-two patients (41 percent) were judged to have had a successful analytic result, five (23 percent) had a limited analytic result, and eight (36 percent) were judged to be unanalyzed. Nonetheless, most of the cases achieved some therapeutic benefits along each of the change and outcome dimensions—affect management, object relationships, and reality testing. Along each dimension the therapeutic benefit achieved exceeded the analytic result in terms of the degree of successfully completed analytic work. Of course, "the better the analytic result, the greater the improvement in the capacity to modulate affect [for example]" (Kantrowitz et al. 1986, 546). But also, "The improvement [in level and quality of object relations] occurred even though approximately one-third of these patients were in treatment which their analysts perceived as having failed to even partially resolve the transference neurosis" (Kantrowitz et al. 1987a, 35). Overall, "in support of the Menninger findings, the Boston study found that change in affect management (availability and tolerance) . . . is associated with at least partial resolution of the transference neurosis; such change can and does occur, however, without a transference neurosis being established or resolved" (Kantrowitz et al. 1986, 551). That is, a consistent and important finding was that therapeutic benefit was achieved by the majority of the patients in excess of what could be accounted for by the evocation and interpretive resolution of the transference neurosis.[6]

Though most of the patients in the Boston studies derived significant therapeutic benefit from their analytic experience, successful outcome could not be predicted from any of the predictor variables. This led the investigators to speculate that "a particularly important omission [from the predictor variables] might have been consideration of the effect of the [therapist-patient] match in shaping the two-person psychoanalytic interaction" (Kantrowitz et al. 1989, 899). By "match" they meant "an interactional concept . . . a spectrum of compatibility and incompatibility of the patient and analyst which is relevant to the analytic work. . . . The interaction may facilitate or impede the engagement in, and resolution of, the analytic process. . . . Match . . . covers a broader field of phenomena in which countertransference is included as one of many types of match. . . . Match . . . can also refer to observable styles, attitudes, and personal characteristics" (894–95), and these are not necessarily rooted in conflict. Though "this mesh of the analyst's personal qualities with those of the patient has rarely been a special focus of attention . . . most analysts when making referrals do consider it; few assume that equally well-trained analysts are completely interchangeable" (Kantrowitz 1986, 273).

This same team conducted follow-up interviews with the same patient cohort in 1987, now five to ten years after the treatment terminations. This time the goodness of the analyst-patient match was included as one of the variables help-

6. This has already been elaborated in the discussion of the findings of the Menninger project (see chapter 8), in which a major focus was on the effort to explicate the operative mechanisms of change on bases other than interpretive resolution of intrapsychic conflict.

ing determine the patient outcomes (Kantrowitz et al. 1990a,b,c). Nineteen of the twenty-two cases were located, and eighteen agreed to the two-hour, sem-istructured interview and open-ended treatment review (audiotaped and later transcribed). There were then four available data sets, the pre- and posttreatment projective tests, the interviews with the analysts at the termination point, the interviews with the patients at the same point, and the 1987 follow-up inter-views with the patients. A variety of change measures was used: global improve-ment ratings, affect tolerance and management, level and quality of object relations, adequacy of reality testing, work satisfaction and accomplishment, and overall self-esteem. At the follow-up point, three patients had consolidated and further improved their state, four remained stable, six had deteriorated some-what from the termination state but were restored with additional treatment, four had deteriorated and remained so despite additional treatment, and one had returned to the original analyst, was still in treatment, and therefore was not counted (Kantrowitz et al. 1990a, 478).

The most striking finding, again, was that "the stability of psychological change five to ten years after termination of psychoanalysis could not be pre-dicted by the analysts' assessment of the development and at least partial reso-lution of the transference neurosis during the analysis" (1990a, 484). That is, "psychological changes were no more stable over time for the group of patients assessed as having achieved a successful analytic outcome concomitant with con-siderable therapeutic benefit than for the other group of patients assessed as having achieved therapeutic benefit alone" (1990a, 493).

When the focus was on the development of the self-analytic function, pre-sumably both a treatment goal and a criterion for termination ("We define self-analysis as the capacity to observe and reflect upon one's own behaviors, feelings, or fantasy life in a manner that leads to understanding the meaning of the phe-nomenon in a new light" [Kantrowitz et al. 1990b, 639–40]), again, though thirteen of the eighteen described a variety of self-analytic processes, there was no direct relationship between the attainment of the self-analytic function and the "working through the transference neurosis, if we accept their analyst's assessments" (1990b, 652).

Last, the authors felt that in twelve of the seventeen cases, the nature of the analyst-patient match (impeding or facilitating) did play a role in the outcome achieved (Kantrowitz et al. 1990c). They gave examples of what they considered facilitating matches with good ultimate outcomes, impeding matches with poor outcomes, and more complex situations in which the kind of match seemed at first to be facilitating to the unfolding of the analytic process, but later in the treatment seemed to have an influence in preventing the completion of the analytic work.

The other third-generation psychoanalytic therapy research study singled out by Bachrach et al. (1991) was the Psychotherapy Research Project of the Menninger Foundation (PRP), the most comprehensive and ambitious such research program ever carried out (Wallerstein 1986a, 1988b; Wallerstein et al. 1956). Aspects of this project have already been described in chapters 5, 8, and 23 above and will not be restated here. Rather, I wish at this point to highlight several major considerations that derive from PRP and make them more explicit within the context of this chapter.

First, PRP was one of only two of the research projects presented in this chapter (along with the Columbia program) to clearly study psychoanalytic psychotherapy side by side with psychoanalysis, with respect to both the outcomes achieved and the processes by which these outcomes came about. This has at times led to misunderstandings of the findings and conclusions of PRP. It was *not* a comparative study of psychoanalysis and psychoanalytic psychotherapy, to see how each could do when applied to comparable patient populations, as would be the case if a reasonably homogeneous patient population were randomly or alternately assigned for treatment by either psychoanalysis or psychotherapy. Rather, the intent was to study an equal number of cases in psychoanalysis and in psychoanalytic psychotherapy, in which each patient had been assigned to the treatment modality felt to be clinically indicated in terms of the nature of the presenting illness and character organization, as set within the framework of the contemporaneously understood indications and contraindications for these technically differing treatment modalities (see chapter 5, pp. 85-87). Thus each modality would be studied in terms of how well, in what ways, and in response to what processes and mechanisms it lived up to, exceeded, or fell short of the expected change and cure *in that modality*. The fundamental question was, Are our understandings of each of these modalities validly based? and where they are not, how should those understandings be altered?

Second, PRP was one of only two studies (along with the Boston study by Kantrowitz and her colleagues) to encompass within one research framework both the outcome questions and the process questions. The rationale for this was stated originally as follows (Wallerstein and Robbins 1958): "We believe that in theory process and outcome are necessarily interlocked and that the hypotheses that will yield the answers sought can only come from an exploratory study paying equal attention to both components. Any study of outcome, even if it only counts a percentage of cases 'improved,' must establish some criteria for 'improvement,' and these in turn derive from some conceptualization of the nature of the course of illness and the process of change, whether or not this is explicitly formulated. Similarly any study of process, in delineating patterns of change among variables, makes at various points in time cross-sectional assessments which, if compared with one another, provide measures of treatment outcome" (118).

This theoretically necessary conjoining of process and outcome study is subject, however, to practical methodological complexities:

> Though process is conceptually not separable from outcome, methods that yield the best judgments in one area or the other are often operationally opposed. For example, judgments of outcome will be scientifically most convincing if bias is minimized and absolute freedom from contamination maintained by keeping those who make the "after" judgments unaware of the "before" judgments and predictions. "Blind" psychological retesting is an obvious way to meet this research goal. Yet truly "blind" clinical interviewing, in which all knowledge of the "before" state is rigorously excluded, is by the nature of clinical interaction hardly possible. Any clinical interview, no matter how closely geared it is to an assessment of current status, will inevitably yield data comparing present states with prior ones. From the point of view of *process* judgments about the *same therapy,* such care to minimize contamination would be unnecessary. Indeed it would be counter to the whole spirit of inquiry into process in which maximum knowledge of all the known determinants, as these have varied through time, is essential in order to understand the changes that occur. In this sense, in terms of relative emphases at different stages of their operations, psychotherapy projects can be designed with greater clarity and efficiency to answer questions about outcome or about process. (118–19)

In this sense, the findings of PRP have thrown more light upon issues of outcome than of process. This is a major impetus to the current organization of PRP II, an effort to redress this imbalance and to focus more specifically on the relationship of the processes of change in the spectrum of therapies under scrutiny to the differing or similar outcomes achieved.

Third, PRP stands alone in its comprehensiveness and detail, cross-sectionally and longitudinally. For each of the forty-two patients selected, the Initial Study data included the regular Menninger Foundation clinical evaluation of approximately two weeks' duration, comprising psychiatric case study (eight to ten hours), projective psychological testing (eight to ten hours), and family and social history gathered from the accompanying responsible family member (eight to ten hours), all integrated into a final clinical synthesis with treatment recommendations, together with the added-on research study. This consisted of the organization of all these clinical data into twenty-eight Patient Variables that together comprehensively describe the patient's illness, character organization, treatment amenability, and seven Life-Situational Variables describing the patient's life context; the synthesis from this of the predicted course and outcome of the differentially indicated treatment approach in relation to the expected interaction of the patient's illness and character, the expectable external life circumstances, and the proposed clinically indicated treatment approach; and the completion, finally, of a variety of research-created forms designed to test the clinical expectations and predictions in a research-safeguarded way.

The Termination Study data comprised all records kept routinely during the clinical treatment course (from as much as detailed daily process notes on psychoanalyses that ranged up to one thousand hours, to as little as monthly one- or two-paragraph progress notes written for the official Menninger Foundation records), plus interview access to the patient, the therapist, the supervisor of the therapy (if there was one), and others instrumental in the patient's life and management (the hospital doctor, for example, if the patient had been hospitalized at any time during the therapeutic course), as well as blind psychological retesting using the identical projective test battery (but a different tester), together with the added-on research study; reassessment of the status of the same twenty-eight Patient Variables and seven Life-Situational Variables; assessment of a comparable array of Treatment and Therapist Variables as these had evolved over the course of the therapy; and the blind completion of the research forms designed to test the predictions made initially as well as to set up the expectations and predictions for consolidation of, maintenance of, or regression from the treatment changes and gains during the period of follow-up inquiry.

The Follow-Up Study comprised the return—at PRP expense—of the patient (together with a responsible family member) for reassessment over a period of several days in a manner as comparable to the Initial Study as possible—given the ex-patient's now-altered circumstance and motivation; that is, psychiatric interviewing, psychological retesting (again, with the same battery), social and family history, together with whatever medical or mental health care records were available from the follow-up period, again together with the research study consisting of the final assessment in light of the follow-up period of the Patient, the Treatment and Therapist, and the Life-Situational Variables as well as the outcomes of all the predictions to the expected or achieved status and functioning at the two- to three-year follow-up point.[7] This comprehensiveness of

7. In keeping with the usual follow-up protocols in the assessment of "cure" in cancer research, PRP had wanted to utilize a five-year period of follow-up study, but the exigencies of time over the already very long project span as well as fiscal strictures even within this very substantially extramurally funded research program, necessitated the compromise of setting the follow-up studies at a point two to three years after termination.

study of so many patients over so long a time has never been matched in any other psychotherapy research program. It required, of course, a large, dedicated research team (between fifteen and twenty members at any one time), divided into small groups according to specific tasks and held together over time despite individually differing central interests, motivations, and career trajectories. Such resources are only rarely available, but the design structure—to follow multiple sets of variables (Patient, Treatment and Therapist, and Life Situation) over multiple points in time (at least Initial, Termination, and Follow-Up)—is perhaps essential to any research program geared to the study of psychoanalytic and psychotherapeutic courses and outcomes.

Fourth and last in this array of considerations stemming from PRP was the effort to build in research *controls,* an expected requirement in formal and systematic research but unique in the studies presented in this chapter. Because PRP was a clinical, naturalistic research project, the manipulations inherent in the usual kinds of clinical research in biomedicine—matched groups of treated and nontreated cases, random assignment to the modalities under study, and so on—were not possible. But this naturalistic approach did not abrogate the responsibility to tackle the thorny problem (both technically and ethically) of controls in clinical psychotherapy research. Rather, it forced fresh consideration of just what to control and how to control it, by what specific methods. The overall premise was that major efforts at control should be based on the appropriate *selection* of clinical material rather than on any *manipulation* of it. Within this framework, four specific control methods were elaborated:

1. Intrapatient control, or the use of each patient as his/her own control, through the device of the individual prediction study and the creation of blind methods for testing the predictions
2. Interpatient control, or the cross-patient comparison of patterns of change over time in the several arrays of variables under study by the modified application of the research method of "paired comparisons" converted into graphic profiles for each patient and then grouped according to similarities and differences, leading to the control of some variables, so that the variability of other factors could be investigated
3. The parallel and independent study of the repeated psychological test batteries, as a concurrent (and independent) check on the changes discerned in the clinical studies over time
4. "Inadvertent controls," in which for reality reasons (finances, geography) the treatment method of choice would not be possible, and one could then determine whether the course and achieved outcome that

> would have been expected in the treatment of choice could nonethe-
> less eventuate under the modified treatment conditions

These various control methods have been described in detail by PRP (see Robbins and Wallerstein 1959, 39–42).

Overall, these characteristics of PRP bolstered our confidence in the findings
and conclusions of the project:

> [that] these distinctive therapeutic modalities of psychoanalysis, expressive
> psychotherapy, supportive psychotherapy, etc., hardly exist in anywhere
> near ideal or pure form in the real world of actual practice; that real
> treatments in actual practice are inextricably intermingled blends of more
> or less expressive-interpretive and more or less supportive-stabilizing el-
> ements; that almost all treatments (including even presumably pure psy-
> choanalyses) carry many more supportive components than are usually
> credited to them; that the overall outcomes achieved by those treatments
> that are more "analytic" as against those that are more "supportive" are
> less apart than our usual expectations for those differing modalities would
> portend; and that the kinds of changes achieved in treatments from the
> two ends of this spectrum are less different in nature and in permanence,
> than again is usually expected, and indeed can often not be easily distin-
> guished. (chapter 8)

Currently, investigations of psychoanalytic treatment processes and outcomes
take two major directions: the first is an effort toward convergence of empirical
psychoanalytic process studies with the outcome studies we have described; the
second is a more clinical concern with the values, both clinical *and* research,
that would accrue from building routine follow-up inquiry more systematically
into regular clinical psychoanalytic practice. The first direction is exemplified
by *Psychoanalytic Process Research Strategies* (1988), edited by Hartvig Dahl, Horst
Kachele, and Helmut Thoma. For approximately two decades, psychoanalytic
researchers, mostly in the United States and Germany, have been studying mo-
ment-by-moment psychoanalytic interactional processes through the use of audiotaped and transcribed treatment hours. Many of these are described in the
Dahl book. Each of the groups has developed its own concepts of the basic units
of the psychoanalytic situation and the psychoanalytic process and its own meas-
uring instruments; each has utilized these in relation to its own available data
base, though there has been some sharing of sample hours from a particular
psychoanalytic patient (Mrs. C) across a number of these groups. The Dahl book
compares findings from these disparate studies in a search for principles of convergence. In the introduction, Dahl expresses the hope that this will be found

in the Principle of Problem-Treatment-Outcome (P-T-O) congruence (7) enunciated in the chapter by Hans Strupp, Thomas Schacht, and William Henry: "The description and representation, theoretically *and* operationally, of a *patient's conflicts,* of the *patient's treatment,* and of the *assessment of the outcome,* must be congruent, which is to say, must be represented in comparable, if not identical terms" (ix). (It is of course my conviction that PRP was conceived and executed within the framework of this principle.)

An effort is currently under way to put this principle to a systematic and comprehensive empirical test. Under the auspices of the American Psychoanalytic Association, Wallerstein is currently organizing a Collaborative Analytic Multi-Site Program (CAMP) of Psychoanalytic Therapy Research, bringing together sixteen ongoing research groups[8] studying psychoanalytic treatment process and/or outcome, including *all* the U.S. groups represented in the book edited by Dahl et al. and the current groups from the third-generation outcome studies (Kantrowitz et al. in Boston and PRP-II in San Francisco). Each group will use its own concepts and instruments upon a consensually agreed-upon data base drawn from audiotaped and transcribed hours from completed as well as new psychoanalytic cases, so that appropriate before and after studies (as well as planned follow-ups) can be prospectively built in. The comparison of findings by these process and outcome study groups will finally enable us to determine the degrees of convergence of the concepts and instruments elaborated by the different groups and also the degree to which the Principle of P-T-O congruence truly holds. This is one direction that what I call fourth-generation studies is taking, one that, if successful, promises to integrate not only the various psychoanalytic process studies carried out more or less independently over the past two decades but also to integrate process studies with outcome studies.

A second current direction of outcome and efficacy studies stems from more directly clinical considerations. This effort has been spearheaded by Joseph Schachter, who organized and chaired a panel at the December 1987 meeting of the American Psychoanalytic Association under the title "Evaluation of outcome of psychoanalytic treatment: Should followup by the analyst be part of the post-termination phase of analytic treatment?" (Johan 1989). Put this way, the question was intended to challenge the established psychoanalytic convention that planned follow-up is inherently counter to the nature of psychoanalysis; that proper termination means the total, permanent relinquishing of all ties between analyst and ex-analysand; with such follow-up information as does accrue representing only happenstance, as in the instances cited at the beginning

---

8. For a one-paragraph overview of each of these participating groups, see *Research in Psychodynamic Therapy* (Wallerstein, unpubl. ms b, 23–29).

of this chapter from Freud and Deutsch. Schachter posed the issue of the value of regular and systematic follow-up for a different—and more valid—perspective on psychoanalytic outcomes. He referred to a questionnaire on this subject that he had distributed to analysts in five institutes and that had yielded a 52 percent return. The results showed that conventional practice characteristically employed a double standard in regard to follow-up contact. It was not expected with our patients, and when it occurred was usually regarded as an expression of unfinished business or something untoward in the prior treatment or treatment termination. However, we all take for granted the continuation of post-termination contact with our own training analysts.

On this panel Luborsky cited the findings of his research studies on the effects of follow-up contact on the maintenance of treatment gains. He found that it was especially useful for patients deficient in the capacity for internalization of a secure representation of the analyst. He also said that it provided a useful opportunity to assess the need for further therapy, but that also negatively, it could hinder the work of termination and separation. Gary Martin, from a clinical context, reported an experience survey which indicated that two-thirds of "successfully" terminated analytic patients nonetheless contacted their former analyst at some time within the first three years after termination (mostly by letter or phone): "Martin pointed out that since we now accept the idea of adult developmental tasks, the door should be more than open for the analysand to return if and when he encounters new developmental tasks which bring him once again into unconscious conflict" (Johan 1989, 817). Schlessinger, speaking on the basis of his research studies, pursued this same developmental theme, stating that every analysis is necessarily incomplete, that the posttermination phase is a period of consolidation of internalizations that constitute the developing self-analytic function, and that this process is consistently facilitated by planned follow-up interviews.

Wallerstein, on the same panel (see also Wallerstein 1989b), began by observing that the reasons psychoanalysis has never developed a tradition of systematic follow-up study are partly theoretical, stemming from the conception that an unfolding transference neurosis and its analytical resolution (so far as it is possible) are the preconditions for cure and that planned postanalytic contact between analyst and analysand could perpetuate transference fantasies and reflect some unanalyzed transference-countertransference residues; and the reasons are partly historical, having to do with the development of psychoanalysis as a private-practice-based discipline, outside the academic setting. Drawing on the PRP experience, Wallerstein focused specifically on the impact of follow-up qua follow-up on the issues of treatment termination and resolution and on the nature of the posttreatment period from three perspectives: (1) the range of conscious reactions to, and degrees of cooperation with, planned follow-up studies with these research patients, (2) the reverberating meanings of the follow-up experience, including its potential for attenuating or delaying the psychological treatment closure or, conversely, facilitating the treatment resolution, and (3) an experience survey of the varieties of continuing contacts with the treating analyst during the follow-up period, including returns to treatment. In conclusion it was stated that "the impact of *planned* followup study on the termination and outcome of psychoanalytic therapies, while not always inconsequential, does not seem to be detrimental and can, in fact, prove helpful and providential to the patient's and the therapist's therapeutic purposes" (Wallerstein 1989b, 939) and that "both our individual patients and our field as a science will profit thereby" (940)—that is, by systematic, planned follow-up built into regular clinical as well as research activities. On the same panel, several other speakers offered cautionary statements. Calder noted that gains could exact a price in transference and countertransference acting out, and Firestein said that the evidence was still unclear as to how best to consolidate treatment gains, follow-up or no follow-up.

Schachter pursued a number of studies inspired by this panel. From returns to a questionnaire distributed to those who attended the panel, he learned that the analysts' attitudes toward follow-up had shifted; more of them now stated that they either hoped to hear from the patient or would like the patient to return to see them at some specified period after treatment termination (1990a). Then, on the basis of a reexamination of the data from *Forty-Two Lives in Treatment*, Schachter challenged Wallerstein's claim that in six of the forty-two cases, the follow-up seemed in some way to attenuate or delay psychological closure of the treatment course (1990b).

At the December 1990 meeting of the American Psychoanalytic Association Schachter chaired a successor panel entitled "Stability of Gain Achieved during Analytic Treatment from a Followup Perspective." The leaders of the two third-generation outcome studies, Kantrowitz and Wallerstein, each presented clinical data from two research-studied psychoanalytic cases—one in which treatment gains were consolidated (and even enhanced) during the posttermination follow-up period and one in which there was regression toward the pretreatment status—to try to determine when follow-up conduces toward consolidation of treatment results, and when toward regression. In my contribution to that panel (Wallerstein 1992c), I first compared the data bearing on what we have learned thus far from follow-up studies and indicated why I felt that the seemingly discrepant findings from the Menninger and the Boston studies—that in the Menninger project outcome at termination tended to be predictive of the subsequent follow-up course, while in the Boston project this seemed not to be so—might be due not to actual discrepant findings, but to the incomparability or inadequacy of the data of the two projects; that is, the apparent discrepancy in findings might have been only a chance event (reflecting, among other things, very small samples). I then turned to a detailed case description of two patients from the Menninger project who were quite similar in character and in illness structure, took seemingly comparable analytic courses, and had seemingly similarly good treatment outcomes, but who had quite different follow-up courses, one experiencing further consolidation, the other serious regressions toward the pretreatment state. I presented what I felt to be some of the determinants of this difference. The overall panel report has been published by Martin (1993).

Clinical and research studies of psychoanalytic therapy, which have already yielded significant knowledge about the nature of treatment outcomes and efficacy as discerned at the termination and follow-up points, are now poised at a new level, with the possibility for real methodological and substantive breakthroughs, integrating both process and outcome research and perhaps research and clinical studies as well—as this current fourth generation of studies is carried through its planned natural cycle.

25 The Current Scene: The Sea Change since the Era of Convergence

The nature of the relationship of psychoanalytic psychotherapy to the psychoanalysis from which it devolved has become more uncertain and ambiguous over the half-century or so since the initial conceptualizations by Knight and his colleagues Gill and Stone (chapter 3). The high-water mark of those once seemingly clear delineations (in America) was the pivotal 1953 paper by Eissler on parameters, the paper in which psychoanalysis was defined as resting on interpretation alone (chapter 7), and also the sequence of three panels on the overall similarities and differences between psychoanalysis and the psychodynamic psychotherapies published in a single 1954 issue of the *Journal of the American Psychoanalytic Association* (chapter 5).

The impetus for the 1953 Eissler paper and the 1954 panels was twofold. First was the effort to clearly demarcate psychoanalysis from all the psychoanalytically derived psychotherapies that were emerging at the time as technical adaptations of psychoanalytic theory to the treatment of a widened array of psychopathological disorders not considered amenable to psychoanalysis proper. Second was the linked effort to refute the contentions of Alexander and his followers that their various technical modifications, especially the conception of the corrective emotional experience—rooted in the technical modifications originated by Ferenczi (chapter 2)—represented the proper evolution of psychoanalysis. Eissler and the majority position crystallized in the debates published in 1954 (especially by Gill, Rangell, Stone, and Bibring) incisively challenged this contention of Alexander, and the corresponding contention of Fromm-Reichmann and her followers that the technical modifications they introduced in order to bring the overtly psychotic within the scope of the psychotherapeutically approachable remained still within the boundaries of the psychoanalytic. The techniques elaborated by the Alexander and Fromm-Reichmann camps were rather declared to be (psychoanalytic) psychotherapy, perhaps necessary and useful under specific clinical circumstances, but no longer psychoanalysis proper (chapter 5).

This clarity of distinction between psychoanalysis and psychoanalytic psychotherapy, subdivided into expressive and supportive variants, was embodied in major texts of that era, notably Dewald's very influential 1964 book *Psychotherapy: A Dynamic Approach* (chapter 6) and also in the major research program of the period, the Menninger Psychotherapy Research Project (chapters 5 and

8). At the same time, it gradually became increasingly evident that the seeming clarity of conception of the early 1950s was being progressively eroded. By now—four decades later—it has all but disappeared. Significant signposts of this shift were the 1961 monograph by Stone, an effort to mitigate the austerity of Eissler's conception of psychoanalysis, and more broadly, a major expression of a larger trend in psychoanalysis, initiated actually by Ferenczi (chapter 2), toward focusing on the multifaceted nature of the psychoanalytic situation and the psychoanalytic relationship as major determinants of therapeutic change (along with interpretation and working through leading to insight) (chapters 7 and 16); and also the sequence of papers by Lipton from 1967 to 1988 challenging Eissler's delineation of classical technique as a distortion, rather than an accurate depiction, of Freud's actual technique (chapter 7).

These contributions were part of a growing concern in the post–World War II period with the psychoanalytic change mechanism beyond the sequence of interpretation (and working through) leading to insight, conflict resolution, change, and new behavior. As we have seen (chapter 1), Freud's great technical effort was to extricate the psychoanalysis he had created from its forebears in hypnosis and suggestion, by attempting to extirpate the vestiges of suggestive influence from analytic technique, and by declaring his more personal and "real" interactions with his patients to be part of civil human relationships and outside the specific boundaries of technique. It is this last step of acknowledging personal interactions—some of which we today would be extremely uncomfortable with—but considering them outside the bounds of technique that Lipton felt Eissler misunderstood in insisting that the austere technique he advocated represented the full expression of the way Freud actually worked. Freud's concern to separate elements of suggestion from psychoanalysis proper was strongly reinforced by Jones and Glover (chapter 1) and came to its fullest expression in Strachey's seminal paper of 1934, "The Nature of the Therapeutic Action of Psycho-Analysis," with his conception of the mutative interpretation and the operation of the transference interpretation as the basic mutative event.[1] Indeed, Strachey's landmark paper has occupied so pivotal a place in the delineation of the therapeutic action of psychoanalysis that Meissner (1991), in describing the

---

1. Strachey's paper can also be read as recognizing and acknowledging the power of suggestion, via the transference influence, in opening the way for the patient's receptivity to the analytic interpretation of the transference. Meissner made precisely this argument in his 1991 book on the nature of therapeutic interaction, a book built around a reconsideration of Strachey's 1934 article in light of all the subsequent clinical and theoretical developments. Nonetheless, the thrust of Strachey's article was properly seen at the time and since to be on the centrality of veridical transference interpretation as *the* mutative event with, pari passu, the concern to clearly demarcate psychoanalysis from all other psychotherapies on that basis.

evolution of psychoanalytic thinking on this issue, devoted the first quarter of his book to reprinting it and the rest to tracing how subsequent thinking has both grown from and progressively broadened the base that Strachey laid down.

The emergence of psychoanalytic psychotherapy as a derivative of psychoanalysis but distinct from it as a technical instrument, primarily in America, set the issue of "else" or "more" in psychoanalysis in a new framework. Implicitly accepting the model of "Freudian" psychoanalysis articulated by Eissler, albeit softened by the contributions of Stone and Anna Freud to the 1954 panels, Knight, Gill, and Stone and also Rangell and Bibring effectively took suggestive influence in all its variants, and now, under the less restrictive and conceptually more encompassing banner of supportive techniques, elaborated the distinctions between the supportive psychoanalytic psychotherapies devoted to the strengthening of weakened ego functioning in patients not amenable to (or able to tolerate) interpretive therapeutic approaches and their opposite, the expressive psychoanalytic approaches—psychoanalysis included—devoted to the interpretive resolution of intrapsychic conflict through analysis of the ego's defenses and resistances.

The gradual fragmenting of the 1954 consensus on these issues has been described in chapters 8 and 9, the latter portraying the contemporary "world without consensus." Two major trends have marked this massive shift from the clarities and seeming certainties of the 1950s to our contemporary sea of divergent and often discordant voices on these issues. One has been the gradual elaboration within psychoanalysis proper of the role of the psychoanalytic relationship (aside from or beyond interpretation) as an equal and interacting determinant, along with veridical interpretation leading to insight, in effecting therapeutic change; and the other, obviously related, has been the growing awareness of and acceptance in America—the heartland of the psychoanalytic psychotherapy enterprise—of the theoretical diversity that has come to characterize psychoanalysis since Freud's day. The increasing focus on the psychoanalytic relationship as a major factor in effecting change in psychoanalysis itself has been considered in this book under a variety of rubrics: in chapter 15, the focus on the treatment alliance (therapeutic alliance, Zetzel, or working alliance, Greenson)—going back in a line to Sterba (1934); in chapters 16 and 17, the focus on the nature of the therapeutic relationship and the role of the "new experience" it affords (Stone and Loewald)—in a line to Balint (1932) and also Gitelson (1951, 1962) and Spitz (1956); in chapter 18, the hierarchical and developmental models, developed varyingly by Gedo and Goldberg and by Tahka, in which the parameters of psychoanalysis proper as conceptualized for classically neurotic patients have been gradually extended "beyond interpretation" as sicker and more disorganized patients have been encompassed within the psychoanalytic purview, it being quite unclear as to where this is considered to cross the border into the realm of psychoanalytic psychotherapy; in chapter 19, the parallel development in Britain by Suttie, Fairbairn, Guntrip, Balint, Bowlby, Winnicott, and their successors of the Middle or Independent Group, with its object-relational focus (an aspect of the other major trend, increasing psychoanalytic pluralism) and the parallel bringing toward the American mainstream of the current-day proponents of the related Sullivanian interpersonal school (Levenson); and in chapter 20, the delineation of the seeming new paradigmatic patients of our time, the narcissistic personality disorders and the evolved self psychology, by Kohut, and the borderline personality organization and the evolved modified psychoanalytic (ego-structural and object-relational amalgamated) approach by Kernberg, both of them declared to be applications of psychoanalysis proper (or "modified" psychoanalysis—or even possibly psychoanalytic psychotherapy?) to these patients with wider and deeper ego disorders. All these ways of conceptualizing the change process in psychoanalysis that are 'beyond' or other than interpretation have made it progressively more difficult to draw distinctions between so-called psychoanalysis proper and psychoanalytic psychotherapy.

The other, counterpart trend, equally responsible for the progressive unraveling of the clear 1954 consensus, was the growing awareness in American psychoanalysis that the ego psychology metapsychological paradigm, long taken for granted as *the* true modern expression of the psychoanalysis created and handed down by Freud, simply did not reflect the state of affairs in worldwide psychoanalysis; rather, we lived in a world of increasing psychoanalytic diversity, of many (and differing) psychoanalys*es,* which then—with their boundaries then drawable in conceptually differing ways—of course makes more difficult any clear overall distinction of psychoanalysis from psychotherapy.

Psychoanalysis was not always characterized by this pluralism; actually, quite the opposite. In fact, perhaps more than any other branch of human knowledge, psychoanalysis has been the singular product of the creative genius of one man. Sigmund Freud's lifetime of work was extraordinarily productive, and if psychoanalysis consisted of nothing more than the corpus of Freud's work, *die Gesammelte Werke,* I think we could readily agree that all the fundamental principles of a fully operating scientific and professional activity would be available to us as students and practitioners.

Freud made strenuous efforts throughout his lifetime to define the parameters of his new science of the mind and to hold it together as a unified enterprise against both destructive or diluting pressures and seductions from without and also against fractious human divisiveness from within. To him, psychoanalysis was not only a science and a profession but also a Movement, with all the calls to a dedicated and disciplined allegiance that word connotes. When divergent tendencies threatened to splinter the unified edifice Freud was trying to build, he created the famous Committee of the seven ring holders to try to guarantee the integrity of his central psychoanalytic doctrines. The story is chronicled in Freud's "On the History of the Psychoanalytic Movement" (1914b): how that first wave of close co-workers who began to differ with him in major ways, Adler and Stekel and Jung, each found it necessary to leave psychoanalysis over the three-year span from 1910 to 1913.

Freud, from his side, declared the psychological deviations of these dissidents to be totally incompatible with the fundamental postulates of psychoanalysis, and when they left the Movement over these differences, he professed himself to be satisfied that they could pursue any psychological and psychotherapeutic bent they wished so long as they did not claim it to be psychoanalysis. Two of them did establish schools or movements of their own: Adler called his Individual Psychology and Jung took the name Analytic Psychology. Of these two new theoretical systems, Freud felt Adler's to be the more important (1914b, 60) and potentially the more enduring. In this his prediction proved faulty; it is the Jungian movement, which has recently even reappropriated the designation "psychoanalysis," that has endured more solidly worldwide as an alternative therapeutic system.

Freud did declare that both Adler and Jung had brought valuable new contributions to analysis, Adler in recognizing the role of the ego in adaptation and the importance of the aggressive drives in mental life, and Jung in tracing the way in which infantile impulses are used to serve our highest social and ethical interests. But Freud felt that these two, each in his own way, had abandoned the central psychoanalytic concepts of the unconscious and repression, of resistance and transference, thereby placing themselves outside Freud's definition of psychoanalysis. Freud had stated in his "History"—actually the first, the most succinct, and the best known of the several such statements he enunciated over the long span of his writings—that any treatment built around "the facts of transference and of resistance" could call itself psychoanalysis, but that any treatment that "avoided these two hypotheses" would be guilty of misappropriating the name if it designated itself that way (1914b, 16). I would add here that the words "transference" and "resistance" imply the concepts of the unconscious, psychic conflict, and defense, the key building stones of our shared psychoanalytic edifice. Since then, of course, several of Adler's central conceptions—for example, those of the ego and adaptation and of the motive power of aggression—have been actively reincorporated into the main body of psychoanalysis, first by Freud and then by others who came after, like Hartmann, and perhaps that is related to the near collapse of Adlerian psychology as a separate therapeutic enterprise. There have been lesser but still substantial reincorporations from Jungian psychology, or at least cognate developments within the psychoanalytic framework, like Erikson's (1959) life span focus, with its shift in emphases to the coequal concern with the second half of the life cycle, or like our focus on unconscious fantasy systems as guides to understanding motivation and behavior—albeit in a different way from the Jungians—and this lesser reappropriation of concepts from Jung's theoretical system may help to explain its continuing greater vigor as a separate psychology and therapy than its Adlerian counterpart.

Within another decade, after the departures of Adler and Stekel and Jung, psychoanalysis was threatened with new deviations, those of Ferenczi and Rank, Ferenczi in his active therapy (chapter 2) and Rank later in his will therapy. Actually, despite the severe strains aroused by these theoretical and technical developments, Ferenczi never left psychoanalysis, though Rank ultimately did and developed a new school in America, more influential in social work than in psychoanalysis, the so-called functional school. But that Rankian deviation has, like Adler's psychology, now mostly faded into history.

The decade of the 1920s also saw the first major new theoretical direction within psychoanalysis, which at the same time fought fiercely to maintain its sense of direct descent from the psychoanalysis of Freud. Indeed, in some respects, such as its unswerving acceptance of Freud's most problematic and controversial theorizing—the introduction of the death instinct theory—and making it a central building block in its own theoretical conceptual development, it could claim even a closer adherence to Freud than members of the Viennese school, who, while closer to Freud personally, yet split sharply on the value of this particular theoretical turn. I refer of course to Melanie Klein and the development of Kleinian analysis.

Riccardo Steiner (1985), reviewing the British Society's so-called Controversial Discussions of 1943 and 1944, traced clearly the political history of the Kleinian theoretical development in England: the original invitation to Melanie Klein to come from Berlin to lecture on her new ideas about theory and technique, the interest aroused by these ideas among the British analysts, the invitation then to locate permanently in London, the early support of the Kleinian views by Jones and other distinguished members of the first generation of British analysts, and finally the adversarial letters around this development between Jones, supporting Melanie Klein, and Freud, supporting his daughter Anna, in the growing controversy over the proper theoretical and technical development of child psychoanalysis, seen as an unhappy divergence between Kleinian and Anna Freudian views or between what were called the London and Vienna schools, representing at that time the two main centers of psychoanalytic influence in Europe, or in the world, actually.

The fundamental difference here, however, was that the Kleinian development did not lead to a split with the International Psychoanalytical Association (IPA). Rather, the Kleinians insisted on their impeccable psychoanalytic credentials, and their movement remained within the British organizational framework and therefore within the IPA. The terms under which the British Society would henceforth operate with a Kleinian group, a Freudian group, and, in between, a Middle or Independent group were not settled until the year-long Controversial Discussions, which took place four to five years after Freud's death.

My point here is that the Kleinian development, still within Freud's lifetime and when his personal leadership in psychoanalysis was unquestioned, nonetheless represented the beginnings of the transition of psychoanalysis from being, or appearing to be, a thoroughly unified theoretical structure evolved around the creative intellectual corpus of its founding genius into the current theoretical diversity in which we have existing side by side with the American ego-psychological (and by now post-ego-psychological) school, the Kleinian, the Bionian, the (British) object-relational sometimes narrowed down to the Winnicottian, or the Lacanian (largely outside but to a considerable extent in Europe and Latin America inside psychoanalytic organizational ranks). Even the United States, long the stronghold of the monolithic hegemony of the ego-psychological paradigm of Hartmann and Rapaport, has recently witnessed the rise of Kohut's self psychology as a major alternative psychoanalytical theoretical perspective and, to a lesser extent as new schools, Mahler's developmental approach and Schafer's new voice or new idiom for psychoanalysis, as well as also the return to consideration by the psychoanalytic mainstream of the Sullivanian interpersonal perspective.[2]

This transition from the theoretical unity of psychoanalysis that Freud tried to embody and enforce in his conception of a shared intellectual movement built around the intellectual charisma of his leadership to today's broad theoretical diversity was hardly a smooth or an uneventful journey. The interpolated momentous event for psychoanalysis, given the nature of our discipline and its

2. And, of course, these various *theoretical* perspectives do not exhaust the divergent conceptual developments within our field. There are also the various philosophy of science positions on the natural science or behavioral science or hermeneutic characterization of the essential nature of the psychoanalytic enterprise as well as the array of cultural and language distinctivenesses, for example, francophone as distinct from anglophone analysis, with all their stylistic differences and differently constraining linguistic and thought conventions. For an elaboration of all these differences, see Wallerstein 1988a, 7–8.

origins, was the death of Freud, which thrust upon analysts the burden of carrying their field beyond the consummate genius of the man who had single-handedly brought it into being on to what now had to become a discipline and a science that built on its past but rested on the from-now-on independent work of its collectivity. This was a truly wrenching task. I have elsewhere (1988a) indicated some of the consequences for our discipline of our unique continuing historic and mythic relationship to Freud as a fantasied continuing presence. Here I want only to speculate about its relationship to the theme of the dialectic between the effort to maintain the theoretical unity of psychoanalysis by extruding those whose new theoretical proposals, whatever their putative value, were or seemed to be linked to the dilution (if not abandonment) of central Freudian psychoanalytic concepts and the contrapuntal effort to accommodate diverging theoretical perspectives within a more generous and elastic definitional framework for psychoanalysis—albeit one that somehow still defines and encompasses what analysts have in common (and what differentiates them from nonanalysts).

Psychoanalytic development after Freud's death could have tilted in either direction, toward an ever-tighter circle of orthodoxy, of required adherence to one mainstream psychoanalytic doctrine, or, oppositely, toward an expanding diversity of theory that could ultimately pose bewildering problems of boundaries, of deviation, of what is then declared to be wild analysis, and what is altogether beyond analysis, problems that seemed much simpler to resolve in Freud's day. For a long time after Freud's death—until the 1970s, in fact—the tilt was in *both* directions, toward diversity in Europe and toward unity within one mainstream in the United States.

The philosophy of the European development was spelled out by Susan Isaacs (1943) during the British Society's Controversial Discussions: "Listening to the selective accounts of Freud's theories offered by some of the contributors to this discussion, and noting their dogmatic temper, I cannot help wondering what would have happened to the development of psychoanalytic thought, if for any reason Freud's work had not been continued after 1913, before his work 'On Narcissism' and 'Mourning and Melancholia'; or after 1919, before 'Beyond the Pleasure Principle' and 'The Ego and the Id.' Suppose some other adventurous thinker had arrived at these profound truths and had dared to assert them! I fear that such a one would have been treated as a backslider from the strict path of psychoanalytic doctrine, a heretic whose views were incompatible with those of Freud, and therefore subversive of psychoanalysis" (151). Certainly this heartfelt cry can be read as a Kleinian plea for tolerance of diverse theoretical viewpoints *within* the body of psychoanalysis, each equally sincerely—and perhaps with equally good reason—feeling itself to be in a direct and logical line of development from the overall corpus of Freud's work, each emphasizing one or another of the main theoretical conceptions for the understanding of the human mind offered by Freud over the span of his life's work, and not all of these conceptions easily reconciled with each of the others.

Sparked by the success of the Kleinian development in England even within Freud's lifetime and perhaps also by the national and linguistic diversity of the European continent, psychoanalytic development in Europe from rather early on was diverse and pluralistic. The Kleinian movement spread to other parts of Europe and as far away as India and Australia, and it became the dominant theory in psychoanalysis all over South America. The role of the British Society, with its powerful Kleinian group, as a main training center for so many of the psychoanalytic pioneers in these countries has been, of course, a central element in that development.

But the post–World War II decades have also seen the rise and flowering of the theoretical work of Lacan and his followers in France, of the extensions of Kleinian thought by Bion and Meltzer in England, and of the whole development by the British Independent Group of the object-relational perspectives in psychoanalysis pioneered by Suttie, Fairbairn, and Guntrip and further developed by Balint, Bowlby, Winnicott, and a host of others. It is this pluralistic theoretical development, to which various other perspectives can be added (see footnote 2 this chapter), that has, despite the professed desire to see psychoanalysis as a body of theory consonant with some unifying perspective on Freud's writings, rather eventuated in the present-day pluralism of perspectives to which psychoanalysts differentially adhere—depending mostly, it should be added, not on inherent logic, plausibility, or heuristic usefulness, but rather on where and how they trained and where they then live and practice. Latin America, once thought to be a monolithic center of Kleinian analysis, has become home to every one of the theoretical developments in analysis emanating from centers in Europe and the United States as well.

By contrast, psychoanalysis in the United States for a long time took a different course. With the rise of Hitler and the collapse of the main psychoanalytic strongholds in central Europe, the main intellective power of psychoanalysis and the majority of the analysts of Freud's generation were transplanted to the United States. And in America, the postwar tilt was in the direction of a unitary and unifying mainstream—heir in this sense to Freud's political-administrative ambitions—in the development and fruition of the ego-psychology metapsychological paradigm, which for long maintained a monolithic hegemony over the psychoanalytic domain in an arena that contained more than half the world's psychoanalysts. And this uniform theoretical structure made possible the counterposed delineation of a distinctive array of psychoanalytic psychotherapies, varyingly expressive and supportive, each defined in terms of similarity to or difference from the unified conceptual and definitional structure of psychoanalysis.

When divergent theoretical directions emerged in the United States, as early as the 1940s—and here the names of Karen Horney, Erich Fromm, Clara Thompson, and Harry Stack Sullivan as well as many others come to mind, all associated under the loose rubrics of either the interpersonal or the culturalist schools of psychoanalysis—the resulting controversy led in America, just as it had in Freud's day in Vienna, to a forced leaving of the affiliation with organized psychoanalysis and the founding of independent schools and training centers. Some, like Frieda Fromm-Reichmann, Sandor Rado, and Abram Kardiner, did manage to remain part of the American Psychoanalytic Association and even to found new institutes and societies within it. But overall the turmoil and departures of the 1940s in America were indeed reminiscent of the departures of Adler and Stekel and Jung three decades earlier in Vienna.

In the end, however, the defined psychoanalytic mainstream was no better able to survive intact in post–World War II America than in post–World War I Europe. The ego-psychological metapsychology edifice, though still the main focal strength of American psychoanalysis, has been gradually transformed into what some today call the post-ego-psychological age, and object relations perspectives have been varyingly incorporated into it by Zetzel, Modell, Kernberg, and others. The natural science model of psychoanalysis, on which Hartmann's and Rapaport's theorizing rested, has been subjected to vigorous attack by some of its once staunchest adherents, among others, with a variety of hermeneutical, phenomenological, totally subjectivistic, and linguistically based perspectives, like those offered by George Klein, Merton Gill, Roy Schafer, and Donald Spence. And aside from the decades-long work of Margaret Mahler and her followers, who have used their child development observations to fashion an explicitly developmental perspective for psychoanalytic theory and praxis, there has been the evolution in America starting in the 1970s of the self psychology of Heinz Kohut and his followers, a psychology with a distinctive metapsychology of the bipolar self and the vision of Tragic rather than Guilty Man, very much an alternative psychoanalytic theory and school.[3]

All this has led to a situation in American psychoanalysis that, though not

3. Thoroughly in keeping with the then-prevailing American assumption of the uniformity of (American) psychoanalysis under the banner of ego psychology, Kohut's self psychology paradigm was attacked, usually as (only) psychotherapy—i.e., not proper psychoanalysis—or as a revival in another form of Alexander's corrective emotional experience, itself originally widely categorized as a retreat to psychotherapy.

yet comparable to the established pluralism of psychoanalysis in Europe and Latin America, is fast approaching it. In addition to the pluralism of theoretical perspectives in psychoanalysis, that is, of metapsychologies—ego (and post-ego) psychological, object-relational, Kleinian, Bionian, Lacanian, self psychological, interpersonal, and so on—there has developed a pluralism of psychoanalytic epistemologies, various philosophy-of-science positions on the essential nature of the psychoanalytic enterprise. Barbara Fajardo (1993) has recently categorized these into three main groups:

1. The "empirical behavioural science perspective," especially characteristic of American ego-psychology of the 1950s and 1960s, a positivistic perspective with the observer/analyst presumably positioned objectively outside the theater of inquiry and attempting to reconstruct a veridical past that is fully explanatory of present functioning and malfunctioning

2. The "hermeneutic empirical perspective," characteristic, for example, of Kohut's self psychology, with the observer/analyst positioned more subjectively within the theater of inquiry, attempting via empathic immersion to better *discover* the nature of the patient's experience of his/her unfolding life story with the long-ago past conceived as metaphorically analogous to the transferential present (for other examples, Winnicott and Loewald)

3. The "hermeneutic constructivist perspective," exemplified, for example, by Schafer, Spence, Robert Stolorow,[4] and Irwin Hoffman, with

---

4. Stolorow (together with his co-workers George Atwood and Bernard Brandchaft) has emerged as a major exponent of "the intersubjective perspective in psychoanalysis" (Stolorow and Atwood 1992, 1), defined as follows: "Intersubjectivity theory is a field theory or systems theory in that it seeks to comprehend psychological phenomena not as products of isolated intrapsychic mechanisms, but as forming at the interface of reciprocally interacting subjectivities (1); and, "we use 'intersubjective' to refer to *any* psychological field formed by interacting worlds of experience" (3). That is, "An intersubjective field is a system of *reciprocal mutual influence*" (3)—i.e., interacting subjectivities. A recent article by Stolorow (1993) has clarified these relationships: "Intersubjectivity theory is a broad methodological and epistemological perspective that I believe can encompass and synthesize the contributions of both self psychology and object relations theory to the understanding of the therapeutic process. . . . Phenomena that have been the traditional focus of psychoanalytic investigation are viewed, from an intersubjective perspective, not as products of isolated intrapsychic processes but as forming at the interface of interacting worlds of experience" (450–51). The central concept is that of "*unconscious organizing principles* as . . . [an] alternative to that of unconscious fantasy" (451), though unconscious organizing principles are never clearly defined. The technical operations seem fully in accord with the precepts of self psychology, albeit with attention to *two* interacting subjectivities. The congenial fit of these views with both the constructivist position of Hoffman

the life story *constructed* interactively out of psychoanalytic attention to the interacting subjectivities in the transference-countertransference interplay.

The first of these as well as mostly the second (the behavioral science and the hermeneutic empirical perspectives are committed to the "correspondence theory of truth" (see Charles Hanly 1992a, chapter 1) with veridical correspondences—albeit with intervening experiential and developmental transformations—sought between the psychological manifestations of the present and their ultimate etiologic instigators in the past. The third perspective (the hermeneutic constructivist) is committed rather to the "coherence theory of truth" (again, Hanly 1992a as well as Michael Sherwood 1969 and Spence 1982, 1987), with truth criteria inhering in the internal consistency, coherence, comprehensiveness, and therapeutic efficacy as well as subjective satisfaction of the life story constructed by the two interacting participants.

Fajardo's overview is that "psychoanalysis is thought by some to be undergoing a profound change . . . as it enters the post-modern era, with some psychoanalysts now espousing constructivist hermeneutic inquiry" (979). She singled out Schafer, Spence, Jay Greenberg, Lewis Aron, Hoffman, and Stolorow, as well as pointing to a "less radically post-modern posture" (i.e., Gill, Evelyne Schwaber, Arnold Modell) that emphasizes "the use of countertransference-transference experiences in the analytic process, seeing psychoanalysis as a mutually experienced dyadic process *coloured by discovery* of the patient's past experiences. This position advocates a dialectic between experience *created vs. discovered* in the psychoanalytic process" (979, italics added). Although the epistemological undergirding of the various theoretical perspectives and its impact on psychoanalysis, psychoanalytic psychotherapy, their evolving interrelationships, and the modus operandi of each have not been explicitly focused on in this book, I think it is clear from all the presentations of viewpoints from chapter 15 through chapter 24 that there has recently been the very significant shift in perspective on these issues that Fajardo has pointed to, as well as continuing advocacy of adherence to the natural science, veridical truth-seeking, theoretical framework for psychoanalysis that was once almost unquestioned.[5]

---

and the hermeneutic posture of Schafer and Spence is readily evident. For a full tracing of the work of Stolorow and his collaborators, including the initial starting point in Kohut's self psychology, see three books, Atwood and Stolorow (1984), Stolorow, Brandchaft, and Atwood (1987), and Stolorow and Atwood (1992).

5. This issue of psychoanalytic epistemologies is a major focus of Carlo Strenger's monograph *Between Hermeneutics and Science* (1991), which was mentioned previously for its perspectives on the major change in psychoanalytic conceptualizing from the "historical" to the "mod-

The fragmentation of the seemingly crystallized consensus (at least in America) of the 1950s on the nature of psychoanalysis, the psychoanalytic psychotherapies, and their similarities and differences can be seen in this present context as an all but inevitable consequence of the two trends I have noted, the gradual elaboration within psychoanalysis proper of the role of the psychoanalytic relationship (beyond interpretation) as a coequal and interacting determinant along with (veridical) interpretation in effecting therapeutic change (chapters 15–20) and the concomitant growing appreciation of the theoretical diversity that was coming to characterize psychoanalysis everywhere—and by extension, therefore, necessarily all the psychoanalytically based psychotherapies. Among the many issues that have in consequence been conceptually recast is that of so-called wild analysis. When Freud was constructing his unitary theoretic edifice for psychoanalysis, he attempted to demarcate its parameters and define its proper practitioners in order to warn against imitators and pretenders. In his essay " 'Wild' Psycho-Analysis" (1910b) he described a well-intentioned physician with a pseudounderstanding of psychoanalysis who had advised a woman complaining of anxiety after a divorce "that the cause of her anxiety was her lack of sexual satisfaction. He said that she could not tolerate the loss of intercourse with her husband, and so there were only three ways by which she could recover her health—she must either return to her husband, or take a lover, or obtain satisfaction from herself. Since then she had been convinced that she was incurable, for she would not return to her husband, and the other two alternatives were repugnant to her moral and religious feelings" (221).

Freud used his consultation with this woman (whom the doctor in question had actually sent to him, telling his patient that Freud was responsible for these discoveries and would confirm the truth of what he had advised) to discuss the technical error—made presumably out of ignorance—in this kind of "wild" application of psychoanalytic ideas: "It is not enough . . . for a physician to know a few of the findings of psycho-analysis; he must also have familiarized himself with its technique if he wishes his medical procedure to be guided by a psycho-analytic point of view. This technique cannot yet be learnt from books, and it certainly cannot be discovered independently without great sacrifices of time, labour, and success. Like other medical techniques, it is to be learnt from those who are already proficient in it" (226). While disavowing the desire to claim a monopoly on psychoanalysis, Freud did attribute his creation of the psychoanalytic "organization" to the dangers of such "wild analysis." He wrote,

---

ernist" perception of the transference. I did not there discuss the wider ramifications of the epistemological issues that were the central thrust of Strenger's argument because these issues have not been an explicit focus in this book.

"In face of the dangers to patients and to the cause of psycho-analysis which are inherent in the practice that is to be seen of a 'wild' psycho-analysis, we have had no other choice. In the spring of 1910 we founded an International Psycho-Analytical Association, to which its members declare their adherence by the publication of their names, in order to be able to repudiate responsibility for what is done by those who do not belong to us and yet call their medical procedure 'psycho-analysis' " (226–27).[6]

However, over the decades after Freud's 1910 paper, the concept of wild analysis took on a connotation far broader than efforts at analytic work by the analytically untrained and unversed. Strachey's then (1934) defining article on the nature of the therapeutic action of psychoanalysis via his elaboration of the conception of the mutative interpretation could, by implication at least, be readily used to consign psychoanalytic endeavors that diminished or slighted the centrality of the *transference* interpretation to the category of wild or improper analysis. Similarly, Eissler's (1953) article on the essence of proper analysis clearly designated what was to be excluded as psychoanalytically improper or wild. That is, during the period of wide acceptance of Eissler's model of psychoanalysis, wild analysis was extended to comprise any "undisciplined" or "deviant" analytic work practiced outside the dimensions defined by Strachey and Eissler and their followers, whether carried out by trained psychoanalysts or by variously trained psychodynamic psychotherapists improperly imitating their understandings of what psychoanalytic work was supposed to be.

This, of course, can all be regarded as a matter of boundaries, of parameters, of widening scope, and ultimately of (possibly differing) opinions. It is clearly also a matter of what is (proper) psychoanalysis and what is (only) psychotherapy. Unhappily, the issue of so-called wild analysis can also simply be a matter of a laissez-faire or an anything goes philosophy. This perspective was discussed, for

6. Freud felt that most such wild analytic activities were simply fruitless. He said (as already quoted), "Attempts to 'rush' him [the patient] at first consultation, by brusquely telling him the secrets which have been discovered by the physician, are technically objectionable. And they mostly bring their own punishment by inspiring a hearty enmity towards the physician on the patient's part and cutting him off from having any further influence" (226). But he also tempered these observations: "As a matter of fact 'wild' analysts of this kind do more harm to the cause of psycho-analysis than to individual patients. I have often found that a clumsy procedure like this, even if at first it produced an exacerbation of the patient's condition, led to a recovery in the end. Not always, but still often." And, "I should say that, despite everything, the 'wild' psychoanalyst did more for her than some highly respected authority who might have told her she was suffering from a 'vasomotor neurosis.' He forced her attention to the real cause of her trouble, or in that direction, and in spite of all her opposition this intervention of his cannot be without some favourable results" (227). Not at all a blanket condemnation of such misguided effort!

example, in Stone's paper "The Influence of the Practice and Theory of Psychotherapy on Education in Psychoanalysis" (1982): "If psychotherapeutic practice is conceived of as a 'do-as-you-please' relaxation from the strict analytic discipline, there might be merit in discarding it from training altogether. But insofar as it is an honest, disciplined effort to utilize psychoanalytic knowledge in a variably different setting, it is difficult to see how this effort can have other than an enriching effect" (111). This Stone contrasted with an earlier characterization of a common enough view (by psychoanalysts) of psychotherapy as comprising only "an endless gamut of ad hoc, or intuitive, or faute de mieux improvisations" (84)—indeed, wild psychoanalysis!

Within this perhaps useful but very imprecise categorization, the concept of wild analysis has come to range (depending on who invokes it) from the slightest departure from the strictest tenets of so-called classical or pure psychoanalysis to an undisciplined potpourri of efforts that are claimed to be analytic or derivative of the analytic. But of course these usages, including the most pejorative, all developed within the context of the understandings of what (proper) psychoanalysis and (proper) psychotherapy consisted of that prevailed in the (American) conceptual climate of the 1950s, with its emphases on clarity of boundaries and distinctness of characteristics, techniques, and mechanisms.

In light of all the changes since then, the issue of wild analysis must today indeed look very different. It was Schafer (1985) who brought to center stage the inevitable and necessary reconsideration of the concept in view of the current acceptance of theoretical pluralism: "If we take seriously this multiplicity of models and the putative technical consequences of each of them, we soon realize that the referents of the concept wild analysis have become uncertain in important respects. This increased uncertainty is not to be passed over lightly, for our ideas of sound technique and appropriate lines of interpretation are necessarily defined by contrast with what is not acceptable. At least implicitly, the concept we have of wild analysis steadily influences the way we work. It also influences the way we teach psychoanalysis and psychoanalytic psychotherapy" (275–76). And "Whereas once upon a time wild analysis referred to idiosyncratic violations of the theoretical premises and technical precepts of a simpler and solitary psychoanalysis, today recourse to the concept wild analysis plunges us into theoretical debate . . . the debate can take place within the Freudian conventions or between these conventions and others" (276). To this reexamination Schafer gave a new name: "comparative analysis, that is to say, seeing how things look from within the perspective of each system [Klein's, Kohut's, etc.] . . . for questions concerning the type, degree, and conventionalization of wildness can only be considered usefully from a systematic position" (276–77).

Schafer began his statement of his updated conceptions by counterposing his views to Freud's: "Freud maintained that analytic interventions are to be considered wild unless two preconditions have been met: First, adequate preparatory analysis of resistance must have been done already to allow the repressed material to come very near to consciousness. Second, the analysand must already have developed a transference attachment to the analyst so that he will not flee from the analysis as the repressed material is brought to light" (279). But in view of our emerging awareness of "the intrinsically and fruitfully dialogical, intersubjective, co-authored nature of all analytic data" (280), Freud's seemingly clearcut defining stance has become more problematic. The conception of the interactive nature of the therapeutic process, which is today so ensconced, Schafer called "interpenetration": "The mere fact of interpenetration establishes not wildness, but the derivation of psychoanalytic meaning through dialogue and mutual influence" (280). Further,

> it continues to be difficult to state explicitly all the criteria to be used in deciding whether a particular method or line of interpretation is sound or wild. For another thing, it is the inevitability of interpenetration in psychoanalytic work that has opened the door to different schools of analytic thought, each with its distinctive methods, phenomena, and clinical processes. Nothing is to be gained by denying that there are numerous ways of transforming apparently senseless phenomena into intelligible aspects of a person's life. We must accept the idea that each of these ways is based on plausible accounts of typical vicissitudes of development, typical conflicts, and standardized criteria of intelligibility. Once we have recognized that this heterogeneity is a fact of psychoanalytic life, we are in a position to discuss profitably the merits and constraints of one or another approach to establishing analytic intelligibility. (280–81)

Within this framework, Schafer proceeded to compare systematically the psychoanalytic perspectives of Melanie Klein, Kohut, and Gill, showing how from within each perspective the work of each of the others could be readily construed as (pejoratively) wild analysis or, at best, a species of psychoanalytic psychotherapy.[7]

7. For reasons not at all clear to me, Schafer, in his most recent book, in a chapter entitled "Psychoanalysis, Pseudoanalysis, and Psychotherapy" (1992), seems to have retreated from this call to substitute the heuristically fruitful conception of comparative analysis for the more ambiguous and potentially mischievous concept of wild analysis, back towards the earlier views that in 1985 he was trying to supersede. Here (1992) he used the word "pseudoanalysis" to encompass two phenomena, what he called "wild" and what he called "insubstantial" psychoanalysis: "I use the term *pseudoanalysis* to refer to a number of cases that share only one

Within this context, what then can we say about the psychoanalytic psycho-therapies today in their similarities to and differences from what we should now call the psychoanaly*ses?* Freud, of course, was never called upon to confront this issue. As Tahka (1993) put it,

> Freud was explicit in his definition of psychoanalysis as "a method for the treatment of *neurotic* disorders." . . . The technique often referred to as "classical" analysis was specifically developed by him for the treatment of neurotic patients, and he never recommended its use in treating other patient categories. On the contrary, he excluded from the indications of psychoanalysis all those patients who were not capable of developing an-alyzable transference neuroses. . . . This was fully consistent with the es-tablished body of psychoanalytic knowledge at that time. Freud never developed a theory of preoedipal development and its failures, that would have allowed a structural and dynamic understanding of the pathogenic conditions underlying psychotic and borderline levels of psychopathology. In the absence of such theory and understanding, no specific psychoan-alytic approach for their treatment could be developed either. (161)

Though none of the recent diverse array of books and articles on the nature of therapeutic action in psychoanalysis and psychoanalytic psychotherapy have had

---

feature: they represent themselves as analysis in form and substance despite their either violating the principles of psychoanalysis in some fundamental way or giving only the appearance of being analysis. In the former group are the varieties of wild analysis; in the latter group, analyses that exist in form but not in active process" (269). Of wild analysis, he reverted to the old familiar description: "The characterization *wild analysis* is usually reserved for the making of interpretations that are neither warranted by the material at hand nor invited by the analysand's basic, even if erratic, acceptance and use of the analytic method. . . . Usually the charge of wild analysis is made when the analyst rapidly makes deep interpretations of unconscious conflict or hastily engages in reductive reconstructions. . . . The crucial factor should be that the intervention is unwarranted by the evidence available and inappropriate to the patient's state of preparation for that kind of intervention" (269–70). Nowhere here does he mention the idea of comparative analysis, though he does ask, "If wild analysis is a form of pseudoan-alysis, how far can we go in making interpretations before being judged 'wild' rather than being accepted as intuitive, or creative, or highly individual in style but still sound?" (267). The other form of pseudoanalysis, insubstantial analysis, Schafer ascribes to those analysands who take readily enough to the psychoanalytic situation but do not develop a discernible psychoanalytic process, do not really learn to free associate, etc. (Joyce McDougall's [1980] "anti-analysands" and Betty Joseph's [1993] "nonresonating patients"): "Analysts say finally of those who take this position unyieldingly that they are unanalyzable" (274); and further, "Fuller discussions of the part played by analysands in developing insubstantial analysis can be found in the extensive literature on resistance; the part played by analysts, in the extensive literature on disruptive countertransference" (275).

the commanding impact that Dewald's 1964 *Psychotherapy: A Dynamic Approach* had (written within the relative certainties and clarities of the consensus articulated a decade earlier), nonetheless I will quote from a variety of these as typical exemplars of the profound shift that has occurred in the psychoanalytic concerns with issues of psychotherapy vis-á-vis psychoanalysis since the perspective of Freud's day described by Tahka, and also as witness to the diversity of contemporary perspectives in our present "world without consensus" on these issues.

Meissner's book *What Is Effective in Psychoanalytic Therapy: The Move from Interpretation to Relation* (1991) first reprints Strachey's seminal 1934 paper on the therapeutic action of psychoanalysis. Despite the focus there on the transference *interpretation* as the truly (and only) mutative event, Meissner indicated that Strachey was himself quick to qualify this stark inference: "The patient's transference has become a motivating force inducing him to give up the resistances and undo the repression. The transference opens the way for the analyst to exercise an influence on the patient, which Strachey was not slow to call 'the power of suggestion.' Suggestion thus operates in the direction of undoing the resistances and facilitating the analytic work" (52). This overly narrow conception of suggestion was then broadened by Meissner to the more felicitous concern with the "relational matrix": "Even if interpretation is the process by which understanding is achieved and insight generated, that process takes place within a relational matrix that both colors the interpretive process and provides those elements that make the process viable and meaningful" (59). Meissner's favored rubric for these concerns is that of the "therapeutic alliance." In fact, he said, "I would argue that interpretations are mutative to the extent that they are developed within the context of the alliance rather than the transference" (70).

Meissner went on to consider concerns with technique for the so-called widening scope patients, which he said took two major directions: increasing attention in our literature (1) to the therapeutic alliance (*relational* factors) and (2) to the *developmental* perspective and models of "developmentally attuned interventions" (157) that are "beyond interpretation" (Gedo 1979). Meissner put the latter concern as follows: "how much, given the legitimacy or at least the unavoidability of dealing with infantile needs, concessions to such needs should be regarded as integral to psychoanalytic technique. Within the last decade, the view that endorses the need for such concessions in principle has assumed a more prominent position in psychoanalytic practice" (157–58). This massive shift has not been without controversy or confusion. "The divergence in viewpoints," according to Meissner,

> raises the question as to what therapeutic emphases are most appropriate or effective in a given case. The question has been posed first in terms of

the differential focus on the intrapsychic versus the interpersonal dimensions. The conflict orientation tends to direct its attention to the intrapsychic, while object relations and self psychology look to the interpersonal primarily. Efforts to align these approaches with developmental strata—intrapsychic with oedipal conflicts and the interpersonal with earlier infant-caretaker interactions—do not seem entirely satisfactory. The conflict approach does not exclude preoedipal pathology, nor does the interpersonal overlook concerns of the oedipal period. Nor does the constriction of the intrapsychic focus to neurotic patients with autoplastic adaptive styles who are treated in psychoanalysis, and of the interpersonal focus to more impaired alloplastically adapting patients [who are treated in psychoanalytic psychotherapy? or in "modified" psychoanalysis?] seem altogether cogent. (171–72)

Meissner went on to express his sense of the overall field today: "We are still in search of a theory of therapeutic change. There is a general agreement that any attempt at a unitary theory will probably prove to be inadequate, so that any useful theory will have to include a multiple causal perspective. . . . Various approaches emphasize insight, emotional experience, and the quality of the therapeutic relationship—all aspects that are compatible with each other and undoubtedly play a mutually influencing and intertwining role in bringing about therapeutic change" (178–79).

Meissner ended his book with a statement of his personal position:

The arguments over the role of interpretation and reconstruction seem to have shifted the ground somewhat in recent years—rather than interpretive resolution of the oedipal transference as the major agent of therapeutic change, emphasis falls on the analytic setting and the relation to the analyst as bearing the major weight of change in successful psychoanalytic treatment. . . . The question has become whether interpretation works because it leads to insight, or because it reflects and/or consolidates something about the analytic relationship. . . . This current of thinking is well reflected in . . . [the] view that, although interpretation is necessary, its content is not necessarily mutative, but that the implementation of the symbolic actualization of the holding environment in the analytic setting makes it possible for transference interpretations to be effective. (183–84)

On this Meissner felt that the field was by and large in accord: "There seems little question that analysts pay more attention to what is going on in their relationships with patients—over and above the transference vicissitudes—than they did a decade ago. They may formulate that shift in emphasis in various ways, but the sensitivity to the potential implications of the analytic relationship is general. . . . It is striking to me in reviewing this field that clinicians from such disparate persuasions arrive at a seemingly common ground of overlapping descriptions and technical modifications" (p. 190).

In his recent book (1992), in a chapter entitled "Psychoanalysis, Pseudo-analysis, and Psychotherapy," Schafer set these same issues specifically in the context of the relationship of the psychoanalyses to the psychoanalytic psychotherapies: "What is sometimes presented as Freudian psychoanalysis proves on close examination to have many of the features of eclectic psychotherapy. What is ostensibly psychoanalytic psychotherapy may prove to have many of the features of Freudian psychoanalysis. Some analysts doing psychotherapy get more analysis done, at least with certain patients, than other analysts do in carrying out conventional analyses. And some patients in psychotherapy get more analysis done, at least with certain therapists, than other patients get done in psychoanalysis proper. . . . There may be advantages, then, in treating the three therapeutic categories in this chapter's title as therapeutic approaches that differ in degree rather than kind" (266). He ended the chapter with, "Suppose that analysis is always a matter of degree, that much of what passes for analysis is pseudoanalysis, that some psychotherapy is very like analysis proper, and so forth: Why not just call any psychoanalytic psychotherapy *psychoanalysis?* Recognizing that psychoanalyses themselves vary in effectiveness, where could we draw the line between them and comparable psychotherapies? . . . In this perspective, psychoanalytic psychotherapy might be characterized as another form of limited or incomplete analysis" (277–78).

Jule Miller, a psychoanalyst much influenced by Alexander and by Kohut, expressed the fullest extension of this tendency toward actual amalgamation of psychoanalysis and psychotherapy in his paper "Can Psychotherapy Substitute for Psychoanalysis?" (1991). Miller began, "After many years of experience doing both analysis and therapy, I continue to believe that they are on a continuum and that there is no sharp dividing line either in theory, technique, goals, or results between psychotherapy and psychoanalysis" (45). Reviewing the papers from the 1954 debates by Rangell and Gill that sought both to define psychoanalysis and to set it off from the psychoanalytic psychotherapies, Miller declared their statements to be examples of "the idealization of analysis" (48) that characterized the period. And in reviewing the distinctions between psychoanalysis and the psychoanalytic psychotherapies advanced in subsequent years (49), Miller wrote, "I believe that each of these distinctions is fallacious . . . that the creation of such lists of dichotomies resulted from an idealization of analysis and an underestimation of the possibilities of psychotherapy" (49–50).

Miller went on to state his own position (within the Kohutian self psychology paradigm): "I believe that the central underlying process in psychotherapy is the formation and maintenance of a self-selfobject bond between patient and analyst. This bond enhances the patient's self-functioning. As it is maintained over time, the effects of this bond are internalized and lead to lasting improvements in the functioning of the patient's personality." This was followed by, "The most essential underlying process is the same in both psychotherapy and psychoanalysis" (52). What then are the differences, if any, between the two? "If one compares a typical analysis with a typical twice-weekly psychotherapy, the self-selfobject bond that is formed in the analysis will usually be deeper, and the explication and understanding of the bond will usually be more extensive, and the internalization more complete, leading to deeper and more far-reaching improvement. However, although these differences may be important, they are only differences of degree. A significant transference formation usually develops in both forms of therapy; this formation is typically more apparent in analysis than in therapy, although at times it may not be very visible in either. The more intense the psychotherapy and the more it is conducted in an analytic fashion, the less the difference between the two modalities" (53).

To his starting question, "Can Psychotherapy Substitute for Psychoanalysis?"—referring of course to patients considered amenable to analysis—Miller responded,

> The answer to the question is yes, if properly conducted. For maximum improvement, patients need to regress to the level of their most central psychopathology. Some patients, who are gifted as patients, may achieve the necessary depth of regression relatively easily because their defenses are pliable and the important issues are relatively accessible. With such patients, several-times-a-week psychotherapy over a prolonged period of time may be fully satisfactory. Most patients are not particularly gifted as patients, however; they are more rigidly constructed, their defenses are more impermeable, and they may need the maximum frequency of meetings, the use of auxiliary techniques (such as the couch, etc.), in order to experience an optimal level of regression. In other words, they will do best in an analysis, or its equivalent. It is the less accessible patients, with ingrained psychopathology, who require either an analysis or a form of intensive psychotherapy that closely approximates it, to obtain the best therapeutic results. (54–55)

These considerations led Miller to call psychoanalysis and psychoanalytic psychotherapy "one procedure with two names," with differences, if any, only in degree and with distinctions usually "made on historical or territorial grounds"

(54), that is, not on scientific grounds, like "the kind of credentials that the therapist possesses" (54).[8]

Kernberg (1993a, 1993c) has undertaken (in his characteristically methodical way) to clarify more precisely just where there are (in his view) real convergences today around issues of technique and the theory of technique (and theory of change), and where there are continuing divergences. He began his fuller statement on this subject (1993c) in the context of "Wallerstein's concept of the common ground of *clinical* theory—as against the marked discrepancies in metapsychological or *theoretical* formulations" (659). After citing numerous recent texts on technique, he said, "What is . . . interesting is that, even in texts that clearly announce their author's own bias, viewpoints of alternative schools are included, and one finds a generally more flexible attitude toward other viewpoints; an indication, in short, that older antagonisms have given way to a concern for communicating differences" (1993c, 659–60).

Kernberg then stated where he now saw convergences on issues of technique and on concepts of therapeutic action:

1. "A general tendency toward earlier interpretation of the transference, and an increased focus on the centrality of transference analysis in all psychoanalytic approaches (except, probably, the Lacanian)" (660)
2. The "focus on the analysis of the patient's habitual—and often unobtrusive yet rigid—behavior patterns in the psychoanalytic situation" (661), that is, character and character analysis
3. An increasing "focus on the unconscious meanings in the 'here and now' " (661)
4. An "increasing focus on translation of unconscious conflicts into object relations terminology" (662)
5. An increasing focus on the countertransference in "the broader sense of the total emotional reaction of the analyst to the patient . . . [which has] signalled a shift from a negative—what one might even call a phobic—attitude toward the countertransference (as an assumed reflection of the analyst's unresolved neurotic conflicts) to . . . an important instrument for investigating the transference and the total patient-analyst interaction" (662); and that, "I think it is fair to say that all analysts utilise the exploration of their own affective responses to

---

8. Miller's position on the actual amalgamation of psychotherapy and psychoanalysis is virtually a restatement of Gill's views as propounded in the 1979 Atlanta Symposium and published in 1984(a). This identity of current positions was arrived at from differing theoretical perspectives in psychoanalysis, Miller's a self psychological and Gill's a (post) ego-psychological framework.

their patients in a consistent and much freer way than earlier clinicians did" (662)

6. Concomitantly, an "increasing focus on [the] patient's affective experience" (663)

7. An emphasis on the "multiplicity of 'royal roads' to the unconscious" (663)

8. An "increasing concern with 'indoctrination' of patients" (664)

9. An "increased questioning of linear concepts of development" (665)

Kernberg then adumbrated what he called still-divergent trends in contemporary psychoanalytic technique, and the list proved to be almost equal in length:

1. The issue of the "real" relationship vis-à-vis the transference, that is, whether the transference concept encompasses the totality of the analytic relationship, as against the conception of the real relationship, the alliance, and so on, as distinct and separable from the transference, albeit interpenetrating with it, or whether the therapeutic effects of analysis derive from interpretation alone, as against the role of new experience; and also whether the transference represents the projected production of the patient or a joint creation of the therapeutic dyad (666–67)

2. The still-unsettled issue of the therapeutic as against the resistance aspects of treatment regressions (667–68)

3. The central problem of this book, the relationship between psychoanalysis and psychoanalytic psychotherapy, with Kernberg here stating two problems: "the boundaries of what may be considered standard analysis, in contrast to its modification or extension for patients who are not able to undergo such treatment, and the question of the 'dilution' of standard technique when a clear distinction between psychoanalysis and psychoanalytic psychotherapy is not maintained, as opposed to those who wish to experiment freely with the elements of the psychoanalytic technique and apply it to new fields" (668)

4. The role of analytic empathy, whether as the primary vehicle of the cure or merely as an essential precondition (668–69)

5. The focus on "historical truth," central to the scientific model of psychoanalysis, as against the focus on "narrative truth," central to the hermeneutic model (669)

6. The issue of "technical neutrality and cultural bias" (669), meaning by the latter unconscious collusions between analysts and patients regarding social, cultural, and political ideologies, and the requirement of their analytic exposure

7. The feasibility and utility of "the reconstruction and recovery of pre-verbal experience" (670)

In the other (1993a) article, Kernberg presented an almost identical list in abbreviated form. He did elaborate a little more fully a plea for the acknowledgment of the coequal status of psychoanalytic psychotherapy with proper psychoanalysis: "There is a tendency to apply stricter and more precise modifications of psychoanalytic technique to the psychotherapies, a tendency to question the traditionally subtle or not so subtle demeaning of psychoanalytic psychotherapies that are less than the 'pure gold' of standard psychoanalytic technique, and less fear that the development of such innovations in method will harm the methodological 'purity' of standard psychoanalysis." What might pass almost unnoticed in a comparison of these articles is that in the fuller statement I quoted first (1993c), the relationship between psychoanalysis and psychotherapy is listed among the areas of divergence in viewpoints whereas in the more abbreviated listing (1993a), it is listed among the areas of convergence and emerging consensus. This split within the mind of a single (major) contributor to these issues perhaps best reflects the state of the field today!

This same issue was George Allison's central topic in his 1992 plenary address to the American Psychoanalytic Association (1994), presented as a cautionary concern over what he felt to be the tendency toward "homogenization" of the two modalities in contemporary psychoanalytic discourse. This, he said, has resulted from the confluence of a number of trends: "the contemporary emphasis on the interactional, interpersonal, and relational factors in psychoanalysis as well as in psychoanalytic psychotherapy where they have always been considered more 'kosher' " (343); the "increasing acceptance of the legitimacy of judicious and introspectively guided attention to issues of attunement, empathy and human responsiveness in the analytic situation"; the greater freedom of analysts "to allow their compassionate, humane, inner responsiveness be evident to their patients. There is less concern that this might compromise neutrality and interfere with interpretation and insight as the primary activity and mode of therapeutic action"; the balancing of this greater freedom "by closer scrutiny of the countertransference with delineations, separation, and interpretive use of the role-responsive aspects of countertransference from the portion based on the analyst's own transferred past" (345), and so forth. It is this recent increase of attention to the interactive and mutually enactive relational aspects of the therapeutic process, with the concomitant oscillating focus on countertransference impulses and enactments along with the transferential impulses and behaviors—all of which, in Eissler's purified model, had once been consigned to psychotherapy, at least in America—that has fostered what Allison calls the tendency toward homogenization of the two modalities. And here Allison has pointed to the diverging camps, those who advocate this homogenization or amalgamation of psychoanalytic psychotherapy to psychoanalysis and those who hold more strictly to a traditional or classical definition of psychoanalysis in its narrower scope, with all those not amenable to psychoanalysis within this framework assigned to one or another approach within the range of varyingly expressive and supportive psychoanalytic psychotherapies. Clearly, both these positions have been represented throughout this book.

Allison stated his own measured position as follows:

> If one holds to the old idea (which I still do) of a continuum of psycho-analytic psychotherapies with psychoanalysis proper at one end and supportive psychotherapy at the other, I posit a similar continuum of different processes and outcomes with insight predominating at one end and un-analyzed interactions at the other. A distinction at the more interpretive end between formal psychoanalysis and interpretive but less frequent and usually sitting-up psychotherapy is also still desirable. *Their* homogenization ignores differences which I believe *exist* among the various processes and their modes of therapeutic action, resulting from differences in the frequency of sessions and the use (or not) of the couch. In psychotherapy, the *experience* of the interaction differs from that of analysis, which suggests that the mode of therapeutic action also differs by virtue of the lessened immersion and of the "reality" of the patient and analyst facing each other. (344)

Implicit in all this is Allison's corollary statement: "Both principal modes of therapeutic action (insight and relational) do occur in both modalities [psychoanalysis and psychoanalytic psychotherapy], although I believe that they are in different proportion" (346).

Allison then elaborated how he saw psychoanalysis and psychotherapy as different—that is, as different mixes of the same ingredients—and therefore related along a continuum and vulnerable to conceptual homogenization: "The model of the mother-infant dyad for both analysis and psychotherapy, and the importance of the analyst's self-perception and availability for the patient's perception as a warm, empathic, trustworthy co-worker are often cited as the foundation for either treatment. The *vis-à-vis* format of psychotherapy brings this 'reality' more to the *foreground* of the interaction, where its supportive meaning is more prominent. In analysis, with the use of the couch and its greater frequency of sessions, the supportive 'holding environment' of the treatment is rather the *background*. In analysis, the replay of old scenarios, dyadic and triadic, including strong negative transference, has a greater opportunity to be manifested and to be successfully interpreted and worked through in the here-and-now" (346).

In terms of different modes of therapeutic action, Allison added, "An increasingly accepted thesis to which I subscribe is that *unanalyzed* interactional, supportive, or relational factors predominate in the therapeutic action of psychotherapy, and that analysis of the interaction with insight and working through of the transference or transference neurosis predominates in the therapeutic action of psychoanalysis" (352). This had actually been stated in a more comprehensive form in an earlier version of this paper: "I believe, as I think most analysts still do, that the idea of a continuum or spectrum is still viable, useful, and consonant with clinical experience. I hold that in this continuum the psychotherapies blend into one another along with a continuum of fundamentally different processes and outcomes . . . with insight predominating at one end and unanalyzed interactions at the other. Some blending and homogenization of psychotherapy and psychoanalysis is inherent in the work we do and psychoanalysis is of course a form of psychotherapy. However, most psychoanalysts believe from their subjective experience that there is a distinction to be noted and maintained, while they also note and ponder its blurring from the pressures towards homogenization." Allison ended his paper with a strong plea for intensified empirical research into psychoanalytic processes and outcomes, citing in that connection *Psychoanalytic Process Research Studies* (edited by Dahl, Kachele, and Thoma 1988), *Forty-Two Lives in Treatment* (Wallerstein 1986a), and the Collaborative Multi-Site Psychoanalytic Therapy Research Program being organized by Wallerstein under the auspices of the American Psychoanalytic Association.

I have accorded Allison's recent statement of his views such place because I feel it to be a reasonable expression of the current American psychoanalytic mainstream on the issues of psychoanalytic psychotherapy vis-à-vis psychoanalysis, granted that there is a wide spectrum of opinion deviating from this view. The current degree of consensus, at least in the American literature, has been in the increasing awareness that the psychoanalyses in all their major variants comprise very significantly relational, affective, and enactive elements once thought to be the distinguishing marks of psychotherapy as technically distinct from psychoanalysis, and that therefore the differences between the two presumably distinct modalities are far less clear today than they were (in America) in the 1950s, more in the realm of variations in quantity and emphasis; and the similarities are far more striking, in almost all the essential qualitative characteristics.[9]

9. That Allison's statement does represent the current American and American-influenced post-ego-psychological mainstream position on these issues is reflected, for example, in an article by Douglas Frayn (1993) in the initial issue of the *Canadian Journal of Psychoanalysis*. Frayn has

In Britain, the other main originating center of psychoanalytic psychotherapy, there has all along been a far greater conceptual closeness of psychotherapy and psychoanalysis; or, put oppositely, greater reluctance to demarcate a distinctive psychotherapy with differing (and explicitly supportive) technical implementation, just because psychoanalysis in Britain under the sway of both the Kleinian and the Independent object-relational perspectives (and the British Contemporary Freudian, as exemplified by Sandler, as well) has always been more relationship-centered than the American mainstream. Consequently, many of the distinctions and conceptions that were so meaningful—and controversial—in America (like the therapeutic and working alliance concepts, for example) were considered tangential and neither useful nor relevant by most workers in Britain. The pull to what Allison calls homogenization has consequently always been stronger in Britain than in America.

How would I, then, express the overall conclusions of this book on the evolution of our understandings of the nature of psychoanalysis or the psychoanalyses, in particular its (their) theory (theories) of therapeutic change, and of the nature of the psychoanalytic psychotherapies, whether or not we still adhere to the particular distinctions among the expressive and the supportive approaches worked out in the 1940s and 1950s? and of our understandings of the differently imbricating relationship in terms of similarities and differences between these related treatment modalities as this has correspondingly evolved? And how similar is my viewpoint to the current views of Meissner and Schafer and Miller and Kernberg and Allison (and Frayn) as well as the host of others quoted in this book? I turn to these issues in the final chapter.

---

noted the same shifts over time to which Allison was calling attention and has espoused the same continuum approach: "The recent emphasis on subjectivity is seen by some analysts as signifying a novel and major psychoanalytic perspective shift, while others feel that the theoretical change is primarily semantic rather than substantive. It is my position that an 'intersubjective approach' . . . is an important feature of all analytic interventions regardless of the theoretical orientation of the analyst" (7). And "Interventions can be conceptualized as taking place along a *continuum* beginning from genetic interpretation of the unconscious through immediate empathic and conscious supportive statements to educational elements of inquiry, suggestion and advice. Gabbard (1990) includes interpretation, confrontation and clarification as primarily classical expressive interventions which aim to engage the analysand in addressing and reformulating his urges and resistance. Elaboration, empathic validation, affirmation and praise are considered as primarily ego supportive activities with supportive/empathic activity predominating when regressive/narcissistic transferences are most significant" (19, italics added).

26 Overview: Conclusions and Directions

For a variety of historical circumstances detailed in chapter 3, the psychoanalytic psychotherapies were first differentiated from psychoanalysis proper in an effort to apply psychoanalytic theoretical understandings to the treatment of a wider array of patients not deemed amenable to classical psychoanalytic treatment—within the then-prevailing ego-psychological metapsychology paradigm. This was a natural science framework (Hartmann), marked by a striving for maximum objectivity, with the analyst as observer and commentator upon the patient's transferences thrown in relief upon the blank analytic screen, except where clouded by the analyst's interfering countertransferences. The ensuing analytic process within the patient would then illuminate the patient's intrapsychic life and conflicts. This was called (mostly by those who developed differing views) a one-body psychology. The technical imprimatur was given by Eissler's 1953 paper on parameters, which sought to define an austere model of psychoanalysis based on veridical interpretation alone and expunged, insofar as possible, of suggestive influence of any kind; this was said to be the proper codification of the psychoanalysis created by Freud, the ultimate expression of Freud's classical analysis. Within and against this technical model, wild analysis could be carefully delineated, and, more important, an array of technical modifications could be introduced, comprised of various suggestive and other supportive elements adapted to the requirements of that wider spectrum of patients not amenable to proper psychoanalysis.

Almost from its inception, this theoretical model and the theories of technique derived from it began to suffer progressive erosion, but it was not till 1977 that a persuasive challenge was mounted (by Lipton) to the notion that this model did indeed reflect Freud's actual technique. But far more important, in a line going back to the technical papers of Ferenczi that were written almost contemporaneously with those of Freud, another perspective on the technique of psychoanalysis, based on the mutative power of the psychoanalytic relationship, beyond interpretation or in interaction with interpretation, emerged as a contrapuntally vital stream of psychoanalytic thinking. In America this first took root as the alliance concepts (called therapeutic by Zetzel and working by Greenson) and as the interpersonal psychiatry of Harry Stack Sullivan and its modern development (Levenson).

In Britain this position was crystallized as the object relations perspective of the Independent or Middle Group, with the central technical conceptions of Balint, the scientific heir to Ferenczi (the "new beginning"), and of Winnicott (the "holding environment"). And Greenberg and Mitchell (1983) made a plausible case for including Kleinian psychoanalysis as an object-relational perspective even though it is drenched in the language of instinctual drive. In America, kindred positions were espoused by Stone and Loewald, albeit in ego-psychological language, and, more forthrightly object-relational in language, by Zetzel, Modell, and Kernberg. The underlying tenets here were of an interactive, two-body psychology, moving seamlessly over the vicissitudes of internalized object relationships across all developmental levels, from the integrated oedipal neuroses, the centerpiece of ego-psychological theorizing, to the most archaic, primitive, and preoedipal vicissitudes. In this framework, therapeutic regression is more accepted, or at least tolerated, with some notable exceptions (cf. Gill and Arlow); enactment and mutual enactment are focused within the transference-countertransference interplay; and within its logical extension there is a leveling of the conceptual distinctions between transference and countertransference (McLaughlin and Gill in the American development of this position) and a conception even of transference (Poland) and resistance (Boesky) as, to a considerable degree, "joint creations" or "new creations" out of the interactional dialogue. All these relational perspectives on the analytic process, originating in Budapest and developed so extensively over many decades in Britain, have gradually infiltrated and effected a sea change in American psychoanalysis, now called by some post-ego-psychological. The most fully developed extensions of this viewpoint are in the "intersubjective perspective in psychoanalysis" of Stolorow and his co-workers and in Owen Renik's recent statement of the "irreducible (and necessary) subjectivity" on both sides of the analytic couch. Along with all this has been the major shift noted most recently by Fajardo in the conception of the epistemological underpinnings of the psychoanalytic enterprise from the objective "empirical behavioural science" perspective of Hartmann, through the "empirical hermeneutic" view of theorists as diverse as Kohut, Loewald, and Winnicott, to the thoroughly "hermeneutic constructivist perspective" of Schafer (at times), Spence, Stolorow, and Hoffman.[1]

---

1. Kimberlyn Leary (1994) has offered a persuasive account of the congruence of the varieties of relational, interactional, interpersonal, intersubjective, and social constructivist conceptualizations of psychoanalysis with what has come to be known, out of its roots in literary criticism and philosophy, as the postmodernist stance toward theory, culture, and knowledge. Leary demonstrates the direct relatedness of the postmodern or deconstructionist perspective, that written texts are but arrangements of words on paper which different readers with different subjectivities will respond to differently, so that the reality of each text is not inherent, to be uniformly retrieved, but will be constructed differently with each reader; the relatedness of this, for example, to Schafer's (1981) conception of analysis as a succession of narrative acts, a

What has brought about these changes in the conceptualization of the theory and the technique of psychoanalytic (and psychotherapeutic) work? To over-simplify, it has been a confluence of two main trends. First, the very austere model of psychoanalysis and of the distinctly demarcated expressive and supportive psychoanalytic psychotherapies simply did not work, did not adequately reflect the events of the therapeutic process and the interacting mutative influences discerned within it. This was very clearly articulated during the era of fragmenting consensus (chapter 8)—for example, by Rangell (1981b) in his report at the 1979 Symposium discussing these issues "twenty-five years later" and by Wallerstein (1986a) in his massive write-up of the thirty-year findings of the Psychotherapy Research Project of the Menninger Foundation. The lack of convincing fit between the model and the therapeutic process and outcome was evident not just with the sicker patients, the narcissistic personality disorders and the borderline personality organizations, but also with the "normal neurotic" patients considered classically the most amenable to unmodified psychoanalysis.

The other trend was the increasing receptivity—worldwide, but most importantly in America, the heartland of psychoanalytic psychotherapy—to the diverse theoretical developments arising in other psychoanalytic centers around the world, particularly the object-relational, Kleinian, Bionian, and even Lacanian perspectives, and to developments finally arising in America as well, especially Kohut's self psychology and also a new mainstream American interest in the Sullivanian interpersonal school. Some, like Kernberg, have been trying to build an overarching drive/structural-object/relational theoretical framework to encompass these shifts and the clinical verities they are designed to explain. Others, like Greenberg and Mitchell (1983), see the two paradigms as mutually exclusive and opt for total replacement of the drive/structural by the object/relational perspective. This issue remains unsettled today, as does our episte-

---

telling of life stories, or to Hoffman (1991) whose "social-constructivist" perspective shifts the task of analysis from a concern with interpreting an objective reality to a focus on the interactive process by which therapist and patient together create and shape a mutual impact on each other, their uniquely constructed reality.

Leary then develops the useful corrective that this "postmodern sensibility" has brought to traditional psychoanalytic perspectives (like a tendency toward a misplaced scientism, or the temptation to an authoritarian stance by the analyst as the arbiter of reality, etc.), but she also points to some of the problematic ingredients that can come with it (including in the extreme, an "anything goes" posture with no constraining limits on the intervention possibilities). A full discussion of these issues and the placing of this sea change that I have been chronicling in our understanding of the analytic enterprise over these recent decades within these overall trends in modern culture and society is beyond the scope of this book.

mological anchoring in a "correspondence" or a "coherence" theory of truth (Hanly 1992a)—another (and correlated) way of organizing the natural science-social science-"hermeneutic science"-hermeneutic spectrum.

Finally, what are the implications of this sea change for the relationship(s) between (now) the psychoanaly*ses* and the psychoanalytic psychotherap*ies?* First, the concept of wild analysis very properly goes by the board and should indeed be replaced by Schafer's felicitous "comparative analysis." Neither "wild analysis" nor "wild psychotherapy," for that matter, has any proper conceptual underpinning in today's analytic world. It is clear that all the strands of development tracing back in heritage to Ferenczi's original foregrounding of the analytic relationship were, early in the development of an explicit psychoanalytic psychotherapy, consigned to the realm of the psychoanalytic psychotherapies. Now that these influences have been reconceptualized as central to our understanding of what psychoanalysis is and how it works, it is indeed far more difficult to draw heuristically useful conceptual lines between psychoanalysis, or modified psychoanalysis, and (only or merely) psychoanalytic psychotherapy. And depending on the theoretical allegiance of the observer or investigator within the range of psychoanalytic theoretical perspectives, that line can be drawn very differently.

Nonetheless, many agree, perhaps only intuitively, with Allison's position that there is a spectrum and the quantitative mix of kinds of interventions changes as one goes along the spectrum from the most expressive-analytic end (for the normal neurotic patients) to the more suggestive-supportive end (for the sicker than neurotic patients) and that somewhere conceptual boundaries do get crossed, though without even as clear nodal crystallizations of predominant therapy modes along the spectrum as I propounded in 1986a in *Forty-Two Lives*. Allison put his faith in empirical research into the nature of psychoanalytic and psychotherapeutic processes and outcomes as the key to the sought-for renewed clarification and specification. Others, not so sanguine, see this less as a scientifically researchable issue than as an administrative and political issue determined by guild interests and by desires to protect the uniqueness of very rigorous and intensive training, training whose graduates are distinguished by their (putatively unique) ability to foster and manage those specific psychoanalytic processes that take place in daily sessions, recumbent on the couch.

Given these varying positions on the distinctions (or not) between the psychoanalyses and the psychoanalytic psychotherapies and given the lack of agreement on the extent to which these issues are truly susceptible to clarification via empirical research or are simply administrative-political (guild) issues (i.e., a vying for material or prestige advantage), or, more basically, issues of philosophical commitments and aesthetic predilections about the nature of the therapeutic enterprise; given all this, I want to make explicit an altered approach to these issues. This entails, first, trying to look afresh at the nature of the questions that have framed and guided this book. Perhaps we can now say, in comfortable hindsight, that from an investigative or research point of view central questions of our inquiry turned out not to have been framed in the heuristically most appropriate or fruitful ways. Perhaps, indeed, the question of the place of the psychoanalytic psychotherapies vis-à-vis the (various) psychoanalyses, although it has framed critical debates over the past four decades, has been but epiphenomenal to the more central question of the nature of psychic *change* and how it is brought about in desired directions via psychological engagements in the consulting room.

Putting the primary question of this book in this way yields several immediate advantages. It transforms some of the perennially vexing issues described in this book into potentially much more manageable form; for example, the question of boundaries between modalities—that is, when have enough departures taken place from whatever model of proper psychoanalysis one holds to warrant designating the treatment a psychoanalytic psychotherapy rather than a psychoanalysis proper? This should be more than simply a semantic or definitional predilection or prejudice, as it so often is. The study of psychic change, of the varying kinds of interventions that lead to change, and of the precise mechanisms according to which those interventions operate to effect change can perhaps generate greater concurrence on which interventions, leading to specific kinds of change in specific categories of patients, should be considered to be within the bounds of psychoanalysis and which within the bounds of psychoanalytic psychotherapy.

Coming at these issues from a primary focus on the problem of change provides a decidedly more manageable (i.e., researchable) and more value-neutral cast, freer of the pejorative convictions, endemic among so many of us, that proper psychoanalysis is the best treatment available and all variations of it are no more than second best. Such value-determined considerations can significantly cloud research efforts by confounding proper empirical questions with covert value predilections and distortions. As a well-known sports metaphor puts it, how level has the playing field been over our decades of scientific preoccupation with these issues? and how much can we help to level the field of scientific inquiry through, among other things, such a shift in the main question at issue to the problem of psychic change, its mechanisms and its determinants, and working from that to our overarching descriptive rubrics, psychoanalysis, psychotherapy, and so on, rather than, as traditionally, starting from our encompassing diagnostic designations with their implicit (even if unwanted and disavowed) value-loadings?

It was natural enough that things developed as they did to this point. The psychoanalysis innovated by Freud a century ago has been, after all, the natural starting point of our inquiry. It was historically the first scientific psychotherapy, dedicated to the amelioration of mental and emotional distress in those individuals sick enough to need it, but equally vital, healthy enough to tolerate its rigorous demands (those with Freud's "hypothetically normal ego," as Eissler put it). In theory the varyingly expressive and supportive psychoanalytically oriented psychotherapies were derived from psychoanalysis proper—a half-century after its creation—as technical applications of psychoanalytic understandings both to those "too healthy" for it, who do not need so deep a probe into their lives and so extensive a reconstruction as psychoanalysis represents and to those less fortunate, "too sick" to tolerate the (regressive) demands of analysis.

Put this way, the indications for the range of psychoanalytic psychotherapies seem value-neutral enough. However, the prevailing bias within psychoanalytic ranks has always been that those healthier patients whose presenting illnesses could be resolved via an expressive psychotherapy with limited probing into the patient's personality functioning well short of the effort at completeness of a thorough psychoanalysis could profit even more from full analysis and would therefore somehow be sold short if the therapist were to simply address the evident distress and its causal instigators. That is, whether they are "healthier" patients who are denied the putative far-ranging benefits of analysis because an expressive psychotherapy could suffice to cope with their complaints or "sicker" patients who are felt to be unable to tolerate analysis and therefore have to be content with the presumably smaller accomplishment of their more supportive therapeutic mode, in either case those not in psychoanalysis would have to settle for a lesser, faute de mieux, result than those fortunate enough to need, be suitable for, and experience a proper psychoanalysis. It is just this bias that has always been inherent in the ostensibly neutral dictum, "Be as expressive [meaning properly psychoanalytic] as you can be; be as supportive as you have to be."

Thus we have always operated (not necessarily self-consciously) with a double (value) standard, that formal psychoanalysis—and whatever we can call psychoanalysis—is better, hard as we may have tried to eschew this bias. A striking example of this predilection is a recent remark reportedly made by one of our most eminent psychoanalytic clinicians and theoreticians, a man who, because of age and infirmity, has ceased taking patients into regular psychoanalysis but is continuing a limited clinical practice with once-a-week patients and has discovered to his happy surprise that he is doing comparably "analytic" work with his patients after all. Certainly we (collectively) have simply not been able, in our considerations of indications and contraindications to the psychoanalyses and the psychotherapies, of similarities and differences, of technical distinctions in suitability, kinds of interventions, goals, and results, to transcend this prevailing conviction that, all else being equal, psychoanalysis is just better. We have consequently never had the level conceptual playing field that best guarantees knowledge accrual via systematic study and conceptual and empirical advance in any scientific discipline. Certainly the whole trend toward reconceptualizing all the relationship and developmental and enactive and intersubjective perspectives, that early on in the development of an explicit psychoanalytic psychotherapy were consigned to the realm of the varyingly expressive and supportive psychotherapies, as now central to the nature of psychoanalysis itself has clearly been given impetus by the tendency to bring whatever we feel is good and useful therapy back within the rubric of psychoanalysis, because that is, after all, the "best" place to be, the best conceptual home in which to stake one's claim.

All this has posed significant difficulties for the attempts to resolve the questions and dilemmas posed throughout this book. It has created precisely the biased playing field, the confounding of truly empirical questions with all the varieties of political, socioeconomic, and even basic philosophical questions that are ultimately matters of predilection and prejudice. It is exactly this set of confoundings and unclarities that I feel has beset the issues dealt with throughout this book. My proposal for the rectification—as much as possible—of this handicap, recasting the central question as that of psychic change and the mechanisms through which it comes about or is brought about, I believe can put the focus of our studies into a more heuristically and empirically manageable frame. It can better set the issues involved in the quest to put our accumulating psychoanalytic knowledge at the service of the full range of patients who seek our aid, whatever the rubrics we feel best characterize the array of technical interventions that mark our therapeutic endeavors and whatever the extent to which the designations that have been employed throughout this book to represent our range of therapeutic modes survive as still useful or are superseded by new names and new definitions embodying refined or altered or more comprehensively integrative conceptions.

An example of the effort to reconceptualize the issues of this book under the central question of the nature of psychic change is the shift in conceptualization from that of the Menninger Psychotherapy Research Project, (PRP) which operated from the early 1950s to the early 1980s, to that of the successor project at the Langley Porter Institute (PRP-II). Basically, in PRP the central question was the kinds of changes (patient *outcomes*) brought about via the differentiated range of proffered therapeutic modalities, psychoanalysis, expressive psychotherapy, and supportive psychotherapy, each in relation to the kinds of patients for which that modality was deemed clinically indicated.

The major finding of this endeavor was that most of the treatments (psycho-therapeutic and psychoanalytic alike) had substantially altered during their course in a supportive direction, that more of the patients (again, psychotherapeutic and psychoanalytic alike) had changed on the basis of designedly supportive interventions and mechanisms than had been expected, and that in many of the more supportive therapies the changes reached seemed frequently just as much "structural change" as the changes reached in the most expressive-analytic cases. In order to explore these findings and conclusions more rigorously, PRP-II was devised to construct Scales of Psychological Capacities, changes in which over the course of therapy could be validly taken to reflect underlying structural changes, and then to relate these changes to the kinds of therapeutic interven-tions that brought them about, under whatever definitional rubrics we would then organize those patterns of intervention on the basis of our accruing enlarged understandings. This of course is precisely the shift in strategy advocated here, though at the time of its construction as the successor to PRP, PRP-II seemed just the logical outgrowth and in no wise was perceived as a shift in research strategy and in the very formulation of the research question.

This altered strategy is evident also in the Collaborative Analytic Multi-Site Program (CAMP), a consortium organized under the auspices of the American Psychoanalytic Association, which, as noted earlier, will bring the concepts and instruments of thirteen process study groups and three outcome study groups to bear on a common data base of audiotaped and transcribed analytic and therapeutic hours from patients with completed treatments, and with before and after assessments. (See Wallerstein, unpubl. ms c for the overall research plan.) And this new direction is fully in accord with my conviction that the new and far more sophisticated empirical research concepts and instruments (see *Psycho-analytic Process Research Strategies* by Dahl, Kachele, and Thoma 1988) developed over recent years promise to further our knowledge—and our capacity to help sufferers of mental and emotional disorders—in the realm of the psychoanalyt-ically based therapeutic approaches significantly beyond the level achieved today by the forty years of cumulated study and conceptual and technical advance chronicled in this book.

All this brings me to a final statement about the place of research in the present and future psychoanalytic scheme of things. I have written about this overall issue in a number of contexts (see especially Wallerstein 1988c). Here I want only to make the point elaborated elsewhere (Wallerstein 1988a) that at the present stage of our development as a discipline, with the pluralism of the-oretical perspectives to which we differentially give allegiance and within which we try to give meaning to our clinical data in the present and to reconstruct the past out of which the present developed, that this pluralism represents only the variety of scientific metaphors we have created to satisfy our variously conditioned needs for closure and coherence and theoretical understanding. By this I mean that the metapsychological concepts that mark our various theoretical perspectives are too experience-distant, too remote from the clinical data of our consulting rooms and from the shared concepts that mark our clinical theory, to be susceptible to scientific inquiry and testing. But I view the formation of clinical theory—the theory of conflict and compromise, of resistance and defense, of transference and countertransference—aided though it is by the symbolisms of our metaphoric (our varying metapsychological) constructions, as nonetheless sufficiently experience-near, anchored directly enough to the data of our consulting rooms, to be amenable to the self-same processes of hypothesis formation, testing, and validation as any other scientific enterprise, albeit by methods adapted to the subjectivistic nature of the essential data. The example just cited from PRP and from PRP-II, with its focus on observable "psychological capacities" as reflectors of underlying structure, is an expression of such a research approach within the common ground of our experience-near clinical theory. And this more value-neutral and therefore more level playing field will help us push the limits of scientific empirical advance in regard to the central issues of this book, whether posed as the problem of change, structure, and of structural change, or ultimately, the further delineation and clarification of the parameters of whatever in the end we encompass within the rubrics of the psychoanalyses and the psychoanalytic psychotherapies.

References

Abend, Sander M. (1989). Countertransference and Psychoanalytic Technique. *Psychoanal. Quart.* 58:374–95.

———— (1990). The Psychoanalytic Process: Motives and Obstacles in the Search for Clarification. *Psychoanal. Quart.* 59:532–49.

———— (1993). An Inquiry into the Fate of the Transference in Psychoanalysis. *J. Amer. Psychoanal. Assn.* 41:627–51.

————, Michael S. Porder and Martin S. Willick (1983). *Borderline Patients: Psychoanalytic Perspectives,* 255. New York: Int. Univ. Press.

Abrams, Samuel (1987). The Psychoanalytic Process: A Schematic Model. *Int. J. Psycho-Anal.* 68:441–52.

———— (1990). The Psychoanalytic Process: The Developmental and the Integrative. *Psychoanal. Quart.* 59:650–77.

———— (1992). Interpretation: A Dialogue. *Psychoanal. Inq.* 12:196–207.

Adler, Gerald (1993). Book Review of *Psychodynamic Psychotherapy of Borderline Patients* by Otto F. Kernberg, Michael A. Selzer, Harold W. Koenigsberg, Arthur C. Carr, and Ann H. Appelbaum. *Psychoanal. Quart.* 62:294–97.

Aichhorn, August (1935). *Wayward Youth,* 236. New York: Viking Press.

Alexander, Franz (1937). *Five Year Report of the Chicago Institute for Psychoanalysis: 1932–1937.* Chicago: Chicago Institute for Psychoanalysis.

———— (1950a). *Psychosomatic Medicine: Its Principles and Applications,* 300. New York: W. W. Norton.

———— (1950b). Analysis of the Therapeutic Factors in Psychoanalytic Treatment. *Psychoanal. Quart.* 19:482–500.

———— (1953). Current Views on Psychotherapy. *Psychiatry* 16:113–22.

———— (1954a). Some Quantitative Aspects of Psychoanalytic Technique. *J. Amer. Psychoanal. Assn.* 2:685–701.

———— (1954b). Psychoanalysis and Psychotherapy. *J. Amer. Psychoanal. Assn.* 2:722–33.

———— (1956). *Psychoanalysis and Psychotherapy: Developments in Theory, Technique and Training,* 299. New York: W. W. Norton.

———— (1961). *The Scope of Psychoanalysis, 1921–1961: Selected Papers,* 594. New York: Basic Books.

———— and Thomas Morton French (1946). *Psychoanalytic Therapy: Principles and Application,* 353. New York: Ronald Press.

———— and ———— (1948). *Studies in Psychosomatic Medicine: An Approach to the Cause and Treatment of Vegetative Disturbances,* 568. New York: Ronald Press.

Allen, Clifford (1935). The Diagnosis and Treatment of the Early Psychotic and Prepsychotic. *Brit. J. Med. Psychol.* 15:140–52.

Allison, George H. (1994). On the Homogenization of Psychoanalysis and Psychoanalytic Psychotherapy: A Review of Some of the Issues. *J. Amer. Psychoanal. Assn.,* 42:341–62.

Alpert, Augusta (1959). Reversibility of Pathological Fixation Associated with Maternal Deprivation in Infancy. *Psychoanal. Study of Child* 14:169–85.

Arlow, Jacob A. (1975). Discussion of Paper by Mark Kanzer: The Therapeutic and Working Alliances. *Int. J. Psychoanal. Psychother.* 4:69–73.

—— (1979). The Genesis of Interpretation. *J. Amer. Psychoanal. Assn.* 27(Suppl.):193–206.

—— (1987). The Dynamics of Interpretation. *Psychoanal. Quart.* 56:68–87.

—— and Charles Brenner (1969). The Psychopathology of the Psychoses: A Proposed Revision. *Int. J. Psycho-Anal.* 50:5–14.

—— and —— (1990). The Psychoanalytic Process. *Psychoanal. Quart.* 59:678–92.

Aron, Lewis, and Therese Ragen (1990). Conference on Sandor Ferenczi held in New York City, May 1991. *The Round Robin,* Division 39, American Psychological Association, December, pp. 3–4.

Atwood, George E., and Robert D. Stolorow (1984). *Structures of Subjectivity: Explorations in Psychoanalytic Phenomenology,* 217. Hillsdale, N.J., and London: Analytic Press.

Bacal, Howard A., and Kenneth M. Newman (1990). *Theories of Object Relations: Bridges to Self Psychology,* 299. New York: Columbia Univ. Press.

Bachrach, Henry M., Robert Galatzer-Levy, Alan Z. Skolnikoff and Sherwood Waldron, Jr. (1991). On the Efficacy of Psychoanalysis. *J. Amer. Psychoanal. Assn.* 39:871–916.

——, John J. Weber and Murray Solomon (1985). Factors Associated with the Outcome of Psychoanalysis (Clinical and Methodological Considerations): Report of the Columbia Psychoanalytic Center Research Project (IV). *Int. Rev. Psycho-Anal.* 12:379–88.

Balint, Michael (1932). Character Analysis and New Beginning. In Michael Balint, *Primary Love and Psycho-Analytic Technique,* 159–73. New York: Liveright Publ., 1953.

—— (1967). Sandor Ferenczi's Technical Experiments. In *Psychoanalytic Techniques: A Handbook for the Practicing Psychoanalyst,* ed. Benjamin B. Wolman, 147–67. New York and London: Basic Books.

—— (1968). *The Basic Fault: Therapeutic Aspects of Regression,* 205. London: Tavistock Publ.

Balter, Leon, and James H. Spencer, Jr. (1991). Observation and Theory in Psychoanalysis: The Self Psychology of Heinz Kohut. *Psychoanal. Quart.* 60:361–95.

Basch, Michael Franz (1980). *Doing Psychotherapy,* 188. New York: Basic Books.

—— (1988a). *Understanding Psychotherapy: The Science Related to the Art,* 329. New York: Basic Books.

—— (1988b). How Does Treatment Help? A Developmental Perspective. In *How Does Treatment Help? On the Modes of Therapeutic Action of Psychoanalytic Psychotherapy,* ed. Arnold Rothstein, 127–33. Madison, Conn.: Int. Univ. Press.

—— (1992). *Practicing Psychotherapy: A Casebook,* 204. New York: Basic Books.

Bass, Anthony (1992). Review Essay of *Psychotic Anxieties and Containment: A Personal Account of an Analysis with Winnicott* by Margaret Little. *Psychoanal. Dial.* 2:117–31.

Berezin, Martin A., and Stanley H. Cath, eds. (1965). *Geriatric Psychiatry: Grief, Loss, and Emotional Disorders in the Aging Process,* 380. New York: Int. Univ. Press.

Berliner, Bernhard (1941). Short Psychoanalytic Psychotherapy: Its Possibilities and Its Limitations. *Bull. Menn. Clinic* 5:204–13.

—— (1945). Short Psychoanalytic Psychotherapy: Second Contribution. *Bull. Menn. Clinic* 9:155–61.

Berman, Leo (1949). Counter-Transferences and Attitudes of the Analyst in the Therapeutic Process. *Psychiatry* 12:159–66.

Bernfeld, Siegfried (1941). The Facts of Observation in Psychoanalysis. *J. Psychol.* 12:289–305.

Bernstein, Stephen B. (1983). Treatment Preparatory to Psychoanalysis. *J. Amer. Psychoanal. Assn.* 31:363–90.

Bibring, Edward (1937). Symposium on the Theory of the Therapeutic Results of Psycho-Analysis. *Int. J. Psycho-Anal.* 18:170–89.

——— (1954). Psychoanalysis and the Dynamic Psychotherapies. *J. Amer. Psychoanal. Assn.* 2:745–70.

Bird, Brian (1972). Notes on Transference: Universal Phenomenon and Hardest Part of Analysis. *J. Amer. Psychoanal. Assn.* 20:267–301.

Blos, Peter (1962). *On Adolescence: A Psychoanalytic Interpretation,* 269. New York: Free Press.

——— (1979). *The Adolescent Passage: Developmental Issues,* 521. New York: Int. Univ. Press.

Blum, Harold P. (1971). On the Conception and Development of the Transference Neurosis. *J. Amer. Psychoanal. Assn.* 19:41–53.

——— (1979). The Curative and Creative Aspects of Insight. *J. Amer. Psychoanal. Assn.* 27(Suppl):41–70.

——— (1983). The Position and Value of Extratransference Interpretation. *J. Amer. Psychoanal. Assn.* 31:587–617.

——— (1989). The Concept of Termination and the Evolution of Psychoanalytic Thought. *J. Amer. Psychoanal. Assn.* 37:275–95.

——— (1992). Psychic Change: The Analytic Relationship(s) and Agents of Change. *Int. J. Psycho-Anal.* 73:255–65.

Boesky, Dale (1988a). The Concept of Psychic Structure. *J. Amer. Psychoanal. Assn.* 36(Suppl): 113–35.

——— (1988b). Comments on the Structural Theory of Technique. *Int. J. Psycho-Anal.* 69: 303–16.

——— (1988c). A Discussion of Evidential Criteria for Therapeutic Change. In *How Does Treatment Help? On the Modes of Therapeutic Action of Psychoanalytic Psychotherapy,* ed. Arnold Rothstein, 171–80. Madison, Conn.: Int. Univ. Press.

——— (1989). The Questions and Curiosity of the Psychoanalyst. *J. Amer. Psychoanal. Assn.* 37:579–603.

——— (1990). The Psychoanalytic Process and Its Components. *Psychoanal. Quart.* 59:550–84.

——— (unpubl. ms). Countertransference and Resistance. Victor Calef Memorial Lecture, San Francisco, 1990.

Bollas, Christopher (1987). *The Shadow of the Object: Psychoanalysis of the Unthought Known,* 283. London: Free Association Books.

——— (1991). *Forces of Destiny: Psychoanalysis and Human Idiom,*223. London: Free Association Books.

——— (1992). *Being a Character: Psychoanalysis and Self Experience,* 294. New York: Hill and Wang.

Bowen, Murray (1978). *Family Therapy in Clinical Practice,* 565. New York and London: Jason Aronson.

Brabant, Eva, Ernst Falzeder, and Patrizia Giamperi-Deutsch, eds., under the supervision of Andre Haynal. Translated by Peter T. Hoffer (1993). *The Correspondence of Sigmund Freud and Sandor Ferenczi, Vol. 1, 1908–1914,* 548. Cambridge: Belknap Press, Harvard Univ. Press.

Brenner, Charles (1979). Working Alliance, Therapeutic Alliance, and Transference. *J. Amer. Psychoanal. Assn.* 27(Suppl):137–57.

——— (1982). *The Mind in Conflict,* 266. New York: Int. Univ. Press.

——— (1987). Working Through: 1914–1984. *Psychoanal. Quart.* 56:88–108.

Buckley, Peter (1989). Fifty Years after Freud: Dora, the Rat Man and the Wolf-Man. *Amer. J. Psychiat.* 146:1394–1403.

Bullard, Dexter M., ed. (1959). *Psychoanalysis and Psychotherapy: Selected Papers of Frieda Fromm-Reichmann,* 350. Chicago: Univ. of Chicago Press.

Busch, Fred (1994). Some Ambiguities in the Method of Free Association and their Implications for Technique. *J. Amer. Psychoanal. Assn.* 42:363–84.

Calef, Victor, and Edward M. Weinshel (1977). Transference Neurosis. *Int. Encyclopedia of Psychiatry, Psychology, Psychoanalysis, and Neurology,* 256–61. Aesculapius Publ.

———— and ———— (1979). The New Psychoanalysis and Psychoanalytic Revisionism: Book Review Essay on Borderline Conditions and Pathological Narcissism. *Psychoanal. Quart.* 48: 470–91.

Carroll, Denis (1938). The Unwilling Patient I. *Brit. J. Med. Psychol.* 17:54–63.

Casement, Patrick J. (1985). *On Learning from the Patient,* 244. London and New York: Routledge.

———— (1990a). *Learning from the Patient,* 386. New York and London: Guilford Press.

———— (1990b). The Meeting of Needs in Psychoanalysis. *Psychoanal. Inq.* 10:325–46.

Chasseguet-Smirgel, Janine (1984). *Creativity and Perversion,* 172. New York: W. W. Norton.

———— (1992). Some Thoughts on the Psychoanalytic Situation. *J. Amer. Psychoanal. Assn.* 40:3–25.

———— and Angela Goyena (1993). Core Fantasy and Psychoanalytic Change. In *Psychic Structure and Psychic Change: Essays in Honor of Robert S. Wallerstein, M.D.,* ed. Mardi J. Horowitz, Otto F. Kernberg, and Edward M. Weinshel, 233–62. Madison, Conn.: Int. Univ. Press.

Chassell, Joseph O. (1955). Panel reporter, Psychoanalysis and Psychotherapy. *J. Amer. Psychoanal. Assn.* 3:528–33.

Chused, Judith Fingert (1992). Interpretations and Their Consequences in Adolescents. *Psychoanal. Inq.* 12:275–95.

Clarkson, Petruska (1990). A Multiplicity of Psychotherapeutic Relationships. *Brit. J. Psychother.* 7:148–63.

Colby, Kenneth Mark (1951). *A Primer for Psychotherapists,* 167. New York: Ronald Press.

Compton, Allan (1990). The Psychoanalytic Process. *Psychoanal. Quart.* 59:585–98.

Cooper, Arnold M. (1987a). Changes in Psychoanalytic Ideas: Transference Interpretation. *J. Amer. Psychoanal. Assn.* 35:77–98.

———— (1987b). The Transference Neurosis: A Concept Ready for Retirement. *Psychoanal. Inq.* 7:569–85.

———— (1988). Our Changing Views of the Therapeutic Action of Psychoanalysis: Comparing Strachey and Loewald. *Psychoanal. Quart.* 57:15–27.

———— (1989). Concepts of Therapeutic Effectiveness in Psychoanalysis: A Historical Review. *Psychoanal. Inq.* 9:4–25.

———— (1992). Psychic Change: Development in the Theory of Psychoanalytic Techniques: 37th IPA Congress Overview. *Int. J. Psycho-Anal.* 73:245–50.

Cooper, Steven H. (1993). Interpretive Fallibility and the Psychoanalytic Dialogue. *J. Amer. Psychoanal. Assn.* 41:95–126.

Coriat, Isador H. (1917). Some Statistical Results of the Psychoanalytic Treatment of the Psychoneuroses. *Psychoanal. Rev.* 4:209–16.

Crichton-Miller, Hugh (1937). The Frontiers of Psychotherapy. *Brit. J. Med. Psychol.* 16:165–83.

Crits-Christoph, Paul, and Jacques P. Barber, eds. (1991). *Handbook of Short-Term Dynamic Psychotherapy*, 365. New York: Basic Books.

Curtis, Homer C. (1979). The Concept of Therapeutic Alliance: Implications for the "Widening Scope." *J. Amer. Psychoanal. Assn.* 27(Suppl):159–92.

Dahl, Hartvig, Horst Kachele, and Helmut Thoma (1988). *Psychoanalytic Process Research Strategies*, 334. Berlin, Heidelberg, New York, London, Paris, and Tokyo: Springer-Verlag.

Davanloo, Habib (1978). *Basic Principles and Techniques in Short-Term Dynamic Psychotherapy*, 555. New York and London: Spectrum Publ.

Deutsch, Felix (1949). *Applied Psychoanalysis: Selected Objectives of Psychotherapy*, 144. New York: Grune and Stratton.

———, ed. (1953). *The Psychosomatic Concept in Psychoanalysis*, 182. New York: Int. Univ. Press.

———, ed. (1959). *On the Mysterious Leap from the Mind to the Body: A Workshop Study on the Theory of Conversion*, 273. New York: Int. Univ. Press.

Deutsch, Helene (1959). Psychoanalytic Therapy in the Light of Follow-Up. *J. Amer. Psychoanal. Assn.* 7:445–58.

Devine, H. (1930). The Psychotherapy of the Psychoses (I). *Brit. J. Med. Psychol.* 10:217–25.

Dewald, Paul A. (1964). *Psychotherapy: A Dynamic Approach*, 307. New York: Basic Books.

——— (1972). The Clinical Assessment of Structural Change. *J. Amer. Psychoanal. Assn.* 20: 302–24.

——— (1978). The Psychoanalytic Process in Adult Patients. *Psychoanal. Study of Child* 33: 323–32.

——— (1990). Conceptualizations of the Psychoanalytic Process. *Psychoanal. Quart.* 59:693–711.

——— (1992). The "Rule" and Role of Abstinence in Psychoanalysis. In *The Technique and Practice of Psychoanalysis. 2: A Memorial Volume to Ralph R. Greenson*, ed. Alan Sugarman, Robert A. Nemiroff, and Daniel P. Greenson, 135–57. Madison, Conn.: Int. Univ. Press.

——— (1993). Psychic Structure and Psychic Change. In *Psychic Structure and Psychic Change: Essays in Honor of Robert S. Wallerstein, M.D.*, ed. Mardi J. Horowitz, Otto F. Kernberg, and Edward M. Weinshel, 117–34. Madison, Conn.: Int. Univ. Press.

——— (unpubl. ms). Psychoanalysis and Psychoanalytic Psychotherapy. Panel presentation at American Psychoanalytic Association, Dec. 1989.

DeWitt, Kathryn N., Dianna E. Hartley, Saul E. Rosenberg, Nathan J. Zilberg, and Robert S. Wallerstein (1991). Scales of Psychological Capacities: Development of an Assessment Approach. *Psychoanal. Cont. Thought* 14:343–61.

Dicks, Henry V. (1970). *Fifty Years of the Tavistock Clinic*, 415. London: Routledge and Kegan Paul.

Dimon, Jim (1992). Review of the Literature. *Psychoanal. Inq.* 12:182–95.

Dorpat, Theodore (1976). Structural Conflict and Object Relations Conflict. *J. Amer. Psychoanal. Assn.* 24:855–74.

Dupont, Judith, ed. (1988). *The Clinical Diary of Sandor Ferenczi*, 227. Cambridge and London: Harvard Univ. Press.

Edelson, Marshall (1984). *Hypothesis and Evidence in Psychoanalysis*, 179. Chicago and London: Univ. Chicago Press.

Ehrenreich, Gerald K. (1958). Personal communication.

Eissler, Kurt R., ed. (1949). *Searchlights on Delinquency: New Psychoanalytic Studies*, 456. New York: Int. Univ. Press.

—— (1950). The Chicago Institute of Psychoanalysis and the Sixth Period of the Development of Psychoanalytic Technique. *J. General Psychol.* 42:103–57.

—— (1953). The Effect of the Structure of the Ego on Psychoanalytic Technique. *J. Amer. Psychoanal. Assn.* 1:104–43.

—— (1958). Remarks on Some Variations in Psycho-Analytical Technique. *Int. J. Psycho-Anal.* 39:222–29.

Ekstein, Rudolf, and Robert S. Wallerstein (1958). *The Teaching and Learning of Psychotherapy*, 334. New York: Basic Books. Reprinted, New York: Int. Univ. Press, 1972, 344.

English, O. Spurgeon (1953). Panel reporter, The Essentials of Psychotherapy as Viewed by the Psychoanalyst. *J. Amer. Psychoanal. Assn.* 1:550–61.

Erikson, Erik H. (1950). *Childhood and Society*, 397. New York: W. W. Norton.

—— (1959). *Identity and the Life Cycle*, 171. Psychol. Issues Monograph 1. New York: Int. Univ. Press.

—— (1982). *The Life Cycle Completed: A Review*, 108. New York: W. W. Norton.

Erle, Joan B. (1979). An Approach to the Study of Analyzability and Analysis: The Course of Forty Consecutive Cases Selected for Supervised Analysis. *Psychoanal. Quart.* 48:198–228.

—— (1990). Studying the Psychoanalytic Process: An Introduction. *Psychoanal. Quart.* 59:527–31.

—— and Daniel A. Goldberg (1979). Problems in the Assessment of Analyzability. *Psychoanal. Quart.* 48:48–84.

—— and —— (1984). Observations on Assessment of Analyzability by Experienced Analysts. *J. Amer. Psychoanal. Assn.* 32: 715–37.

Esman, Aaron H. (1991). Book Review of *The Technique at Issue: Controversies in Psychoanalysis from Freud and Ferenczi to Michael Balint*, by Andre Haynal. *J. Amer. Psychoanal. Assn.* 39: 290–92.

Etchegoyen, R. Horacio (1991). *The Fundamentals of Psychoanalytic Technique*, 863. London and New York: Karnac Books.

Ezriel, Henry (1950). A Psycho-Analytic Approach to Group Treatment. *Brit. J. Med. Psychol.* 23:59–74.

—— (1952). Notes on Psycho-Analytic Group Therapy: Interpretation and Research. *Psychiatry* 15:119–26.

Fajardo, Barbara (1993). Conditions for the Relevance of Infant Research to Clinical Psychoanalysis. *Int. J. Psycho-Anal.* 74:975–91.

Federn, Paul (1952). *Ego Psychology and the Psychoses*. Edited and with an Introduction by Edoardo Weiss, 375. New York: Basic Books.

Feldman, Fred (1968). Results of Psychoanalysis in Clinic Assignments. *J. Amer. Psychoanal. Assn.* 16:274–300.

Fenichel, Otto (1930). Statisticher Bericht uber die Therapeutische Tatigkeit 1920–1930. In Zehn Jahre Berliner Psychoanalytisches Institut. *Int. Psychoanal. Verlag* 13–19.

—— (1941a). *Problems of Psychoanalytic Technique*, 130. Albany: Psychoanal. Quart.

—— (1941b). The Ego and the Affects. In *Collected Papers*, Second Series, 215–27. New York: W. W. Norton, 1954.

—— (1945). *The Psychoanalytic Theory of Neurosis*, 703. New York: W. W. Norton.

Ferenczi, Sandor (1912). Suggestion and Psycho-Analysis. In *Further Contributions to the Theory and Technique of Psycho-Analysis*, 55–68. London: Hogarth Press, 1926.

—— (1919a). On the Technique of Psycho-Analysis. In *Further Contributions to the Theory and Technique of Psycho-Analysis*, 177–89. London: Hogarth Press, 1926.

—— (1919b). Technical Difficulties in the Analysis of a Case of Hysteria. In *Further Contributions to the Theory and Technique of Psycho-Analysis*, 189–97. London: Hogarth Press, 1926.

—— (1920). The Further Development of an Active Therapy in Psycho-Analysis. In *Further Contributions to the Theory and Technique of Psycho-Analysis*, 198–217. London: Hogarth Press, 1926.

—— (1925). Contra-Indications to the 'Active' Psycho-Analaytical Technique. In *Further Contributions to the Theory and Technique of Psycho-Analysis*, 217–30. London: Hogarth Press, 1926.

—— (1928). The Elasticity of Psycho-Analytic Technique. In *Final Contributions to the Problems and Methods of Psychoanalysis*, 87–101. New York: Basic Books, 1955.

—— (1930). The Principle of Relaxation and Neocatharsis. In *Final Contributions to the Problems and Methods of Psychoanalysis*, 108–25. New York: Basic Books, 1955.

—— (1933). Confusion of Tongues between Adults and the Child. In *Final Contributions to the Problems and Methods of Psychoanalysis*, 156–67. New York: Basic Books, 1955.

—— and Otto Rank (1924). *The Development of Psycho-Analysis*, 68. Reprinted, Madison, Conn.: Int. Univ. Press, 1986.

Fisher, Charles P. (1987). Panel reporter, Conversion of Psychotherapy to Psychoanalysis. *J. Amer. Psychoanal. Assn.* 35:713–26.

Fleischmann, Otto, Paul Kramer, and Helen Ross (1964). *Delinquency and Child Guidance: Selected Papers by August Aichhorn*, 244. New York: Int. Univ. Press.

Fogel, Gerald I. (1989). The Authentic Function of Psychoanalytic Theory: An Overview of the Contributions of Hans Loewald. *Psychoanal. Quart.* 58:419–51.

—— (1993). Transitional Phase in Our Understanding of the Psychoanalytic Process: A New Look at Ferenczi and Rank. *J. Amer. Psychoanal. Assn.* 41:585–602.

Fonagy, Peter, and George S. Moran (1991). Understanding Psychic Change in Child Psychoanalysis. *Int. J. Psycho-Anal.* 72:15–22.

Fosshage, James L. (1994). Toward Reconceptualising Transference: Theoretical and Clinical Considerations. *Int. J. Psycho-Anal.* 75:265–80.

Foulkes, S. H. (1948). *Introduction to Group-Analytic Psychotherapy: Studies in the Social Integration of Individuals and Groups*, 181. London: Wm. Heinemann Medical Books.

Fox, Richard P. (1989). Towards a Revised Model of Psychoanalytic Technique: The Impact of Freud's Self-Analysis on Model Technique. *Int. Rev. Psycho-Anal.* 16:473–82.

Frank, Jerome D. (1961). *Persuasion and Healing: A Comparative Study of Psychotherapy*, 282. Baltimore: Johns Hopkins Univ. Press.

Frank, Kenneth A. (1992). Combining Action Techniques with Psychoanalytic Therapy. *Int. Rev. Psycho-Anal.* 19:57–79.

Frayn, Douglas (1993). Contemporary Considerations Influencing Psychoanalytic Interventions. *Canadian J. Psychoanal.* 1:7–25.

Freedman, Norbert, and Michael Berzofsky (unpubl. ms). The Shape of the Communicated Transference in Difficult and Not So Difficult Patients: The Symbolized and Desymbolized Transference. Presented at Society for Psychotherapy Research, 1992: submitted for publication.

Freud, Anna (1936). *The Ego and the Mechanisms of Defense*, 196. New York: Int. Univ. Press, 1946.

—— (1954). The Widening Scope of Indications for Psychoanalysis: Discussion. *J. Amer. Psychoanal. Assn.* 2:607–20.

———— (1962). The Theory of the Parent-Infant Relationship: Contributions to Discussion. *Int. J. Psycho-Anal.* 43:240–42.

Freud, Sigmund (1893–95). Studies on Hysteria (with Josef Breuer). *Standard Edition* 2:1–335, 1955.

———— (1900). The Interpretation of Dreams. *Standard Edition* 4:1–338, 1953, and *Standard Edition* 5:339–627, 1953.

———— (1905a). Fragment of an Analysis of a Case of Hysteria. *Standard Edition* 7:1–122, 1953.

———— (1905b). On Psychotherapy. *Standard Edition* 7:255–68, 1953.

———— (1905c). Psychical (or Mental) Treatment. *Standard Edition* 7:281–302.

———— (1909a). Analysis of a Phobia in a Five-Year-Old Boy. *Standard Edition* 10:1–147, 1955.

———— (1909b). Notes upon a Case of Obsessional Neurosis. *Standard Edition* 10:151–318, 1955.

———— (1910a). The Future Prospects of Psycho-Analytic Therapy. *Standard Edition* 11:139–51, 1957.

———— (1910b). 'Wild' Psycho-Analysis. *Standard Edition* 11:219–27, 1957.

———— (1911–15). Papers on Technique. *Standard Edition* 12:83–173, 1958.

———— (1912a). The Dynamics of Transference. *Standard Edition* 12:97–108, 1958.

———— (1912b). Recommendations to Physicians Practicing Psycho-Analysis. *Standard Edition* 12:109–20, 1958.

———— (1913). On Beginning the Treatment (Further Recommendations on the Technique of Psycho-Analysis I). *Standard Edition* 12:121–44, 1958.

———— (1914a). Remembering, Repeating, and Working Through (Further Recommendations on the Technique of Psycho-Analysis II). *Standard Edition* 12:145–56, 1958.

———— (1914b). On the History of the Psycho-Analytic Movement. *Standard Edition* 14:1–66, 1957.

———— (1914c). On Narcissism: An Introduction. *Standard Edition* 14:67–102, 1957.

———— (1915). Observations on Transference Love. *Standard Edition* 12:157–71, 1958.

———— (1916–17). Introductory Lectures on Psycho-Analysis. *Standard Edition* 15:1–239, 1963, and *Standard Edition* 16:241–496, 1963.

———— (1917). Mourning and Melancholia. *Standard Edition* 14:237–58, 1957.

———— (1918). From the History of an Infantile Neurosis. *Standard Edition* 17:1–122, 1955.

———— (1919). Lines of Advance in Psycho-Analytic Therapy. *Standard Edition* 17:157–68, 1955.

———— (1920a). Beyond the Pleasure Principle. *Standard Edition* 18:1–64, 1955.

———— (1920b). The Psychogenesis of a Case of Homosexuality in a Woman. *Standard Edition* 18:145–72, 1955.

———— (1922). Postscript to Analysis of a Phobia in a Five-Year-Old Boy. *Standard Edition* 10:148–149, 1955.

———— (1923). The Ego and the Id. *Standard Edition* 19:1–66, 1961.

———— (1925a). Preface to Aichhorn's *Wayward Youth*. *Standard Edition* 19:271–75, 1961.

———— (1925b). An Autobiographical Study. *Standard Edition* 20:1–74, 1959.

———— (1926). Inhibitions, Symptoms and Anxiety. *Standard Edition* 20:75–174, 1959.

———— (1937a). Analysis Terminable and Interminable. *Standard Edition* 23:209–53, 1964.

———— (1937b). Constructions in Analysis. *Standard Edition* 23:255–69, 1964.

———— (1940). An Outline of Psycho-Analysis. *Standard Edition* 23:139–207, 1964.

Friedman, Lawrence (1969). The Therapeutic Alliance. *Int. J. Psycho-Anal.* 50:139–53.

—— (1978). Trends in the Psychoanalytic Theory of Treatment. *Psychoanal. Quart.* 47: 524–67.

—— (1988). *The Anatomy of Psychotherapy,* 601. Hillsdale, N.J., and London: Analytic Press.

—— (1992). How and Why Do Patients Become More Objective? Sterba Compared with Strachey. *Psychoanal. Quart.* 61:1–17.

Fromm-Reichmann, Frieda (1950). *Principles of Intensive Psychotherapy,* 246. Chicago: Univ. of Chicago Press.

—— (1954). Psychoanalytic and General Dynamic Conceptions of Theory and of Therapy: Differences and Similarities. *J. Amer. Psychoanal. Assn.* 2:711–21.

Gabbard, Glen O. (1990). *Psychodynamic Psychiatry in Clinical Practice,* 505. Washington, D.C., and London: American Psychiatric Press.

Gardiner, Muriel, ed. (1971). *The Wolf Man by the Wolf Man: The Double Story of Freud's Most Famous Case,* 370. New York: Basic Books.

—— (1983). The Wolf Man's Last Years. *J. Amer. Psychoanal. Assn.* 31:867–97.

Gaskill, Herbert S. (1980). The Closing Phase of the Psychoanalytic Treatment of Adults and the Goals of Psychoanalysis. 'The Myth of Perfectibility.' *Int. J. Psycho-Anal.* 61:11–23.

Gediman, Helen K. (1990). The Pure Gold in Psychoanalytic Psychotherapy. *Round Robin* (Newsletter of Section I, Division 39, American Psychological Assn.) 6, no.2:6–10.

Gedo, John E. (1964). Concepts for a Classification of the Psychotherapies. *Int. J. Psycho-Anal.* 45:530–39.

—— (1966). The Psychotherapy of Developmental Arrest. *Brit. J. Med. Psychol.* 39:25–33.

—— (1979). *Beyond Interpretation: Toward a Revised Theory for Psychoanalysis,* 280. New York: Int. Univ. Press.

—— (1986). *Conceptual Issues in Psychoanalysis,* 243. Hillsdale, N.J.: Analytic Press.

—— and Arnold Goldberg (1973). *Models of the Mind: A Psychoanalytic Theory,* 220. Chicago and London: Univ. of Chicago Press.

Gill, Merton M. (1951). Ego Psychology and Psychotherapy. *Psychoanal. Quart.* 20:62–71.

—— (1954). Psychoanalysis and Exploratory Psychotherapy. *J. Amer. Psychoanal. Assn.* 2: 771–97.

—— (1979). The Analysis of the Transference. *J. Amer. Psychoanal. Assn.* 27(Suppl):263–88.

—— (1980–81). The Analysis of Transference: A Critique of Fenichel's *Problems of Psychoanalytic Technique. Int. J. Psychoanal. Psychother.* 8:45–56.

—— (1982). *Analysis of Transference: Volume I. Theory and Technique,* 193. Psychol. Issues Mono. 53. New York: Int. Univ. Press.

—— (1983a). The Point of View of Psychoanalysis: Energy Discharge or Person? *Psychoanal. Cont. Thought* 6:523–51.

—— (1983b). The Interpersonal Paradigm and the Degree of the Therapist's Involvement. *Cont. Psychoanal.* 19:200–37.

—— (1984a). Psychoanalysis and Psychotherapy: A Revision. *Int. Rev. Psycho-Anal.* 11: 161–79.

—— (1984b). Transference: A Change in Conception or Only in Emphasis? *Psychoanal. Inq.* 4:489–523.

—— (1988). Converting Psychotherapy into Psychoanalysis. *Cont. Psychoanal.* 24:262–74.

—— (1991). Indirect Suggestion: A Response to Oremland's *Interpretation and Interaction.*

In *Interpretation and Interaction: Psychoanalysis or Psychotherapy?* by Jerome D. Oremland, 137–63. Hillsdale, N.J.: Analytic Press.

————— (1994). *Psychoanalysis in Transition: A Personal View,* 179. Hillsdale, N.J., and London: Analytic Press.

————— and Irwin Z. Hoffman, (1982). *Analysis of Transference: Volume II. Studies of Nine Audio-Recorded Psychoanalytic Sessions,* 236. Psychol. Issues Mono. No. 54. New York: Int. Univ. Press.

————— and Hyman L. Muslin, (1976). Early Interpretation of Transference. *J. Amer. Psychoanal. Assn.* 24:779–94.

Gitelson, Maxwell (1951). Psychoanalysis and Dynamic Psychiatry. *Arch. Neurol. & Psychiat.* 66:280–88.

————— (1952). The Emotional Position of the Analyst in the Psycho-Analytic Situation. *Int. J. Psycho-Anal.* 33:1–10.

————— (1956). Psychoanalyst USA. In *Psychoanalysis: Science and Profession* by Maxwell Gitelson, 239–53. New York: Int. Univ. Press, 1979. Reprinted from *Amer. J. Psychiat.* 112:700–05, 1956.

————— (1962). The Curative Factors in Psychoanalysis I. The First Phase of Psycho-Analysis. *Int. J. Psycho-Anal.* 43:194–205.

————— (1963). The Present Scientific and Social Position of Psycho-Analysis. *Int. J. Psycho-Anal.* 44:521–27.

Glover, Edward (1924). 'Active Therapy' and Psychoanalysis: A Critical Review. *Int. J. Psycho-Anal.* 5:269–311.

————— (1930). The Psychotherapy of the Psychoses (II). *Brit. J. Med. Psychol.* 10:226–34, 248–52.

————— (1931). The Therapeutic Effect of Inexact Interpretation: A Contribution to the Theory of Suggestion. *Int. J. Psycho-Anal.* 12:397–411.

————— (1954). The Indications for Psycho-Analysis. *J. Mental Sc.* 100:393–401.

————— (1955). *The Technique of Psycho-Analysis,* 404. New York: Int. Univ. Press.

————— (1960a). *The Roots of Crime: Selected Papers on Psychoanalysis: Volume 2,* 422. New York: Int. Univ. Press.

————— (1960b). Psychoanalysis and Psychotherapy. *Brit. J. Med. Psychol.* 33:73–82.

Glover, James (1926). Divergent Tendencies in Psychotherapy. *Brit. J. Med. Psychol.* 6:93–109.

Goldberg, Arnold, ed. (1978). *The Psychology of the Self: A Casebook,* 460. New York: Int. Univ. Press.

————— (1980–81). Self Psychology and the Distinctiveness of Psychotherapy. *Int. J. Psychoanal. Psychother.* 8:57–70.

————— (1988). *A Fresh Look at Psychoanalysis: The View from Self Psychology,* 175–88. Hillsdale, N.J., and London: Analytic Press.

Goldman, George (1956). Reparative Psychotherapy. In *Changing Concepts of Psycho-analytic Medicine,* ed. Sandor Rado and George Daniels, 101–13. New York: Grune & Stratton.

Grand, Carole, and Daniel Hill, eds. (1994). The Clinical Use of Multiple Models: Possibilities and Dangers in the Approaches of Fred Pine, PhD, and John Gedo, MD. *Psychoanal. Inq.* 14:157–318.

Gray, Paul (1973). Psychoanalytic Technique and the Ego's Capacity for Viewing Intrapsychic Activity. *J. Amer. Psychoanal. Assn.* 21:474–94.

——— (1982). Developmental "Lag" in the Evolution of Technique for Psychoanalysis of Neurotic Conflict. *J. Amer. Psychoanal. Assn.* 30:621–55.

——— (1986). On Helping Analysands Observe Intrapsychic Activity. In *Psychoanalysis: The Science of Mental Conflict: Essays in Honor of Charles Brenner,* ed. Arnold D. Richards, and Martin S. Willick, 245–62. Hillsdale, N.J.: Analytic Press.

——— (1987). On the Technique of Analysis of the Superego—An Introduction. *Psychoanal. Quart.* 56:130–54.

——— (1988). On the Significance of Influence and Insight in the Spectrum of Psychoanalytic Psychotherapies. In *How Does Treatment Help? On the Modes of Therapeutic Action of Psychoanalytic Psychotherapy,* ed. Arnold Rothstein, 41–50. Madison, Conn.: Int. Univ. Press.

——— (1990). The Nature of Therapeutic Action in Psychoanalysis. *J. Amer. Psychoanal. Assn.* 38:1083–97.

——— (1991). On Transferred Permissive or Approving Superego Functions: The Analysis of the Ego's Superego Activities. Part II. *Psychoanal. Quart.* 60:1–21.

——— (1994). *The Ego and Analysis of Defense,* 254. Northvale, N.J., and London: Jason Aronson.

Greenacre, Phyllis (1954). The Role of Transference: Practical Considerations in Relation to Psychoanalytic Therapy. *J. Amer. Psychoanal. Assn.* 2:671–84.

——— (1959). Certain Technical Problems in the Transference Relationship. *J. Amer. Psychoanal. Assn.* 7:484–502.

Greenberg, Jay R., and Stephen A. Mitchell, (1983). *Object Relations in Psychoanalytic Theory,* 437. Cambridge and London: Harvard Univ. Press.

Greenson, Ralph R. (1965). The Working Alliance and the Transference Neurosis. *Psychoanal. Quart.* 34:155–81.

——— (1967). *The Technique and Practice of Psychoanalysis. Volume I,* 452. New York: Int. Univ. Press.

——— (1972). Beyond Transference and Interpretation. *Int. J. Psycho-Anal.* 53:213–17.

——— and Milton Wexler (1969). The Non-Transference Relationship in the Psychoanalytic Situation. *Int. J. Psycho-Anal.* 50:27–39.

Grinker, Roy R., Sr. (1959). A Transactional Model for Psychotherapy. *Arch. Gen. Psychiat.* 1:132–48.

——— (1961). A Transactional Model for Psychotherapy. In *Contemporary Psychotherapies,* ed. Morris I. Stein, 190–213. New York: Free Press of Glencoe.

Grubrich-Simitis, Ilse (1986). Six Letters of Sigmund Freud and Sandor Ferenczi on the Interrelationship of Psychoanalytic Theory and Technique. *Int. Rev. Psycho-Anal.* 13:259–77.

Grunbaum, Adolf (1984). *The Foundation of Psychoanalysis: A Philosophical Critique,* 310. Berkeley, Los Angeles, and London: Univ. of Calif. Press.

Gumbel, Erich (Chair) (1970). Discussion of 'The Non-Transference Relationship in the Psychoanalytic Situation.' *Int. J. Psycho-Anal.* 51:143–50.

Guttman, Samuel A., Randall L. Jones, and Stephen M. Parrish (1980). *The Concordance to the Standard Edition of the Complete Psychological Works of Sigmund Freud,* 6 volumes. Boston: G. K. Hall & Co.,

Hamburg, David A., Grete L. Bibring, Charles Fisher, Alfred H. Stanton, Robert S. Wallerstein, Harry I. Weinstock, and Ernest Haggard (1967). Report of ad hoc Committee on Central Fact-Gathering Data of the American Psychoanalytic Association. *J. Amer. Psychoanal. Assn.* 15:841–61.

Hamilton, N. Gregory (1989). A Critical Review of Object Relations Theory. *Amer. J. Psychiat.* 146:1552–60.

Hanly, Charles (1992a). *The Problem of Truth in Applied Psychoanalysis,* 236. New York and London: Guilford Press.

—— (1992b). Reflections on the Place of the Therapeutic Alliance in Psychoanalysis. *Brit. Psychoanal. Soc. Bull.* 28:Nov. 1992, 1–8.

—— (1994). Reflections on the Place of the Therapeutic Alliance in Psychoanalysis. *Int. J. Psycho-Anal.* 75:457–67.

Harrison, Saul I. (1970). Is Psychoanalysis "Our" Science? Reflections on the Scientific Status of Psychoanalysis. *J. Amer. Psychoanal. Assn.* 18:125–49.

Hartmann, Heinz (1939). *Ego Psychology and the Problem of Adaptation,* 121, New York: Int. Univ. Press, 1958.

—— (1951). Technical Implications of Ego Psychology. *Psychoanal. Quart.* 20:31–43.

Hawthorne, Nathaniel E. (1962–88). *The Centenary Edition of the Works of Nathaniel Hawthorne,* 20 vols., Vol. I. *The Scarlet Letter,* ed. H. Pearce, C. Simpson et al. Columbus: Ohio State Univ. Press.

Hayley, Tom (1990). Charisma, Suggestion, Psychoanalysts, Medicine-Men, and Metaphor. *Int. Rev. Psycho-Anal.* 17:1–10.

—— (1991). Obituary: Thomas Forrest Main (1911–1990). *Int. J. Psycho-Anal.* 72:719–22.

Haynal, Andre (1988). *The Technique at Issue: Controversies in Psychoanalysis from Freud and Ferenczi to Michael Balint,* 202. London: Karmac Books. (Also published as *Controversies in Psychoanalytic Method: From Freud and Ferenczi to Michael Balint,* 202. New York: New York Univ. Press, 1989.)

Heimann, Paula (1950). On Counter-Transference. *Int. J. Psycho-Anal.* 31:81–84.

Hernandez, Max (unpubl. ms). Analysis, Overdetermination, Narrative. Presented at 1st Int. Psychoanal. Assn. Conference on Literature and Psychoanalysis, Univ. Coll. London, Nov. 1992, p. 15. Forthcoming, Yale Univ. Press.

Hoch, Samuel (1992). Panel reporter, Psychoanalysis and Psychoanalytic Psychotherapy—Similarities and Differences: Conceptual Overview. *J. Amer. Psychoanal. Assn.* 40:233–38.

Hoffer, Axel (1990). Book Review of *The Clinical Diary of Sandor Ferenczi,* ed. Judith Dupont. *Int. J. Psycho-Anal.* 71:723–27.

—— (1991). The Freud-Ferenczi Controversy—A Living Legacy. *Int. Rev. Psycho-Anal.* 18:465–72.

Hoffer, Willi (1956). Transference and Transference Neurosis. *Int. J. Psycho-Anal.* 37:377–79.

Hoffman, Irwin Z. (1983). The Patient as Interpreter of the Analyst's Experience. *Cont. Psychoanal.* 19:389–422.

—— (1987). The Value of Uncertainty in Psychoanalytic Practice. *Contemp. Psychoanal.* 23:205–15.

—— (1990). In the Eye of the Beholder: A Reply to Levenson. *Cont. Psychoanal.* 26:291–99.

—— (1991). Discussion: Toward a Social-Constructivist View of the Psychoanalytic Situation. *Psychoanal. Dial.* 1:74–105.

—— (1992a). Expressive Participation and Psychoanalytic Discipline. *Cont. Psychoanal.* 28:1–14.

—— (1992b). Some Practical Implications of a Social-Constructivist View of the Psychoanalytic Situation. *Psychoanal. Dial.* 2:287–304.

—— (1992c). Reply to Orange. *Psychoanal. Dial.* 2:567–70.

—— (1993). The Intimate Authority of the Psychoanalyst's Presence. *Psychologist Psycho-analyst* 13:15–23.

—— (1994). Dialectical Thinking and Therapeutic Action in the Psychoanalytic Process. *Psychoanal. Quart.* 63:187–218.

—— and Merton M. Gill (1988). Critical Reflections on a Coding Scheme. *Int. J. Psycho-Anal.* 69:55–64.

Holinger, Paul C. (1989). A Developmental Perspective on Psychotherapy and Psychoanalysis. *Amer. J. Psychiat.* 146:1404–12.

Horowitz, Mardi J. (1976). *Stress Response Syndromes,* 366. New York: Jason Aronson.

—— (1979). *States of Mind: Analysis of Change in Psychotherapy,* 282. New York and London: Plenum Books.

—— ed. (1991). *Person-Schemas and Maladaptive Interpersonal Patterns,* 433. Chicago and London: Univ. of Chicago Press.

——, Charles Marmar, Janice Krupnick, Nancy Wilner, Nancy Kaltreider, and Robert S. Wallerstein (1984). *Personality Styles and Brief Psychotherapy,* 349. New York: Basic Books.

Horwitz, Leonard (1974). *Clinical Prediction in Psychotherapy,* 372. New York: Jason Aronson.

Hughes, Judith M. (1989). *Reshaping the Psychoanalytic Domain: The Work of Melanie Klein, W. R. D. Fairbairn and D. W. Winnicott,* 244. Berkeley, Los Angeles, and London: Univ. of Calif. Press.

Isaacs, Susan (1943). Conclusion of Discussion on her paper, "The Nature and Function of Phantasy." *Scientific Bull. Brit. Psychoanaly. Soc.* 17:151, 153, 1967. Quoted by Steiner (1985), 49.

Jacobs, Theodore J. (1986). On Countertransference Enactments. *J. Amer. Psychoanal. Assn.* 34:289–307.

—— (1988). Notes on the Therapeutic Process: Working with the Young Adult. In *How Does Treatment Help? On the Modes of Therapeutic Action of Psychoanalytic Psychotherapy,* ed. Arnold Rothstein, 61–80. Madison, Conn.: Int. Univ. Press.

—— (1990). The Corrective Emotional Experience—Its Place in Current Technique. *Psychoanal. Inq.* 10:433–54.

—— (1991). *The Use of the Self: Countertransference and Communication in the Analytic Situation,* 237. Madison, Conn.: Int. Univ. Press.

Jacobson, Jacob G. (1994). Signal Affects and Our Psychoanalytic Confusion of Tongues. *J. Amer. Psychoanal. Assn.* 42:15–42.

Jaffe, Daniel S. (1991). Beyond the What, When, and How of Transference: A Consideration of the Why. *J. Amer. Psychoanal. Assn.* 39:491–512.

Johan, Morton (1989). Evaluation of Outcome of Psychoanalytic Treatment: Should Followup by the Analyst be Part of the Post-Termination Phase of Analytic Treatment? *J. Amer. Psychoanal. Assn.* 37:813–22.

Johns, Jennifer (1989). Historical Background. In *The Ailment and Other Psychoanalytic Essays,* by Tom Main, 1–4. London: Free Association Books,

Jones, Ernest (1910). The Action of Suggestion in Psychotherapy. In *Papers on Psychoanalysis* by Ernest Jones, 318–59. New York: Wm. Wood & Co., 1918.

—— (1930). Decannual Report of the London Clinic of Psychoanalysis, 1926–36.

—— (1946). Book Review of *Psychoanalytic Therapy* by Franz Alexander and Thomas Morton French. *Int. J. Psycho-Anal.* 27:162–63.

de Jonghe, Frans, Piet Rijnierse, and Rob Janssen (1991). Aspects of the Analytic Relationship. *Int. J. Psycho-Anal.* 72:693–707.

————, ————, and ———— (1992). The Role of Support in Psychoanalysis. *J. Amer. Psychoanal. Assn.* 40:475–99.

————, ————, and ———— (1994). Psychoanalytic Supportive Psychotherapy. *J. Amer. Psychoanal. Assn.* 42:421–46.

Joseph, Betty (1992). Psychic Change: Some Perspectives. *Int. J. Psycho-Anal.* 73:237–43.

———— (1993). A Factor Militating against Psychic Change: Nonresonance. In *Psychic Structure and Psychic Change: Essays in Honor of Robert S. Wallerstein, M.D.* ed. Mardi J. Horowitz, Otto F. Kernberg, and Edward M. Weinshel, 311–25. Madison, Conn.: Int. Univ. Press.

Kantrowitz, Judy L. (1986). The Role of the Patient-Analyst "Match" in the Outcome of Psychoanalysis. *Ann. Psychoanal.* 14:273–97.

————, Ann L. Katz, Deborah A. Greenman, Humphrey Morris, Frank Paolitto, Jerome Sashin, and Leonard Solomon (1989). The Patient-Analyst Match and the Outcome of Psychoanalysis: A Pilot Study. *J. Amer. Psychoanal. Assn.* 37:893–919.

————, ————, and Frank Paolitto (1990a). Followup of Psychoanalysis Five to Ten Years after Termination: I. Stability of Change. *J. Amer. Psychoanal. Assn.* 38:471–96.

————, ————, and ———— (1990b). Followup of Psychoanalysis Five to Ten Years after Termination: II. Development of the Self-Analytic Function. *J. Amer. Psychoanal. Assn.* 38:637–54.

————, ————, and ———— (1990c). Followup of Psychoanalysis Five to Ten Years after Termination: III. The Relation between Resolution of the Transference and the Patient-Analyst Match. *J. Amer. Psychoanal. Assn.* 38:655–78.

————, ————, ————, Jerome Sashin and Leonard Solomon (1987a). Changes in the Level and Quality of Object Relations in Psychoanalysis: Followup of a Longitudinal, Prospective Study. *J. Amer. Psychoanal. Assn.* 35:23–46.

————, ————, ————, ————, and ———— (1987b). The Role of Reality Testing in Psychoanalysis: Followup of 22 Cases. *J. Amer. Psychoanal. Assn.* 35:367–85.

————, Frank Paolitto, Jerome Sashin, Leonard Solomon and Ann L. Katz (1986). Affect Availability, Tolerance, Complexity, and Modulation in Psychoanalysis: Followup of a Longitudinal, Prospective Study. *J. Amer. Psychoanal. Assn.* 34:529–59.

Kanzer, Mark (1975). The Therapeutic and Working Alliances. *Int. J. Psychoanal. Psychother.* 4:48–68.

Kernberg, Otto F. (1966). Structural Derivatives of Object Relationships. *Int. J. Psycho-Anal.* 47:236–53.

———— (1975). *Borderline Conditions and Pathological Narcissism*, 361. New York: Jason Aronson.

———— (1976). *Object Relations Theory and Clinical Psychoanalysis*, 299. New York: Jason Aronson.

———— (1980). *Internal World and External Reality: Object Relations Theory Applied*, 359. New York and London: Jason Aronson.

———— (1983). Expressive and Supportive Psychotherapy: Mutual Differentiation and Hypothesized Differential Effects. In *Psychotherapy Research*, 256–58. New York: Guilford Press (publ. of American Psychopathological Association).

———— (1984). *Severe Personality Disorders: Psychotherapeutic Strategies*, 381. New Haven and London: Yale Univ. Press.

———— (1988). Psychic Structure and Structural Change: An Ego Psychology-Object Relations Theory Viewpoint. *J. Amer. Psychoanal. Assn.* 36(Suppl):315–37.

———— (1992). *Aggression in Personality Disorders and Perversions*, 316. New Haven and London: Yale Univ. Press.

———— (1993a). The Current Status of Psychoanalysis. *J. Amer. Psychoanal. Assn.* 41:45–62.

———— (1993b). Nature and Agents of Structural Intrapsychic Change. In *Psychic Structure and Psychic Change: Essays in Honor of Robert S. Wallerstein,* ed. Mardi J. Horowitz, Otto F. Kernberg and Edward M. Weinshel, 327–44. Madison, Conn.: Int. Univ. Press.

———— (1993c). Convergences and Divergences in Contemporary Psychoanalytic Technique. *Int. J. Psycho-Anal.* 74:659–73.

————, Esther D. Burstein, Lolafaye Coyne, Ann Appelbaum, Leonard Horwitz and Harold Voth (1972). Psychotherapy and Psychoanalysis: Final Report of the Menninger Foundation's Psychotherapy Research Project. *Bull. Menn. Clinic* 36:1–275.

————, Michael A. Selzer, Harold W. Koenigsberg, Arthur C. Carr and Ann Appelbaum (1989). *Psychodynamic Psychotherapy of Borderline Patients,* 210. New York: Basic Books.

Kessel, L., and H. Hyman (1933). The Value of Psychoanalysis as a Therapeutic Procedure. *J. Amer. Med. Assn.* 101:1612–15.

Knapp, Peter H., Sidney Levin, Robert H. McCarter, Henry Wermer and Elizabeth Zetzel (1960). Suitability for Psychoanalysis: A Review of One Hundred Supervised Analytic Cases. *Psychoanal. Quart.* 29:434–46.

Knight, Robert P. (1939). Psychotherapy in Acute Paranoid Schizophrenia with Successful Outcome: A Case Report. *Bull. Menn. Clinic* 3:97–105.

———— (1941). Evaluation of the Results of Psychoanalytic Therapy. *Amer. J. Psychiat.* 98: 434–46.

———— (1945). The Relationship of Psychoanalysis to Psychiatry. *Amer. J. Psychiatry* 101:777–82. Reprinted in *Clinician and Therapist: Selected Papers of Robert P. Knight,* ed. Stuart C. Miller, 121–30. New York: Basic Books, 1972.

———— (1946). Psychotherapy of an Adolescent Catatonic Schizophrenic with Mutism: A Study in Empathy and Establishing Contact. *Psychiatry* 9:323–39.

———— (1949). A Critique of the Present Status of the Psychotherapies. *Bull. NY Acad. Med.* 25:100–14. Reprinted in *Clinician and Therapist: Selected Papers of Robert P. Knight,* ed. Stuart C. Miller, 177–92. New York: Basic Books, 1972.

———— (1952). An Evaluation of Psychotherapeutic Techniques. *Bull. Menn. Clinic* 16:113–24. Reprinted in *Clinician and Therapist: Selected Papers of Robert P. Knight,* ed. Stuart C. Miller, 193–207. New York: Basic Books, 1972.

———— (1953a). The Present Status of Organized Psychoanalysis in the United States. *J. Amer. Psychoanal. Assn.* 1:197–221.

———— (1953b). Borderline States. *Bull. Menn. Clinic* 17:1–12. Reprinted in *Clinician and Therapist: Selected Papers of Robert P. Knight,* ed. Stuart C. Miller, 208–23. New York: Basic Books, 1972.

Kohon, Gregorio, ed. (1986). *The British School of Psychoanalysis: The Independent Tradition,* 429. New Haven and London: Yale Univ. Press.

Kohut, Heinz (1959). Introspection, Empathy, and Psychoanalysis. *J. Amer. Psychoanal. Assn.* 7:459–83.

———— (1966). Forms and Transformations of Narcissism. *J. Amer. Psychoanal. Assn.* 14:243–72.

———— (1971). *The Analysis of the Self: A Systematic Approach to the Psychoanalytic Treatment of Narcissistic Personality Disorders,* 368. New York: Int. Univ. Press.

———— (1972). Thoughts on Narcissism and Narcissistic Rage. *Psychoanal. Study Child* 27: 360–400.

———— (1977). *The Restoration of the Self,* 345. New York: Int. Univ. Press.

——— (1984) (Edited by Arnold Goldberg with the collaboration of Paul E. Stepansky). *How Does Analysis Cure?* 240. Chicago and London: Univ. of Chicago Press.

Kramer, Maria K. (1959). On the Continuation of the Analytic Process after Psychoanalysis (A Self-Observation). *Int. J. Psycho-Anal.* 40:17–25.

Kris, Anton O. (1977). Either–Or Dilemmas. *Psychoanal. Study Child* 32:91–117.

——— (1982). *Free Association: Method and Process,* 113. New Haven and London: Yale Univ. Press.

——— (1983). The Analyst's Conceptual Freedom in the Method of Free Association. *Int. J. Psycho-Anal.* 64:407–11.

——— (1984). The Conflicts of Ambivalence. *Psychoanal. Study Child* 39:213–34.

——— (1985). Resistance in Convergent and in Divergent Conflicts. *Psychoanal. Quart.* 54: 537–68.

——— (1988). Some Clinical Applications of the Distinction between Divergent and Convergent Conflicts. *Int. J. Psycho-Anal.* 69:431–41.

——— (1990a). Helping Patients by Analyzing Self-Criticism. *J. Amer. Psychoanal. Assn.* 38: 605–36.

——— (1990b). The Analyst's Stance and the Method of Free Association. *Psychoanal. Study Child* 45:25–41.

——— (1992). Interpretation and the Method of Free Association. *Psychoanal. Inq.* 12:208–24.

——— (1993). Support and Psychic Structural Change. In *Psychic Structure and Psychic Change: Essays in Honor of Robert S. Wallerstein, M.D.* ed. Mardi J. Horowitz, Otto F. Kernberg and Edward M. Weinshel, 95–115. Madison, Conn.: Int. Univ. Press.

——— (1994). Freud's Treatment of a Narcissistic Patient. *Int. J. Psycho-Anal.* 75:649–64.

Kris, Ernst (1947). The Nature of Psychoanalytic Propositions and Their Validation. In *Freedom and Experience: Essays Presented to Horace M. Kallen,* ed. Sidney Hook and Milton R. Konvitz, 239–59. Ithaca and New York: Cornell Univ. Press. Reprinted in *The Selected Papers of Ernst Kris,* 3–23. New Haven and London: Yale Univ. Press, 1975.

——— (1951). Ego Psychology and Interpretation in Psychoanalytic Therapy. *Psychoanal. Quart.* 20:15–30.

——— (1956). On Some Vicissitudes of Insight in Psycho-Analysis. *Int. J. Psycho-Anal.* 37: 445–55.

Kubie, Lawrence S. (1943). The Nature of Psychotherapy. *Bull. NY Acad. Med.* 199:183–94.

——— (1974). The Drive to Become Both Sexes. *Psychoanal. Quart.* 43:349–426.

Lampl-de Groot, Jeanne (1975). Vicissitudes of Narcissism and Problems of Civilization. In *Man and Mind,* 319–31. New York: Int. Univ. Press, 1985.

Langs, Robert (1976). *The Bipersonal Field,* 468. New York: Jason Aronson.

Laplanche, Jean, and J-B. Pontalis (1973). *The Language of Psychoanalysis,* 510. London: Hogarth Press.

Lasch, Christopher (1978). *The Culture of Narcissism: American Life in an Age of Diminishing Expectations,* 268. New York: W. W. Norton.

Laufer, Moses (1992). Personal communication.

——— and M. Egle Laufer (1984). *Adolescence and Developmental Breakdown: A Psychoanalytic View,* 225. New Haven and London: Yale Univ. Press.

Leary, Kimberlyn (1994). Psychoanalytic "Problems" and Postmodern "Solutions." *Psychoanal. Quart.* 63:433–65.

Lederer, Wolfgang (1964). *Dragons, Delinquents, and Destiny: An Essay on Positive Superego Functions*, 83. Psychol. Issues Mono. No. 15. New York: Int. Univ. Press.

Leites, Nathan (1977). Transference Interpretation *Only? Int. J. Psycho-Anal.* 58:275–87.

Levenson, Edgar A. (1972). *The Fallacy of Understanding: An Inquiry into the Changing Structure of Psychoanalysis*, 236. New York and London: Basic Books.

——— (1983). *The Ambiguity of Change: An Inquiry into the Nature of Psychoanalytic Reality*, 180. New York: Basic Books.

——— (1988). Show and Tell: The Recursive Order of Transference. In *How Does Treatment Help? On the Modes of Therapeutic Action of Psychoanalytic Psychotherapy*, ed. Arnold Rothstein 135–43. Madison, Conn.: Int. Univ. Press.

——— (1991). *The Purloined Self: Interpersonal Perspectives in Psychoanalysis*, 266. New York: William Alanson White Institute.

Levine, Frederic J. (1979). On the Clinical Application of Kohut's Psychology of the Self: Comments on Some Recently Published Case Studies. *J. Phila. Assn. Psychoanal.* 6:1–19.

Levine, Howard B. (1994). The Analyst's Participation in the Analytic Process. *Int. J. Psycho-Anal.* 75: 665–676.

Levine, Maurice (1942). *Psychotherapy in Medical Practice*, 320. New York: Macmillan.

Levy, Steven T., and Inderbitzin, Lawrence B. (1990). The Analytic Surface and the Theory of Technique. *J. Amer. Psychoanal. Assn.* 38:371–91.

——— and ——— (1992). Interpretation. In *The Technique and Practice of Psychoanalysis. 2. A Memorial Volume to Ralph R. Greenson,* ed. Alan Sugerman, Robert A. Nemiroff, and Daniel P. Greenson, 101–15. Madison, Conn.: Int. Univ. Press.

Lewin, Bertram D. (1955). Dream Psychology and the Analytic Situation. *Psychoanal. Quart.* 24:169–99.

Lewy, Ernst (1941). The Return of the Repression. *Bull. Menn. Clinic* 5:47–55.

Lichtenberg, Joseph D. (1988). A Discussion. In *How Does Treatment Help? On the Modes of Therapeutic Action of Psychoanalytic Psychotherapy*, ed. Arnold Rothstein, 181–87. Madison, Conn.: Int. Univ. Press.

——— (1992). Interpretive Sequence. *Psychoanal. Inq.* 12:248–74.

Limentani, Adam (1989). *Between Freud and Klein: The Psychoanalytic Quest for Knowledge and Truth*, 281. London: Free Association Books.

Lipton, Samuel D. (1967). Later Developments in Freud's Technique (1920–1939). In *Psychoanalytic Technique: A Handbook for the Practicing Psychoanalyst*, ed. Benjamin B. Wolman, 51–92. New York and London: Basic Books.

——— (1977). The Advantages of Freud's Technique as Shown in His Analysis of the Rat Man. *Int. J. Psycho-Anal.* 58:255–73.

——— (1979). An Addendum to "The Advantages of Freud's Technique as Shown in His Analysis of the Rat Man." *Int. J. Psycho-Anal.* 60:215–16.

——— (1988). Further Observations on the Advantages of Freud's Technique. *Annual Psychoanal.* 16:19–32.

Little, Margaret (1951). Counter-transference and the Patient's Response to It. *Int. J. Psycho-Anal.* 32:32–40.

——— (1958). On Delusional Transference (Transference Psychosis). *Int. J. Psycho-Anal.* 39: 134–38.

——— (1990). *Psychotic Anxieties and Containment: A Personal Account of an Analysis with Winnicott.* Northvale, N.J.: Jason Aronson.

Loewald, Hans W. (1960). On the Therapeutic Action of Psycho-Analysis. *Int. J. Psycho-Anal.* 41:16–33.

——— (1970). Psychoanalytic Theory and the Psychoanalytic Process. *Psychoanal. Study Child* 25:45–68.

——— (1971). The Transference Neurosis: Comments on the Concept and the Phenomenon. *J. Amer. Psychoanal. Assn.* 19:54–66.

——— (1979). Reflections on the Psychoanalytic Process and Its Therapeutic Potential. *Psychoanal. Study Child.* 34:155–67.

——— (1986). Transference-Countertransference. *J. Amer. Psychoanal. Assn.* 34:275–87.

——— (1988). On the Mode of Therapeutic Action of Psychoanalytic Psychotherapy. In *How Does Treatment Help? On the Modes of Therapeutic Action of Psychoanalytic Psychotherapy*, ed. Arnold Rothstein, 51–59. Madison, Conn.: Int. Univ. Press.

Loewenstein, Rudolph M. (1951). The Problem of Interpretation. *Psychoanal. Quart.* 20:1–14.

London, Nathaniel J. (1987a). Prologue. *Psychoanal. Inq.* 7:457–63.

——— (1987b). Discussion: In Defense of the Transference Neurosis Concept: A Process and Interactional Definition. *Psychoanal. Inq.* 7:587–98.

Luborsky, Lester (1976). Helping Alliances of Psychotherapy. In *Successful Psychotherapy*, ed. J. P. Claghorn, 92–116. New York: Brunner/Mazel.

——— (1984). *Principles of Psychoanalytic Psychotherapy: A Manual for Supportive-Expressive Treatment*, 270. New York: Basic Books.

——— and Paul Crits-Christoph (1990). *Understanding Transference: The CCRT Method*, 313. New York: Basic Books.

———, ———, Jim Mintz, and Arthur Auerbach (1988). *Who Will Benefit from Psychotherapy? Predicting Therapeutic Outcomes*, 416. New York: Basic Books.

Ludwig, Alfred O. (1954). Panel reporter, Psychoanalysis and Psychotherapy: Dynamic Criteria for Treatment Choice. *J. Amer. Psychoanal. Assn.* 2:346–50.

McDougall, Joyce (1980). *Plea for a Measure of Abnormality* (Chap. 5. The Anti-Analysand in Analysis), 213–46. New York: Int. Univ. Press. Also in *Psychoanalysis in France*, ed. Serge Lebovici and Daniel Widlocher, 333–54. New York: Int. Univ. Press, 1980.

——— (1989). *Theatres of the Body: A Psychoanalytic Approach to Psychosomatic Illness*, 181. London: Free Association Books.

McLaughlin, James T. (1981). Transference, Psychic Reality, and Countertransference. *Psychoanal. Quart.* 50:639–64.

McNutt, Edith R. (1992). Panel reporter, Psychoanalysis and Psychoanalytic Psychotherapy— Similarities and Differences: Indications, Contraindications, and Initiation. *J. Amer. Psychoanal. Assn.* 40:223–31.

Macalpine, Ida (1950). The Development of the Transference. *Psychoanal. Quart.* 19:501–39.

Main, Tom (1989). *The Ailment and Other Psychoanalytic Essays*, 256. London: Free Association Books.

Malan, David H. (1963). *A Study of Brief Psychotherapy*, 312. Springfield, Ill.: Charles C Thomas. (Also London, Mind and Medicine Monographs, Tavistock).

Malin, Arthur (1990). Converting Psychotherapy to Psychoanalysis: Epilogue. *Psychoanal. Inq.* 19:135.

Mann, James (1973). *Time-Limited Psychotherapy*, 202. Cambridge: Harvard Univ. Press.

Martin, Gary C. (1993). Panel reporter, Stability of Gains Achieved during Analytic Treatment from a Followup Perspective. *J. Amer. Psychoanal. Assn.* 41:209–17.

Marty, Pierre, and Michel de M'Uzan (1963). La Pensée Operatoire. *Rev. franc. Psychoanal.* 27, Special no., 345–55.

Mayes, Linda C., and Donald P. Spence (1994). Understanding Therapeutic Action in the Analytic Situation: A Second Look at the Developmental Metaphor. *J. Amer. Psychoanal. Assn.* 42:789–817.

Meisel, Perry, and Walter Kendrick, eds. (1985). *Bloomsbury/Freud: The Letters of James and Alix Strachey 1924–1925,* 360. New York: Basic Books.

Meissner, W. W. (1991). *What Is Effective in Psychoanalytic Therapy: The Move from Interpretation to Relation,* 217. Northvale, N.J., and London: Jason Aronson.

———— (1992). The Concept of the Therapeutic Alliance. *J. Amer. Psychoanal. Assn.* 40:1059–87.

Menninger, Karl A. (1958). *Theory of Psychoanalytic Technique,* 206. New York: Basic Books.

Michels, Robert (1985). The Evolution of Psychodynamic Psychotherapy. *Strecker Monograph Series of Institute of Pennsylvania Hospital,* 22:22.

———— (1986). Oedipus and Insight. *Psychoanal. Quart.* 50:599–617.

Miller, Ira (1969). Interpretation as a Supportive Technique in Psychotherapy. *Bull. Menn. Clinic* 33:154–64.

Miller, Jule P., Jr. (1987). The Transference Neurosis from the Viewpoint of Self Psychology. *Psychoanal. Inq.* 7:535–50.

———— (1990). The Corrective Emotional Experience: Reflections in Retrospect. *Psychoanal. Inq.* 10:373–88.

———— (1991). Can Psychotherapy Substitute for Psychoanalysis? In *Progress in Self Psychology, Vol. 7,* ed. Arnold Goldberg, 45–58. Hillsdale, N.J.: The Analytic Press.

Miller, Stuart C., ed. (1972). *Clinician and Therapist: Selected Papers of Robert P. Knight,* 322. New York: Basic Books.

Mitchell, Stephen A. (1988). *Relationship Concepts in Psychoanalysis: An Integration,* 326. Cambridge and London: Harvard Univ. Press.

Modell, Arnold H. (1968). *Object Love and Reality: An Introduction to a Psychoanalytic Theory of Object Relations,* 181. New York: Int. Univ. Press.

———— (1976). "The Holding Environment" and the Therapeutic Action of Psychoanalysis. *J. Amer. Psychoanal. Assn.* 24:285–307.

———— (1984). *Psychoanalysis in a New Context,* 284. New York: Int. Univ. Press.

———— (1988a). The Centrality of the Psychoanalytic Setting and the Changing Aims of Treatment: A Perspective from the Theory of Object Relations. *Psychoanal. Quart.* 57:577–96.

———— (1988b). Changing Psychic Structure through Treatment: Preconditions for the Resolution of the Transference. *J. Amer. Psychoanal. Assn.* 36 (Suppl):225–39.

———— (1988c). On the Protection and Safety of the Therapeutic Setting. In *How Does Treatment Help? On the Modes of Therapeutic Action of Psychoanalytic Psychotherapy,* ed. Arnold Rothstein, 95–104. Madison, Conn.: Int. Univ. Press.

———— (1989). The Psychoanalytic Setting as a Container of Multiple Levels of Reality: A Perspective on the Theory of Psychoanalytic Treatment. *Psychoanal. Inq.* 9:67–87.

———— (1990). *Other Times, Other Realities: Toward a Theory of Psychoanalytic Treatment,* 190. Cambridge and London: Harvard Univ. Press.

Morris, James L. (1992). Panel reporter, Psychoanalysis and Psychoanalytic Psychotherapy—Similarities and Differences: Therapeutic Technique. *J. Amer. Psychoanal. Assn.* 40:211–21.

Myerson, Paul (1981). The Nature of the Transactions that Occur in Other than Classical Analysis. *Int. Rev. Psycho-Anal.* 8:173–89.

Neubauer, Peter B. (1979). The Role of Insight in Psychoanalysis. *J. Amer. Psychoanal. Assn.* 27 (Suppl):29–40.

Newman, Kenneth (1991). Book Review of *Other Times, Other Realities: Towards a Theory of Psychoanalytic Treatment* by Arnold H. Modell. *Int. J. Psycho-Anal.* 72:739–42.

Norman, Haskell F., Kay H. Blacker, Jerome D. Oremland, and William G. Barrett (1976). The Fate of the Transference Neurosis after Termination of a Satisfactory Analysis. *J. Amer. Psychoanal. Assn.* 24:471–98.

Novalis, Peter N. (1989). What Supports Supportive Therapy. *Jefferson J. Psychiat.* 7:17–29.

Nunberg, Herman (1926). The Will to Recovery. In *Practice and Theory of Psychoanalysis, Vol. I,* 75–88. New York: Int. Univ. Press, 1948.

——— (1928). Problems of Therapy. In *Practice and Theory of Psychoanalysis, Vol. I,* 105–19. New York: Int. Univ. Press, 1948.

——— (1931). The Synthetic Function of the Ego. *Int. J. Psycho-Anal.* 12:123–40.

——— (1932). *Principles of Psychoanalysis: Their Application to the Neuroses,* 382. New York: Int. Univ. Press, 1955.

Obholzer, Karin (1980). *The Wolf-Man: Sixty Years Later,* 250. London, Melbourne and Henley: Routledge & Kegan Paul, 1982.

Offenkrantz, William, and Arnold Tobin. (1974) Psychoanalytic Psychotherapy. *Arch. Gen. Psychiat.* 30:593–606.

Oremland, Jerome D. (1991). *Interpretation and Interaction: Psychoanalysis or Psychotherapy?* 184. Hillsdale, N.J.: Analytic Press.

———, Kay H. Blacker, and Haskell T. Norman, (1975).Incompleteness in "Successful" Psychoanalyses: A Follow-up Study. *J. Amer. Psychoanal. Assn.* 23:819–44.

Ornstein, Paul H. (1988). Multiple Curative Factors and Processes in the Psychoanalytic Psychotherapies. In *How Does Treatment Help? On the Modes of Therapeutic Action of Psychoanalytic Psychotherapy,* ed. Arnold Rothstein, 105–26. Madison, Conn.: Int. Univ. Press.

——— and Anna Ornstein, (1977). On the Continuing Evolution of Psychoanalytic Psychotherapy: Reflections and Predictions. *Annual Psychoanal.* 5:329–55.

Orr, Douglass W. (1954). Transference and Countertransference: A Historical Survey. *J. Amer. Psychoanal. Assn.* 2:621–70.

Paul, Louis. (1963). The Operations of Psychotherapy. *Comprehensive Psychiat.* 4:281–90.

——— (1965). Repeated Emotionally-Toned Interpretations: A Parameter of Basic Psychoanalytic Technique. *Comprehensive Psychiat.* 6:61–64.

Payne, Sylvia M. (1936). Post-War Activities and the Advance of Psychotherapy. *Brit. J. Med. Psychol.* 16:1–15.

Pedder, Jonathan (1989). How Can Psychotherapists Influence Psychiatry? *Psychoanal. Psychother.* 4:43–54.

——— (1990a). Lines of Advance in Psychoanalytic Psychotherapy. *Psychoanal. Psychother.* 4: 201–17.

——— (1990b). News from the Maudsley Psychotherapy Unit. *Bull. Brit. Psychoanal. Soc.* 26: Nov., 15.

Pfeffer, Arnold Z. (1959). A Procedure for Evaluating the Results of Psychoanalysis: A Preliminary Report. *J. Amer. Psychoanal. Assn.* 7:418–44.

——— (1961). Follow-up Study of a Satisfactory Analysis. *J. Amer. Psychoanal. Assn.* 9:698–718.

———— (1963). The Meaning of the Analyst after Analysis: A Contribution to the Theory of Therapeutic Results. *J. Amer. Psychoanal. Assn.* 11:229–44.

Pine, Fred (1984). The Interpretive Moment: Variations on Classical Themes. *Bull. Menn. Clinic* 48:54–71.

———— (1988a). On the Four Psychologies of Psychoanalysis and the Nature of the Therapeutic Impact. In *How Does Treatment Help? On the Modes of Therapeutic Action of Psychoanalytic Psychotherapy*, ed. Arnold Rothstein, 145–55. Madison, Conn.: Int. Univ. Press.

———— (1988b). The Four Psychologies of Psychoanalysis and Their Place in Clinical Work. *J. Amer. Psychoanal. Assn.* 36:571–96.

———— (1990). *Drive, Ego, Object, and Self: A Synthesis for Clinical Work*, 279. New York: Basic Books.

———— (1992). From Technique to a Theory of Psychic Change. *Int. J. Psycho-Anal.* 73:251–54.

———— (1993). A Contribution to the Analysis of the Psychoanalytic Process. *Psychoanal. Quart.* 62:185–205.

———— (1994). Some Impressions Regarding Conflict, Defect, and Deficit. *Psychoanal. Study of Child* 49:222–240.

Pines, Malcolm (1990). An English Freud? *Psychoanal. Psychother.* 5:1–9.

———— (1991a). A History of Psychodynamic Psychotherapy in Britain. In *Textbook of Psychotherapy in Psychiatric Practice*, ed. Jeremy Holmes, 31–55. London: Churchill Livingstone.

———— (1991b). The Development of the Psychodynamic Movement. In *150 Years of British Psychiatry, 1841–1991*, ed. German E. Berrios and Hugh Freeman, 206–81. London: Gaskell Press, Royal College of Psychiatrists.

Poland, Warren S. (1988). Insight and the Analytic Dyad. *Psychoanal. Quart.* 57:341–69.

———— (1992). Transference: "An Original Creation." *Psychoanal. Quart.* 61:185–205.

Pulver, Sydney E. (1992). Psychic Change: Insight or Relationship? *Int. J. Psycho-Anal.* 73: 199–208.

Racker, Heinrich (1968). *Transference and Countertransference*, 203. New York: Int. Univ. Press.

Rado, Sandor (1956). Adaptational Development of Psychoanalytic Therapy. In *Changing Concepts of Psychoanalytic Medicine*, ed. Sandor Rado, and George E. Daniels, 89–100. New York and London: Grune & Stratton.

Rangell, Leo (1954a). Panel reporter, Psychoanalysis and Dynamic Psychotherapy—Similarities and Differences. *J. Amer. Psychoanal. Assn.* 2:152–66.

———— (1954b). Similarities and Differences between Psychoanalysis and Dynamic Psychotherapy. *J. Amer. Psychoanal. Assn.* 2:734–44.

———— (1963a). The Scope of Intrapsychic Conflict: Microscopic and Macroscopic Considerations. *Psychoanal. Study Child* 18:75–102.

———— (1963b). Structural Problems in Intrapsychic Conflict. *Psychoanal. Study Child* 18:103–38.

———— (1966). An Overview of the Ending of an Analysis. In *Psychoanalysis in the Americas*, ed. Robert E. Litman, 141–65. New York: Int. Univ. Press.

———— (1968). The Psychoanalytic Process. *Int. J. Psycho-Anal.* 49:19–26.

———— (1981a). From Insight to Change. *J. Amer. Psychoanal. Assn.* 29:119–41.

———— (1981b). Psychoanalysis and Dynamic Psychotherapy: Similarities and Differences Twenty-Five Years Later. *Psychoanal. Quart.* 50:665–93.

———— (1989). Structural and Interstructural Change in Psychoanalytic Treatment. *Psychoanal. Inq.* 9:45–66.

—— (1990). *The Human Core: The Intrapsychic Basis of Behavior. Vol. I. Action within the Structural View. Vol. II. From Anxiety to Integrity*, 1–468, 469–959. Madison, Conn.: Int. Univ. Press.

—— (1992). The Psychoanalytic Theory of Change. *Int. J. Psycho-Anal.* 73:415–28.

—— (1993). The Psychoanalytic Theory of Change. In *Psychic Structure and Psychic Change: Essays in Honor of Robert S. Wallerstein, M.D.*, ed. Mardi J. Horowitz, Otto F. Kernberg, and Edward M. Weinshel, 159–90. Madison, Conn.: Int. Univ. Press.

—— (unpubl. ms). Psychoanalysis and Psychoanalytic Psychotherapy: Similarities and Differences—Evolution of the Conceptual Issues since 1954. Presented at American Psychoanalytic Association, New York, Dec. 1989.

Rapaport, David (1945 and 1946). *Diagnostic Psychological Testing: The Theory, Statistical Evaluation, and Diagnostic Application of a Battery of Tests*, 2 Vols, 573 and 516. Chicago: Year Book Publishers.

—— (1960). *The Structure of Psychoanalytic Theory: A Systematizing Attempt*, 158. Psychol. Issues Mono. No. 6. New York: Int. Univ. Press.

Rawn, Moss L. (1991). The Working Alliance: Current Concepts and Controversies. *Psychoanal. Rev.* 78:379–89.

Rayner, Eric (1989). Introduction to *The Ailment and Other Psychoanalytic Essays* by Tom Main, 256. London: Free Association Books.

—— (1990). *The Independent Mind in British Psychoanalysis*, 345. London: Free Association Books.

Redl, Fritz, and David Wineman (1951). *Children Who Hate: The Disorganization and Breakdown of Behavior Controls*, 253. Glencoe, Ill.: Free Press.

——, —— (1952). *Controls from Within: Techniques for the Treatment of the Aggressive Child*, 332. Glencoe, Ill.: Free Press.

Reed, Gail S. (1987a). Rules of Clinical Understanding in Classical Psychoanalysis and in Self Psychology: A Comparison. *J. Amer. Psychoanal. Assn.* 35:421–46.

—— (1987b). Scientific and Polemical Aspects of the Term *Transference Neurosis* in Psychoanalysis. *Psychoanal. Inq.* 7:465–83.

—— (1993). On the Value of Explicit Reconstruction. *Psychoanal. Quart.* 62:52–73.

Renik, Owen (1992). Prologue and Epilogue. *Psychoanal. Inq.* 12:175–81, 368–69.

—— (1993a). Countertransference Enactment and the Psychoanalytic Process. In *Psychic Structure and Psychic Change: Essays in Honor of Robert S. Wallerstein, M.D.*, ed. Mardi J. Horowitz, Otto F. Kernberg and Edward M. Weinshel, 135–58. Madison, Conn.: Int. Univ. Press.

—— (1993b). Analytic Interaction: Conceptualizing Technique in Light of the Analyst's Irreducible Subjectivity. *Psychoanal. Quart.* 62:553–71.

Richfield, Jerome (1954). An Analysis of the Concept of Insight. *Psychoanal. Quart.* 23:390–408.

Ricoeur, Paul (1970). *Freud and Philosophy: An Essay on Interpretation*, 573. New Haven and London: Yale Univ. Press.

Robbins, Lewis L., and Robert S. Wallerstein (1959). The Research Strategy and Tactics of the Psychotherapy Research Project of the Menninger Foundation and the Problem of Controls. In *Research in Psychotherapy*, ed. Eli A. Rubinstein and Morris B. Parloff, 27–43. Washington, D.C., American Psychological Association.

Rockland, Lawrence H. (1989). *Supportive Therapy: A Psychodynamic Approach*, 308. New York: Basic Books.

Rosen, John N. (1953). *Direct Analysis: Selected Papers*, 184. New York: Grune and Stratton.

Rosenblatt, Allan D. (1987). Change in Psychotherapy. *Annual Psychoanal.* 15:175–90.

Rosenfeld, David (1992). *The Psychotic: Aspects of the Personality*, 318. London and New York: Karmac Books.

Rosenfeld, Herbert A. (1954). Considerations Regarding the Psycho-Analytic Approach to Acute and Chronic Schizophrenia. *Int. J. Psycho-Anal.* 35:135–40.

—— (1965). *Psychotic States: A Psychoanalytical Approach*, 263. New York: Int. Univ. Press.

Rothstein, Arnold (1983). Panel reporter, Interpretation: Toward a Contemporary Understanding of the Term. *J. Amer. Psychoanal. Assn.* 31:237–45.

——, ed. (1988). *How Does Treatment Help? On the Modes of Therapeutic Action of Psychoanalytic Psychotherapy*, 232. Madison, Conn.: Int. Univ. Press.

Roughton, Ralph E. (In Press). Nathaniel Hawthorne: A Pre-Freudian 'Psychoanalyst.' Presented at IPA Conference on Psychoanalysis and Literature. London, Univ. Coll. London, Nov. 1992, 28.

Rumney, David (1992). The Portman Clinic. In *Let Justice Be Done: A History of the Institute for the Study and Treatment of Delinquency*, ed. Eve Saville and David Rumney. London: The Portman Clinic.

Sachs, David M. (1979). On the Relationship between Psychoanalysis and Psychoanalytic Psychotherapy. *J. Phila. Assn. Psychoanal.* 6:119–45.

—— (unpubl. ms). Similarities and Differences between Psychoanalysis and Psychoanalytic Psychotherapy: Implications for Training. Presented to Division 39, American Psychological Association, Phila., April 1992.

Sampson, Harold (1992). The Role of "Real" Experience in Psychopathology and Treatment. *Psychoanal. Dial.* 2:509–28.

Sandler, Joseph (1960). The Background of Safety. *Int. J. Psycho-Anal.* 41:352–56.

—— (1974). Psychological Conflict and the Structural Model: Some Clinical and Theoretical Implications. *Int. J. Psycho-Anal.* 55:53–62.

—— (1976a). Countertransference and Role-Responsiveness. *Int. Rev. Psycho-Anal.* 3:43–47.

—— (1976b). Actualization and Object Relationships. *J. Phila. Assn. Psychoanal.* 3:59–70.

—— (1982). Psychoanalysis and Psychotherapy: The Training Analyst's Dilemma. In *Psychotherapy: Impact on Psychoanalytic Training*, ed. Edward D. Joseph and Robert S. Wallerstein, 39–47. New York: Int. Univ. Press.

—— (1986). Reality and the Stabilizing Function of Unconscious Fantasy. *Bull. Anna Freud Centre* 9:177–94.

—— (1988). Psychoanalysis and Psychoanalytic Psychotherapy: Problems of Differentiation. *Brit. J. Psychother.* 5:172–77.

——, Christopher Dare and Alex Holder (1973). *The Patient and the Analyst: The Basis of the Psychoanalytic Process*, 150. London: George Allen & Unwin.

—— and Anne Marie Sandler (1983). The "Second Censorship," the "Three Box Model" and Some Technical Implications. *Int. J. Psycho-Anal.* 64:413–25.

—— and —— (1984). The Past Unconscious, the Present Unconscious, and Interpretation of the Transference. *Psychoanal. Inq.* 4:367–99.

—— and —— (1992). Psychoanalytic Technique and Theory of Psychic Change. *Bull. Anna Freud Centre* 15:35–51.

—— and —— (1993). Psychoanalytic Technique and Theory of Psychic Change. In *Psychic Structure and Psychic Change: Essays in Honor of Robert S. Wallerstein, M.D.*, ed. Mardi

J. Horowitz, Otto F. Kernberg and Edward M. Weinshel, 57–75. Madison, Conn.: Int. Univ. Press.

Sargent, Helen D. (1958). Personal communication.

Sashin, Jerome I., Stanley H. Eldred and Suzanne T. van Amerongen (1975). A Search for Predictive Factors in Institute Supervised Cases: A Retrospective Study of 183 Cases from 1959–1966 at the Boston Psychoanalytic Society and Institute. *Int. J. Psycho-Anal.* 56:343–59.

Schachter, Joseph (1990a). Does a Panel Discussion on Analytic Technique Have Any Effect on an Audience of Analysts? *J. Amer. Psychoanal. Assn.* 38:733–41.

—— (1990b). Post-Termination Patient-Analyst Contact. I. Analyst's Attitudes and Experience. II. Impact on Patients. *Int. J. Psycho-Anal.* 71:475–86.

Schafer, Roy (1981). *Narrative Actions in Psychoanalysis.* Heinz Werner Lecture Series 14. Worcester, Mass.: Clark Univ. Press.

—— (1985). Wild Analysis. *J. Amer. Psychoanal. Assn.* 33:275–99.

—— (1992). *Retelling a Life: Narration and Dialogue in Psychoanalysis.* Chapter 16, Psychoanalysis, Pseudoanalysis, and Psychotherapy, 266–80. New York: Basic Books.

Scheidlinger, Saul (1952). *Psychoanalysis and Group Behavior: A Study of Freudian Group Psychology,* 245. New York: W. W. Norton.

—— (1982). *Focus on Group Psychotherapy: Clinical Essays,* 264. New York: Int. Univ. Press.

Schlesinger, Herbert J. (1969). Diagnosis and Prescription for Psychotherapy. *Bull. Menn. Clinic* 33:269–78.

—— (1988). A Historical Overview of Conceptions of the Mode of Therapeutic Action of Psychoanalytic Psychotherapy In *How Does Treatment Help? On the Modes of Therapeutic Action of Psychoanalytic Psychotherapy,* ed. Arnold Rothstein, 7–27. Madison, Conn.: Int. Univ. Press.

—— (unpubl. ms). Psychoanalysis and Psychoanalytic Psychotherapy. Presented at American Psychoanalytic Association, New York, Dec. 1989.

Schlessinger, Nathan and Fred P. Robbins (1974). Assessment and Follow-Up in Psychoanalysis. *J. Amer. Psychoanal. Assn.* 22:542–67.

—— and —— (1975). The Psychoanalytic Process: Recurrent Patterns of Conflict and Changes in Ego Functions. *J. Amer. Psychoanal. Assn.* 23:761–82.

—— and —— (1983). *A Developmental View of the Psychoanalytic Process: Follow-up Studies and Their Consequences,* 228. New York: Int. Univ. Press.

Schwaber, Evelyne Albrecht (1981). Empathy: A Mode of Analytic Listening. *Psychoanal. Inq.* 1:357–92.

—— (1983a). A Particular Perspective on Analytic Listening. *Psychoanal. Study Child* 38:519–46.

—— (1983b). Psychoanalytic Listening and Psychic Reality. *Int. Rev. Psycho-Anal.* 10:379–92.

—— (1986). Reconstruction and Perceptual Experience: Further Thoughts on Psychoanalytic Listening. *J. Amer. Psychoanal. Assn.* 34:911–32.

—— (1987). Models of the Mind and Data-Gathering in Clinical Work. *Psychoanal. Inq.* 7:261–75.

—— (1988). On the Mode of Therapeutic Action: A Clinical Montage. In *How Does Treatment Help? On the Modes of Therapeutic Action of Psychoanalytic Psychotherapy,* ed. Arnold Rothstein, 81–93. Madison, Conn.: Int. Univ Press.

―――― (1990). Interpretation and the Therapeutic Action of Psychoanalysis. *Int. J. Psycho-Anal.* 71:229–40.

―――― (1992a). Countertransference: The Analyst's Retreat from the Patient's Vantage Point. *Int. J. Psycho-Anal.* 73:349–61.

―――― (1992b). Psychoanalytic Theory and Its Relationship to Clinical Work. *J. Amer. Psychoanal. Assn.* 40:1039–57.

Schwing, Gertrud (1954). *A Way to the Soul of the Mentally Ill,* 158. New York: Int. Univ. Press.

Searles, Harold F. (1965). *Collected Papers on Schizophrenia and Related Subjects,* 797. New York: Int. Univ. Press.

―――― (1986). *My Work with Borderline Patients,* 409. Northvale, N.J.: Jason Aronson.

Sechehaye, Marguerite A. (1951). *Symbolic Realization: A New Method of Psychotherapy Applied to a Case of Schizophrenia,* 184. New York: Int. Univ. Press.

Segal, Hanna (1990). Some Comments on the Alexander Technique. *Psychoanal. Inq.* 10:409–14.

Segel, Nathan P. (1981a). Book Review of *Borderline Conditions and Pathological Narcissism* and of *Object-Relations Theory and Clinical Psychoanalysis,* both by Otto Kernberg. *J. Amer. Psychoanal. Assn.* 29:221–36.

―――― (1981b). Narcissism and Adaptation to Indignity. *Int. J. Psycho-Anal.* 62:465–76.

Shane, Morton and Estelle Shane (1992). Transference, Countertransference, and the Real Relationship: A Study and Reassessment of Greenson's Views of the Patient/Analyst Dyad. In *The Technique and Practice of Psychoanalysis, 2, A Memorial Volume to Ralph R. Greenson,* ed. Alan Sugarman, Robert A. Nemiroff and Daniel P. Greenson, 285–303. Madison, Conn.: Int. Univ. Press.

Shaw, Ronda R. (1991). Panel reporter, Concepts and Controversies about the Transference Neurosis. *J. Amer. Psychoanal. Assn.* 39:227–39.

Sherwood, Michael (1969). *The Logic of Explanation in Psychoanalysis,* 276. New York: Academic Press.

Sifneos, Peter E. (1972). *Short-Term Psychotherapy and Emotional Crisis,* 299. Cambridge: Harvard Univ. Press.

Simons, Richard C. (1990). Our Analytic Heritage: Ideals and Idealizations. *J. Amer. Psychoanal. Assn.* 38:5–38.

Skolnikoff, Alan Z. (1993). The Analyst's Experience in the Psychoanalytic Situation: A Continuum between Objective and Subjective Reality. *Psychoanal. Inq.* 13:296–309.

―――― (1995). Paradox and Ambiguity in the Reactions of the Analyst at Work. *Psychoanal. Inq.* 15: In press.

Slavson, Samuel Richard (1943). *An Introduction to Group Therapy,* 351. New York: Commonwealth Fund.

――――, ed. (1947). *The Practice of Group Therapy,* 271. New York: Int. Univ. Press.

―――― (1950). *Analytic Group Psychotherapy with Children, Adolescents and Adults,* 275. New York: Columbia Univ. Press.

Socarides, Charles W. (1968). *The Overt Homosexual,* 245. New York and London: Grune and Stratton.

―――― (1975). *Beyond Sexual Freedom,* 181. New York: Quadrangle/New York Times.

―――― (1978). *Homosexuality,* 642. New York and London: Jason Aronson.

―――― (1988). *The Preoedipal Origin and Psychoanalytic Therapy of Sexual Perversions,* 639. Madison, Conn.: Int. Univ. Press.

Spence, Donald P. (1982). *Narrative Truth and Historical Truth: Meaning and Interpretation in Psychoanalysis*, 320. New York and London: W. W. Norton.

—— (1986). When Interpretation Masquerades as Explanation. *J. Amer. Psychoanal. Assn.* 34:3–22.

—— (1987). *The Freudian Metaphor: Toward Paradigm Change in Psychoanalysis*, 230. New York and London: W. W. Norton.

Spitz, Rene A. (1956). Countertransference: Comments on Its Varying Role in the Analytic Situation. *J. Amer. Psychoanal. Assn.* 4:256–65.

Stein, Martin H. (1981). The Unobjectionable Part of the Transference. *J. Amer. Psychoanal. Assn.* 29:869–92.

Steiner, Riccardo (1985). Some Thoughts about Tradition and Change from an Examination of the British Psychoanalytical Society's Controversial Discussions (1943–1944). *Int. Rev. Psycho-Anal.* 12:27–71.

Sterba, Richard (1934). The Fate of the Ego in Analytic Therapy. *Int. J. Psycho-Anal.* 15:117–26.

Stewart, Harold (1987). Varieties of Transference Interpretation: An Object-Relations View. *Int. J. Psycho-Anal.* 68:197–205.

—— (1990). Interpretation and Other Agents for Psychic Change. *Int. Rev. Psycho-Anal.* 17:61–69.

Stolorow, Robert D. (1990). Converting Psychotherapy to Psychoanalysis: A Critique of the Underlying Assumptions. *Psychoanal. Inq.* 10:119–30.

—— (1993). An Intersubjective View of the Therepeutic Process. *Bull. Menn. Clinic* 57:450–57.

—— and George E. Atwood (1992). *Contexts of Being: The Intersubjective Foundation of Psychological Life*, 145. Hillsdale, N.J., and London: Analytic Press.

——, Bernard Brandchaft, and George E. Atwood (1987). *Psychoanalytic Treatment: An Intersubjective Approach*, 187. Hillsdale, N.J., and London: Analytic Press.

Stone, Leo (1951). Psychoanalysis and Brief Psychotherapy. *Psychoanal. Quart.* 20:215–36.

—— (1954). The Widening Scope of Indications for Psychoanalysis. *J. Amer. Psychoanal. Assn.* 2:567–94.

—— (1957). Book Review of *Psychoanalysis and Psychotherapy: Developments in Theory, Technique and Training* by Franz Alexander. *Psychoanal Quart.* 26:397–405.

—— (1961). *The Psychoanalytic Situation: An Examination of Its Development and Essential Nature*, 160. New York: Int. Univ. Press.

—— (1981a). Notes on the Noninterpretive Elements in the Psychoanalytic Situation and Process. *J. Amer. Psychoanal. Assn.* 29:89–118.

—— (1981b). Some Thoughts on the "Here and Now" in Psychoanalytic Technique and Process. *Psychoanal. Quart.* 50:709–33.

—— (1982). The Influence of the Practice and Theory of Psychotherapy on Education in Psychoanalysis. In *Psychotherapy: Impact on Psychoanalytic Training*, ed. Edward D. Joseph, and Robert S. Wallerstein, 75–118. IPA Mono. No. 1. New York: Int. Univ. Press.

Strachey, James (1934). The Nature of the Therapeutic Action of Psycho-Analysis. *Int. J. Psycho-Anal.* 15:127–59.

Strenger, Carlo (1989). The Classic and the Romantic Vision in Psychoanalysis. *Int. J. Psycho-Anal.* 70:593–610.

—— (1991). *Between Hermeneutics and Science: An Essay on the Epistemology of Psychoanalysis*, 234. Psychol. Issues Mono. No. 59. Madison, Conn.: Int. Univ. Press.

Suttie, Ian D. (1935). *The Origins of Love and Hate,* 275. Reprinted London: Free Association Books, 1988.

Symposium on the Theory of the Therapeutic Results of Psycho-Analysis (1937). Edward Glover, Otto Fenichel, James Strachey, Edmund Bergler, Herman Nunberg, and Edward Bibring. *Int. J. Psycho-Anal.* 18:125–95.

Szurek, Stanislaus A. (1958). *The Roots of Psychoanalysis and Psychotherapy: A Search for Principles of General Therapeutics,* 134. Springfield, Ill.: Charles C Thomas.

Tahka, Veikko (1979). Psychotherapy as Phase-Specific Interaction: Towards a General Psychoanalytic Theory of Psychotherapy. *Scand. Psychoanal. Rev.* 2:113–32.

—— (1993). *Mind and Its Treatment: A Psychoanalytic Approach* 490. Madison, Conn.: Int. Univ. Press.

Tarachow, Sidney (1962). Interpretation and Reality in Psychotherapy. *Int. J. Psycho-Anal.* 43:377–87.

—— (1963). *An Introduction to Psychotherapy,* 376. New York: Int. Univ. Press.

Thoma, Helmut, and Horst Kachele, (1987). *Psychoanalytic Practice, Vol. 1, Principles,* trans. M. Wilson and D. Roseveare, 421. Berlin: Springer-Verlag.

Ticho, Gertrude (1967). On Self-Analysis. *Int. J. Psycho-Anal.* 48:308–18.

Treurniet, Nikolaas (1993). Support of the Analytical Process and Structural Change. In *Psychic Structure and Psychic Change: Essays in Honor of Robert S. Wallerstein, M.D.,* ed. Mardi J. Horowitz, Otto F. Kernberg, and Edward M. Weinshel, 191–232. Madison, Conn.: Int. Univ. Press.

Tyson, Robert L. (1986). Countertransference Evolution in Theory and Practice. *J. Amer. Psychoanal. Assn.* 34:251–74.

Valenstein, Arthur F. (1962). The Psychoanalytic Situation: Affects, Emotional Reliving, and Insight in the Psycho-Analytic Process. *Int. J. Psycho-Anal.* 43:315–24.

—— (1979). The Concept of "Classical" Psychoanalysis. *J. Amer. Psychoanal. Assn.* 27(Suppl):113–36.

—— (1983). Working Through and Resistance to Change: Insight and the Action System. *J. Amer. Psychoanal. Assn.* 31(Suppl):353–73.

—— (unpubl.). Remarks at International Scientific Colloquium at the Anna Freud Centre, London, Oct. 1989.

Viederman, Milton (1991). The Real Person of the Analyst and His Role in the Process of Psychoanalytic Cure. *J. Amer. Psychoanal. Assn.* 39:451–89.

Waelder, Robert (1960). *Basic Theory of Psychoanalysis,* 273. New York: Int. Univ. Press.

—— (1967). *Progress and Revolution: A Study of the Issues of Our Age,* 372. New York: Int. Univ. Press.

Wallerstein, Robert S. (1963). The Problem of the Assessment of Change in Psychotherapy. *Int. J. Psycho-Anal.* 44:31–41.

—— (1964). The Role of Prediction in Theory Building in Psychoanalysis. *J. Amer. Psychoanal. Assn.* 12:675–91.

—— (1965). The Goals of Psychoanalysis: A Survey of Analytic Viewpoints. *J. Amer. Psychoanal. Assn.* 13:748–70.

—— (1966). The Current State of Psychotherapy: Theory, Practice, Research. *J. Amer. Psychoanal. Assn.* 14:183–225.

—— (1967). Reconstruction and Mastery in the Transference Psychosis. *J. Amer. Psychoanal. Assn.* 15:551–83.

———— (1969). Introduction to Panel on Psychoanalysis and Psychotherapy: The Relationship of Psychoanalysis to Psychotherapy—Current Issues. *Int. J. Psycho-Anal.* 50:117–26.

———— (1972). Transactional Psychotherapy. In *Modern Psychiatry and Clinical Research: Essays in Honor of Roy R. Grinker, Sr.,* ed. Daniel Offer and Daniel X. Freedman, 120–35. New York: Basic Books.

———— (1974). Herbert S. Gaskill and the History of American Psychoanalysis in American Psychiatry. *The Denver Psychoanal. Society Newsletter* 1, no. 3, Dec., 1–9.

———— (1976). Psychoanalysis as a Science: Its Present Status and Its Future Tasks. In *Psychology versus Metapsychology: Psychoanalytic Essays in Memory of George S. Klein,* ed. Merton M. Gill and Philip S. Holzman, Psychol. Issues Mono. 36:198–228.

———— (1980). Psychoanalysis and Academic Psychiatry—Bridges. *Psychoanal. Study Child* 35: 419–48.

———— (1981). The Bipolar Self: Discussion of Alternative Perspectives. *J. Amer. Psychoanal. Assn.* 29:377–94.

———— (1983a). Self Psychology and "Classical" Psychoanalytic Psychology: The Nature of Their Relationship. *Psychoanal. Cont. Thought* 6:553–95.

———— (1983b). Some Thoughts about Insight and Psychoanalysis. *Israel J. Psychiat. and Related Sciences* 20:33–43.

———— (1984). The Analysis of the Transference: A Matter of Emphasis or of Theory Reformulation? *Psychoanal. Inq.* 4:325–54.

———— (1985). How Does Self Psychology Differ in Practice? *Int. J. Psycho-Anal.* 66:391–404.

———— (1986a). *Forty-Two Lives in Treatment: A Study of Psychoanalysis and Psychotherapy,* 784. New York: Guilford Press.

———— (1986b). Psychoanalysis as a Science: A Response to the New Challenges. *Psychoanal. Quart.* 55:414–51.

———— (1986c). Book Review of *Severe Personality Disorders: Psychotherapeutic Strategies* by Otto Kernberg. *J. Amer. Psychoanal. Assn.* 34:711–22.

———— (1987). Book Review of *The Psychoanalytic Process: Theory, Clinical Observations, and Empirical Research* by Joseph Weiss, Harold Sampson, and the Mount Zion Psychotherapy Research Group. *Int. J. Psycho-Anal.* 68:565–67.

———— (1988a). One Psychoanalysis or Many? *Int. J. Psycho-Anal.* 69:5–21.

———— (1988b). Psychoanalysis and Psychotherapy: Relative Roles Reconsidered. *Annual Psychoanal.* 16:129–51.

———— (1988c). Psychoanalysis, Psychoanalytic Science, and Psychoanalytic Research—1986. *J. Amer. Psychoanal. Assn.* 36:3–30.

———— (1988d). Assessment of Structural Change in Psychoanalytic Therapy and Research. *J. Amer. Psychoanal. Assn.* 36(Suppl):241–61.

———— (1989a). Psychoanalysis and Psychotherapy: A Historical Perspective. *Int. J. Psycho-Anal.* 70:563–91.

———— (1989b). Followup in Psychoanalysis: Clinical and Research Values. *J. Amer. Psychoanal. Assn.* 37:921–42.

———— (1990a). Psychoanalysis: The Common Ground. *Int. J. Psycho-Anal.* 71:3–20.

———— (1990b). The Corrective Emotional Experience: Is Reconsideration Due? *Psychoanal. Inq.* 10:288–324.

———— (1990c). Book Review of *The Anatomy of Psychotherapy* by Lawrence Friedman. *Int. Rev. Psycho-Anal.* 17:510–13.

——— (1991). The Future of Psychotherapy. *Bull. Menn. Clinic* 55:421–42.
———, ed. (1992a). *The Common Ground of Psychoanalysis*, 320. Northvale, N.J., and London: Jason Aronson.
——— (1992b). The Goals of Psychoanalysis Reconsidered. In *The Technique and Practice of Psychoanalysis 2. A Memorial Volume to Ralph R. Greenson,* ed. Alan Sugarman, Robert A. Nemiroff, and Daniel P. Greenson, 63–99. Madison, Conn.: Int. Univ. Press.
——— (1992c). Followup in Psychoanalysis: What Happens to Treatment Gains? *J. Amer. Psychoanal. Assn.* 40:665–90.
——— (1993). On Transference Love: Revisiting Freud. In *On Freud's "Observations on Transference-Love,"* ed. Ethel Spector Person, Aiban Hagelin, and Peter Fonagy, 57–74. IPA Educational Monograph No. 3. New Haven and London: Yale Univ. Press.
——— (unpubl. ms a). The Relation of Theory to Therapy: An Alternative Vision. Forthcoming, *Psychoanalytic Inquiry.*
——— (unpubl. ms b). Research in Psychodynamic Therapy. Forth coming in *Psychodynamic Concepts in General Psychiatry,* ed. Harvey J. Schwartz, with Efrain Bleiberg and Sidney Weissman. Washington, D.C.: American Psychiatric Association Press.
——— (unpubl. ms c). Proposal to the Ludwig Foundation for a Collaborative Analytic Multi-Site Program of Psychoanalytic Therapy Research.
——— (unpubl. ms d). Supportive Interventions, from Psychotherapy Research Project II.
———, in collaboration with John W. Chotlos, Merril B. Friend, Donald W. Hammersley, Ellis A. Perlswig, and G. M. Winship, (1957). *Hospital Treatment of Alcoholism: A Comparative, Experimental Study,* 212. New York: Basic Books.
——— and Lewis L. Robbins (1956). Concepts: The Psychotherapy Research Project of the Menninger Foundation. *Bull. Menn. Clinic* 20:239–62.
——— and ——— (1958). Further Notes on Design and Concepts. *Bull. Menn. Clinic* 22: 117–25.
———, ———, Helen D. Sargent and Lester Luborsky (1956). The Psychotherapy Research Project of the Menninger Foundation: Rationale, Method and Sample Use. *Bull. Menn. Clinic* 20:221–78.
——— and Harold Sampson (1971). Issues in Research in the Psychoanalytic Process. *Int. J. Psycho-Anal.* 52:11–50.
——— and Edward M. Weinshel (1989). The Future of Psychoanalysis. *Psychoanal. Quart.* 58:341–73.
Weber, John J., Henry M. Bachrach, and Murray Solomon (1985a). Factors Associated with the Outcome of Psychoanalysis: Report of the Columbia Psychoanalytic Center Research Project (II). *Int. Rev. Psycho-Anal.* 12:127–41.
———, ———, and ——— (1985b). Factors Associated with the Outcome of Psychoanalysis: Report of the Columbia Psychoanalytic Center Research Project (III). *Int. Rev. Psycho-Anal.* 12:251–62.
———, Murray Solomon, and Henry M. Bachrach (1985c). Characteristics of Psychoanalytic Clinic Patients: Report of the Columbia Psychoanalytic Center Research Project (I). *Int. Rev. Psycho-Anal.* 12:13–26.
Webster's Third New International Dictionary (1965). Springfield, Mass.: G. & C. Merriam.
Weigert, Edith (1954). The Importance of Flexibility in Psychoanalytic Technique. *J. Amer. Psychoanal. Assn.* 2:702–10.
Weinshel, Edward M. (1971). The Transference Neurosis: A Survey of the Literature. *J. Amer. Psychoanal. Assn.* 19:67–88.

———— (1984). Some Observations on the Psychoanalytic Process. *Psychoanal. Quart.* 53:63–92.

———— (1988). Structural Change in Psychoanalysis. *J. Amer. Psychoanal. Assn.* 36(Suppl):263–80.

———— (1990a). How Wide Is the Widening Scope of Psychoanalysis and How Solid Is Its Structural Model? Some Concerns and Observations. *J. Amer. Psychoanal. Assn.* 38:275–96.

———— (1990b). Further Observations on the Psychoanalytic Process. *Psychoanal. Quart.* 59:629–49.

———— (1992). Therapeutic Technique in Psychoanalysis and Psychoanalytic Psychotherapy. *J. Amer. Psychoanal. Assn.* 40:327–47.

———— and Owen Renik, (1991). The Past Ten Years: Psychoanalysis in the United States, 1980–1990. *Psychoanal. Inq.* 11:13–29.

Weiss, Joseph (1992). The Role of Interpretation. *Psychoanal. Inq.* 12:296–313.

————, Harold Sampson, and the Mount Zion Psychotherapy Research Group (1986). *The Psychoanalytic Process: Theory, Clinical Observation and Empirical Research*, 423. New York and London: Guilford Press.

Werman, David S. (1984). *The Practice of Supportive Psychotherapy* 192. New York: Brunner/Mazel.

———— (1988). On the Mode of Therapeutic Action of Psychoanalytic Supportive Psychotherapy. In *How Does Treatment Help? On the Modes of Therapeutic Action of Psychoanalytic Psychotherapy*, ed. Arnold Rothstein, 157–67. Madison, Conn.: Int. Univ. Press.

———— (1989). The Idealization of Structural Change. *Psychoanal. Inq.* 9:119–39.

———— (1990). Supportive Psychotherapy. *Highland Highlights* 13:17–24.

Wheelis, Allen (1950). The Place of Action in Personality Change. *Psychiatry* 13:135–48.

———— (1956). Will and Psychoanalysis. *J. Amer. Psychoanal. Assn.* 4:285–303.

Whitehorn, John C. (Chairman of the Editorial Board) (1953). *The Psychiatrist, His Training and Development*, 214. Washington, D.C.: American Psychiatric Association.

Winnicott, Donald W. (1958). *Collected Papers: Through Paediatrics to Psycho-Analysis*, 350. New York: Basic Books.

———— (1965). *The Maturational Process and the Facilitating Environment*. New York: Int. Univ. Press.

Wolff, Heinz (1988). The Relationship between Psychoanalytic Psychotherapy and Psychoanalysis: Attitudes and Aims. *Brit. J. Psychother.* 5:178–85.

Woodcock, O. H. (1938). The Unwilling Patient IV. *Brit. J. Med. Psychol.* 17:71–75.

Zetzel, Elizabeth R. (1953). Panel reporter, The Traditional Psychoanalytic Technique and Its Variations. *J. Amer. Psychoanal. Assn.* 1:526–37.

———— (1956). Current Concepts of Transference. *Int. J. Psycho-Anal.* 37:369–75.

———— (1965). The Theory of Therapy in Relation to a Developmental Model of the Psychic Apparatus. *Int. J. Psycho-Anal.* 46:39–52.

———— (1966). The Analytic Situation. In *Psychoanalysis in the Americas*, ed. Robert E. Litman, 86–106. New York: Int. Univ. Press.

Zilberg, Nathan J., Robert S. Wallerstein, Kathryn N. DeWitt, Dianna E. Hartley, and Saul R. Rosenberg (1991). A Conceptual Analysis and Strategy for Assessing Structural Change. *Psychoanal. Cont. Thought* 14:317–42.

Zilboorg, Gregory (1952). The Emotional Problem and the Therapeutic Role of Insight. *Psychoanal. Quart.* 21:1–24.

Index

Obholzer, Karin, 482
Object need, 98–99
Object relations, xvii, 62, 64, 192, 315, 317, 318, 325, 372–74, 456–57, 515, 516, 534–35, 536
Objectivity (neutrality) of analyst, 302–03, 322n, 370, 394n8, 428, 430–31, 478, 534
Obsessive-compulsives, 108
Offenkrantz, William, 102–03n
Optimal disillusionment as a therapeutic technique, 339–40, 341
Oremland, Jerome, 91, 145, 155–61, 259–60, 330, 479
Ornstein, Paul, 382–83, 388–89
Orr, Douglass, xiv, 209–10, 225, 253
Outcomes: control methods in outcome research, 501–02; current directions in research on, 502–06; definitional, conceptual, methodological, and practical considerations in research on, 480–81; of Deutsch's cases, 483–84; first-generation studies, 485–87, 486n; fourth-generation studies, 506; of Freud's cases, 481–83; and "Pfeffer phenomenon," 492–93; of psychoanalysis, 480–95, 503–06; of psychoanalytic psychotherapy, 495–504; second-generation studies, 487–95; third-generation studies, 495–502. See also Psychotherapy Research Project (PRP)

Pacification as a therapeutic technique, 339, 341
"Palliative psychotherapy," 35
Parameters of psychoanalysis, 107–11, 107n, 119, 161, 176n, 295, 331, 341, 342, 473, 507, 519, 534
Paul, Louis, 97n, 126, 176n
Payne, Sylvia, 367, 369–70
Pedder, Jonathan, 363, 365, 371
Personality, as hierarchy of personal aims, 340–41
Perspectivism, 437–38
Pfeffer, Arnold, 446, 492–93

"Pfeffer phenomenon," 492–94
Phobia, 15, 107–08
Pine, Fred, 143–44, 187–88, 315–17, 342n, 353–54
Pines, Malcolm, 358–61, 361n
Poland, Warren, 190–91, 196, 236–37, 238, 448, 535
Pontalis, J.-B., 322
Portman Clinic, 361, 365–66, 370
POST. See Psychodynamically oriented supportive therapy (POST)
Postanalytic phase, 494
Postmodernism, 535–36n
Primal transference, 307–08
Primary transference, 210–11
Prince, Morton, 360
Projective tests, 88
Proust, Marcel, 236, 237
PRP. See Psychotherapy Research Project (PRP)
Pseudoanalysis, 522–23n
PSP. See Psychoanalytic supportive psychotherapy (PSP)
Psychiatry: in America, 34, 34n, 36–37, 40–41n, 46; in Great Britain, 357–67
Psychoanalysis: "classical" technique of, 4n2, 14, 48, 60n, 61–62, 107–23, 161, 267, 283, 293, 294–95, 298, 299, 341, 391, 393–94n8, 414, 508, 509, 520, 530, 534, 536; conversion of psychotherapy to, 473–79; couch used in, 133–34; early distinctions between psychoanalytic psychotherapies and, 42–49, 61–62, 96–97, 313; empirical behavioral science perspective on, 517, 518, 535; fitting patient to treatment versus fitting treatment to patient, 88; frequency and length of, 133–34, 150, 156; S. Freud on, 3–7, 5n, 21–24, 28–32, 32n, 42, 48–49, 74, 110, 134, 189–90, 203–07, 390, 473, 508, 510–11, 519, 523, 534, 539; S. Freud's "actual technique" of, 5n, 16, 48–49, 60n, 107–09, 112–17, 121–22, 393–94n, 428, 482–83, 508, 534; S. Freud's definition of, 74, 77, 523;

analyst as teacher/parent, 303–07,
322–23; Bibring on, 326n; Blum on,
329–30; Brenner on, 299–300, 450–
51; Casement on, 64–65; and
charismatic authority of psychoanalyst,
13–14; Chasseguet-Smirgel on,
330; Clarkson on, 322–23; A. Cooper
on, 318–19; and corrective emotional
experience, 52–54, 54n5; developmental metaphor for, 303–07, 306n;
ego dissociation during, 268–69, 268n,
280n; Ferenczi on, 19, 19n, 27, 267,
269n, 291, 298, 322–23, 325, 534,
537; focus on, 509–10; A. Freud on,
118–19; S. Freud on, 112, 117, 118,
267, 295–96, 325, 443, 445, 457;
Gitelson on, 292–94, 306, 307, 317;
Hamilton on, 317; "humanness" of
analyst-patient relationship, 286–87,
294–300, 301; Jacobs on, 313–14;
Jacobson on, 330–31; Jonghe, Rijnierse, and Janssen on, 322, 323–28,
328–29n; Kohut on, 319; Levenson
on, 314–15; Lipton's critique of,
114–15; Loewald on, 291, 300–09,
315, 316, 319, 445–46n; Meissner on,
326–27n; Modell on, 310–11;
"mother-tenderness" in, 24, 28–29,
59; "mutual" or "reciprocal" analysis,
19, 23, 27; objectivity or neutrality of
analyst, 302–03, 322n, 370, 394n8,
428, 430–31, 478, 534; Oremland on,
330; patient's experience of, 63;
Pine on, 315–17; as primary relationship, 325–26; as process and resistance, 443–58; "professional
hypocrisy" in, 19, 19n, 27; Pulver on,
329; Rangell on, 81, 317–18, 444;
Segal on, 63–64; Spitz on, 291–92,
317, 325; Sterba on, 267–69, 268n1,
324; Stone on, 60, 291, 294–300,
307, 316; and subjectivity of analyst,
434, 455–56, 456n, 478, 479, 533n,
535; Tahka on, 68; Tarachow on,
98–99; and technical mistakes of
analyst, 276, 276n; therapeutic and
working alliances, 270–90; and "two-

body" psychology, 21, 28, 63, 321n;
typologies of relationship patterns in,
322–28; Viederman, 320–22;
Weinshel on, 444–45. *See also*
Countertransference; Empathy;
Insight; Interpretation; Transference
Psychoanalytic supportive psychotherapy
(PSP), 328–29n
Psychoanalytically oriented psychotherapy,
157–58, 160
Psychodynamically oriented supportive
therapy (POST), 104–05
Psychological capacities, 465–66, 541
Psychopathic Clinic, 365
Psychoses, 4, 4n2, 22, 26, 27, 27n, 37,
37n, 39n, 46, 73–76, 78, 89–90, 205–
06, 245, 245n, 270n, 276–77, 339,
347–48, 349–51, 350nn4–5, 368–69.
See also Schizophrenia
Psychotherapeutic counseling, 85–86
Psychotherapeutic relationship: anabolic
versus analytic therapies, 334; Basch
on, 342–45; for borderline states,
348, 349, 351, 397–405; Casement on, 372–74; for current
developmental crises, 332–34; for
developmental arrests, 332–34;
Gedo on, 332–34, 336–42; Gill on,
426, 427–30; Gray on, 413–21;
hierarchical and developmental model
of, 332–56; Hoffman on, 427, 430–
39, 439n; Holinger on, 345–46;
introspection versus, 340; Levy and
Inderbitzin on, 440–42; Loewald on,
354; and models of the mind, 336–
37, 341; for narcissistic personality
disorders, 339–40; for neurotic
disorders, 340, 348–49, 351–52; Pine
on, 353–54; for psychotic patients,
339, 347–48, 349–51, 351nn;
resistances and therapeutic process,
443–58; Schwaber on, 421–27, 422n;
Tahka on, 346–53; Tarachow on,
98–99; for traumatic states, 339;
Zetzel's developmental model of,
334–36. *See also* Psychoanalytic
psychotherapies